Learning Disabilities,
Literacy, and Adult Education

Learning Disabilities, Literacy, and Adult Education

edited by

Susan A. Vogel, Ph.D.
Northern Illinois University
De Kalb, Illinois

and

Stephen Reder, Ph.D.
Portland State University
Portland, Oregon

·P A U L·H·
BROOKES
PUBLISHING C?

Baltimore • London • Toronto • Sydney

Paul H. Brookes Publishing Co.
Post Office Box 10624
Baltimore, Maryland 21285-0624

www.pbrookes.com

Typeset by Barton Matheson Willse & Worthington,
Baltimore, Maryland.
Manufactured in the United States of America by
The Maple Press Co., York, Pennsylvania.

Library of Congress Cataloging-in-Publication Data

Learning disabilities, literacy, and adult education / [edited] by Susan A. Vogel and
    Stephen Reder.
        p.   cm.
    Includes bibliographical references.
    ISBN 1-55766-347-5
        1. Learning disabled—Education—United States.   2. Adult education—United States.
    3. Learning disabled—United States—Identification.   4. Functional literacy—United States.
    I. Vogel, Susan Ann.   II. Reder, Stephen M.
    LC4818.5.L436   1998
    371.9'0475—dc21   98-7641
                                                                                                                                            CIP

British Library Cataloguing in Publication data are available from the British Library.

Contents

About the Editors

Susan A. Vogel, Ph.D., Educational Psychology, Counseling, and Special Education Department, Graham Hall 145, Northern Illinois University, De Kalb, IL 60115

Susan A. Vogel is Professor of Special Education in the Educational Psychology, Counseling, and Special Education Department at Northern Illinois University in De Kalb, Illinois. She has published more than 50 articles as well as several handbooks, chapters, and books on adults with learning disabilities (LD) that have concentrated on factors contributing to student success; postsecondary support services; and, most recently, adults with severe difficulties with literacy. The 1997 edition of her handbook, *College Students with Learning Disabilities*, which is distributed by the Learning Disabilities Association of America, has sold more than 45,000 copies in the United States and Canada.

In 1992, Dr. Vogel was appointed by President George Bush and confirmed by the U.S. Senate to serve as a founding member of the Advisory Board of the National Institute for Literacy in Washington, D.C. and served on the national advisory boards of the International Dyslexia Association and HEATH (a national clearinghouse for information on adults with disabilities). In addition, she was the founding editor of *Learning Disabilities Research and Practice* and serves as consulting editor for six journals, including *Annals of Dyslexia, Journal of Developmental Education*, and the *Journal of Learning Disabilities*.

Presently, Dr. Vogel serves as President of the International Academy for Research in Learning Disabilities, which is composed of 300 elected fellows from around the world. The Academy is involved in cutting-edge research on LD. Dr. Vogel's research interests include the prevalence of adults with LD in formal and informal educational settings; literacy proficiency; educational attainment; employment; financial and occupational status; gender differences; and support services, accommodations, and faculty attitudes toward students with LD in higher education.

Stephen Reder, Ph.D., Portland State University, Post Office Box 751, Portland, OR 97207

Stephen Reder is University Professor at Portland State University in Portland, Oregon. Dr. Reder is Co-director of Development, Education and Work, an interdisciplinary research group at Portland State University. Dr. Reder is the author of numerous articles, chapters, and reports on various aspects of adult literacy, learning, and development. He has studied adult literacy in a wide variety of environments, including native villages in West Africa and Alaska, immigrant and migrant communities in the United States, and other diverse workplaces. He specializes in combining qualitative and quantitative research methods to gain new understanding about how adults develop and apply literacy skills in everyday activities and how individuals with different information-processing abilities work together to reach shared goals.

Dr. Reder's research has focused on profiling self-reported LD among adults and analyzing the lifespan results of LD on social, economic, and educational outcomes. His research focuses on studies of adult literacy growth and learning across these individuals' life spans and on techniques for facilitating learning in the workplace. Dr. Reder has served on numerous state and national committees and advisory groups concerned with adult education, adult literacy, and work force development throughout the United States.

Dr. Reder is currently the West Coast coordinator for the National Center for the Study of Adult Literacy and Learning, a federally funded research and development center based at Harvard University.

Contributors

Diane S. Bassett, Ph.D.
Associate Professor
Division of Special Education
University of Northern Colorado
McKee 29
Greelay, CO 80639

Hugh Catts, Ph.D.
Associate Professor
Department of Speech-Language-Hearing
University of Kansas
Lawrence, KS 66045

Rob Crawford, M.Ed.
President
Life Development Institute
1720 East Monta Vista
Phoenix, AZ 85006

Mary E. Cronin, Ph.D.
Professor of Special Education and
   Habilitative Services
University of New Orleans
ED 246
New Orleans, LA 70148

Angela J. Fawcett, Ph.D.
Department of Psychology
University of Sheffield
Western Bank
Sheffield, Yorks
ENGLAND S10 2TP

Melinda Giovengo, Ph.D.
Learning Disabilities Project Director
State of Washington Department of Social
   and Health Services
7051 14th Avenue, NW
Seattle, WA 98117

Gregory A. Holliday, Ph.D.
Director
Assessment and Consultation Clinic
University of Missouri
223 Townsend
Columbia, MO 65211

James R. Koller, Ph.D.
Professor
Department of Educational and Counseling
   Psychology
University of Missouri
16 Hill Hall
Columbia, MO 65211

Keith Lenz, Ph.D.
Senior Research Scientist
University of Kansas Center for Research on
   Learning
3061 Dole Human Development Center
Lawrence, KS 66045

Elizabeth J. Moore, Ph.D.
Research Consultant
University of Washington
3937 15th Avenue, NE
Seattle, WA 98105

Roderick I. Nicolson, Ph.D.
Professor
Department of Psychology
University of Sheffield
Western Bank
Sheffield, Yorks
ENGLAND S10 2TP

James R. Patton, Ed.D.
Executive Editor
PRO-ED
Post Office Box 26897
Austin, TX 78755

Nancie A. Payne, M.S.
Senior Consultant
Payne & Associates
Northwest Center for the Advancement of
   Learning
205 Lilly Road, NE
Building B, Suite A
Olympia, WA 98506

Blanche Podhajski, Ph.D.
President
Stern Center for Language and Learning
20 Allen Brook Lane
Williston, VT 05495

Marshall H. Raskind, Ph.D.
Director of Research
The Frostig Center
971 North Altadena Drive
Pasadena, CA 91107

Stephen Reder, Ph.D.
University Professor
Portland State University
Post Office Box 751
Portland, OR 97207

Henry B. Reiff, Ph.D.
Associate Professor of Special Education
Western Maryland College
2 College Hill
Westminster, MD 21157

Jovita M. Ross-Gordon, Ed.D.
Associate Professor of Developmental and
    Adult Education
Department of Educational Administration
    and Psychological Services
Southwest Texas State University
San Marcos, TX 78666

Laura F. Rothstein, J.D.
Law Foundation Professor of Law
Law Center
University of Houston
Houston, TX 77204

David Scanlon, Ph.D.
Assistant Professor
Teacher Education Department
Boston College
Campion Hall
Chestnut Hill, MA 02167

Neil Sturomski, M.S.
Sturomski & Associates
1732 S Street, NW
Washington, D.C. 20009

Susan A. Vogel, Ph.D.
Professor of Special Education
Educational Psychology, Counseling, and
    Special Education Department
Graham Hall 145
Northern Illinois University
De Kalb, IL 60115

Laura P. Weisel, Ph.D.
Executive Clinical Consultant
The TLP Group
1179 Farview Avenue
Columbus, OH 43212

Barbara A. Wilson, B.A.
Director
Wilson Training Program
Wilson Training Corporation
175 West Main Street
Millbury, MA 01527

Glenn Young, M.P.A.
Learning Disabilities Specialist
National Institute for Literacy
800 Connecticut Avenue, NW
Suite 200
Washington, D.C. 20006

Foreword

Learning Disabilities, Literacy, and Adult Education deals with the long-neglected problem of learning disabilities (LD) and the relationship of LD to difficulties in the acquisition of literacy. I recall while teaching at Sangamon State University (now the University of Illinois at Springfield) that I had a student who would repeat words several times when responding to questions on exams, and each time he would spell the same word differently. For instance, on a single question, he might spell the word *pedestrian* first as *padestrian*, then as *pidestrian*, and then finally spell it correctly. As far as I could determine, apart from this characteristic, the student was neither illiterate nor experiencing any other difficulties in understanding the material. I asked the student whether he had ever been tested for a learning disability, and he said not to his knowledge. I decided to call his parents, who lived in an upper–middle-income Chicago suburb, and ask them whether their son had ever been tested–for LD. They said he had not.

At this point, I suggested that he be formally evaluated, and the results confirmed what I sensed: He was diagnosed as having a learning disability. Although the diagnosis of a learning disability alone did not make the student's difficulties disappear, he could begin to receive the appropriate accommodations and services to best promote his success.

Since this experience at Sangamon State University, I have encountered adults with undiagnosed LD a number of times. The most striking example that I recall was with Dexter Manley, a former star defensive player for the Washington Redskins football team. Manley had contacted me after I held a hearing on illiteracy. He wanted to come and speak before a U.S. Senate subcommittee. It was at this time that Manley told me about his history. He went through grade school and high school without learning to read. However, because of his great athletic ability, he was recruited by Oklahoma State University, where he played football for 4 years. Manley then was drafted into the National Football League.

It was not until Manley was standing on the sidelines watching as the Redskins' quarterback, Joe Theisman, broke his leg that Manley asked himself what would happen if he broke his own leg. Manley, who at the time was making $600,000 per year, made a courageous decision—a decision that took great strength and that few adults with LD at the height of their careers ever make. He contacted a school and admitted that he needed help. The school tested Dexter Manley and determined that he read at the second-grade level. After 8 years of elementary school, 4 years of high school, and 4 years at a collegiate institution, he could still read at only the second-grade level! The school also told Manley that he had a learning disability. By the time Manley testified before the U.S. Senate subcommittee, he had made huge progress and even spent part of his time studying Japanese.

This particular story does not have a happy ending. Unfortunately, before Manley began to face his learning disability, he developed a drug problem. My amateur analysis suggests that this happened because of an insecurity that grew out of his failure to receive the assistance needed to cope with his learning disability. Manley has tried to rid himself of his drug habit, but the last I heard was that he still had great difficulties. My instinct says that if someone had discovered his learning disability earlier, he would be doing much better today.

Learning Disabilities, Literacy, and Adult Education focuses on the difficulties surrounding LD, with scholars from the United States and the United Kingdom providing their insights. Although the book may not make *The New York Times* best-seller list, it will probably contribute more to society than 90% of the books that are on that list.

I hope that literacy providers, adult educators, LD teachers, academicians, policy makers, and parents will hear about this book and profit from it. If that happens, then society as a whole will profit.

Paul Simon
U.S. Senator
Southern Illinois University
Carbondale, Illinois

Preface

The concept underlying *Learning Disabilities, Literacy, and Adult Education* grew out of a chance meeting in 1992 at the National Institute for Literacy in Washington, D.C. Although the professionals who contributed to this book had read one another's work prior to this meeting, we were simply names to one another. Once introduced, however, we sat down and talked for hours, sharing our teaching experiences and research interests. It was immediately apparent that, although we come from different fields, we were all attempting to help the same individuals. Unfortunately, we had been working mostly in isolation.

The dialogue that began at the National Institute for Literacy led to a deeper understanding of one another's problems and goals, and together we learned from each other and acquired new insights. As a result of acquiring this experience, we realized that other adult educators and learning disabilities (LD) specialists could benefit from such an interchange. Our first attempts to spread this interchange were a series of symposia at various LD and literacy conferences in which literacy instructors and adult educators (many of whom contributed chapters to this book) came together and presented their programs leaving ample time for discussion. We learned that many professionals in formal and informal literacy education settings, developmental reading classes, adult education and adult secondary education courses, and workplace literacy classes were experiencing frustration because many of their students dropped out of their classes after only a few sessions.

These educators recognized that many of their students were capable and highly intelligent in spite of their reading, spelling, and writing difficulties. Because several of their students appeared to share some of the same characteristics as younger individuals with diagnosed LD, many instructors wondered whether some of their adult students also might have LD. The symposia participants expressed the desire to learn more about identifying adults with LD and helping these individuals in their attempts to acquire literacy skills.

Adult educators were not the only ones to express frustration at these symposia. A limited number of LD specialists who had experience working with adolescents with LD found themselves teaching adult education classes or developmental education courses in community colleges. Although these specialists were familiar with the field of LD, most of the information they possessed was relevant only for teaching younger individuals. These teachers were unfamiliar with adult developmental life stages and did not know how to adapt their instructional programs and materials to meet the needs of adults wishing to acquire functional literacy skills. In addition, the teachers were not aware of the assessment measures appropriate for this age bracket and level of proficiency. Moreover, literacy instructors and adult educators wanted to know how to screen their students for possible LD, where to refer them for assessment if they wanted a full evaluation, and how to modify their instructional programs to meet their needs.

OUR PURPOSE IN WRITING THIS BOOK

The major purpose of this book is to share cutting-edge developments and information from individuals in the forefront of their fields of LD, literacy, and adult education. The contributors represent this voice. They have contributed to both the formulation of the basic questions posed in each section as well as the book's content. They have established and deepened the dialogue regarding the questions that have been asked most frequently by literacy providers, adult educators, and learning disability teachers. The contributors came together eager to learn from each other, and we want to share this excitement with a wider audience.

THE UNDERLYING ASSUMPTIONS OF THE BOOK

1. Based on breakthroughs in brain and genetics research funded by the National Institute on Child Health and Human Development, it is now possible to demonstrate the existence of the most common type of learning disability—namely, reading disabilities (i.e., dyslexia)—to even the most skeptical audiences.
2. Although alternative definitions of learning disability exist, there is general consensus regarding the concept of learning disability as defined by the National Joint Committee on Learning Disabilities.
3. Identifying LD in adults is an important first step toward self-understanding, and this can empower individuals with this diagnosis to set and achieve their goals.
4. Learning in adults is in some respects similar to and in some respects different from learning in children. Some needs apply to individuals of all ages: learning to read, write, spell, and solve basic mathematical problems.
5. Adult educators must be cognizant of the fundamentally different nature of the relationship between adult learners and teachers and the relationship between school children and their teachers.
6. Learning disability specialists working with adults who have LD must be cognizant of the following:
   • Adults' purposes and/or goals in wanting to learn
   • The immediacy of the endeavor
   • The need to teach efficiently
   • The need for adults to apply new learning to their employment settings and/or to their personal lives
   • The necessity to view learning in a broader context, including much more than academic skills
7. Time must be allocated for immediate application of learning to the individual's own needs (e.g., employment concerns, helping children with schoolwork, negotiating bureaucratic systems, gaining access to and understanding written materials about personal interests and hobbies).

ORGANIZATION AND CONTENT: AN OVERVIEW

This book is divided into five sections. Each section begins with a section opener that helps the reader to identify the main themes and content of each chapter in that section.

The chapters in Section I address some of the most basic questions surrounding LD, including the definition, cause, prevalence, and characteristics of the disorder. Three additional questions round out this section:

1. What laws safeguard individuals with LD against discrimination in educational settings and in employment?
2. What is known about the educational attainment of adults with LD?
3. What do LD teachers need and want to know about adult literacy education?

The chapters in Section II address, from various vantage points, the basic questions of whether and how adult education students with LD should be identified. Chapter 5 describes the standards, criteria, and procedures that can be used to evaluate screening measures or procedures. Chapter 6 focuses on the rationale, components, and usefulness of informal assessment. Chapter 7 offers a description of a computer-assisted procedure to screen adults in literacy education settings, and Chapter 8 gives a brief overview of a screening procedure developed in the United Kingdom. Chapter 9 describes a project undertaken in Washington state to validate a widely used screening procedure.

The chapters in Section III address the question of how adult education students with LD should be taught. Chapters 10 and 11 address the question of reading instruction, and Chapter 12 addresses the question of mathematics. Chapter 13 considers an alternative approach to helping adults to augment their basic skills—namely, by using assistive technology.

The chapters in Section IV address various important issues beyond the classroom for adults with LD: career counseling, job training, and transition to employment. Chapter 14 describes a highly successful employment program that is developed on a community-based residential model. Chapter 15 describes a range of field-tested effective practices in assessment and training for employment. Chapter 16 draws on case studies of adults with LD who have achieved a high degree of success in the workplace.

Chapter 17 in Section V is a capstone chapter that reviews the complete book from an adult literacy education perspective. Chapter 17 addresses what has been learned and what remains to be learned about essential questions raised in the book. The critical questions that this book raises include the prevalence of LD among adult education students, whether and how adult literacy students should be screened for LD, whether those students identified as having LD should be taught differently from other adult literacy students, and the most effective types of instructional and noninstructional interventions for adults with LD. Chapter 17 concludes with various recommendations for future directions in research, policy, and practice.

Following Section V are three appendices. Appendix A provides a list of accommodations that may be helpful when a student has a suspected or identified learning disability. Appendix B provides a product resource list of technology for adults with LD. Appendix C provides an information resource and clearinghouse list of major sources of information in the fields of LD, literacy, and adult education.

IN CLOSING

We hope that this book will stimulate more dialogue and collaboration between the fields of LD and adult education as well as between researchers and practitioners in these two fields. If this interaction occurs, then many adults with LD will benefit. By helping adult students with LD capitalize on their strengths and compensate for their weaknesses, we will enable them to take fuller advantage of many more opportunities for learning.

Acknowledgments

We wish to acknowledge our heartfelt appreciation to a number of individuals who contributed to the preparation and completion of this book. We extend our sincere gratitude to Elaine Niefeld, Editorial Director at Paul H. Brookes Publishing Co., who gave us the opportunity to persevere and bring this book to fruition. Her expertise was invaluable. We are also indebted to Seth G. Morrison, Book Production Editor, who worked tirelessly on the editorial content and production of this book. We are grateful to these two individuals for their encouragement, wise counsel, and expertise throughout the process.

In addition, we are indebted to Deborah Holderness and Marion Gilbert, whose expertise was invaluable in the preparation of this book. Last, we would like to acknowledge our many friends, colleagues, adult learners, and adults with learning disabilities who inspired us to pull together the thoughts, knowledge, experiences, and research presented in this book. They confirmed for us the need for such a book as well as encouraged and affirmed us in our endeavors.

To our mothers and fathers—Natalie and Louis Sugarman and Edna and Melvin Reder—whose sharp minds; natural curiosity; love of learning; and dedication to their families, friends, and students have served to inspire us throughout our lives

Learning Disabilities,
Literacy, and Adult Education

Introduction

Section I is designed to bridge the knowledge gap that exists among professionals from the fields of learning disabilities (LD), adult education, and literacy instruction. Professionals in the field of LD often know a lot about children and youth with LD; however, they need more information about the distinct characteristics of adults with LD, about the legislation that mandates reasonable accommodations in postsecondary education and employment settings, about adult development, and about adult education alternatives. Adult educators have expertise in adult development and literacy education but may be unable to distinguish the differences between adults with poor literacy skills and those with LD—namely, the characteristics of adults with LD; the cutting-edge research regarding the causes of LD, especially the most widespread type of learning disability (i.e., reading disabilities); and the legislation that mandates program accessibility and reasonable accommodations that must be provided for adults with documented LD.

Regardless of the background and expertise of many professionals, until the 1990s no one quite knew how widespread LD were among adults with low levels of literacy, the educational levels that adults with LD had achieved, the causes of reading disabilities, or how adults with LD should be identified and taught. Section I addresses these topics and attempts to bring together the most up-to-date information on LD for all professionals who work with adults who have diagnosed or suspected LD.

In Chapter 1, Susan A. Vogel sets the tone for this book by explaining the various definitions of LD. Vogel focuses her attention on describing the laws that protect those with LD, the characteristics and prevalence of LD, the causes of the most common type of LD (i.e., reading disabilities, or dyslexia), and the rationale for identifying adults with LD in adult literacy education settings. Vogel offers several cost-effective models for identifying and documenting LD in adulthood.

In Chapter 2, Laura F. Rothstein describes the significant legislation that protects the rights of individuals with LD in educational and employment settings. Through a careful review of case law (beginning with the passage of Section 504 of the Rehabilitation Act of 1973 [PL 93-112]), Rothstein provides the most up-to-date information regarding learning disability legislation and accommodations in postsecondary educational settings as well as learning disability licensing and professional examinations. Rothstein provides a series of strategies to ensure compliance with learning disability legislation, including strategies that address inappropriate attitudes, lack of knowledge or incorrect information, and the development of learning disability policies and procedures. Many of these recommendations are useful in postsecondary education and adult literacy settings that offer adult education courses, in state agencies that administer learning disability licensing examinations and in the trades/unions/apprenticeships.

In Chapter 3, Susan A. Vogel and Stephen Reder provide an in-depth review of the educational attainment of adults with school-identified, clinic-identified, and self-reported LD in national samples and smaller regional, clinic, and specific private school samples. In these samples (in which the ratio of males to females differed), the high school dropout rates, postsecondary enrollment patterns, and degree completion rates differed. Some of the factors that had an impact on these variations were differences in age range, gender distribution, ethnic background, and the passage of significant legislation (e.g., the Education for All Handicapped Children Act of 1975 [PL 94-142]). Corresponding with the findings regarding the prevalence of LD in adults that Vogel presented in Chapter 1, Vogel and Reder conclude that there is no definitive answer regarding the educational attainment or gender ratio among adults with LD but rather a range depending on the age and literacy proficiency of the group and whether the group members were self-identified, school-identified, or research-identified.

In Chapter 4, Jovita Ross-Gordon provides an overview of adult education and literacy education for the benefit of those readers who are new to the field—mainly those readers who come to this book with background and expertise in LD. This overview is followed by a description of the increased awareness regarding LD among adult educators. This increase in awareness has come to the fore as a result of the increasing number of opportunities for staff development through printed materials, workshops, and interactive videotaped materials. Ross-Gordon provides a description of the various curriculums and program developments that have accompanied several of these growth opportunities. Ross-Gordon also addresses several questions that bridge the fields of adult literacy, adult education, and LD.

REFERENCES

Education for All Handicapped Children Act of 1975, PL 94-142, 20 U.S.C. §§ 1400 *et. seq.*
Rehabilitation Act of 1973, PL 93-112, 29 U.S.C. §§ 701 *et seq.*

1

Adults with Learning Disabilities

What Learning Disabilities Specialists, Adult Literacy Educators, and Other Service Providers Want and Need to Know

Susan A. Vogel

The impetus for this book can be attributed to Goal Five of the National Education Goals 2000, which stated that "by the year 2000 every adult American will be literate and will possess the knowledge and skills necessary to compete in a global economy and exercise the rights and responsibilities of citizenship" (National Education Goals Panel, 1991, p. 113).

Literacy was first given front and center attention by Senator Paul Simon when he spearheaded the effort to raise the literacy level of all adults in the United States by crafting the National Literacy Act of 1991 (PL 102-73). This Act defined *literacy* in Section 3 as "the ability to read, write, and speak in English, and compute and solve problems at levels of proficiency necessary to function on the job and in society, to achieve one's goals, and develop one's knowledge and potential." It was enacted because of the widespread and serious problems of illiteracy among adults; because literacy problems are intergenerational and are closely associated with poverty (Reder, 1995; Reder & Vogel, 1997); and because present literacy programs reach only a small portion of the U.S. population who need to improve their literacy proficiency (Reder, 1995; Vogel & Reder, in press), and many of those who participate make only very modest gains (Reder, 1995).

The National Literacy Act also mandated the creation of the National Institute for Literacy, whose initial funding priorities included a mandate to develop projects for adults with English as a Second Language (ESL) and those with learning disabilities (LD). At that time, not much was known regarding the prevalence of LD among adults in the United States, but some estimated the prevalence of LD in adults in adult education classes to be as high as 80% (Travis, 1979). More conservative estimates were made by leaders in the field of adult literacy, such as Peter Waite (1991), President of Laubach Literacy Action, who concluded that between 25% and 50% of adults in local Laubach programs have LD. According to Waite, some of these adults, if not most, are unaware that they have LD, for a variety of reasons including their having been enrolled in elementary or secondary school prior to passage of the Education for All Handicapped Children Act of 1975 (PL 94-142), which mandated that school districts must screen children and youth for disabilities and that the public schools must provide a free appropriate public education for all children and youth, including those with disabilities.

In order to teach adults with identified or suspected LD most effectively, the National Institute for Literacy established the National Adult Literacy and Learning Disabilities Center to raise the level of awareness, knowledge, and expertise of LD specialists and adult literacy educators about LD in adults; to identify or to develop validated screening tools to identify those adults who are at high risk for LD; to identify effective teaching strategies and materials to teach adults with LD; and to prepare adult literacy providers and LD specialists in the use of these strategies and tools. This book was conceived to assist LD and adult literacy providers in learning about the progress that has been made to date in accomplishing these goals.

CHARACTERISTICS OF ADULTS WITH LEARNING DISABILITIES

A very important basic assumption of this book is that LD are not just a difficulty of childhood nor are they specific to school settings and academic endeavors. There has been growing awareness and increased understanding among LD specialists, adult literacy educators, and other professionals that LD, although their manifestations may change, persist into adulthood and affect all aspects of life, even among those who have overcome their reading disabilities or are gifted, highly educated, and recognized in their professions (Blalock, 1981, 1982; Bruck, 1987, 1990, 1992; Dinklage, 1971; Fink, 1997; Frauenheim, 1978; Gerber, 1997; Gerber, Ginsberg, & Reiff, 1992; Gerber & Reiff, 1991; Johnson & Blalock, 1987; Rawson, 1968; Reder, 1995; Rogan & Hartman, 1990; Simpson, 1979; Vogel, 1985, 1997b).

More specifically, the focus of this chapter is on the most common type of LD— namely, language-based LD or difficulties in oral language, reading, and/or writing, often referred to as dyslexia. Moreover, another basic assumption is that LD occur on a continuum from mild to severe; this chapter and, in fact, this book focuses mainly on adults with significant problems in acquiring functional literacy skills because of LD. We begin by providing a chronological overview of the definitions of *learning disabilities*, the laws that protect adults with LD, and the prevalence of LD in adults in different segments of the U.S. population. This information provides the backdrop for a description of the characteristics of adults with LD; the causes of reading disabilities; the rationale for identification and assessment of adults with LD; and several different national models for providing assessment, documentation, and determination of eligibility for services and accommodations.

DEFINITIONS OF LEARNING DISABILITIES

The earliest and most widely used definition of LD was incorporated into the original Education for All Handicapped Children Act (U.S. Office of Education, 1977) and each subsequent version through the Individuals with Disabilities Education Act (IDEA) Amendments of 1997 (PL 105-17). It is the definition that all subsequent statutes refer to, and it states the following:

> The term "specific learning disability" [SLD] means those children who have a disorder in one or more of the basic psychological processes involved in understanding or in using language, spoken or written, which disorder may manifest itself in imperfect ability to listen, think, speak, read, write, spell, or to do mathematical calculations. The term includes such conditions as perceptual handicaps, brain injury, minimal brain dysfunction, dyslexia, and developmental aphasia. The term does not include a learning problem which is primarily the result of visual, hearing, or motor handicaps, of mental retardation, or emotional disturbance, or of environmental, cultural, or economic disadvantage. (U.S. Office of Education, 1977, p. 65083)

The second part of the definition includes regulations that enable the identification of SLD in those students who did not achieve in one or more of the seven listed areas commensurate with their age and ability level despite having been given the opportunity to learn and who demonstrated a severe discrepancy between intellectual ability and one or more of the seven areas. The foundational concepts that were incorporated into the definition and the implementing regulations are still widely accepted:

1. An individual with a SLD has to have a "disorder in one or more of the basic psychological processes," which include auditory and visual memory, perception, discrimination, analysis, synthesis, sequencing, and figure–ground.
2. The "seven areas of disability" include listening comprehension, speaking, written language, basic reading skills, reading comprehension, mathematical calculations, and mathematical reasoning.
3. "A severe discrepancy" has to exist between intellectual ability and one of the seven areas of disability.

One of the major criticisms of the IDEA definition is that it refers to children rather than individuals of all ages. Certainly the Association for Children with Learning Disabilities (ACLD), the organization whose members (mostly parents of individuals with LD) spearheaded the efforts to include LD in the federal law, was one of the first groups to raise the level of awareness regarding the persistence of LD into adulthood. This awareness was reflected in the change of the name of the ACLD in March 1988 to the Learning Disabilities Association of America (LDA). Following are four other definitions.

National Joint Committee on Learning Disabilities Definition of Learning Disabilities

The first widely accepted revision of the definition of LD was developed in 1981 and revised in 1988 by the National Joint Committee on Learning Disabilities (NJCLD), a committee composed of representatives of the major professional organizations concerned with LD. The revised definition states that

> Learning disabilities is a general term that refers to a heterogeneous group of disorders manifested by significant difficulties in the acquisition and use of listening, speaking, reading, writing, reasoning, or mathematical abilities. These disorder are intrinsic to the individual, presumed to be due to central nervous system dysfunction, and may occur across the life span. Problems in self-regulatory behaviors, social perception, and social interaction may exist with learning disabilities but do not by themselves constitute a learning disability. Although learning disabilities may occur concomitantly with other handicapping conditions (for example,

sensory impairment, mental retardation, social and emotional disturbance) or with environmental influences (such as cultural differences, insufficient/inappropriate instruction, psychogenic factors), it is not the result of those conditions or influences. (1994, pp. 65–66)

The NJCLD definition was the first to acknowledge that LD affect individuals of all ages, not just children; that LD are a heterogeneous group of disorders; that the cause of LD is intrinsic to the individual and is a "presumed central nervous system dysfunction"; and that LD can occur concomitantly with other disabilities.

Interagency Committee on Learning Disabilities Definition

At about the same time that the NJCLD definition first appeared, the U.S. Congress appointed a 12-member committee representing 12 agencies within the U.S Department of Health and Human Services and the U.S. Department of Education for the express purpose of developing a definition of LD. This committee, referred to as the Interagency Committee on Learning Disabilities (ICLD), produced a definition very similar to that of the NJCLD, with one significant addition: Social skills difficulties were included as one of the manifestations in the list of significant areas of difficulty (ICLD, 1987). Although it gained considerable support at that time from the LDA, the Rehabilitation Services Administration (RSA), and the National Adult Literacy and Learning Disabilities Center, the ICLD definition was considered problematic. It was criticized by professionals in the field of LD because of opposition to the inclusion of social skills difficulties in the absence of one or more of the other areas of difficulty and by professionals in social-emotional disorders because of the possibility of a blurring of the distinction between LD and social-emotional disorders in both diagnosis and treatment.

Association of Children with Learning Disabilities Definition

The leadership within the ACLD resonated to the inclusion of social skills difficulties in the ICLD definition and incorporated this concept into the definition that it approved in 1984 (Association for Children with Learning Disabilities [ACLD], 1986). This definition also emphasized the chronicity of LD and the impact of LD on employment and daily living. The LDA definition reads

> Specific Learning Disabilities is a chronic condition of presumed neurological origin which selectively interferes with the development, integration, and/or demonstration of verbal and/or non-verbal abilities. Specific Learning Disabilities exists as a distinct handicapping condition and varies in its manifestations and in degree of severity. Throughout life, the condition can affect self-esteem, education, vocation, socialization, and/or daily living activities. (ACLD, 1986, p. 15)

In light of our present understanding of LD, the acknowledgment that SLD can affect "vocation, . . . and/or daily living activities" and not just language functioning and academic achievement makes the ACLD definition an important addition to the development of the field.

Vocational Rehabilitation Services Definition

The mid-1980s brought about another important change to the legislation that governed identification (Mulkey, Kopp, & Miller, 1984) and services for individuals in the workforce and gave rise to yet another important definition of LD. Perhaps as a result of the strong protest and advocacy of leaders of the self-help organizations for adults with LD, along with that of professionals (Gregg & Phillips, 1996) and the increase in awareness of the impact of such disabilities on employment success, the RSA in 1980 revised its policy of recognition of LD (RSA, Task Force on Learning Disabilities, 1980; RSA, 1980). No longer was it necessary for a learning disability to be diagnosed as a medical disability according to the criteria of the American Psychiatric Association (1980) or the U.S. Department of Health and Human Services (1980) (Gerber, 1981). In 1985, the federal and state vocational rehabilitation (VR) system was required to comply with the revised RSA definition of *learning disability*, which read

> A specific learning disability is a specific disorder in one or more of the central nervous system processes involved in perceiving, understanding and/or using concepts through verbal (spoken or written) language or nonverbal means. This disorder manifests itself with a deficit in one or more of the following areas: attention, reasoning, processing, memory, communication, reading, writing, spelling, calculation, coordination, social competence and emotional maturity.

Similar to the ICLD definition, the RSA definition recognized the importance of social skills on the job. Because of the observations of VR counselors that, when problems on the job occur, they are often the result of attentional problems, social immaturity, and nonverbal communication skills impairments (Koller, 1997; see also Chapter 15), the RSA definition included these additional concepts. Since these major revisions were put in place, the percentage of consumers with LD who received VR services and were gainfully employed increased from 1.3% of all VR consumers in 1983 to 7.95% in 1994 (Koller, 1997). An increase in training opportunities for VR personnel in assessment and services for adults with SLD has also occurred (Dowdy & Smith, 1994; Koller, 1994, 1997; Koller, Holliday, & Multon, 1996; McCue, 1984, 1987; Vogel, 1989a; Zwerlein, Smith, & Diffley, 1984: see also Chapter 15).

LEARNING DISABILITIES AND THE LAW

LD also have a legal reality (Gregg, Johnson, & McKinley, 1996). Adults diagnosed with LD are protected from discrimination under two specific laws: The Rehabilitation Act of 1973 (PL 93-112), specifically its most applicable provision Section 504, and the Americans with Disabilities Act (ADA) of 1990 (PL 101-336). Both of these statutes acknowledge the existence and persistence of LD throughout life. Section 504 has its most profound impact on adults with disabilities in educational environments, that of the ADA, on adults in employment. Because these two statutes protect individuals with disabilities from discrimination, provide equal educational and employment opportunities, and utilize much of the same terminology, they are discussed together here. First, it may be helpful to clarify some of the key concepts in both of these statutes:

1. "Accommodations" to be provided for individuals with LD in an educational environment include equal opportunity for acceptance in the application process, providing or modifying equipment, and modifying instructional methodology and examination procedures to ensure that individuals with a disability have an equal opportunity to learn and to be evaluated on the basis of their knowledge and skills rather than on the basis of their disability.
2. "Reasonable" refers to accommodations that do not impose undo hardship on an institution.
3. According to these statutes, a person with a disability has a "physical or mental impairment which substantially limits one or more major life activities, has a record of such an impairment, or is regarded as having such an impairment" (ADA § 1613.702 [b][2]).

4. "Physical or mental impairments" include mental retardation, organic brains syndrome, emotional or mental illness, and specific learning disabilities (ADA § 1613.702 [b][2]).

5. Because LD affect learning, they are included under Section 504. However, it is not sufficient that the individual has a learning disability; this disability must be severe enough to substantially limit one or more major life activities. "Major life activities" are defined as including caring for oneself; being able to hear, see, speak, walk, and work; and also being able to learn.

6. A "substantial limitation" is interpreted to mean that the person is either unable to perform the task or is substantially restricted as compared with the average person.

7. The concept "otherwise qualified" pertains to adults with LD in literacy environments, job-training, adult education and adult secondary education (ASE) classes, and postsecondary institutions who meet the criteria for admission and participation in education programs or activities.

8. A "program or activity" is defined as all education programs that receive federal subsidies and grants and, therefore, includes all public elementary and secondary schools; adult educational environments, such as adult education and ASE programs; and postsecondary vocational, trade, and military schools, and public independent colleges and universities.

Some of the instructional and examination accommodations most frequently requested of instructors include providing assignments in writing after going over them orally in class; explaining technical vocabulary, specific terminology, or foreign words; reading aloud what is written on the chalkboard or overhead transparencies; and providing extra time, a quiet environment, or both for those students who are easily distracted (Vogel, 1997b; see other accommodations listed in Appendix A at the end of this book). In literacy and adult education classes, these types of accommodations do not usually present a problem. In some courses or programs (e.g., ASE and postsecondary settings), however, the instructor may be concerned that the requested accommodation may modify the objectives or essential competencies of the course/program, or both. In order to address this question, it is incumbent on instructors to identify the essential content, skills, and competencies of each program and inform applicants/participants of them (Rothstein, 1993).

Section 504 and the ADA give decision-making authority and responsibility to determine the essential functions, skills, and/or competencies to the instructional staff, employer, or accrediting organization. Requests for accommodations must be accompanied by documentation indicating that the presence of a disability interferes with the individual's ability to perform a task in the same manner as individuals without disabilities. Both the type of accommodation and the intensity must be described explicitly. For example, individuals with dyslexia may need prerecorded, objective examination questions and alternative multiple choices so they can listen, and re-listen if necessary, just as someone would reread a particularly complex question. In addition, because listening comprehension and processing rates may be slower for individuals with LD as compared with those without such disabilities, individuals with LD may request extended time. The exact amount of time requested should be based on a comparison of performance on a standardized reading comprehension test administered under timed versus untimed conditions. However, if performing a task quickly is an essential objective or aspect of the job, then it would be inappropriate to give extended time. The underlying rationale for provision of extended time is that the goal of evaluation is to determine the level of mastery of the objectives rather than the level of mastery under specific time constraints. That is not to say that there are not some specific skills and competencies that must be performed under strict time conditions (e.g., performing a tracheotomy when the windpipe is occluded). In such instances, competence must include rapidity of decision making and performance to avoid loss of life, and therefore extended time is an unacceptable accommodation. In most situations and work environments, time is not as essential to performance as in this example. In fact, in a 15-year follow-up study of 50 adults ages 30–59 with LD regarding the impact of the disability on the job and how they compensate, 46% indicated that they spend more time at their own expense to get the job done (Vogel & Adelman, 1997).

Although these laws cover adults with LD in slightly different arenas of life functioning, their message is clear: LD are not a myth. LD, similar to sensory loss and physical disabilities, alter the learning process and can have a profound impact on the acquisition of literacy skills and essential knowledge needed to be gainfully employed and economically self-sufficient. Given that individuals with LD are protected under several different statutes and that the awareness of the persistence of LD into adulthood has increased dramatically, what do we know about how widespread the problem of LD is in adults?

PREVALENCE RATE

There is a growing body of reliable data indicating that LD in adults are a widespread problem. Previously, we have only had estimates of the prevalence rate of adults with LD in specific segments of the population, including various formal and informal educational and workplace training environments. Some estimates have been alarmingly high. For example, Travis (1979) was one of the first to speculate that the prevalence of LD in adult education settings was high, possibly as high as 80%. In contrast, the U.S. Employment and Training Administration (1991) estimated that between 15% and 23% of Job Training Partnership Act Title IIA (PL 97-300) recipients may have a learning disability. Based on Department of Labor observations, the percentage of adults with LD increased to 50% and 80% among those reading below the seventh-grade level (U.S. Employment and Training Administration, 1991). Ryan and Price (1993) asked directors of ABE programs in the 50 states and two American territories to estimate the prevalence of adults with LD in ABE classes. The estimates ranged from less than 10% to more than 50%, with 21% of the ABE directors estimating that more than 50% of students were suspected of having LD while only 19% said that less than 10% were at such risk.

Prevalence of Self-Reported Learning Disabilities

Additional perspectives on the prevalence of LD in adults are provided by the U.S. Department of Education, National Center for Education Statistics (NCES), and the American Council on Education (ACE). The NCES and the ACE regularly report national statistics regarding the incidence of self-reported learning disabilities (SRLD) in a national representative sample. The NCES reports on full-time freshmen with SRLD as well as graduate/professional school students (U.S. Department of Education, 1994), whereas the ACE reports only on full-time, first-time college freshmen (Henderson, 1995). The ACE data are part of a larger study of college freshmen conducted every 3 years by the Cooperative Institutional Research Program at the University of

California–Los Angeles. Although the percentage of students with self-reported disabilities other than LD has remained almost constant since 1978, the percentage of students with SRLD increased from 1.6% in 1985 to 3.0% in 1994. When the prevalence was examined according to the type of degree-granting institution, both Henderson and the U.S. Department of Education reported a much higher rate of students with SRLD in 2-year colleges than in public or private universities. According to Henderson, 54.4% of the full-time freshmen with SRLD attended a 2-year college, compared with only 11.8% who attended a university, thus confirming that there is a higher prevalence rate of students with SRLD in community colleges. There is also a growing awareness that the students with LD enrolled in community colleges have more severe disabilities.

The increase in students with SRLD has been attributed to several factors, including increased awareness among professionals, parents, and individuals with LD of the increased availability of support services in higher education (Vogel et al., 1998) and awareness of college and university faculty of the needs of students with documented LD (Leyser, 1989; Leyser, Vogel, Brulle, & Wyland, in press; Vogel, Leyser, Brulle, & Wyland, 1997). In addition, we cannot rule out the possibility of genuine demographic changes and medical advances resulting in an increase in the incidence of postsecondary students with other disabilities (e.g., closed head injuries) and the resulting complications, including LD.

Prevalence of Documented Learning Disabilities

A third national collegiate database—the National Learning Disabilities Data Bank (Vogel et al., in press)—was designed to determine the incidence of students with documented LD (Vogel, 1987) enrolled in a nationally representative sample of 502 postsecondary institutions drawn randomly from the total list of approximately 3,000 such institutions divided by Carnegie classification (e.g., size, type, independent/public, degrees granted, grant money). The sample included undergraduate, graduate, and professional schools ranging from the most highly selective to those with open admission. The purpose of this survey was to determine the prevalence of students with LD, to describe the available support services, and to identify institutional and support services characteristics that may have influenced the proportion of students with LD on these campuses. Unlike the ACE and the NCES databases, the prevalence of LD in this survey was not based on self-report because all participating institutions required documentation of a disability in order to provide accommodations and services (Vogel et al., in press). Although these institutions reported that, on average, 2.6% of the student body had documented LD, the percentage of such students on these campuses varied from 0.5% in the most highly selective institutions to 10% in open admission colleges. Using this national database and that of the ACE, it is clear that prevalence rates vary significantly by institution type, size of student body, and degrees offered (Vogel et al., in press). However, it is very important to keep in mind that one of the limitations of national collegiate databases is precisely that they represent only one segment of the total population of adults with LD: those who enroll in a postsecondary institution. What do we know about the prevalence of LD in adults in the United States?

Prevalence in the General Population

The first national database on adults with LD in the general U.S. population was compiled in response to the Adult Education Amendments of 1988 (PL 100-297), which required that the U.S. Department of Education assess the literacy proficiency and practices of adults in the nation. The NCES was then charged with the task of concretely identifying the basic education skills needed for literate functioning and, in conjunction with the Education Testing Service, developed the National Adult Literacy Survey (NALS). The survey (Kirsch, 1993) was administered to a nationally representative sample of 26,000 individuals ages 16 years or older. It included direct assessment of literacy skills and activities; language background; educational and work experiences; health problems; and disabilities, if any. In regard to health problems and disabilities, participants were asked whether they had a physical, mental, or other health condition that kept them from participating fully in work, school, housework, or other activities. The 12% of respondents who said "yes" to this question were then asked a series of follow-up questions to determine the specific disability. In response, 3% of these participants said that they had a learning disability (Kirsch, Jungeblut, Jenkins, & Kolstad, 1993).

Based on the previously reviewed estimates of LD in adults, the percentage of adults in the United States with SRLD who responded to the NALS on first glance seems very low, especially in light of the annual national child count statistics, in which the percentage of school-age individuals (6–17 years old) with LD who received services in the 1993–1994 school year was 5.27% (U.S. Department of Education, 1995). Given that the adults in the NALS database were ages 16 and older and many of them were not in school when IDEA mandated "search and screen" for children with disabilities, many of these adults were probably unaware that their reading difficulties were a result of a learning disability, which may account for the discrepancy in the prevalence rates. Likewise, a similar although less dramatic increase in the prevalence rate was found when the SRLD group who responded to the NALS was segmented by literacy proficiency and educational attainment. The prevalence rate among those with the poorest literacy skills and those who completed less than 8 years of school increased four- to fivefold to between 10% and 15%, respectively, which is similar to the 15%–20% prevalence estimates of dyslexia based on clinical and research identification (Lyon, 1995; Reder, 1995; Vogel & Reder, in press; see also Chapter 3).

Prevalence by Gender

Finally, what do we know about the prevalence of SRLD and school-identified LD among males and females? It is a common observation that, in school-identified groups of students with LD, there is a 4:1 ratio of boys to girls. In contrast, in research and self-identified samples there is almost an equal number of men and women with LD (Lyon, 1994; Moats & Lyon, 1993; Shaywitz, Shaywitz, Fletcher, & Escobar, 1990; Vogel, 1990). This gender ratio is very similar to that found among the adults with SRLD who responded to the NALS, in which an almost equal number of men and women indicated that they had a learning disability. The reason for the sharp contrast in gender ratio in school-identified samples and research or self-identified samples pertains to referral bias in school-identified samples and higher prevalence of attention-deficit/hyperactivity disorder (ADHD) and LD in males, resulting in males being referred for assessment and found eligible for special services more frequently than females (Shaywitz et al., 1990; Vogel, 1990).

Summary

We have seen that there is neither one prevalence rate, nor one definitive gender ratio, for LD in adults but rather a variety of rates and ratios based on which segment and which age range of the adult group are scrutinized and in which environment they are located. The NALS database made it possible to determine the prevalence of SRLD in adults grouped in addition by literacy proficiency, educational attainment, and gender.

The National Learning Disabilities Data Bank made it possible to compare the prevalence of students with LD in different types of colleges and universities; both undergraduates and graduate students (e.g., community colleges, 4-year colleges/universities); and some of the pioneering work of adult literacy educators and LD specialists provided us with estimates of the prevalence of LD among participants in ABE, Aid to Families with Dependent Children (AFDC), and Job Opportunities and Basic Skills literacy education settings. Just as there is no one type of severity of learning disability, there is no one prevalence rate or gender ratio but rather a range depending on the parameters described previously. Thus, by comparing the different databases, we are now in a better position to understand the reasons for the differences in reported prevalence rates.

CHARACTERISTICS OF ADULTS WITH LEARNING DISABILITIES

When adults enroll in adult education or ASE classes, developmental education classes in postsecondary education settings, job training or literacy classes, or postsecondary vocational education programs, they bring with them a history of past difficulties, failure experiences, and present frustrations.

A comprehensive listing of the manifestations or characteristics of adults with LD that have been reported in the literature (Vogel, 1985) in the areas of oral language, reading, written language, math, study skills, and attentional problems appears in Table 1.1. Through careful analysis of the literature (Blalock, 1981, 1982; Bruck; 1987, 1990, 1992; Gottesman, 1994; Johnson, 1994, 1995; Johnson & Blalock, 1987; Vogel, 1985, 1997b; Vogel & Adelman, 1993; see also Chapter 3) and detailed case histories (Vogel, 1985), the most frequently mentioned characteristics (strengths and limitations) of adults with LD were identified and grouped into six domains: oral language, reading, written language, mathematics, study skills, and attentional difficulties.

Within this master list, Vogel (1985) developed a checklist and identified the areas of greatest difficulty, defined as those identified by 50% or more of adults with LD enrolled in a college setting. From the highest to the lowest percentage, the difficulties were concentrating in a noisy environment (72%); reading comprehension, reading fast, spelling, learning the rules of grammar, and working math word problems (62%); and learning a foreign language, learning the rules of punctuation and capitalization, taking essay exams, writing compositions, recognizing misspelled words, and reading in front of a group (52%–55%). It is not surprising that almost half of the adults still had difficulties in mastery of multiplication (45%), and one third had difficulties with keyboarding. It is interesting to note that 12 of the 15 areas of difficulty identified by half or more of the adults with LD have a language basis. The exceptions included the item mentioned the most frequently, auditory distractibility or difficulty filtering out extraneous noise in the environment; keyboarding; and long-term auditory memory for number facts. These tasks and the percentages of individuals who identified them as a difficulty in the past or present appear in Table 1.2.

It is important to note that individuals with LD have varying strengths and difficulties. Areas of difficulty for some adults are areas of strength for others. It is also important to keep in mind that LD are not a generalized problem of learning but are specific to certain domains. It is this characteristic jagged profile of abilities that led to the concept of discrepancy between one or more of the six areas of achievement and intelligence in the identification process.

The requirement of determination of a severe discrepancy in order to establish the presence of a learning disability and eligibility for K–12 special services has been

Table 1.1.   Specific difficulties of adults with learning disabilities

Oral language

- Difficulty perceiving sounds or syllables within words in the correct sequence
- Incomplete or imprecise comprehension of affixes
- Difficulty understanding abstract words, idioms, or complex syntax
- Difficulty correctly perceiving similar-sounding words (e.g., *lent* for *tent* or *rent*)
- Difficulty segmenting a word into its individual sounds/syllables, especially multisyllabic words
- Difficulty comprehending oral language presented at a rapid rate
- Difficulty providing synonyms for a word
- Difficulty providing precise definition of a word without a lot of circumlocution
- Vocabulary weaknesses
- Inaccurate comprehension of transition words
- Difficulty following a long speech or lecture
- Difficulty expressing ideas succinctly
- Difficulty relaying a series of events in the correct sequence
- Difficulty using new terminology or technical language correctly
- Grammatical errors; usage unlike the community in which he or she grew up
- Word-finding difficulties (e.g., *exhilarated* for *accelerated*) or use of nonspecific words (e.g., *thingamajig*)
- Pauses in spoken language while searching for a word or name
- Difficulty pronouncing multisyllabic words (e.g., *stastistics* for *statistics, amonymity* for *anonymity*)

- Slightly slurred speech even when not fatigued
- Difficulty learning a foreign language
- Slow rate of expression
- Incorrect use of prepositions
- Difficulty pronouncing certain words (e.g., *flustration* for *frustration*)
- Oral language is far superior to written language, especially when writing under pressure of time, without the use of assistive technology, or both
- Overuse of self-correction, revision, and "empty" words (e.g., *uh, unh, mmm*)
- Problems with the pragmatics of oral language, including
  - knowing how to initiate, sustain, and break into a conversation or ask a question
  - knowing how to enter into an ongoing conversation without interrupting someone
  - knowing how personal or impersonal to be
  - knowing how to modify/vary the linguistic code based on audience, conversational partner, and setting
  - difficulty understanding and using humor and catching on to jokes
  - knowing how to tell jokes, when a joke is appropriate and when it is not, and which joke is appropriate in which setting
  - difficulty with idiomatic language
  - inappropriate vocal intensity for setting and relationship
  - inappropriate distance maintained between speaker and listener
  - difficulty understanding intonation patterns (e.g., sarcasm, teasing)

Reading

- Inaccurate decoding
- Inaccurate comprehension
  - difficulty understanding sentences with complex syntax structure (e.g., double negatives)
  - vocabulary weaknesses
  - difficulty remembering details (e.g., specific names, dates, places)
  - difficulty understanding the main ideas
  - comprehends at only a very literal level
  - difficulty with inferential comprehension

- Poor retention of what is read
- A passive reader
- Slow reading rate
- Does not read for pleasure
- Subvocalizes audibly when reading in order to comprehend
- Cannot understand what is read when reading aloud
- When reading aloud, ignores punctuation marks
- Does not vary reading rate when reading for different purposes

Written language

- Poor penmanship, especially in cursive
- Preference for manuscript (printing) rather than cursive
- Occasional use of manuscript letters (lower or upper case) when writing in cursive, even in the middle of a word, as a strategy to minimize letter reversals and inversions
- Overuse of the upper case, even in the middle of a word or a sentence
- Overly large or cramped handwriting
- Poorly formed or illegible letters
- Difficulty initiating work on a written assignment or report

- Frequent spelling errors, including transpositions of letters (e.g., *ro* for *or*), omissions, additions, or substitutions of sounds/syllables, attempts at phonetic spelling for nonphonetic words, and/or confusion of homonyms
- Memos, reports, letters limited in length
- Sentence structure difficulties, varying from an abundance of short, simple sentences, sentence fragments, and run-ons to overly long, complex sentences and unacceptable syntax
- Missing inflectional endings, such as / s / for plural and / ed / for past tense
- Inappropriate use of prepositions and transition words

(continued)

Table 1.1.   *(continued)*

Written language—*(continued)*
- Difficulty in overall organization and development of ideas
- Inappropriate or infrequent use of transition words, or both

- Uses vocabulary inappropriate for formal written language

Mathematics
- Incomplete mastery of basic facts, in particular the multiplication tables
- Difficulty recalling the sequence of steps in an operation
- Difficulty understanding and retaining terms representing quantitative concepts
- Number and symbol reversals, transpositions, or both in the order of numbers in a sequence when copying or writing numbers to dictation (as is necessary in taking a phone message)

- Computational skill difficulties
- Reasoning impairments
- Difficulty in copying problems and in alignment of numbers in columns
- Associated nonverbal disorders (e.g., difficulties in left–right, time, spatial, and compass orientation; recognizing familiar faces; reading a map; "reading" body language)

Study skills
- Difficulty organizing papers, time, and space
- Difficulty initiating effort on a task
- Notetaking and outlining difficulties
- Difficulty in integrating information from various sources
- Poor test-taking strategies
- Difficulty in memorizing and self-rehearsal strategies

- Difficulty using a dictionary, thesaurus, and other self-help handbooks, software, or both
- Library and research skills impairments
- Poor mastery of word-processing and other assistive technology software and devices
- Limited repertoire of reading, study skills, proofreading, and test-taking strategies

Attentional difficulties
- Interrupts frequently
- Becomes distracted during a conversation and changes the subject
- Response in a conversation does not follow logically
- Blurts out an inappropriate remark out of context

- Changes the subject without warning
- Gets up and moves around, starting to do other things, during a conversation
- Shifts from one task to another before completion of job
- Does not maintain eye contact

challenged (Lyon, 1995). Some of the same difficulties apply to the identification of adults at high risk for LD as apply to children:

- Depending on the method or formula used, the same individual will sometimes be eligible for services and sometimes not.
- Rigid use of a mathematical formula by some school districts and psychologists does not allow important qualitative information such as observational data, informal assessment information, clinical judgment, and teacher observations to be considered in the decision-making process.
- Individuals with low-average intelligence quotients (IQs) are less likely to be identified because the low IQ score predicts low levels of literacy, and therefore the discrepancy does not reach the required level of significance.
- In the case of adults who are in the gifted range in IQ score or have grown up in an advantaged environment, there may no longer be a significant discrepancy between achievement and IQ score. However, these individuals often remain slow readers, inaccurate decoders, and poor spellers. They may also have significant impairment in written expression and foreign language learning ability, necessitating certain accommodations and services. These adults have sometimes been referred to as "compensated" adults and often manifest residual difficulties with phonological analysis, speech–sound perception, and rapid recognition of phonetically regular nonsense words (Fletcher, Francis, Rourke, Shaywitz, & Shaywitz, 1992).

Table 1.2.   Difficulties in the past and present for adults with learning disabilities (N = 71)

Areas of difficulty	Past (percent)	Present (percent)
Oral language		
Learning to speak a foreign language	59	52
Reading		
Reading comprehension	69	62
Reading fast	72	62
Reading orally in front of a group	76	55
Writing		
Spelling	72	62
Recognizing misspelled words	62	52
Writing compositions	69	52
Learning rules of grammar	69	62
Learning rules of punctuation and capitalization	55	52
Taking notes	86	45
Taking essay exams	76	55
Learning to type/keyboard	48	34
Mathematics		
Learning multiplication table	66	45
Solving word problems	79	62

Secondary Problems Caused by Learning Disabilities

LD can have a significant impact on psychological well-being, social-emotional adjustment, achievement motivation, and self-esteem. Because of their history of failure as youngsters, many adults with LD have a pattern of procrastination, even though they know time-management strategies, and also have trouble taking the initiative. The lack of self-confidence sometimes causes these individuals to ascribe their successes to luck rather than taking credit where credit is due. When things do not go well, they have difficulty in taking responsibility for their behavior and analyzing what they could have done differently rather than ascribing their failure to an external cause. This phenomenon has been referred to as *external locus of control* (Bell, Feraios, & Bryan, 1991).

Mithaug and Horiuchi (1983) reported that almost half of the adults in their cohort were socially inactive. Other studies have reported that individuals with LD have few friends and remember having been teased or rejected by about 50% of their peers in the past (LaGreca & Stone, 1990; Vaughn, Zaragoza, Hogan, & Walker, 1993). Not surprising, Hoffman and colleagues (1987) reported that the adults in their study were afraid of intimacy, socially isolated, and lonely. They may have limited ability to share personal data because of their fear of criticism. Many adults have also reported mild chronic depression, which may have a basis in reality because of their isolation and because they have not achieved the educational goal, employment, or financial status commensurate with their level of intelligence (Forness, 1988; Rourke, Young, & Leenaars, 1989; Vogel & Forness, 1992).

Their lives of loneliness, lack of fulfillment, and mild depression may lead some adults with LD to overuse mood-altering legal substances such as caffeine and alcohol, leading to dependence. In addition, some have experimented with unvalidated treatments for individuals with LD or ADHD or with illicit substances that have the potential to be harmful (Karacostas & Fisher, 1993). For these reasons, medical consultation, individual therapy, and support groups have been found to be very effective in assisting adults with LD in coping with these problems (Johnson, 1994; Price, 1988). Some adults have taken a leadership role in forming their own self-help groups in various parts of the United States (Gregg & Phillips, 1996).

What Learning Disabilities Are Not

Because of the difficulty in understanding the complex nature of LD and its many sub-types, there is a great deal of misinformation that must be dispelled. Therefore, it is important to state clearly that *learning disability* is not synonymous with *mental retardation*. In fact, there is good evidence that reading disabilities occur in individuals of average and above-average intelligence, as well as in those who are intellectually gifted (Fink, 1995, 1997; Siegel, 1989). Although some of the diagnoses of giftedness and language-based learning disability have been questioned because the data were anecdotal and analyzed posthumously, Fink (1997) conducted an interesting study in which she interviewed and evaluated a group of gifted adults with dyslexia, some of whom are Nobel Laureates and/or members of the National Academy of Sciences. The groundbreaking work of Gerber and Reiff (1991) also confirmed the disassociation of dyslexia and intelligence.

THE NATURE OF READING DISABILITIES

A third way in which the existence of LD in adults has been validated is based on newly acquired knowledge regarding the nature of dyslexia. In the 1990s, the National Institute of Child Health and Human Development (NICHD) of the National Institutes of Health has invested approximately $80 million in eight research centers and program projects to investigate the prevalence and causes of dyslexia and the identification and treatment of dyslexia. What have they learned?

Prevalence

Based on the NICHD research, dyslexia appears to be even more widespread than previously thought. Approximately 15%–20% of school-age individuals are affected by this disorder (Lyon, 1991, 1995; Shaywitz, Escobar, Shaywitz, Fletcher, & Makuch, 1992; Shaywitz et al., 1990).

The Nature of Dyslexia

First, dyslexia occurs on a continuum from mild to severe impairment (Fletcher et al., 1994; Shaywitz et al., 1992). (For our purposes, adults with severe reading disabilities are those reading at the fourth-grade level or below.) Second, it is a language-based, auditory processing difficulty that persists even in people who have learned to read and comprehend with accuracy. Third, even for those individuals with dyslexia who have learned to read and comprehend, rapid and accurate decoding of unfamiliar, multisyllabic, and/or foreign language words remain inaccurate and rate of decoding often remains slow. Although they remain slow readers, with appropriate instruction some will become good comprehenders, especially when reading material in their area of expertise.

The Core Limitation Hypothesis

The core limitation in dyslexia has been identified as difficulty in hearing distinct sounds within words and segmenting words into syllables and sounds or phonemes (Fletcher et al., 1994; Lyon, 1994, 1995). Such skills are considered critical because they are prerequisite skills for accurately decoding and spelling unfamiliar words, especially multisyllabic words. Reading comprehension, the ultimate goal of reading instruction, is also dependent on accurate, automatic (i.e., rapid) decoding of single words.

Genetics and Brain Differences in Individuals with Reading Disabilities

The major investigations in genetics and brain differences have been done by the Colorado Reading Project (DeFries et al., 1997). The findings indicated that reading disability or dyslexia is an inherited trait; and, more specifically, the ability to segment words into their discrete sounds (phoneme awareness), rapid phonological decoding, and word recognition are the subskills that are limiting (Olson, Forsberg, & Wise, 1994). One of the locations of this genetic marker has been found to be on chromosome 6 in the vicinity of the gene related to autoimmune disorders (the human leukocyte antigen marker) (Cardon et al., 1994, 1995, 1997), which perhaps explains why there is a higher prevalence of autoimmune disorders such as allergies, diabetes, and thyroid diseases in people who have dyslexia (DeFries et al., 1997). In addition, Galaburda (1997) and colleagues found specific signs of brain pathology (e.g., cell loss, abnormalities in the area between the two hemispheres called the corpus callosum) and atypical neural organization altering the usual pattern of asymmetry (i.e., left hemisphere equal to right hemisphere rather than left being greater than right) in one specific area of the brain called the temporal lobe. In addition, Shaywitz (1998) found differences in activity levels when using functional magnetic resonance imaging to compare the brains of individuals who have dyslexia with the brains of individuals who do not have dyslexia during various reading tasks. When the tasks that the individuals without dyslexia performed increased in difficulty from simple to complex, the activity levels in their brains also increased in the area of the brain called the *angular gyrus*. (This area of the brain is considered important for cross-medial associations such as vision and language.) In contrast, there was underactivation in this area of the brain in the individuals with dyslexia when they performed the same tasks. Shaywitz's findings confirmed earlier research on acquired reading disorders in which there was damage to the same area of the brain and provided evidence to support the presence of a functional disruption in neural systems within developmental reading disorders. Finally, differences in activity level (sometimes more and sometimes less than normal activation, depending on the area of the brain) have been seen in regional blood flow and positron emission tomography studies (Wood, Flowers, Buchsbaum, & Tallal, 1991).

THE PROS AND CONS OF ASSESSMENT OF ADULTS AT HIGH RISK FOR LEARNING DISABILITIES

Recognition of LD in legislation, accessibility of educational opportunities, protection against discrimination, and availability of vocational instruction to enhance employment success are some of the prerequisites for adults with LD to achieve at the level of their highest abilities. However, the key that determines who is protected under the law; who is eligible for entrance or licensing examination accommodations; and who receives instructional and test accommodations, support services, and/or vocational rehabilitation services is establishing the diagnosis. In order to do this, the adult must undergo a formal diagnostic evaluation.

Arguments Against Assessment

Aside from the dilemmas of the scarcity of well-qualified diagnosticians and the expense of assessment, some adult literacy, job-training, adult education, ASE, and postsecondary educators have argued that establishing the presence of a learning disability in adults who are already burdened with unemployment/underemployment, financial insecurity, and significant limitations in literacy skills places an unnecessary burden on them without sufficient benefit (Alderson-Gill & Associates, 1989). Furthermore, they suggested that learning disability assessments do not use measures that lead to further self-understanding or recommended teaching strategies for adult literacy educators. These professionals argued that, when adults are evaluated, they may experience further frustration and difficulty. If these adults are diagnosed as having a learning disability, then the argument continues that the diagnosis may lead to feelings of even greater inadequacy because they now have a known disability in addition to all of their other difficulties. The disability "label" is therefore much more ominous than having garden-variety reading, spelling, or math difficulties of unknown origin. In addition, the determination of a disability carries with it the burden of permanence and may result in a defeatist attitude or, at the very least, diminished motivation to improve in the areas of difficulty.

The diagnostic testing may also provide a perspective on their abilities and achievement in relation to other adults that these tested adults did not have previously, and they may become even more discouraged knowing how severe their reading, spelling, or math disability is. Again, seeing themselves in relation to other adults may serve to increase their feelings of inadequacy. If after discussing their educational, developmental, and family history, adults with LD realize that the same symptoms may have been present in a parent, uncle or aunt, or grandparent, they may become concerned about the possibility that their present or future children or grandchildren will have a learning disability. Finally, to confuse the issue even more, two noted reading disability specialists argued that most, if not all, very poor readers in adult education and literacy education settings manifest the same characteristic error patterns as adults with LD, which makes differentiating those with LD from those with "garden-variety reading difficulties" very difficult (Fowler & Scarborough, 1993). What these authors do not acknowledge is that these poor readers may manifest the same characteristics because they also have LD. Unfortunately, the solution they suggested was to bypass the evaluation step and instead teach all adults in adult education, literacy education settings, and other programs as if they had a learning disability. One footnote is added to this recommendation, however: A diagnostic evaluation to determine if a person has a learning disability is justifiable and meaningful for those adults who want to exercise their legal rights to accommodations or support services and need to provide appropriate documentation of their LD.

Arguments for Assessment

It is my position that the personal, economic, and societal arguments in favor of a diagnostic evaluation and identification of adults with severe difficulties in literacy resulting from a learning disability far outweigh the arguments against being evaluated and diagnosed. First, it is important to state at the outset that adults referred for evaluation should have been screened for LD and been identified as being in the high-risk category (see Section II). Second, during the screening process, mental retardation, ESL, and visual acuity problems should have been ruled out as possible causes for severe literacy difficulties. Third, the evaluators must be well trained and experienced in assessment of adults at risk for LD (Association of Higher Education and Disability, 1997) and understand intimately the fears that adults bring to the evaluation process, how to establish a supportive relationship in the evaluation process, and how to sensitively conduct an in-depth interview regarding developmental, medical, personal, educational, and employment history (Hawks, 1996; Johnson, 1987; Johnson & Blalock, 1987; Vogel, 1985, 1989a, 1989b).

Knowing versus Not Knowing   Adults who have struggled with acquiring literacy skills all of their lives have a deep-seated fear that perhaps, in fact, they really are "retarded" or in some way to be blamed for their learning difficulties. They begin to doubt their innate intelligence and their expenditure of effort and wonder whether maybe there really is something dreadfully wrong with them. In the backs of their minds they still see themselves as the "class dummies" or wonder whether perhaps they are not really very smart after all or really did not listen hard enough or work hard enough in school.

In establishing the diagnosis of a learning disability, diagnosticians can lay to rest the fear of mental retardation by sharing with adults the results of the cognitive abilities testing—for example, showing individuals that they fell in the average or above-average range on the verbal and nonverbal sections of the intelligence test administered. In addition, seeing the profile of their cognitive abilities will give adults insight as to their strengths and how those strengths relate to aspects of life in which they excel in comparison to areas of impairment. Understanding their strengths will also enable these adults to develop compensatory strategies that minimize the impact of their processing limitations. Using these strategies will help them acquire greater self-confidence and increased self-esteem. Understanding one's pattern of cognitive abilities and literacy strengths and weaknesses is an important step in exploring alternative employment directions, identifying appropriate assistive technology, setting goals, and charting progress.

Finally, learning about their pattern of strengths and weaknesses helps such adults to acquire a perspective on their own LD and allows them to understand that there are other adults with LD who have similar degrees of impairment and have "made it" in school and employment. Many adults with LD have found it helpful to participate in a support group, share personal histories and strategies that have worked for them, and become change agents by speaking publicly either individually or as part of a panel to different audiences such as high school students, employers, and teachers/faculty with limited experience working with adults with LD (Price, 1988).

Establishing the diagnosis of a learning disability is the beginning of the process of recognition, acceptance, and self-understanding. Many adults report feeling an immediate sense of relief on learning that they have a learning disability. It gives a name to their struggles. It legitimizes their efforts and the obstacles they face. At the same time, it serves as the first opportunity for them to go over the test results with a knowledgeable and understanding specialist/diagnostician and to understand thoroughly the nature of their disabilities, the underlying processing limitations, their profile of abilities, and how they learn best using their areas of strength.

According to Gerber and Reiff (1991, 1994), understanding follows recognition and acceptance of one's learning disability and leads to a "reframing" process that entails reconceptualizing the learning disability in a positive light. Once having accepted their LD, these adults can benefit from counseling to assist them in identifying appropriate employment in which they utilize their strengths and there is minimal impact from their weaknesses (referred to by Gerber as "goodness of fit") and to identify or to create a work environment in which they have a strong support system (referred to as "social ecology"). At this level, adults with LD can use their self-understanding regarding the importance of a strong support system and mentoring relationships to be successful on the job.

Acceptance of the Disability   Is it better for individuals with LD not to know about having such disabilities because they will never go away or be entirely overcome, or is it better for them to know? We have learned from longitudinal studies that have followed groups of adults with LD into their 30s and beyond that individuals with such disabilities can be born at risk for negative outcomes (Keogh & Weisner, 1993; Werner, 1993) and succeed against the odds (Bruck, 1987, 1990; Rawson, 1968; Rogan & Hartman, 1990; Spekman, Goldberg, & Herman, 1993; Werner & Smith, 1992). Vogel, Hruby, and Adelman (1993) and Spekman, Herman, and Vogel (1993) identified many of the same characteristics in successful adults with LD in which success was defined in terms of educational attainment, career attainment, job satisfaction, and financial status commensurate with that of their peers without LD. Factors identified that were within the individuals' ability to control included a high level of self-awareness, under-standing, and acceptance of their LD, and a high level of motivation and persistence in achieving their goals. The critical importance of accepting one's learning disability and viewing it as a strength was expressed very well by one of the participants in a 15-year follow-up study, who described her learning disability in this way: "It is a part of me. It is what makes me unique. It is what makes me who I am, and is something I would never want to give up" (Vogel, 1997a).

The Genetic Link and Early Intervention   As noted previously, there is a growing body of evidence that certain aspects of reading tend to be genetic. However, having the genetic marker does not mean that the individual will inevitably have a reading disabil-ity because the reading and language environment contributes significantly to the risk factor. However, if one or more of the parents has dyslexia, this should serve as an early warning signal and the children should be monitored carefully and screened as preschoolers. If the child is at risk, the language and reading environment could then be immediately enriched at an early age (Foorman, Francis, Beeler, Winikates, & Fletcher, 1997). Validated preventative and remedial reading instruction can also be implemented in the child's classroom to minimize the risk and perhaps even avoid the negative impact of failure to learn to read (Torgesen, Wagner, Rashotte, Alexander, & Conway, 1997).

Intervention   What does the literature tell us about reading instruction? Unfortu-nately, there is very little research on the way adults with LD learn to read, but empir-ical studies that have been done (Guyer, Banks, & Guyer, 1993; Guyer & Sabatino, 1989) confirm that they learn the same way that children learn. First, the overriding principle is that instruction must be intensive, skill focused, and systematic. It should incorporate elements of language beginning with the building blocks of sound (pho-nemes) and teach first to the level of phonological awareness, followed by morpholog-ical awareness (e.g., roots, prefixes, suffixes). Simultaneously, letter–sound correspon-dences are taught in a systematic, logical order to the level of mastery, using intensive practice, computer-assisted instruction, and speeded practice to assist the reader to become a fluent and rapid reader. As soon as possible, reading comprehension materi-als should be introduced using controlled vocabulary, and opportunities for written expressive activities are then integrated into the curriculum (Bell & Lindamood, 1992; Foorman et al., 1997; Lewkowicz, 1987; Liberman, Shankweiler, Camp, Blachman, & Werfelman, 1980; Torgesen et al., 1997; see also Chapters 10 and 11).

FUTURE DIRECTIONS

The recognition of the continuing needs of adults with LD in adult education, ASE, job-training, postsecondary education, and literacy education settings has increased dra-matically in the 1990s. We have made progress in determining the answers to some very basic questions about prevalence, characteristics, causation, and intervention. However, there are major gaps in our knowledge that we need to close. As can be seen in the en-suing chapters, we are making progress toward developing and validating screening instruments that can identify adults at high risk for having a learning disability and in developing instructional approaches that are effective in teaching adults with severe reading disabilities (see Sections II and III). The step we have neglected to address is that between screening and instruction—namely, diagnosis/evaluation. This critical component is the missing link leading to self-understanding, acceptance, reframing, goal setting, educational attainment, gainful satisfying employment, and self-sufficiency. How can we close this gap?

There are four models that have begun to address the need to provide assessment at no cost to adults seeking to determine whether they have a learning disability and to document it for purposes of eligibility for services and accommodations. One of these, in which AFDC consumers who are identified as being at high risk for LD are then evaluated under a grant from the Washington State Department of Social and Health Services, is described in Chapter 9.

Another model—in fact, the very first—was developed between 1982 and 1987 by the California Community College System in conjunction with the Kansas Institute for Research in Learning Disabilities (Mellard, 1990; Mellard & Byrne, 1993). This model is based on quantitative data, self-reported information, and the clinical judgment of the LD diagnostician. The diagnosis of learning disability and determination of eligibility are made using a discrepancy model and clinical judgment according to specific guidelines and criteria.

A third model was established in the state of Georgia in 1993 that created three regional Georgia Learning Disorders Centers (Gregg, Heggoy, Stapleton, Jackson, & Morris, 1996). These three regional centers provide a variety of services, including on student request, a review of previous documentation against a well-defined set of criteria, student assessment, assistance in development of academic policies as they pertain to students with LD, and technical assistance to colleges and universities to train faculty and service providers to use specific instructional strategies, assistive technology, and accommodations (Gregg, Heggoy, et al., 1996).

A fourth model is now being developed in the United Kingdom in response to the Disability Discrimination Act of 1995 (Pumfrey, 1997). This act requires each higher education institution to develop and publish a Disability Statement that delineates its formal policy and practices regarding students with documented disabilities, including how the institution meets the need for review of documentation for those students who were already identified or who might need to be assessed (Pumfrey, 1997). It will be important for U.S. researchers to keep abreast of the developments in the United Kingdom.

Other important areas to investigate include the following:

- What is the validity of the diagnostic measures presently in widespread use?
- Are these instruments able to discriminate between individuals with LD and those without such disabilities but who have very low literacy proficiency because they are non-native English speakers, slow learners or mildly retarded, previously unmotivated learners, or educationally disadvantaged?
- What is the prevalence of adults with LD in adult education, ASE, literacy, job-training, and adult literacy settings?
- What is the relationship between assessment and instructional methodology/intervention, and outcome?
- What information or combination of information from formal and informal testing, history (developmental, educational, and vocational), personality and motivational factors, and social and vocational competence will be the best predictors of successful outcome?

- How can the predictive validity of the present screening and diagnostic instruments, informal checklists, and achievement measures be improved and made more time and cost efficient?
- How can present and/or new instruments be developed to assess the impact of intervention on literacy proficiency, educational attainment, employability, financial status, social competence, emotional maturity, daily living, and quality of life?

It is hoped that this book and these questions will facilitate a deepening dialogue among LD professionals, adult literacy educators, adult educators, adult secondary and developmental educators, vocational rehabilitation experts, mental health professionals, diagnosticians, researchers, and others who work with adults with LD in helping them achieve their educational, economic, and personal goals.

REFERENCES

Adult Education Amendments of 1988, PL 100-297, 20 U.S.C. §§ 1201 *et seq.*

Alderson-Gill & Associates. (1989). *Study of literature and learning disabilities.* Ottawa, Ontario: Learning Disabilities Association of Canada.

American Psychiatric Association. (1980). *Diagnostic and statistical manual of mental disorders* (3rd ed.). Washington, DC: Author.

Americans with Disabilities Act of 1990, PL 101-336, 42 U.S.C. §§ 12101 *et seq.*

Association for Children with Learning Disabilities (ACLD). (1986, September–October). ACLD Description: Specific learning disabilities. *ACLD Newsbriefs, 15–16.*

Association of Higher Education and Disability. (1997). *Guidelines for documentation of a learning disability in adolescents and adults.* Columbus, OH: Author.

Bell, B., & Lindamood, P. (1992). Issues in phonological awareness assessment. *Annals of Dyslexia, 42, 242–259.*

Bell, D., Feraios, A.J., & Bryan, T. (1991). Learning disabled adolescent's knowledge and attitudes about AIDS. *Learning Disabilities Research and Practice, 6, 94–111.*

Blalock, J. (1981). Persistent problems and concerns of young adults with learning disabilities. In W. Cruickshank & A. Silver (Eds.), *Bridges to tomorrow: The best of ACLD* (Vol. 2, pp. 35–55). Syracuse, NY: Syracuse University Press.

Blalock, J. (1982). Persistent auditory language deficits in adults with learning disabilities. *Journal of Learning Disabilities, 15, 604–609.*

Bruck, M. (1987). The adult outcomes of children with learning disabilities. *Annals of Dyslexia, 37, 252–263.*

Bruck, M. (1990). Word recognition skills of adults with childhood diagnoses of dyslexia. *Developmental Psychology, 26, 439–454.*

Bruck, M. (1992). Persistence of dyslexics' phonological awareness deficits. *Developmental Psychology, 28, 874–886.*

Cardon, L.R., Smith, S., Fulker, D., Kimberling, W., Pennington, B., & DeFries, J. (1994). Quantitative trait locus for reading disability on chromosome 6. *Science, 266, 276–279.*

Cardon, L.R., Smith, S., Fulker, D., Kimberling, W., Pennington, B., & DeFries, J. (1995). Quantitative trait locus for reading disability: A correction. *Science, 268, 5217.*

DeFries, J.C., Filipek, P.A., Fulker, D.W., Olson, R.K., Pennington, B.F., Smith, S.D., & Wise, B.W. (1997). Colorado Learning Disability Research Center. *Learning Disability Quarterly, 8, 7–19.*

Dinklage, K. (1971). Inability to learn a foreign language. In G. Blaine & C. McArthur (Eds.), *Emotional problems of the student* (2nd ed; pp. 185–206). New York: Appleton-Century-Crofts.

Dowdy, C., & Smith, T.E.C. (1994). Serving individuals with specific learning disabilities in the vocational rehabilitation system. In P.F. Gerber & H.B. Reiff (Eds.), *Learning disabilities in adulthood: Persisting problems and evolving issues* (pp. 171–178). Boston: Andover Medical Publishers.

Education for All Handicapped Children Act of 1975, PL 94-142, 20 U.S.C. §§ 1400 *et seq.*

Fink, R.P. (1995). Successful dyslexics: A constructivist study of passionate interest reading. *Journal of Adolescent and Adult Literacy, 39*(4), 268–280.

Fink, R. (1997). Successful dyslexia: A constructivist study of passionate interest reading. In C. Weaver (Ed.), *Reconsidering a balanced approach to reading* (Vol. 1). Urbana, IL: The National Council of Teachers of English.

Fletcher, J.M., Francis, D.J., Rourke, B.P., Shaywitz, S.E., & Shaywitz, B.A. (1992). The validity of discrepancy-based definitions of reading disabilities. *Journal of Learning Disabilities, 25,* 555–561, 573.

Fletcher, J.M., Shaywitz, S.E., Shankweiler, D.P., Katz, L., Liberman, I.Y., Stuebing, K.K., Francis, D.J., Fowler, A.E., & Shaywitz, B.A. (1994). Cognitive profiles of reading disability: Comparisons of discrepancy and low achievement definitions. *Journal of Educational Psychology, 86,* 6–23.

Foorman, B., Francis, D., Beeler, T., Winikates, D., & Fletcher, J.M. (1997). Early intervention for children with reading problems: Study designs and preliminary findings. *Learning Disabilities: A Multidisciplinary Journal, 8*(1), 63–71.

Forness, S. (1988). School characteristics of children and adolescents with depression. *Monographs in Behavioral Disorders, 10,* 177–203.

Frauenheim, J.G. (1978). Academic achievement characteristics of adult males who were diagnosed as dyslexic in childhood. *Journal of Learning Disabilities, 11*(8), 476–483.

Galaburda, A.M. (1997). Neurobiology of developmental dyslexia: Results of a ten-year research program. *Learning Disabilities: A Multidisciplinary Journal, 8*(1), 43–50.

Gerber, P. (1981). Learning disabilities and eligibility for vocational rehabilitation services: A chronology of events. *Learning Disability Quarterly, 4*(4), 422–425.

Gerber, P.J. (1997). Life after school: Challenges in the workplace. In P.F. Gerber & D.S. Brown (Eds.), *Learning disabilities and employment* (pp. 3–18). Austin, TX: PRO-ED.

Gerber, P.J., Ginsberg, R., & Reiff, H.B. (1992). Identifying alterable patterns in employment success for highly successful adults with learning disabilities. *Journal of Learning Disabilities, 25,* 475–487.

Gerber, P.J., & Reiff, H.B. (1991). *Speaking for themselves: Ethnographic interviews with adults with learning disabilities.* Ann Arbor: The University of Michigan Press.

Gottesman, R.L. (1994). The adult with learning disabilities: An overview. *Learning Disabilities: A Multidisciplinary Journal, 5*(1), 1–14.

Gregg, N., Heggoy, S., Stapleton, M., Jackson, R., & Morris, R. (1996). Eligibility for college learning disabilities services: A system-wide approach. *Learning Disabilities: A Multidisciplinary Journal, 7*(1), 29–36.

Gregg, N., Johnson, Y., & McKinley, C. (1996). Learning disabilities policy and legal issues: Consumer and practitioner user-friendly guide. In N. Gregg, S. Hoy, & A. Gay (Eds.), *Adults with learning disabilities* (pp. 329–367). New York: Guilford Press.

Gregg, N., & Phillips, C. (1996). Adults with learning disabilities: Empowering networks of inclusion, collaboration, and self-acceptance. In N. Gregg, S. Hoy, & A. Gay (Eds.), *Adults with learning disabilities* (pp. 1–20). New York: Guilford Press.

Guyer, B.P., & Sabatino, D. (1989). The effectiveness of a multidisciplinary alphabetic phonetic approach with college students who are learning disabled. *Journal of Learning Disabilities, 22,* 430–434.

Guyer, B.P., Banks, S.R., & Fuyer, K.E. (1993). Spelling improvement for college students who are dyslexic. *Annals of Dyslexia, 43,* 186–193.

Hawks, R. (1996). Assessing adults with learning disabilities. In N. Gregg, S. Hoy, & A. Gay (Eds.), *Adults with learning disabilities* (pp. 144–161). New York: Guilford Press.

Henderson, C. (1995). *College freshmen with disabilities: A triennial statistical profile.* Washington DC: American Council on Education and HEATH Resource Center.

Hoffman, T.J., Sheldon, K.L., Minskoff, E.H., Sautter, S.W., Steidle, E.F., Baker, D.B., Bailey, M.B., & Echols, L.D. (1987). Needs of the learning disabled adult. *Journal of Learning Disabilities, 20,* 43–52.

Individuals with Disabilities Education Act (IDEA) Amendments of 1997, PL 105-17, 20 U.S.C. §§ 1400 *et seq.*

Interagency Committee on Learning Disabilitie (ICLD). (1987). *Learning disabilities: A report to the U.S. Congress.* Washington, DC: U.S. Department of Health and Human Services.

Johnson, D. (1987). Principles of assessment and diagnosis. In D. Johnson & J. Blalock (Eds.), *Adults with learning disabilities* (pp. 9–30). Orlando, FL: Grune & Stratton.

Johnson, D.J. (1994). Clinical studies of adults with severe learning disabilities. *Learning Disabilities: A Multidisciplinary Journal, 5*(1), 43–50.

Johnson, D.J. (1995). An overview of learning disabilities: Psychoeducational perspectives. *Journal of Child Neurology, 10*(Suppl. 1), S2–S5.

Johnson, D., & Blalock, J. (Eds.). (1987). *Adults with learning disabilities.* Orlando, FL: Grune & Stratton.

Karacostas, D.D., & Fisher, G.L. (1993). Chemical dependency in students with and without learning disabilities. *Journal of Learning Disabilities, 26,* 491–495.

Keogh, B., & Weisner, T. (1993). An ecocultural perspective on risk and resilience factors in children's development: Implications for learning disabilities. *Learning Disabilities Research and Practice, 8,* 3–10.

Kirsch, I.S., Jungeblut, A., Jenkins, L., & Kolstad, A. (1993). *Adult literacy in America: A first look at the results of the National Adult Literacy survey.* Princeton, NJ: Educational Testing Service.

Koller, J.R. (1994, Summer). Improving transition outcomes for persons with specific learning disabilities. *Journal of Rehabilitation,* 37–42.

Koller, J.R. (1997). Vocational rehabilitation: Current practices for work preparation. In P.J. Gerber & D.S. Brown (Eds.), *Learning disabilities and employment* (pp. 165–186). Austin, TX: PRO-ED.

Koller, J.R., Holliday, G.A., & Multon, K.D. (Eds.). (1996). *Koller Adolescent and Adult Behavior Scale–Revised (KAABS–R).* (Available from the Assessment and Consultation Clinic, University of Missouri–Columbia, 223 Townsend Hall, Columbia, MO 65211)

La Greca, A.M., & Stone, W.L. (1990). LD status and achievement: Confounding variables in the study of children's social status, self-esteem, and behavioral functioning. *Journal of Learning Disabilities, 23,* 483–490.

Learning Disabilities Association of America. (1986, September–October). LDA definition: Specific learning disabilities. *LDA Newsbriefs,* 15–16.

Lewkowicz, N. (1987). On the question of teaching decoding skills to older students. *Journal of Reading, 31,* 50–57.

Leyser, Y. (1989). A survey of faculty attitudes and accommodations for students with disabilities. *Journal of Postsecondary Education and Disabilities, 7*(3–4), 97–108.

Leyser, Y., Vogel, S.A., Brulle, A., & Wyland, S. (in press). Faculty attitudes and practices regarding students with disabilities: Two decades after implementation of Section 504. *Journal of Postsecondary Education and Disability.*

Liberman, I.Y., Shankweiler, D., Camp, L., Blachman, B., & Werfelman, M. (1980). Steps toward literacy: A linguistic approach. In P. Levinson & C. Sloan (Eds.), *Auditory processing and language: Clinical and research perspectives* (pp. 189–215). New York: Grune & Stratton.

Lyon, G.R. (1991). *Research in learning disabilities* (Tech. Rep.). Bethesda, MD: National Institute of Child Health and Human Development.

Lyon, G.R. (1994). *Frames of reference for the assessment of learning disabilities: New views on measurement issues.* Baltimore: Paul H. Brookes Publishing Co.

Lyon, G.R. (1995). Research initiatives in learning disabilities: Contributions from scientists supported by the National Institute of Child Health and Human Development. *Journal of Child Neurology, 10*(Suppl. 1), S120–S126.

McCue, M. (1984, May). Assessment and rehabilitation of learning-disabled adults. *Rehabilitation Counseling Bulletin,* 281–290.

McCue, M. (1987, April). *The role of assessment in the vocational rehabilitation of adults with SLD.* Paper presented at the State-of-the-Art conference on Learning Disabilities for the National Institute on Disability and Rehabilitation Research, Washington, DC.

Mellard, D.F. (1990). The eligibility process: Identifying students with learning disabilities in California's community colleges. *Learning Disabilities Focus, 5,* 75–90.

Mellard, D.F., & Byrne, M. (1993). Learning disabilities referrals, eligibility outcomes, and services in community colleges: A four-year summary. *Learning Disability Quarterly, 16,* 199–218.

Mithaug, D.E., & Horiuchi, C.N. (1983). Colorado statewide follow-up survey of special education students. *Exceptional Children, 51,* 397–404.

Moats, L.C., & Lyon, G.R. (1993). Learning disabilities in the United States: Advocacy, science, and the future of the field. *Journal of Learning Disabilities, 26,* 282–294.

Mulkey, S., Kopp, K., & Miller, J. (1984). Determining eligibility of learning disabled adults for vocational rehabilitation services. *Journal of Rehabilitation, 50*(2), 53–58.

National Education Goals Panel. (1991). *The national goals report: Building a nation of learners.* Washington, DC: U.S. Printing Office.

National Joint Committee on Learning Disabilities (NJCLD). (1994). Learning disabilities issue on definition. In *Collective perspectives on issues affecting learning disabilities: Position papers and statements* (pp. 61–66). Austin, TX: PRO-ED.

National Literacy Act of 1991, PL 102-73, 20 U.S.C. §§ 12089a *et seq.*

Olson, R.K., Forsberg, H., & Wise, B. (1994). Genes, environment, and the development of orthographic skills. In V.W. Berninger (Ed.), *The varieties of orthographic knowledge I: Theoretical and developmental issues* (pp. 27–71). Dordecht, The Netherlands: Kluwer Academic Publishers.

Price, L. (1988). LD support groups work! *The Journal of Counseling and Human Services Professions,* *21*(1), 35–46.

Pumfrey, P. (1997, September). *Dyslexia in higher education in the United Kingdom (UK): Obstacles and opportunities.* Paper presented at the Fourth World Congress on Dyslexia, Macedonia, Greece.

Rawson, M. (1968). *Developmental language disability: Adult accomplishment of dyslexic boys.* Baltimore: The Johns Hopkins University Press.

Reder, S. (1995). *Literacy, education, and learning disabilities.* Portland, OR: Northwest Regional Educational Laboratory.

Reder, S., & Vogel, S.A. (1977). Life-span employment and economic outcomes for adults with self-reported learning disabilities. In P. Gerber & D. Brown (Eds.), *Learning disabilities and employment* (pp. 371–394). Austin, TX: PRO-ED.

Rehabilitation Act of 1973, PL 93-112, 29 U.S.C. §§ 701 *et seq.*

Rehabilitation Services Administration. (1981, July 27). *Memorandum from the task force on learning disabilities* (Information memorandum RSA-IV-81-39).

Rehabilitation Services Administration. (1985, March 5). *Operational definition of specific learning disabilities for VR purposes* (Program Policy Directive, RSA-OOD-85-7). Washington, DC: Author.

Rehabilitation Services Administration, Task Force on Learning Disabilities. (1980). *Action plan on learning disabilities.* Washington, DC: U.S. Department of Education.

Rogan, L., & Hartman, L. (1990). Adult outcome of learning disabled students ten years after initial follow-up. *Learning Disabilities Focus, 5,* 91–102.

Rothstein, L. (1993). Legal issues. In S.A. Vogel & P.B. Adelman (Eds.), *Success for college students with learning disabilities* (pp. 21–35). New York: Springer-Verlag.

Rourke, B.P., Young, G.C., & Leenaars, A.A. (1989). A childhood learning disability that predisposes those afflicted to adolescent and adult depression and suicide risk. *Journal of Learning Disabilities, 22,* 169–175.

Ryan, A., & Price, L. (1993). Learning disabilities in adult education: A survey of current practices. *Journal of Postsecondary Education and Disability, 10*(3), 31–40.

Shaywitz, S.E. (1998). Functional disruption in the organization of the brain for reading in dyslexia. *Proceedings of the National Academy of Sciences, 95*(5), 2636–2641.

Shaywitz, S.E., Escobar, M.D., Shaywitz, B.A., Fletcher, J.M., & Makuch, R. (1992). Evidence that dyslexia may represent the lower tail of a normal distribution of reading ability. *New England Journal of Medicine, 326,* 145–150.

Shaywitz, S.E., Shaywitz, B.A., Fletcher, J.M., & Escobar, M.D. (1990). Prevalence of reading disability in boys and girls: Results of the Connecticut Longitudinal Study. *JAMA, 264,* 998–1002.

Siegel, L.S. (1989). I.Q. is irrelevant to the definition of learning disabilities. *Journal of Learning Disabilities, 22,* 469–479.

Simpson, E. (1979). *Reversals: A personal account of victory over dyslexia.* Boston: Houghton Mifflin.

Spekman, N.J., Goldberg, R.J., & Herman, K.L. (1993). An exploration of risk and resilience in the lives of individuals with learning disabilities. *Learning Disabilities Research and Practice, 8*(1), 11–18.

Spekman, N.J., Herman, K.L., & Vogel, S.A. (1993). Risk and resilience in individuals with learning disabilities: A challenge to the field. *Learning Disabilities Research and Practice, 8*(1), 59–65.

Torgesen, J.K., Wagner, R.K., Rashotte, C., Alexander, A.W., & Conway, T. (1997). Preventive and remedial interventions for children with severe reading disabilities. *Learning Disabilities: A Multidisciplinary Journal, 8*(1), 51–62.

Travis, G. (1979). An adult educator views learning disabilities. *Adult Literacy and Basic Education, 3,* 85–92.

U.S. Department of Education. (1994). National Center for Education Statistics. *The 1992–93 National postsecondary student aid study.* Washington, DC: Author.

U.S. Department of Education. (1995). *Seventeenth annual report to Congress on the implementation of the Individuals with Disabilities Education Act.* Washington, DC: Author.

U.S. Department of Health and Human Services. (1980). *The international classification of diseases, 9th revision, clinical modification* (2nd ed.). Washington, DC: Author.

U.S. Employment and Training Administration. (1991). *The learning disabled in employment and training programs* (Research and Evaluation Series 91-E). Washington, DC: U.S. Department of Labor.

U.S. Office of Education. (1977). Assistance to states for education of handicapped children: Procedures for evaluating specific learning disabilities. 42 *Federal Register* 65082–65095.

Vaughn, S., Zaragoza, N., Hogan, Z., & Walker, J. (1993). A four-year longitudinal investigation of the social skills and behavior problems of students with learning disabilities. *Journal of Learning Disabilities, 26*(6), 404–412.

Vogel, S.A. (1985). Learning disabled college students: Identification, assessment, and outcomes. In D. Duane & C.K. Leong (Eds.), *Understanding learning disabilities: International and multidisciplinary views* (pp. 179–203). New York: Plenum Press.

Vogel, S.A. (1987). Eligibility and identification considerations. In S. Vaughn & C. Bos (Eds.), *Research in learning disabilities: Issues and future directions* (pp. 121–137). Boston: College-Hill.

Vogel, S.A. (1989a). Adults with language learning disorders: Definition, diagnosis, and determination of eligibility for postsecondary and vocational rehabilitation services. *Rehabilitation Education, 3*, 77–90.

Vogel, S.A. (1989b). Models for diagnosis of adults with learning disabilities. In L.B. Silver (Ed.), *The assessment of learning disabilities* (pp. 111–134). Boston: Little, Brown.

Vogel, S.A. (1990). Gender differences in intelligence, language, visual-motor abilities, and academic achievement in students with learning disabilities: A review of the literature. *Journal of Learning Disabilities, 23*(1), 44–52.

Vogel, S.A. (1997a, September). *Adults with learning disabilities: A fifteen-year follow-up study.* Paper presented at the International Academy for Research in Learning Disabilities Conference, Macedonia, Greece.

Vogel, S. (1997b). *The college student with a learning disability: A handbook for college LD students, admissions officers, faculty, and administrators.* Lake Forest, IL: Author.

Vogel, S.A., & Adelman, P.B. (Eds.). (1993). *Success for college students with learning disabilities.* New York: Springer-Verlag.

Vogel, S.A., & Adelman, P.B. (1997, September). *Adults with learning disabilities: A fifteen year follow-up study.* Paper presented at the International Dyslexia Association Conference, Minneapolis.

Vogel, S.A., & Forness, S. (1992). Social functioning in adults with learning disabilities. *School Psychology Review, 21*(3), 374–385.

Vogel, S.A., Hruby, P., & Adelman, P.B. (1993). Educational and psychological factors in successful and unsuccessful college students with learning disabilities. *Learning Disabilities Research and Practice, 8*(1), 35–43.

Vogel, S.A., Leonard, F., Scales, W., Hayeslip, E., Hermanson, J., & Donnels, L. (1998). The National Learning Disabilities Data Bank: An overview. *Journal of Learning Disabilities, 31*(3), 234–247.

Vogel, S.A., Leyser, Y., Brulle, A., & Wyland, S. (1997, February). *Faculty attitude toward university students with learning disabilities.* Paper presented at the International Learning Disabilities Association of America Conference, Chicago.

Vogel, S.A., & Reder, S. (in press). Literacy proficiency of adults with self-reported learning disabilities. In M.C. Smith (Ed.), *Literacy for the 21st century: Research, policy, practices, and the National Adult Literacy Survey.* Westport, CT: Greenwood Press.

Waite, P. (1991, Fall). Adult literacy programs now see learning disabilities as a critical component to deal with. *Counterpoint,* 24–26.

Werner, E.E. (1993). Risk and resilience in individuals with learning disabilities: Lessons learned from the Kauai Longitudinal Study. *Learning Disabilities Research and Practice, 8*(1), 28–34.

Werner, E.E., & Smith, R.S. (1992). *Overcoming the odds: High-risk children from birth to adulthood.* Ithaca, NY: Cornell University Press.

Wood, F., Flowers, L., Buchsbaum, M., & Tallal, P. (1991). Investigation of abnormal left temporal functioning in dyslexia through CBF, auditory evoked potentials, and positron emission tomography. *Reading and Writing: An Interdisciplinary Journal, 3*, 379–393.

Zwerlein, R., Smith, M., & Diffley, J. (1984). *Vocational rehabilitation for learning disabled adults: A handbook for rehabilitation professionals.* Albertson, NY: National Center on Employment of the Handicapped at Human Resources Center.

2

The Americans with Disabilities Act, Section 504, and Adults with Learning Disabilities in Adult Education and Transition to Employment

Laura F. Rothstein

HISTORICAL BACKGROUND

Before the passage of the Americans with Disabilities Act (ADA) of 1990 (PL 101-336), most of the legal attention focused on the issue of discrimination against individuals with learning disabilities (LD) in the context of education related to students in public schools, kindergarten through high school graduation. This is because the Individuals with Disabilities Education Act (IDEA) of 1990 (PL 101-476), which was a reenactment of the original legislation on education for people with disabilities—the Education for All Handicapped Children Act of 1975 (PL 94-142)—provided comprehensive legal protection for students with LD. Although Section 504 of the Rehabilitation Act (PL 93-112), which prohibits discrimination on the basis of disability and covers many postsecondary institutions, had been passed in 1973, its protections were slow to be applied to adult education contexts. About the same time that the ADA was enacted in 1990, the legal attention to this issue grew substantially.

Postsecondary education is usually closely tied to the transition to the workplace. The primary goal of such education is to prepare for a trade or profession or other employment. In many cases, some process of certification by a state agency or other licensing agency is a follow-up and may even be tied in with the education program. The ADA applies to many more workplaces than the Rehabilitation Act. In addition,

A comprehensive overview of disability law relating to education, professional certification, and employment can be found in Rothstein (1997). Appreciation is expressed to the M.D. Anderson Foundation for its research support.

the ADA applies to most certifying agencies. Because the ADA applies more comprehensively to the workplace, there is greater attention to the interpretation of disability discrimination law by the courts and regulatory agencies. For this reason, greater legal guidance is now available than before the ADA was passed.

OVERVIEW OF THE STATUTES AND REGULATIONS

The following are the legal requirements for adult education that are found in statutes, regulations, and federal agency guidelines.

Individuals with Disabilities Education Act

IDEA generally has little application to postsecondary education because of its age eligibility requirements and its limitation to public education that is available to all. It is nonetheless important to understand its requirements and how it compares with and relates to the ADA and Section 504 of the Rehabilitation Act. In addition, if community college and other public postsecondary education programming is part of a state or local public education program and is open to all, then there may be applicable requirements under IDEA.

IDEA was originally enacted as the Education for All Handicapped Children Act of 1975. (The title was changed in 1990 to be more consistent with currently preferred terminology.) This legislation provides both procedural and substantive protections for students with certain conditions, including LD. The principles of IDEA are that all age-eligible students are to be provided a free appropriate public education in the least restrictive environment. Their educational programs are to be individualized, and they are entitled to detailed procedural safeguards, including notice and hearing opportunities. The availability of remedies such as compensatory education, reimbursement, injunctive relief, and attorneys' fees has helped to ensure the enforcement of IDEA. IDEA includes mandates related to identifying students entitled to protection and ensuring personnel preparation to address the educational needs of these students.

Section 504 of the Rehabilitation Act

Section 504 of the Rehabilitation Act was passed in 1973. Section 504 mandates that programs receiving federal financial assistance may not discriminate on the basis of disability (the original use of *handicap* was changed to reflect preferred terminology).

A substantial part of the employment sector was not covered by Section 504, nor by Section 501 (applying to federal agency employment) or Section 503 (applying to federal contractor employment). Most postsecondary education institutions, however, were recipients of federal financial assistance, through federal grants or through federal student aid programs, and were thus covered. Perhaps because most employment was exempt or because of lack of awareness of the Section 504 mandates, few postsecondary students brought court cases to enforce the requirements before 1990.

Section 504 provides for a three-part test of who is entitled to be protected from discrimination on the basis of disability. In order to be protected, one must have a *substantial* impairment to one or more major life activities, have a record of such an impairment, or be regarded as having such an impairment. Whereas major life activities are defined to include caring for oneself, performing manual tasks, walking, seeing, hearing, speaking, breathing, learning, and working, nothing in the statute or in the regulations specifies that having a learning disability automatically qualifies one as "disabled" within Section 504.

Although Section 504 does not provide the same level of substantive programming that is required by IDEA, it does require reasonable accommodations. Basically, the accommodations relevant to postsecondary education and students with LD include auxiliary aids and services and program modification. The regulations also provide guidance about certain actions that might be viewed as discriminatory in the admissions process and once the student is enrolled (Rehabilitation Act Regulations, 1977).

Americans with Disabilities Act

Congress was able to draw on 17 years of experience with the Rehabilitation Act when it passed the ADA in 1990. Unlike Section 504 of the Rehabilitation Act, which is a very short statute, the ADA is lengthy and much more detailed. Many of the regulatory provisions and judicial interpretations relating to the definition of who is protected, what actions are discriminatory, and other issues were incorporated directly into the statutory language.

There are three primary sections of the ADA relevant to postsecondary students with LD. All three sections prohibit discrimination against otherwise qualified individuals with disabilities on the basis of their disabilities. Title I of the ADA applies to employers with 15 or more employees, Title II applies to state and local government agencies (including postsecondary education institutions), and Title III applies to private providers of public accommodations (including private postsecondary institutions). The remedies and procedures applicable to these sections vary, so it can matter which section applies. Title I requires an individual complaining of discrimination to first seek redress through administrative agency enforcement. Titles II and III allow an individual to go directly to court without exhausting administrative remedies, but one cannot recover damages under Title III in most cases.

Section 504 and the ADA may overlap in their application. For example, a private technical school may receive federal financial assistance through a grant or student financial aid assistance and thus be covered by both Title III (private provider of public accommodations) and Section 504 (recipient of federal financial assistance). Employees of the school would also be protected by Title I and Section 504. Although the substantive protections of the statutes are fairly consistent, the remedies and procedures can make a difference. For that reason, it is important to know whether more than one statute might apply in a given situation.

One significant aspect of the ADA that relates to postsecondary students with LD is the application to certifying agencies. Most of these agencies are state government entities, which were not subject to the Rehabilitation Act but which are subject to Title II of the ADA. Private certifying agencies or private entities that provide standardized testing services (e.g., the Educational Testing Service) are subject to Title III of the ADA.

The definition of who is protected under the ADA is virtually identical to that in the Rehabilitation Act. A three-part test protects individuals with substantial impairments to one or more major life activities, those with records of such impairments, or those who are regarded as having such impairments. The ADA also directly includes language that was developed through judicial interpretation of the Rehabilitation Act. Although most courts would find a learning disability to be a protected disability, a few have held that it is not a condition protected under the ADA or the Rehabilitation Act (*Dubois v. Alderson-Broaddus College, Inc.*, 1997; *Ellis v. Morehouse School of Medicine*, 1996; *Riblett v. The Boeing Co.*, 1995; *Sherman v. Optical Imaging Systems*, 1994). Some courts have found that conditions such as inability to organize material and attention-deficit/hyperactivity disorder (ADHD) are not disabilities entitling the individual to accommodations (*Argen v. New York State Board of Law Examiners*, 1994; *Pandazides v. Virginia Board of Education*, 1992; *Price v. National Board of Medical Examiners*, 1997; *Tips v. Regents of Texas Tech University*, 1996). The condition of adult ADHD is controversial within the health profession, with little judicial attention to whether this condition is to be treated as a disability (Ranseen & Campbell, 1996).

To be protected, individuals must be otherwise qualified to carry out the fundamental requirements of the program with or without reasonable accommodation (*Duke University*, 1993; *Ellis v. Morehouse School of Medicine*, 1996; *Emory University*, 1993; *Schartle v. Motorola, Inc.*, 1994; *Sedor v. Frank*, 1994; *United States International University*, 1994; *University of Massachusetts Medical Center*, 1993; *University of Minnesota*, 1995; *University of Santa Cruz*, 1993; *Vanderbilt University*, 1993; *Washington & Lee University*, 1993). Individuals who pose a direct threat to self, property, or others are not protected. For example, one court has held that a lawyer with ADHD should not, because of his disability, be excused from disciplinary measures relating to unethical conduct (*Oklahoma Bar Association v. Busch*, 1996). Another court found that an applicant with dyslexia who sought employment as a structural firefighter would compromise safety because of the requirement to read and identify words and symbols in a wide variety of emergency and nonemergency situations. Being able to know if there were hazardous materials in a building and dealing with elevator emergencies require reading skills (*DiPompo v. West Point Military Academy*, 1991).

The statute specifies that reasonable accommodations are required to ensure nondiscrimination. Perhaps because model regulations had already been promulgated pursuant to Section 504, and the statutes are generally intended to have consistent substantive requirements, no new regulations have yet been developed under the ADA specific to postsecondary institutions. There is, however, regulatory guidance related to certifying agencies and standardized test administrators that is useful to students with LD. The ADA regulations require that examination reflect abilities that the exam is intended to measure and that modifications be provided that do not fundamentally alter the measurement of skills or knowledge or result in an undue burden. The regulations list tape-recorded examinations, readers for individuals with LD, and other services (ADA Regulations, 28 C.F.R., § 36.309 [1994]).

JUDICIAL AND ADMINISTRATIVE AGENCY INTERPRETATIONS

Adult education programs may not discriminate in admissions and must provide reasonable accommodations in programming once the student is enrolled (*University of Minnesota*, 1995).

Admissions

Although there is a general prohibition against mandatory self-identification, when an education program has a special program specifically for individuals with a particular disability, it is permissible in that instance to *require* self-identification and that the applicant provide supporting documentation (*Fruth v. New York University*, 1993).

Identifying Individuals with Learning Disabilities   Requiring self-identification in the admissions process, however, is legal only when application to a special program is an option, and the individual with a learning disability can apply to the general program without making the disclosure.

Using Standardized Test Scores   There are a number of admissions practices that are not intentionally discriminatory but that may have a disparately negative impact on individuals with disabilities, including those with LD. The consideration of standardized test scores for admissions purposes is one of those practices and one that has been subject to evaluation in light of federal mandates on nondiscrimination.

The standardized test administration programs do not receive federal financial assistance and therefore are not subject to Section 504 of the Rehabilitation Act. They are, however, subject to Title III of the ADA and therefore have been required to provide reasonable accommodations on the tests. Even before the passage of the ADA, however, most standardized test programs provided accommodations because virtually all of the education programs to which scores were sent were subject to Section 504 (Sherman & Robinson, 1982). Accommodations on standardized tests have been provided by virtually all of the major national testing companies since the 1980s. These accommodations include extra time, use of scratch paper, and other accommodations that may enable a test taker with LD to demonstrate ability.

Although the major national companies, such as the Educational Testing Service, the Law School Admission Council, and others, are fairly adept at providing appropriate accommodations, some of the standardized testing programs at the state level are newer at providing accommodations, and legitimate complaints are more likely to occur regarding whether the test takers have been appropriately accommodated. For this reason, education programs requiring scores from these test administrators may be subject to challenge along with the test administrator. There is not yet a well-developed legal response to complaints about the smaller and newer test administrators, so guidance on this issue is difficult.

Accommodating the Enrolled Student

Students with disabilities in postsecondary education are not entitled to special education intended to meet their individualized needs. They are, however, entitled to *reasonable accommodations*. What this phrase means for students with LD has been the subject of some guidance in federal regulations and judicial and agency interpretations of those regulations.

Identifying the Individual Needing Accommodations   Federal law is clear that one need accommodate only *known* disabilities (*Barry v. City of Madison*, 1994; *Illingworth v. Nestle U.S.A., Inc.*, 1996). Generally speaking, it is the individual's obligation to make the disability known, to provide the documentation to support the provision of accommodations, and to do so in a timely manner (*Dubois v. Alderson-Broaddus College, Inc.*, 1997; *Temple University [PA]*, 1995; *University of California, Los Angeles*, 1996). Students in community colleges and vocational training programs, however, may be more accustomed to last-minute or even late enrollment. This practice may be an obstacle to the student needing accommodations in a course or in preplacement exams, which are increasingly being required in community colleges (*Community College of Vermont*, 1993). The education or testing program, however, must ensure that it has a system set up to facilitate this self-identification.

In one case, a court found that a job applicant for a custodial position had not given adequate notice of her learning disability and the need for an oral exam simply by indicating that she had taken special education courses in school. The county employer had indicated the procedure for requesting accommodations in the job announcement. Therefore, it was not a violation of the ADA to refuse her request for an oral exam on the day of the exam without provision of any documentation of her condition or an advance request for accommodation (*Morisky v. Broward County*, 1996).

Once the student has been admitted, there is no prohibition at that point against inviting students to self-identify *if they need accommodations*. In fact, it is advisable to do so. It is essential that education programs have a person who is responsible for coordinating services for students with disabilities. Service coordination need not be that administrator's sole function, but there must be a clearly identified individual or office where such services are provided.

Student admissions publications, student handbooks, and other general student literature should provide this information. The program might even wish to encourage admitted students needing accommodations to self-identify as early as in the acceptance letter or in enclosed flyers. The sooner the need for an accommodation is known, the easier it will be to facilitate.

A number of disputes have arisen in the courts or in the federal Department of Education Office for Civil Rights (OCR) about whether a student gave sufficient notice of the need for accommodations. The OCR and the courts have been quite reasonable in investigating and resolving these disputes and looking at each individual case (*University of California, Los Angeles,* 1996).

It is impossible to set guidelines for most accommodation issues. Each institution must evaluate requests on a case-by-case basis. Publishing the deadlines for making certain requests will put the institution in the best position when a denial is challenged. For example, if a program provides adequate notice through publications that a student requesting special exam accommodations must provide documentation of the need at least 2 weeks (or some other reasonable time, depending on the size of the program, the number of students with disabilities, and/or the ability to evaluate the documentation within the time frame), the student who shows up on the morning of the exam and asks for extra time is not in a good position to challenge the denial.

Care should be taken in giving individual faculty members discretion about what accommodations are to be given in various situations. Most faculty members do not have the expertise to evaluate a student's request for extra time on an exam (*Dinsmore v. University of California, Berkeley,* 1990). For that reason, a more systematic approach is essential. Conversely, central offices for students with disabilities should not be given the final word on whether an accommodation should be provided. The recommendations of those with expertise should be given deference, but a procedure for evaluating a faculty member's or a department's recommendation that the accommodation not be given should be in place.

It is also important to have a procedure for addressing grievances when an accommodation is refused. This procedure need not be a full-blown legal hearing, but it should provide for some reasonable mechanism for all sides to be heard and have their viewpoints considered.

It is not entirely clear what is required when the learning disability is unknown even to the individual at the time of the deficient performance. There seems to be some guidance from the courts and OCR that a later-identified learning disability should be a factor taken into account in a readmission or reconsideration request (*DePaul University,* 1993; *Illingworth v. Nestle U.S.A., Inc.,* 1996; Milani, 1996; *Riedel v. Board of Regents,* 1993).

Fundamental Requirements, Essential Aspects, and Undue Burden   The statutes and the courts have made clear that education programs are neither required to waive fundamental requirements or essential aspects of their programs in accommodating students with disabilities (*Bennett College [NC],* 1995) nor are they required to lower standards or provide accommodations that would be unduly burdensome (either financially or administratively). Attendance requirements need not be waived just because a student has a disability, and failure to attend may justify the denial of certain accommodations (*North Carolina Central University,* 1994).

A growing body of law, however, is also clarifying that although educational insti-tutions (particularly those involving law enforcement, teacher training, and health care professions) are given substantial deference in determining which requirements are fundamental, which aspects are essential, and which standards are to be applied, education programs are not automatically deferred to in making these decisions. These programs must demonstrate that alternative means—their feasibility, cost, and effect—were considered by appropriate individuals in refusing to provide requested accom-modations (*Wynne v. Tufts University School of Medicine*, 1991).

For example, one court found that a medical student with dyslexia could not be accommodated in such a way as to overcome his deficiencies. His performance diffi-culties included lack of cognitive abilities necessary for complex clinical diagnosis and inefficient processing of visually obtained information. These were deemed essential functions of the medical school by the professors, and the court deferred to this judg-ment (*Ellis v. Morehouse School of Medicine*, 1996).

One court, in addressing whether an applicant to take the bar exam should be given double time and other accommodations for her LD, determined that taking tests under time constraints and reading visually are not essential functions of being a lawyer (*Bartlett v. New York State Board of Law Examiners*, 1997). Another court required a university to reconsider its policy of not allowing waiver of a foreign language requirement, although the university has upheld the requirement to take core math courses (*Guckenberger v. Boston University*, 1997). It is not clear, however, whether such holdings will become a trend or are isolated decisions.

Auxiliary Aids and Services   Auxiliary aids and services might include tape-recorded texts, readers, and notetakers. Services of a personal nature, such as tape-recorded texts for personal reading, need not be provided (*Northern Arizona University*, 1994; *Oregon State University*, 1993). Although services such as specialized tutoring and counseling for students with LD *may* be provided, these are not generally considered to be reasonable accommodations that must be provided. Programs that provide tutoring and counseling to students generally, however, may not deny such services to students who have LD.

In addition to services, the availability of certain equipment, such as a Kurzweil machine or a computer in the library, may be considered auxiliary aids that should be available. Programs may not be required to provide such equipment to the student individually, but they may be required to have it available, depending on the factors discussed later.

The weight of judicial authority is that education programs *are* obligated to pay the costs of auxiliary aids and services when other outside sources are not available. Stu-dents may not be required to use insurance or other personal resources for such ser-vices (*United States v. Board of Trustees of the University of Alabama*, 1990).

Education programs are permitted to work with the student to facilitate funding by outside sources, such as state vocational rehabilitation, but they may not put the burden to gain access to these sources on the students themselves. For this reason, the early invitation to self-identify becomes important. The earlier a program knows that tape-recorded texts may be needed by the student, the earlier the program can con-sider allowing the student early enrollment to ensure placement in classes in which such texts are available; these texts can be obtained from programs such as Recording for the Blind rather than having to rely on in-house tape recording.

If an education program can demonstrate *undue burden* in providing a particular aid or service, then the service will not be considered a reasonable accommodation that must be provided by the program. Such a burden can be either administrative or financial. For example, a student may request to have a class tape recorded and the tapes transcribed and available within 24 hours. The program may be able to demonstrate that the cost of such transcription is prohibitive, that there are no personnel available to ensure such a turnaround, or both.

Modification of Programs and Services   Program modifications that might be considered by an adult education program include giving instructions orally, reduced courseloads, additional time on exams or special exam scheduling, different exam or evaluation format, separate classrooms for exams, advance registration to ensure placement in appropriate classes, extensions of time for assignments, and even waiver of courses or requirements within a course. Whether any of these modifications must legally be made in a particular instance can be evaluated only on a case-by-case basis. Most OCR rulings and judicial decisions have not required waiver of required work, such as math requirements (*Bennett College*, 1995; *Northern Illinois University*, 1995; *University of Texas at San Antonio*, 1995).

An interesting case involved a plumber who had been in the plumbing business for 23 years. When a county implemented a new licensing requirement involving a written exam, he failed to pass. A settlement between the Department of Justice and the licensing board required that the exam be administered orally and that the county develop and publicize a policy related to accommodations (*United States v. Rockland County Board of Plumbing, Heating, and Cooling Examiners*, 1995). A court in another case held that unlimited time for a teacher certification exam was not required (*Pandazides v. Virginia Board of Education*, 1992).

It should be remembered that institutions are not required to fundamentally alter their programs or to eliminate essential requirements that would lower academic or other performance standards (*Betts v. Rector & Visitors of the University of Virginia*, 1995; *In re Applicant 5*, 1995). The institution will usually bear the burden of demonstrating that a requested accommodation, for which there is supporting documentation, is not reasonable because of one of these factors or because it would be unduly burdensome to provide the accommodation (*Wynne v. Tufts University School of Medicine*, 1991). Although it may be good policy in some instances to require individuals declining accommodations that have been offered to verify this in writing, care should be taken not to go overboard. In one instance, a college was found to have violated the Rehabilitation Act when an instructor repeatedly and publicly asked a student with a learning disability to confirm that instructions were understood (*Columbia Basin College*, 1995).

Policies that have a disparate impact on individuals with LD might be challenged if there is not some opportunity for individualized evaluations. This is the case with respect to challenges of high school athletes who have been denied National Collegiate Athletic Association (NCAA) college scholarships because they had not taken the requisite core courses and did not have the required standardized test scores. Although the courts have thus far held that the NCAA need not lower standards, they have indicated in preliminary rulings that individualized assessments may be appropriate in some circumstances (*Butler v. NCAA*, 1996; *Ganden v. NCAA*, 1996).

Internships, Externships, and Noncredit and Free Programs   As postsecondary institutions have become more aware of the mandates of disability discrimination law, many of their questions related to on-campus activities have been addressed. Newer questions have begun to arise with respect to less traditional programming. These questions relate to internships, externships, and noncredit and free programs.

When a student is placed in an internship or externship for credit, the institution has an obligation to ensure that the host for the placement is in compliance with the applicable law (*San Jose State University*, 1993). The student, of course, still has the obligation to make known the need for accommodations. For example, a student who did not give adequate notice of the need for accommodating a learning disability in a social work field placement did not succeed in alleging a violation of Section 504 and the ADA (*University of California, Los Angeles*, 1996). Problems occur, however, when the student is not sure whether to make known the need to the host or to the postsecondary institution. For example, a student might be placed in a work-study–type setting at an office where the placement involves use of a computer. The student might need certain features of the computer adapted for a learning disability. When the postsecondary institution knows of the need for accommodations in advance of the placement, it is that institution's obligation to advise the internship program of the needs. This may require the institution to engage in some preparation or training.

The Need for Documentation   If an individual wants to receive accommodations in the admissions process or after enrollment, or special consideration in a readmissions context, then he or she is required to provide documentation of the learning disability (*Community College of Vermont*, 1993; *Morisky v. Broward County*, 1996; *University of Alaska Anchorage*, 1993).

Although some legal decisions and OCR opinions indicate that documentation must be reasonably recent, usually within the past 3–5 years (*Northwestern College [Ohio]*, 1995), a highly publicized case involving Boston University's withdrawal of services to students with LD resulted in a different standard. The court decided that the university's policy requiring documentation to be no more than 3 years old was invalid. Instead, documentation should be recent and appropriate (*Guckenberger v. Boston University*, 1997).

It is not uncommon for an adult learner with a learning disability to protest the need for recent documentation. Even those students who have not been evaluated may object because of the high cost of evaluating an individual for the presence of LD. Students with limited means may find this hurdle prohibitive. Nevertheless, the cost of the initial evaluation is to be paid by the student or applicant.

The Credentials of Evaluators   To identify the presence of a learning disability and the accommodations needed for that individual, an expert with appropriate credentials is required. Evaluation should be made by someone with specific training in LD. Court guidance indicates that evaluation should be made by someone with comprehensive training and appropriate experience (*Bartlett v. New York State Board of Law Examiners*, 1997; *Guckenberger v. Boston University*, 1997).

Once such documentation has been received by a postsecondary institution, there should be a mechanism for evaluating and assessing the legitimacy of the requests for accommodations. For that reason, the institution should refer these requests either to in-house staff or to outside consultants for assessment. Like the initial evaluator, the person assessing the evaluation should have training in LD, preferably LD in adult learners.

Timing of Evaluation   Postsecondary institutions have legitimate reasons for requesting that reasonable notice be given by students seeking accommodations such as additional time on exams and other accommodations previously discussed. The students should be given a reasonable deadline for requesting the accommodation and providing the documentation to justify the request. The institution must both evaluate the documentation and implement the staffing or other support needed to provide the accommodation. In one instance, however, because the policy on make-up exams was found to be unduly vague with respect to students with disabilities, the OCR found that

Section 504 had been violated by denying a student's petition to take a make-up exam when she had just learned of her disability (*Harvard University*, 1994).

TRANSITION TO THE WORKPLACE: PROFESSIONAL LICENSING

Professional licensing, although not directly the responsibility of a postsecondary institution, frequently involves such academic institutions in one significant way to students with disabilities.

Standardized Certifying Exams

The first area in which there can be academic institutional involvement relates to the standardized tests that an individual must frequently pass for entry into a profession. Such exams are common for admission to the practice of law (*Argen v. New York State Board of Law Examiners*, 1994; *Christian v. New York State Board of Law Examiners*, 1995; *Fowler v. New York State Board of Law Examiners*, 1994; *In re Rubenstein*, 1994; *Weintraub v. Board of Bar Examiners*, 1992), most health care professions (*Wynne v. Tufts University School of Medicine*, 1991), and teaching (*Florida Department of Education*, 1993; *Pandazides v. Virginia Board of Education*, 1992). Many trades also have standardized tests that must be passed (*United States v. Rockland County Board of Plumbing, Heating, and Cooling Examiners*, 1995).

For the student entering a licensed profession following a postsecondary program, the agency administering the program may request that the academic institution provide information about the accommodations the student received in the academic program. This is because licensing agencies may be inexperienced in knowing which types of accommodations they should grant to students with disabilities, particularly those with LD. For example, the agencies often rely on the academic institution to indicate that a student needs time and a half on the exam. These agencies often require validation of the existence of the disability. They want to ensure that the student is not suddenly discovering a disability to gain an advantage by having additional time on the exam.

Caution should be exercised in providing information about disabilities and accommodations to licensing agencies administering such tests. First, of course, the academic institution should obtain a release from the student allowing this information to be provided (Family Education Rights and Privacy Act, 1974). Second, the academic institution should be aware of the fact that a student may have received an accommodation in an academic program does not necessarily indicate whether the student needs such an accommodation on a licensing exam. In addition, the accommodations received in the academic program are not necessarily appropriate to the licensing exam. For example, a student in a teacher education course with short essay–type tests at the end of each unit of study may not have required significant accommodations, such as additional time to take the exam. That same student, however, may need additional time on a lengthy multiple-choice exam given over more than one day.

This is not to say that the accommodation record from the academic program may not be of value to the licensing agency. It is just that the agency should evaluate it in light of the limitations previously mentioned, and the institution should remind the licensing agency of the limitations (*Bartlett v. New York State Board of Law Examiners*, 1997; *Pandazides v. Virginia Board of Education*, 1992; *Price v. National Board of Medical Examiners*, 1997).

STRATEGY FOR ENSURING COMPLIANCE

If a postsecondary institution's goal is compliance with nondiscrimination laws, then a plan to ensure compliance is needed. One of the key elements of such a plan is a positive attitude and sensitivity toward students with LD.

Attitudes

Just as doctors are less likely to be sued for malpractice when they have a good bedside manner and communicate well with patients and staff, it is probable that the academic institution with a proactive and positive attitude toward students with LD will be less likely to be subject to challenges by these students. In a highly publicized case, a court commented on statements about students with LD but did not require the university to pay damages to plaintiffs who claimed that changed administrative policies had created a hostile learning environment (*Guckenberger v. Boston University*, 1997).

Knowledge of Learning Disabilities and the Law

Faculty members and key administrators should be sensitized to what a learning disability is and how it should be accommodated. In-service programming to educate these individuals about what it means to have a learning disability and what the law requires with respect to students who have LD is therefore beneficial.

Developing Policies and Procedures

Although most postsecondary institutions should have engaged in self-evaluation and prioritization under Section 504, the ADA, or both, if such an evaluation has not been done or if it has not focused on issues relating to LD, then such an assessment would be useful. Students with LD and others with expertise on the issue should be involved.

If an ADA compliance coordinator has not been designated, then this should be done. This individual should have a clear understanding of his or her responsibilities. The coordinator should also develop a network of experts and support services providers. Such a network might include individuals in the state vocational rehabilitation agency, the counseling and testing service on campus or a similar program in the community, expert consultants with knowledge of LD in adults, and legal counsel.

Policies and procedures should be developed and should include a procedure for obtaining reasonable accommodations and a grievance procedure to resolve disputes (*San Francisco Community College District [CA]*, 1996). The requirements for documentation of a learning disability should be clearly spelled out. It is important to determine whether state law defines learning disability in a particular way that would be applied at least to public institutions. Once policies and procedures have been developed, they should be communicated to students, staff, and faculty.

Admissions materials should not ask impermissible questions about the presence of LD. Admissions professionals should have awareness about nondiscrimination on the basis of disabilities. Admissions materials and student handbooks should indicate the nondiscrimination policy and where to obtain information about services. Faculty members should be encouraged to indicate on their syllabi and orally how to go about obtaining reasonable accommodations. Policies and procedures should ensure appropriate confidentiality protection for students with disabilities. These policies should be made known to appropriate staff and faculty, as well as to students.

A procedure should be in place to encourage students needing accommodations to self-identify as early as possible. Deadlines should be reasonable and should be clearly stated. It is also useful to maintain some type of centralized process for recording accommodations that have been made. Having such a record will help to demonstrate compliance, and it will also help to ensure consistency.

Having an ongoing ADA compliance workgroup that includes students with disabilities can be a valuable tool for ensuring continued success. The goal is not simply technical, legal compliance. Communicating to protected parties about the policies and practices and exhibiting a positive and proactive attitude will help avoid challenges. An institution that successfully defends a challenge by the OCR or in court has still undergone substantial administrative time and effort and oftentimes adverse publicity as a result. For this reason, good attitudes cannot be stressed enough.

CONCLUSION

Although federal law has required nondiscrimination against individuals with LD since 1973, it is only since the early 1990s that the application of these requirements to adult learners with LD has begun to develop. Difficulties in identifying who is protected by federal law and in knowing how to appropriately accommodate LD have caused legal challenges to practices and policies of educational institutions, professional licensing programs, and employers. Such challenges have required these entities to focus more specifically on the fundamental requirements of their programs and activities.

Although a better understanding is beginning to emerge as to how to comply with federal law, there is still much confusion in this area. Programs in the best position to respond to these difficult challenges are those with positive attitudes. In addition, those programs that will find themselves having the least difficulty will be those that take a proactive approach toward compliance through good faith efforts to understanding their legal responsibilities and that have implemented reasonable policies and procedures as a response.

REFERENCES

Americans with Disabilities Act of 1990, PL 101-336, 42 U.S.C. §§ 12101 *et seq.*
Americans with Disabilities Act Regulations, 28 C.F.R. § 36.309 (1994).
Argen v. New York State Board of Law Examiners, 860 F. Supp. 84 (W.D.N.Y. 1994).
Barry v. City of Madison, 5 NDLR ¶ 156 (W.D. Wis. 1994).
Bartlett v. New York State Board of Law Examiners, 1997 WL 375689 (S.D.N.Y. 1997).
Bennett College (NC), 7 NDLR ¶ 26 (OCR 1995).
Betts v. Rector & Visitors of the University of Virginia, 939 F. Supp. 461 (W.D. Va. 1996).
Butler v. NCAA, C.A. No. 96-1656D (W.D. Wash. 1996).
Christian v. New York State Board of Law Examiners, 899 F. Supp. 1254 (S.D.N.Y. 1995).
Columbia Basin College (WA), 7 NDLR ¶ 188 (OCR 1995).
Community College of Vermont, 4 NDLR ¶ 406 (1993).
Community Colleges and Students with Disabilities. (1993). *National Clearinghouse on Postsecondary Education for Individuals with Disabilities,* 12(1), 1, 6–7.
DePaul University, 4 NDLR ¶ 157 (OCR 1993).
DiPompo v. West Point Military Academy, 770 F. Supp. 887 (S.D.N.Y. 1991).
Dinsmore v. University of California, Berkeley (N.D. Cal., September 23, 1990) (settlement).
Dubois v. Alderson-Broaddus College, Inc., 950 F. Supp. 754 (N.D. W. Va. 1997).
Duke University, 4 NDLR ¶ 488 (1993).
Education for All Handicapped Children Act of 1975, PL 94-142, 20 U.S.C. §§ 1400 *et seq.*

Ellis v. Morehouse School of Medicine, 925 F. Supp. 1529 (N.D. Ga. 1996).

Emory University 5, NDLR ¶ 79 (1993).

Family Education Rights and Privacy Act of 1974, PL 93-380, 20 U.S.C. § 1232g.

Florida Department of Education, 4 NDLR ¶ 333 (1993).

Fowler v. New York State Board of Law Examiners, 885 F. Supp. 66 (W.D.N.Y. 1994).

Fruth v. New York University, 2 AD Cas (BNA) 1197 (S.D.N.Y. 1993).

Ganden v. NCAA, 1996 U.S. Dist. LEXIS 17368 (N.D. Ill. 1996).

Guckenberger v. Boston University, 974 F. Supp. 106 (D. Mass. 1997).

Harvard University (MA), 6 NDLR ¶ 58 (1994).

Illingworth v. Nestle U.S.A., Inc., F. Supp. (D.N.J. 1996).

Individuals with Disabilities Education Act (IDEA) of 1990, PL 101-476, 20 U.S.C. §§ 1401 *et. seq.*

In re Applicant 5, 6 NDLR ¶ 357 (Del. 1995).

In re Rubenstein, 637 A.2d 1131 (Del. 1994).

Milani, A. (1996). Disabled students in higher education. *Journal of College and University Law,* *22*(4), 989, 1004–1008.

Morisky v. Broward County, 5 AD Cases 737 (11th Cir. 1996).

North Carolina Central University, 6 NDLR ¶ 205 (1994).

Northern Arizona University, 5 NDLR ¶ 284 (1994).

Northern Illinois University, 7 NDLR ¶ 392 (OCR 1995).

Northwestern College (Ohio), 6 NDLR ¶ 261 (1995).

Oklahoma Bar Association v. Busch, 919 P.2d 1114 (Okla. Sup. Ct. 1996).

Oregon State University, 5 NDLR ¶ 19 (1993).

Pandazides v. Virginia Board of Education, 804 F. Supp. 794 (E.D. Va. 1992).

Price v. National Board of Medical Examiners, 966 F. Supp. 419 (S.D.W. Va. 1997).

Ranseen, J.D., & Campbell, D.A. (1996). Adult attention deficit disorder: Current concepts & controversies. *The Bar Examiner,* 65(1), 49–56.

Rehabilitation Act of 1973, PL 93-112, 29 U.S.C. §§ 701 *et seq.*

Rehabilitation Act Regulations, 34 C.F.R. Part 104 (1977).

Riblett v. The Boeing Co., 1995 WL 580053 (D. Kan. 1995).

Riedel v. Board of Regents, 1993 WL 500892 (D. Kan. 1993).

Rothstein, L.F. (1997). *Disabilities and the law* (2nd ed.). Rochester, NY: Westgroup Publishing Company.

San Francisco Community College District (CA), 8 NDLR ¶ 281 (1996).

San Jose State University, 4 NDLR ¶ 358 (1993).

Schartle v. Motorola, Inc., 1994 WL 323281 (N.D. Ill. 1994).

Sedor v. Frank, 42 F.3d 741 (2d Cir. 1994).

Sherman v. Optical Imaging Systems, 843 F. Supp. 1168 (E.D. Mich. 1994).

Sherman, S., & Robinson, N. (Eds.) (1982). *Ability testing of handicapped people: Dilemma for government, science, and the public.* Washington, DC: National Academy Press.

Temple University (PA), 8 NDLR ¶ 125 (1995).

Tips v. Regents of Texas Tech University, 8 NDLR ¶ 48 (N.D. Tex. 1996).

United States v. Board of Trustees of the University of Alabama, 908 F.2d 740 (11th Cir. 1990).

United States v. Rockland County Board of Plumbing, Heating, and Cooling Examiners, N.Y. Settlement (8/28/95).

United States International University, 6 NDLR ¶ 232 (1994).

University of Alaska Anchorage, 5 NDLR ¶ 39 (1993).

University of California, Los Angeles, 8 NDLR ¶ 314 (1996).

University of Massachusetts Medical Center, 4 NDLR ¶ 314 (1993).

University of Minnesota, 6 NDLR ¶ 295 (OCR 1995).

University of Santa Cruz, 5 NDLR § 37 (1993).

University of Texas at San Antonio, 7 NDLR ¶ 447 (OCR 1995).

Vanderbilt University, 4 NDLR ¶ 382 (1993).

Washington & Lee University, 5 NDLR ¶ 78 (1993).

Weintraub v. Board of Bar Examiners, SJC-06058 (S. Jud. Ct. Mass. 1992).

Wynne v. Tufts University School of Medicine, 932 F.2d 19 (1st Cir. 1991).

3

Educational Attainment of Adults with Learning Disabilities

Susan A. Vogel and Stephen Reder

A well-known reality for decades among individuals with learning disabilities has been that learning disabilities (LD) are a lifelong condition. However, most earlier studies have focused on private school, school district, regional, or state samples of adults with LD who were, for the most part, out of high school for only 5 years or less. Many of these studies have reported very contradictory findings that can be understood in light of methodological differences, including criteria for identification as having LD, sample selection criteria, type of school attended, size and gender distribution of the sample, racial and ethnic composition, socioeconomic status of sample and/or school district, cognitive abilities, and severity of learning disability (Vogel, 1996). Nonetheless, they are foundational studies in the field regarding adult outcomes in the field of LD.

For example, the findings varied based on what schools the individuals attended, including a private preparatory school (Rawson, 1968); private schools designed specifically for children and adolescents with LD (Rogan & Hartman, 1976, 1990; Spekman, Goldberg, & Herman, 1992); and a small, private, liberal arts college with comprehensive support services for adults with LD (Vogel & Adelman, 1990a, 1990b). The findings also varied based on where an individual's learning disability was identified—for example, in a hospital or a university-affiliated evaluation center (Blalock, 1982, 1987; Gottesman, 1994; Johnson, 1994; Johnson & Blalock, 1987; Silver & Hagin, 1964, 1985); a public school (Affleck, Edgar, Levine, & Kortering, 1990; Blackorby & Wagner, 1996;

This research was supported by a grant from the ACLD Foundation to the authors and contract number R117Q0003 to the National Center on Adult Literacy from the U.S. Department of Education, Office of Educational Research and Improvement. The findings and opinions expressed here are those of the authors and do not necessarily reflect the views of the foundation or any institution or agency.

43

Nourse, 1995; Scuccimarra & Speece, 1990; Sitlington & Frank, 1990); or a college/university (Shaywitz & Shaw, 1988; Vogel & Adelman, 1990a). In addition, some follow-up studies consisted of all students with LD who were receiving support services in high school at the time of data collection (Blackorby & Wagner, 1996; Fairweather & Shaver, 1991; Scuccimarra & Speece, 1990), whereas others included in their follow-up only high school or college/university graduates (Affleck et al., 1990; Bruck, 1985; Greenbaum, 1993; Nisbet & Lichtenstein, 1993; Nourse, 1995; Sitlington & Frank, 1990; Vogel & Adelman, 1990a).

Other significant differences could be attributed to variability in cognitive functioning, severity of learning disability, or both. Frauenheim and Heckerl (1983), Gottesman (1994), and Johnson (1994) reported on a subgroup who had very severe reading disabilities. Other samples, such as Rawson's (1968), were in the gifted range in intellectual abilities and had high socioeconomic status and mild LD. The impact of these factors on outcomes can be seen in Rawson's landmark follow-up study of 20 men with dyslexia who attended a small private preparatory school in which not only did 100% graduate from high school but 80% also graduated from college, and many completed graduate and professional degrees.

As students with LD have matured, concern regarding the high school dropout rate has also increased. Two of the earliest follow-up studies focused on individuals who attended specific urban or semirural school districts (deBettencourt, Zigmond, & Thornton, 1989; Zigmond & Thornton, 1985). According to Zigmond and Thornton (1985), the dropout rate for students with LD in an urban school district was an alarming 54%. In contrast, deBettencourt et al. (1989) found the high school dropout rate for such students in a semirural district was only 36%. Based on the national statistics that are reported each year in the United States, the dropout rate has remained close to 36%. In the *Sixteenth Annual Report to Congress on the Implementation of the Individuals with Disabilities Education Act* (U.S. Department of Education, 1994), the high school dropout rate was reported to be 12.3%; when combined with the additional 17.7% who left school for "unknown reasons" (usually also considered dropouts), the dropout rate can be estimated to be approximately 30%. Even this relatively low dropout rate has led to an increase in concern regarding what happens to adolescents with LD after they leave high school, whether by dropping out, receiving a certificate of completion, or becoming too old to attend. There has also been concern about the limited number of high school dropouts who enroll in adult secondary education (ASE) and receive their General Equivalency Diploma (GED) as well as the limited number of high school graduates with LD who enroll in postsecondary programs, and even more concern about the minuscule number who graduate from a postsecondary institution.

EDUCATIONAL ATTAINMENT BEYOND HIGH SCHOOL FOR ADULTS WITH LEARNING DISABILITIES: RESULTS OF EARLY STUDIES

Until the late 1980s, there was very limited information (other than from the foundational studies based on clinical groups of individuals or individuals who attended specific private schools) regarding postschool outcomes of adults with LD. In 1978, the implementation regulations of Section 504 of the Rehabilitation Act of 1973 (PL 93-112) were passed and the American Council on Education (ACE) collected the first data regarding enrollment of students with disabilities in higher education (Henderson, 1995). It was not until 1988, however, that ACE collected benchmark data regarding postsecondary enrollment for college and university freshmen with self-reported learning disabilities

(SRLD). There were no shock waves created when ACE reported that slightly more than 1% of all first-year college students had SRLD (Henderson, 1995); this number represented 15% of all students with disabilities in the nation. Neither did it come as a surprise when Bursuck, Rose, Cowen, and Yahaya (1989) reported that only 20 institutions (representing 10% of the 197 institutions that returned the surveys) responded to the item asking for the number of students with LD who graduated from their postsecondary institution—indicative, perhaps, of the unavailability of such information at that time.

The first type of postsecondary data to be collected, therefore, concerned enrollment patterns for high school graduates. Some of these findings were based on follow-up studies conducted by specific high school districts, colleges, or universities; others were from follow-up studies conducted regionally, statewide, or both. One of the first follow-up studies on postsecondary enrollment was conducted by Sitlington and Frank (1990). They reported the results of a survey sent to almost 1,000 high school graduates with LD in the state of Iowa and reported that, although 50% had enrolled in a postsecondary program immediately after graduating, 1 year later only 7% were still enrolled. In order to further examine the question of postsecondary degree completion, Vogel and Adelman (1990a, 1992) followed a group of 107 college students with documented LD and a random stratified sample of 153 of their peers without LD matched on gender and year of entrance to a small, liberal arts, competitive private college that offered comprehensive learning disability support services. They reported that 37% of the students with LD as compared with 39% of the students without LD had graduated and that each group took 6$^1/_2$ years to graduate (Vogel & Adelman, 1990a).

Two years later, Vogel and Adelman (1992) compared the students who had LD with a traditional college-age group of students without LD matched on the American College Testing composite score. This measure was selected for matching the groups in order to control for differences in high school preparation as well as age. In this study, they also found no significant differences in graduation rates. In fact, for students with LD, the graduation rate (33%) was slightly (although not significantly) higher than that of the matched group without LD (26%). In summary, the undergraduate degree completion rate for students with LD was high (between 33% and 37%), and there was no significant difference in the graduation rate for students with and without LD.

In an attempt to address this same issue, Edgar and his colleagues (Affleck et al., 1990, Edgar & Levine 1988) initiated the First Decade after Graduation Study in the state of Washington in 1985, comparing groups of high school graduates with school-identified learning disabilities (SILD) with those with mental retardation and with a group of students without disabilities. Of particular interest are the study results of Levine and Edgar (1995) and Nourse (1995), who traced the postsecondary enrollment and graduation patterns of 892 adults with SILD who had graduated from high schools in 13 districts in Washington state. As did earlier researchers, they found a decline in enrollment for the SILD group in postsecondary school each consecutive year. In the first year after graduation, 37% of the men and 26% of the women were enrolled in a postsecondary setting, as compared with 79% of men and 71% of women without disabilities. Two years after high school graduation, the percentages among those with SILD declined to 28% of the men and 11% of the women but remained relatively stable for men and women without disabilities (Levine & Edgar, 1995). Although they found highly significant differences between those individuals with and without LD, the authors reported only minimal gender differences. However, this may have been a result of a very small sample size, apparent on visual examination of the published tables, and the fact that more than twice as many men as women with SILD were enrolled in postsecondary school 2 years after graduation.

These findings may also be related to Levine and Edgar's (1995) broad definition of *postsecondary education*—which included business, vocational, and trade schools; the Job Corps; community colleges; and universities—and to the way they reported postsecondary enrollment and graduation data in the aggregate for all of these settings. In contrast, postsecondary completion rate, grouped under the umbrella of "credentials," was divided into three categories: 1) certificate or license, 2) Associate in Arts (A.A.) degree, and 3) Bachelor of Arts (B.A.) degree (Levine & Edgar, 1995). Because of the size of the total group of individuals, the breakdown by type of postsecondary completion/degree, and the limited number of adults with LD who completed an A.A. or B.A. degree, the resulting subgroups in the higher education degree completion categories were quite small. In reporting these data by subgroup, the number of adults with LD enrolled in a postsecondary setting at the last two data collection periods (6 and 7 years after graduating or exiting from high school) was 12 of 61 men and 0 of 27 women in Year 6; in Year 7, 9 of 62 men and 2 of 21 women with LD were enrolled in postsecondary education. When the data were broken down by type of degree earned, 7% (4/62) of the men received an A.A. degree, as compared with 11% (3/27) of the women. However, of the 62 men, only 1 had earned a B.A. degree, while no women had done so. These findings must be interpreted cautiously because of the very small subgroup size.

One nationwide study to date, the National Longitudinal Transition Study (NLTS) conducted by SRI International, addressed the question of postsecondary enrollment and completion, as well as the aspects of secondary school education that contributed to high school graduation, successful transition to full-time employment, and living a satisfying life after high school (Blackorby & Wagner, 1996; Marder & D'Amico, 1992; Wagner, 1989, 1992; Wagner, Blackorby, Cameto, Hebbeler, & Newman, 1993; Wagner et al., 1991). This database included data collected on students less than 2 years after exiting from high school and then again on a subset of the total sample 3–5 years after exiting from high school. The study utilized a nationally representative sample of 8,000 young adults from the 13 disability categories as defined by federal law at that time. Participants were 13–21 years old in the 1985–1986 school year and were receiving special education services (Wagner et al., 1993). They came from a sample of 300 school districts stratified by region of the country, wealth, and size, and 22 private secondary special education schools for deaf, blind, and/or deafblind students. This comprehensive study provided descriptive information regarding individual and family characteristics, schools attended, special services received, high school graduation rate, ASE enrollment and completion of the GED, postsecondary enrollment and completion, employment, and postschool life experiences such as living arrangements and trouble with the law. The gender ratio was 73.2% male and 26.8% female, or 2.7:1, a gender ratio typical of SILD samples. Among the participants with LD, 24% were African American, as compared with 12% among the sample without disabilities. The findings were compared with data available on a cohort of youth without disabilities who participated in the National Longitudinal Survey of Youth (Wagner et al., 1991).

Because we have noted that the number of years since exit from high school has a significant impact on findings, we are focusing on the follow-up study conducted 3–5 years after exiting high school, in which Wagner, D'Amico, Marder, Newman, and

Blackorby (1992) contacted a subsample of 327 adults with LD who were ages 26 or younger. The major findings relevant to the present discussion were

1. The high school graduation rate for students with LD was 63.6%.
2. The high school dropout rate for these students was 35.6%.
3. The percentage of high school dropouts with SILD who enrolled in ASE was 29.1%; however, only 2.8% obtained their GED certificates.
4. A total of 30.5% had enrolled in some type of postsecondary program.
5. Of the 30.5%, 19.0% attended a vocational school, 13.7% enrolled in a community college, and 4.4% attended a 4-year college.
6. Eleven percent completed a program in a vocational school, 2.9% completed a 2-year degree, and 0.4% completed a 4-year degree, yielding an average for postsecondary program or degree completion of 3.3%.

One of the limitations of the NLTS database is obviously that the adults exited from high school *only* 3–5 years before the last data collection. In fact, age of participants was identified as one of the important variables that have an impact on outcomes (Vogel, 1996), and Polloway, Smith, and Patton (1984) emphasized the importance of having a life-span approach in the study of adults with LD. A significantly older group of adults with SRLD responded to a questionnaire inserted in the Winter 1995 issue of *LDA Newsbriefs*. (Although the survey could have been filled out by adults with LD, their parents, or their teachers, in order to control for differences in informants, we are reporting here only the findings from the 332 respondents who filled out the survey themselves.) This survey was designed to determine educational attainment, vocational history, mental and physical health, income and income management, living arrangements, interaction with the justice system, and prevalence of learning and other disabilities in the families of respondents (Kissire, 1996). Among those who responded, the gender distribution was 43% male and 57% female, and the ethnic composition, albeit reported by only two thirds of the sample, was 1% each for African American, Asian, and Native American and 2% "other." Fifty-two percent were 37 years of age or older, making this an older sample than that in the NLTS. Fourteen percent of the respondents reported that they had never been formally diagnosed as having a learning disability. The findings of special interest here are that the high school graduation rate was similar to that of students living in a semirural community reported previously (i.e., two thirds of the respondents had completed high school) (Fleischner, 1996). Moreover, 22% had earned a 4-year college degree, and 15% had completed graduate school (Fleischner, 1996). It is difficult to determine the impact of outcomes on willingness to respond, but we cannot preclude the possibility that the respondents volunteered to fill out the survey because they felt proud of their accomplishments and were more willing to disclose positive outcomes. Nonetheless, this is an important study because this is a considerably older sample, and it has addressed one of the major questions about adults with LD—namely, what happens to them more than 5 years beyond exit from high school. However, although much has been learned from this study, these findings, too, must be interpreted with caution because the respondents volunteered to respond to the survey.

In summary, it appears as though there are uncertain if not contradictory findings regarding the educational attainment of adults with LD, and limited data exist regarding completion of a postsecondary certificate, degree, or both and the interaction of gender and LD on educational attainment. However, in general, the statewide and national studies reported significantly lower educational attainment for adults with LD.

The range in reported high school graduation rate was between 32% and 66%, whereas high school dropout rate was as high as 54%. At least for the present, the only national database we have regarding 2- and 4-year degree completion presents a very dismal picture indeed, with a 2-year degree completion rate of approximately 3% and a 4-year completion rate of 0.4% (Affleck et al., 1990; Blackorby & Wagner, 1996; Fairweather & Shaver, 1991; Frank, Sitlington, & Carson, 1995; Levine, 1993; Scuccimarra & Speece, 1990; Sitlington & Frank, 1990). Some of the possible reasons for contradictory findings were the result of limitations of prior studies—namely, the limited age range of the participants, differences in how the samples were drawn (volunteers versus school identified, clinic referred, or random, stratified samples), small sample size, and the restricted number of years following exit from high school (Vogel, 1996).

NATIONAL ADULT LITERACY SURVEY DATABASE ON ADULTS WITH SELF-REPORTED LEARNING DISABILITIES

Findings from an adult database that avoided some of these methodological problems are described in this section. We report the findings relevant to educational attainment among adults with SRLD as compared with adults without SRLD who responded to the National Adult Literacy Survey (NALS). Following this discussion, we explore the interaction of learning disability and gender on educational attainment and the implications of these findings that are especially germane for learning disability specialists, adult educators, and literacy providers in curriculum and program planning in formal and informal educational settings (elementary, junior high/middle school, secondary school, and postsecondary).

Methodology

The primary purpose of the NALS was to identify the skills needed to function in a literate society and to measure the functional English literacy skills of adults in the United States using tasks involving everyday life situations and written materials. It utilized an assessment framework that combined the methodologies of item-response theory and large-scale group surveys (Kirsch, Jungeblut, Jenkins, & Kolstad, 1993) and employed a literacy profiling approach developed by Irwin Kirsch and his colleagues (Campbell, Kirsch, & Kolstad, 1992; Kirsch et al., 1993; Mosenthal & Kirsch, 1994). The participants responded to open-ended questions (rather than multiple- choice items). These assessment methods were used to profile the literacy proficiency distributions of various subgroups of adults on prose, document, and quantitative scales. Because the three literacy proficiencies as measured by the NALS are so highly intercorrelated as to be effectively unidimensional, the prose, document, and quantitative scores were averaged for each individual into a composite literacy score for the purposes of this chapter (Reder, 1995).

In addition to these three literacy domains, the participants were asked a set of questions about their demographic characteristics, years of schooling and educational experiences, employment and training experiences, economic status, self-assessment of reading and writing abilities, perceptions and uses of literacy, various languages spoken in the home, whether they received any assistance with literacy tasks from family or friends, their political and social participation, and literacy activities. Survey respondents also carried out a series of simulated everyday functional literacy tasks requiring literacy proficiency and problem-solving ability, such as completing a form, locating information on a map, summarizing information from newspaper articles, and solving mathematics problems from information provided on maps, charts, graphs, and diagrams. Based on their performance on these tasks and background information provided, individuals were assigned a set of plausible values ranging from 0 to 500 points.

The NALS Participants

The NALS was administered during 1-hour in-home interviews of a stratified random sample of adults ages 16 years and older (referred to as the *household sample*). (Technical details about the survey design, assessment techniques and instruments, and administration procedures are described in Kirsch et al., 1993.) The data examined came from the household sample of the NALS, which included 24,944 randomly selected Americans, none of whom were institutionalized.

The Target Group The target group for the analyses reported was defined as a subgroup of individuals living in the United States who met five conditions: 1) born in the United States, 2) spoke English before entering school, 3) did not report having mental retardation, 4) were not students at the time of the survey, and 5) were between the ages of 25 and 64. The target group of individuals was restricted to native-born individuals who spoke English before entering school because of the concern that individuals who first attended foreign schools would not have spoken English at the time they started school in the United States, and their literacy proficiency may have been adversely affected. Finally, individuals who were students at the time of participation were excluded from the study because their educational attainment would have still been in a state of flux. Of the 24,944 individuals in the household sample (drawn from a group of 191 million adults in the nation), 14,495 satisfied the five selection criteria and had no missing data (referred to as the *target sample*); this group consisted of 8,231 women and 6,264 men between 25 and 64 years of age. This target sample represented a group of 100.6 million individuals that included 48.2 million men (48%) and 52.2 million women (52%).

The SRLD Participants NALS participants were asked if they currently had a learning disability. Those respondents answering "yes" to this question were designated as the SRLD group in this study. Despite the frequent use of self-identification as an indicator of LD, the false-positive and false-negative rates of misclassification in the general adult participants of this indicator with respect to other assessment techniques is unknown. In addition, neither the reliability nor the validity of the measure has been established. Within the target sample, 392 individuals (representing 2.8 million adults) indicated that they had a learning disability. Among those with SRLD, there were more men than women (56% compared with 44%).

Racial/Ethnic Background The prevalence of SRLD among the 25- to 64-year-old target group was 3.6% for African Americans and 2.7% for non–African Americans. Alternatively, the percentage of African Americans in the SRLD participants was 11.5% versus 15.1% among the non-SRLD population. The overall percentage of African Americans was 11.6%. A likelihood-ratio chi-square test of independence was conducted, and no significant effect was found ($\chi^2 = 2.26_1$; $p = 13$); that is, there was no significant difference in the incidence of SRLD between the African American and non–African American participants. Therefore, for the purposes of this chapter, no other disaggregation-by-race analyses were conducted.

Data Analysis Strategies

The basic data for this study are reported in terms of SRLD status (the non-SRLD participants and the SRLD participants) and by gender—that is, for men and women with and without SRLD. Descriptive statistics (e.g., SRLD prevalence rates, gender ratios, averages of such variables as educational attainment by categories of another variable) are estimated for the subgroups using the NALS survey case weights. Several inferential statistics were utilized to carry out significance tests: likelihood ratio t-tests were used to compare the means of a variable in the two groups, such as male and female; likelihood-ratio chi-square tests of independence were carried out to examine the possible interaction of SRLD and gender; and analyses of variance (ANOVAs) were conducted to examine the effects of SRLD and gender on educational attainment. All such inferential tests were conducted using "design-weighted" data in which the NALS survey weights are rescaled to sum to one half of the target sample or subsample size for a given analysis; this rescaling effectively compensates for the complex hierarchical sampling design of NALS, which is less efficient than simple random samplings (D. Rock, personal communication, 1994).

Definition of Variables

Age   Although the total NALS sample age range was 16 years of age and older, only individuals between the ages of 25 and 64 were included in this study. The participants at the time of the interview were divided into four age groupings (25–34, 35–44, 45–54, and 55–64 years).

Educational Attainment   When used as an independent variable, educational attainment was treated as an ordinal variable as follows:

1. Completion of 0–8 years of schooling
2. Completion of 9–12 years of education without having graduated or having received the GED
3. Graduation from high school or completion of the GED
4. Some college without having received a degree
5. Graduation from a 2-year, 4-year, graduate, or professional school

When used as a dependent variable in ANOVAs, educational attainment was treated as a continuous variable and coded as the number of years of schooling: the number of the highest grade completed for Grades 0–11; 12 for high school graduation or GED; 13 for some college (no degree); 14 for a 2-year degree; 15 for more than 2 years of college without having completed a degree; 16 for a bachelor's degree; 17 for having attended graduate school without completing a degree; and 18 for having completed a graduate degree.

Results

Prevalence of SRLD and Gender Distribution   Of the target group meeting the five selection criteria, 2.9% self-reported having a learning disability. As can be seen in Figure 3.1, the gender distribution in the non-SRLD participants was 48% men and 52% women, corresponding to a male/female ratio of 0.9:1.1. Given that in most twin studies and samples of self-referred and research-identified individuals there is approximately a 1.3:1 male/female ratio, it was not surprising that the same pattern was seen among the adults with SRLD in the NALS participants. As can also be seen in Figure 3.1, there were slightly more men (56%) than women (44%) self-reporting a learning disability, representing a 1.3:1 male/female ratio.

Educational Attainment in the Non-SRLD and SRLD Participants   In an effort to determine the interaction of LD and gender on educational attainment, a two-way

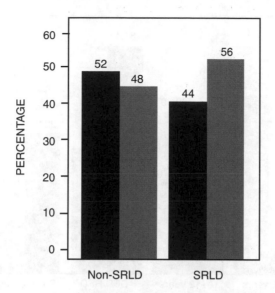

Figure 3.1.   Gender distribution for self-reported learning disabilities (SRLD) compared with the non-SRLD participants. (*Key:* ■ = Women; ■ = Men.)

ANOVA was performed on years of schooling as a continuous dependent variable. Findings indicate that there was a significant two-way interaction of group by gender on the number of years of schooling completed ($F = 11.611_{7, 244}$; $p < .001$). In regard to educational attainment, both LD and gender had a significant main effect on educational attainment. As was to be expected, having a learning disability had a profound impact on the number of years of schooling an individual completed ($F = 189.48_1$; $p < .001$). Although the impact of gender was much less apparent, it nonetheless was also significant ($F = 4.5_{1, 7244}$; $p = .033$) at the two extremes of the continuum, with more men with SRLD completing fewer years of schooling and slightly more women with SRLD completing a higher education degree.

The percentages of individuals in the two groups who completed 0–8 years of schooling, 9–12 years of schooling, high school or the GED, some college, or an undergraduate or graduate degree are shown in Figure 3.2. Adults with SRLD are more highly represented in the two lowest groupings; the largest difference between the non-SRLD and SRLD participants occurred among those who completed 0–8 years of schooling (4.2% compared with 27.1%, respectively). In the other four categories, high school completion and beyond, the reverse pattern was apparent, with the next largest discrepancy between the non-SRLD and SRLD participants occurring among those who completed an undergraduate or graduate degree (27.4% in the non-SRLD participants as compared with 8.7% in the SRLD participants).

Gender Differences in Educational Attainment   When educational attainment was examined for women and men in the non-SRLD group, very few differences were apparent (see Figure 3.3). Within the educational categories other than college degree completion, there was a discrepancy of only one or two percentage points. In postsecondary degree completion, there was a 4-point discrepancy favoring the men.

In the SRLD participants there were slightly larger discrepancies, with a 7- to 8-percentage-point difference at the lowest and highest educational categories (0–8 years and college degree completion) (see Figure 3.4). More men with SRLD reported com-

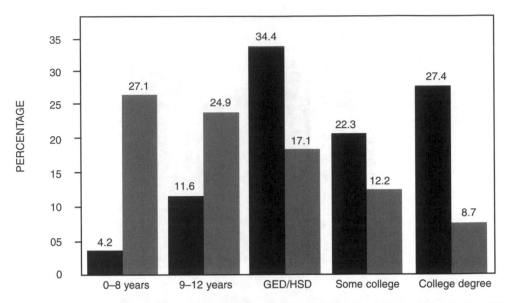

Figure 3.2.   Educational attainment in the self-reported learning disabilities (SRLD) and non-SRLD participants. (*Key:* GED = General Equivalency Diploma; HSD = high school diploma; ■ = No learning disability; ■ = SRLD.)

pleting 0–8 years of schooling as compared with women with SRLD (31% compared with 23%). The educational attainment of men and women in the SRLD group as compared with men and women in the non-SRLD group seemed to differ in that men with SRLD more frequently completed fewer years of schooling than women with SRLD. The reverse pattern from that seen in the non-SRLD participants was observed in the higher education degree completion category; that is, the percentage of women who completed a college or graduate degree (13%) was more than twice that of men (6%). Moreover, more women with SRLD than men with SRLD completed a postsecondary degree, whereas in the non-SRLD participants, the percentages of men and women were almost identical except at the highest level. This latter finding regarding SRLD participants should be considered with caution, given the small sample size in the highest educational category.

Prevalence and Gender Distribution by Educational Attainment   An alternative way of examining the impact of LD on educational attainment is to examine the prevalence of SRLD within each educational category. Because of the frustration of failing to achieve in school and of having difficulty in learning to read and spell, we anticipated that there would be a higher rate of SRLD among those adults who had completed the least amount of schooling. As expected, 15% of the adults who completed 8 years of schooling or less had SRLD (see Table 3.1). In addition, there is a sharp decrease in the prevalence rate among adults with SRLD completing 9–12 years of schooling (6%), followed by a gradual decline in the prevalence rate. What is surprising is that there were adults in the highest level of educational attainment who self-reported having a learning disability, just as there were some adults scoring in the highest literacy level with SRLD (Vogel & Reder, in press). In other words, these adults seemed to have a clear understanding that their LD did not disappear once they had achieved a high level of education; rather, having a learning disability is a lifelong condition that permeates their existence across the life span and is not just a difficulty that children experience in school.

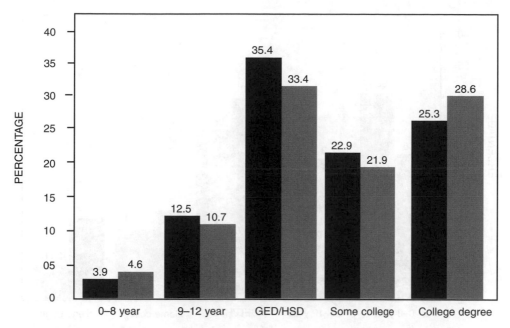

Figure 3.3. Educational attainment for women and men without learning disabilities. (*Key*: GED = General Equivalency Diploma; HSD = high school diploma; ■ = Women; ■ = Men.)

When these data were examined by gender, a pattern emerged that is similar to the pattern seen in the gender distribution among adults with SRLD when grouped by literacy proficiency (Vogel & Reder, in press). More men with SRLD completed 8 years or less of schooling as compared with women with SRLD (18% versus 12%), indicative of a trend for men with SRLD to have completed fewer years of formal education than women with SRLD, perhaps because of (or, alternatively, contributing to) the larger percentage of men with severe literacy deficiencies. The reverse pattern, although less well defined, was apparent at the highest level of educational attainment in that slightly more women with SRLD completed a college degree than men with SRLD (1% versus 0.6%). Again, this latter finding must be interpreted cautiously, given the limited sample size and small proportions in some of the cells.

High School/GED Completion and Dropout Rate   In order to interpret the NALS data in relation to findings based on other national databases, such as the NLTS, we calculated high school/GED completion rate or beyond as well as educational attainment. The percentage of adults in the non-SRLD population who completed high school/GED was 84%, compared with 48% among those with SRLD (see Figure 3.5). Although the percentages of men and women in the non-SRLD population who completed high school/GED were almost identical (84% for women versus 85% for men), among those with SRLD, more women (55%) than men (42%) completed high school/GED.

The percentage of adults in the non-SRLD population of individuals who did not complete high school or a GED was 16% as compared with 52% in the SRLD participants (see Figure 3.6). Although there was no difference in dropout rate between men and women in the non-SRLD participants, the reverse pattern of that observed in high school/GED completion rate for men and women with SRLD was found. More men with SRLD (58%) did not complete high school or earn a GED than women with SRLD

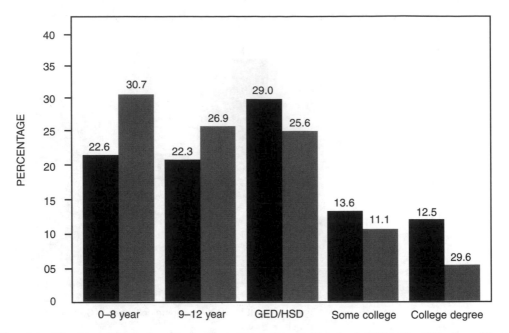

Figure 3.4.   Educational attainment for women and men without self-reported learning disabilities. (*Key*: GED = General Equivalency Diploma; HSD = high school diploma; ■ = Women; ■ = Men.)

(45%). Moreover, the same pattern was observed in men and women with SRLD who completed 8 years or less of schooling (18% of men versus 12% of women).

DISCUSSION

In summary, the high school/GED graduation rate was 48% in the SRLD group as compared with 84% in the non-SRLD group. Although there were no significant differences in the percentages of men and women in the non-SRLD group (85% versus 84%, respectively), among those with SRLD, there were more women (55%) than men (42%) who had completed either high school/ASE, college, or a graduate/professional school degree. The discrepancy was slightly smaller among those who completed 8 years or less of schooling (27% of adults with SRLD versus 4% of the non-SRLD group), and more men with SRLD dropped out of school than women (58% versus 45%). In the SRLD group, more men completed only 8 years or less of schooling as compared with women (31% versus 23%), whereas no difference was observed for the non-SRLD group (5% of men versus 4% of women). The reverse pattern was seen for the SRLD group at the three highest levels of educational attainment, with slightly

Table 3.1.   Prevalence of self-reported learning disabilities (SRLD) by educational attainment

Group	Level of educational attainment (percent)				
	0–8 years	9–12 years	High school/GED	Some college	College degree
All SRLD	15.1	5.6	2.1	1.5	1.0
Men with SRLD	18	7.7	2.4	1.6	.6
Women with SRLD	11.7	4.0	1.9	1.4	1.2

Note: GED = General Equivalency Diploma.

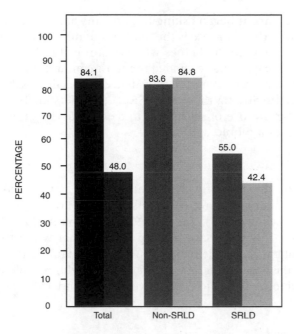

Figure 3.5.   High school diploma or general equivalency diploma completion rates for the self-reported learning disabilities (SRLD) and non-SRLD participants (by group and by gender). (*Key*: ■ = Female; ■ = Male; ■ = Non-SRLD; ■ = SRLD.)

more women at each level. The major finding of importance was that there is a significant interaction of both learning disability and gender on educational attainment, with a tendency for men with SRLD to have completed fewer years of schooling and women with SRLD to have completed more years of schooling in spite of the fact that the genders did not differ in literacy proficiency.

Use of Self-Report in the Field of Learning Disabilities

Self-report has been used in several other national surveys. For example, the ACE national database (Henderson, 1995) in particular has relied exclusively on self-reported

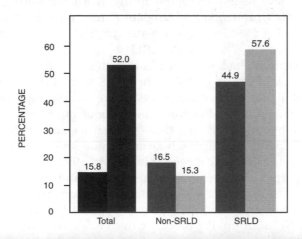

Figure 3.6.   Rates of dropout in high school or earlier for the self-reported learning disabilities (SRLD) and non-SRLD participants (by group and by gender). (*Key*: ■ = Female; ■ = Male; ■ = Non-SRLD; ■ = SRLD.)

disabilities in adults since it began asking respondents about the presence of a disability in 1978. Moreover, this database is the most frequently cited source for determining the number of students with disabilities who are enrolled in U.S. colleges and universities (Henderson, 1995) and has provided the most comprehensive national, regularly updated statistics to date regarding the prevalence of specific disabilities in college and university freshmen, including those with SRLD (Henderson, 1995). Therefore, there is good precedent for the use of self-report to determine the prevalence of disabilities in the United States as a whole.

Prevalence Rate

There is no question that the prevalence rate of 2.9% is much lower than expected based on the observations of adult educators (Ryan & Price, 1993; Travis, 1979), the U.S. Department of Labor (1993), and the 1996 child count of the U.S. Department of Education. However, it is important to keep in mind that when the SRLD group was disaggregated by literacy proficiency or educational attainment, the prevalence rate among those with the poorest literacy skills and those who completed less than 8 years of school increased four- to fivefold to between 10% and 15%, respectively (Vogel & Reder, in press).

Educational Attainment

The NALS data set is the first nationally representative group of adults with SRLD across the life span who can be compared with the non-SRLD group. It not only provides data on high school dropout and graduation rates but also includes information about how many actually dropped out of school prior to high school. These individuals are typically not included in high school follow-up studies because they have already dropped out of the system, thus providing an even more optimistic picture than is actually the case. Thus, the NALS has provided the first opportunity to determine the school dropout rate, including those who actually drop out before beginning high school, as well as those who enroll in and graduate from vocational, trade school, college, and graduate/professional school well beyond their mid- to late 20s. Many adults, especially women in their 30s, 40s, and 50s, return to school to complete their formal education that may have been interrupted during their childbearing years.

High School/GED Graduation and Dropout Rate   In order to compare the NALS database with that of the NLTS, we calculated high school/GED graduation rate or beyond and found that 48% among the SRLD NALS participants, as compared with 61% in the NLTS database, had graduated from high school, went on to postsecondary education, or both, and 51% and 32% in the NALS and NLTS databases, respectively, had dropped out of high school (Wagner, 1990). We can only speculate as to why the high school/GED graduation and beyond and dropout rates were discrepant in these two databases. One hypothesis is that the NALS participants were significantly older than the NLTS participants, and high school graduation for someone born in the 1930s was perhaps more equivalent to college graduation in 1998. Also, there are now many more publicly supported higher-education institutions and certainly a proliferation of community colleges; thus, there are many more postsecondary enrollment options for those born in the 1960s and after, perhaps resulting in a higher rate of postsecondary enrollment for the NLTS group. However, we need to exercise caution regarding these explanations because one of the limitations of the NALS database is that it is a cross-sectional rather than longitudinal data set. Therefore, imposing an historical interpretation on the findings is hard, if not impossible because, when situations change historically, they inevitably get confounded with age factors as well.

Even if these explanations were to be validated, are they sufficient to explain that only 12% of the SRLD group, in contrast to 30% of the NLTS LD subgroup, had enrolled in postsecondary settings? An additional factor that may have resulted in a higher proportion of NLTS participants with LD having enrolled in postsecondary school is the definition of postsecondary education. Apparently, the NLTS database included vocational and trade schools and Job Opportunities and Basic Skills program participants within the category of postsecondary education, whereas we selected for inclusion only college and university degree-granting settings. A third factor that could be related to this discrepancy is the fact that the NLTS participants were significantly younger than the NALS respondents and could have had the advantage of an individualized transition plan (ITP) on file, whereas none of the 25- to 43-year-olds (i.e., the youngest NALS age group included in this study) would have had an ITP on file because they would have completed their high school diplomas or GEDs before the ITP was mandated. Finally, there are many more opportunities and higher expectations for young adults with LD reaching maturity in the 1980s and 1990s (e.g., the NLTS sample) to enroll in a wide variety of postsecondary settings than was the case for adults now ages 45 and older.

Postsecondary Graduation Rate A surprising finding regarding postsecondary graduation rate is that, in spite of the fact that fewer adults with SRLD in the NALS participants enrolled in postsecondary settings than adults with LD in the NLTS sample, more than twice as many (8%) earned either a 2-year, 4-year, or graduate degree, compared with only 3% of the NLTS participants. This finding could be related to the age of the NALS and NLTS participants. At least one follow-up study has reported that many individuals with LD are older when they graduate from college as compared with their peers without LD and take on average 6 years instead of 5 years to complete their undergraduate degrees (Vogel & Adelman, 1992), for three reasons:

1. They started or returned to school at an older age. The pattern that was observed was that they started their college career at one school and dropped out when the going got tough, they were in danger of academic failure, or they had too many financial or child care responsibilities that interfered with their ability to pursue a formal education program.
2. When they were ready to return to school, they may have been unaware that they had a learning disability or unaware of Section 504 and the variety of higher-education support services and accommodations made for students with documented LD. As they acquired more experience and learned about these services as well as their own needs, they often found themselves having to transfer from one school to another until they found an environment and program that met their needs. Transferring multiple times often leads to lost credit because not all coursework transfers, and institutional requirements and programs vary in different postsecondary institutions (Ratcliff & Associates, 1995).
3. In addition, oftentimes they took a lighter load in college in order to enhance their chances of success and fulfill other obligations.

As a result of these factors, an accurate estimate of postsecondary outcomes cannot be determined until participants are older than the traditional-age college students who participated in the last NLTS data collection (ages 21–26). In summary, although considered only a tentative finding given the small sample size, it appears that more than twice as many adults with SRLD in the NALS group graduated from an institution of higher education as compared with adults with LD in the NLTS participants, which is considered to be related to the inclusion of adults across the life span in the NALS data set.

Gender Differences in Educational Attainment

We posed the question as to why more men with SRLD (31%) completed only 0–8 years of education than women with SRLD (23%). Second, we asked why the reverse pattern was found at the highest level of educational attainment, where, at least tentatively, we reported that more women with SRLD (13%) completed a higher-education degree as compared with men (6%). These findings again are contradictory to earlier studies in which data were analyzed by gender. In previous studies, women with LD completed fewer years of schooling, contradicting the picture that emerges from the NALS participants, in which women with SRLD completed more years of schooling than their male counterparts.

We can only speculate as to possible reasons for this interesting finding. One hypothesis relates to the difference in sample ascertainment in the NALS a compared with previous studies. As will be recalled, the learning disability sample in the NLTS data set was school identified, in contrast to the SRLD group in the NALS data set, who self-identified from within the representative sample of all adults in the nation. In an extensive review of the literature, Vogel (1990) found that, in order to be identified in the schools, women with LD must 1) be significantly lower in intelligence, 2) have more significant impairments in their reading and written language abilities, and 3) have a greater aptitude–achievement discrepancy than their male counterparts. In fact, the mean IQ score in the SILD respondents in the NLTS was reported to be 87, and approximately 9% of the respondents had an IQ score of less than 70, which according to the federal definition of learning disability would have disqualified them for LD services (Wagner et al., 1992). Confirmation of this reasoning has come from comparisons of school-identified and research-identified cohorts studied in Connecticut and Wisconsin (Flynn & Rahbar, 1994; Shaywitz, Shaywitz, Fletcher, & Escobar, 1990). Finally, we speculated that the more favorable outcomes for NALS women with SRLD may be related to Vogel and Adelman's (1990a, 1992) and Werner's (1993) findings that women with LD often have higher achievement motivation, fewer concomitant emotional problems, and a more favorable attitude toward teachers and the teaching–learning process than their male counterparts, resulting in higher educational attainment in spite of the finding that there were no substantial gender differences in literacy proficiency (Kirsch et al., 1993; Vogel & Reder, in press).

IMPLICATIONS

The findings that only 48% of adults with SRLD completed high school/GED as compared with 84% of the non-SRLD group and, moreover, that 27% of the SRLD group dropped out of school before ever reaching high school, as compared with 4% of the non-SRLD group have important implications for elementary, junior high/middle school, and high school/GED teachers, and adult educators. The implications are even more significant in light of the findings of Reder and Vogel (1997) indicating that adults with SRLD are employed more frequently in part-time jobs, earn significantly lower wages, and have significantly lower occupational status as compared with the non-SRLD group.

It is well known that, for the SRLD participants, staying in school and completing high school/GED and beyond have major benefits for later employment and financial status. According to Murphy and Welch (1989), unemployment among high school dropouts in the non-SRLD group is two times greater than that among high school graduates, and the unemployment rate for high school graduates is two times that of college graduates. In terms of salary benefits, Murphy and Welch reported that high school graduates earn 14% more than dropouts but that the real financial benefits accrue to college graduates, who earned 40% more than high school graduates. With a high school dropout rate of 52% and a 27% dropout rate prior to entering ninth grade, is it any wonder that the employment and economic outcomes for the SRLD participants were so discouraging?

Therefore, the major implication of these findings regarding educational attainment is that we have to keep students with LD in school longer, hopefully until they graduate from high school. If all such efforts fail, we have to be persuasive to motivate them to enroll in ASE, and, once they are enrolled, we must make that environment one in which they can succeed and graduate with their GED. Two questions must be addressed first:

1. What are the problems that youth and adolescents with LD face that contribute to their high dropout rate?
2. How can these problems be addressed so that youth and adolescents with LD will be motivated to stay in school longer?

When adolescents with LD enter high school, they face a change in emphasis from a basic skills, student-oriented curriculum to a content or subject matter orientation (Levine & Swarz, 1995). This change introduces a special challenge to students with LD, who still experience basic skills impairments, especially in written expression and spelling (Manheimer & Fleischner, 1995; Vogel & Konrad, 1988; Vogel & Moran, 1982); have experienced problems in the past with subject matter–oriented courses (Wagner, 1990); and are passive learners who lack motivation (Luther, 1993), study skills such as notetaking and test-taking strategies (Zigmond, 1990), and adequate interpersonal skills (Bryan, 1991; Rieth & Polsgrove, 1994; Vaughn, 1991; Vaughn, McIntosh, & Spencer-Rowe, 1991). In addition, the educational reform movement has resulted in increased demands for uniform, higher standards of academic excellence and increased numbers of requirements in the core curriculum of English, math, foreign language, science, and social studies (Zigmond, 1990; Zigmond & Baker, 1994). These demands create additional problems for students with LD (National Joint Committee on Learning Disabilities, 1994) as a result of the increased pressure on high school teachers for their students to meet these higher expectations and teachers' reduced flexibility in teaching strategies and curriculum alternatives.

We suggest that there are at least three avenues for exploration that address these problems in order to enhance the educational attainment of adults with LD: 1) Create a meaningful school environment, 2) improve the transition process, and 3) increase the number of adults with LD who enroll in and complete ASE programs and receive their GEDs.

Create a Meaningful School Environment

From the research on college minority student dropout rates, we have learned that one of the hallmark characteristics of an effective college climate is a validating environment (Ratcliff & Associates, 1995). Students experience validation when they are made to feel that students like themselves have succeeded in their environment. This same principle should be applied in the earlier years. High school graduates with LD can serve as role models and be invited to return to school as speakers, to share with the current students the nature of their LD and how they succeeded in school and work experiences (Polloway, Schewel, & Patton, 1992). These individuals could then serve as mentors and informal "job coaches" during summer internships, work–study experiences, or both during the regular school year.

A validating environment is one in which students are successful in their coursework. In order to enhance their chances of success, intensive basic skills instruction in reading, written expressive language, and mathematics can be integrated into subject matter tutoring utilizing the student's textbook, written assignments, and test preparation as the basis for one-to-one tutoring (Adelman, O'Connell, Konrad, & Vogel, 1993; Rieth & Polsgrove, 1994; Zigmond, 1990). Motivation is enhanced when the students see that they are accomplishing the assignment; preparing for exams; and, instead of failing courses, achieving a passing grade and credit toward graduation.

Alongside the emphasis on intensive basic skills instruction, adolescents need to be familiar with the newest and most powerful technology that can help them to bypass their disability and function independently. Computer-assisted technology and instructional coaches must be available so that students can learn how to use a variety of software and hardware to assist them in daily living; in their present and future classes, whether they will attend postsecondary school now or later; and in employment. This technology can be divided into several categories: written expressive language, reading, personal data managers, and listening aids (Raskind & Scott, 1993) (see Appendix B at the end of this book for a list of resources that should be helpful in obtaining further information on assistive technology and LD) and, based on the purpose, demands of the task, and type and severity of learning disability, the individual can decide what is the most appropriate software, hardware, or both and become proficient in using it.

Improve the Transition Process

Wagner (1991a) reported that only 39% of seventh- and eighth-grade youth with LD had taken a vocational education course, whereas 67% of the eleventh and twelfth graders had taken such a course. Moreover, one of the most important findings from recent transition and follow-up studies during the 1990s has been that students who took vocational courses found them to be very helpful in finding the right career path, getting a job, and meeting success on the job (Payne, 1996). Therefore, one of the most important aspects of the junior high and high school curriculum is the vocational education curriculum. Given that there is a dropout rate by eighth grade or earlier of about one third based on the NALS database and that another one fourth drop out before graduating from high school, it is critical that students enroll in vocational courses before eighth grade if not earlier.

The first vocational courses should focus on career exploration so that students can identify jobs/professions that allow them to function at the level of their highest abilities. Students should be exposed to a wide variety of job lists, inventories, and occupational indexes. Speakers in different employment settings could then be invited to address the class and describe their job responsibilities; prerequisite skills needed at the entry level and beyond; how, if at all, their LD affect them on the job; and, if so, how they compensate or use assistive technology to minimize the impact of the LD on the job. Having these speakers share information with the class about how they got their present jobs will be a critical component for the students. The speakers could also address how students might best prepare for this type of career, explain what employers are looking for in the hiring process, and describe the application process. Sample applications, questions that students might be asked or would want to ask, and sample employment examinations could also be provided. The presentation should prepare the students in the class to visit the speaker on the jobsite. Following jobsite visits and discussion in class, interested students may opt to explore a job shadowing experience or a summer internship.

Assessment is an important part of the early phase of career exploration. Students should be introduced to the local vocational rehabilitation (VR) counselor and become familiar with VR eligibility requirements and the necessary steps to follow to determine if they are eligible. One of the most valuable services that VR can provide is assessment, which could include interest inventories, aptitude testing, functional literacy testing, knowledge of career search strategies and job requirements, and job search strategies (Koller, 1997; Koller, Holliday, & Multon, 1996; see also Chapter 9). It is important that career counseling be broad enough to provide direction for not only those who may not graduate from high school but also for those who will be considering a 4-year college degree and beyond. In addition, the recommendations should be free of gender bias; that is, young women with the appropriate aptitude and who indicate an interest should be provided information regarding previously male-dominated fields such as forestry, public safety, and the trades, and young men to fields such as early childhood, elementary education, and secretarial services (Fourquean, 1994).

Another important component of the transition curriculum is for students to become knowledgeable about the laws that protect employees and students with LD in the application process, on the job, in the classroom, and in acquiring the necessary credentials to qualify for employment in certain careers, including those that require taking certain examinations (e.g., the trades, teaching, real estate, law, medicine). Many adults with LD are unaware of the Americans with Disabilities Act of 1990 (PL 101-336) and Section 504 of the Rehabilitation Act of 1973 (PL 93-112) and are, therefore, reluctant to disclose their LD if they anticipate that they will need, or when they find that they need, accommodations (Adelman & Vogel, 1990; Greenbaum, Graham, & Scales, 1996). Rather than disclose, some adults have changed jobs, majors, or colleges in order to avoid failure, often resulting in abandoning lifelong career aspirations and making career compromises (Adelman & Vogel, 1990). There is a need for both knowledge of and assistance with the decision-making process regarding disclosure, if it is appropriate; what the alternatives and risks are; and when, how, and to whom to disclose if they decide on that route. Role playing the various scenarios that may occur can be helpful prior to disclosure as well. Throughout this process, skillful counselors/teachers can also facilitate improvement of the necessary interpersonal skills needed in the work environment, which adults with LD often lack (Price, 1997).

The transition curriculum also must match the student's post–high school goals, identified ideally during junior high school. It is hard to overestimate the importance of matching the courses and experiences with the setting desired following exit from high school. Too often students who intend to work following high school are placed in a majority of basic skills courses rather than vocational courses and work experiences (Blackorby & Wagner, 1997). It has also been suggested that literacy (i.e., basic skills) be taught with specific goals in mind—for example, literacy for specific employment settings, literacy for survival, literacy for family life, literacy for recreation and entertainment, and literacy for higher education (Fourquean, 1994). Students who aspire to higher education also must have the prerequisite core courses in high school to perform well on college entrance examinations or in college-level courses (Vogel & Adelman, 1990a). Students with disabilities whose high school program included appropriate school-to-work planning, who had appropriate reading, writing, and math skills, who had two or more meaningful work experiences in the last 2 years of high school, and who had highly developed job search skills and career awareness were two to three times more likely to be competitively employed 1 year after exiting from high school (Benz, Yovanoff, & Doren, 1997).

Postsecondary Decision Making An important aspect of the transition curriculum is for students and adults to become familiar with the variety and types of postsecondary options available to them (National Joint Committee on Learning Disabilities, 1994; Vogel, 1993b). The process involves assisting students to become aware of the variety of formal and informal postsecondary options that are available, such as non–college-degree programs based on college campuses; vocational and trade schools; apprenticeships; community college certificate, license, and degree programs; and 4-year undergraduate degree programs. Within these settings, there is a wide range of awareness of the needs of students with LD and of support services, accommodations, and programs designed to meet the needs of such students. This plethora of options may be very confusing for students with LD, and these students need assistance in evaluating the options and determining which program and setting might be the right one for them.

In order for students to make a well-informed decision, they need to have an understanding of their own learning needs, as well as a profile of their cognitive abilities, academic achievement, processing strengths and weaknesses, problem-solving strategies, level of independent functioning, and interpersonal skills. The self-understanding that can emerge from postsecondary transition planning is one of the many benefits of postsecondary counseling, and although this process of self-knowledge can take many months or years, with added maturity it can result in the identification of short-term and long-term goals, a career focus, and an increase in motivation to complete high school and later to enroll in and graduate from a postsecondary program.

A third aspect of the transition-planning process regarding postsecondary decision making is for students to become knowledgeable about Section 504 of the Rehabilitation Act and its implications for students with LD in higher education. Unlike the "search and screen" mandate of the Individuals with Disabilities Education Act (IDEA) of 1990 (PL 101-476), Section 504 does not mandate that postsecondary institutions screen students for LD. Rather, students with diagnosed LD who want support services, accommodations, or both must request services and provide documentation that makes them eligible for the services/accommodations they seek. Students need to know what documentation they should bring with them to the postsecondary setting and procure these documents prior to entrance to the postsecondary setting. For example, many institutions require that students have the results of current diagnostic testing (i.e., no older than 3 years). For this reason, many high school students have the school psychologist administer the testing during their junior year. Additional materials that they may be asked to provide include an unaided writing sample; developmental, educational, and medical history; high school and prior college transcripts; and results of college admissions testing. Students who have used accommodations in a previous educational setting or on the job will have an easier time receiving similar accommodations in the new postsecondary setting if they can document the prior use, and therefore the transition portfolio should include letters of documentation regarding accommodations received in the past. For traditional-age college students, an individualized education program may serve this purpose.

When provision of accommodations and support services is inadequate to over-come the severity of the learning disability and the student is in danger of not being able to meet a specific requirement of the university (e.g., 2 years of a foreign language), he or she should inquire about the petition process for granting a course substitution or waiver. Many institutions of higher education have written policies regarding the peti-tion process. If they do not, this would be an appropriate avenue for exploration dur-ing a campus visit and, depending on the response, may play an important role in the final decision.

Once students have decided on their academic interests and goals, as well as needed accommodations/support services, and have reviewed the literature from a variety of institutions that seem able to meet their needs, they need to verify the infor-mation by making a campus visit and meeting with admissions officers, faculty, and students with LD on campus. Students need to be prepared to ask and respond to appropriate questions (Vogel, 1987) and then be assisted in evaluating and comparing the institutions following their visits.

The next stage in the postsecondary decision-making process is completing the application process. Institutions have different application and admissions procedures and requirements depending on the comprehensiveness of the support services and the philosophy of the program. Vogel (1993a) described these differences on a con-tinuum from procedures identical to the process for students without disabilities to an autonomous and distinct process for students with LD. Regardless, just as students without disabilities often require assistance from the college guidance counselor, stu-dents with LD need even more assistance because they often experience organiza-tional and written language difficulties. The rule of thumb for all students is to apply to at least three schools: an "insurance school" (i.e., one they are sure will accept them), one that will most likely accept them, and a "reach school" (i.e., one they are hoping will accept them). Students with LD are advised to do the same and, in addi-tion, to be aware that they can always begin their college career at an open-admissions community college in their geographic location. Regardless of where they choose to apply, application is a complex, multistep process involving multiple forms and dead-lines. Vogel (1993b) described the step-by-step process for students with LD and their teacher, college counselor, or parent to follow to complete the application process. Fol-lowing notification of acceptance, students, teachers, and family members have to weigh the alternatives and come to a final decision.

Personal Transition Portfolio   Completion of the application process is an advan-tageous moment to also complete the process of compiling the personal transition port-folio. The transition portfolio will help students keep track of important documents regarding their learning disability should they decide to disclose, to document their strengths and special talents, and to monitor progress and can be used in the event they decide to transfer to a different college or university, to apply to graduate school, or to disclose their learning disability in an employment setting (Vogel, 1993a). This process, begun in junior high, should be a gradual shifting of responsibility for record keeping and decision making from a parent or guardian to the individual with LD. This process can serve as the catalyst for the counseling component of the transition program, in which youth and adolescents with LD review the results of assessment and come to an understanding of the nature of their disabilities, their strength and weaknesses, and appropriate compensatory strategies and assistive technology (Vogel, 1989). Building these understandings is a long-term endeavor, lays the foundation for goal setting and career decision making, and can serve as a motivating factor in high school graduation and postsecondary enrollment.

Increase the Number of Adults with Learning Disabilities Who Enroll in and Complete Adult Secondary Education Programs and Receive a GED

When adolescents drop out of school, a follow-up plan should be put in place immediately that includes establishing telephone contact with the students and their parents, offering assistance in the students' job search, and providing information about alternative opportunities to complete their high school education. Although approximately 30% of high school dropouts enrolled in ASE classes 3–5 years after exiting high school (Wagner et al., 1992), only approximately 3% completed the program and received their GEDs. We can only speculate as to why the remaining 27% did not. One obvious reason is that the time that had elapsed since their exit from high school may have been insufficient and that more adults will have finished their GED after another 5 years. Alternatively, it could be that ASE is not responsive to the needs of adult learners with previously diagnosed or unidentified LD.

In recognition of this need, the National Institute of Developmental Disabilities Research funded the Kansas Institute for Research in Learning Disabilities to prepare ASE instructors to be better able to recognize and teach adults with LD. The National Institute for Literacy also recognized the need for validated screening measures in order to identify adults at high risk for having a learning disability and funded the Academy for Educational Development to identify or develop and validate screening and instructional "tool kits" to identify and teach those adults with suspected LD. Chapters in Section II of this book address these topics from a variety of vantage points to bring the reader up to date on the progress that has been made in response to these identified needs.

One of the major implications of having a documented learning disability is that such students should be eligible for test accommodations on the GED. Unfortunately, however, in 1994 only 0.2% of those students who took the GED test requested special accommodations because of a learning disability (that percentage increased to 0.3% in 1995) (Baldwin, 1996). Given that the learning disability prevalence rate is between 10% and 15% among those with low literacy proficiency and less than a high school diploma (Vogel & Reder, in press), this must be only a minute fraction of those students with LD enrolled in ASE classes. Two factors may have contributed to the very low percentage of adults taking the GED with accommodations: 1) Many adults do not know they have a learning disability or, if they do know, have not been informed that they are eligible to request accommodations when taking the GED exam; and 2) the process for requesting accommodations is either unknown to their teachers and therefore to the adult learners as well, is too complex and daunting a chore, or is itself flawed.

In response to criticism regarding the underrepresentation of adults with LD taking the GED, the GED Testing Service of The Center for Adult Learning and Educational Credentials sponsored by the American Council on Education directed their attention to reexamine the procedures for qualifying for testing accommodations for those with documented LD. ASE teachers and administrators need to become knowledgeable regarding changes in the procedures for processing the application for accommodations, in the forms, in the deadlines, and in the location of testing centers for special administration of the GED as they become known. All of these have proved to be major hurdles in the past. Learning disability and ASE instructors will also need to keep updated on changes in the application procedures for requesting accommodations on college admissions tests; licensing examinations; and professional and union/trade examinations because they too may change as more research becomes available.

Given that adolescents with LD are at high risk for dropping out of school, for not entering ASE or postsecondary settings and graduating, and for remaining underemployed or unemployed, we face the challenge, therefore, to incorporate these recommendations and those of others in this book into the education programs for youth, adolescents, and adults with LD. The measure of our success will be an increase in the high school and postsecondary graduation rate and in the percentage of adults with LD employed full time in occupations that are equivalent to their educational attainment, literacy proficiency, and preparation. If we can succeed in achieving these goals, adults with LD will no longer be in jeopardy of unemployment, underemployment, low status occupations, and a life of poverty.

REFERENCES

Adelman, P.B., O'Connell, J., Konrad, D., & Vogel, S.A. (1993). The integration of remediation and subject-matter tutoring: Support at the college level. In S.A. Vogel & P.B. Adelman (Eds.), *Success for college students with learning disabilities* (pp. 206–239). New York: Springer-Verlag.

Adelman, P.B., & Vogel, S.A. (1990). College graduates with learning disabilities: Employment attainment and career patterns. *Learning Disability Quarterly, 13*(3), 154–166.

Affleck, J.Q., Edgar, E., Levine, P., & Kortering, L. (1990). Postschool status of students classified as mildly mentally retarded, learning disabled, nonhandicapped: Does it get better with time? *Education and Training in Mental Retardation, 25*(4), 315–324.

Americans with Disabilities Act (ADA) of 1990, PL 101-336, 42 U.S.C. §§ 12101 *et seq.*

Baldwin, J. (Ed.). (1996). *Who took the GED?* Washington, DC: American Council on Education.

Benz, M., Yovanoff, P., & Doren, B. (1997). School-to-work components that predict postschool success for students with and without disabilities. *Exceptional Children, 63*(2), 151–165.

Blackorby, J., & Wagner, M. (1996). Longitudinal postschool outcomes of youth with disabilities: Findings from the National Longitudinal Transition Study. *Exceptional Children, 62*(5), 399–413.

Blackorby, J., & Wagner, M. (1997). The employment outcomes of youth with learning disabilities: A review of findings from the NLTS. In P. Gerber & D. Brown (Eds.), *Learning disabilities and employment* (pp. 57–74). Austin, TX: PRO-ED.

Blalock, J. (1982). Persistent auditory language deficits in adults with learning disabilities. *Journal of Learning Disabilities, 15*, 604–609.

Blalock, J. (1987). Intellectual levels and patterns. In D. Johnson & J. Blalock (Eds.), *Young adults with learning disabilities* (pp. 47–65). Orlando, FL: Grune & Stratton.

Bruck, M. (1985). The adult functioning of children with specific learning disabilities: A follow-up study. In I. Siegel (Ed.), *Advances in applied developmental psychology* (pp. 91–129). Norwood, NJ: Ablex.

Bryan, T. (1991). Social problems and learning disabilities. In B. Wong (Ed.), *Learning about learning disabilities* (pp. 190–231). San Diego: Academic Press.

Bursuck, W.D., Rose, E., Cowen, S., & Yahaya, M.A. (1989). Nationwide survey of postsecondary education services for students with learning disabilities. *Exceptional Children, 56*(3), 236–245.

Campbell, A., Kirsch, I.S., & Kolstad, A. (1992). *Assessing literacy: The framework for the National Adult Literacy Survey.* Washington, DC: National Center for Education Statistics, U.S. Department of Education.

deBettencourt, L.U., Zigmond, N., & Thornton, H. (1989). Follow-up of postsecondary-age rural learning disabled graduates and dropouts. *Exceptional Children, 56*(1), 40–49.

Edgar, E., & Levine, P. (1988). *A longitudinal follow-along study of graduates of special education.* Seattle: University of Washington, Experimental Education Unit.

Fairweather, J.S., & Shaver, D. (1991). Making transition to postsecondary education and training. *Exceptional Children, 57*(3), 264–270.

Fleischner, J. (1996). Interventions reported by adults with learning disabilities. In *They speak for themselves: A survey of adults with learning disabilities* (pp. 13–25). Pittsburgh: Learning Disabilities Association of America, Adult Issues Committee.

Flynn, J.M., & Rahbar, M.H. (1994). Prevalence of reading failure in boys compared with girls. *Psychology in the Schools, 31*, 66–71.

Fourqurean, J.M. (1994). The use of follow-up studies for improving transition planning for young adults with learning disabilities. *Journal of Vocational Rehabilitation, 4*(2), 96–104.

Frank, A.R., Sitlington, P.L., & Carson, R. (1995). Young adults with behavioral disorders: A comparison with peers with mild disabilities. *Journal of Emotional and Behavioral Disorders, 3*(3), 156–164.

Frauenheim, J., & Heckerl, J. (1983). A longitudinal study of psychological and achievement test performance in severe dyslexic adults. *Journal of Learning Disabilities, 16,* 336–347.

Gottesman, R. (1994). The adult with learning disabilities: An overview. *Learning Disabilities: A Multidisciplinary Journal, 5*(1), 1–14.

Greenbaum, B.L. (1993). *A follow-up survey for students with learning disabilities after exiting a postsecondary institution.* Unpublished doctoral dissertation, University of Maryland, College Park.

Greenbaum, B.L., Graham, S., & Scales, W. (1996). Adults with learning disabilities: Occupational and social status after college. *Journal of Learning Disabilities, 29*(2), 167–173.

Henderson, C. (1995). *College freshmen with disabilities: A triennial statistical profile.* Washington, DC: American Council on Education, HEATH Resource Center.

Individuals with Disabilities Education Act (IDEA) of 1990, PL 101-476, 20 U.S.C. §§ 1400 *et seq.*

Johnson, D. (1994). Clinical study of adults with severe learning disabilities. *Learning Disabilities: A Multidisciplinary Journal, 5*(1), 43–50.

Johnson, D., & Blalock, J. (Eds.). (1987). *Young adults with learning disabilities.* Orlando, FL: Grune & Stratton.

Kirsch, I.S., Jungeblut, A., Jenkins, L., & Kolstad, A. (1993). *Adult literacy in America: A first look at the results of the National Adult Literacy Survey.* Washington, DC: National Center for Education Statistics, U.S. Department of Education.

Kissire, P. (1996). Design of the survey. In *They speak for themselves: A survey of adults with learning disabilities* (pp. 1–6). Pittsburgh: Learning Disabilities Association of America, Adults Issues Committee.

Koller, J. (1997). Vocational rehabilitation: Current practices for work preparation. In P.J. Gerber & D.S. Brown (Eds.), *Learning disabilities and employment* (pp. 165–186). Austin, TX: PRO-ED.

Koller, J.R., Holliday, G.A., & Multon, K.D. (Eds.). (1996). *Koller Adolescent and Adult Behavior Scale–Revised (KAABS-R).* (Available from the Assessment & Consultation Clinic, University of Missouri–Columbia, 223 Townsend Hall, Columbia, MO 65211)

Levine, M., & Swarz, C. (1995). The unsuccessful adolescent. In Learning Disabilities Association of America (Ed.), *Secondary education and beyond: Providing opportunities for students with learning disabilities* (pp. 3–12). Pittsburgh: Learning Disabilities Association of America.

Levine, P. (1993). *Gender differences in long-term postschool outcomes for youth with mild mental retardation, learning disabilities and no disabilities: Myth or reality?* Doctoral dissertation, University of Washington, Seattle.

Levine, P., & Edgar, E. (1995). An analysis by gender of long-term postschool outcomes for youth with and without disabilities. *Exceptional Children, 61*(3), 282–300.

Luther, S. (1993). Methodological and conceptual issues in research in childhood resilience. *Journal of Child Psychology and Psychiatry and Allied Disciplines, 34,* 441–453.

Manheimer, M.A., & Fleischner, J.E. (1995). Helping students with learning disabilities meet the new math standards. *Secondary education and beyond: Providing opportunities for students with learning disabilities* (pp. 149–158). Pittsburgh: Learning Disabilities Association of America.

Marder, C., & D'Amico, R. (1992). *How well are youth with disabilities really doing? A comparison of youth with disabilities and youth in general.* Menlo Park, CA: SRI International.

Mosenthal, P.P., & Kirsch, I.S. (1994, December). *Defining the proficiency standards of adult literacy in the U.S.: A profile approach.* Paper presented at the National Reading Conference, San Diego.

Murphy, K., & Welch, F. (1989). Wage premiums for college graduates: Recent growth and possible explanations. *Educational Researcher, 18*(4), 17–26.

National Joint Committee on Learning Disabilities. (1994). *Secondary to postsecondary education transition planning for students with learning disabilities.* Austin, TX: PRO-ED.

Nisbet, J., & Lichtenstein, S. (1993). Gender differences in the postschool status of young adults with mild disabilities. *Fact Sheet: Following the Lives of Young Adults, 4*(1), 1–5. (Available from Institute on Disability at the University of New Hampshire).

Nourse, S.W. (1995). *Special education students who attend postsecondary education programs: What programs are attended, who graduates, and does it help?* Unpublished doctoral dissertation, University of Washington, Seattle.

Payne, N. (1996). Interventions reported by adults with learning disabilities. In *They speak for themselves: A survey of adults with learning disabilities* (pp. 26–32). Pittsburgh: Learning Disabilities Association of America, Adults Issues Committee.

Polloway, E.A., Smith, J.D., & Patton, J.R. (1984). Learning disabilities: An adult development perspective. *Learning Disability Quarterly, 7,* 179–186.

Polloway, E.A., Schewel, R., & Patton, J.R. (1992). Learning disabilities in adulthood: Personal perspectives. *Learning disabilities and employment* (pp. 275–306). Austin, TX: PRO-ED.

Price, L. (1997). Psychological issues of workplace adjustment. In P. Gerber & D. Brown (Eds.), *Learning disabilities and employment* (pp. 275–306). Austin, TX, PRO-ED.

Raskind, M., & Scott, N. (1993). Technology for postsecondary students with learning disabilities. In S.A. Vogel & P.B. Adelman (Eds.), *Success for college students with learning disabilities* (pp. 240–279). New York: Spring-Verlag.

Ratcliff & Associates. (1995). *Realizing the potential: Improving postsecondary teaching, learning, and assessment.* University Park: Pennsylvania State University, National Institute of Postsecondary Education, Libraries, and Lifelong Learning.

Rawson, M. (1968). *Developmental language disability: Adult accomplishments of dyslexic boys.* Baltimore: The Johns Hopkins University Press.

Reder, S. (1995). *Literacy, education, and learning disabilities.* Portland, OR: Northwest Regional Educational Laboratory.

Reder, S., & Vogel, S.A. (1997). Lifespan employment and economic outcomes for adults with self-reported learning disabilities. In P. Gerber & D. Brown (Eds.), *Learning disabilities and employment* (pp. 371–394). Austin, TX: PRO-ED.

Rehabilitation Act of 1973, PL 93-112, 29 U.S.C. §§ 701 *et seq.*

Rieth, H., & Polsgrove, L. (1994). Curriculum and instructional issues in teaching secondary students with learning disabilities. *Learning Disabilities Research and Practice, 9*(2), 118–126.

Rogan, L.L., & Hartman, L.D. (1976). *A follow-up study of learning disabled children as adults: Final report.* Evanston, IL: Cove School. (ERIC Document Reproduction Service No. ED 163-728)

Rogan, L.L., & Hartman, L.D. (1990). Adult outcome of learning disabled students 10 years after initial follow-up. *Learning Disabilities Focus, 5*(2), 91–102.

Ryan, A., & Price, L. (1993). Learning disabilities in adult basic education: A survey of current practices. *Journal of Postsecondary Education and Disability, 10*(3), 31–40.

Scuccimarra, D.J., & Speece, D.L. (1990). Employment outcomes and social integration of students with mild handicaps: The quality of life two years after high school. *Journal of Learning Disabilities, 23*(4), 213–219.

Shaywitz, S.E., & Shaw, R. (1988). The admissions process: An approach to selecting learning disabled students at the most selective colleges. *Learning Disabilities Focus, 3*(2), 81–86.

Shaywitz, S.E., Shaywitz, B.A., Fletcher, J.M., & Escobar, M.D. (1990). Prevalence of reading disability in boys and girls. *Journal of the American Medical Association, 264*(8), 998–1002.

Silver, A.A., & Hagin, R.A. (1964). Specific reading disability: Follow-up studies. *American Journal of Orthopsychiatry, 34,* 95–102.

Silver, A.A., & Hagin, R.A. (1985). Outcomes of learning disabilities in adolescence. *Annals of the American Society for Adolescent Psychiatry, 12*(14), 197–213.

Sitlington, P.L., & Frank, A.R. (1990). Are adolescents with learning disabilities successfully crossing the bridge into adult life? *Learning Disabilities Research and Practice, 8*(4), 244–252.

Spekman, N.J., Goldberg, R.J., & Herman, K.L. (1992). Learning disabled children grow up: A search for factors related to success in the young adult years. *Learning Disabilities Research and Practice, 7*(3), 161–170.

Travis, G. (1979). An adult educator views learning disabilities. *Adult Literacy and Basic Education, 3,* 85–92.

U.S. Department of Education. (1994). *Sixteenth annual report to Congress on the implementation of Individuals with Disabilities Education Act.* Washington, DC: Office of Special Education Programs.

U.S. Department of Education. (1996). *Eighteenth annual report to Congress on the implementation of IDEA.* Washington, DC: Office of Special Education Programs.

U.S. Department of Labor. (1993). *Workplace literacy and the nation's unemployed workers* (Research and Evaluation Report Series 93-F). Washington, DC: Author.

Vaughn, S. (1991). Social skills enhancement in students with learning disabilities. In B. Wong (Ed.), *Learning about learning disabilities* (pp. 408–440). San Diego: Academic Press.

Vaughn, S., McIntosh, R., & Spencer-Rowe, J. (1991). Peer rejection is a stubborn thing: Increasing peer acceptance of rejected students with learning disabilities. *Learning Disabilities Research and Practice, 6,* 83–88.

Vogel, S.A. (1987). Issues and concerns in LD college programming. In D. Johnson & J. Blalock (Eds.), *Adults with learning disabilities: Clinical studies* (pp. 239–275). Orlando, FL: Grune & Stratton.

Vogel, S.A. (1989). Adults with language learning disabilities: Definition, diagnosis and determination of eligibility for postsecondary and vocational rehabilitation services. *Rehabilitation Education, 3,* 77–90.

Vogel, S.A. (1990). Gender differences in intelligence, language, visual-motor abilities, and academic achievement in students with learning disabilities: A review of literature. *Journal of Learning Disabilities, 23*(1), 44–52.

Vogel, S.A. (1993a). The continuum of university responses to Section 504 for students with learning disabilities. In S.A. Vogel & P.B. Adelman (Eds.), *Success for college students with learning disabilities* (pp. 83–113). New York: Springer-Verlag.

Vogel, S.A. (1993b). *Postsecondary decision-making for adults with learning disabilities.* Pittsburgh: Learning Disabilities Association of America.

Vogel, S.A. (1996). Adults with learning disabilities: Research questions and methodological issues in planning a research agenda for 2000 and beyond. *Canadian Journal of Special Education, 11*(2), 33–54.

Vogel, S.A., & Adelman, P.B. (1990a). Extrinsic and intrinsic factors in graduation and academic failure among LD college students. *Annals of Dyslexia, 40,* 119–137.

Vogel, S.A., & Adelman, P.B. (1990b). Intervention effectiveness at the postsecondary level for the learning disabled. In T. Scruggs & B. Wong (Eds.), *Intervention research in learning disabilities* (pp. 329–344). New York: Springer-Verlag.

Vogel, S.A., & Adelman, P.B. (1992). The success of college students with learning disabilities: Factors related to educational attainment. *Journal of Learning Disabilities, 25*(7), 430–441.

Vogel, S.A., & Konrad, D. (1988). Characteristic written expressive language deficits of the learning disabled: Some general and specific intervention strategies. *Journal of Reading, Writing, and Learning Disabilities International, 4,* 88–99.

Vogel, S.A., & Moran, M. (1982). Written language disorders in learning disabled college students: A preliminary report. In W. Cruickshank & J. Lerner (Eds.), *Coming of age: The best of ACLD* (Vol. III, pp. 211–225). Syracuse, NY: Syracuse University Press.

Vogel, S.A., & Reder, S. (in press). Literacy proficiency among adults with self-reported learning disabilities. In M.C. Smith (Ed.), *Literacy for the 21st century: Research, policy, practices, and the National Adult Literacy Survey.* Westport, CT: Greenwood Press.

Wagner, M. (1989). *Youth with disabilities during transition: An overview of descriptive findings from the National Longitudinal Transition Study.* Menlo Park, CA: SRI International.

Wagner, M. (1990). The school programs and some school performance of secondary students classified as learning disabled: Findings from the National Longitudinal Transition Study of Special Education Students. Prepared for presentation to Division G, American Educational Research Association annual meetings, Boston.

Wagner, M. (1991). *Dropouts with disabilities: What do we know? What can we do?* Menlo Park, CA: SRI International.

Wagner, M. (1992, April). *Being female: A secondary disability? Gender differences in the transition and experiences of young people with disabilities.* Paper presented at the annual meeting of the American Educational Research Association, San Francisco, CA.

Wagner, M., Blackorby, J., Cameto, R., Hebbeler, K., & Newman, L. (1993). *The transition experiences of young people with disabilities: A summary of findings from the National Longitudinal Transition Study of Special Education Students.* Menlo Park, CA: SRI International.

Wagner, M., D'Amico, R., Marder, C., Newman, L., & Blackorby, J. (1992). *What happens next? Trends in postschool outcomes of youth with disabilities: The second comprehensive report from the National Longitudinal Transition Study of Special Education Students.* Menlo Park, CA: SRI International.

Wagner, M., Newman, L., D'Amico, R., Jay, E.D., Butler-Nalin, P., Marder, C., & Cox, R. (1991). *Youth with disabilities: How are they really doing? The first comprehensive report from the National Longitudinal Transition Study of Special Education Students* (pp. 1–15). Menlo Park, CA: SRI International.

Werner, E.E. (1993). Risk and resilience in individuals with learning disabilities: Lessons learned from the Kauai longitudinal study. *Learning Disabilities Research and Practice, 8*(1), 28–34.

Zigmond, N. (1990). Rethinking secondary school programs for students with learning disabilities. *Focus on Exceptional Children, 23,* 1–22.

Zigmond, N., & Baker, J. (1994). Is the mainstream a more appropriate setting for Randy? A case study of one student with learning disabilities. *Learning Disabilities Research and Practice, 9,* 108–117.

Zigmond, N., & Thornton, H. (1985). Follow-up of postsecondary age learning disabled graduates and dropouts. *Learning Disabilities Research, 1*(1), 50–55.

4

Literacy Education for Adults with Learning Disabilities

Perspectives from the Adult Education Side of the Mirror

Jovita M. Ross-Gordon

UNDERSTANDING THE CONTEXT

Adult education is a thriving enterprise in an era when continuing education and life-long learning are imperative. Acknowledging that definitions of *adult education* are myriad, depending on one's position on what "counts" as adult education, Merriam and Brockett defined *adult education* as "activities intentionally designed for the purpose of bringing about learning among those whose age, social roles, or self-perception define them as adults" (1997, p. 8). Within this definition, they included those activities that are self-planned as well as those aided by an adult educator. Numerous forces have been cited as driving participation by today's adults in various forms of formal and informal learning. Surely high on every list is technology. Its impact is multifaceted. Technology has made adult education more accessible, as seen in the person-to-person and network-to-network learning that is facilitated by the World Wide Web. Educational institutions also have been quick to make use of technology to enhance the teaching–learning environment and to deliver education in ways not confined by space and time. Technology forces people to participate in adult education, especially in the workforce, lest they be steamrolled under the wheels of change. Job obsolescence is a common artifact of technological change. Adult education programs aimed at amelio-rating its results are often categorized under the title *job retraining*.

Other social forces driving the increase in participation in adult education can be linked to technological change. For instance, many speak of the changing nature of the economy. American society is said to have shifted from an industrial economy

69

based on production of goods to an information economy in which a premium is placed on knowledge production. In such an economy, the individuals who can easily gain access and contribute to a steadily growing body of knowledge are advantaged. The logarithmic growth in available information has often been referred to as the *knowlege explosion*. Its impact on adult education is seen most vividly in the proliferation of continuing education programs for groups ranging from physicians to elevator repairpersons.

The Broad Context of Adult Education

The contexts of adult education are even more diverse than the forces driving participation. The broad scope of adult education has inspired numerous authors since Lyman Bryson to attempt to typologize it. Writing in 1936, Bryson traced the roots of adult education to four major providers (lyceums, chautauquas, women's clubs, and correspondence schools) and referred to nine "contemporary" agencies: 1) public schools, 2) national public programs, 3) federal emergency programs, 4) colleges and universities, 5) libraries, 6) museums, 7) religious organizations, 8) workers' groups, and 9) parent–teacher groups. Two typologies are presented here to help impress on the reader the continuing ubiquity of adult education and the complexity that awaits any person who would attempt to develop certification standards for the adult educator.

One of the most frequently cited typologies of adult education was proposed by Wayne Shroeder in the *Handbook of Adult Education* (1970). He described four categories of adult education agencies:

Type I—Adult education as a central function: Agencies established to serve the educational needs of adults. These are relatively rare and include agencies such as proprietary schools and residential conference centers.

Type II—Adult education as a secondary function: Agencies established to serve the educational needs of youth but assume the added responsibility of at least partially serving the needs of adults. Public school programs serving adults would be included here, as would continuing education divisions; universities and evening colleges; and community outreach programs in junior colleges, colleges, and universities.

Type III—Adult education as an allied function: Agencies established to meet the needs of the community but are also employed to fulfill some of the needs that agencies recognize as their responsibility. Agencies such as libraries, museums, and social groups often fit this category, as when a Head Start program offers parent education as part of fulfilling its overall mission.

Type IV—Adult education as a subordinate function: Agencies established to serve the special interests of the agency itself. Examples include training; staff development; and human resource development programs in the military, business and industry, churches, and voluntary associations. (1970, p. 37, summarized in Apps, 1989)

Those who have studied adult education extensively will recognize that most agency-based adult education occurs in settings in which adult education is not the primary focus—Types II, III, and IV. As discussion in this chapter continues, it becomes apparent that adult literacy and basic education most often occur within Type II agencies, those founded to serve youth (e.g., evening adult education programs at public schools, programs in community colleges); however, they are also sometimes found in Type III agencies (e.g., public library–sponsored literacy programs, family literacy programs sponsored by human services agencies) and Type IV agencies (e.g., workplace literacy programs, programs sponsored by labor unions). This has significant implications for understanding the place of adult education within organizational priorities and understanding staffing patterns related to adult education programs as compared with education of youth, which takes place in the school, an institution in which education is the primary mission and for which the state has a primary interest in the standardized certification of instructors.

Apps (1989) proposed a typology of adult education based on four categories of providers of educational opportunities for adult education. Apps's framework assumes that most adult learners exercise choice in selecting learning opportunities. This typology is valuable in that it looks at the sources of financial support for adult education programs as a key dimension of categorization:

> *Type I—Fully or partially tax-supported agencies and institutions*: These include public school adult education, adult education programs in 4-year colleges and universities, community and technical colleges, cooperative extension, armed forces, correctional institutions, libraries and museums, and state and federal public adult education agencies.
> *Type II—Nonprofit, self-supporting agencies and institutions*: These include religious institutions, health institutions, community-based agencies (e.g., YMCA/YWCA), service clubs, voluntary organizations, professional organizations, worker education programs (e.g., union leadership programs), and national adult education clearinghouses (e.g., the Educational Resources Information Center [ERIC]) and conference providers.
> *Type III—For-profit providers*: These include correspondence schools; proprietary schools; private tutors; for-profit, degree-granting colleges; on-line data base services; business and industry human resources development programs; and conference centers.
> *Type IV—Nonorganized learning opportunities*: These include television viewing and other mass media, the family, travel, recreational and leisure-time activities, and informal learning in the workplace. (Apps, 1989, pp. 280–281)

A review of this typology indicates that much of the adult education for adults with learning disabilities (LD) described in this book occurs within the first of Apps's four provider contexts, that of fully or partially tax-supported agencies and institutions. Although this category reflects a relatively small proportion of adult education activity overall, adult education aimed at developing literacy and educational skills typically acquired by students in K–12 education is interpreted as falling within the Adult Education Act of 1966 (PL 89-750, as amended). Although monetary resources to support programs subsumed within this act are never adequate to meet the demand, this is one of the few domains of adult education not driven by the ability of adult users or service providers to cover costs. Within higher education, for instance, adults traditionally are limited in their ability to make full use of tax support because many financial aid programs are still targeted at full-time students. The reader should note that although this text concentrates on these publicly supported domains of adult education, the adult with LD may well require educational assistance in the nonprofit and for-profit sectors of adult education.

Diverse Contexts of Literacy Education for Adults

Because this book is concerned with literacy education for adults with LD, the remainder of this chapter focuses on those segments of adult education most concerned with literacy education. Similar to adult education in general, literacy education takes many forms and occurs in many settings. Four primary systems of literacy education can be identified: 1) tutor-based volunteer literacy programs sponsored by large nonprofit organizations, such as Laubach Literacy Action (LLA) and Literacy Volunteers of America (LVA); 2) community-based literacy programs; 3) privately sponsored workplace literacy programs; and 4) the largest system, publicly funded literacy programs. This fourth system was established in 1966 by the Adult Education Act, which has since been amended 16 times (Beder, 1991). Three primary components compose the adult literacy system established by this act and its amendments: 1) Adult Basic Education (ABE), 2) adult secondary education (ASE), and 3) English as a second language (ESL). Despite the urgings of many to define *adult literacy* in functional terms rather than in terms related to school-based grade equivalents, ABE programs are generally aimed at adults assessed as functioning below the ninth-grade level in basic skills (reading, writing, computation). ASE includes programs preparing students for the general educational development (GED) test, high school credit programs for adults, and external diploma programs (Merriam & Brockett, 1997), although in most states ASE is geared to preparing adults to pass the GED test (Beder, 1991).

Newman (1994) presented a concise history of the key legislation that has supported literacy education in the United States since the 1960s as well as its dominant forms and providers. Her overview included discussion of the primary volunteer organizations (LLA and LVA); expansions of the Adult Education Act to include programs such as Literacy Training for Homeless Adults and Literacy Programs for Prisoners; the growth and expansion of workplace literacy programs, such as those represented in the National Coalition for Literacy; and the emergence of intergenerational and family literacy programs such as Even Start. For a critical analysis of the history of literacy education in the United States and the assumptions undergirding contemporary literacy policy initiatives and their portrayal in the media, the reader is referred to Beder (1991), Illsley and Stahl (1993), Quigley (1997), and Stuckey (1991). These authors encourage us to think carefully about the rhetoric through which public support for literacy efforts are garnered and raise important questions about gaining access to literacy education, structural variables influencing participation in literacy programs, and sociocultural factors influencing student recruitment and retention.

The diversity of contexts for adult literacy education makes it difficult to describe with specificity the education program that awaits the adult with LD who seeks involvement with an adult literacy program. It may be more fruitful to acknowledge a few principles of adult education that are commonly espoused by adult literacy educators and to discuss briefly some of the philosophical and contextual variables that influence the nature of program content and pedagogical practices. Beder (1991), for instance, described common professional norms of literacy education. First, he mentioned the role of the teacher as a guide who assists the adult in gaining access to both literacy knowledge and the broader society. Recognizing the frequently troubled relationship some literacy learners have had with the education system and observing that teachers are acutely aware of the voluntary nature of participation in adult literacy education, he noted that many literacy educators subscribe to the "ideology of minimum failure," making every effort to maximize opportunities for success in the teaching–learning interaction. In line with assumptions about the learner who is motivated but likely to be lacking in self-confidence, a professional norm of nurturing is common to many programs. These norms are only partially consistent with principles that have been advocated for working with adult learners in general. For instance, Brookfield (1986) offered the following principles of effective practice in facilitating adult learning:

- Participation in learning is voluntary—intimidation or coercion have no place in motivating adult participation.

- Effective practice is characterized by respect among participants for each other's self-worth.
- Learners and facilitators share responsibility for setting objectives and evaluating learning.
- Praxis is at the heart of effective facilitation, with learners and facilitators involved in a continual cycle of collaborative activity and reflection on activity.
- Facilitation aims to foster in adults a spirit of critical reflection. Educational encounters should assist adults to question many aspects of their personal, occupational, and political lives.
- The aim of facilitation is to nurture self-directed adults who will function as proactive individuals.

Comparing this list of principles with the one provided by Beder (1991), it is possible to see how the "deficit" perspective that colors perceptions of adult illiteracy (Illsley & Stahl, 1993) can lead to altered expectations for this group of individuals. In actuality, the content and pedagogy of adult literacy programs will be significantly influenced by the philosophical underpinnings of the program. Wrigley (1993) described varying approaches used in ESL programs based on six common philosophical orientations:

1. *Common educational core*—reflected in the "basic skills" approach and designed to provide all students with a common set of educational experiences, including basic literacy skills, a command of standard English, and an understanding of common cultural knowledge
2. *Social and economic adaptation*—designed to help adults acquire the skills and knowledge to be self-sufficient and function effectively in the dominant culture
3. *Development of cognitive and academic skills*—stressing process over content, strategies over skills, and understanding over memorization, this approach encourages adults to make their own meaning while interacting with text
4. *Personal relevance*—grounded in humanism, this approach emphasizes enabling adult learners to identify their personal goals, work toward achieving those goals, and assess their own programs
5. *Social change*—assuming that traditional literacy approaches ignore the cultural, linguistic, societal, and political issues surrounding literacy and its uses, programs with this orientation emphasize participatory practices, with learners taking a key role in the classroom and program design
6. *Technological management of education*—with origins in the scientific, social efficiency movement, this approach is exemplified in curriculum models that stress predetermined objectives, well-structured activities, and pre- and posttests to determine mastery of objectives

Looking back to the broader field of adult education, we can see the correspondence between these six orientations and those philosophies of adult education labeled by Merriam and Brockett (1997) as liberal, progressive, constructivist, humanist, and critical. They suggested that although constructivist and critical perspectives are increasingly reflected in adult education programs today, programs based on more traditional philosophies associated with liberal, progressive, humanist, and behaviorist traditions are more common. Their observations seem accurate in describing the dominant skills-based (liberal, progressive, and behaviorist) and learner-oriented (humanistic) emphases most common in descriptions of adult education programs. As they suggested is true of literacy programs based on the philosophies of Paulo Freire, an increasing number of adult literacy programs reflect a critical philosophy.

Staffing Patterns in Adult Education and Adult Literacy Education

Several differences exist between staffing patterns in adult education and K–12 schooling. Whereas teachers of youth tend to be full-time professionals trained and certified by the state, the historically diverse contexts of adult education have not developed a similar system. Frequently cited in describing the personnel issue in adult education is Houle's (1970) pyramid of leadership. At the base of the pyramid are the numerous volunteers who lead groups of adults or tutor other adults. At the middle of the pyramid are those who are paid on an hourly basis for their work and those who are full-time workers with part-time responsibility for adult education. At the top of the pyramid are the full-time adult educators, including program administrators, professors of adult education, training directors, and the like. According to Merriam and Brockett (1997), it is the people in the group at the top who are most likely to identify with being in an adult education career and, indeed, to have access to anything close to a career ladder.

Although some individuals object to the elitism conveyed by this hierarchical conceptualization of workers in the field, Houle's (1970) pyramid provides a useful tool for analyzing staffing patterns in the area of adult literacy education. For instance, program directors and literacy coordinators are likely to be among the few employed full time in literacy work. In most ABE, ASE, and ESL programs, part-time teachers—many who also work as schoolteachers during the day—serve a vital function of direct delivery of services to adult learners; they are frequently aided in this work by volunteers. Part-time teachers make up as much as 90% of the work force in ABE (Kutner et al., 1992). Although some have argued in favor of increasing professionalization and certification in the broad field of adult education, others question the feasibility of creating universal certification standards that would apply equally well across the entire field and argue against trends that would serve to exclude many experienced and able adult educators (James, 1981, 1992). ABE represents one segment of the field in which there has been significant movement toward certification, with certification requirements in one half of the states in the United States (Kutner et al., 1992); however, of the 25 states requiring certification of teachers in ABE and ESL education, only 11 states have certification requirements that include special preparation or training in adult education, with certification in elementary or secondary education serving as the primary certification requirement in 14 others.

Educational preparation for those who educate adults differs from the training of schoolteachers in ways linked to the staffing patterns described previously. Given the rarity of undergraduate programs in adult education and the corresponding infrequency with which individuals begin their careers as adult educators, few enter the field with prior formal training. Graduate programs in adult education have existed since the 1930s, but those who enter them typically first begin working as adult educators and subsequently choose to improve their practice and career opportunities through formal studies. Although those who engage in the academic study of adult education as professors and graduate students would argue its benefits for the professional adult educator, most who work as educators of adults acquire their skills as teachers, program planners, administrators, and counselors through experiential learning and continuing education opportunities (Galbraith & Zelenak, 1989). The subfield of adult literacy education is no exception in this regard. Aside from learning needs related to adult LD, many of the volunteer and paid staff members begin their work with staff development needs related to basic principles of adult learning and education. Ongoing staff development programs organized by state-funded ABE programs and tutor-training programs offered to volunteer tutors are developed to address these needs and are often the primary modes of learning through which the volunteer and part-time educators of adults involved in these programs are oriented to and upgraded in their work. The structures and resources already in place to supply such training provide a vehicle for the introduction of information on identification, assessment, and intervention with adults with LD, although the financial resources for staff development are recognized to be limited relative to the identified need. The other work commitments held by ABE teachers and volunteer instructors and tutors also create scheduling challenges (Kutner et al., 1992).

RESPONDING TO THE PRESENCE OF ADULTS WITH LEARNING DISABILITIES IN ADULT LITERACY EDUCATION: SIGNS OF CHANGE

Elsewhere (Ross-Gordon, 1996), I have traced the earliest discussions of adults with LD in the context of adult education to a flurry of articles appearing in the late 1970s and early 1980s (Bowren, 1981; Gold, 1981; Hamilton, 1983; O'Donnel & Wood, 1981; Travis, 1979). These articles pointed to questions regarding prevalence of LD among adult education students as well as issues regarding appropriate procedures and practices for identification, assessment, curriculum and program development, and intervention approaches. Although articles and chapters written in the 1990s suggested these questions remain with us as of 1998 (Anderson, 1994; Ross-Gordon, 1992; Ryan & Price, 1993; Sturomski, 1996), significant progress has been made in the recognition and delineation of the problems. There is also evidence to suggest that even as scholars and policy makers representing several fields continue to grapple with the issues of how best of identify and meet the needs of the adult with LD in literacy programs, those working in the trenches are increasingly making efforts to gain access to and use whatever information is available, and program administrators increasingly are responding to the needs of their staff members by providing resources and staff development. Progress can be noted in two major areas: 1) staff development and 2) program and curriculum development.

Staff Development

Limited research conducted on the perceived staff development needs of adult education workers on the subject of adult LD (Ross & Smith, 1990; Ryan & Price, 1993) confirms what is easily observable in attendance at staff development programs and conference sessions on the topic: Workers in adult basic and literacy education are eager to learn about this topic. Initially this staff development was most apparent in the form of print resource materials. An example from 1984 is found in a series of documents developed by Hoy and Gregg (1984a, 1984b, 1984c, 1984d, 1984e) for adult education staff in Georgia. These documents *separately* covered a range of topics, including description and definition of LD (1984e); appraisal and assessment (1984a); and assessment and remediation of mathematics (1984b), reading (1984c), and written language (1984d). Development of this guide was supported by project development monies of the Adult Education Section of the state of Georgia. Additional handbooks or resource guides on adult LD and adult literacy have subsequently been developed with support from other states, including Kansas (Hebert, 1988), Maryland (Hawkins, 1991), and Mississippi (Hutto, 1995). Development of similar comprehensive handbooks and resource guides has been supported by organizations including the Learning Disabilities

Association of Canada (Karassik, 1989) and the ERIC Clearinghouse on Adult, Career, and Vocational Education (Ross-Gordon, 1989). In addition, Literacy Volunteers of America has incorporated suggestions for working with adults with suspected LD in its primary training manual (Vogel, 1993). During the 1990s, the National Adult Literacy and Learning Disabilities Center (see Chapter 5) has played a key role in the development and dissemination of print resource materials on LD to the literacy community.

Obviously, staff development cannot depend on print materials alone. To provide technical support for local staff development, the federal Office of Vocational and Adult Education has commissioned development of a training packet on LD as one of nine such packets for ABE/ESL staff development (Osher, Webb, & Koehler, 1993). Aimed at embodying good adult education practice as well as at teaching it, these training materials employ theory, demonstrations, practice, structured feedback, and applications with follow-up exercises. Topics covered include the definition of a learning disability; attitudes, barriers, and accommodations; planning for learning; teacher research and collaboration; developing a monitoring plan; and gaining access to and using resources. The packet provides a complete set of materials for use in delivery of a three-session workshop series, including agendas, overheads, and sample supplementary readings for participants. At the state level, Florida (Dean, 1995) and Pennsylvania (Cooper, 1994)—among others—have also shown a continuing effort in the 1990s to bring staff development programs on LD to literacy workers. A report on the results of a survey of state directors of adult education regarding the priority areas for new training activities and demonstration projects afforded by an amendment to Section 353 of the Adult Education Act indicated that certain recurring training programs were emphasized in the responses—including those on individuals with LD (Ryan & Price, 1993).

Although some staff development efforts, such as the workshops described by Dean (1995), have been designed in such a fashion as to incorporate literacy tutors with paid staff, select staff development programs have been aimed specifically at tutors. One such program has been developed and delivered by the Stern Center for Language and Learning via interactive television to 100 ABE tutors throughout the state of Vermont and included follow-up visits to 17 ABE sites (Podhajski, 1995; see also Chapter 10). Its content includes definition and identification of LD, discussion of the language continuum, and approaches to instruction (with an emphasis on synthetic phonics).

Program and Curriculum Development

As interest and understanding of LD among educators in the context of ABE have increased, a growing number of curriculum development projects and special intervention programs have also been reported. In a number of instances, these projects have been supported by what are referred to as 353 funds (monies flowing from funding of Section 353 of the Adult Education Act). These project development funds are administered by the states as a way of encouraging innovative program development, such as the Head Start for Learning Disabled Students program funded by the Pennsylvania Department of Education (Reading Area Community College, 1990). The Office of Vocational and Adult Education has also supported program development in the area of workplace literacy, as illustrated by a project housed at Hampden Papers, Inc., in Massachusetts (Massachusetts State Department of Education, 1993). Yet another area of program development supported by Section 353 funds is curriculum development. For instance, in the state of Pennsylvania, development of curricular materials has been supported in the areas of math (Cooper, 1988) and reading (Cooper, 1989).

UNRESOLVED ISSUES IN SERVING ADULTS WITH LEARNING DISABILITIES IN ADULT LITERACY EDUCATION

As the preceding section suggests, significant progress has been made in attention to LD among learners in adult literacy education since the early 1980s. At the same time, a number of fundamental issues have only partially been addressed. Several of these are the focus of the work of the National Adult Literacy and Learning Disabilities Center (NALLD) (see Chapter 5 for an update of the center's activities, particularly in developing a tool kit for literacy practitioners to use in identification, assessment, and educational planning with the adult with learning disabilities). The remainder of this chapter is devoted to the delineation of practice-related questions in the late 1990s. These are presented as a series of questions for which answers are evolving as research and experience grows.

Are the Best Interests of Previously Unidentified Adults with LD Always Best Served by Identification?

Professionals in the field of LD are likely to favor identification of LD on the assumption that diagnosis is necessary to appropriate service delivery. This has been historically true within the special education system. Adults with LD themselves have in some cases argued the benefits of labeling (Hatt, 1991). However, literacy professionals have questioned the appropriateness and necessity of labeling (Alderson-Gill & Associates, 1989; Coles, 1980; Ross-Gordon, 1989; Sturomski, 1996). A study sponsored by the Learning Disabilities Association of Canada (Alderson-Gill, 1989) pointed to the discrepancy between learning disability professionals and literacy professionals on this point and attempted to provide some explanation. Objections to routine diagnosis by literacy experts were framed in doubts about the presumed "good" to come of labeling, possible negative effects on self-esteem associated with the term *disability*, concerns about subjecting adults to testing given their history of failure with similar situations, and arguments that a well-trained literacy tutor or instructor can effectively plan a course of instruction to address a learner's individual strengths and weaknesses without having knowledge of a label (Alderson-Gill & Associates, 1989). A counterargument can be made that students will not be able to gain access to services to which they are entitled, such as GED testing or workplace accommodations, without a documented disability. One can also argue that the empowered adult learner needs an accurate understanding of his or her learning strengths and weaknesses in order to act as his or her own best advocate. Acknowledging the merits of both arguments, a sensible response may be seeking a diagnosis only when it is apparent that there is some likely benefit that cannot otherwise be obtained. Where such a benefit is thought to be likely, a discussion with the adult student is warranted, presenting possible merits of diagnosis and leaving the decision in his or her hands as to whether testing is desired (Fowler & Scarborough, 1993; Ross-Gordon, 1989).

What Are the Appropriate Tools for Assessment of Adults Suspected of Having Learning Disabilities?

The paucity of validated screening procedures and diagnostic instruments that are appropriate for use with adult literacy students continues to be an issue. Focus groups conducted by the NALLD have identified a number of features desired by participants from the literacy community (see Chapter 5). As part of the evaluation process, diagnosticians should be sure to incorporate interviews with learners about their histories, needs, and goals. This information may be of value in focusing the formal testing process so that only tests essential to the determination of disability and those that will provide information useful to the adult and his or her literacy provider are selected, thus minimizing the hours devoted to testing. Instruments must be selected that have been standardized with adults, although there may be conditions under which other instruments might be useful to collect informal assessment information without assigning a score. Whatever mix of interviews, informal testing, and formal testing is used, it is critical that evaluation reports produce summaries and recommendations that are interpretable by literacy providers and can be shared with adult learners.

Which Sociocultural Issues Must Be Considered in Identifying and Serving Adults with Learning Disabilities?

Scarce attention has been devoted to the sociocultural dimensions of LD assessment in adults who are returning to the adult literacy programs (Ross-Gordon, 1996). Literature on younger individuals with LD has been more likely to raise issues related to possible biases in the identification process linked to gender, race, and primary language. For instance, to the extent that gender-related bias in teacher referrals partially accounts for the consistent data showing greater rates of LD among boys than among girls (Hassitt & Gurian, 1984; Vogel, 1990), women may be more likely to arrive in adult literacy programs undiagnosed. At the point of referral, such bias can contribute to either over-identification or underidentification of cultural or linguistic minority students. This may occur because of a lack of understanding of cultural or linguistic differences on the part of a classroom teacher. For instance, a teacher may have reduced expectations of certain students because of race or may assume that a student's difficulties are a result of not having English as his or her primary language, which leads to a reduced likelihood of referring the student for appropriate testing. In the same vein, a tutor may interpret a student's use of Ebonics in language-experience stories as a sign of a linguistic impairment and inappropriately refer him or her for evaluation of spoken and written language disorders. At the stage of formal evaluation, cultural bias inherent to instruments may influence the likelihood that the student will be identified as having LD (Rydell, 1990; Wolfram, 1990). This is particularly likely in cases in which a rigid intelligent quotient (IQ) cutoff or discrepancy score criterion is adhered to, despite controversies over cultural bias in IQ score testing (de la Cruz, 1996; LaGrow & Prochnow-LaGrow, 1985), the adequacies of traditional measures of intelligence (Naglieri & Reardon, 1993), the construct and measurement of ability–achievement discrepancy (Kavale & Forness, 1994), and even the construct of general intelligence underlying traditional IQ score measurement (Gardner, 1983; Sternberg, 1985, 1988).

Is There Equitable and Affordable Access to Quality Diagnostic Services?

The cost of private diagnostic services is prohibitive to many adult learners involved in literacy education. No doubt in an attempt to address this problem, half of the state directors of adult education surveyed by Ryan and Price (1993) indicated that they would refer students to state agencies such as Rehabilitative Services, and 27% reported that diagnostic assessment would likely occur on-site free of charge. Only 4% reported that students would be directed to private agencies. This leaves many adults dependent on publicly supported diagnostic services, such as those sponsored by vocational rehabilitation (VR) services. Restrictive eligibility criteria can be a barrier in some locales where stretched-thin VR services budgets force allocation of even diagnostic services to those assumed to possess the most severe employment-related disabilities. Where resources do support allocation of evaluation services to the as-yet-undiagnosed adult with possible LD, another issue may be the variability in diagnostic services offered by the providers with whom VR services contract locally. Literacy providers will not find a report that summarizes test scores without offering implications for instructional and compensatory strategies.

What Considerations Should Be Made Regarding Linguistic and Cultural Group Status?

Special concern is warranted in the effort to provide fair evaluations and appropriate interventions for students from nondominant culture groups—two such cases are those students belonging to linguistic and racial/ethnic minorities. Some of the same issues related to biases inherent to commonly used assessment instruments such as IQ tests prevail when considering adults in ESL programs as with children in Limited English Proficiency classes. Language differences between teacher or tutor and student may make it difficult to determine the extent of the student's basic literacy skills in his or her native language. Thus it becomes unclear whether difficulties are related primarily to language difference, learning disability, or mere lack of acquisition of written language literacy skills. Although questions about this learner group are common at conferences, little has been written about these individuals' needs and how to serve them effectively.

In an ERIC Digest on access to literacy education for adults who are members of a linguistic minority, Cumming (1992) discussed the following situational barriers that may complicate the pursuit of literacy for these adults:

- Lack of on-site child care by trusted members of their own culture
- Unfamiliarity with institutional practices and government services
- Responsibilities to extended-family members
- Schedule conflicts with family responsibilities

Although some of these variables may be similar to those faced by other adults in literacy programs, other barriers may be unique. Cumming (1992) described, for example, the particular barriers to participation in adult education for women of some cultures and the negative reactions to literacy education manifested by Mayan refugees and aboriginal peoples in Canada who act in ways consistent with cultural traditions of resistance to assimilation and oppression. Denny (1992) suggested similar barriers may exist for some African American adults, who, like others described by Ogbu (1978) as nonvoluntary minorities, may have adopted expressive responses of identity and culture to cope with a subordinate economic and social status, including a skepticism regarding the benefits of literacy and suspicion of some literacy providers. Personal and familial experience with the effects of disproportionate special education labeling (Harry, 1992) also may make these adults particularly suspicious of diagnoses aimed at providing such a label, no matter how well intended the tutor or educator.

What Services Are Needed to Facilitate Psychosocial Adjustment of Adults with Learning Disabilities and Literacy Needs?

Although many literacy programs focus on the acquisition of basic skills in reading, writing, and numeracy, adult education program staff are accustomed to working with a clientele whose needs go beyond a focus on academics. In looking at the needs of adults with LD, it becomes immediately clear that these adults often require more extensive services than those provided by the literacy educator alone. Although Ryan and Price (1992) wisely warned against overgeneralizing that all individuals with LD have low self-esteem and other psychosocial problems; they and others (Johnson &

Blalock, 1987; Ross-Gordon, 1989) noted that such needs are important to address for many adults with LD. Citing the work of numerous researchers documenting psychosocial adjustment characteristics, including depression, anger, excessive dependency, shyness, impulsivity, and lack of motivation, they pointed to the role of these characteristics in difficulties in communicating with others, dysfunctional interactions with spouses and children, and inappropriate social skills.

Given the impact such difficulties can have on adults in the areas of independent living, family life, and work (Ross-Gordon, 1989), it is no wonder that, when asked to rank the areas in which they needed assistance, 560 adults surveyed by the Association for Children with Learning Disabilities (prior to organizational name change to the Learning Disabilities Association of America) ranked in the first three places social relationships and skills, career counseling, and self-esteem. More traditional academic areas, such as reading and spelling, ranked nearer the bottom of their list (Chesler, 1982). The greatest personal and social impact may be observed in those individuals referred to in discussion of links between LD and welfare (Cohen, Golonka, Ooms, & Owen, 1995; National Institute for Literacy, 1994), corrections (Ohio State Legislative Office of Education Oversight, 1994: Tevis & Orem, 1985), and unemployment ("Another Chance," 1991).

Numerous intervention strategies in the domain of psychosocial adjustment have been discussed, including transitional living facilities, individual and family counseling, LD self-help/support groups, vocational rehabilitation and job training, and job clubs (Ross-Gordon, 1989; Ryan & Price, 1992). Yet the degree to which adults with LD are referred to such services remains variable, depending on the sensitivity of educational providers to the need and their awareness of existing local services.

What Are the Staff Development Needs of Special Educators Working in Literacy Education with Adults with Learning Disabilities?

An increasing amount of attention is being paid to the staff development needs of teachers and tutors in adult education, ASE, ESL, and literacy programs with regard to LD, and this attention is well warranted. There has, however, been no parallel call for staff development on adult learning and education for an increasing number of professionals who were trained in LD and special education of youth and have moved into roles serving adult learners. Many are acquiring a basic understanding of the differences between youth and adult learners through direct experience, and scholarly literature in the field of LD devotes increasing attention to the adult with LD. The value of staff development programs targeted at increasing the awareness among learning disability professionals of theories and practices in adult learning and education does not appear to be mentioned in this literature, however, leaving one to conclude its value has yet to be recognized. Yet, similar to others who come to the role of adult educator in midcareer, this group of professionals would be enriched by exposure to both the theoretical and practice traditions of adult education. Aside from assisting individuals in their own reflective practice, professional development opportunities of this kind might help decrease the conceptual distance between the fields, which often intersect in their interest in serving adults known or suspected to have LD as a contributing factor to literacy difficulties.

How Can Principles of Adult Education Most Effectively Be Incorporated into Teacher–Learner Relationships with Adults with Learning Disabilities?

Because of the orientation toward a focus on the impairments of adult learners with low levels of literacy and those with LD, it is easy for administrative staff, teachers, and tutors to put aside basic principles of adult education and shift toward educational practices customary with younger, more dependent learners. The literature on education for literacy with adults who have LD, whether originating in special education or adult education professional sources, has seldom given attention to strategies for ensuring that basic tenets of adult education are honored. Contrary to the diagnostic-prescriptive educational model, which leaves nearly all power in the educational relationship in the hands of the trained professional, tenets of adult education would suggest that adults should be integrally involved in the design and implementation of the educational programs, at every step from identifying learning needs to evaluating success of the learning activity. This suggests an instructor role familiar to many in adult education, placing the teacher at the side of the learner as a guide or facilitator rather than in front of the learner as director of the learning experience. As has been found with adults in other arenas of adult education practice, not every learner will come equally well prepared or enthusiastic about taking a more active role in his or her own learning. While taking student and situational variables into account to determine appropriate amounts of structure and support, the effective adult educator can help guide the learner toward taking greater personal responsibility for his or her learning (Grow, 1991; Pratt, 1988, 1993).

What Instructional Strategies Are Effective with Adults with Learning Disabilities?

A simple answer to this question is not likely to be forthcoming, given the diversity of LD and the fact that no two individuals are likely to have exactly the same array of learning strengths and weaknesses. Lists of general strategies have been offered (Ross-Gordon, 1989; Vogel, 1993) and are likely to be helpful to either the adult or special education professional. Such lists are useful in helping the educator create a learning environment that is characterized by 1) a positive and supportive climate, 2) minimal distraction, 3) appropriate levels of structure and feedback, and 4) tailored to the learning style preferences of learners. In addition, the suggestions in these lists are aimed at helping the learner develop personal learning and metacognitive strategies that may be used when the tutor or teacher is not present. Beyond this level, diverse kinds of LD require different strategies. Guides differentiated according to type of learning difficulty, such as those developed by Hoy and Gregg (1984a, 1984b, 1984c, 1984d, 1984e), are likely to be of greater utility once the teacher or tutor has information regarding the nature of the specific LD and strengths to be drawn on in instruction.

The general question of whether there are distinct strategies *specifically* appropriate for use with adult learners with LD elicits different responses according to the professional group being asked (Alderson-Gill & Associates, 1989). Findings from an interview study conducted for the Learning Disabilities Association of Canada with representative experts from the literacy and learning disability fields found common ground in recommending flexible and individualized instruction and a success-oriented, eclectic approach, employing materials appropriate for adult learners (Alderson-Gill & Associates, 1989). Learning disability experts were more likely to agree that LD required diagnosis through standardized testing, that adults with LD are likely to require literacy programs distinct from those offered to the general population, and that literacy teachers and tutors need to be trained in the body of knowledge on LD and in associated interventions. Literacy experts, in contrast, were more likely to agree that labeling and the testing required to determine a label might do more harm than good and that a well-trained tutor, with expert support in challenging situations, would be sensitive enough to recognize a learning difficulty and develop an approach to combat that difficulty.

What Is the Place of Accommodation, versus Remediation, in Literacy Education for Adults with Learning Disabilities?

Reference is made previously in this chapter to the dominant skills-based orientation of literacy programs. With the emphasis on the role of the educator or the tutor in helping the adult acquire literacy skills in most literacy programs, it is not uncommon for attention to development of compensatory learning strategies to be neglected. These may be viewed as something the learner acquires naturally or as coping strategies that will no longer be needed once the adult can strengthen his or her basic skills. Therefore, one is probably more likely to find the adult with severe dyslexia in the postsecondary setting learning through the use of audiotapes as an alternative or supplement to texts than one is to find the adult secondary student studying for the GED test in this fashion. This relates to the fundamental question facing the adult literacy educator regarding the primary purposes of literacy education. An answer will not necessarily be found by looking to the definition of literacy, of which Quigley (1997) reported counting 150 variations since 1880. To the extent that literacy educators see adult literacy as focused on the acquisition of reading and writing skills, they are likely to be reluctant to allocate scarce instructional time to assisting students to develop modes of learning not based on print media. To the extent that literacy is viewed in a broader perspective—possessing the skills needed to acquire and critically analyze information and to function effectively in a variety of contexts of adult life—literacy education is likely to be viewed as encompassing all instruction aimed at assisting adults to become independent learners through whichever modes are available to them. A literacy educator with the latter viewpoint is more likely to see as legitimate the learning that a student may do through listening to audiotapes or using multimedia instructional programs and is more likely to allocate time to helping adults identify and expand their repertoire of learning strategies to include those that utilize the audio, video, and multimedia resources that are increasingly relied on by adult learners who are not thought to have a low level of literacy or learning disability.

What Kind of Balance Is Desirable Among Various Intervention Options?

The model of intervention historically used in the field of special education has placed a specialist in direct contact with a learner, although in this postinclusion era the specialist has increasingly played the role of consultant to a classroom teacher. Therefore, learning disability professionals may be inclined to assume that the most effective way to serve adults with LD in literacy education programs is through special programs bringing students and learning disability specialists together. In adult literacy programs, adults have typically been served by a general education teacher or by a tutor who may have had varying degrees of support from a professional. Accustomed to this model, adult literacy educators may assume that all adults with LD can be effectively served by a tutor or a teacher who has some prior training in working with such students. Each of these models has flaws that are linked to feasibility based on cost in the first case and linked to difficulties faced by the insufficiently prepared tutor or teacher in the second.

Elsewhere a more differentiated model of intervention has been described (Ross & Smith, 1990; Ross-Gordon, 1992) and is recapped briefly here. This model has been referred to simply as the Multilevel Model of Intervention. *Level one* focuses on the literacy teacher or the tutor and includes *preservice training and staff development*. It begins when teachers are hired or tutors are selected to instruct within ABE/ASE and literacy programs. Teachers and tutors should be taught to modify their instructional strategies to fit a variety of learning styles. Supplementary instruction should address identification and screening for LD and accommodations for students with LD that can be made in the classroom. *Level two*, still providing service through the literacy teacher or the tutor, includes *ongoing consultation*. Initially, specialists should consult with teachers to help them interpret diagnostic information. Later, as needed, professionals trained in LD assist the teacher or tutor in developing an intervention plan based on diagnostic information and modifying that plan as suggested by initial results. (This often occurs in a diagnostic or clinical teaching model.) As appropriate, other specialists, including physicians, psychologists, neurologists, rehabilitation counselors, and others who have demonstrated a specific interest in applying the knowledge and skills of their disciplines to LD, might be consulted by the teacher or the tutor coordinator.

Finally, *Level three* includes ongoing *direct services by specialists*. In a limited number of instances for students whose situations suggested needs beyond those that could be addressed by the teacher or the tutor even with specialist consultation, this option could be utilized. The most frequent form of direct service would be diagnostic evaluation for LD. With some students, an extended period of diagnostic teaching might proceed with the learning disability specialist in order to identify instructional strategies to be used by the literacy teacher or tutor. In a limited number of situations, ongoing assistance from a learning disability specialist would be recommended. As appropriate, the adult learner would also be referred for direct services to be provided by other specialists, including psychologists, social workers, and rehabilitation counselors.

Analysis of the literature reviewed for this chapter suggests that since the time when this model was first proposed, increasing activity has occurred at Level one (i.e., preservice training and staff development). Reports by learning disability specialists of their work with adult literacy students also suggest that activity continues to increase at Level three (i.e., direct services by specialists). The apparent missing link is that of Level two (i.e., ongoing consultation). Rarely are descriptions provided of instances in which literacy educators and tutors who have already been provided basic training in identifying and responding to adult LD are then provided ongoing support as they apply their new teaching skills. The reader should refer to Chapters 12 and 14 for models for working with both learners and teachers.

CONCLUSION

Writing as an educator who was first trained in the field of LD but now most closely identifies with the field of adult education, I have attempted to present an overview that can be useful to adult or special educators. Speaking first to special educators and others who have come into roles as educators of adults with a limited academic background in the field, I have presented a brief orientation to the broad field of adult education as well as to adult education literature on literacy education. Next, I have outlined what I saw as encouraging trends indicating growing attention to LD by adult educators engaged in or writing about literacy education. These trends are reported in terms of a growing body of literature, increasing availability of staff development on LD, and a growing number of curricular and program development efforts funded through the Adult Education Act. Last, I have discussed a series of practice-oriented questions for which answers are evolving.

The reader will no doubt find that more questions have been raised than answered. Such is the status of the field. What is encouraging, however, is the fact that many professionals and volunteers coming from various theoretical and practical orientations are engaged in the effort to understand the needs of the adult who learns differently. Critical to the attempt to meet these needs is the involvement of the learners themselves. The field of adult education offers a long tradition and rich experience in learner-centered education that has much to offer in this endeavor.

REFERENCES

Adult Education Act of 1966, PL 89-750, 20 U.S.C. §§ 1201 *et seq.*

Alderson-Gill & Associates. (1989). *Study of literacy and learning disabilities.* Ottawa, Ontario: Learning Disabilities Association of Canada.

Anderson, C. (1994). Adult literacy and learning disabilities. In P.G. Gerber & H.B. Reiff (Eds.), *Learning disabilities in adulthood: Persisting problems, and evolving issues* (pp. 121–129). Boston: Andover Medical Publishers.

Another chance: The comprehensive learning program for adults with learning disabilities. (1991). Bronx, NY: Fordham University, Graduate School of Education (ERIC Document Reproduction Service No. ED 335 817)

Apps, J.W. (1989). Providers of adult and community education: A framework. In S.B. Merriam & P.M. Cunningham (Eds.), *Handbook of adult and continuing education* (pp. 275–286). San Francisco: Jossey-Bass.

Beder, H. (1991). *Adult literacy: Issues for policy and practice.* Malabar, FL: Krieger Publishing Co.

Bowren, W.F. (1981). Teaching the learning disabled to read. *Adult Literacy and Basic Education, 5*(3), 179–184.

Brookfield, S. (1986). *Understanding and facilitating adult learning.* San Francisco: Jossey-Bass.

Bryson, L. (1936). *Adult education.* New York: American Book.

Chesler, B. (1982). ACLD vocational committee completes survey on LD adult. *ACLD Newsbriefs, 146*(5), 20–23.

Cohen, E., Golonka, S., Ooms, T., & Owen, T. (1995). *Literacy and welfare reform: Are we making the connection?* (NCAL Brief #BP95-01) Philadelphia: National Center on Adult Literacy (ERIC Document Reproduction Service No. ED 387 675)

Coles, G. (1980). Can ABE students be identified as learning disabled? *Adult Literacy and Basic Education, 4*(3), 170–181.

Cooper, R. (1988). *Tic Tac Toe Math: Instructional Guide.* Bryn Mawr, PA: Center for Alternative Learning. (ERIC Document Reproduction Service No. ED 376 358)

Cooper, R. (1989). *Sight/Sound System.* Bryn Mawr, PA: Center for Alternative Learning. (ERIC Document Reproduction Service No. ED 376 357)

Cooper, R. (1994). *Staff development workshops about learning disabilities.* Bryn Mawr, PA: Center for Alternative Learning. (ERIC Document Reproduction Service No. ED 376 356)

Cumming, A. (1992). *Access to literacy for language minority adults.* Washington, DC: National Clearinghouse on Literacy Education. (ERIC Document Reproduction Service No. ED 350 886)

Dean, K. (1995). *We're sold: Strategies for overcoming learning differences. A Section 353 Training Project.* Clearwater, FL: Pinellas County School Board. (ERIC Document Reproduction Service No. ED 391 046)

de la Cruz, R. (1996). *Assessment-bias issues in special education: A review of literature.* (ERIC Document Reproduction Service No. ED 390 246)

Denny, V.H. (1992). Access to literacy programs: Perspectives of African-American adults. *Theory into Practice, 31*(4), 337–341.

Fowler, A.E., & Scarborough, H.S. (1993). *Should reading-disabled adults be distinguished from other adults seeking literacy instruction? A review of theory and research.* (NCAL Technical Report TR93-07). Philadelphia: University of Pennsylvania. (ERIC Document Reproduction Service No. ED 363 732)

Galbraith, M.W., & Zelenak, B.S. (1989). The education of adult and continuing education practitioners. In S.B. Merriam & P.M. Cunningham (Eds.) *Handbook of adult and continuing education* (pp. 125–133). San Francisco: Jossey-Bass.

Gardner, H. (1983). *Frames of mind: The theory of multiple intelligences.* New York: Basic Books.

Gold, P.C. (1981). The DL-LEA: A remedial approach for nonreaders with a language deficiency handicap. *Adult Literacy and Basic Education, 5*(3), 185–192.

Grow, G. (1991). Teaching learners to be self-directed: A stage approach. *Adult Education Quarterly, 41*(3).

Hamilton, E. (1983). Language and reading comprehension: A strategy for planning programs with learning-disabled adults *Adult Literacy and Basic Education, 7*(3), 129–137.

Harry, B. (1992). *Cultural diversity, families, and the special educational system.* New York: Teachers College Press.

Hassitt, I.D., & Gurian, A. (1984). *The learning disabled girl: A profile.* Paper presented at the Annual Convention of the American Psychological Association, Toronto, Canada. (ERIC Document Reproduction Service No. ED 250 872)

Hatt, P. (1991). Learning disabilities: To label or not to label. *Literacy/Alphabétisation, 15*(3), 4–5. (ERIC Document Reproduction Service No. ED 350 394)

Hawkins, D. (1991). *Retaining the learning disabled adult: A handbook for adult basic education instructors.* Frederick, MD: Frederick County Public Schools. (ERIC Document Reproduction Service No. ED 377 389)

Hebert, J. (1988). *Project Upgrade: Working adults who have learning disabilities.* Manhattan, KS: Manhattan Adult Learning and Resource Center.

Houle, C.O. (1970). *The educators of adults.* In R.M. Smith, G.F. Aker, & J.R. Kidd (Eds.), *Handbook of adult education* (pp. 109–120). New York: Macmillan.

Hoy, C.A., & Gregg, K.N. (1984a). *Appraisal and Assessment of Learning Disabilities, Including a Special Bibliography. Academic assessment of remediation of adults with learning disabilities: A resource series for adult basic education teachers.* Athens, GA: Clarke County Board of Education. (ERIC Document Reproduction Service No. ED 285 352)

Hoy, C.A., & Gregg, K.N. (1984b). *Asssessment and remediation of mathematics. Academic assessment of remediation of adults with learning disabilities: A resource series for adult basic education teachers.* Athens, GA: Clarke County Board of Education. (ERIC Document Reproduction Service No. ED 285 356)

Hoy, C.A., & Gregg, K.N. (1984c). *Assessment and remediation of reading. Academic assessment of remediation of adults with learning disabilities: A resource series for adult basic education teachers.* Athens, GA: Clarke County Board of Education. (ERIC Document Reproduction Service No. ED 285 355)

Hoy, C.A., & Gregg, K.N. (1984d). *Assessment and remediation of written language. Academic assessment of remediation of adults with learning disabilities: A resource series for adult basic education teachers.* Athens, GA: Clarke County Board of Education. (ERIC Document Reproduction Service No. ED 285 354)

Hoy, C.A., & Gregg, K.N. (1984e). *Description and definition of learning disabilities. Academic assessment of remediation of adults with learning disabilities: A resource series for adult basic education teachers.* Athens, GA: Clarke County Board of Education. (ERIC Document Reproduction Service No. ED 285 351)

Hutto, M. (1995). *Adults who have a learning disability: A guide for the ABE instructor.* Mississippi State: Mississippi State University. (ERIC Document Reproduction Service No. ED 393 266)

Illsley, P.J., & Stahl, N.A. (1993). Reconceptualizing the language of adult literacy. *Journal of Reading, 37*(1), 20–27.

James, W.B. (1981). Certification is unfeasible and unnecessary. In B.S. Kreitlow & Associates (Eds.), *Examining controversies in adult education* (pp. 84–95). San Francisco: Jossey-Bass.

James, W.B. (1992). Professional certification is not needed in adult and continuing education. In M.W. Galbraith & B. Sisco (Eds.), *Confronting controversies in challenging times: A call for action.* (New Directions for Adult and Continuing Education, No. 54). San Francisco: Jossey-Bass.

Johnson, D.J., & Blalock, J.W. (Eds.). (1987). *Adults with learning disabilities: Clinical studies.* Orlando, FL: Grune & Stratton.

Karassik, J.W. (1989). *Literacy and learning disabilities: A handbook for literacy workers.* Ottawa, Ontario: Learning Disabilities Association of Canada.

Kavale, K.A., & Forness, S.R. (1994). Learning disabilities and intelligence: An uneasy alliance. *Advances in Learning and Behavioral Disabilities, 8,* 1–63.

Kutner, M., Sherman, R., Webb, L., Herman, R., Tibbetts, J., Hemphill, D., Terdy, D., & Jones, E. (1992). *Study of ABE/ESL instructor training approaches: Phase I report.* Washington, DC: Pelavin Associates, Inc. (ERIC Document Reproduction Service No. ED 344 054)

LaGrow, S.J., & Prochnow-LaGrow, J.E. (1985). Consideration of bias in the assessment and placement process of exceptional children. In A.F. Rotarori & R. Fox (Eds.), *Assessment for regular and special education teachers: A case study approach* (pp. 31–51). Austin, TX: PRO-ED.

Massachusetts State Department of Education. (1993). *Learning differently in adult education: Development of a learning disabilities component at Hampden Papers, Inc.* Washington, DC: National Workplace Literacy Program. (ERIC Document Reproduction Service No. ED 363 742)

Merriam, S.B., & Brockett, R.G. (1997). *The professional practice of adult education: An introduction.* San Francisco: Jossey-Bass.

Naglieri, J., & Reardon, S.M. (1993). Traditional IQ is irrelevant to learning disabilities—intelligence is not. *Journal of Learning Disabilities, 26*(2), 127–133.

National Institute for Literacy. (1994). *What kind of adult literacy policy do we need if we are serious about ending welfare as we know it?* Washington, DC: Author. (ERIC Document Reproduction Service No. ED 372 279)

O'Donnel, N.O., & Wood, M. (1981). Adult learning problems: A critique of the London Procedure. *Adult Literacy and Basic Education, 5*(4), 243–249.

Ogbu, J.U. (1978). *Minority education and caste: The American system in cross-cultural perspective.* New York: Academic Press.

Ohio State Legislative Office of Education Oversight. (1994). *Education behind bars: Opportunities and obstacles.* Columbus, OH: Author. (ERIC Document Reproduction Service No. ED 392 942)

Osher, D., Webb, L., & Koehler, S. (1993). *Learning disabilities: Learner-centered approaches. Training packet.* Washington, DC: Pelavin Associates. (ERIC Document Reproduction Service No. ED 368 943)

Podhajski, B. (1995). *Teaching adults with learning disabilities. A model training program for ABE tutors.* Williston, VT: Stern Center for Language and Learning. (ERIC Document Reproduction Service No. ED 385 774)

Pratt, D.D. (1988). Andragogy as a relational construct. *Adult Education Quarterly, 36*(3), 160–181.

Pratt, D.D. (1993). Andragogy after twenty-five years. In S. Merriam (Ed.), *An update on adult learning theory: New directions for adult and continuing education,* No. 57 (pp. 15–23). San Francisco: Jossey-Bass.

Quigley, B.A. (1997). *Rethinking literacy education: The critical needs for practice-based change.* San Francisco: Jossey-Bass.

Reading Area Community College. (1990). *Head Start for learning disabled students: Final report 1990–1991.* Harrisburg, PA: PA Department of Education. (ERIC Document Reproduction Service No. ED 342 908)

Ross, J.M., & Smith, J.O. (1990). Adult basic educator's perceptions of learning disabilities. *Journal of Reading, 33*(5), 340–347.

Ross-Gordon, J.M. (1989). *Adults with learning disabilities: An overview for the adult educator* (Information Series No. 337). Columbus, OH: ERIC Clearinghouse on Adult, Career and Vocational Education. (ERIC Document Reproduction Service No. ED 315 664)

Ross-Gordon, J.M. (1992). Literacy and the adult with specific learning disabilities. In A.M. Scales & J.E. Burley (Eds.), *Perspectives from adult literacy to continuing education* (pp. 103–115). Dubuque, IA: William C. Brown.

Ross-Gordon, J.M. (1996). Sociocultural issues affecting identification and service delivery models for adults with learning disabilities. In N. Gregg, C. Hoy, A.F. Gay (Eds.), *Adults with learning disabilities: Theoretical and practical perspectives* (pp. 85–126). New York: The Guilford Press.

Ryan, A.G., & Price, L.P. (1992). Adults with LD in the 1990s. *Intervention in School and Clinic, 28*(1), 6–20.

Ryan, A.G., & Price, L. (1993). Learning disabilities in adult basic education: A survey of current practices. *Journal of Postsecondary Education and Disability, 10*(3), 31–40.

Rydell, L. (1990). *Crosscultural Special Education Series: Vol. 4. The least biased assessment: Implications for special education.* Sacramento, CA: Resources in Special Education. (ERIC Document Reproduction Service No. ED 337 945)

Schroeder, W.O. (1970). Adult education defined and described. In R.M. Smith, G.F. Aker, & J.R. Kidd (Eds.), *Handbook of adult education* (pp. 25–43). New York: Macmillan.

Sternberg, R.J. (1985). *Beyond IQ: A triarchic theory of human intelligence.* New York: Cambridge University Press.

Sternberg, R.J. (1988). *Triarchic mind: A new theory of human intelligence.* New York: Viking.

Stuckey, J.E. (1991). *The violence of literacy.* Portsmouth, NH: Boynton/Cook.

Sturomski, N. (1996). Literacy needs for adults who have learning disabilities. In N. Gregg, C, Hoy, & A.F. Gay (Eds.), *Adults with learning disabilities: Theoretical and practical perspectives* (pp. 261–276). New York: The Guilford Press.

Tevis, M.P., & Orem, R.A. (1985). The learning disabled adult offender. *Adult Literacy and Basic Education, 9*(1), 24–34.

Travis, G.Y. (1979). An adult educator views learning disabilities. *Adult Literacy and Basic Education, 3*, 85–93.

Vogel, S.A. (1990). Gender differences in intelligence, language, visual motor abilities, and academic achievement in students with learning disabilities: A review of literature. *Journal of Learning Disabilities, 23*(1), 44–52.

Vogel, S.A. (1993). Teaching suggestions for adults with suspected learning disabilities/differences. In J.B. Cheatham, R.J. Colvin, & L.L. Laminack (Eds.), *Tutor: A collaborative approach to literacy instruction*, (pp. 188–189). Syracuse, NY: Literacy Volunteers of America, Inc.

Wolfram, W. (1990). *Dialect differences and testing* (ERIC Digest, EDO-FL-90-7). (ERIC Document Reproduction Service No. ED 323 813)

Wrigley, H.S. (1993). One size does not fit all: Educational perspectives and practices in the U.S. *TESOL Quarterly, 27*, 449–465.

II

Screening and Assessment

Section II addresses the difficult problem of screening adults who are at high risk for or who have learning disabilities (LD). The basic assumption underlying Section II is that although screening cannot confirm the presence of a learning disability, it can identify those individuals at high risk for having LD and be informative for those who may have a learning disability, their families, and their instructors.

For individuals with suspected LD, the self-knowledge and understanding that can come from screening can lead to a discussion in terms of their particular learning disability. This discussion may enable them to understand some of the possible reasons for the severe learning difficulties (usually with reading and written expression) that they have experienced in the past. Such a discussion can also lead to sources of more information about LD, including employment laws that mandate on-the-job accommodations, on licensing and/or admission examinations, or in educational settings and that can lead to referral to clinics or agencies should they want to pursue a full assessment. Determining the presence of a learning disability is especially important in order to receive accommodations on state or national examinations or to gain entry to a profession (e.g., building trades, cosmetology, real estate) or a postsecondary institution.

In Chapter 5, Neil Sturomski, Keith Lenz, David Scanlon, and Hugh Catts describe the activities of the National Adult Literacy and Learning Disabilities (NALLD) Center since it was established in 1993. The NALLD's mandate is to develop a "took kit" to screen and teach adults in literacy education settings who are high risk for or who have LD. (As this book goes to press, the results of field testing the NALLD "tool kit," now called "Bridges to Understanding," are being reviewed.) One of the first goals of the NALLD was to facilitate the development of a set of standards that practitioners could use when determining "best practices" in screening and teaching. The second goal was to train practitioners in the application of these standards. Chapter 5 concentrates on the first nine stages in developing and applying these standards to evaluate available screening procedures and instructional programs.

In Chapter 6, Nancie A. Payne focuses directly on *informal assessment*. After an in-depth analysis of the differences and similarities between formal and informal assessment, Payne delineates the major components of informal assessment. The first source of information in this screening process is provided through structured observations of the adult learner's auditory and visual acuity, memory difficulties, listening comprehension, spoken language, and attentional and organizational abilities.

Checklists and surveys are used in informal assessment to acquire additional information regarding an individual's specific learning difficulties as well as his or her learning style. In-depth interviews are used in order to avoid the areas of impairment—namely reading and written expression—and provide a great deal of insightful information. Last, observing students' interactions in class, group, or independent work environments provides valuable input into their difficulties with reading, written language, and/or math. The integration of this information may reveal patterns of behavior that closely resemble the characteristics of adults with LD and is considered the first step toward a formal assessment.

Chapter 7 provides an alternative procedure for screening individuals who are at high risk for or who have LD. This procedure, entitled PowerPath to Adult Basic Learning, was developed by Laura P. Weisel. Both the Payne System (see Chapter 6) and PowerPath were selected for inclusion in this book because of the empirical studies (either already conducted or under way) to validate the ability of these programs to correctly identify a large portion of those adults with previously unidentified LD. The PowerPath software includes an intake interview, checklists, inventories of learning and behavior, and assessment measures; it generates teacher, student, and administrative individual reports. The PowerPath system was designed for adults reading at the seventh-grade level or lower and takes approximately 90 minutes to administer. Included in the reports generated for the teacher and learner are an overview of the results, an indication of the severity of the learning disability, recommendations regarding services and learning accommodations that may be needed, a personal learning plan (i.e., an agreement) between the learner and the teacher regarding the basic skills program, and referral forms. The program also provides detailed information on the development of the PowerPath system and validation studies conducted since the mid-1970s.

Great ideas seem to develop simultaneously in different parts of the world. While Weisel was hard at work in the United States, Angela J. Fawcett and Rod I. Nicolson were also developing a computer-supported screening procedure, The Dyslexia Adult Screening Test (DAST), in the United Kingdom. DAST, which is detailed in Chapter 8, was envisaged as the preliminary step leading to a full assessment for those individuals who were at high risk for or who had LD. The first step in the development of DAST was to review the literature about adult literacy and dyslexia, followed by a series of interviews with dyslexia experts, and culminating in the development and distribution of a survey. DAST, which is still in the process of being validated, consists of 11 tasks (two reading and two spelling tasks, three rapid naming tasks, a verbal fluency measure, a phonological segmentation task, postural stability, and auditory memory for numbers) that are difficult for individuals with dyslexia to perform and two tasks (nonverbal reasoning and semantic fluency) that are often areas of strength for these individuals. The performance on these 11 tasks was evaluated and a "risk" score identified those adults at high risk for LD and in need of full assessment.

In Chapter 9, Melinda Giovengo, Elizabeth J. Moore, and Glenn Young explain a project in Washington state that set out to 1) determine the prevalence of LD among individuals receiving Aid to Families with Dependent Children (AFDC), 2) provide instructional accommodations and medical assistance to these individuals, and 3) validate a screening tool to identify AFDC recipients at high risk for LD. This research serves as an exemplary model because it is the first time that a screening procedure has been validated against a full diagnostic assessment in the United States. The findings indicated that 36% of AFDC consumers had diagnosed LD. Approximately 33% of the individuals with LD recalled having been previously identified as having LD. One troubling finding, however, was that approximately 20% of individuals not diagnosed as having LD also remembered having been previously identified as "learning disabled." This is indicative of the overidentification and misdiagnosis of LD in school identification. Clearly, when there is previous identification of LD, the documentation (if available) has to be reviewed by a qualified professional. Last, in validating The Payne Screening System, Giovengo and her colleagues reported that 71% of those with diagnosed LD had been correctly identified. The authors delineate the next steps to further refine the screening process. Clearly, major progress has been made in the 1990s in the awareness of the importance of identification of LD and in screening adults at high risk for LD.

5

The National Adult Literacy
and Learning Disabilities Center

Standards, Criteria, Procedures, and Strategies
for Screening and Teaching Adults with Learning Disabilities

Neil Sturomski, Keith Lenz, David Scanlon, and Hugh Catts

Adults with limited literacy skills often meet roadblocks in their day-to-day activities, resulting in frustration and failure that can significantly limit their quality of life. Although literacy programs are designed to reduce that frustration and failure by building enabling skills, not all adults can profit from traditional literacy programs; such programs often are not equipped to deal with adults with learning disabilities (LD). For many of these adults, frustration and failure become a way of life, often with little hope for meaningful change.

Providing a means for adults with LD to experience success has become a major challenge for the literacy community. One effort to address the challenge is represented by the work of the National Adult Literacy and Learning Disabilities (NALLD) Center. The NALLD Center was established in October 1993 to address the needs of literacy providers who work with adults with LD. Funded by the National Institute for Literacy, the NALLD Center, a collaborative project of the Academy for Educational Development and the University of Kansas Institute for Research in Learning Disabilities, is an important component of a larger venture—the National Institute for Literacy's efforts to promote, enhance, and coordinate literacy programs for U.S. citizens.

FOCUS OF THE WORK OF THE NATIONAL
ADULT LITERACY AND LEARNING DISABILITIES CENTER

The focus of activities at the NALLD Center has been on 1) enhancing awareness among literacy practitioners, policy makers, researchers, and adult learners about the nature of LD and their impact on the provision of literacy services; 2) designing a tool kit with guidelines and information for selecting screening tools and instructional materials and approaches for improving services for adults with LD in adult literacy programs; and 3) empowering state systems to train and provide technical assistance to literacy practitioners in their use and refinement of these best practices.

To accomplish these activities, the NALLD Center has 1) created an easily accessible National Information Exchange Network that brings together research and the latest thinking on LD related to adult literacy services, 2) developed a tool kit for use by literacy practitioners that includes information on a variety of materials related to screening and instruction, and 3) developed a training plan to support and assist practitioners who teach adults with LD. The NALLD Center staff have concentrated their efforts on producing and refining knowledge by reviewing research on practices for teaching adults with LD, providing instruction and technical assistance in recommended practices related to screening and instruction to literacy practitioners, and creating linkages and partnerships among programs and agencies concerned with adults with LD. The National Information Exchange Network was developed for the sharing of information, research, and resources regarding the relationship between adult literacy and LD. It includes resource files, a library, a national database, and a Listserv (a "chat" area that is part of the National Information Exchange Network of the NALLD Center) to facilitate accurate and quick exchange of information.[1]

WHAT WE KNOW ABOUT BEST PRACTICES
RELATED TO ADULTS WITH LEARNING DISABILITIES

What Is Best Practice?

An early task that NALLD Center staff faced was to struggle with the meaning of *best practice*. During the early stages of project activities, center staff found little consensus in the fields of LD and adult literacy regarding a definition of *best practice*. Drawing from different perspectives, center staff defined *best practice* as using a screening or instructional material, program, or activity that has a defensible record of success in guiding a literacy practitioner assisting an adult with a learning disability to attain literacy goals in an efficient manner. A *defensible record of success* was defined as the existence of one or more studies, including studies with experimental or quasiexperimental research designs, showing positive outcomes when a specific practice was used.

Available Research on Practices Related to Adults with Learning Disabilities

The staff at the NALLD Center conducted a comprehensive review of published research related to literacy practices for adults with LD (see Scanlon et al., 1998).[2]

---

[1]An inquirer can contact the National Adult Literacy and Learning Disabilities (NALLD) Center by writing to the NALLD Center c/o AED, 1875 Connecticut Avenue, NW, Washington, D.C. 20009-1202; by calling 1-800-953-2553 or 202-884-8185; or by e-mailing to info@nalldc.aed.org.
[2]The general findings of this literature review are presented here in summary form. Individuals wishing to obtain copies of the research report describing the details and summary of the literature review should contact the University of Kansas Center for Research on Learning or the NALLD Center.

Scanlon et al. reported that four computerized databases were searched: *Dissertation Abstracts International,* Education Resources Information Center, Psychological Abstracts, and Social Sciences Citation Index. These databases were selected because they have comprehensive cross-listings of publications relevant to adult literacy and LD, and they and the majority of materials they reference can be obtained from libraries throughout the United States. The search included all posted materials dated from January 1982 to September 1995. Search results clearly showed a lack of information regarding what works with adults with LD. This lack of information is what has frustrated the adult education and literacy communities regarding adult literacy and LD. This frustration stems from two main factors: 1) the amount of information that exists is limited, and 2) the information that does exist is not easily accessible.

The search initially yielded more than 500 references. Three relatively liberal inclusion criteria were used to determine which of the 500 references generated from the four databases were eligible for representation in the set of reviewable literature. First, the publication had to be either a specific research study or a review of research studies. All forms of research were accepted (e.g., qualitative, quantitative, experimental, quasiexperimental). Theoretical and reflective pieces were not included. Second, the studies had to address some aspect of literacy services for adults with LD. Third, the research study had to be available to the public. Public access included publications that could be purchased or secured through libraries or clearinghouses. A total of 87 of the 500 publications were found to satisfy these three criteria. Of the 87 eligible studies, 14 were categorized as addressing screening; 19 addressed interventions; and 58 addressed characteristics of adult education staff, students, and/or programs. Several of the studies fell into multiple categories.

Research on Adult Education Program Staff The studies on adult education staff were broadly grouped by whether they addressed characteristics of staff or staff training. All of these studies focused on staff preparedness to serve students, including those with LD. Each of these studies involved practitioners with direct responsibility for educating adult students. Across the studies' findings, there was a strong indication that educators of adults believed that they were prepared to meet the needs of their students with LD. However, none of these studies sought the views of students with LD.

Studies consistently found that adult educators received training in a variety of areas in education, and they tended to have training and credentials such as teacher certification or baccalaureate degrees. Whereas Adult Basic Education and General Equivalency Diploma (GED) educators (teachers, counselors, and administrators) generally have confidence in their ability to serve students with LD and welcome having these individuals as students, they reported a desire for more training in LD and in providing services to individuals with LD. More than one study found that adult educators professed that they were willing to provide more services for their students with LD than they actually provided. However, few of the studies sought to independently verify the staff's preparedness.

Research on Characteristics of Adult Education Students Studies on the characteristics of adult education students involved either the effect on students or the degree of student participation in adult education. Consistent with what has been found for school-age groups of individuals with LD, adults with LD participating in adult education or rehabilitation programs were often found to have negative self-affect that researchers claimed contributed to poor literacy learning. Adults with LD who completed a literacy program were more likely to have a positive self-affect than those who did not complete the program. Those who completed the program often reported confidence in their abilities and indicated that they had been resourceful in seeking out the assistance they needed to be successful.

Adults with LD were found to be generally less likely than their peers without such disabilities to participate in and complete postsecondary education. Those who did participate in postsecondary education tended to be unprepared; appeared disinterested to instructors; and had low program participation rates, especially in programs that did not take into consideration their LD.

Research on Screening   Studies on screening addressed either the appropriateness of specific screening practices or how they were used. For example, although a significant aptitude–achievement discrepancy is most frequently used as the basis for determining LD, the review found that few tests are appropriate for assessing aptitude or achievement in individuals in community colleges and that those that may be appropriate are susceptible to bias for certain groups of individuals. Findings also showed little difference between adults with LD and those who were low achievers (i.e., most adults in literacy programs have a significant discrepancy between aptitude and achievement). Consequently, the aptitude–achievement discrepancy formula may not be appropriate for assessing LD in adults.

The authors of some of the studies included in the review expressed concern regarding how assessment is being conducted in some literacy programs. Although the studies demonstrated that a variety of areas have been examined as part of screening efforts (e.g., language and communication skills, math, reading, visual perception skills), many programs did not assess all areas pertinent to the characteristics associated with LD. In several instances, the tests being used as part of the assessment process had not been normed on adults. Potential age, gender, and language biases in assessment practices also were found in several of the studies.

Research on Interventions   The studies included in the research review that concerned intervention practices addressed specific intervention practices or approaches to intervention. The majority of the published research in the intervention category (on both practices and approaches) focused on reading practices. This general finding is indicative of the degree to which reading is a pervasive area of need for adult literacy and the importance of learning to read in the lives of adults with LD.

A review of the reading-based intervention studies revealed what the adult literacy research community considers to be the most important approaches to reading instruction. Almost without exception, the studies reflected an orientation toward skills-based approaches to reading, both for understanding the reading abilities of the adult student and for providing reading interventions. Direct instructional approaches that allow for overlearning and compensatory strategies were found to be more common than experiential learning–type approaches. Only a few of the intervention studies specifically studied the teaching or learning processes that occurred during instruction.

Overall, the published studies of interventions should be very useful to those interested in literacy practices. Many of them could be accessed in a literature search using terms such as *reading, daily living skills,* or *tutoring.* They tend to identify a very specific group of adults with LD and literacy needs (e.g., community college students, those reading below a fifth-grade level). Most describe the intervention studied in sufficient detail for the reader to replicate the practice. Also, they typically provide pre- and postintervention performance data that may be useful for comparison if an intervention is replicated.

Conclusions   Overall, the review of research on best practices associated with adult literacy and LD indicated that there are few practices that could be recommended as best practices from published research. In addition, the research that has been conducted on LD, in general, has not found its way into programs. However, the problem of validated practices finding their way into programs is not unique to the field of adult literacy.

Despite support for research and development activities on behalf of individuals with LD and limited literacy skills in the K–12 educational system, the knowledge of effective practice generated has only sporadically found its way into instructional practice (e.g., Malouf, 1993). Furthermore, less than 10% of the materials and methods being used across instructional settings have been validated through any type of research. Researchers at the National Center to Improve the Tools of Educators highlighted the problem presented by the gap between practice and research by drawing an analogy between the practice of using medicines that have not undergone rigorous research and testing with the practice of using nonvalidated educational procedures with students (Carnine, 1993). Although untested medicines are not tolerated in health care, the use of nonvalidated instructional practices seems to be commonly accepted across a variety of educational settings, including adult literacy settings.

Other Sources for Identifying Best Practices

Several dilemmas arise from using existing research on adults with LD as the criteria for identifying best practices. First, as we found through our literature review, little research has been conducted that actually identifies best practices for adults with LD. Although this reality provides an excellent rationale for developing a research and development agenda for investigating practices, it leaves literacy practitioners with little guidance in terms of what to do with the adults whom they are serving. Second, although practitioners may want to feel more confident about their practices, many practitioners report feeling uncomfortable with using only research-based criteria to guide practice. Research-based criteria ignore the value of practitioner experience in working with adults with LD. Indeed, the development of new practices largely depends on experienced practitioners generating new ideas, materials, and approaches that can serve as the basis for research and development activities. Third, practitioners are not easily able to take advantage of what we do know about the construct of LD and to apply these principles to adults with LD. Fourth, regardless of the amount of research that has been conducted, simply identifying best practices does not provide a framework that can assist practitioners to scrutinize evolving practices and changes in the fields of adult literacy and LD.

In response to these dilemmas, it became clear that a more dynamic perspective on best practices needed to be developed. Therefore, the task of simply identifying existing best practices had to shift to one of ongoing program development and evaluation. In completing a set of tasks targeted toward developing a process through which best practices can emerge, the staff of a literacy program must perform specific activities as part of ongoing program development and evaluation. To accomplish this, several factors become important. First, standards are needed that can be used to evaluate the potential for success in various practices. Second, practitioners in both literacy and LD must be involved in developing these standards. Third, in addition to the standards being used to evaluate practices, literacy practitioners must be taught to independently apply and use the standards to guide decision making related to the use of practices in the design of services for adults with LD.

HOW DO WE ACKNOWLEDGE BEST PRACTICES?

Why Standards for Best Practices Must Be Identified

Standards are the criteria by which practices are judged and selected. A literacy practitioner will select a practice if it meets the criteria that he or she has personally developed for what he or she believes will work best. These standards are the guidelines that a person uses to obtain information needed to make good decisions related to the best way to reach screening or intervention goals. If the standards that are used are based on vague or wrong information or are not tied to desired outcomes, the chances that poor decisions will be made and ineffective practices will be implemented dramatically increase.

When practitioners in a program meet and begin to discuss what they individually value in a practice and then work to gain consensus on what they collectively value, they are developing standards for selecting and implementing best practices in their program. The information associated with the standards that a staff collects and processes about a practice will be weighed by program size, staff, resources, location, program goals, participant characteristics, and the like. Therefore, some standards may become more important for some programs than for other programs. However, although program variables may influence how the standards are used to make decisions, the basic standards that practitioners establish as being important in decision making usually remain fairly constant.

For the diverse national literacy community, the challenge of building a framework for thinking about, discussing, and addressing the needs of adults with LD presents an excellent context for developing standards for guiding practice. Furthermore, to accomplish the task of creating a tool kit of literacy best practices for adults with LD, given the research available on these adults, a set of guidelines for gauging best practices is critical.

How Best Practices Standards Are Developed

To accomplish the task of developing a set of standards that could serve as the basis for building a best practices tool kit, the NALLD Center's research staff adapted Stufflebeam's (1983) Context, Input, Process, Product (CIPP) program evaluation model to guide the standards development process. The CIPP model was chosen for three reasons. First, this model has applicability to both formative and summative evaluation activities. Second, this evaluation approach recognizes that training and dissemination activities have equal importance to the development of best practices tools. Third, it allows for different cycles of research to be developed as new information emerges from the research. There are five stages to the process that NALLD Center staff initially planned to use to develop and apply the best practices standards in the construction and field testing of the best practices tool kit:

Stage 1: Identify issues—identify the goals, dimensions, and values related to best practices in serving adults with LD

Stage 2: Develop and adopt standards—adopt a set of standards that could serve as minimum evaluation guidelines that should be applied nationwide to judge practices

Stage 3: Gather standards data on practices—collect data on practices and how well practices meet the minimum adopted standard

Stage 4: Synthesize data—determine which practices could be recommended as best practices

Stage 5: Plan and revise—examine how well the goals associated with developing standards and identifying best practices have been met and then determine additional
research and development priorities

A graphic of this plan is shown in Figure 5.1. This plan served as the major framework
for guiding and evaluating the NALLD Center's first few years of work. It became clear
after the standards were applied to various literacy practices, however, that very few
practices being used in the field or even available to the field met the high standards
desired by literacy practitioners. Therefore, it became important to expand the evaluation plan for the development activities to once again identify issues and determine
how the standards could be applied in the form of a useful tool kit for literacy practitioners. As a result, the research and development plan eventually took on the form
depicted in Figure 5.2. Finally, as the standards and the procedures for applying the
standards evolved into the final tool kit form, the development and evaluation efforts
shifted to developing and implementing a comprehensive and useful training plan.
This effort is depicted in Figure 5.3. A description of the activities for each of the 14
stages shown in Figure 5.3 is provided next.

Identifying Standards

Stage 1: Identify Issues   Because a major goal of the NALLD Center was to design
a tool kit for literacy practitioners, the center needed to identify what stakeholders—
professionals in the fields of adult education, literacy, and LD—liked and disliked about
materials that were already available. Thus, during its first year, the center conducted

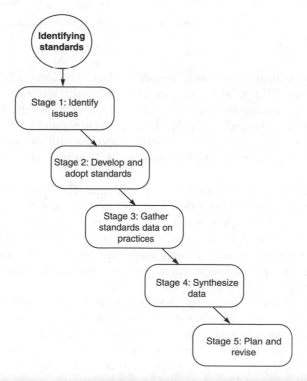

Figure 5.1.   National Adult Literacy and Learning Disabilities Center's five stages for identifying standards for best practices
(Phase 1).

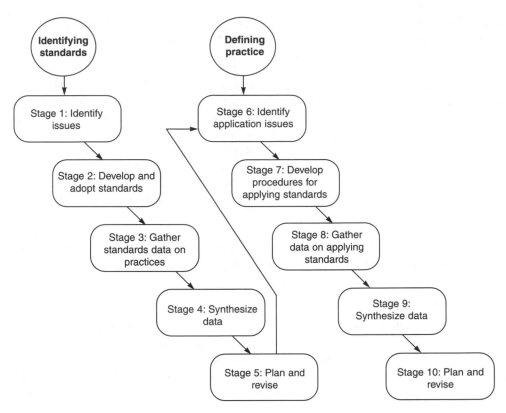

Figure 5.2.   National Adult Literacy and Learning Disabilities Center's research and development evaluation plan for identifying best practices (Phase 2).

eight focus group meetings to answer these and other questions. These meetings were held in Washington, D.C.; Atlanta; Kansas City, Missouri; and San Francisco. Participants from diverse backgrounds came from almost every state in the United States. The focus group members included researchers; GED administrators and teachers; correctional literacy educators; English as a second language professionals; librarians; and others in the fields of literacy, adult education, and LD. Adults with LD also participated in the meetings.

The focus groups were facilitated by Bev Schwartz, the Director of Social Marketing at the Academy for Educational Development and an expert in focus group methodology. Each meeting was taped and later transcribed. In these meetings, participants were asked to share their opinions on 1) screening processes used to determine the likelihood of LD, 2) intervention methods used with adults with suspected LD, 3) staff training to use screening and intervention methods, and 4) dissemination of materials to adult literacy programs.

The results from the focus group meetings were used to further define the need for standards to evaluate best practices when working with adults with LD. As a whole, the focus group members stated that the standards needed to 1) be practitioner oriented, 2) take into account the "whole" individual, 3) be practical, and 4) integrate screening and intervention. These groups' conversations also revealed participants' uncertain knowledge about LD yet relayed their experience-based perspectives about what worked with individuals whom they suspected of having LD. Finally, they showed

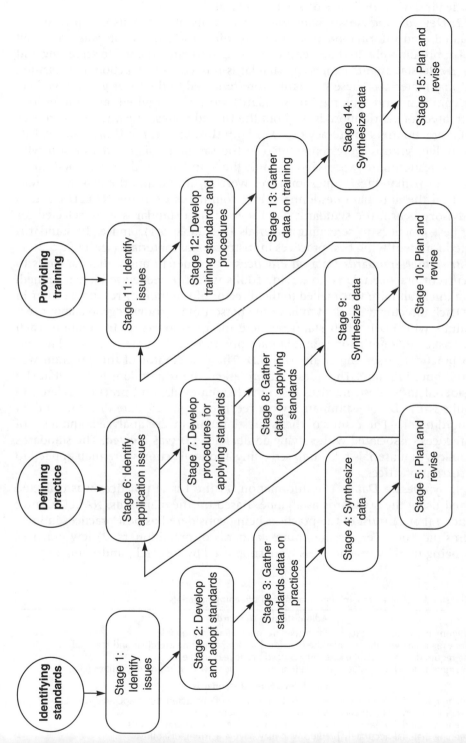

Figure 5.3. National Adult Literacy and Learning Disabilities Center's research and development evaluation plan for identifying best practices (Phase 3).

concern for the lack of available resources, trained staff, and a professional knowledge base when dealing with the issues of adult literacy and LD.

Stage 2: Develop and Adopt Standards   Transcripts of the focus group meetings were evaluated, and information related to screening and instruction was organized into a set of approximately 20 statements expressing standards related to screening and approximately 20 statements expressing standards related to instruction as presented by instructional materials. These standards were returned to the focus group members for further comment and ranking. The standards were then revised, and a questionnaire was created for distribution throughout the United States. The questionnaire was sent to 1,200 practitioners in literacy or LD or both throughout the United States. Different stakeholder groups were represented in the sampling plan. Each person who received the questionnaire was asked to rank the standards and provide additional comments. Approximately 370 questionnaires were returned, and the data were analyzed. Based on the national questionnaire and comments from the NALLD Center's national advisory board, the standards were revised. Ten standards were selected for identifying best practices in screening materials (see Table 5.1), and eight standards were selected for identifying best practices in instructional materials (see Table 5.2).

Stage 3: Gather Standards Data on Practices   In order to apply the standards to practices, current practice related to serving adults with LD needed to be determined. Therefore, a questionnaire was mailed to the director of the literacy resource center in each state. Each director was asked to have the person most knowledgeable about services for adults with LD in their state complete the questionnaire. In addition, each director was asked to identify one adult literacy program in the state considered to represent best practices in serving adults with LD. The coordinator of this program was then sent the questionnaire. The questionnaire asked the respondent to list what she or he considered to be best practices instruments, materials, and practices related to serving adults with LD. Questionnaires were returned from 25 state directors and 24 program coordinators. The results of these questionnaires were analyzed, and a set of "current practices" associated with serving adults with LD was created. The standards for best practices in materials related to screening and instruction were then applied to the list of current practices.

Stage 4: Synthesize Data   The information on the list of practices was collected and reviewed using the standards as a guide. Based on the standards, NALLD Center staff concluded that 1) most of the practices being considered as best practices in literacy programs did not meet the minimum standards of practitioners, 2) few practices commonly being used by practitioners were supported by research, and 3) many prac-

Table 5.1.   Ten standards for identifying best practices in screening materials

Administration standards

1. The requirements for learning to use the screening material are reasonable.
2. Guidelines regarding whether to refer the individual for further testing are clear and reasonable.
3. The time required to conduct the screening procedures is reasonable.
4. The screening material allows accommodations for individuals with learning disabilities (LD).

Technical development standards

5. The screening material adequately represents the full range of characteristics associated with LD.
6. The screening material is consistent with what is known about LD.
7. The screening material reliably measures the individual's learning characteristics.
8. The screening material accurately predicts who may have a learning disability.
9. The screening material accurately predicts a learning disability, regardless of a person's age, gender, race, ethnicity, or primary language.
10. Research supports the links between screening procedures and instructional materials.

Table 5.2.   Eight standards for identifying best practices in instructional materials

1. The instructional material is effective for teaching adults with learning disabilities (LD).
2. The instructional material is appropriate for an adult, regardless of the person's age, gender, race, ethnicity, or primary language.
3. The instructional principles used to promote learning are clearly stated and consistent with what is known about LD.
4. The learning outcomes that can be expected are clearly described.
5. The instructional material's results can be used to make decisions regarding further instruction.
6. The procedures for checking the learner's progress are clear and easy to use.
7. The requirements for literacy practitioners to learn to use the instructional material are reasonable.
8. The instructional material can be used in a variety of instructional situations within the literacy program.

tices being used in literacy programs had limited potential for having an impact on the success and motivation of adults with LD.

Stage 5: Plan and Revise   After reviewing the data, the original plan to simply provide lists of best practices was abandoned. It became apparent that an important goal for improving services for adults with LD being served in literacy programs was to focus on helping adult literacy providers become critical consumers of available materials. This became an important goal because 1) literacy programs do not have sufficient resources to invest in marginally effective materials and 2) the literacy provider has a relatively short period of time to provide instruction, show the adult learner that he or she can learn, and motivate the learner to stay with the program. As a result, NALLD Center staff shifted their attention to helping the adult literacy providers define best practices based on their programs' needs and resources by teaching them how to 1) apply the standards for selecting materials related to screening and instruction, 2) make improved decisions about services based on these standards, and 3) plan for the implementation of decisions regarding adults with LD in the context of what we do know about providing services for individuals with LD.

Defining Practice

Stage 6: Identify Application Issues   Project staff reviewed the standards and identified problems and issues that literacy practitioners might have in applying them. Several literacy programs served as pilots and were asked to apply the standards. In addition, NALLD Center staff held 10 preliminary training events related to teaching practitioners how to apply the standards. These training events were organized through local literacy organizations as full-day preconference workshops at state-level and national literacy conferences, and through state literacy resource centers. The training events were run by the NALLD Center's director with the assistance of Christopher Lee, Training Director of the Learning Disabilities Research and Training Center, housed at the University of Georgia. Lee is himself an adult with a learning disability. During the training, the standards were applied to materials related to screening and instruction to determine whether these materials were consistent with best practices according to the standards for working with adults with LD. The training events provided the NALLD Center with further feedback from adult educators and literacy practitioners on the standards. It also provided the center with information on the ability of adult educators and literacy practitioners to apply the standards to materials during and following training. Based on the internal review, application of the standards with program staff in pilot sites, and the preliminary training events, a list of application issues was identified.

Stage 7: Develop Procedures for Applying Standards   The list of application issues was used to develop procedures for literacy practitioners to apply the standards to materials related to screening and instruction that they might be reviewing or using in literacy programs. Information was written defining each standard, explaining what the practitioner should look for in determining whether the standard had been met, and providing examples of what the practitioner should find if the standard had been met. This information was included in a draft of the tool kit that also included general information about LD. This draft of the tool kit was field tested in eight literacy programs across the states of Maryland, Minnesota, and Washington. Program staff attended a workshop on applying the standards and then were expected to review screening and instructional materials independently in their programs during a period of several months. Program staff were interviewed at the end of the field test. Based on the feedback from the field test, the procedures for applying the standards were revised. The tool kit was once again revised, and additional information related to decision making and integration of best practices information was incorporated into the revised draft of the tool kit.

Stage 8: Gather Data on Applying Standards   The revised tool kit was field tested for 6 weeks in literacy programs in Florida, Kansas, Minnesota, and Washington. A variety of program types were included. Program staff were provided with a 1-day workshop that focused on 1) understanding LD in adults, 2) applying the best practices standards to materials related to screening and instruction, 3) using the implementation guidelines and resources included in the tool kit, and 4) planning for improving services for adults with LD. The focus of the field test was to determine whether literacy practitioners could apply the standards and would use the information gleaned from the tool kit to plan improved services for adults with LD.

Stage 9: Synthesize Data, and Stage 10: Plan and Revise   The data from the second field test were being collected as this chapter went to press. The analyzed data will be used to guide the final production of the tool kit for use in the national training and dissemination effort planned for the next phase of the NALLD Center's activities.

Providing Training

The focus of the final set of activities related to preparing the tool kit will relate to providing training to literacy practitioners in the use of the tool kit. Early attempts in the field testing indicated that a significant amount of training is required if the tool kit is to have the intended impact related to improving services to adults with LD. Therefore, NALLD Center staff will work through stages similar to the ones described in the previous sections. These stages, depicted in Figure 5.3, will likely include *Stage 11: Identify Issues; Stage 12: Develop Training Standards and Procedures; Stage 13: Gather Data on Training; Stage 14: Synthesize Data; and Stage 15: Plan and Revise.* When activities related to the completion of these stages are concluded, procedures for conducting training and disseminating the tool kit to literacy programs throughout the United States will be developed and implemented.

CONCLUSION

To accomplish the NALLD Center's goals, the tool kit that is developed and disseminated by the center must provide a vehicle that will promote a common perspective on the condition of adults with LD and a model that can be used to identify and create a continuum of related services and resources. This common understanding will be useful for all service providers as well as for adults with LD as they address primary literacy needs. We believe that this common understanding must emerge from 1) an awareness of the unique nature of the adult learner and the range of personal issues associated with limited literacy; 2) a shared vision of support built on the development of partnerships among agencies, groups, and individuals concerned with adult learners; and 3) a set of policies, research standards, and activities that ensure the integrity of the assistance provided to adults with LD. Building the work of the NALLD Center on these premises will result in more confidence in how we in the literacy community use our time, energy, and dollars to enhance the learning of adults who attend literacy programs.

REFERENCES

Carnine, D. (1993). *Criteria for developing and evaluating instructional standards*. Eugene, OR: National Center to Improve the Tools of Educators.

Malouf, D. (1993). *Practice and research in special education*. (Paper on the federal role in improving practice in special education.) Washington, DC: U.S. Office of Special Education, Division of Innovation and Development, Directed Research Branch.

Scanlon, D., Mellard, D., Garrison, S., Lancaster, S., Mellard, J., & Rausch, T. (1998). *What we know about literacy practices for adults with LD: A review of published research* (Research Report). Lawrence: The University of Kansas Center for Research on Learning.

Stufflebeam, D.L. (1983). The CIPP model for program evaluation. In G. Madaus, M. Scriven, & D. Stufflebeam (Eds.), *Evaluation models* (pp. 117–141). Boston: Kluwer-Nijhoff Publishing.

6

The Rationale, Components, and Usefulness of Informal Assessment of Adults with Learning Disabilities

Nancie A. Payne

As research continues to provide evidence that learning disabilities (LD) are lifelong conditions, more emphasis is placed on the value of adult assessment and diagnosis. Research indicates that 15%–80% of the eligible population of adults within adult education, literacy, and basic skills environments are affected by LD (Nightingale, Yudd, Anderson, & Barnow, 1991; Ross-Gordon, 1989; Sturomski, 1996). As adults enter these programs, there is an overwhelming need for instructors and volunteers to collect, understand, and apply assessment information in an effort to plan for and provide appropriate services to students who may be at high risk of having LD or special learning needs (Anderson, 1993; Sturomski, 1996).

Some adults are identified or diagnosed in elementary or secondary environments. If such information is available, then it does not typically address adult student needs and goals (Learning Disabilities Association of America, 1996). Those adult students who have been diagnosed as having a learning disability, regardless of whether the diagnosis is recent, frequently cannot describe what that diagnosis means (Silver, 1995). More important, however, is the fact that the majority of struggling adult students have never been diagnosed and usually do not recognize that a hidden disability may be affecting their education, instruction, or employment progress (National Adult Literacy and Learning Disabilities Center, 1995).

If a diagnosis is available, then most practitioners in adult education, literacy, and basic skills programs neither have the expertise or background to review psychological, neuropsychological, psychiatric, or other clinically based diagnostic reports, nor do they have the time. Even if a practitioner has the expertise and time, generally, the data do not specify information helpful for student-centered instruction, academic adjustments, or accommodations.

What about those adult students who do not know there is something—perhaps a learning disability—affecting their skills acquisition and advancement? What about those who are experiencing significant difficulty in acquiring skills and performing in life because they have never had the opportunity to gain access to diagnostic services? Adult education and basic skills instructors and literacy providers are asking how to be more efficient, save money, and distribute limited resources among the numerous students with special learning needs as they concurrently strive to reduce time factors, false starts, and recidivism.

For the adult learner who is at high risk of having a learning disability or a special learning need, the best response to these questions may well be *informal assessment*. Adult education, basic skills, and literacy providers need informal methods for determining the special learning needs of students. Those methods must be well defined and must promote a structured, objective process that addresses the goals set by both the student and the program (Anderson, 1993; National Adult Literacy and Learning Disabilities Center, 1995).

There are numerous ways to define *informal assessment*. For the purposes of this discussion, *informal assessment* is defined by comparing the distinctions between informal and formal assessment methods as applied to the process of identifying students who are at high risk of having LD or special learning needs.

Holistically, assessment should be a goal-focused process the results of which are used to make decisions as to the needs of an individual and to provide the individual with the opportunity to accomplish the goal successfully (Anderson, 1993; Brinckerhoff, 1992; Johnson, 1987; Payne & Robins, 1994; Zwerlein, Smith, & Diffley, 1984). The process of identifying students with possible LD or special learning needs should incorporate several elements, including screening, intensive interviewing, psychological or neuropsychological examination, functional evaluation, situational assessment, and clinical observation, as well as career and academic testing when appropriate (Anderson, 1993; Johnson, 1987; McCue, 1994; National Adult Literacy and Learning Disabilities Center, 1995; Payne & Robins, 1994; Sturomski, 1997).

Formal assessment methods, referred to as *diagnostic assessment*, are defined as those techniques that provide information using diagnostic criteria (McCue, 1994) that are typically based on standardized criteria or normative, statistically valid, age- or grade-determined research. This process assists in determining whether a learning disability, or the likelihood of such, exists.

Informal assessment techniques, sometimes referred to as *screening* or *functional assessment* (McCue, 1994), use methods usually based on research and secondary data. Secondary or historical data are data that were previously collected and assembled for some other process or project but that, when analyzed, have meaning or worth to processes other than the original ones (Zikmund, 1988). These processes are used to determine whether a student is "at risk" of having a special learning need or a learning disability (Payne & Robins, 1994; Sturomski, 1996).

Full assessment of LD should be viewed as a process, constant and flowing, that includes a strong mix of informal and formal assessment (Anderson, 1993). As each element of the process is completed, goal-related information and data are shared with the student to assist him or her in making meaningful choices that promote opportunities for success.

THREE PHASES OF ASSESSMENT

Globally speaking, there are three predominant phases in special learning needs and LD assessment processes. Consisting of medical, formal, and informal assessment, the phases are not mutually exclusive but rather must be incorporated as part of a comprehensive assessment process (Ross-Gordon, 1989). McCue (1994) referred to similar assessment measures by describing assessment as that which includes functional interviewing, rating scales, questionnaires, psychological and neuropsychological tests, situational assessments and simulations, and direct observation. Additional key components are medical history, related illness, and medical or physical conditions (Accardo, 1996; Vogel, 1989). McCue stated, "Information gathered in this [assessment] process constitutes data on which inferences are made about an individual's ability to meet the demands of work, vocational training, higher education, and daily living" (1994, p. 63). These inferences also apply to an adult student's ability to acquire basic and literacy skills.

Sometimes the manifestations of what appears to be a learning disability on the surface actually result from other medical conditions. Medical assessment should include but not be limited to comprehensive screening of vision and hearing (Accardo, 1996; Johnson, 1987; National Adult Literacy and Learning Disability Center, 1995). A complete review of previously or recently sustained concussions or acquired brain injuries, frequent or prolonged headaches, psychiatric or mental health disorders, diabetes, allergies, seizure or convulsive disorders, attention-deficit or attention-deficit/hyperactivity disorders, central nervous system disorders, neurosurgical disorders, or other serious health problems should be conducted as well (Accardo, 1996; Anderson, 1993). The existence of these conditions may require medical treatment combined with learning interventions.

Formal assessment or a differential diagnosis is critical in the identification of factors interfering with learning (Johnson, 1987; National Joint Committee on Learning Disabilities, 1987/1994; Vogel, 1989). Diagnosis should include the specific type of learning disability as well as the individual's strengths and limitations (Payne & Robins, 1994) and must be comprehensive enough to span the depth of psychological factors evident in students with LD (McCue, 1994). Vogel specifically stated, "The examiner [conducting the formal assessment] should integrate extensive information from a variety of sources into a meaningful whole" (1989, p. 117). Formal assessment should involve standardized methods to understand the psychological and cognitive capabilities and aptitudes of the student in order to provide better services and opportunities for success in adult education, basic skills, or literacy programs.

Informal assessment or screening seeks to identify whether a student is at risk of having a special learning need or a learning disability (Payne & Robins, 1994; Sturomski, 1996, 1997) or whether the observed difficulty in learning is due to a lack of educational exposure or opportunity. Although informal assessment alone cannot be used to make a diagnosis, it is an integral part of gathering relevant data and should include observations, interviews, and student self-reports as well as a complete review of available medical, psychological, school, instruction, and/or employment records (National Adult Literacy and Learning Disabilities Center, 1995). Another part of informal assessment is an intensive interview to look at background, medical data, strengths, weaknesses, and needs (Sturomski, 1997). This method of interviewing is described in more depth later.

In review, these three phases of the assessment process must not stand alone if comprehensive and accurate diagnosis of special learning needs or LD is to occur. McCue (1994) specified that a sound assessment practice encompasses clinical diagnostic and functional assessment approaches. For students encountering significant learning difficulties in adult education, basic skills, and literacy programs, a multidisciplinary set of assessment and referral procedures that go beyond psychometric analysis of special learning needs and LD is necessary.

INFORMAL ASSESSMENT BY DESIGN

Prior to designing or selecting and implementing any informal assessment protocols, the following questions must be given serious consideration:

- Who is being assessed?
- Who will do the informal assessment?
- When should the informal assessment process begin?
- What is the goal or purpose of informal assessment?
- Why is informal assessment necessary?
- What will an informal assessment identify or provide?
- When will the informal assessment information be used?
- How will the informal assessment results be used?
- Where and how will the informal assessment take place?
- Who will need and benefit from the informal assessment information?

Who Is Being Assessed?

In the adult education, basic skills, or literacy program arena, the answer to the question of whom to assess is youth and adults who have low literacy or basic skills, lack high school diplomas or General Equivalency Diplomas (GEDs), or have trouble in instruction or in work, usually as a result of limitations in reading, spelling, mathematics, and writing. Major factors that could include age, culture, education exposure, instruction or employment experiences, family background, and life events must be identified and analyzed as possible influences on students. Of extreme importance is recognizing the characteristics of the overall group as well as the program environment. Program-specific assessment methods and protocols for use within adult prisons or jails, youth correction or detention facilities, alternative schools, shelters, learning centers, colleges, adult schools, libraries, churches, group homes, family centers, or worksites may need to be developed.

Who Will Do the Informal Assessment?

Selection of assessment protocols should be partially based on who will be responsible for implementation and management of the informal assessment process. This could be an instructor, education assistant, program manager, volunteer, counselor, receptionist, or program secretary or a combination of several of these individuals. Identification of who will begin the informal screening process with the student may denote the structure of the process as well.

When Should the Informal Assessment Process Begin?

Many students provide enough clues or information early on to warrant beginning an informal assessment process. Examples include full disclosure of a learning disability, recognition of difficulties as a result of recent identification of a child or other family member as having significant difficulty with learning, discussion of prolonged trouble in learning in various settings, extremely low placement scores, or history of special education or related services. Equally, when a student is not progressing satisfactorily as measured by a set of indicators or criteria, additional assessment may be important to the stability of the student's progress. As a student is engaged in the learning process, the instructor or volunteer should continually evaluate progress and identify problem areas (Adelman & Taylor, 1991; Sturomski, 1997).

What Is the Goal or Purpose of Informal Assessment?

The sole goal or purpose of an informal assessment process should be to assist students who appear to be at high risk of having a learning disability or special learning need in the accomplishment of specific learner-centered objectives by, first, identifying difficulties or conditions affecting progress and performance and, second, providing interventions or adjustments that in turn facilitate student success. Assessment processes should never be engaged in based on a goal of "screening out" or excluding students who are judged unable to benefit from services. Furthermore, informal assessment methods should never seek to label or to affix "conditions" related to ability or disability (Johnson & Croasmun, 1991). Identification of a specific disability should be made only through a comprehensive formal assessment process (Johnson, 1987; McCue, 1994). The promotion and facilitation of student success should be the baseline goal or purpose for beginning the informal assessment process.

Why Is Informal Assessment Necessary?

In evaluating human functions, especially learning characteristics and behaviors, no two individuals are alike. This is certainly true within the ranks of students. Without informal assessment methods, practitioners cannot determine what each student requires to be successful. In addition, because life experiences and successes are a constant combination of performance and evaluation, the informal assessment model sets the stage for students to imitate some or all of the processes in other environments in which learning may be difficult. Swanson stated that

> It may be difficult to define [solely through formal assessment measures] the mental processes necessary for effective learning, to identify subprocesses underlying academic tasks, as well as global processes required for school learning, and to provide a link between theories of learning and educational practice. (1991, p. 3)

Moreover, many students may not require formal assessment or may need a different formal strategy than anticipated prior to informal assessment. Thus, the informal methods may reduce access and cost factors of diagnosis by assisting in the creation of better plans and referrals. Furthermore, many times the informal assessment process will result in disclosure of previous diagnoses or educational strategies. At completion of the process, the instructor or volunteer may ask the student why he or she did not share the pertinent data prior to the time of assessment. The student's reply to this question is usually one of three: "I didn't know who to tell," "I didn't know when to tell," or "I didn't know that it was important to tell."

What Will an Informal Assessment Identify or Provide?

A comprehensive informal assessment process provides insight about the current state and concerns of the student, possible intervention techniques, and specific methods for student-based planning and instruction in literacy, adult education, and instruction environments (Adelman & Taylor, 1991; Johnson, 1987; Sturomski, 1996). The process also provides an opportunity for students to explore and learn about their unique style of learning. All too often, this foundation of basic learning information is missing. Anderson stated, "Providing a process whereby students can become aware of the manifestations of the difficulty and strengths is crucial to accessing future academic adjustments, auxiliary aids, modifications and interventions in all education, training, and employment environments" (1993, p. 101).

When Will the Informal Assessment Information Be Used?

The information collected from an informal assessment can be used even as it is being gathered. Envision an instructor or counselor finding out during screening that a student has a significant hearing loss in the right ear. As soon as the information is realized, the instructor or counselor can make necessary adjustments to the assessment process. Now imagine that a student has just finished an assessment process and has responded "Yes, most definitely!" to the question "Do you have trouble filling out forms?" Immediately, the instructor or counselor can make an adjustment by presenting the printed intake form orally and recording the student's verbal responses. A second question "Do you get turned around or lost in places that should be familiar?" also receives an emphatic "Yes!" When these responses are combined with the response from a third question, "When someone gives you directions to a new place or location, how would you prefer to get them?", immediate adjustments may be made. For example, whenever the instructor or counselor refers the student to outside services, he or she prepares a "landmark-specific" color-coded map. The advantage and perhaps major attraction of informal assessment information is that it can be used immediately in virtually every setting.

How Will the Informal Assessment Results Be Used?

As stated previously, if the purpose of informal assessment is to assist the student in accomplishing specific goals through identification of needs, then the results should be used to facilitate the student's goals. For example, if remediation of learning difficulties is the goal of the informal assessment, then the results should be used to refine the remediation plan (Sturomski, 1996, 1997; Swanson, 1991). Of course, more than one course of action can be identified through an informal assessment process. Suppose a student has extreme difficulty with reading comprehension and retention; after an informal assessment, remediation techniques as well as specific accommodations (i.e., audiocassette version of the text and the use of a color-coded, symbol-based outline) are identified. In addition, the informal assessment identifies the need for instructional support (a volunteer tutor) and a mutual agreement for referral for formal assessment and diagnosis. Results of informal assessment may be used to change instructional methods, add interventions and accommodations, provide better substantiation for referral, and facilitate student goals more effectively and efficiently.

Where and How Will the Informal Assessment Take Place?

Given the varied environments within adult education, basic skills, and literacy programs, several key issues should be addressed. The location and implementation of informal assessment processes is crucial for ensuring the validity of the information gathered. A private environment is required to ensure reliability of information. If screening or intensive information collection occurs in open settings, such as at the back of the classroom while other students are present; in the staff lunch or lounge area while other practitioners are coming and going; in a public portion of a library or restaurant where strangers can overhear; or in other, similar nonprivate environments, then the chances are good that, because the student is uncomfortable with the lack of privacy, the information gathered will not be as reliable. The data should be collected using a multisensorial method combining visual, auditory, and verbal strategies in a one-to-one interview process. These protocols ensure all parts of the informal assessment process are clearly understood and allow for follow-up questioning and observation when necessary.

Who Will Need and Benefit from the Informal Assessment Information?

First and foremost, the person who will benefit most from the information gathered from informal assessment is the student. By providing direct and immediate feedback, an informal assessment starts the student down a pathway of self-awareness leading to improved self-esteem. By having more information about him- or herself, the student can recognize specific personal learning needs and learn to self-advocate (Silver, 1995; Smith, 1994). After the student has some understanding of the information generated, then, with the student's authorization, other instructors, counselors, and literacy tutors can also benefit from the data. The potential benefits of informal assessment appear to be numerous. However, without longitudinal research, only speculation based on practical and authentic application can be discussed. In classrooms and literacy programs throughout the United States, there is agreement that both the practitioner and the student benefit greatly from the knowledge acquired through the process (National Adult Literacy and Learning Disabilities Center, 1995). Reports of lower stress and frustration on both the student's and practitioner's parts as well as increases in learning, improvements in self-esteem, higher levels of motivation, and decreases in absenteeism and recurring enrollment are all experiences many participants are attributing to the results of informal assessment processes. Although the true values of the process are unknown, primarily because of the lack of research, anecdotes from students and practitioners alike strongly suggest that a major factor in the success of students with special learning needs or LD is the existence of a comprehensive, informal assessment process.

Summary

The adult education, basic skills, and literacy programs are laying the foundation for the design of an objective-informal assessment process by identifying who is being assessed and why; the goal of the assessment; when, where, and how an assessment should begin; who should conduct the assessment; what information should be collected and how it will be used; and what the value of the assessment will be to whom. When combined, these elements allow the selection of the best-suited informal assessment protocols to garner the maximum amount of information from the student. Applying this strategy before development or implementation ensures that the primary goal—providing a learning environment in which all students, especially those at risk of having LD or special learning needs, can succeed—is first and foremost.

FOUR ELEMENTS OF INFORMAL ASSESSMENT IN LEARNING ENVIRONMENTS

Within the learning environment, there are four skill areas in which adult education, basic skills, and literacy program practitioners must become proficient. The four areas are 1) observation of student characteristics and manifestations within the classroom or learning environment, 2) use of checklists and surveys to gather information that helps to identify a need for further informal assessment, 3) analysis of authentic skill or task demonstration to evaluate student performance, and 4) implementation of an intensive interview or self-report questionnaire.

Classroom and Learning Environment Observations

Ongoing observation in the learning environment can serve as a platform for identifying instructional techniques, interventions, and support needs (McCue, 1994). Practitioners must develop strong observation skills that allow them to look for characteristics and manifestations common among students with special learning needs or LD. These manifestations are often embedded in student behavior and performance and can be misread as lack of motivation, self-esteem, self-discipline, or educational opportunity. Practitioners should exercise observation skills in teams to ensure that they recognize characteristics and manifestations as well as contributing behaviors and performance issues while guarding against misinterpreting or missing prevalent signs. The premise of every practitioner should be this: There is a reason for every behavior or performance issue observed, and it is usually not "bad attitude" or "lack of motivation." If attitude or motivation were true factors, why would the student bother to attend classes? Listed are some of the more predominant classroom or learning environment behaviors and performance issues grouped by characteristics or manifestations.

Auditory or Receptive Abilities   Auditory or receptive abilities govern the way a student responds to oral directions, questions, and group work. Does he or she interrupt frequently or respond inaccurately? Does he or she regularly request that verbally presented information be repeated or give indications of accurate interpretation but not perform in the way he or she was instructed or as expected? Does the student tip or turn his or her head when listening to the instructor, tutor, or another student? Can she or he track or follow conversations? Does the student hesitate frequently before responding in conversation? Each of these examples may relate to either auditory processing or physically based hearing difficulties.

Oral Expressive Language Abilities   Oral expressive language abilities relate to the level of expressive language used, tonal quality, and comfort or ease of oral expression as well as appropriate or inappropriate use of words within the culture. What is the level of conversation presented by the student? Is the level equal to or lower or higher than other performance or skill areas? These and other conditions might relate to oral or expressive language difficulties.

Visual Abilities   Visual ability encompasses what is seen or processed through the eyes or visual modality. How does the student track print in books, forms, and tests? What is the student's ability to process printed text in comparison with verbal expression? Is the student wearing eyeglasses? Has the student mentioned the need for eyeglasses or that he or she has eyeglasses but they do not fit, do not work, or have never made a difference? If the student reads out loud, does she or he frequently skip a partial or full line of print? Is the student repeatedly on the wrong number, response, or column when using a bubble answer sheet? Each of these conditions, in combination or in isolation, might relate to visual processing difficulties as well as possible physical acuity or central vision difficulties.

Memory Abilities   Memory abilities may be demonstrated by the ability to retain past events that are or should be important. Is the student able to describe, either in writing or orally, previous educational history, varied learning experiences, and other experiences in a logical, clear manner? Does she or he have difficulty in remembering a personal address, important telephone numbers, automated teller machine (ATM) personal identification numbers, names of people important to him or her, notable events, and so forth? These and other related conditions may relate to memory processing and retention difficulties.

Sequencing Abilities   When observing a student's patterns, watch how he or she responds to questions about past events. Is the information presented in a natural or appropriate event order? Does the student approach directions and instructions sequentially? Can he or she identify the beginning and the end of certain events? In the expressive process, is there excessive verbal wandering? Does the writing sample contain good concepts that are out of order? These and other issues may relate to trouble integrating and organizing sequences.

Organizational Abilities   Organizational abilities are best noticed by observing study or work habits together with the ability to transfer information and skills from one task or process to another. Does the student have difficulty with abstract reasoning and conceptualization? Does he or she have difficulty with organizing or demonstrate inadequate organization patterns? Can the student prioritize? Does he or she have difficulty with following through or completing tasks or assignments? Is the difficulty a result of not knowing where or how to start? These and a host of other examples may be related to special learning needs or LD.

Visual-Motor Abilities   Visual-motor abilities are best observed through the completion of activities that require eye–hand coordination. How does the student complete the program application or intake form? Does he or she display inconsistent writing patterns or have difficulty in doing mathematical calculations on paper? Does he or she demonstrate difficulty in copying information from a book to a paper or from a chalkboard to a paper? Are writing patterns inconsistent? Is there difficulty in transferring information or answers from a test booklet to an answer sheet? These observations and others involving eye–hand coordination could be linked to visual-motor processing difficulties.

Gross and Fine Motor Abilities   When observing the student's patterns, take note of how the student manages motor-related functions in the classroom or environment. Overall, how does the student present when moving around the learning space? Is a level of clumsiness exhibited? Is the student always bumping into things or tripping? Can he or she manipulate scissors, a stapler, small books, folders, papers, pens, and pencils? These manifestations as well as others may relate to gross or fine motor difficulties.

Tactile and Kinesthetic Abilities   The student with difficulties with tactile and kinesthetic abilities might touch everything, not in an inquisitive manner but just for the sake of touching. The student may rub his or her fingers a lot or play with small objects and items within reach. Does the student always stand up to talk, take frequent breaks, or explain concepts and answer questions with a high level of movement? Is he or she very active or a participant in team sports, aerobics, or routine exercise? These behaviors and others, if observed frequently, could indicate the student needs a higher level of tactile, kinesthetic, or haptic involvement.

Temporal and Spatial Relations Abilities   Temporal and spatial relations abilities pertain to the ability of the student to orient or manage him- or herself in space and time. Does the student forget what time it is or when appointments are scheduled? Does he or she complain of getting lost frequently? Does the student have difficulty with managing time or comprehending the length of time needed to complete a task or assignment? Can the student identify the correct time and understand the concept of time? Does he or she have difficulty with finding places within buildings or at the mall?

These and many other observations could be related to difficulty with orienting oneself in time and space.

Attention Abilities   Attention abilities are best surveyed by observing the student's capacity to sustain attention during specific activities and/or tasks. Does the student have a span of focus that is short or irregular? Is he or she easily distracted by auditory and visual stimuli, such as too many books on the shelf, noise from other students or outside the environment, fluorescent lighting, windows, and so forth? Is the student's concentration erratic or inadequate? Is he or she easily pulled off task? Is there a high level of impulsiveness demonstrated socially, verbally, visually, or functionally? These and many more characteristics could relate to attention-processing difficulties or attention-deficit disorders.

Social Interaction Abilities   Social interaction abilities relate to the student's capacity to interact with other people. Without imposing personal value systems and considering culture and language differences, does the student present differently? Does he or she have difficulty with social interaction during breaks or group work? Is there a demonstrated level of anxiety and frustration in various learning situations? Does the student view him- or herself as a poor learner? Are there self-esteem issues? Is the student a loner, seldom socializing during breaks or participating in fun activities? Again, these and other related manifestations may point to social problems prompted by special learning needs or LD.

Comment   These behaviors and performance issues are frequently noticeable during the entry or beginning stages of services, including reception; eligibility processing; intake; initial interview; orientation; testing; or the first few weeks of class, tutoring, or training. *(A cautionary note: When reviewing and improving observation skills, it is very important to remember that there is typically a display of multiple behaviors and performance issues that can be identified through consistent observation with the characteristics and manifestations prevalent in students with special learning needs and LD.)*

Use of Checklists and Surveys

A variety of checklists and surveys addressing specific learning difficulties as well as learning characteristics can also be useful to practitioners. Dowdy and Smith stated, "The most important area to assess might well be the student's learning style" (1984, p. 174). Learning styles or unique learning methods are defined or identified within a student's chosen or preferred processing style, which includes cognitive, conceptual, and affective characteristics (Payne, 1995). There are a number of well-developed checklists and surveys that can assist the practitioner in identifying specific learning styles, characteristics, and related difficulties. Some are standardized; some are not. Many tools are available in a self-report format: Students complete the survey themselves. Others are intended to be completed by teachers, tutors, education assistants, support staff, spouses or partners, friends, parents, supervisors, or counselors.

Checklists and surveys are most useful when the information collected is validated with the student. Without this important step, the process is seen as biased and subjective. Another relevant factor is the reading and comprehension level needed to complete the checklist or survey. If the student has difficulty with reading and interpreting the information, the reliability of the data collected is affected. In addition, practitioners should identify whether the student can track printed text, transfer data (many tools require the use of a separate answer page), process visually, and write well enough to present accurate and complete information. Having students with special learning needs or LD respond independently to a printed checklist or survey without assistance can lead to inconsistent or inaccurate information.

Sometimes having practitioners, family, or friends who "know the student" complete checklists or surveys produces another level of inconsistency or inaccuracy resulting from "bias" or lack of knowledge. Faulty information is collected if the practitioner, family member, or friend has difficulty in interpreting behaviors or performance because of his or her own learning difficulties, lack of knowledge, or assumptions that the behaviors and performance issues are the result of a lack of motivation or not paying attention. Finally, important information is lost if a checklist or survey format is used without follow-up to validate results and assist the practitioner in interpretation and relationship of responses to special learning needs, LD, or other related impairments.

Authentic Skill or Task Demonstration and Analysis

Sometimes referred to as *diagnostic-prescriptive teaching*, Sturomski (1997) described this process as instruction involving "constant evaluation." He continued by describing an instructor–student or tutor–student relationship that involves observation and evaluation. The fundamental distinction is the student's role in the partnership: He or she is responsible for providing input and feedback when a process or method is or is not working. As authentic skill or task demonstration and analysis continues, instructors and tutors look for concrete signs or manifestations of special learning needs and LD in class, group, or independent work. For example, a student may present signs of visual discrimination difficulties by frequently reversing letters when writing or spelling (e.g., *bog/dog, was/saw*) or by exchanging words that look similar (e.g., *medal/metal, picture/pitcher*). Students with auditory processing difficulties may confuse or mix similar-sounding words (e.g., *clock/block, crashing/clashing*). Still other students may write a paragraph leaving endings and small words out of the text but, when asked to read the work out loud, read back the missing elements without hesitation. This type of authentic skill or task demonstration and analysis requires the instructor or tutor to observe how the student accomplishes similar tasks, consistently evaluate for error patterns, and note what is and what is not working (Johnson, 1987; Sturomski, 1997).

Specific skill or task analysis also provides a performance or competency-based analysis of skills and tasks necessary to reach specified goals. The instructor or tutor can clearly identify areas of accomplishment and areas requiring targeted, specific instruction by observing the manner in which the student approaches a task or skill and then evaluating whether the student can perform adequately. Task or skill analysis requires clear, structured identification of prerequisite skills as well as specifications for the task or skill (Lloyd & Blandford, 1991). Measurement is based on the degree of competence needed to perform the skill or task competently. Task or skill analysis can be extremely useful in identifying student-specific instructional methodologies and targeted interventions within adult education, basic skills, or literacy programs. By evaluating the tasks or skills (academic or nonacademic) that the student does well, practitioners can frequently determine which learning characteristics and styles are more prevalent in or more comfortable for the student. This information can then be applied to other learning situations in which acquisition of knowledge is more difficult because of a special learning need or a learning disability. Also known as *situational assessments* and *simulations*, these are exceptional methods of determining needs and accommodations for individuals with LD in instruction and work environments (McCue, 1994).

Intensive Interview or Self-Report Questionnaires

"Some of the most valuable information is provided by the adults themselves during the intake interview or from questionnaires" (Vogel, 1989, p. 121). How true this statement is. All too often adults who have special learning needs or LD have made statements such as the following: "If only they [supervisors or administrators] would ask me what would work better, I could tell them," or "Why hasn't anyone asked me these questions? This stuff really makes sense," or "Learning about my learning needs has really helped me sort out the difference between 'lack of interest' or 'not trying' [phrases that the author of this chapter used to hear all the time] and the need to learn differently because school is set up for the other learner." Of course, there are those students who are convinced that they cannot learn or have such low self-esteem that their responses are very different. All responses, however, present extremely valuable information for student-based goal development.

As a means of informal assessment for a youth or adult student in adult education, basic skills, and literacy programs, intensive inventories or self-report questionnaires are probably the most effective. The purpose should be to intensively look at the student's processing style and learning characteristics as well as specific strengths, weaknesses, and limitations (Sturomski, 1997). This method is an effective protocol to gather data related to the student's family, education, instruction, and employment background; medical history and circumstances; preferred or necessary learning style; memory difficulties; reading, spelling, writing, and mathematical limitations; organizational difficulties; metacognitive skills; receptive and expressive language skills; study skills and work habits; social skills and personal presentation skills; other personal issues; and self-esteem, as well as previous learning strategies that have and have not worked and effective teaching methods. In addition, this method helps the student share his or her perception of specific limitations and strengths (Anderson, 1993; Lloyd & Blandford, 1991; McCue, 1994).

Brinckerhoff (1992) asserted that students should be actively involved in the assessment process. When using inventories or self-report questionnaires, the information-gathering process engages and involves the student in an objective manner. By using this method of informal assessment, practitioners never risk operating or providing services based on assumptions. The student has the opportunity to follow responses with a "for instance" or to give specific examples with more descriptive detail than many formal assessment protocols allow. Equally important, the practitioner has the opportunity to prod through surface responses to the internal thinking, learning, and doing processes of the student. The quality of information obtained is far more substantial than realized at first glance.

An important element of inventories and self-report questionnaires is developing a rapport with the student. This can be accomplished by setting a positive tone at the beginning of the process. Practitioners should explain that, in the program in which the student is participating, learning is thought of differently. That is, in this program everyone is treated as a learner, and it is the instructor's or tutor's responsibility to teach in ways and methods by which each student learns best.

Oftentimes the dilemma is not what to ask but where to stop or what could be pursued later. This occurs because engaging students in an intensive interview affords opportunities for information gathering that are rarely available. Students begin to take charge of their own learning experience. They reflect on past experiences and recognize that the instructor, counselor, or tutor really cares about them as a learner and is interested in their progress and success in the program. This "bonding" process creates a desire in students to learn more while diminishing hopelessness and feelings of being unsuccessful learners—the evolving processing of self-awareness.

Inventories and self-report questionnaires should take the guesswork out of interpretation and the relationship of responses gathered from observation methods, surveys and checklists, and authentic skill or task analysis. The process is structured so that all students exhibiting a set of predetermined characteristics and manifestations specifically related to LD or special learning needs are interviewed. This ensures that all students receive equal services within adult education, basic skills, and literacy programs.

DEVELOPING STRUCTURED SELF-REPORT INVENTORIES

Many different informal assessment tools are available that can be used by practitioners working with students who have LD or special learning needs. Each of these tools has varying degrees of usefulness, and practitioners must become familiar with their attributes in order to select those that are most appropriate for individual use. The National Adult Literacy and Learning Disabilities Center in Washington, D.C., maintains a complete list of researched and referenced screening and informal assessment tools.

Since 1980, Payne & Associates has been developing structured, self-report informal assessment tools for use in various programs, organizations, and businesses that assist in identifying those students or consumers who are at high risk of having a learning disability or a special learning need. A sample of these informal assessment tools is provided in the appendix at the end of this chapter. Referred to as Payne Learning Needs Inventories, these tools have been implemented in postsecondary and secondary environments; adult education, basic skills, and literacy programs; employment and training projects; correctional facilities; human services operations; and businesses in 11 states (see Chapter 7). In each instance, prior to identification or selection of a specific Learning Needs Inventory, an evaluation of organizational goals and structure, student or consumer demographics, risk factors for prevalence of special learning needs and LD, student or consumer needs and goals, and existing formal and informal assessment protocols is completed by a team or focus group consisting of personnel from the organization or entity involved and Payne & Associates.

The next step is to select a structured, objective, informal assessment process that meets the goals and needs of the student and the program or business. The protocols selected should assist in determining whether a student is at high risk because of a suspected learning disability or a special learning need or whether other fundamental issues such as limited access to school, transiency, poor study habits, or social or emotional concerns exist (Anderson, 1993). After these factors are eliminated, the primary goal of the Payne Learning Needs Inventory is to identify specific learning needs, instruction or tutoring interventions and accommodations, and necessary referrals. In addition, the results of the inventory help develop a better rapport with the student and produce a more stable educational experience, thus minimizing recurring enrollment. Simply stated, the goal is to identify a struggling student's learning characteristics and strengths early in the delivery of basic education, literacy services, or skill advancement and match them with appropriate interventions and accommodations in instruction, tutoring, or program design as well as to identify a process for diagnosis of LD or special learning needs when necessary. By identifying special learning needs and providing interventions, the opportunities for success can be realized, thus enhancing self-esteem, maximizing potential, and *creating learning power* for the student as well as *instructional power* for the instructor or tutor.

Payne & Associates has developed several versions of the Learning Needs Inventory; each is structured to meet the needs of students or consumers in specific programs within organizations and businesses. Each version has been developed by using focus groups consisting of a full representation of the organization or business staff involved in the student's or consumer's learning-based program. For example, the inventories designed for use in the adult education, basic skills, and literacy environments had focus groups consisting of adult education and literacy coordinators, instructors and tutors, counselors, students, program and state administrators, disability service representatives, and appropriate referral representatives (e.g., vision, audiology, training directors, educational psychologists). After a specific inventory was designed, practitioners serving that group of students or consumers then informally field tested the design, questions, and flow of the tool. After a reasonable period of time, usually on completion of 50–100 interviews, results were summarized and incorporated as appropriate into the final inventory.

The need for several versions of the inventory is substantiated by preliminary assessment of the group to be served. Contributing factors include the student's or consumer's background and exposure to education, instruction, or employment; current learning environment; and primary goals. For example, questions on the corrections facility version ask what the student does in the structured free time available each day, whereas the basic skills version asks the student what he or she does in his or her spare time for fun. Inventories and developed screening processes include versions that can be used in universities and colleges, adult education and literacy programs, workplace education training facilities, programs serving youth at risk, short-term and long-term correctional facilities, dislocated worker projects, employment and training operations, and human services settings. Each version asks specific questions that elicit responses about how students or consumers who are at risk of having LD or special learning needs think or know they learn best. This is accomplished by the identification of strengths, weaknesses, and limitations. This process promotes multiple opportunities to provide direct feedback and ask follow-up questions during both the interview and the learning process.

Rationale for Choice of Questions and Domains

The questions on the Payne Learning Needs Inventories are based on four global areas: background information, medical data, manifestations and behaviors, and preferred modality and processing methods. Descriptive in nature, each question has been identified based on the markers cited in research on special learning needs, LD, and related disorders. The appendix at the end of this chapter presents a sample of questions in each area. Background information covers areas such as elementary, secondary, and postsecondary education experiences; training and workshop opportunities; employment history; incarceration data (when appropriate); family learning history and learning needs; frustration and anger issues; and goals (both previous and present). Medical data cover information related to medical history, such as past and current health; eye, ear, and sinus conditions; allergies; substance abuse; brain injuries, seizures, or convulsions; family health; previous and current medications; special needs or learning disability diagnosis; left–right dominance; genetic learning difficulties; mental health disabilities; and other related physical conditions. Manifestations and behaviors are related to impairments known to be common markers of special learning needs, especially LD and attention disorders. These questions address limitations and areas of weakness. Preferred modalities and processing methods are revealed by questions covering methods that the student identifies as the best ways to learn: the student's strengths and talents.

Questions regarding manifestations and behaviors and preferred modality and processing methods are broken into several cognitive and metacognitive domains, including attention, reasoning and processing, memory, oral communication, reading, writing, spelling, calculations, gross and fine motor coordination, social competence, emotional maturity and self-esteem, time orientation, and spatial orientation. Each question focuses on prior learning experiences in a variety of settings that incorporate parenting, social activities, church activities, safety training, work, school experiences, vocational instruction, driving, volunteer work, recreation, on-the-job training programs, and community activities. One interesting phenomenon is the distinctions discovered when students with special learning needs describe how they learn in an academic environment versus a nonacademic environment. Their personal learning methods used in the academic setting are usually depicted as more traditional (e.g., reading, writing, listening, taking notes), whereas the same students frequently describe personal learning methods in nonacademic settings as hands-on methods integrated with discussion and nonprint data. This factor speaks to the value of having inventory questions that address learning in more than one environment.

The Learning Needs Inventory has another component not usually seen on other inventories and self-report questionnaires. Each question and subpart has a described rationale or domain (see the appendix at the end of this chapter). This assists the practitioner in recognizing the value of the student's response and knowing whether follow-up questioning is required. The rationale or domain also serves as a prompter or reminder, defining questions that need clarification as well as providing a short explanation about the functions identified within the question or subpart. Finally, it specifies critical information such as cultural impact or confidentiality of specific questions. Some versions have space to note behavioral observations such as personal presentation, concentration, attention, and distractibility. A condensed cross-section of the type of questions asked and accompanying rationale or descriptors is presented in Table 6.1.

Table 6.1.   Learning Needs Inventory cross section of questions

Question	Rationale/domain
How many jobs have you had since high school or instruction?	Background information; substantiates difficulties in learning in multiple settings
What is the highest grade you completed?	Education history
Do time limits bother you?	Time orientation, integration, stress and anxiety
Do you like to write?	Visual acuity, visual print, visual-motor, visual integration
Do you have difficulty with following oral instructions?	Auditory processing, sequencing, and organizing
How do you remember important telephone numbers?	Association, memory, sequencing, modality-based processing
Are you easily distracted or bothered by fluorescent lighting?	Visual and/or auditory distortion or distraction
Do you experience difficulty in finishing a task or a project?	Attention, concentration, distractibility, and organization
Do you have difficulty with expressing your ideas out loud?	Verbal, expressive problems
When using the computer, do you like to learn using the pictures, icons, and graphs?	Visual, visual nonprint, visual-motor, visual integration
Do you like to use the mouse on the computer or play a computer game on your television?	Visual, visual-motor, tactile, eye–hand coordination.
Describe how you would remember how to spell an important word.	Memory and modality processing

Note: Cross-section of questions included on the Payne Learning Needs Inventory, a structured, self-report assessment tool developed by Payne & Associates (©1991); reprinted by permission.

This type of informal assessment interview is conducted in a private setting. The practitioner presents all of the questions orally, clarifies any unknowns, and records the student's verbal responses. For ease in tracking, students are provided with a large-print version of the questions that does not include accompanying rationale or domains. This is the student's personal copy, and, even if he or she has extreme difficulty in reading, the student is encouraged to take it home and review the data with a family member who has no reading difficulty. This copy also addresses some students' need for visual input or a combined visual and auditory input. Students are encouraged to think about their responses, and if, in the course of a few days, they realize that some of their responses do not totally reflect their strengths or limitations, they are welcome to change their responses, sharing the additional or new information with the practitioner. Sometimes students do investigative work and present more medical, psychological, or mental health data. Again, when an actual interview is in process, the practitioner always pursues more in-depth information, requesting clarification and additional information or descriptions.

Summarizing Data

After completing the inventory, strengths and possible limitations are grouped by the following cognitive areas: attention, auditory, verbal, orientation, sequencing, tactile and kinesthetic, memory, physical visual, visual print, visual nonprint, and visual-motor. At this point, it is extremely important to recognize the routine multiplicity of cognitive and metacognitive factors in each question and subpart. In the appendix at the end of this chapter, Question 1 clearly presents these factors. If a student responds that she learns best by watching someone give a demonstration (d), doing something hands-on or working with my hands (e), and looking at pictures/graphs (f), the summary data would denote the following cognitive and metacognitive factors. Summarizing subpart 1d, watching someone give a demonstration, would include attention (attention span, concentration), visual (acuity, tracking, figure–ground), and visual nonprint (perception, discrimination, visual memory processing) factors. Adding subpart 1e, doing something hands-on or working with my hands, would include such factors as attention (attention span, concentration), orientation (spatial), tactile/kinesthetic (hands-on, demonstration, experiential), visual (acuity, tracking, figure–ground), visual nonprint (perception, discrimination, visual memory processing), and visual-motor (eye–hand coordination). Finally, if subpart 1f, looking at pictures/graphs, is summarized, factors included would be attention (attention span, concentration), orientation (sequencing, spatial), visual (acuity, tracking, figure–ground), and visual nonprint and visual print (perception, discrimination, visual memory processing). This simple example points out that none of the inventory questions is mutually exclusive of another question. Just as learning is complex, so is identification of strengths and limitations. However, by summarizing responses in this manner, the practitioner can quickly identify the predominance of true self-reported weaknesses or limitations as well as predominant strengths when the student is engaged in learning activities.

After the responses are summarized, feedback is provided, including referrals and resources for further assessment or diagnosis if warranted. A structured plan is developed with suggested accommodations, teaching techniques, and interventions specific to the student's or consumer's needs. In addition, the student or consumer is encouraged to identify personal learning strategies and create a personal plan for implementation.

An interview process should follow standard protocols so that each student feels secure and comfortable when responding to questions. Some of the more important protocols include a private interview space, acceptance of data presented without regard to personal values or morals; a one-to-one interview format with a verbal exchange and follow-up discussion; and, above all, respect of confidential issues.

QUALITATIVE RESULTS OF INFORMAL ASSESSMENT

There are few research data quantitatively supporting the use of informal assessment processes, including intensive inventory protocols, for use with students suspected of having significant LD or special learning needs. Anderson (1993) cited a few institutions that have developed screening procedures after several years of providing in-house testing. Evaluation of those individuals referred for formal testing on the basis of informal assessment protocols revealed a 25%–39% higher diagnoses accuracy rate than those referred previously without the use of informal screening. Research conducted by the state of Washington Division of Employment and Social Services, Learning Disabilities Initiative, suggested in an interim report (Washington State Division of Employment and Social Services, 1997) that the use of a structured screening process appears to result in a more accurate referral process for diagnosis (see Chapter 7). As noted previously, the National Adult Literacy and Learning Disabilities Center in Washington, D.C., continues to study the use of informal assessment procedures. Other studies point to reduction of cost and time as well as increased efficiency and access to resources, especially diagnostic services, as benefits of informal screening and assessment (Carlton & Knapke, 1992; Vogel, 1989).

What can be legitimately discussed are a sampling of the qualitative results of informal assessment and screening protocols. With regard to the Payne Learning Needs Inventory, Maher stated, "In my opinion, this Inventory is one of my most valuable teaching tools. In just about an hour, I gain a wealth of information regarding the learning style and personal/educational background of the student" (Carter & Maher, 1995, p. 6). In one example, she cited a student who had been coming to the program off and on for approximately 3 years. She explained that, during the course of the interview, she learned the student was deaf in one ear and had blurred vision, which affected his ability to discriminate letters on a page. After appropriate referrals and interventions, the student began to make significant progress in class.

Carter spoke about informal assessment processes within a workplace basic skills program to identify those at high risk of having LD or special learning needs. She commented, "Through this project I have witnessed lives blossoming and changing direction where once frustration and despair with learning had otherwise stymied good, capable people" (Carter & Maher, 1995, p. 6). One student reported, "When I started taking classes in a program for adults with learning disabilities, I had a difficult time opening up to the teachers" (Copps, 1994, p. 8). The remainder of her story highlighted the knowledge she had gained from the assessment and intervention process. She concluded,

> Just as I was determined to help myself, I am determined to help those who may not know how to help themselves. I will use that same self-love and determination to stay motivated to study to get my GED so I can become a teaching assistant. (Billie Kenner, in Copps, 1994, p. 8)

Another student stated,

> Now that I understand and can better accept that I have learning disabilities, I have a whole new attitude about life. As for my future, I would really like a job that will allow me to use more of my mind and less of my body. (Tim King, in Sturomski, 1994, p. 10)

After administering a Payne Learning Needs Inventory to a student who had been particularly difficult to teach, one instructor stated that the information collected was
invaluable. He went on to describe the student's educational and family background as
extremely dysfunctional and noted that he had always thought the student lacked
motivation. His conclusion after completion of the informal assessment process was
that the student had never received the opportunity to learn and that he (the instructor) was going to make "darn sure" the opportunity occurred.

Finally, maybe the most enlightening story comes from a student who had been
struggling for months in a basic skills class. The instructor had decided to do an interview, and, after listening to a long history of special education, private tutoring, and
numerous diagnostic experiences, she asked the student why she had never mentioned
any of these experiences before this. The student replied, "I didn't know you wanted
or needed to know, and if I had known that, I'm not sure I'd have known when or how
to tell you."

CONCLUSION

Johnson stated, "Diagnosis [or assessment] in any field is a complex process that
involves a search for patterns" (1987, p. 9). The elements of an informal assessment
begin that process. Informal assessment provides an opportunity to recognize and
honor the accomplishments, hidden talents, and strengths of the student who has special learning needs or a possible learning disability. Informal assessment processes put
the student in charge by promoting an effective way of acknowledging talents and
strengths; identifying limitations; and, after applying interventions and accommodations, remediating weaknesses into strengths. Determination of methods, strategies,
and interventions should never be made on the basis of a single test score but must instead be based on patterns of strengths and abilities as well as difficulties and errors
(Dowdy & Smith, 1984; Johnson, 1987; Vogel, 1989).

Informal assessment processes are paramount in the efforts to answer the basic
question of whether interventions and accommodations for students who have special
learning needs and LD are effective (Adelman & Taylor, 1991). This chapter attempts
to address at least a portion of the answer to this question. Informal assessment methods should use and build on information from multiple processes. They should be implemented when the objective is to clarify whether a student is at risk of having LD or
special learning needs in an effort to assist the student in meeting his or her goals.
Assessment information should present objective data pertinent to the student's needs
or goals as well as answer a specific set of referral questions (McCue, 1994).

The informal assessment of students with special learning needs and LD provides
a means for helping the student live life more fully (Ross-Gordon, 1989). By embrac-
ing informal assessment processes in adult education, basic skills, and literacy programs, practitioners agree to promote student success by helping students increase
their awareness of how they learn best; recognizing their strengths and limitations;
understanding their education, basic skills, or literacy needs; assisting them in the
development and use of strategies and accommodations for the identified special learning needs or LD; and creating the foundation for self-advocacy (Andresen, 1994). This
process begins to establish a climate in which students can develop the confidence in
their own potential that underlies self-esteem (Krupp, 1994). Silver (1995) best summarized what the expected results of informal and formal assessment processes for students with special learning needs or LD should be. Simply defined, the result should be

knowledge, both for the student and the practitioner. Silver asserted, "First comes knowledge. Knowledge is the key to self-esteem and the ability to self advocate" (p. 233). Practitioners gain knowledge from the informal assessment process that allows them to provide better instruction, thus increasing their self-esteem as practitioners and improving their ability to advocate for more instruction and skill development. This knowledge, when shared through the process of informal assessment, feedback, and application, results in improved self-esteem and enhanced self-advocacy skills for the student.

A final note for practitioners must be added regarding informal assessment. Sometimes, after an informal assessment is completed, the feedback from adult education, basic skills, or literacy providers is, "I know she didn't give me accurate information" or "Even though he responded this way, I know that's not really how he learns." Practitioners must believe that each student's response is vitally important and valuable. All too often someone has trivialized or minimized what the student believed were insurmountable conditions when trying to learn. Practitioners must become facilitators of significant change for students by closing the textbook of narrow-mindedness and assumptions and opening the book entitled, "Meeting Your Students Where They Are." The adult education, basic skills, and literacy systems are like cocoons, warm and supportive of eager students wanting to learn. All programs should strive to equalize knowledge acquisition by recognizing each student's unique and distinct learning characteristics as an integral part of the diversities within our communities that expand our capacity to broaden that base of knowledge. Students with special learning needs and LD come to our programs because deep in their inner beings they hope they can be successful. Comprehensive, ongoing informal assessment processes, which begin at student entry and end at student exit, identify the possibilities and turn hope into pathways of opportunity. Through these pathways, there is truth in the statement "everyone is a learner."

REFERENCES

Accardo, P. (1996). *The invisible disability: Understanding learning disabilities in the context of health and education.* Washington, DC: National Health & Education Consortium.

Adelman, H.S., & Taylor, L. (1991). Issues and problems related to the assessment of learning disabilities. In H.L. Swanson (Ed.), *Handbook on the assessment of learning disabilities* (pp. 21–43). Austin, TX: PRO-ED.

Anderson, P.L. (1993). Issues in assessment and diagnosis. In L.C. Brinckerhoff, S.F. Shaw, & J.M. McGuire (Eds.), *Promoting postsecondary education for students with learning disabilities* (pp. 89–136). Austin, TX: PRO-ED.

Andresen, L. (1994, Summer). Stacking the deck: Four aces of self-esteem. *Linkages: Linking Literacy & Learning Disabilities, 1,* 4–5.

Brinckerhoff, L. (1992). Diagnostic considerations for students with learning disabilities at selective colleges. In M.L. Farrell (Ed.), *Support services for student with learning disabilities in higher education: A compendium of readings* (Book 3, pp. 83–86). Columbus, OH: Association on Higher Education and Disability. (Reprinted from Brinckerhoff, L.C. [Ed.]. [1989, Fall]. *Latest developments: Learning Disabilities Special Interest Group Newsletter*)

Carlton, P.M., & Knapke, D. (1992). Case history factors that correlate with a learning disability diagnosis. In M.L. Farrell (Ed.), *Support services for students with learning disabilities in higher education: A compendium of readings* (Book 3, pp. 87–88). Columbus, OH: Association on Higher Education and Disability. (Reprinted from Ellis, D. [Ed.]. [1990]. *In tune with the future: Selected proceedings of the 1990 AHSSPPE conference.* Columbus, OH: Association on Higher Education and Disability.)

Carter, J., & Maher, P. (1995, Spring). Joint efforts in training. *Linkages: Linking Literacy & Learning Disabilities, 2*(1), 4–6.

Copps, K. (1994, Summer). No more pity parties. *Linkages: Linking Literacy & Learning Disabilities*, *1*(1), 6–8.

Dowdy, C.A., & Smith, T.E.C. (1984). Serving individuals with specific learning disabilities in the vocational rehabilitation system. In P.J. Gerber & H.B. Reiff (Eds.), *Learning disabilities in adulthood: Persisting problems and evolving issues* (pp. 171–178). Boston: Andover Medical.

Johnson, D.J. (1987). Principles of assessment and diagnosis. In D.J. Johnson & J.W. Blalock (Eds.), *Adults with learning disabilities: Clinical studies* (pp. 9–30). Orlando, FL: Grune & Stratton.

Johnson, D.J., & Croasmun, P.A. (1991). Language assessment. In H.L. Swanson (Ed.), *Handbook on the assessment of learning disabilities* (pp. 229–248). Austin, TX: PRO-ED.

Krupp, J. (1994, Summer). Breaking the low self-esteem cycle. *Linkages: Linking Literacy & Learning Disabilities, 1,* 3–4.

Learning Disabilities Association of America. (1996). *They speak for themselves: A survey of adults with learning disabilities.* Pittsburgh: Author.

Lloyd, J.W., & Blandford, B.J. (1991). Assessment for instruction. In H.L. Swanson (Ed.), *Handbook on the assessment of learning disabilities* (pp. 45–58). Austin, TX: PRO-ED.

McCue, M. (1994). Clinical diagnostic and functional assessment of adults with learning disabilities. In P.J. Gerber & H.B. Reiff (Eds.), *Learning disabilities in adulthood: Persisting problems and evolving issues* (pp. 55–71). Boston: Andover Medical.

National Adult Literacy and Learning Disabilities Center. (1995, Summer). *Screening for adults with learning disabilities.* Washington, DC: Author.

National Joint Committee on Learning Disabilities. (1994). Issues in learning disabilities: Assessment and diagnosis. In *Collective perspectives on issues affecting learning disabilities: Position papers and statements* (pp. 49–55). Austin, TX: PRO-ED. (Original work published 1987)

Nightingale, D., Yudd, R., Anderson, S., & Barnow, B. (1991). *The learning disabled in employment and training programs* (Research & Evaluation Report Series 91-E). Washington, DC: U.S. Department of Labor, The Urban Institute.

Payne & Associates. (1997). *Payne Learning Needs Inventory.* Olympia, WA: Author.

Payne, M.D., & Robins, E. (Eds.). (1994). *National resources for adults with learning disabilities.* (Available from HEATH Resource Center, One Dupont Circle, Suite 800, Washington, DC 20036).

Payne, N. (1995, Spring). The connection between learning culture and learning disabilities. *Linkages: Linking Literacy & Learning Disabilities, 2,* 7.

Ross-Gordon, J.M. (1989). *Adults with learning disabilities: An overview for the adult educator.* Columbus: The Ohio State University, Center on Education and Training for Employment.

Silver, L.B. (1995). Knowledge of self: The key to self-esteem and self advocacy. In *Secondary education & beyond: Providing opportunities for students with learning disabilities* (pp. 223–233). Pittsburgh: Learning Disabilities Association of America.

Smith, S.L. (1994, Summer). How not to feel stupid when you know you're not: Self-esteem and learning disabilities. *Linkages: Linking Literacy & Learning Disabilities, 1,* 1–2.

Sturomski, N.A. (1994, Summer). Tim's story. *Linkages: Linking Literacy & Learning Disabilities, 1*(1), 8–10.

Sturomski, N.A. (1996). Literacy needs for adults who have learning disabilities. In N. Gregg, C. Hoy, & A.F. Gay (Eds.), *Adults with learning disabilities: Theoretical and practical perspectives* (pp. 261–276). New York: The Guilford Press.

Sturomski, N.A. (1997). In N.A. Sturomski & N. Payne (Eds.), *Supporting adults with learning disabilities and other special learning needs* (pp. 4–7). Oklahoma City: Oklahoma State Department of Education, Lifelong Learning Section.

Swanson, H.L. (1991). Introduction: Issues in the assessment of learning disabilities. In H.L. Swanson (Ed.), *Handbook on the assessment of learning disabilities* (pp. 1–19). Austin, TX: PRO-ED.

Vogel, S.A. (1989). Special considerations in the development of models for diagnosis of adults with learning disabilities. In L.B. Silver (Ed.), *The assessment of learning disabilities: Preschool through adulthood* (pp. 111–134). Austin, TX: PRO-ED.

Washington State Division of Employment and Social Services. (1997). *Learning disability initiative: An interim report.* Seattle: Author.

Zikmund, W.G. (1988). *Business research methods.* New York: Dryden Press.

Zwerlein, R.A., Smith, M., & Diffley, J. (1984). *Vocational rehabilitation for learning disabled adults.* Albertson, NY: Human Resources Center.

Appendix

Payne Learning Needs Inventory

The Payne Learning Needs Inventory (Payne & Associates, ©1997) is an informal assessment tool that can be used by practitioners to identify special learning needs, recommend instruction or tutoring interventions and accommodations, and make necessary referrals for individuals with learning disabilities or special learning needs.

The questions presented are representative of actual questions used within the inventory. (No part of any question or rationale may be copied or used without written permission.) Responses to all questions are always confidential in nature and should be treated as such. The term *learning differences* may be substituted for the term *learning difficulties*.

RATIONALE FOR QUESTIONS	QUESTIONS	STUDENT RESPONSE	COMMENTS
Learning method involving modality and memory process a. visual—eyes (print) b. listening—ears c. verbal—oral (interactive) d. visual—eyes/see (nonprint) e. tactile/kinesthetic/visual/visual-motor—activity f. visual—eyes (nonprint) g. listening—ears h. verbal—oral to hearing i. visual—eyes (nonprint) j. visual/motor—eye-hand	**1. How do you think you learn best when you are learning something new?** (Check all that apply.) a. [ ] reading print b. [ ] listening to a lecture c. [ ] discussing with someone d. [ ] watching someone give a demonstration e. [ ] doing something hands-on or working with my hands f. [ ] looking at pictures/graphs g. [ ] listening to others h. [ ] saying it out loud i. [ ] observing j. [ ] writing it down k. [ ] other	S	
Number association and processing a. aural processing b. visual to visual–motor processing c. aural/auditory processing d. visual to visual–motor (nonprint processing) e. aural to verbal processing f. tactile or touch processing g. other	**8. How do you remember telephone numbers?** a. [ ] mentally, by listening b. [ ] write them down c. [ ] sound of the touch-tone keys d. [ ] recalling a visual pattern e. [ ] repeating the telephone number out loud f. [ ] by where the buttons are located/by touch on the telephone g. [ ] other	S	

		S/W
Common manifestations of special learning needs may require immediate accommodations. a. visual acuity, visual discrimination, and visual figure–ground b. tracking and visual discrimination c. visual acuity and visual discrimination d. visual acuity and visual discrimination e. visual acuity, tracking, and eye coordination/discrimination f. visual discrimination/tracking acuity	**12. Which do you have difficulty in or experience problems with?** (Check all that apply.) a. [ ] finding a number in the telephone book b. [ ] keeping your place when you read c. [ ] words looking different each time you see them d. [ ] blurring or fading of words when you try to read e. [ ] skipping lines, words, or letters f. [ ] mixing or reversing letters	W
Comprehension processing method a. visual processing b. verbal/aural processing c. aural processing d. aural/visual processing	**17. When you are reading, which ways seem to work best?** a. [ ] reading silently to yourself b. [ ] reading aloud c. [ ] having someone else read to you d. [ ] having someone else read to you while you follow along	S
Visual discrimination and acuity; visual health	**18. After reading, do you look up and notice that distant objects are momentarily blurred?** [ ] yes [ ] no [ ] sometimes Describe:	W

Key: S, strength; W, weakness; B, background. [x]. yes (checked); [ ], no (blank); [s], sometimes.

RATIONALE FOR QUESTIONS	QUESTIONS	STUDENT RESPONSE	COMMENTS
Learning disabilities (LD) can be acquired; also may not be learning problem but a medical need a. auditory/phonics problems b. auditory/phonics problems c. may present as LD d. may induce acquired LD e. may induce acquired LD f. may present as LD g. may induce acquired LD h. may induce acquired LD i. may induce acquired LD j. may affect memory for a period of time k. may be medical in nature	**21. Have you had any of the following?** (Check all that apply.) a. [ ] multiple ear infections b. [ ] multiple sinus problems c. [ ] diabetes d. [ ] serious accident e. [ ] convulsions or seizures f. [ ] severe allergies g. [ ] prolonged high fevers h. [ ] concussion or head injury i. [ ] frequent headaches j. [ ] anesthesia in the last 6 months k. [ ] serious health problems	B	
Visual/verbal association and memory processing a. visual processing (print) b. visual processing (print/non-print) c. aural processing (listen) d. visual processing (nonprint) e. visual processing (nonprint) f. visual processing (print) g. verbal/aural processing and speaking/listening h. aural/visual–motor processing (listen/eye–motor) i. visual non-print/aural processing	**24. How do you like to get directions to a new place?** (Check all that apply.) a. [ ] written directions b. [ ] a map c. [ ] oral directions d. [ ] pictures e. [ ] landmarks f. [ ] streets/highway signs or names g. [ ] repeat the directions h. [ ] hearing and writing them i. [ ] point and gesture with verbal directions	S	

#	Question	Code	Note
28.	**How would you put together a ready-to-assemble bookshelf?** (Check all that apply.) a. [ ] look at the diagram or pictures b. [ ] read the directions c. [ ] do it without either d. [ ] talk about it with someone	S	Organizing and sequencing processing modality a. visual—non-language based b. visual—language based c. visual—tactile/kinesthetic d. verbal—language based
36.	**Were you ever in a special program or given extra help in school?** [ ] yes [ ] no Describe:	B	Most "special services" are based on some element of assessment of special learning needs
38.	**Were you ever diagnosed or thought to have:** a. [ ] a learning disability b. [ ] attention-deficit/hyperactivity disorder c. [ ] hyperactivity d. [ ] dyslexia When? By whom? Can you get that information?	B	Learning disability diagnosis; possible education or medical records available Attention-deficit/hyperactivity disorder symptoms should be noticed prior to age 6/7. Medical diagnosis required. Impulsive, easily distracted, short attention span.
39.	**As a learner, do you suspect that you have a learning difficulty or something that interferes with learning?** [ ] yes [ ] no] Explain:	B	Informal self-identification. Most know and can describe symptoms or behaviors.

Key: S, strength; W, weakness; B, background. [x], yes (checked); [ ], no (blank); [s], sometimes.

7

PowerPath to Adult Basic Learning

A Diagnostic Screening System for Adults Who
Are at High Risk for Being Diagnosed as Having Learning Disabilities

Laura P. Weisel

PowerPath to Adult Basic Learning is an intake, diagnostic screening, and intervention system for adults entering basic skills and literacy programs. Whereas other assessments focus on what an individual knows, PowerPath seeks to identify how an individual learns by screening for difficulties in processing information. Based on an individual's assessment profile, the system's software prescribes personalized strategies that can be helpful in building academic, life, and vocational skills. The process is completed when the instructor and student together design a plan that combines skills to be learned with recommended learning accommodations.

PowerPath has been developed over the years by drawing on aggregate principles and research findings spanning a variety of disciplines. The foundations of the system are grounded in the areas of adult learning, neuropsychology, cognitive psychology, transformational counseling, human behavior, learning disabilities (LD), reading, and organizational development. PowerPath is being used in a variety of basic skills and literacy settings. Sites include

- Adult basic skills and literacy education programs
- Community-based organizations providing adult and family literacy services
- Community colleges
- Job Opportunities and Basic Skills (JOBS) programs
- Jobs Training Partnership Act (JTPA)/Private Industry Councils programs
- Criminal justice/correctional education programs—adult and juvenile

- Workplace education and basic skills programs
- Mental health treatment facilities

This chapter describes the development and use of the PowerPath system. The first section describes the concepts integral to the system. The second section describes the system's historical development in a series of previous studies. Next an overview of the PowerPath system is given and the five steps of the PowerPath process are detailed, along with specific information about test administration. Finally, plans for the future are discussed.

POWERPATH: A HOLISTIC TOOL TO SUPPORT ADULTS WITH LEARNING DIFFICULTIES

PowerPath is designed to be a structured and easy-to-use intake and diagnostic screening system for adults entering basic skills and literacy programs. The system includes a guided interview; a standardized diagnostic screening of information processing; a computer-generated analysis of screening, results, and recommended accommodations based on an individual's learning strengths and weaknesses; and an intervention process to implement accommodations. The software also produces administrative reports. The data in these reports can be used to profile a program's learners (demographics and screening scores). The administrative reports were designed to support the trend for data that can be used to increase program accountability, more easily complete funding reports, and prepare for writing grants.

The components of the PowerPath system include User's Guide, Test Plates, Vision Screening Kit, audiometer, Personal Profile folders, Response Booklets, Crib Sheets, Personal Learning Plans, and software (see Figure 7.1). The software creates three reports, including the Individual Report, Service Summary, and Annual Report. By following the guided interview on the outside of the Personal Profile folder along with administering and scoring the diagnostic screening using the Test Plates' step-by-step instructions, an instructor can administer PowerPath in approximately 90 minutes. The various assessments can also be separated and administered at different times. Training, although not required, is recommended for personnel unfamiliar with administration of vision and hearing screenings, psychological testing, and integrating accommodations into learning or instruction curriculums.

The PowerPath system screens for difficulties in specific aspects of information processing that, on the basis of early statistical studies, are linked to success with learning basic academic skills (Weisel, 1993). Based on the individual's assessed diagnostic profile, the system's software describes a person's learning strengths and weaknesses, prescribes a variety of personalized accommodations, and includes a framework in which the instructor and consumer can work together to design a learning plan using recommended accommodations.

Importance of Promoting a Learning Partnership

In too many instances, adults who are struggling learners become dependent on instructors for all aspects of learning. This dependency continues to promote helplessness. Without an instructor's attention, adult learners in basic skills programs who were previously unsuccessful in meeting their educational goals cannot seem to ask for the help they need, often drop out of basic skills and literacy programs, and do not meet their stated learning goals (Quigley, 1994). To stay committed and to move

Figure 7.1.   Components of PowerPath to Adult Basic Learning system.

toward achieving the stated learning outcomes, the adult learner needs to be actively involved with the instructor in an interdependent partnership (Fowler & Scarborough, 1992; Imel, 1994; Mace, 1992; Perin, 1994).

PowerPath addresses this problem by making the consumer and the instructor partners. From the initial intake interview to developing a learning plan, the system integrates the individual learner into the learning process as an active participant. Individuals are integral partners in developing learning plans to meet their needs and in evaluating their own progress. The partnership between the instructor and the consumer broadens the role of instructor, moving beyond that of a traditional teacher to one of a facilitator of learning. The instructor is guided in this process by a variety of suggested approaches listed in the Individual Report targeting the emotional, social, and instruction supports needed by the consumer to become an active partner in the learning process.

Importance of Learning How to Learn

In the fast-paced society of the United States, change is a given. Today's state-of-the-art technology is quickly replaced by tomorrow's cutting-edge developments. Knowing how to learn has become more essential than what one knows. Individuals who know how to learn, how to work with other people, how to accomplish tasks, and how to ask for help when they need it are the people whom employers want to hire (Carnevale, Gainer, & Meltzer, 1990). Adults struggling to learn basic skills generally have little insight into how they need to learn and master new information or new skills (Brier, 1994). PowerPath provides such insight by profiling both learning strengths *and* learning weaknesses. These strengths and weaknesses help identify how a person learns and are used as the basis for the prescribed accommodations included in the Individual Report. When followed, these accommodations assist in making learning easier and the learning process more effective and efficient (Osher & Webb, 1994; Paris & Parecki, 1993). Equally important, PowerPath also identifies approaches to learning that should be avoided because the individual's information-processing weaknesses can have a direct impact on learning efficiency.

HISTORICAL DEVELOPMENT OF POWERPATH

PowerPath (Weisel, 1993) builds on the Adult Basic Education (ABE) screening known as the London Procedure (Jordan, 1993; Travis, 1979; Travis, Weisel, & White, 1979; Weisel, 1977, 1979, 1980). In 1974, when the London Procedure was conceived, numerous tools were available to screen for and diagnose LD in children, but none was designed either to screen for or assess LD in adults. It was the author's central hypothesis that, as children with LD became adults, these LD would continue.

From 1976 to 1981, the London Procedure was widely used throughout the United States. Instructors and administrators from basic skills programs in 33 states were trained in the administration and implementation of the procedure. The London Procedure attempted to be comprehensive rather than specific, covering multiple facets of information processing and including both a screening of visual and auditory functions and a screening for breakdowns in visual, auditory, and language processing. It sampled a broad spectrum of abilities instead of only one or two domains. Offering a standardized and reliable assessment battery, the procedure screened adult learners for breakdowns in information processing, produced a profile of learning strengths and weaknesses, and recommended instructional interventions based on the adult's assessed strengths and weaknesses.

The London Procedure was not intended to take the place of a traditional evaluation of LD, nor was it designed to offer a precise description of an individual's disability or degree of impairment. Rather, it was intended as a measure that offered a systematic, standardized approach for identifying adults at risk for being clinically diagnosed as having LD (Travis, 1979; Weisel, 1979). As the London Procedure evolved into Power-Path, the basic premise did not change. Therefore, PowerPath does not diagnose LD. Instead, through a statistically determined weighting of assessment scores, the system can be used to predict which adults may be diagnosed as having a learning disability if tested by a licensed clinician (Weisel, 1987).

Developmental Phases, Pilot Tests, and Additional Studies

The developmental phases of the 1979 version of the London Procedure included three pilot tests with participants in Ohio ABE programs. These pilot studies were important in shaping the battery of tests and the initial strategies used to assess adult students in their efforts in building basic reading, writing, and math skills. Developmentally, the strategies grew from a combination of good teaching practices; secondary reviews of research in the field of LD; a review of the literature on adult learning, cognitive psychology, and behavior modification; and trial and error. Intervention strategies began to accumulate with the first versions and continued throughout the development of PowerPath. The strategies evolved from remedial and compensatory techniques to include holistic accommodations that support the learner's emotional, social, and learning needs (Brier, 1994; Jordan, 1996a, 1996b; Osher & Webb, 1994).

   Phase One: Screening Tool Development (1974–1975)   Phase one included substantiation of the need for a diagnostic and planning tool for adults with learning difficulties. A review of the literature and a series of strategic key informant interviews revealed that most often LD (not resulting from a lack of education) were defined as dysfunctions within the neurological system. Based on a review of the literature and the key informant interviews, an advisory team consisting of researchers and practitioners defined an initial set of constructs. The advisory team represented the fields of adult learning, LD, reading, optometry, speech and hearing, neuropsychology, and cognitive psychology.

   The task of the advisory team was to develop a broad-based, standardized, and reliable screening tool that could be administered by practitioners for the purposes of 1) detecting individuals who were at risk for being diagnosed as having LD, 2) identifying individuals who had significant weaknesses in aspects of processing information that led to learning difficulties, 3) locating areas of learning strengths and learning weaknesses, and 4) recommending interventions based on the results of the screening that could expedite learning (Weisel, 1977).

   An information-processing model (Luria, 1973; Valett, 1973) was recommended by the advisory team as the basic framework on which to build the screening. The basic components involved in processing information were considered to be the core components involved in the learning process. In general, these include the following:

Input modalities	Vision
	Auditory
	Kinesthetic
	Tactile
Mediation processes	Receive
	Decode
	Perceive
	Analyze
	Integrate
Output modalities	Verbal
	Nonverbal gestures
	Movement

During the first years of the project, the advisory team recommended five domains as assessment areas that could be the broad base of a screening for breakdowns in information processing. These were visual functioning, auditory functioning, reading encoding and decoding (language processing), visual processing, and auditory processing. These five general domains extended over multiple aspects of information processing. The initial constitutive definition (and corresponding operations definition) of key elements in the screening contained approximately 30 different components within the five main domains that were thought to be critical for successful learning (Weisel, 1977).

The process of developing a screening battery to reflect the five domains and assess adults included a variety of initiatives. Several standardized assessments were available for many of these components. The advisory team researched and identified tests that would assess each of the critical components and be easily administered by an instructor. Considering the resource issues (human and fiscal) related to the administration of lengthy assessments in ABE programs, the goal was to reduce the number of tests and test items so that each item and test would provide the maximum amount of information in the least amount of time. In some instances, a complete test was recommended; in other instances, only part of a test was identified as fitting into the battery. The content validity of each measure was assessed by members of the advisory team in relation to the specific aspects of the total construct. Face validity, content validity, and procedural authenticity were assessed by those team members with experience related to adults with low-level academic skills.

Phase Two: Pilot Testing   Only one of the tests, the Visual Function Screening, was developed and standardized separately so that it could be part of the trial battery (Saladin, 1975). In the following sections, the development of the visual functions screening is reviewed along with a description of pilot tests one, two, and three, conducted with adults attending ABE programs in multiple locations throughout Ohio.

Visual Function Validity Study (1975)   During the summer of 1975, Dr. James Saladin, Director of the Orthoptics Clinic at The Ohio State University College of Optometry, created a vision screening for adults that could be administered by a nonclinician. After initial, minor modification, the Visual Function Screening battery provided a valid vision screening with approximately a 10% overreferral and underreferral rate. These results compare more favorably than any other vision-screening procedure conducted by nonprofessional visual examiners.

After completion of this study, the Visual Function Screening was added to the other assessments that had been selected for pilot testing.

Pilot Test One: Initial Trial (1975–1976)   A sample of 81 randomly selected adults was used to conduct the first pilot test. The sample was drawn from five ABE programs in Ohio. The age range of the sample was 18–60+ years, with most of the sample being between 21 and 40 years of age. The test battery in the first pilot, containing 31 tests, was administered to the sample. On the basis of the analysis of the responses from the 81 tested adults in pilot test one, the entire procedure was modified and the number of items per test was altered. The subsequent battery included 22 tests with a total of 329 items. Several tests were dropped from the battery, whereas others were modified based on whether the test significantly correlated with a subject's academic ability (or lack thereof). An item analysis was then performed on each significant test to determine the item's relationship to the participant's overall academic ability. Some test items were altered to improve the test's reliability. These changes were based on a statistical review of each test and each test item. The review included the following procedures: item analyses, factor analyses, explorations of correlations between and among test items and tests, a review of individual test results with results from academic assessments, and participant and examiner evaluations of the tests (Weisel, 1977, 1979). These tests and test items were considered as key or critical aspects of information processing that should be included in a diagnostic screening to identify adults at high risk of being clinically diagnosed as having LD (Weisel, 1993).

Pilot Test Two: Revised Version Trial Plus Internal Consistency (1976–1977)   The revised collection of tests and items was used in pilot test two with a group of 30 adults randomly sampled from four additional ABE programs in Ohio. This sample had demographics similar to those of the participants in pilot test one. Reliability, descriptive statistics, and correlations were computed by combining data from the samples of pilot tests one and two (Weisel, 1977). The results of these analyses, combined with the advisory team's review of preliminary data, determined the final selection of 22 tests that made up the 1977 version of the London Procedure, which has, with little modification, become the current diagnostic screening component of PowerPath.

Pilot Test Three: Utilization of Pretest–Posttest Analysis for Identification of Alterable Test Scores (1977–1978)   The 22 tests selected in pilot test two were used in the third pilot test. This test included 196 adults from nine Ohio ABE programs referred based on an instructor's use of an observation checklist (Jordan, 1977). The checklist was created to identify adults with possible LD. Examiners in each site were trained, monitored, and observed for interrater and intrarater reliability in test administration and scoring. All of the adults referred and tested with the London Procedure were noted as having multiple areas of information-processing weaknesses.

The third pilot was a one-group pretest–posttest design. Because some participants dropped out between the administration of the pretests and posttests, the final number of individuals used in the data analysis was 110 of the original 196. The purpose of the pretest–posttest design was to determine the extent to which the characteristics measured by the London Procedure would remain stable. The participants were administered the screening, were offered an average of 53 contact hours of instruction in basic skills (as determined by an academic assessment) using recommended strategies within the London Procedure to support learning strengths while accommodating weaknesses, and then were retested. Results suggested that many of the characteristics were addressable and did change (Weisel, 1979). As might be expected, those test results that remained mostly consistent were functional assessments, including the plus lens, near acuity, and auditory functioning. The tests on which the most gains were noted were in visual-motor integration, auditory comprehension and sequencing, reading encoding and decoding, and binocularity.

Internal consistency reliability, using Cronbach's alpha, was determined from data collected from all three pilot studies (except for the visual function scales of distance acuity and plus lens test, which used only data from pilot tests one and two). The internal consistency reliability was generally good, with coefficients ranging from .52 (auditory comprehension) to .67 and .69 (eye–hand motor coordination and motor free test), .74 (auditory functions), .79 (random numbers), .80 (binocularity), .82 and .83 (words in context and visual-motor integration, respectively), .95 (distance acuity, right eye), .98 (distance acuity, left eye; near acuity, right and left eyes), and .99 and 1.00 (plus lens, right and left eyes, respectively). Tests in the area of reading encoding and decoding were not a consistent part of the battery when the studies were compiled (Weisel, 1979). On the basis of these results, the test of auditory comprehension was altered by rewording several questions that appeared possibly ambiguous and by changing some of the vocabulary in the test passage. Although a statistical analysis was not conducted on the test, qualitative reports indicate that the results are far more consistent.

The London Procedure: Associated Studies

Job Corps: Determining the Strength–Weakness Criterion (1978–1979)   In 1978, the London Procedure was selected by the U.S. Department of Labor to determine the prevalence of learning difficulties and potential disabilities in Job Corps consumers. The study included 404 randomly selected consumers from 10 Job Corps sites (Travis et al., 1979). The scores correlated positively, providing statistically significant coefficients with the Reading Job Corps Screening and the Mathematics Job Corps Screening scores.

Job Corps' London Procedure data were used to further strengthen previously established criteria for determining test scores as a strength or a weakness. In addition, a level of severity was determined based on the number of tests that did not meet criteria (Travis et al., 1979). The levels ranged from none to low, moderate, high, and extreme. These levels of difficulty were further refined in the 1983–1985 study with the Ohio Department of Rehabilitation and Corrections and The Ohio State University (Weisel, 1987).

Dropout Validation Study: Methodological Considerations for Administration of the London Procedure (1979–1980)   The Ohio Department of Education provided funding for a 1-year study of ABE program "dropouts." The purpose of this project was to identify students at high risk as well as key program variables that increase the probability of student retention and goal attainment. The findings of this study indicated that several key variables had an impact on student retention and goal attainment. Those critical elements of a basic skills program were use of an in-depth intake process, use of multimodality materials and equipment, and variable time options for attending the ABE program (Weisel, White, & Travis, 1980).

Central Ohio Psychiatric Hospital; Use of the London Procedure with an Inpatient Psychiatric Population and the Development of an Intake Interview (1980–1985)   During the years 1980–1985, the author was the Director for Educational Therapy at the Central Ohio Psychiatric Hospital. Individuals requesting and receiving educational services were assessed academically and vocationally before having the London Procedure administered. Through clinical observation, it was determined that many individuals entering the interview possessed a high degree of anxiety. When questioned, individuals (young and old) stated that the anxiety centered on returning to an educational setting. The intake procedure was therefore refined so that it was separate from the actual testing procedures. Second appointments were scheduled for assessments. At these appointments, individuals were more at ease and stated they had less anxiety than at the first interview.

Rehabilitation and Corrections: Construct Validity Assessment and Weighting of Subscale for the Total London Procedure Score (1983–1985)   From 1983 to 1985, the Ohio Department of Rehabilitation and Corrections, in cooperation with The Ohio State University, supported a research project to determine the prevalence of learning difficulties in male prisoners. A sample of 98 inmates between the ages of 18 and 35 was selected at the Ohio State Reformatory in Mansfield. Ten instructors were trained to administer both the London Procedure (Weisel, 1979) and the Woodcock-Johnson Psycho-Educational Battery, Parts I and II (Woodcock & Johnson, 1977). The Woodcock-Johnson often has had widespread acceptance as a psychometric instrument used as part of a clinical diagnostic process for determining the presence or absence of LD (Hessler, 1982).

An analysis of the relationship between the Woodcock-Johnson and the London Procedure is described in Weisel (1987) and has helped to develop construct validity for the screening. Each of the Woodcock-Johnson subscales was correlated with the tests from the London Procedure. Twenty-one of the Woodcock-Johnson's 22 subscales correlated significantly with 18 of the London Procedure's 22 tests at significance levels of .01 or better. The outcome of this analysis led to the development of a weighting for London Procedure tests that could predict an individual's degree of learning difficulty as determined by the criteria developed for the full-scale score on the Woodcock-Johnson battery. Score weightings were used as a means to determine the final degree-of-difficulty score found in PowerPath to Adult Basic Learning and, optionally, for using PowerPath to predict individuals at risk of being clinically diagnosed as having LD (Weisel, 1993).

Juvenile Justice Study: Utilization of the Weighting Criteria for the Total London Procedure Score (1988–1989)   The Foundation for Children with Learning Disabilities provided funding to the Consortium, Inc.'s, Sentenced to Read program, in conjunction with the JTPA and juvenile court system in Morehead, Kentucky. This grant was awarded to conduct a study of the prevalence of learning difficulties in a sample of youth offenders (Bailey, 1989). The project was set up as a demonstration model to identify and implement a LD screening procedure to serve the juvenile courts and young offenders. The target group served through the program was made up of economically disadvantaged youth ages 14–21 who were at risk for learning difficulties.

The project sample included 28 individuals who did not complete high school. Seventy-five percent of the group had not previously been tested or received help for learning difficulties. This sample was used to test the degree-of-learning-difficulty weightings (London Procedure scores weighted to predict a Woodcock-Johnson full-scale score) as identified in the correction study (Weisel, 1987). Results indicated that 77% of the youth functioned at the mild difficulty level and that 35% had moderate to severe learning difficulties and would benefit by having a full clinical assessment for suspected LD.

Transforming the London Procedure into PowerPath

In 1990, the Ohio Department of Education funded the Literacy Initiative of Central Ohio to develop a centralized intake system for multiple literacy programs. The London Procedure was implemented as the core of the intake system, targeting vision and hearing functions, reading encoding and decoding, and visual and auditory processing. The present author, who consulted with the project, was able to pilot test new aspects for a revised version of the London Procedure, building on the research findings of the 1970s and 1980s. A formal in-depth intake interview was added (later becoming Step 1 of the PowerPath process) to address the immediate emotional needs of these new individuals, reduce anxiety, offer needed attention, begin a partnership, and enhance learner retention.

In 1991–1992, this effort was expanded to include basic skills sites in Kentucky and Nevada. This three-state pilot test included the revised intake interview, the Personal Profile, and a newly developed software system. In addition to the revisions described here, the site staff recommended that the program name be changed to connote a different approach to initiating literacy/basic skills services. Hence the name PowerPath to Adult Basic Learning was derived.

THE POWERPATH PROCESS

PowerPath offers a standardized process that includes an intake interview, a diagnostic screening, and a systematic framework for interventions. The PowerPath Process has evolved into five steps that lead the instructor and consumer from interview to intervention. The process helps the instructor to build a new model for working with adults who struggle with learning difficulties. The five steps work together to build a learning partnership between the consumer and the instructor:

Step 1: Build a personal profile.
Step 2: Screen for learning difficulties.

Step 3: Complete the power behind the process.
Step 4: Build the partnership.
Step 5: Set the path.

Here is a snapshot of how the PowerPath process works: A first-time consumer receives an orientation to the education program and schedules a time to complete an intake interview and screening. At the intake session (Steps 1 and 2), the intake interview is guided by the information and questions on the outside of the Personal Profile Folder. The diagnostic screening is administered using the Test Plates, Response Booklet, Vision Screening Kit, and audiometer. The screening is scored on the inside of the Personal Profile Folder. At the end of the intake session, the instructor provides some preliminary feedback to the consumer and schedules a follow-up session to review the complete results of the screening and recommended accommodations to improve learning success.

After the intake session, the instructor enters intake information and tests results into a computer loaded with PowerPath's software (Step 3). Using the data, Power-Path's software constructs an Individual Report containing an analysis of assessment results along with recommended strategies to accommodate learning difficulties and to maximize learning. Prior to printing the report, the instructor can (on screen) modify the report to add or delete accommodations, modify the analysis, or add comments.

At the follow-up session, the instructor and consumer review and annotate the Individual Report (Step 4). In reviewing the report, accommodations are selected and listed on a Crib Sheet. These strategies target interventions for "how to learn" and are used in developing Personal Learning Plans. If the consumer's vision or hearing has been identified as an impairment, then the Individual Report will print out a referral form. The final page in the Individual Report is a Partnership Contract. In completing the contract, the instructor and consumer determine how they will work together and set mutual expectations.

Using the strategies listed on the Crib Sheet, the instructor and consumer develop the first of many Personal Learning Plans (Step 5). The Personal Learning Plan combines the skills that need to be learned (results from skill-based or informal assessments) with PowerPath's strategies. Tasks are created to learn needed skills and materials are selected that will support how the consumer needs to learn. As part of this intervention process, the consumer determines dates for task completion and evaluates his or her own work. In developing and implementing the Personal Learning Plan, the consumer has a structured approach for *learning how to learn* and a path for building successful learning experiences. Once completed, a Personal Learning Plan can be updated and altered as needed. The interventions (selecting and using accommodations and practicing planning, organizing, and making judgments with the Personal Learning Plan) become the ongoing structure for building additional skills. With this overall picture in mind, the steps to the PowerPath process can be reviewed in more detail.

Step 1: Build a Personal Profile

The purpose of the intake interview is to collect information about the consumer and build rapport. The applicant is placed in the role of the expert about his or her own life. He or she is asked to give basic demographic and referral information and to identify his or her goal in attending the program (see Figures 7.2a and 7.2b). In addition, the consumer is asked about his or her educational, vocational, and health history; living

Personal Profile

1 Intake Information

Intake Date _____ / _____ / _____

Examiner _____

Agency _____

Service Site _____

Service Location (Select one)

1 ☐ School Bldg.   7 ☐ Work Site
2 ☐ Comm. College   8 ☐ Library
3 ☐ University   9 ☐ Com. Based Org.
4 ☐ Learning Center 10 ☐ Home/Homebase
5 ☐ Correctional Facility 11 ☐ Other _____
6 ☐ Facility for Disabled

Instruction Level (Select one)

Beg 0 - 5.9   Int 6 - 8.9   Adv 9 - 12.9

ABLE   1 ☐   2 ☐   3 ☐
       4 ☐   5 ☐   6 ☐

Exit Information

Circle N=No Y=Yes

Total hours of instruction _____

Movement to a higher level: N   Y

Objectives completed: N   Y

Instruction Level (Select one)

Beg 0 - 5.9   Int 6 - 8.9   Adv 9 - 12.9

ABLE   1 ☐   2 ☐   3 ☐
       4 ☐   5 ☐   6 ☐

ESOL

Reasons for separation (Mark all that apply)

N Y Health   N Y Moved
N Y Child care   N Y Became employed
N Y Transportation   N Y Other: _____
N Y Family   N Y End of service year
N Y Class location   N Y Unknown
N Y Lack of interest   N Y Completed goal
N Y Class time/schedule N Y Instruction not helpful

2 Complete the following information with the applicant

Last Name _____ First Name _____ Mid. Initial _____ S S # _____

Street Address _____ Apt. # _____

City _____ State _____ Zip Code _____

Day Phone # (_____) _____ Preferred Contact Time _____ : _____ ☐ AM ☐ PM   Eve. Phone # (_____) _____

Emergency Contact: _____ Emergency Phone: (_____) _____

Sex   ☐ M   ☐ F
Glasses ☐ No ☐ Yes
Handed   ☐ L   ☐ R

Date of Birth _____ / _____ / _____
(Month/Day/Year)

Age _____

Ethnic Group

1 ☐ Am. Indian/Alaskan Native   4 ☐ Hispanic
2 ☐ Asian/Pacific Islander   5 ☐ White
3 ☐ Black   6 ☐ Mult-Ethnic

Citizenship

1 ☐ U.S.   2 ☐ Other: _____

Circle N=No Y=Yes

N Y New to this program   N Y In correctional program
N Y Returning to this program   N Y Institutionalized
N Y In a job training program   N Y Immigrant
N Y Employed   N Y Limited English proficiency
N Y Unemployed (but looking)   N Y Receives public assistance
N Y Unemployed (not available) N Y Family literacy
N Y Homeless   N Y Urban
N Y Workplace Literacy   N Y Rural
N Y Disabled   N Y Migrant farm worker
N Y Veteran

Goals Achieved
(Mark all that apply)

N Y Passed GED / in process   N Y Entered other ed. / training program   N Y Advanced in job status
N Y Obtained a High School diploma   N Y Received US citizenship   N Y Removed from public assistance
N Y Maintained employment   N Y Registered to vote / or voted the first time   N Y Received a driver's license
                                           N Y Improved life skills   N Y Other: _____ (Specify)
                                           N Y Became employed

3

Referred By

1 ☐ Individual _____ (please specify)
2 ☐ Agency _____ (please specify)

Primary Reason for Referral (Select one)

1 ☐ Intake into basic skills program   4 ☐ Screening for adult learning problems
2 ☐ Intake into continuing ed. program   5 ☐ Other
3 ☐ Intake into literacy program

What is your single most important reason for coming to this program? (Select one)

1 ☐ Get a job as a _____   6 ☐ Get a better job
2 ☐ Feel better about myself   7 ☐ Help children
3 ☐ Read the Bible   8 ☐ Become more independent
4 ☐ Obtain GED   9 ☐ Go to college
5 ☐ Get into a job training/education program for _____   10 ☐ Improve English
                                           11 ☐ Get off public assistance
                                           12 ☐ Other

Figure 7.2a. Front side of the PowerPath Personal Profile folder, which is filled out by the instructor and the consumer.

143

4 | Ask the next set of questions open-ended and select the best response.
Circle N=No Y=Yes

Educational History

What is the highest level of school you completed?
1☐ 2☐ 3☐ 4☐ 5☐ 6☐ 7☐ 8☐ 9☐ 10☐ 11☐ 12☐
13☐ GED 14☐ some College 15☐ Other:

Were you ever tested for having difficulty in learning?
1☐ No   3☐ Yes - in a vocational school
2☐ Yes - in a public school 4☐ Yes (other) -

N Y Were you ever told you have a "learning disability?"
If YES, when were you told and who told you?
Approx. year:
Relationship of person:

N Y When in school, were you in Special Education classes?

N Y As an adult, have you ever been in a program to help you improve your basic skills?

If YES, where did you attend?
N Y Community Literacy Program   N Y ABLE   N Y Other
N Y Job Training Program   N Y Community College

Vocational History

N Y Are you currently employed?
If YES, complete the following:
Job type
Company name
Length of stay _____ (round off to the nearest number of years)

Have you worked any other jobs?
Job type:
Length of Stay: (round off to the nearest number of years) _____
Job type:
Length of Stay: (round off to the nearest number of years) _____
Job type:
Length of Stay: (round off to the nearest number of years) _____

Have you had any special job training:
1 ☐ No 2 ☐ Yes, as a _____   But did not complete training
        3 ☐ Yes, as a _____   Training completed

Health History

N Y Do you have any health problems that might interfere with your learning?
If Yes (specify)

N Y Have any of your immediate family members been identified as having a learning problem?
If Yes (specify relationship)

Have you had a check-up in the last three years?
N Y Medical   N Y Dental
N Y Vision   N Y Hearing

Living Arrangements

Including yourself, how many people are currently living in your home? _____ (number)

How many children are currently living with you? _____

How old are they ?
(Insert # into appropriate category)
1- 5 years _____ 6 - 10 years _____ 11 -15 years _____ 1 6 - 20 years _____

How long have you lived in your current home?
1☐ 1-12 months 2☐ 1 -2 years 3☐ 3 - 5 years 4☐ 6 + years

Social Support

N Y When you have problems in your life is there someone you can turn to for help?
If YES, Who is it? _____ (Relationship of person identified)

Who knows you are coming to this program?
N Y No one   N Y Family   N Y Employer   N Y Friends   ☐ Other

Community Involvement

N Y Do you have a library card?
N Y Are you registered to vote?
N Y Do you have a driver's license?

What do you like to do BEST when you have some free time?
(select one)
1 ☐ No free time   3 ☐ Mechanics   5 ☐ Social activities   7 ☐ Hunting/fishing
2 ☐ Self-improvement 4 ☐ Watch TV   6 ☐ Physical activity   8 ☐ Hobby 9 ☐ Other

Service Supports

What days and times do you have available to be in a program to improve your basic skills?
(check appropriate boxes for time of day)

N Y Monday   ☐ Morning ☐ Afternoon ☐ Evening
N Y Tuesday   ☐ Morning ☐ Afternoon ☐ Evening
N Y Wednesday ☐ Morning ☐ Afternoon ☐ Evening
N Y Thursday   ☐ Morning ☐ Afternoon ☐ Evening
N Y Friday   ☐ Morning ☐ Afternoon ☐ Evening
N Y Saturday   ☐ Morning ☐ Afternoon ☐ Evening
N Y Sunday   ☐ Morning ☐ Afternoon ☐ Evening

What transportation is available to you to get to this program?
1 ☐ None 2 ☐ Car 3 ☐ Bus 4 ☐ Family/Friend 5 ☐ Other _____

Do you have any child care needs in coming to this program?
☐ No   ☐ Yes... (Specify) _____

Figure 7.2b. Back side of the PowerPath Personal Profile folder, which is filled out by the instructor and the consumer. (© 1996. The TLP Group. All rights reserved.)

arrangements; social supports; community involvement; and service supports needed for retention (e.g., transportation, childcare).

Step 2: Screen for Learning Differences

In Step 2, the applicant is given a set of tests to determine his or her strengths and weaknesses in key areas of information processing that have been correlated to academic success. The Test Plates (see Figure 7.3) include easy-to-follow instructions and guidelines for accurate administration and test scoring. Tests responses are noted on the Diagnostic Screening Form located on the inside of the Personal Profile Folder. The entire diagnostic screening can be administered in 90 minutes or less. Assessments can be separated by test area and administered in multiple sessions without affecting reliability or validity. The screening includes visual and auditory functions, reading encoding and decoding, and visual and auditory processing.

Visual Functions   Good vision is a critical component in learning basic skills. The eyes must align, focus, work together, and sustain clear vision for basic reading, writing, and computation. Without good vision, building basic skills can be both frustrat-

Figure 7.3.   Example of Test Plates for PowerPath system.

ing and difficult. The vision screening identifies individuals needing a referral to a licensed vision specialist.

The Vision Screening Kit (see Figure 7.4) contains all equipment necessary to screen visual functioning for distance acuity (at a distance of 20 feet), near acuity (at reading distance), and binocularity (using both eyes for focusing, moving, aligning, and at reading distance). Once test data are entered into the program, the software will include an analysis of the consumer's vision function strengths and weaknesses in the Individual Report. Specific accommodations will be included if any weaknesses are noted. A Vision Referral Form is printed listing the specific tests on which the consumer did not meet passing criteria.

Auditory Functions   Adequate hearing is an important element of processing information in a learning environment. Listening to instructions, participating in discussions, socializing with instructors and peers, and using tape-recorded materials all require a basic level of auditory functioning. Screening of auditory functions can identify individuals unable to hear a range of standard sounds. The audiometer included in the PowerPath Starter Kit is both high-quality and durable. When screening results are entered into the software, the Individual Report provides an analysis of the consumer's auditory strengths and weaknesses. If a weakness is noted, an Auditory Functions Referral Form is generated as part of the Individual Report.

Figure 7.4.   Vision Screening Kit for PowerPath system.

Reading Encoding and Decoding   The tests included for the area of reading encoding and decoding are not designed to be an extensive assessment of reading ability. Instead, the consumer's reading and writing samples are used to identify strengths and weaknesses in *how* language sounds and symbols are processed. The five tests in this area are Reading of Single Words, Alphabet, Days of the Week, Months of the Year, and Auditory to Motor (Jordan, 1977, 1989). A diagnostic error analysis (Weisel, 1993) is used to evaluate a consumer's reading and writing samples. Based on the patterns of errors and level of reading, the PowerPath's software recommends accommodations and strategies to most effectively improve reading skills.

Visual Processing   Although it is important to accurately see images, it is critical to be able to accurately process and interpret what is seen. Processing visual information requires the ability to decode, perceive, analyze, organize, integrate, and interpret visual information. In most situations, this highly complex process happens within seconds. The visual processing assessments identify strengths and weaknesses in spatial relations, short-term visual memory, figure-ground relationships, visual motor integration, position in space, visual discrimination, and eye–hand motor coordination.

Auditory Processing   Just as visual functioning and visual processing are different levels of "seeing," the ability to hear and the ability to understand what is heard are different levels of "hearing." Auditory processing includes the ability to analyze, organize, understand, and recall information that is heard. The screening assesses strengths and weaknesses in auditory comprehension, including recall of facts and making inferences, sequential short-term memory (random numbers), and short-term memory with comprehension (words in context).

Completion of Step 2   When the assessments are finished, the consumer takes a short break while the instructor totals correct responses, completes the strength/weakness profile, and prepares a simple overview of the screening results. The Response Booklet contains the format and structure for providing this personal feedback to the consumer. Used to build insight and dispel fears of failure, the feedback is positive, upbeat, hopeful, and looks to begin to build the partnership between the program staff and the consumer. A future date is set to meet and review the complete Individual Report and begin developing a Personal Learning Plan.

Step 3: Complete the Power Behind the Process

PowerPath employs a proprietary, user-friendly software that analyzes all intake and screening data and produces a personalized Individual Report. Entering data for a single consumer can be completed in 5 minutes or less. Once a consumer's data has been entered into the computer, the software will analyze the data and display on the computer screen an Individual Report. A special software feature allows the user to easily edit the Individual Report prior to printing. With this feature, additional recommendations, observations, and comments can be added to the Individual Report.

Two copies of the Individual Report are automatically printed—one for the program/instructor and one for the consumer. Each report includes the following:

- Personal Profile—a recap of the information collected during the intake interview
- Diagnostic Screening Summary—a one page summary of the consumer's strengths and weaknesses
- Degree of Learning Difficulty Score—a weighted score used to predict required service accommodations and levels of learning difficulty
- Diagnostic Screening Analysis—an explanation of assessment results

- Service Accommodations—the emotional, social, and structural supports and strategies needed for the consumer to build self-esteem as a learner, develop independent (interdependent) learning skills, and transfer "learning how to learn" skills from academic to real life situations
- Learning Accommodations—recommended strategies that build on strengths, compensate for weaknesses, and target the development of basic skills in academic and workplace environments
- Partnership Contract—a guide for setting mutual expectations toward a successful learning experience
- Referral Forms—for necessary follow-ups on vision and/or hearing weaknesses uncovered in the screening

The Individual Report is a powerful piece of information for consumers. Using the principles of empowerment, it validates their strengths, offers insight into how they learn, and provides ways to help them learn. The report is a document the consumer may keep and share with anyone or any organization he or she chooses. The Response Booklet contains a Release of Information Form that, when completed, allows the program to share the report with anyone designated by the consumer.

Steps 4 and 5: Build the Partnership and Set the Path

Adults with learning difficulties demand structure, involvement, and practice planning and critical thinking skills (Deshler, Schumaker, Lenz & Ellis, 1984; Brookfield, 1986; Juromo, 1989). Steps 4 and 5 promote the learning partnership, offer insight, and provide a systematic intervention for the learning process. By participating in this part of the process, the consumer has an opportunity to practice critical thinking skills in addition to a structure for planning. Steps 4 and 5 target modeling, building, and practicing the skills involved in "learning how to learn."

The Individual Report   The instructor meets with the consumer to review the analysis of the screening results and recommended accommodations. The Individual Report has been designed for the instructor and the consumer to review together. Reviewing with the consumer and annotating the report with the consumer's comments is an essential part of the PowerPath Process. In this process, the consumer is presented with information that can be used to gain personal insight into how he or she learns and feel validated that his or her input is an important part of the learning process. As the report is reviewed, the instructor can use a pen or marker to annotate the report with comments made by the consumer and highlight accommodations to adapt the learning environment to meet the consumer's needs. Selected accommodations are then listed on the Crib Sheet (see Figure 7.5).

The Individual Report includes at least one additional form and possibly two. If the consumer showed a weakness in either visual or auditory functioning, a referral form is printed noting the specific area(s) of weakness. A Partnership Contract is also printed as part of the Individual Report. This contingency-based contract outlines expectations for both the consumer and the instructor. The open-ended outline offers the opportunity for a dialogue around the key elements of participating in a skill building program. The process of discussing expectations and putting them into writing helps to tune both partners into how they will work together to achieve the consumer's long-term and short-term goal.

The Personal Learning Plan   The intervention portion of the PowerPath Process is modeled in the form of a Personal Learning Plan (see Figure 7.6). This structured

PowerPath   *Crib Sheet*

Name   *David Buckles*
Date   *3/5/97*

Page	Service	Learning	Strategy	Date Used
1	√		*Build on strengths "math, autos, sports, energy"*	
2	√		*Use 'actions learning' -- see, say, write*	
2	√		*Work with a friend or friends*	
3	√		*Celebrate every Friday -- bring a magazine to read!*	
4		√	*Keep work times short -- take a break every 15 min*	
4		√	*Use a marker to keep place when reading*	
6		√	*Read out loud -- read with a friend*	
7		√	*Use the 'chunk' approach for spelling*	
7		√	*Keep desk area clear of extra papers and books*	
8		√	*Write in books and on work pages -- don't copy*	
8		√	*Use a computer when possible*	
9		√	*Have directions written out for you*	
9		√	*After reading -- talk about what you have read*	
9		√	*"Did you say.." Check out what you heard!*	

Figure 7.5.   Sample Crib Sheet for PowerPath system.

approach for identifying 1) skills to be learned, 2) selecting strategies to learn the needed skills, 3) choosing tasks and materials to support the strategy and build needed skills, 4) determining a time frame, and 5) evaluating the learner's efforts is intentionally similar to executive brain functioning (planning, organizing, carrying out behaviors, and making judgments). Simply stated, the plan develops the framework to organize the steps in learning that often elude the learner who is experiencing difficulties. To build a Personal Learning Plan, the instructor and consumer work together using results from academic assessments with the learning strategies listed on the Crib Sheet. Activities and materials are selected to build needed skills in the ways that the consumer can most effectively learn. By involving the consumer in developing the plan,

PowerPath

Personal Learning Plan

Name: _Armando_

Long-Term Goal: _To become a truck driver_

Short-Term Goal: _improve reading/writing to get driver's license and read orders_ **Dates:** _9/10_ **to** _9/25_

Personal Learning Strengths: _Good at fixing cars, friendly, pretty good at seeing and hearing, can copy pictures and words, good with remembering what words look like, good at listening_

Skill *What*	Strategy *How*	Materials	Complete by	√	How I did	What I learned
Reading: "*Vocabulary*" learn lots of new words Use new words to read and write Life words	Write and read stories together. - Make cards of new words.	Paper, Pencil, cards Tape recorder	9/15	√	pretty good	names of streets names of friends
	Type words onto computer. - Make sentences using the new words.	Computer and cards	9/25	√	not so good	typing is hard I have to take my time
Trucking words	Work with team to find 25 important words in truck magazines	Truck magazines highlighter	9/13	√	good	lots of words to learn
	Write down words on cards Practice reading	Pencil and cards Tape recorder	9/25	√	real good	I get stuck and can ask for help
Driving words/signs	Put road signs on cards Study cards Tell what the road signs mean.	Driver's License book sissors and tape	9/25	---	Didn't get book	Couldn't get to pick up a book yet
Word attack skills *Comprehension*	Practice reading with Tutor	Building Skills Books	9/25	√	Did Book 1 Started book 2	I'm getting good!

Figure 7.6. Sample Personal Learning Plan for PowerPath system. (From the TLP Group (© 1994. All rights reserved.))

the consumer begins to learn the skills the consumer needs to work through new learning situations. The Personal Learning Plan offers a short-term, time-limited approach that breaks learning new skills into manageable bits. Based on the consumer's degree of learning difficulty, learning plans should be written for periods of 1–2 days and up to 1–2 weeks.

In addition to the initial five steps of the PowerPath process, administrators can find PowerPath to be very useful in providing two additional reports. These reports, the Service Summary and the Annual Report, add to program accountability and give an accurate profile of consumers. The Service Summary (see Figure 7.7) is an aggregate report of intake and diagnostic screening results for all individuals entered into the system's software. The data are reported in percentages. At the top of each report page is the total number of consumers (N) on which the data are based. A Service Summary can be produced for each individual program site. Information provided in the summary can be used by an organization to prepare program reports, to brief advisory boards, and to advocate for additional resources within a community. Many PowerPath sites use the information contained in the Service Summary for developing grant proposals.

The Annual Report can be generated only after exit data on consumers has been entered into the software. When the Annual Report is generated, it will include only data about individuals who meet the U.S. Office of Education's program consumer criteria (i.e., attending 12 or more hours of instruction or achieving personal objectives). Consumer data are combined and presented both in percentages and in table formats corresponding to standard table formats requested by most federal and state funding authorities. An Annual Report can be generated for each site, allowing for multisite statistics.

Administration of PowerPath

PowerPath is a process that includes a variety of assessments and steps. Some of these steps may be familiar to staff in basic skill and literacy programs. If the individual using PowerPath is not familiar with psychological testing, counseling and developing learning plans with consumers, then he or she will most likely benefit from attending a PowerPath training session. Those individuals that are familiar with the process included in PowerPath will still need to practice the process to achieve the skills that are required for accurate administration and implementation of the PowerPath process. The User's Guide, Test Plates, Personal Profile Folder, Diagnostic Screening Form, Response Booklet, Crib Sheets, and Personal Learning Plans have been designed to lead both the new and experienced user through the assessment and intervention process to achieve maximum success.

Are the Assessments Administered Individually or in Groups? PowerPath differs from most standardized adult assessments in that it is individually administered and requires personal interaction between the examiner and the consumer. Most of the adults coming to basic skills programs have anxieties about learning, lack positive past experiences (Osher & Webb, 1994), and need personalized attention. PowerPath provides a personalized setting with personalized attention. PowerPath can be given in segments to meet the needs of the program and the consumers. For example, the information on the outside of the Personal Profile Folder might be collected as part of the initial orientation, whereas the Diagnostic Screening (on the inside of the folder) can be completed at the second meeting. Some programs might prefer to screen vision and auditory functions all at one time for all consumers.

How Much Time Will the Process Take? PowerPath can be administered in approximately 90 minutes. The actual amount of time the process takes will vary based

Average age	37.5	Native American	5.70%
16–24	11.4%	Asian/Pacific Islander	5.70%
25–44	65.7%	African American	22.9%
45–59	20.0%	Hispanic	17.1%
60+	2.90%	Caucasion	40.0%
		Missing	8.60%
Sex	51.4% (female)		
Glasses	22.9%		
Handed	45.7% (right)		

62.9% New to this program	2.90% In correctional program
22.9% Returning to this program	2.90% Institutionalized
11.4% In job-training program	8.60% Immigrant
42.9% Employed	5.70% Limited English proficiency
28.6% Unemployed (but looking)	14.3% Receving public assistance
5.70% Unemployed (not available)	14.3% Family literacy
5.70% Homeless	57.1% Urban
8.60% With disability	25.7% Rural
5.70% Veteran	5.70% Migrant worker

Referred by: 40.0% An agency

Primary referral reason (percent):

31.4	Intake in basic skills program
17.1	Intake into continuing education program
11.4	Intake into literacy program
25.7	Screen for adult learning problems
2.90	Other reasons
11.4	Missing

Most improtant reason for coming to program (percent):

14.3	Get a job	5.70	Help my children
8.60	Feel better about self	17.1	Be more independent
5.70	Read the bible	5.70	Go to college
11.4	Obtain GED	5.70	Improve English
5.70	Get into job training	2.90	Other reasons
2.9	Get better job	5.70	Get off public assistance
		11.4	Missing

Educational History
Highest grade (percent)

5.70	Less than 7th grade	0.00	GED
25.7	7th, 8th, or 9th grade	2.90	Some college
45.7	10th or 11th grade	0.00	Other
8.60	High school graduate	11.4	Missing

Tested for difficulty with learning (percent)

74.3	No	0.00	GED
25.7	Yes (public school)	11.4	Missing
0.00	Yes (vocational school)		

Told had a learning disability: 20%   Special education: 28.6%

Figure 7.7.   Example of PowerPath Service Summary.

on a number of factors—the comfort of the examiner, the care taken in following the recommended procedures, the uniqueness of the individual being assessed, and the assessment environment. The *length* of time to administer the intake and diagnostic screening is not nearly as important as the *quality* of the time spent. Used as an intake system, PowerPath establishes the first important step in building a meaningful partnership among the examiner, the program, and the adult learner.

Who Can Administer PowerPath?   The PowerPath system can be administered by a wide variety of personnel. These include intake staff members, teachers, volunteer tutors, and counselors. Although administering the system does demand strong interpersonal skills, a background in psychometrics (i.e., formal training in test administration) is not required to administer or score the diagnostic assessment. PowerPath is highly structured, with specific instructions for both administering and scoring the diagnostic screening assessments. Following the specific instructions listed in the User's Guide and the wording noted on the Test Plates ensures high interrater reliability and assessment accuracy (Weisel, 1993). Although not mandatory, it is recommended that individuals administering PowerPath attend a certification training program and complete the case study requirements for certification. Certification is granted after an individual attends a 20-hour training program and completes and submits a specified case study. The training includes an overview of adult LD, accurate administration of the Diagnostic Screening, utilization of the software and reports, implementation of the interventions and accommodations, a special section on the neurological and cognitive constructs underlying learning and LD, effective practices for working differently with adults who learn differently, and a strategic plan for implementing PowerPath into adult education programs. Certification is initially granted for a 1-year period. Annual renewals are awarded when ongoing assessment information is provided. These structured requirements maintain the integrity of the certification and ensure that individuals who obtain certification retain a base level of competency.

CONCLUSION AND FUTURE DIRECTIONS

Developed as a screening system for use by adult educators to identify adults who are at high risk for being diagnosed as having LD, PowerPath to Adult Basic Learning has evolved since its inception as the London Procedure. During this time, the screening for breakdowns in information processing has become a more complete system that integrates a variety of multidisciplinary strategies and interventions into a comprehensive process that engages and empowers the consumer. Together the consumer and instructor collaborate to develop a learning plan based on a profile of assessed learning strengths and personal goals. In the PowerPath process, it is ultimately the consumer who evaluates the effectiveness of the selected accommodations and his or her own learning successes.

As the historical development of PowerPath has shown, the procedures are under constant review and refinement. A Spanish version of the procedures is being developed and standardized. In addition, new screening systems are being explored for the following:

- Attention-deficit/hyperactivity disorder screening and accommodations
- Scotopic sensitivity and visual tracking
- Workplace accommodations

REFERENCES

Bailey, C.J. (1989). *The LD connection: An incidence of learning problems in a sample study of youth offenders—project report.* Morehead, KY: The Consortium, Inc.

Brier, N. (1994). Psychological adjustment and adults with severe learning difficulties: Implications of the literature on children and adolescents with learning disabilities for research and practice. *Learning Disabilities, 5*(1), 15–27.

Brookfield, S.D. (1986). *Understanding and facilitating adult learning.* San Francisco: Jossey-Bass.

Carnevale, A.P., Gainer, L.J., & Meltzer, A.S. (1990). *Workplace basics: The essential skills employers want.* San Francisco: Jossey-Bass.

Deshler, D.D., Schumaker, J.B., Lenz, B.K., & Ellis, E. (1984). Academic and cognitive interventions with LD adolescents: Part II. *Journal of Learning Disabilities, 17,* 170–179.

Fowler, A., & Scarborough, H. (1992). *Adult literacy and learning disabilities: A summary and review* (Final Report, Year 2). Philadelphia: University of Pennsylvania, National Center on Adult Literacy.

Hessler, G.L. (1982). *Use and interpretation of the Woodcock-Johnson Psycho-Educational Battery.* Cambridge, MA: Teaching Resources.

Imel, S. (1994). *Guidelines for working with adult learners* (ERIC Digest 154). Columbus, OH: Center on Education and Training for Employment.

Jordan, D. (1977). *Dyslexia in the classroom.* Columbus, OH: Charles E. Merrill.

Jordan, D. (1989). *Jordan prescriptive tutorial reading program.* Austin, TX: PRO-ED.

Jordan, D. (1993). *Foreword.* In L.P. Weisel (Ed.), *PowerPath to adult basic learning.* Columbus, OH: The TLP Group.

Jordan, D. (1996a). *Overcoming dyslexia.* Austin, TX: PRO-ED.

Jordan, D. (1996b). *Teaching adults with learning disabilities.* Malabar, FL: Krieger Publishing Co.

Jurmo, P. (1989). The case for participatory literacy education. In A. Fingeret and P. Jurmo (Eds.), *Participatory literacy education* (pp. 17–28). San Francisco: Jossey-Bass.

Luria, A.R. (1973). *The working brain.* London: Penguin Books Ltd.

Mace, J. (1992). *Talking about literacy: Principles and practice of adult literacy education.* London: Routledge.

Osher, D., & Webb, L. (1994). *Adult literacy, learning disabilities and social context: conceptual foundations for a learner-centered approach.* Washington, DC: U.S. Department of Education, Office of Vocational and Adult Education.

Paris, S., & Parecki, A. (1993). *Metacognitive aspects of adult literacy* (Technical Report TR93-9). Philadelphia: University of Pennsylvania, National Center on Adult Literacy.

Perin, D. (1994). Adult students help shape their own education: active learner participation in a workplace basic education program. *Adult Basic Education, 4*(2), 94–104.

Quigley, A.B. (1994). *Understanding and overcoming resistance to adult literacy education.* University Park, PA: Institute for the Study of Adult Literacy.

Saladin, J. (1975). *A report on the validity study of the Visual Function Assessment screening battery.* Columbus: The Ohio State University College of Optometry.

Travis, G.Y. (1979). An adult educator views learning disabilities. *Adult Literacy and Basic Education, 8,* 79–85.

Travis, G.Y., Weisel, L.P., & White, A.L. (1979). *Job Corps Learning Problems Screening Project.* Washington, DC: U.S. Department of Labor.

Valett, R.E. (1973). *Learning disabilities.* Belmont, CA: Fearon Publishers, Inc.

Weisel, L.P. (1977). *The London Procedure: A screening, diagnostic, and teaching guide for adult learning problems.* Columbus: The Ohio Department of Education.

Weisel, L.P. (1979). *The London Procedure: A screening, diagnostic, and teaching guide for adult learning problems—Revised.* Columbus: The Ohio State University, Instructional Materials Lab.

Weisel, L.P. (1980). *Adult learning problems: insights, instruction, and implications* (Information Series 214). Columbus, OH: ERIC Clearinghouse for Adult, Career, and Vocational Education.

Weisel, L.P. (1987). *A comparative analysis of two diagnostic procedures for identification of adult learning problems in a male prison population.* Columbus: The Ohio State University.

Weisel, L.P. (1993). *PowerPath to adult basic learning.* Columbus, OH: The TLP Group.

Weisel, L.P., White, A.L., & Travis, G.Y. (1980). *Who is the ABE "high-risk" dropout student?* Columbus: The Ohio Department of Education.

Woodcock, R.W., & Johnson, M.B. (1977). *Woodcock-Johnson Psycho-Educational Battery.* Hingham, MA: Teaching Resources Corp.

8

Screening and Diagnosis of Dyslexia in Adults in the United Kingdom

Angela J. Fawcett and Roderick I. Nicolson

In this information age, fluent literacy skills are becoming even more important than they were for previous generations. Aaron, Chall, Durkin, Goodman, and Strickland (1990) estimated that the level of functional literacy required in the United States has risen to the equivalent of grade 12. They suggested that this reflects the increased demands for sophisticated skills within the workplace, in place of the simple life skills that would once have been adequate. However, it has been estimated that approximately 20% of adults in the United States are unable to understand or use printed materials that they encounter as part of their work or leisure (Stedman & Kaestle, 1987, cited in Fowler & Scarborough, 1993). The U.S. National Adult Literacy Survey (Kirsch, Jungeblut, Jenkins, & Kolstad, 1993) showed that almost a quarter of the adults tested performed at the lowest of five levels of proficiency. Similar difficulties have been found in the United Kingdom, where research showed that 24% of a large, nationally representative sample of 21-year-olds could not find basic information in a videotape recorder manual (Ekinsmyth & Bynner, 1994). Furthermore, there is a strong familial pattern in literacy disabilities. The U.K. National Child Development Study (Adult Literacy and Basic Skills Unit, 1993) noted that 48% of children with family histories of reading disabilities fell in the lowest quartile of reading performance[1]; this number rose to 72% for those who also came from an impoverished background. The impact of reading disabilities is compounded by the increasing need for literacy in employment, to the extent that many adults with learning disabilities

---

Names that are presented within the case studies for this chapter have been changed to preserve participant confidentiality.

[1]It has now been clearly established that there is a genetic component in reading (Pennington, 1995), with a marker on chromosome 6 and possibly one on chromosome 15.

(LD) may never find suitable employment. This situation places an even heavier responsibility on the education and employment systems to attempt to identify and remediate such difficulties (for reviews of factors in success, see Adelman & Vogel, 1990, 1993; and Vogel & Adelman, 1992).

It has been estimated that 5%–15% of individuals have dyslexia and therefore show unexpected difficulties in literacy (Badian, 1984; Jorm, Share, McLean, & Matthews, 1986; Lyon, 1994; Shaywitz, Shaywitz, Fletcher, & Escobar, 1990). A further 15% have a generalized literacy difficulty together with low intelligence—sometimes referred to as "garden variety" poor readers (Stanovich, 1988). In the United Kingdom, there is a legal requirement to provide support in education and employment for anyone with LD, but the nature of support in education depends on the individual need. Formal assessment usually requires testing by a fully trained psychologist, who in the United Kingdom must be licensed by the British Psychological Society to perform assessments of this type. Full psychometric testing takes between 3 and 4 hours and costs approximately $300. Unfortunately, the adults who are most in need of assessment and support are typically those least financially well placed to obtain help. Moreover, many adults with poor literacy skills lack the initiative to seek appropriate help, having acquired "learned helplessness" from their experiences of failure. Literacy difficulties for adults have frequently been compounded by the lack of recognition of dyslexia when they were at school. Most adults with dyslexia received no specialist support in school and were exposed to a watered-down curriculum leading to a progressive decline in motivation, opportunity, and skill—the so-called Matthew effect, based on a biblical reference to the poor becoming poorer (Stanovich, 1986).

Experienced practitioners have also noted that many adults and children with dyslexia have unusual styles of interaction and performance, probably linked to limitations in working memory and skill automatization (Gilroy & Miles, 1995; McLoughlin, Fitzgibbon, & Young, 1994). These difficulties may lead to problems with both interpersonal and organizational skills and thus to difficulties in holding down a job. The problem is clearly described by Augur, former Education Officer for the British Dyslexia Association:

> So many dyslexic people can't work for other people, because they're out of step with them and they have no concept of time, so they'd be late getting to work, or when they get to work they haven't got on with the job as fast as other people. You know these things are so important, particularly in adult life, these are the things you get sacked for, and they extract themselves from this painful situation and work for themselves. (1993, p. 17)

In view of these limitations and differences and their difficulties in successfully completing application forms, many adults with dyslexia find themselves in long-term unemployment. Even here, difficulties with literacy may prevent an unemployed adult from claiming the benefits to which he or she is entitled. The problem is again highlighted by Augur:

> "Look at the forms required to be filled in to get your benefits!" I said to one of the people at the Department of Health and Social Security, "How do you fill it in?" I mean, *I* would have problems filling it in, and I'm supposed to be an intelligent woman who can read. It may be easier to go and pinch money than it is to fill the form in to get it. (1993, p. 16)

However, many adults with dyslexia are gifted in other ways, for example, in terms of their creativity and spatial skills (West, 1991). Consequently, they could make a significant contribution to the nation, once given the support needed to allow them to improve their literacy. This could lead to substantial enhancements in quality of life for both the adults involved and their children.

THE ADULT DYSLEXIA SCREENING FEASIBILITY STUDY

Clearly, there is an acknowledged need to be able to assess adults for dyslexia more systematically and more effectively. Our approach to this problem benefited greatly from an international survey (Nicolson, Fawcett, & Miles, 1993) designed to assess the feasibility of large-scale screening for dyslexia in adults. The scenario that the respondents were asked to consider was initial testing by trained professionals in a job center (probably with computer support), probably involving subsequent referral to an appropriately qualified psychologist or adult literacy specialist for further testing and support. The project involved a complete literature survey of the field of adult literacy and diagnosis of dyslexia, a series of interviews with British experts on theoretical and applied aspects of dyslexia, and finally an international questionnaire study conducted with a wide range of dyslexia practitioners and researchers.

Two items are of particular significance here. It is interesting to note that although there was reasonable satisfaction overall with diagnosis in children, there was general dissatisfaction with diagnosis in adults. One major reason for this dissatisfaction is that reading ages on tests of single-word reading typically level off at about 17 years of age. Few tests are normed beyond school age, and so for adults it is not meaningful to calculate a discrepancy between the reading age obtained on such tests and that predicted from IQ scores. A further problem for diagnosis is that many children with dyslexia continue to improve at reading into adulthood, with the result that their reading level improves to within the typical range in terms of single-word reading. Yet they continue to experience difficulties in terms of rate and fluency, which means that their performance is impaired compared with that of their peers.

A second question was whether it might be possible to complete the testing in a single session. The respondents were near-unanimous on this issue: The vast majority preferred a two-stage process. There was also clear agreement that the first stage might possibly be achievable by a support professional (rather than a highly qualified psychologist) given an appropriate screening instrument, whereas it was vital that the second stage be undertaken by a suitably qualified and experienced psychologist or adult literacy specialist who would be able not only to undertake a detailed diagnosis but also to determine an appropriate support regimen.

In short, the survey established a clear consensus in the dyslexia community that was particularly impressive, given that the respondents were specialists whose opinions spanned the spectrum of approaches to dyslexia and adult literacy. There was consensus that new developments in computer technology made it feasible to introduce computer-supported testing procedures that do not require the direction of a trained clinician/diagnostician and could therefore be carried out cost-effectively in sites such as adult literacy centers, units for young offenders, or job centers, subject to the provisos that a follow-up second-stage testing procedure was available and that the screening was integrated within a support framework.

The survey was carried out in 1991; but we consider that its main conclusions remain valid, and we have used this guidance in the design of our research program for adult assessment and support. In particular, it is vital to derive a cost-effective yet valid method for large-scale screening of adults for dyslexia. It is equally vital to develop a support system that enables an adult with dyslexia to obtain the help needed to achieve his or her current objectives.

Overview of the Proposed Solution

Figure 8.1 presents an overview of a proposed solution to the need for better assessment of adults for dyslexia. The framework involves a three-stage procedure. The first stage is a quick and simple screening test, which can be carried out by support professionals (with minimal extra training) in the adult's workplace (for large organizations) or at educational centers, employment centers, or a medical practitioner's office. The screening test gives an indication of whether the adult is at risk for dyslexia or other LD. If the likelihood is high, then it may be worth obtaining a diagnostic assessment for dyslexia, in that in many countries this is the key to formal support of various types. A diagnostic assessment requires a fully trained psychologist and is expensive. Regardless of whether the likelihood of dyslexia is high (or whether a formal diagnosis is made), it is important to provide an effective follow-up support service. We envisage that this would require the involvement of a literacy service provider, together with a support representative from the adult's workplace (or a career advisor for unemployed adults). This "support assessment" would lead to the design of an agreed-on individual development plan tailored to meet the individual's perceived needs and aspirations. The final support stage involves the delivery of the support needed to implement this plan. This is, of course, an uncertain and potentially costly process, but the high costs involved reinforce the need for a systematic approach initially. We believe that, given a systematic screening and assessment procedure, it is now feasible to develop coherent support procedures that provide cost-effective yet individualized support.

The remainder of this chapter outlines the progress made toward the overall goal. We start by outlining the screening tool we are developing, then move on to assessment and support. It should be stressed that this research is very much in progress as of 1998, and the work is described as an indication of how a coherent framework might be implemented, rather than a specification of a finished product. Having outlined the processes involved, we attempt to illustrate the potential by means of three case studies: screening using adults known to have dyslexia; screening of young offenders for

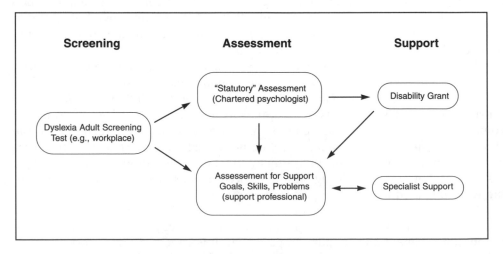

Figure 8.1.   A screening–assessment–support system for adults with dyslexia.

LD; and preliminary work toward the introduction of a complete system for screening, assessment, and support of students with learning difficulties and disabilities.

SCREENING

Although our research has primarily been directed toward adults with dyslexia, a similar analysis applies to the needs of all adults with learning or literacy disabilities. We do not consider that a screening system need necessarily attempt to differentiate fully between dyslexia and other LD. The screening tests, as described in this chapter, have been designed to identify LD of any type, rather than being specifically targeted for dyslexia. They would therefore be expected to identify adults with attention-deficit/hyperactivity disorder (ADHD) or language disabilities as well as "garden variety" poor readers, although they have been particularly tailored to the profile of dyslexia. An advantage of the two-stage diagnostic method is that more skilled differential diagnoses may be made at the second stage by a more fully trained tester. Our plan for screening overall would be that adults should be screened in the appropriate environment (in educational institutions, in employment, in job centers, in young offenders programs, or even in prison). We are developing a test—the Dyslexia Adult Screening Test (DAST)—for this purpose.

The Dyslexia Adult Screening Test

The DAST has evolved out of related research we have undertaken in screening for dyslexia in children that has led to the publication of the Dyslexia Screening Test (DST; Fawcett & Nicolson, 1996a) for children ages 6 years, 6 months to 16 years, 5 months. This test is designed to be administered by school professionals with minimal extra training and to take no more than 30 minutes to produce a profile of performance on a range of tests known to be positive indicators of dyslexia, adopting an approach similar to that pioneered by Miles (1983). The DAST was based on the DST, which was normed on a sample of more than 1,000 British schoolchildren and validated on a panel of children with dyslexia. The DST has 11 subtests and derives an overall quantitative "at-risk" index. The subtests were based on a range of skills for which children with dyslexia are known to show difficulties, including literacy measures (e.g., reading, writing, spelling), measures of phonological skill (see Bradley & Bryant, 1983), naming speed (see Denckla & Rudel, 1976), balance (Fawcett & Nicolson, 1996b; Nicolson & Fawcett, 1990), and verbal fluency (Frith, Landerl, & Frith, 1995). The scores on each subtest are aggregated to give the composite overall at-risk index and can also be used as an "ability profile" to aid the development of an appropriate support plan. Because many of the subtests do not tap taught skills, they also have the potential for identifying limitations throughout the life span.

Screening adults for dyslexia is very different from screening children, not least because adults may have an extensive history of difficulty and thus considerable sensitivity is required (Fawcett, 1995a). It is for this reason that screening must be seen as only the first step in the development of an individual development plan designed to help overcome the specific difficulties identified. Furthermore, for many adults, the simple realization that they are not "stupid" has a particularly beneficial effect, spurring them on to extra effort to overcome their difficulties. Therefore, despite the difficulties involved, we consider that screening adults is a particularly worthwhile endeavor.

Our approach in developing the DAST was first to ask experts in the field of adult support to evaluate the DST and suggest how it should be modified for adults. We then modified the DST in line with their suggestions—for example, removing a test of bead threading—to produce a prototype DAST, which we then evaluated. Following an extensive series of trials with various adults user groups and professionals associated with adult literacy testing, we derived the set of subtests outlined in Table 8.1. Note that the majority of tests are intended to identify specific weaknesses of the individual, but two (Tests 8 and 11) are intended to assess strengths. This is a valuable aspect both to avoid deliberate underachieving by the individual and to allow a more representative pattern of strengths and weaknesses to be identified.

An example of the DAST scoring system is shown in Figure 8.2. Each subtest performance is graded into one of five categories based on population norms: "+" (above average performance; percentile 76–100); 0 (average performance; percentile 25–75); and three minus categories (−, −−, −−−) that indicate increasingly severe "at-risk" performance. A single-minus score indicates performance within percentiles 15–25; a double-minus score performance within percentiles 5–15; and a triple-minus score performance within the bottom 5 percentiles). In order to determine the overall at-risk score, each minus score is allotted a number (3 for triple minus, 2 for double minus, and 1 for single minus), with the + and 0 scores valued as 0. These values are then totaled and divided by the number of subtests (9)[2] that are indicative of dyslexia to find the overall at-risk score. A score of 1 or more indicates increasingly severe at-risk performance. Note that the adult represented in Figure 8.2 has highly at-risk performance (triple minus) on segmentation and naming speed, with above-average performance only on verbal fluency. The overall at-risk index is 1.22 (11 divided by 9), leading to a diagnosis of "at risk." This adult did not take the nonverbal reasoning test.

In the remaining sections of this chapter, we illustrate the development of the DAST with case studies of the test in use with different groups of individuals. Information on the validation of the DAST with two diverse groups (high-achieving and underachieving adults with dyslexia) is provided in the second case study (see also Nicolson & Fawcett, 1996b). For the time being, we note that the DAST has proved popular with those tested, provides a positive "at-risk" indicator for dyslexia that correlates well with the formal diagnostic procedures for adult dyslexia, takes only 30 minutes to complete, and can be administered by professionals with only minimal training in its use. As a result, we consider that the DAST demonstrates the feasibility of producing a quick but effective screening tool. We turn now to the next phase in the framework: assessment.

ASSESSMENT

As was shown in Figure 8.1, we consider there to be two independent requirements for assessment: a formal diagnostic assessment for dyslexia, which must be undertaken by a suitably qualified psychologist; and a "support assessment," which is intended to lead to the creation of an individual development plan tailored to the specific goals of the individual and probably best created in an interview between a support specialist and the adult together with a representative of the adult's workplace (or, e.g., employment office).

Formal Diagnostic Assessment

The traditional method for assessing dyslexia in adults is to administer an adult intelligence test (typically the Wechsler Adult Intelligence Scale–Revised [WAIS–R; Wechsler,

---

[2]The index is derived by dividing by 9 tests, rather than the full set of 11, because adults with dyslexia are expected to achieve at the average level or above on semantic fluency and nonverbal reasoning (thus scoring 0). These two tests are included to measure strengths, and they therefore do not count as evidence of risk.

Table 8.1.   Components of the Dyslexia Adult Screening Test

Test	Description	Skills tapped
Test 1: Rapid naming	Time taken to name all the simple pictures on a card	Speed of lexical access and articulation
Test 2: 1-minute reading test	The number of words read correctly in 1 minute	Reading fluency
Test 3: Postural stability	The disturbance in balance caused by a calibrated push in the back	Balance
Test 4: Phonemic segmentation	The ability to split a word up into its constituent phonemes	Phonological skill
Test 5: 2-minute spelling test	The number of words spelled correctly in 2 minutes (tester speaks them)	Spelling fluency
Test 6: Backward digit span	The maximum number of digits that can be correctly repeated in the reverse order	Working memory
Test 7: Nonsense passage reading	The score on a jabberwocky-type passage	Grapheme/phoneme translation fluency
Test 8: Nonverbal reasoning	A short nonverbal IQ test	Nonverbal reasoning (OK for adults with dyslexia)
Test 9: 1-minute writing test	The number of words of a sentence transcribed correctly in 1 minute	Transcription fluency
Test 10: Verbal fluency	The number of words beginning with s that can be thought of in 1 minute	Verbal fluency
Test 11: Semantic fluency	The number of animals that can be thought of in 1 minute	Semantic fluency (OK for adults with dyslexia)

1986]) to check that the adult has an IQ score of 90 or higher, and then to administer a test of single-word reading (a suitable modern test would be the Wechsler Objective Reading Dimension [WORD] test [Wechsler, 1993]). A WORD reading age of 14 years or younger together with an IQ score of 90 or higher might then be taken as a reasonable indicator of dyslexia. Unfortunately, the WAIS–R is a restricted test (it can be used only by psychologists, rather than the support specialists who would naturally be involved with adults), and its administration is a lengthy and skilled procedure. Therefore, this method of assessment is costly (because it can only be administered by highly trained professionals) as well as unsatisfactory (because of the overlay of learned skills in reading for adults). In designing the Adult Dyslexia Index (ADI), we wanted to augment this traditional procedure in a principled manner to improve its validity without adding substantially to the testing time.

We achieved this by first assessing four positive indicators for adult dyslexia (see Table 8.2): the WAIS–R Arithmetic, Coding/Digit Symbol, Information and Digital Span (ACID)[3] profile, WORD spelling, nonsense passage reading, and previous diagnosis of dyslexia. It is also valuable to combine these four indicators into a single, objective composite score that gives an index of severity (the ADI), and this can be done simply

---

[3]Note that women with dyslexia may show superior performance on the Coding subtest of the ACID profile (Vogel, 1982). In our sample, only 32% of the women showed impairments, compared with 45% of the men. However, women show equally poor performance as men on the Arithmetic, Information, and Digit Span components. This means that they can still generate a score of 1.0 on the ACID profile.

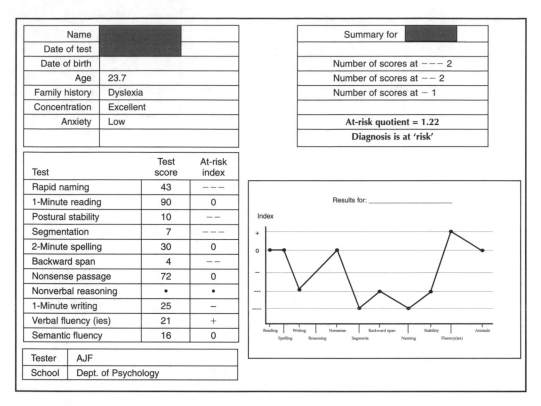

Name	
Date of test	
Date of birth	
Age	23.7
Family history	Dyslexia
Concentration	Excellent
Anxiety	Low

Summary for	
Number of scores at − − −	2
Number of scores at − −	2
Number of scores at −	1
At-risk quotient = 1.22	
Diagnosis is at 'risk'	

Test	Test score	At-risk index
Rapid naming	43	− − −
1-Minute reading	90	0
Postural stability	10	− −
Segmentation	7	− − −
2-Minute spelling	30	0
Backward span	4	− −
Nonsense passage	72	0
Nonverbal reasoning	•	•
1-Minute writing	25	−
Verbal fluency (ies)	21	+
Semantic fluency	16	0

Tester	AJF
School	Dept. of Psychology

Figure 8.2. Illustration of the Dyslexic Adult Screening Test (DAST) scoring system (see text for explanation). (*Note*: Because full norms through the adult age range were not at the time of writing, the norms used for this figure were the DAST norms for 16-year-olds. Adult performance would be slightly better than average; so if adult norms were used, performance would be judged as somewhat more at risk.)

by adding them. This procedure leads to a score of 0, 0.5, or 1 on each of the four measures and a composite ADI (Fawcett & Nicolson, 1993) ranging from 0 to 4 in increments of 0.5 (see Table 8.2 for an illustrative example of the procedure). It should be noted that a detailed history is also collected to reinforce the diagnosis and contribute to the development of support programs (see the discussion of support issues later). The ADI data in Table 8.2 are those of the man whose scores on the DAST were presented in Figure 8.2. It may be seen by comparison of scores derived from the DAST (1.22) and the ADI (4) that both show strong evidence of dyslexia.

An adequate psychometric test should be valid, objective, and reliable. Naturally the ADI is reliable, in that its components are based on existing psychometric tests for which the reliability is established. Objectivity is an important strength of the ADI—the diagnosis follows directly from the scores on the test components, without any need for expert judgment. The issue of validity is less clear cut, not least because the question of how to diagnose dyslexia in adults is not fully resolved. There are two aspects to consider here: theory and practice. The ADI is a composite score, each component of which provides a known positive indicator for dyslexia, and so one would expect that the validity of the overall score should be at least as great as that of any of the components. Theoretically, therefore, its validity is a least as good as that of any extant diagnostic test. In further tests of validity in practice, Nicolson and Fawcett (1997) compared the outcomes of the ADI with previous expert diagnoses of 105 students referred for diagnostic assessment at the University of Sheffield and established complete agree-

Table 8.2.   Illustrative use of the four tests to derive the Adult Dyslexia Index (ADI)

Criterion measure	Score	ADI score	Scoring criterion
Previous diagnosis of dyslexia	Yes	1	1 for psychologist's report (0 otherwise)
WORD spelling scale (age equivalent)	14	1	0.5 for 16–17 1 for <16
Nonsense word passage			
Error score	9	0.5	0.5 for >7 errors
Completion time	68 seconds	0.5	0.5 for >59 seconds
WAIS–R ACID profile			0.5 for discrepancy (≥3 points) in one of
Average WAIS–R score (non-ACID)	11.11		the ACID subtests compared with
Arithmetic	8	0.5	non-ACID mean; 1 for two or more
Digit Symbol	5	0.5	discrepancies
Digit Span	9		
Information	11		
WAIS–R IQ scores			
Full-Scale IQ	100		IQ score must be 90 or more
Performance IQ	96		for diagnosis of dyslexia
Verbal IQ	103		
Overall ADI		4	>2.5 points: dyslexic >1 point: nondyslexic
Overall diagnosis	*Strong evidence of dyslexia*		

Note: ACID = arithmetic, coding/digital symbol, information, digit span; IQ = intelligence quotient.

ment with the expert decisions in all but two of the instances. In order to assess the validity of the algorithmic ADI approach compared with the clinical judgments, each of the 105 clinical decisions was categorized as dyslexic ($n = 47$), borderline ($n = 43$), or nondyslexic ($n = 15$), and this classification was then compared with the ADI method. There was an exact match for 103 of 105 instances. In both instances of disagreement, the ADI gave a "not dyslexic" diagnosis, whereas the expert gave a "borderline dyslexic" diagnosis. In each instance, a borderline dyslexic diagnosis of 2 would have been obtained if the ACID discrepancy had been even 0.10 greater. In order to assess the likelihood of false results, a further 25 control students were tested. None of these 25 students produced a score of greater than 0.5. The percentage of false positives was therefore zero, and the percentage of false negatives 2.6%, with the two discrepant cases representing borderline diagnoses that could in reality have gone either way. This analysis therefore provides strong support for the ADI method of objectively combining the scores into a composite dyslexia index. It is clear, therefore, that the ADI satisfies the three major criteria for formal diagnosis of dyslexia in adults.

Unfortunately, despite the lengthy testing procedure involved, the ADI in itself gives little or no explicit guidance on which types of support an adult with dyslexia should receive. Consequently, for support purposes, we consider that the ADI must be augmented or even substituted by an assessment that is geared to development of a support program for the adult in question. Components of such an assessment should include objective measures of reading, writing and spelling *fluency*[4] on tests appropriate for adults, coupled with an in-depth interview to analyze the strengths and weaknesses of the adult and his or her goals.

---

[4]This aspect of skilled performance is overlooked in many tests of literacy skills. We address this omission by administering components of our DAST test, including 1-minute reading, 1-minute writing, and 2-minute spelling, in addition to a structured interview.

Informal Assessment for Support

Even if one wished to augment the diagnostic assessment with items relevant to support, the licensed psychologist administering the test will not typically have an equivalent level of instruction in the support of adults with dyslexia. Providing such support is an equally demanding role requiring extensive experience together with current knowledge of support tools and interaction methods.

An ideal support assessment session would involve at least four people: the adult with dyslexia (the consumer), able to outline his or her requirements for support in terms of which goals he or she wishes to achieve; a dyslexia specialist, able to comment on the implications of the formal assessment; a support specialist, able to advise on possible methods for supporting the achievement of the goals; and a representative of the consumer's work environment (e.g., a university tutor, an office manager, a career advisor, a prison counselor), able to advise on the particular requirements of the consumer's work environment. Following collaborative discussions between these experts, an individual development plan might then be derived that identifies the key objectives for the consumer and provides a blueprint of the steps needed to achieve those objectives, together with a means of checking that the individual was on track at subsequent stages of the development plan. This plan would then form the backbone of the subsequent support program, with reasonably frequent subsequent meetings available to monitor progress and revise the development plan as appropriate. This framework is in fact that prescribed by the 1994 U.K. Code of Practice for children with special educational needs (Department for Education, 1994), and this framework seems equally appropriate for adults. However, the two critical differences between supporting children and adults are, first, that the requirements of children are relatively stereotyped—acquisition of literacy skills and appropriate knowledge—whereas the needs of adults are diverse; and, second, that there is a well-established educational system that needs merely to be adapted to fit the special needs of exceptional children, whereas for adults there is typically no system available.

In short, therefore, assessment for support is a difficult process requiring not only excellent interactional skills and insight on the part of the support assessor but also a knowledge of the types of support available and how these might be tailored to the individual's particular goals. Furthermore, continual monitoring of progress should be available. Consequently, although there are aspects of support assessment that are generic, the assessment should be seen as an integral part of the support process, rather than as an independent stage. We turn now to a discussion of support methods.

SUPPORT

Any adequate support system needs to address both the general difficulties likely to occur for adults with dyslexia and the specific difficulties obtaining for each individual, in terms of both their specific profile of abilities and aspirations and their specific circumstances at work or on unemployment. Difficulties in literacy are frequently accompanied by a tendency for poor presentation of work and deteriorating performance under time pressure. On an intermediate level, established difficulties in dynamic working memory make it difficult for adults with dyslexia to hold information in mind while they manipulate it and can lead to a range of difficulties. Perhaps the most significant general difficulties are in organizational skills and in checking work. These difficulties may well result from reduced mental "resources" caused both by limitations in working memory and by likely difficulties in speed of processing and in skill automatization (Nicolson & Fawcett, 1990). McLoughlin et al. (1994) argued strongly (see also Vogel & Adelman, 1992) that an even higher level of difficulty—a metacognitive failure to realize one's own strengths and weaknesses, and in particular the effects that dyslexia will have on one's performance—is perhaps the most fundamental difficulty, and one that should be addressed as soon as possible. It is clear, however, that any attempt to remedy just one source of difficulties is likely to lead only to partial success.

The use of well-written self-help books, such as Gilroy and Miles's (1995) text on dyslexia at college, together with talks on study skills, are of potential value, but theory is of limited use without a strong hands-on practical component. This is especially important for adults with dyslexia, who will have good grounds for distrusting generic advice and may not have the self-confidence to put the advice into practice. Instruction ideally should be based on one-to-one support from a sympathetic and knowledgeable expert, involving both hands-on involvement and insightful feedback. Unfortunately, this type of support is extremely expensive (Higgins & Zvi, 1995), and few experts have both the knowledge of dyslexia and the subject knowledge across the range of topics to fulfill this role adequately.

It is important also to acknowledge the relative intractability of literacy-related disabilities in adults with dyslexia, who will have suffered a decade or more of literacy difficulty, and one should therefore not expect rapid progress on all fronts. The encouraging aspect is that adults can make significant strides; in fact, we have worked with adults who have progressed from literacy courses to university entrance, but such cases are unusual and are characterized by these adults' determination to succeed. Improvement is typically a lengthy process that demands high levels of motivation and commitment from the consumer. It is for this reason that it is important to prioritize each consumer's requirements and to attempt to tailor support to high-priority but achievable targets. Adults may well need more generalized support than children with disabilities because the difficulties they experience affect all aspects of their life and work. In terms of a general analysis, one can distinguish between literacy-related skills and life-related skills (especially work-related skills). We shall consider each briefly in turn.

Literacy-Related Support

As noted previously, literacy-related skills such as reading and spelling are likely to have received considerable (albeit not necessarily very good) support throughout an individual's school days. Consequently, in order to achieve significant improvement, well-tuned individual support is necessary, targeted to the skills of the individual. However, many adults have become demotivated by their lack of success and thus would benefit from a fresh approach to their disabilities in addition to the more traditional support. Our belief is that the best opportunities for literacy-related support derive from the planned use of computer-based methods, especially using the multimedia capabilities of modern microcomputers. However, there are many facets of skilled reading, and extant computer programs do not, in our view, provide the systematic and wide-ranging support, targeted to the pattern of strengths and weaknesses of the user, that is potentially available with skilled individual human teaching. We consider that one of the most pressing issues for the application of computer-based learning theory to practical education is the development of a complete system for supporting the acquisition of literacy.

The reason for failure to develop such a system is that the difficulties involved are formidable. Consider the approach that might ideally be adopted by an experienced teacher when approached by an adult with literacy difficulties. Open learning principles (e.g., Lewis, 1984, 1987) advise that the teacher should start with a discussion of the learner's wishes in general terms, followed by an outline discussion of how these aims might be achieved, followed by more detailed discussions that break down the general aims into a series of fully specified objectives; then a plan is developed for the attainment of each objective (starting with the current profile of skills and knowledge and moving to the desired profile of skills and knowledge). Such an approach requires formidable expertise (interviewing expertise, for establishing what the learner would really wish to achieve; planning expertise, for determining an appropriate and achievable development plan to achieve these aims; assessment expertise, for assessing the learner's current skills and knowledge; and teaching expertise, for working out a method for achieving each objective). The teacher must also have access to a wide range of teaching resources—preferably a fully developed, complete teaching system that prescribes a method for helping the learner progress from the current state of knowledge/skill to the required next stage as specified on the development plan.

We believe that computers can provide very significant help at all stages in this process: in the presentation of literacy support programs, such as spelling and reading programs; in routine matters such as keeping records and compiling progress reports; in providing semiautomatic methods for assessing the learner's current profile of skills and knowledge; and in providing advice to the teacher on which resources might be applicable at which stages, how to structure objectives, and the like. The approach we advocate is based on the Teaching Assistant (Nicolson, 1990; Nicolson & Fawcett, 1994), a computer system that helps rather than replaces the teacher. The key to the approach is to consider the issue of support from the point of view of an experienced teacher and to construct an integrated support package that provides help where appropriate for all aspects of the teacher's task.

We are working toward a support system of this type, which we have dubbed the Readers' Interactive Teaching Assistant (RITA), intended to address the needs of individuals with persistent and severe disabilities in literacy in adolescence and adulthood. RITA involves an established system for automatically maintaining progress records in a workbook for each learner and providing immediate access to a range of teaching resources in a resource book that can be used directly by the teacher to specify, say, a half-hour computer-based session. However, we consider that adult support is best seen in a wider context than literacy alone. Consequently, we hope to add a range of further options for computer-based support for adults with dyslexia, as outlined next.

Wider Support

Adults with dyslexia may have pressing difficulties with life skills only indirectly related to literacy (or, in the case of organizational skills and working memory limitations, not related at all). Consequently, although the general procedure for constructing a development plan on the basis of an initial interview with a support specialist remains appropriate, it is necessary to consider much wider ranging support. Here we outline one promising approach to this problem: the use of computer-based video material for "learning by observation." We hope to exploit this approach in the development of support systems well tuned to the requirements of the adult learner.

Learning by Observation—the Visual Technique   Children take it for granted that television and videotapes are an important source of information. Videotapes are also an important method of learning skills—if one wants to install a new bathtub, one can go down to the local hardware or home products shop and purchase a videotape giving detailed, step-by-step instructions. Unfortunately, although videotapes are excellent for creating interest, it is by no means clear that they are an effective means of fostering learning because they tend to force a passive attitude on the learner; they sweep the viewer along inexorably, giving no time for reflection; they create a high working memory load; and, unlike a book, they are impossible to index or to skim. Furthermore, a videotape is of only limited teaching use unless the student is made aware of the critical points for which to watch, and although interactive videos have been produced, there is no evidence that they are more effective than standard computer-assisted learning (CAL) programs (McNeil & Nelson, 1991). A particularly promising new technological development in this area is the use of digitization techniques; videotape can be digitized and stored in compressed format on disc, and then replayed at normal speed on a window of a computer screen independently of the specific hardware platform used. Crucially, it is then possible to gain access to each frame of the videotape directly, thereby giving the freedom to select which clips to play and when.

Arguably the first major attempt to marry CAL and QuickTime video was the ViSuAL (Video-Supported Active Learning) prototype (Nicolson, Syder & Freeman, 1994). In effect, the ViSuAL shell provides a method of superimposing a text-based, semantic indexing system on videotape material, thereby facilitating the selection, integration, and dynamic resequencing of videotape material. The significance of this innovation cannot be overemphasized. It is valuable for all users but especially for adults with dyslexia because it allows a completely natural form of viewing and is able to provide the opportunities for replay and reanalysis that real life does not provide. Furthermore, ViSuALs can be continually upgraded—the videotape is of considerable value; the digitized videotape is of much more value, in that it is much easier to replay specific segments; the ViSuAL record, which includes transcript plus navigational and selection facilities, is much better, and the addition of tutorial material can make the ViSuAL record more valuable still.

We consider that ViSuAL techniques will be of value in a range of situations—the "watch the expert" format is ideal for instruction (one videotapes, for example, a support assessment interview, then ViSuALizes the videotape, creating a stand-alone resource for training a support assessor) and for creating learning packages (an expert gives a seminar on, say, organizational skills, and this then is ViSuALized for use in subsequent years or in other institutions). It is also very good for motivation; successful adults with dyslexia give interviews showing how they have been able to use their skills to best effect, and how they have been able to use strategies to minimize their difficulties. We sketch some planned uses in the third case study (see next section).

CASE STUDIES OF THE SCREENING–ASSESSMENT–SUPPORT SYSTEM

The previous discussion justifies and outlines our general framework for screening, assessment, and support; but we are aware that it appears very general and that readers may wonder how it could possibly be adapted to their own particular interests and requirements. Consequently, in this section, we present three case studies in which the approach is applied to a specific target group of adults. The case studies are presented roughly in order of occurrence. The first explored the feasibility of using the DAST for rapid screening of young offenders (adolescents convicted of criminal offenses) for LD. The screening proved successful in that it was acceptable to this group of individuals, further strengthening the case for development of an integrated support system as well. The second study, which is described only briefly, validated (against the findings of a full formal assessment) the DAST screening for a group of students referred for dyslexia testing together with a group of adults with dyslexia. Again, the DAST screening proved successful not only in appropriately identifying as at risk those students who were indeed at risk but also in providing valuable further information that could be used as a part of a support process. The third case study, again with students, provides an outline of how we envisage a full screening–assessment–support system might operate for university education.

Case Study 1: Screening Young Offenders for Learning Disabilities

A potential link between dyslexia and crime has been highlighted by controversial media claims that approximately 50% of young offenders have dyslexia (Poseidon Film Productions, 1994). There are several reasons why one might expect relatively high proportions of adults with dyslexia in the prison population. First, the consensus is that dyslexia is constitutional in origin (Critchley, 1964) and therefore persists in some form throughout life. Clearly, therefore, we would expect the prevalence of dyslexia in adults to be similar to that identified in childhood, approximately 5%. Second, literacy disabilities at school can lead to psychological trauma that may be manifested as alienation, disruption, and general refusal to conform, which may lead in turn to petty criminal activities. Third, LD are often associated with ADHD—a 30% comorbidity with dyslexia was cited in one study (Pennington, 1991). One of the major symptoms of ADHD is problems in inhibiting impulsive behavior, which may lead to delinquency and crime. When we consider the combined impact of these factors, it would not be surprising if the prevalence of dyslexia in young offenders was significantly higher than in the general population. Nevertheless, we would not predict that the prevalence of dyslexia in offenders would be 50%, because this figure undoubtedly includes a large proportion of "garden variety" poor readers as well as persistent school nonattenders.

We should stress that this analysis of dyslexia and crime should be balanced with our belief that we would also find higher than expected numbers of people with dyslexia in any "unusual" career, such as the creative arts. This is particularly true of the media, where we have found at least one cameraman with dyslexia in the four camera crews we have met. It also has been suggested that adults with dyslexia may well be represented among the world's innovators (West, 1991), although much of this evidence is anecdotal.

We consider that appropriate screening and support for young offenders with dyslexia is perhaps the most important and cost-effective of the interventions available in the prison service. The alternative is clear—failure to provide support will lead to the prison or young offenders program becoming a "finishing school" for crime, in which useful contacts are made, criminal techniques learned, and antiestablishment attitudes hardened (Chasty & Friel, 1993). By contrast, the diagnosis of dyslexia by itself can lead to an important insight into both the causes of previous difficulties and the existence of large numbers of similarly affected adults who together form one of the largest possible support groups. This moment of insight presents the opportunity for an alert prison counselor to "convert" the young offender to a more constructive view of life. The opportunity probably will not come again (or at best will take much more effort to engineer subsequently), and so it is critical to develop an appropriate screening and support procedure for such individuals.

The study reported here was an initial attempt to assess the feasibility of large-scale screening of the young offenders for LD—this is, of course, a prerequisite for the development of screening and support systems. We piloted the prototype DAST test with 34 young offenders (Lynch, 1995), with the twin intentions of assessing its acceptability and also assessing prevalence of LD in the group. This study was not intended as a validation study for the DAST (two validation studies are presented in Case Study 2).

In this study, we used a group of 9 young offenders serving in an "alternative to youth custody" program and a group of 25 young offenders in prison. Both groups showed high incidences of at-risk scores (compared with our DST norms for 16-year-olds) of 67% and 48%, respectively. The overall prevalence (53%) that we identified is thus very much in line with the figures quoted in the media, which suggests that the level of LD *is* high among these individuals. However, it should be noted that this figure (like the original research) includes adults with more generalized disabilities, as well as those who have persistently truanted and have therefore missed out on the opportunity to learn in school. It therefore should not be accepted as an estimate of dyslexia in the offending population. Considering individual tests for the at-risk group, incidences of impairment were 94%, 89%, 78%, and 61% for segmentation, 1-minute reading, nonsense word reading, and 2-minute spelling, respectively. The mean at-risk index values (scoring as described previously) were 2.1, 1.9, 1.8, and 1.3 for segmentation, 1-minute reading, nonsense word reading, and 2-minute spelling, respectively.

Both groups of offenders were cooperative and keen to participate in the screening tests. The experimenter was able to strike up a rapport with both groups and received some interesting feedback. One of the most striking aspects of this feedback for us was the relief that the more able offenders reported on having their problems finally recognized. No one refused to participate in the study or reported any negative responses to any of the tests we gave. It should be noted that it was not possible in this study to conduct full formal assessment of the individuals for dyslexia, and so we were not able to distinguish between dyslexia and more general impairment. This was because there was a reluctance on the part of the prison authorities to allow psychometric testing with this group. This is one reason why we have introduced a test of nonverbal reasoning in subsequent versions of the DAST, which is under evaluation. Taken with the test of semantic fluency, this measure will provide a rough estimate of intelligence.

In summary, the prototype test proved completely acceptable to young offenders, and the incidence of at-risk scores is in line with estimates of approximately 50% prevalence of LD in this group. The study therefore highlights the importance of developing a full screening and support system for young offenders.

Case Study 2: Screening Adults with Dyslexia

Since the mid-1980s, we have worked with several groups of children with dyslexia, many of whom are now young adults. We are very familiar with their negative views regarding standard tests of literacy, and these views have informed our construction of the screening tests. In this study, we noted whether they found the DAST tests acceptable and also validated the "hit rate" of the DAST against the known diagnoses of dyslexia in this study group.

The Individual Subtests   The DAST nonverbal reasoning subtest was not administered, but full psychometric data were available for the adults with dyslexia in this study. The DAST includes four literacy-related subtests (see Table 8.1): the 1-minute reading test (the number of words read correctly in 1 minute from a long list); the 2-minute spelling test (the number of words spelled correctly in 2 minutes, with the experimenter dictating a new word as soon as the subject finishes the previous one); the 1-minute writing test (the number of words of a sentence transcribed correctly in

1 minute—a test of writing speed rather than literacy), and nonsense passage reading (the number of words read correctly in 1 minute from a nonsense passage containing 30 normal words and 10 nonsense words, with greater weight placed on reading the nonsense words). All of the study group members found these literacy tests more acceptable than standardized reading tests (which are clearly designed for younger children). They particularly liked the 1-minute reading test, which emphasizes fluency as well as accuracy and allows the reader to say "pass" if unable to read any given word. One of the points they particularly emphasized was that all the literacy tests we designed were more acceptable than the standard tests because they were relatively short.

The 1-minute reading test is based on rapid reading of single words presented in a list format, in contrast to the usual single-word reading tests, such as the Schonell, the British Ability Scales or the WORD, which allow several seconds for each word. It is possible to achieve a spuriously high reading age on untimed tests such as these by reading in a very labored fashion that is in no way adequate for normal performance. The 1-minute reading test captures the essence of skilled reading—the development of automaticity in reading (Adams, 1990; Laberge & Samuels, 1974), which allows readers to progress beyond the novice level to attain higher levels of adult reading ability and speed. This fluency is particularly difficult for people with dyslexia to attain (Yap & Van der Leij, 1993). Despite the large number of errors he generated on this test, Stuart[5] (age 19) noted, "Quite like this, could just read down and it was nonthreatening." The study participants were also intrigued by our nonsense word passage, a jabberwocky passage that interweaves real and nonsense words, our version of the type of passage used by Finucci, Guthrie, Childs, Abbey, and Childs (1976), which is problematic even for high-achieving adults with dyslexia (Felton, Naylor, & Wood, 1990). Our participants did not find it humiliating to not be able to read nonsense words because they thought it quite likely that everyone would find them equally difficult. As Rachel (age 18) noted, "Weird, didn't mind doing it, but stopped on the weird ones. I think everyone would."

Let us now consider the reactions of individual members of our study group to the DAST test overall, illustrating this with two case histories. Our motivation here is to examine differences in the responses of individuals to the difficulties they have experienced. Mark (age 19) is an exceptionally bright young adult whose confidence had largely been destroyed by the intervention he received in school. Naturally enough, this has made him angry, and, although he has a good, dry sense of humor, Mark does not tolerate fools gladly. The humiliation he has experienced and the bitterness he feels are clearly evident in the following quote regarding the DAST:

> Alright, compared to some other tests (not ones I've done here) which have "cat," "dog," "rat," this tries to take you at the level you're at. Not like the scheme at school, primary school reading for secondary education. I wouldn't take anything out [of the DAST]. (Fawcett, 1995b)

Tim (age 16) is a young man who has spent many years trying to overcome his embarrassment at his limitations but in his final year at school has become very angry and uncooperative. He has an IQ score in the average range, which has recently fallen to a borderline slow learner (88), a clear illustration of "Matthew" effects. He is bored with the restricted curriculum he receives, and recently he has been in trouble at school because his hot temper causes him to flare up at other pupils and teachers. He

---

[5]In the quotations presented here, we have changed the names to preserve confidentiality.

is hoping to go into the army, but it seems unlikely that he will have a high enough level of literacy to cope with the demands. His comments on the DST/DAST were particularly revealing: "Might be good for my age, because not humiliating or embarrassing. Some were hard, some alright—good compared with other reading tests, because some hard to start with."

The participants in our study, however, were very familiar with our approach and confident of our support. What would the response be from other adults who were less familiar with our work? Following a presentation, Fawcett discussed these issues at length with a number of extremely able and vocal adults with dyslexia, who are themselves now involved in postsecondary education. This group resented the apparent emphasis standardized tests place on impairments, objecting to the concept of focusing on areas of shortcoming rather than strength, although they recognized that screening tests by their very nature must focus on areas of difficulty. In the DAST, we attempt to counterbalance the standard emphasis on impairments by including tests on which we would anticipate that adults with dyslexia would score well (semantic fluency and nonverbal reasoning). Nevertheless, the nature of screening tests is such that some people, in particular adults with more generalized LD, will come out as low achievers. The perceived value of this analysis is much greater if the screening is seen as the first step in support.

The previous section provided reassurance that the DAST was likely to be acceptable to a range of groups. A key issue, therefore, in the validation of the DAST was the accuracy rate in correctly identifying dyslexia. As previously noted, we obtained feedback by administering the test to our group of young adults between ages 17 and 20, with a long-standing diagnosis of dyslexia. This group ($N = 7$) has formed part of our research panel during the late 1980s and early 1990s, and all of them still fulfill standard criteria for diagnosis. Analysis of their scores on the DAST allows us to check how useful these tests are for identifying dyslexia by using our standard scoring system. All seven of this group screened as having dyslexia on the DAST, with a mean score of 1.8 and a range between 1 and 2.5. An analysis of their performance and the prevalence of limitations is presented in Table 8.3. It may be seen from Table 8.3 that segmentation, spelling, and nonsense passage reading produced impairment prevalence rates of 100%. All the tests used produced substantial evidence of impairment in the group members with dyslexia, ranging from 71% incidence upward.

Using the DAST for Screening Students

In 1996, we administered prototype versions of the DAST as well as the ADI to many students referred for dyslexia assessment. Comparison of the DAST screening with the

Table 8.3.   Performance on the Dyslexia Adult Screening Test of adults with dyslexia

Subtest	Mean panel	Impairment prevalence (%)
Rapid naming	1.71 (1.16)	71
1-minute reading test	1.86 (0.99)	86
Postural stability	1.71 (1.16)	71
Phonemic segmentation	3.0 (0.0)	100
2-minute spelling test	2.14 (1.16)	100
Backward digit span	1.71 (1.16)	71
Nonsense passage reading	2.57 (0.49)	100
1-minute writing	N/A	N/A

Note: Norms used were the Dyslexia Screening Test 16-year-old norms. Standard deviations are in parentheses.

(definitive) assessment produced by the ADI permits the analysis of the DAST "hit rate" (the proportion of those individuals identified as having dyslexia by the ADI who were screened as at risk by the DAST) and its false-positive rate (the proportion of those individuals identified as not having dyslexia by the ADI who were screened as at risk by the DAST). This represents the second validation study of the DAST. An ideal screening test would have a high hit rate and a low false-positive rate.

In order to estimate the hit and false-positive rates for the prototype version of the DAST, we collected control data on approximately 150 students without dyslexia on the DAST subtests. The mean and standard deviation for each subtest from this database were used to derive a rough at-risk measure for the DAST-assessed students. Each score on each subtest of the DAST was allocated an index of 0, 1, 2, or 3 (with 0 indicating typical or above-typical performance, and the 1, 2, and 3 categories indicating increasing danger of an at-risk classification.[6] The average of the individual subtest indices was taken as the overall DAST index, and an overall index of 1.0 or more was taken as an at-risk indicator for dyslexia (by analogy with the procedures used in the DST). Table 8.4 presents the analysis of the scores of the 15 students who were tested on both the ADI and the DAST and who scored 2.5 or more on the ADI (diagnosis of "dyslexia"). As may be seen from the bottom line of Table 8.4, the results of this analysis are encouraging. Fourteen of the fifteen students identified by the ADI as having dyslexia were also screened as at-risk by the student DAST—a hit rate of 94%. The right-hand column of Table 8.4 gives an indication of the false-positive rate for the control group of 150 students from whom the norms were derived. It may be seen that none of those students had an at-risk DAST score; in fact, the majority showed very little evidence of impairments (range 0.0 to 0.3), with the highest risk score being 0.6. Therefore, the DAST does an excellent job of discriminating between students who clearly have dyslexia and those who clearly do not (hit rate of 94%; false-positive rate of 0%). With students for whom the ADI diagnosis is less clear cut, the prototype DAST tends to give an at-risk assessment, which suggests the need for a full ADI test. In such instances, the DAST results may then be used in conjunction with the ADI to support the recommendations made.

It is also possible to undertake an equivalent analysis of hits and false positives for each individual subtest. It can be seen from Table 8.4 that every subtest yields a fairly high mean at-risk index (1.0–2.63) and high impairment prevalence (63%–100%) for the students with dyslexia compared with the control students (mean at-risk index 0.08–0.24 and deficit prevalence 5%–17%). The 100% prevalence of impairment for adults with dyslexia on the 2-minute spelling test is particularly striking and leads to the question of whether it alone (or possibly a combination of spelling and 1-minute reading) would be sufficient for an initial screening. The relatively high false-positive rate (11%) makes the use of spelling alone unsatisfactory—indeed, most academics are well aware of the high prevalence of poor spelling in students. We therefore do not recommend using the spelling test alone, because some students without dyslexia show minor difficulties in spelling, with no other positive indicators of dyslexia. A further difficulty is the obvious opportunity for a student to "cheat" by deliberately scoring low on these literacy tests. This suggests that the use of a screening test that covers a wider range of skills, such as the DAST, is more effective than reliance on any single test in isolation. Note that none of the 150 control students showed any evidence of risk on the DAST test overall.

---

[6]An index of 3 indicates performance at least 3 standard deviations below the mean (a Z-score of −3 or worse); an index of 2 indicates a Z-score of −2.0 to −2.99; an index of 1 indicates a Z-score of −1.0 to −1.99; and an index of 0 indicates a Z-score better than −1.

Table 8.4.   Performance of students on the Dyslexia Adult Screening Test (DAST)

DAST Subtest	Students with Dyslexia (n = 15)		Control students (N = 150)	
	Mean	Impairment prevalence	Mean	Impairment prevalence
Rapid naming	1.00 (0.97)	69	0.22 (0.56)	16
1-minute reading test	2.00 (0.89)	94	0.17 (0.46)	11
Postural stability	1.44 (1.36)	63	0.19 (0.70)	8
Phonemic segmentation	2.06 (1.18)	81	0.08 (0.34)	5
2-minute spelling test	2.25 (0.77)	100	0.16 (0.52)	11
Backward digit span	1.00 (0.73)	75	0.14 (0.39)	12
Nonsense passage reading	2.63 (1.02)	88	0.24 (0.60)	17
1-minute writing	2.00 (1.41)	75	0.21 (0.57)	14
Overall mean	**1.72 (0.52)**	**94**	**0.18 (0.52)**	**0**

Note: Scores are standardized relative to the mean and standard deviation (in parentheses) of the control data, with positive scores reflecting impairments. A score of 1.0 or more is considered "at-risk" performance on the subtest in question. See text for further details of the scoring procedure. Data were available only for 8 of the DAST subtests.

Analysis of the hit and false-positive rates allows one to see which tests would benefit from fine tuning, and the relatively low hit rates of the phonemic segmentation, postural stability, and backward span subtests have led us to redesign these tests somewhat to make them more challenging. For example, we have included a number of spoonerisms to make the phonemic test more complex and increased the force applied in the postural stability task to 4 kg. Similarly, the relatively high false-positive rates for nonsense passage reading and rapid naming have also led to redesign of these tests, including 50% more nonsense words to make the nonsense task more complex. We are now gathering norms on the revised prototype test.

Overall, therefore, this study confirms the validity of the DAST in a group of adults with dyslexia and justifies the use of a range of subtests on the DAST rather than merely using a subset of DAST tests.

Case Study 3: Development of a Complete Screening–Assessment–Support System for University Students

The previous two case studies demonstrated the feasibility of introducing large-scale, low-cost screening for dyslexia in adults. We now turn to the possibility of building on such a screening process to create a complete screening–assessment–support system for university students (Figure 8.3). The specific context discussed here is the British university system, but we wish to emphasize that similar analyses are equally applicable in a range of scenarios, including prisons, employment centers, and large firms.

University education in the United Kingdom has seen fundamental changes, with the inclusion of former polytechnics within the university system, together with a substantial increase in the numbers of students enrolling. This has led to significant increases in the numbers of mature students who may not have achieved the necessary grades for university entry on leaving school and may have little experience in writing essays or coping with examination pressures. Many universities have established a systematic approach to diagnosis and support of students with dyslexia, but previously the approaches adopted have been piecemeal. As of 1994, U.K. Disability Discrimination Act requires that all higher education institutions must publish a Disability Statement explaining how they will identify and support students with disabilities (Singleton, 1996).

Implementation of the Screening–Assessment–Support System   In a proposal to the U.K. Higher Education Funding Council (Nicolson & Fawcett, 1996a), we outlined

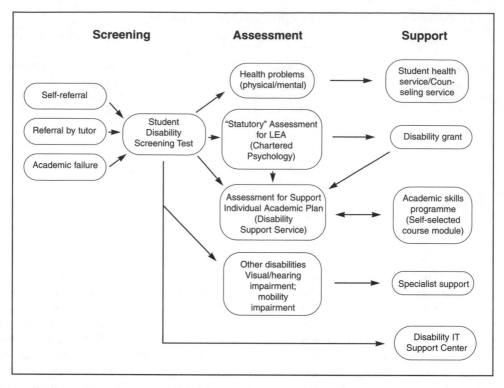

Figure 8.3.   Proposed screening–assessment–support system for university students. (LEA, Local Education Authority; IT, information technology.)

the following scenario for implementing a full screening–assessment–support system for university use. The system is intended for all students with learning difficulties and LD but is especially valuable for students with dyslexia. It follows the staged procedure discussed earlier in the chapter.

Entry   A student enters the system either by self-referral, referral by a tutor, or academic failure (e.g., failing an examination).

Stage 1   The proposed first stage is then a quick, low-cost screening (the Student Disability Screening Test, [SDST]), which is administered by staff in the Disability Support Centre. The SDST will be based on the DAST and will be a 30-minute screening test available free or at low cost. It will indicate general areas of strength and weakness, but its main function is to determine whether it is advisable to refer the student for a full diagnostic assessment of disability.

Stage 2   The SDST will indicate the profile of strengths and weaknesses, together with the likelihood of a diagnosis of dyslexia, but (regardless of the need for a formal diagnostic assessment) a further, more detailed assessment of support needs will be available via the Disability Support Centre, again using computer-based testing procedures, this time designed (if appropriate) to construct an Individual Academic Development Plan (IADP) tailored to the student's profile of attainments and aspirations.

Stage 3   Students with mental or physical health difficulties will be referred to the Student Health Service for treatment and/or counseling as appropriate. Students with an IADP will participate in a structured academic skills program designed to fulfill their IADPs.

Assessment of Academic Needs   This assessment adapts the informal support assessment procedure outlined previously and is intended to be undertaken by a suitably trained disability tutor. In brief, the objective of this assessment is the specification of an IADP developed in consultation among the student, the disability tutor, and a representative of the student's degree course. The IADP should include an Academic Skills Profile plus a set of clearly defined and agreed-on objectives, together with clearly laid down methods for achieving the objectives and for evaluating whether the student has attained them. The Academic Skills Profile will indicate areas of strength and weakness on key academic skills (including cognitive variables such as working memory, reading and writing fluency, and self-insight; study skills variables such as organization, planning, and examination performance; and subject-specific variables such as specific attainments in different topics and skills).

Support   A key requirement is to have a supportive yet formal system to guide the students to achieve their IADPs. We propose to create an Academic Skills Program that has a series of units, each based around an important skill known to be of value for students with disabilities and each of which involves a planned total of about 10 hours of work. Planned units include dyslexia and success, self-analysis and self-monitoring, organizational skills, report writing, intellectual skills (two units), examination skills, career choice, information retrieval, and use of information technology support. We hope to make the system completely computer based using the ViSuAL technique for making tutorials from videos (Nicolson et al., 1993), as discussed previously. Our aim, of course, would be to support the disabilities tutor, rather than the individual students. In due course, we hope to create a whole range of this type of resources for supporting tutors.

A similar system might be envisaged in job centers or in industry, whereby workers with difficulties would self-refer or be referred by management to human resources for assessment and support. In this situation, assessment for learning support would specify training modules and assessment for work-related support would identify ways in which the working environment could be modified to meet the specific needs of the individual worker.

CONCLUSION

There is a pressing need to develop valid and objective methods of diagnosing dyslexia and other LD for people of all ages. A two-stage diagnostic process may be the most cost-effective solution to this need. The first stage of a typical two-stage diagnostic process involves an initial low-cost screening undertaken by a support specialist. In the second stage, those individuals screened as being "at risk" should then be offered a more thorough assessment of their current levels of functional literacy through an adult literacy program. There is limited value in assessing for dyslexia or other LD unless this leads naturally into a systematic support system suitable for that individual. In this chapter, we have outlined progress toward our proposed three-stage screening–assessment–support system. The DAST fulfills the requirements for a quick but informative screening test. We have also described assessment via the ADI and evaluated the discriminative power of the prototype DAST for students, in comparison with scores on the ADI. The assessment procedure should lead in turn to the development of an individual development program tailored to the individual's profile of strengths, weaknesses, and objectives. We consider that there is the most scope for a computer-based multimedia system that aids the support specialist in all the stages of assessment and support. We are working on such systems for assisting in the development of reading skills as well as more general skills, This approach can be used in a variety of groups of individuals, from young offenders to adult literacy classes to general personnel selection and employee support. We consider that such systems, even in prototype form, are highly cost-effective and that their cost-effectiveness will increase significantly as the systems become more systematic and more coherent. A complete screening–assessment–support system has the potential to transform the opportunities for any adult with dyslexia.

REFERENCES

Aaron, I.E., Chall, J.S., Durkin, D., Goodman, K., & Strickland, D.S. (1990). The past, present and future of literacy education: Comment from a panel of distinguished educators, Part 1. *The Reading Teacher, 43*(4), 302–311.

Adams, M.J. (1990). *Beginning to read: Thinking and learning about print.* Cambridge, MA: MIT Press.

Adelman, P.B., & Vogel, S.A. (1990). College graduates with learning disabilities: Employment attainment and career patterns. *Learning Disability Quarterly, 13*, 154–166.

Adelman, P.B., & Vogel, S.A. (1993). Issues in the employment of adults with learning disabilities. *Learning Disability Quarterly, 16*, 219–232.

Adult Literacy and Basic Skills Unit. (1993). *Parents and their children: The intergenerational effect of poor basic skills.* London: Author.

Badian, N.A. (1984). Reading disability in an epidemiological context: Incidence and environmental correlates. *Journal of Learning Disabilities, 17*, 129–136.

Bradley, L., & Bryant, P.E. (1983). Categorising sounds and learning to read: A causal connection. *Nature, 301*, 419–421.

Chasty, H., & Friel, J. (1993). *Children with special needs: Caught in the act* (2nd ed.). London: Jessica Kingsley.

Critchley, M. (1964). *Developmental dyslexia.* London: Heinemann.

Denckla, M.B., & Rudel, R.G. (1976). Rapid "automatized" naming (R.A.N.): Dyslexia differentiated from other learning disabilities. *Neuropsychologia, 14*, 471–479.

Department for Education. (1994). *The code of practice on the identification and assessment of special educational needs.* London: Author. (Available from Her Majesty's Stationery Office, [ISBN 0 85522 444].)

Ekinsmyth, C., & Bynner, J. (1994). *The basic skills of young adults: Some findings from the 1970 British Cohort Study.* London: Adult Literacy and Basic Skills Unit.

Fawcett, A.J. (1995a). Case studies and some recent research. In T.R. Miles and V. Varma (Eds.), *Dyslexia and stress* (pp. 43–55). London: Colin Whurr.

Fawcett, A.J. (1995b). [Structured interview on DAST]. Internal report at the University of Sheffield, Sheffield, England. Unpublished raw data.

Fawcett, A.J., & Nicolson, R.I. (1993). *Validation of the Adult Dyslexia Index* (Internal report LRG 93/16). Sheffield, England: University of Sheffield, Department of Psychology.

Fawcett, A.J., & Nicolson, R.I. (1996a). *The Dyslexia Screening Test.* London: The Psychological Corporation (Europe).

Fawcett, A.J., & Nicolson, R.I. (1996b). Impaired performance of children with dyslexia on a range of cerebellar tasks. *Annals of Dyslexia, 46*, 259–283.

Felton, R.H., Naylor, C.E., & Wood, F.B. (1990). Neuropsychological profile of adult dyslexics. *Brain and Language, 39*, 485–497.

Finucci, J.M., Guthrie, J.T., Childs, A.L., Abbey, H., & Childs, B. (1976). The genetics of specific reading disability. *Annals of Human Genetics, 50*, 1–23.

Fowler, A.E., & Scarborough, H.S. (1993). *Should reading-disabled adults be distinguished from other adults seeking literacy instruction?* (Technical Report TR 93-7). Philadelphia: University of Pennsylvania, National Center on Adult Literacy.

Frith, U., Landerl, K., & Frith, C. (1995). Dyslexia and verbal fluency: More evidence for a phonological deficit. *Dyslexia, 1*, 2–11.

Gilroy, D.E., & Miles, T.R. (1995). *Dyslexia at college* (2nd ed.). London: Routledge.

Higgins, E.L., & Zvi, J.C. (1995). Assistive technology for postsecondary students with learning disabilities: From research to practice. *Annals of Dyslexia, 45,* 123–142.

Jorm, A.F., Share, D.L., McLean, R., & Matthews, D. (1986). Cognitive factors at a school sentry predictive of specific reading retardation and general reading backwardness: A research note. *Journal of Child Psychology and Psychiatry and Allied Disciplines, 27,* 45–54.

Kirsch, I.S., Jungeblut, A., Jenkins, L., & Kolstad, A. (1993). *Executive summary from "Adult Literacy in America": A first look at the results of the National Adult Literacy Survey.* Princeton, NJ: Educational Testing Service.

LaBerge, D., & Samuels, S.J. (1974). Toward a theory of automatic information processing in reading. *Cognitive Psychology, 6,* 293–323.

Lewis, R. (1984). *How to tutor and support learners* (Open Learning Guide 3). London, CET.

Lewis, R. (1987). *How to help learners assess their progress* (Open Learning Guide 2). London: CET.

Lynch, L.H.J. (1995). *Dyslexia and crime: A prevalence study.* Unpublished dissertation, Department of Psychology, University of Sheffield, England.

Lyon, G.R. (Ed.). (1994). *Frames of reference for the assessment of learning disabilities: New views on measurement issues.* Baltimore: Paul H. Brookes Publishing Co.

McLoughlin, D., Fitzgibbon, G., & Young, V. (1994). *Adult dyslexia: Assessment, counselling and training.* London: Colin Whurr.

McNeil, B.J., & Nelson, K.R. (1991). A meta-analysis of interactive video instruction: A 10 year review of achievement effects. *Journal of Computer-Based Instruction, 18,* 1–6.

Miles, T.R. (1983). *Dyslexia: The pattern of difficulties.* London: Granada.

Nicolson, R.I. (1990). The case for intelligent-based hypermedia. In C. Green & R. McAleese (Eds.), *Hypermedia.* Oxford, England: Hypermedia Intellect Books.

Nicolson, R.I., & Fawcett, A.J. (1990). Automaticity: A new framework for dyslexia research? *Cognition, 35,* 159–182.

Nicolson, R.I., & Fawcett, A.J. (1994). Spelling remediation for dyslexic children: A skills approach. In G.D.A Brown & N.C. Ellis (Eds.), *Handbook of spelling: Theory, process and intervention* (pp. 505–528). Chichester, England: Wiley.

Nicolson, R.I., & Fawcett, A.J. (1996a, September). Special initiative to encourage high quality provision for students with learning difficulties and disabilities. (Proposal for the Higher Education Funding Council). Sheffield, England: University of Sheffield.

Nicolson, R.I., & Fawcett, A.J. (1996b). *The Dyslexia Early Screening Test.* London: The Psychological Corporation (Europe).

Nicolson, R.I., & Fawcett, A.J. (1997). Dyslexia in adults: New developments in diagnosis and screening. *Journal of Research in Reading, 20,* 77–83.

Nicolson, R.I., Fawcett, A.J., & Miles, T.R. (1993). *Feasibility study for the development of a computerised screening test for dyslexia in adults* (Report OL176). Sheffield, England: Employment Department.

Nicolson, R.I., Syder, D., & Freeman, M. (1994). Construction of a ViSuAL (VIdeo-SUpported Active Learning) resource. *Computers and Education, 22,* 91–97.

Pennington, B.F. (1991). *Diagnosing learning disabilities: A neuropsychological framework.* New York: Guilford Press.

Pennington, B.F. (1995). Genetics of learning disabilities. *Journal of Child Neurology, 10,* 69–77.

Poseidon Film Productions. (1994). *Dyslexia and crime.* London: Channel 4.

Shaywitz, S.E., Shaywitz, B.A., Fletcher, J.M., & Escobar, M.D. (1990). Prevalence of reading disability in boys and girls: Results of the Connecticut Longitudinal Study. *Journal of the American Medical Association, 264,* 998–1002.

Singleton, C. (1996). Dyslexia in higher education: Issues for policy and practice. In C. Stephens (Ed.), *Proceedings of "Skill" conference: "Dyslexic student in higher education: Practical responses to student and institution needs"* (pp. 10–16). Huddersfield, England: University of Huddersfield/National Bureau for Students with Disabilities.

Stanovich, K.E. (1986). Matthew effects in reading: Some consequences of individual differences in the acquisition of literacy. *Reading Research Quarterly, 21,* 360–406.

Stanovich, K.E. (1988). Explaining the differences between the dyslexic and the garden variety poor reader: The phonological-core variable-difference model. *Journal of Learning Disabilities, 21,* 590–612.

Stedman, L.C., & Kaestle, C.F. (1987). Literacy and reading performance in the United States, from 1880 to the present. *Reading Research Quarterly, (22)*1, 8–46.

Vogel, S.A. (1982). On developing LD college programs. *Journal of Learning Disabilities, 15*(9), 518–527.

Vogel, S.A., & Adelman, P.B. (1992). The success of college students with learning disabilities: Factors related to educational attainment. *Journal of Learning Disabilities, 25*, 430–441.

Wechsler, D. (1986). *The Wechsler Adult Intelligence Scale–Revised (UK edition).* Sidcup, Kent, England: The Psychological Corporation.

Wechsler, D. (1993). *The Wechsler Objective Reading Dimension.* Sidcup, Kent, England: The Psychological Corporation.

West, T.G. (1991). *In the mind's eye.* New York: Prometheus.

Yap, R.L., & Van der Leij, A. (1993). Word processing in dyslexics: An automatic decoding deficit? *Reading and Writing: An Interdisciplinary Journal, 5*, 261–279.

9

Screening and Assessment Results of the Learning Disabilities Initiative

Identification of Individuals with Learning Disabilities in the Job Opportunities and Basic Skills Program

Melinda Giovengo, Elizabeth J. Moore, and Glenn Young

In November 1994, Washington State's Department of Social and Health Services (DSHS) implemented a Learning Disabilities Initiative (LDI) project designed to examine the prevalence of learning disabilities (LD) among people receiving Temporary Assistance for Needy Families (TANF).[1] Under the standard Job Opportunities and Basic Skills (JOBS) program model, JOBS participants lacking a high school diploma or General Equivalency Diploma (GED) are tested during the employability or social services assessment to determine their literacy levels. However, literacy testing instruments are not designed to detect the possible existence of a learning disability or other special learning need.

The accurate identification of JOBS program participants who have LD is critical for the success of any program designed to funnel participants into the employment arena. As resources diminish, each inaccurate screen carries with it distinctive risk for both the program and the individual. False positives cost the programs valuable resources in unnecessary and costly psychological evaluations, thus cutting the available funding for critical services in other areas. False negatives place participants into the cycle of continued difficulty and lack of services that will appropriately address the

---

The use of non–person-first language throughout this chapter is to keep findings from the screening and assessment consistent with the results of the Learning Disabilities Initiative.

[1]Prior to the enactment of the Personal Responsibility Act of 1993 (PL 104-93), the Temporary Assistance for Needy Families program was named Aid to Families with Dependent Children (AFDC).

barriers they bring to being successful in the job market. Additional costs to programs accrue through the recycling of participants through services and participants' additional time in public welfare programs.

Goals of the Project

The following goals were established for the LDI project:

- To estimate the prevalence of LD within the Washington State TANF group
- To provide instructional accommodations and medical interventions
- To develop a brief screening tool to be used to identify individuals receiving TANF who may need further assessment
- To increase workers' awareness of the specific needs of people with LD
- To encourage the development of new program strategies and instructional techniques to promote self-sufficiency within the group of individuals receiving TANF with LD

The following are anticipated outcomes of the LDI project:

- Determining prevalence estimates of LD in the TANF/JOBS program group of individuals
- Determining the accuracy of the Payne Learning Needs Inventory in identifying participants who have LD
- Developing a methodology to better serve people with LD

Definitions

Consistent definitions, terminology, assessment, and remediation have not been established for the LD field (e.g., Torgesen & Wong, 1986). Many different definitions have been proposed, from that of the National Joint Committee for Learning Disabilities to the specific disorders related to learning in the *Diagnostic and Statistical Manual of Mental Disorders, Fourth Edition* (American Psychiatric Association, 1994). Such a lack of consensus in the field has led to substantial differences of opinion regarding how to identify children and adults with LD. The following definition of *learning disability* was adopted for the study presented in this chapter:

> A learning disability is a neurological condition that impedes a person's ability to store, process, and/or produce information. Learning disabilities can affect one's ability to read, write, speak, or compute math and can impair socialization skills. Individuals with LD are of average or above average intelligence, but the disability creates a gap between ability and performance. (National Center for Learning Disabilities, 1996–1997, p. 1)

This definition is measured through a discrepancy diagnostic model looking at the differences between the individual's expected performance and his or her actual performance as measured on an academic achievement test. This definition allows for the inclusion of adults and is compatible with the Education for All Handicapped Children Act of 1975 (PL 94-142).

DESCRIPTION OF THE LEARNING DISABILITIES INITIATIVE PROJECT

Participants

The Capitol Hill Community Services Office in Seattle, Washington, serving an urban population, and the Wenatchee Community Services Office in eastern Washington state, serving a rural population, were chosen as pilot sites. A total of 193 individuals receiving TANF who volunteered to be part of the JOBS program were recruited to participate in the study and, if they agreed, were screened to identify LD and then evaluated by a contracted clinical educational psychologist for diagnostic evaluation.

Learning Disabilities Identification Process

Evaluation information was shared with the participant, Department of Social and Health Services (DSHS) worker, and education/instruction provider. With an understanding of the reasons for previous difficulties with learning, the participant is in a better position to assume responsibility for developing social skills, follow through on educational activities, and use resources in a self-directed manner. Educators/instructors used the information to design appropriate accommodations in the education or instruction activity to ensure that the participant received quality instruction. Accommodations included but were not limited to alternative testing methods, alternative instructional techniques, access to libraries for the blind and those with dyslexia, and individual tutoring. In addition, all participants who were found to have a learning disability or whose IQ score fell within the 70–79 range were included in a special Group Training Program designed by the Learning Disabilities Association (LDA) of Washington State. LDA designed the Lifeskills, Employment, Accommodation, and Development (LEAD) program[2] to address the needs of the low-income population with LD and act as a catalyst for individuals reentering educational or job-training activities.

Service coordination services include provisions for personal, academic, career, and employment counseling. Other services are participant-centered and include semimonthly conferences to monitor progress and ensure that appropriate accommodations are being provided.

Screening   The Payne & Associates Payne Learning Needs Inventory was tested for use as a screening tool with the group of individuals receiving TANF. This is a two-part inventory designed to identify strengths and weaknesses of learning styles in its recipients and "red flag" any learning difficulties in the participants. It uses a system of color flagging in which red indicates the need for further assessment, orange indicates potential difficulties that may be less severe, and pink indicates no difficulty identified. This screening tool was administered through an oral interview format with a large-print copy to allow participants to follow along if appropriate. Payne & Associates developed the Payne Learning Needs Inventory (see Chapter 6) so that it can be administered by DSHS social workers after limited training. The inventory was chosen for field testing in the Washington State pilot projects because of its use in many other settings and states.

The purpose of the screening step is to identify individuals who *may* have LD and to alert practitioners to the possibility of a special learning need in the individual. In the LDI study, all participants were referred for a diagnostic evaluation. On validation of the screening tool as an effective and reliable indicator of LD, diagnostic evaluations will be necessary only for those who screen positive.

Psychological Evaluation   A clinical educational psychologist with a background in identifying LD for the public schools administered standardized intelligence quotient (IQ) and educational achievement testing and, when appropriate, additional assessment of adaptive functioning and freedom from distractibility. The formal assessment involved the administration of the Wechsler Adult Intelligence Scale–Revised (Wechsler, 1981)

---

[2]The curriculum is available through LDA of Washington, 7819 159th Place NE, Redmond, WA 98052.

and the Woodcock-Johnson Revised Tests of Achievement Battery, Part B (Woodcock, 1977).

The purpose of the psychological evaluation step is to confirm or deny the presence of a learning disability; establish the actual prevalence of special learning needs in the group receiving TANF; and to assess the validity of the screening tool, that is, its ability to correctly distinguish between those participants who are likely to have a special learning need and those who are not. For those participants diagnosed as having a learning disability, the evaluation further identifies the specific type of learning disability, resulting in recommendations as to the type of instructional techniques that would be most beneficial to the participant based on his or her disability.

Diagnosis

The diagnosis of a learning disability is made if an individual's actual achievement falls significantly short of his or her expected achievement, based on ability. The definition of "significant" in this context has been disputed (Stanovich, 1989). Although this criterion is not without its detractors, most states require a statistically significant (minimum 15-point) difference between intellectual functioning as measured by IQ testing and academic achievement (excluding those individuals with IQ scores falling below 85) (Frankenberger & Harper, 1987; Hammill, 1990), and the GED Testing Services requires a 15-point (1 standard deviation) discrepancy between verbal and performance IQ scores on a standard test (American Council on Education, 1992). The disadvantage of this method is that it becomes more difficult to demonstrate a learning disability as one approaches the lower end of the IQ score spectrum because of the increasingly restricted range for qualifying achievement scores. To address this issue, Washington state's Office of Special Education implemented the use of a regression-based discrepancy formula (see Table 9.1) for calculating severe discrepancies between overall ability and achievement to determine learning disability eligibility (Washington Administrative Code § 392-172-130, 1995). This method requires smaller discrepancies as one approaches the lower end of the IQ score spectrum and greater discrepancies at the higher end of the spectrum. This formula takes into account the statistical relationship that exists between IQ score and achievement, which is typically not accounted for in the standard discrepancy model (Hallahan, Kaufman, & Lloyd, 1996). In addition, the criterion attempts to account for part of the cultural bias that is inherent in standardized tests.[3] The criteria established by the regression formula were selected as the criteria for identification for this study.

Validity of the Screening Tool

The validity of the screening tool was assessed by comparing its results (positive or negative screen) with those of the formal psychological evaluation (positive or negative diagnosis). This allowed us to determine the rates of false positives and false negatives that occur in using the Payne Learning Needs Inventory. Using the three scaling variables provided by the Payne Inventory (red, orange, and pink) and four LD diagnostic criteria (professional judgment, regression formula discrepancy, IQ–achievement discrepancy of 15 points, and verbal IQ–performance IQ split of 15 points), in addition to an overall scale assigned a positive score if any of the four diagnostic criteria yielded a positive score, two-way frequency tables were constructed to identify the sensitivity

---

[3]Please see full technical report of the Washington State Learning Disabilities Initiative, available through DSHS WorkFirst Division, LD Project Director, 3600 South Graham Street, Seattle, WA 98118.

Table 9.1.   State of Washington severe discrepancy tables

Intelligence quotient	Criterion score	Intelligence quotient	Criterion score	Intelligence quotient	Criterion score
69	62	88	75	107	87
70	62	89	75	108	88
71	63	90	76	109	88
72	64	91	76	110	89
73	65	92	77	111	89
74	65	93	78	112	90
75	66	94	78	113	91
76	67	95	79	114	91
77	67	96	80	115	92
78	68	97	80	116	93
79	69	98	81	117	93
80	69	99	82	118	94
81	70	100	82	119	95
82	71	101	83	120	95
83	71	102	84	121	96
84	72	103	84	122	97
85	73	104	85	123	97
86	73	105	86	124	98
87	74	106	86	125	99

Note: Table presents criterion discrepancy scores, ages 6–21 years.

(rate of correct positive identification), specificity (rate of correct ruling out), false positives (rate of incorrect positive identification), and false negatives (rate of incorrect ruling out) produced by the screening tool.

STUDY FINDINGS

Demographics of the Project Sample

Of the 193 participants who received TANF and agreed to participate in the study, 171 completed the initial interview *and* the psychological evaluation. Participants were given a modest honorarium to complete the screening portion ($10.00) and the formal psychological assessment ($25.00). Although this encouraged some participation, it should be noted that, at the time of this study, the entire JOBS program was contingent on voluntary participation. In addition, this voluntary participation and the instability of housing for this group of individuals accounted for any attrition that was experienced during the project period. Data are computed based on complete information available for the particular data point. Some participants did not complete the final phase of assessment (*n* = 22), and no data were available for follow-up.

Table 9.2 summarizes the demographic characteristics of the sample. The table shows that the study participants were predominantly Caucasian (59%) or African American (33%) single mothers (86%) with an average of 1.8 children among those with any children. They ranged in age from 17 to 58 years, with an average age of 29 years. Thirty-seven percent of the participants were younger than 25 years of age at the time they were recruited into the study. About half already either had received a high school diploma (34%) or had completed their GED (17%),[4] and 41% reported making no effort to obtain a diploma or a GED. On average, the participants had com-

---

[4]The longer that participants were on assistance, the greater their educational attainment. This educational attainment could have occurred as a result of participation in the state JOBS program.

Table 9.2.   Demographics of sample

Demographic characteristics	Number	Percentage
Gender: female	164	(88.2%)
Single-parent household	156	(86.2%)
Number of children	1.8	
Ethnicity		
Caucasian	107	(59.1%)
African American	59	(32.6%)
Hispanic	8	(4.4%)
Asian/Pacific Islander	3	(1.7%)
Native American/Alaska Native	4	(2.2%)
Age		
Average age	29	
25 years and younger	67	(37.4%)
25 years and older	112	(62.6%)
Education		
Years of education	10.6	
High school diploma	60	(33.9%)
GED[a]	30	(16.9%)
GED in progress	15	(8.5%)
No diploma, no GED action	72	(40.7%)
Education by age group		
25 years and younger		
High school diploma or GED	28	(43.1%)
GED in progress	7	(10.8%)
No diploma, no GED action	30	(46.2%)
25 years and older		
High school diploma or GED	60	(57.1%)
GED in progress	7	(6.7%)
No diploma, no GED action	38	(36.2%)
Dropped before psychological evaluation	22	(11.4%)
Months on TANF		
Overall	65.8	
25 years and younger	36.2	
25 years and older	82.8	
Months on food stamps		
Overall	46.6	
25 and younger	24.9	
25 and older	55.9	

Note: Overall sample (*N* = 193)
[a]GED, General Equivalency Diploma.

pleted 10.6 years of school. These participants had received TANF for an average of 66 months and food stamps for an average of 47 months. Almost half of the participants younger than 25 years of age had not received a high school diploma and had not obtained or were not currently working on a GED, compared with 36% of the 25 and older age group.

Overall, the group of individuals included in the pilot study matched the statewide population, with the exception of African Americans who were more heavily represented because of the urban pilot site choice. It was very important to the DSHS that the LDI look at both the rural and urban groups. This preference was the deciding factor in the choice of the two pilot site locations. The Seattle and Wenatchee sites serve different types of communities. Seattle is a large, relatively densely populated urban community, whereas Wenatchee is a less densely populated agricultural community where some seasonal employment is available.

Learning Characteristics of the Sample

Figure 9.1 displays the prevalence of special learning needs among the participants. This figure shows that more than half of the study participants were assessed as having some type of special learning need: 36% were diagnosed as having a learning disability; 13% as "slow learners," with IQ scores between 70 and 79; and 5% as having mild mental retardation (MMR; IQ score below 70). This figure represents discrete categories of individuals with special learning needs as defined for the project.

Table 9.3 summarizes the learning characteristics of the participants. The table shows that, overall, 35.5% of the project participants were diagnosed as having a learning disability using Washington state's regression method. The average IQ score in this sample is 86.6%. Achievement scores indicate that the participants are producing written work at about the sixth-grade level, using math at the seventh-grade level, reading at the eighth-grade level, and understanding language at the ninth-grade level.

Overall, more than half of the study participants were identified as having some special learning need (MMR, 5%; slow learner, 13%; learning disability, 36%). The existence of a special learning need is evidenced in educational status. Of those without an identified special learning need, 63.5% had obtained a high school diploma or GED. Among those with an identified learning need, however, the number obtaining a high school diploma or GED declines to 39%. These figures indicate that participants with special learning needs are more likely than their peers to have unsuccessful school experiences and drop out of the system.

Basic Demographics by Diagnosis

Of the 193 participants who agreed to participate, 178 (92%) completed at least part of the Payne instrument, and 171 (88.6%) completed the psychological evaluation. Basic demographic data were collected during both interviews. Table 9.4 summarizes the demographic distribution of the study participants by diagnosis (presence or absence of learning disability).

There is no significant difference between participants with and without LD in number of children, years of education, single-parent status, or months on public assis-

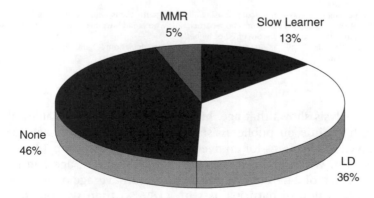

Figure 9.1.   Prevalence of learning needs among recipients of Temporary Assistance for Needy Families. (*Key:* ■ = None; ■ = MMR; ■ = Slow learner; □ = LD; LD, learning disabilities; MMR, mild mental retardation.)

Table 9.3.   Learning characteristics of participants

Learning characteristics	Number	Percentage
Prevalence of LD	59	(37.3%[a])
IQ score		
Average IQ score	85.6	(SD = 11.8)
MMR (below 70)	8	(4.70%)
"Slow learner" (70–79)	49	(28.7%)
80 or higher	114	(66.7%)
Prevalence of LD by IQ category		
80 or higher	34	(30.6%)
70–79	25	(53.2%)
Achievement (grade equivalents and standard scores)		
Writing	6.3	78.9
Mathematics	7.3	83.8
Comprehension	9.0	83.6
Broad reading	9.2	86.7
Basic reading	8.0	84.7
Learning need		
MMR	8	(4.80%)
Slow learner, not LD	22	(13.3%)
LD (by regressional method)	59	(35.5%)
IQ score 80 or higher and not a learning disability	77	(46.4%)
Learning need by educational status		
MMR		
Diploma or GED	1	(14.3%)
GED in progress	1	(14.3%)
No diploma, no GED progress	5	(71.4%)
Slow learner		
Diploma or GED	8	(40%)
GED in progress	1	(05%)
No diploma, no GED action	11	(55%)
Learning disability		
Diploma or GED	23	(41.8%)
GED in progress	6	(10.9%)
No diploma, no GED action	26	(47.3%)
IQ score 80 or higher and not a learning disability		
Diploma or GED	47	(63.5%)
GED in progress	6	(8.10%)
No diploma, no GED action	21	(28.4%)

Note: Overall sample (*N* = 162). The numbers in this table differ slightly as a result of missing data. Percentages are based on actual available data.

[a] A 36% rate of learning disability was calculated using all of the participants who received a psychological examination; the 37.3% rate was calculated using only those participants who could have been diagnosed with a learning disability (i.e., those individuals with an IQ score of 70 or higher).

LD, learning disabilities; MMR, mild mental retardation; *SD*, standard deviation; IQ, intelligence quotient; GED, General Equivalency Diploma.

tance. Further analysis shows that age, but none of the other variables of interest, is related to length of time on public assistance. Those participants ages 25 years and older had received food stamps for an average of 55.9 months and TANF for an average of 82.8 months, whereas those younger than 25 years of age had received food stamps for an average of 24.9 months and TANF for an average of 36.2 months.

A greater proportion of participants with (18.6%) than without (8.1%) LD are men, and three quarters of the participants without LD are ages 25 and older, compared with 57.1% of the participants with LD. The average full-scale IQ score for all

Table 9.4.   Demographic description of project participants with and without learning disabilities (LD)

Description	Without LD	With LD	Total mean/percent
Number of children	1.6	1.8	1.7 children
Ethnicity			
African American	25%	39.7%	32.6%
Asian/Pacific Islander	2.1%	0%	1.7%
Caucasian	66.7%	53.4%	59.1%
Hispanic/Latino	4.2%	6.9%	4.4%
Native American/Alaska Native	2.1%	0%	2.2%
Male $(\chi^2_1 = 3.9^a)$	8.1%	18.6%	11.8%
Female	91.9%	81.4%	88.2%
Age (mean years) $(\chi^2_1 = 4.9^a)$	28.9	30.4	29.5
17–24 years	42.9%	25%	37%
25 and older	57.1%	75%	63%
Case type			
Two parents in household	10.3%	19.3%	13.8%
Single parent in household	89.7%	80.7%	86.2%
IQ score			
Full-scale IQ[b]	88.8	82.8	86.6
Verbal subtest[c]	87.2	79.6	84.4
Performance subtest	91.6	87.5	90.0
Months on public assistance			
TANF (n = 137 available)	61.0	79.1	67.6
Food stamps (n = 136 available)	42.9	52.5	46.4
Ever diagnosed LD $(\chi^2_1 = 4.2^a)$	20.9%	36.4%	26.7%
Grade in school	10.6	10.4	10.5
Educational status			
High school diploma	34%	36.4%	33.9%
GED completed	24.5%	5.5%	16.9%
GED in progress	7.4%	10.9%	8.5%
No diploma, GED, or progress	34%	47.3%	40.7%

[a] $p < .05$; [b] $p < .01$; [c] $p < .001$

TANF, Temporary Assistance for Needy Families (formally AFDC); GED, General Equivalency Diploma.

participants is 86.6, with verbal IQ score averaging 84.4 and performance IQ score averaging 90. Participants with LD scored significantly lower on both the full-scale IQ and the verbal portion. These differences may reflect true differences in intelligence or may indicate that individuals with significant LD may achieve lower IQ test scores because of their learning difficulty.

About one third of both groups have completed their high school diploma, and an additional one fourth of participants without LD (compared with only 5% of participants with LD) have completed their GEDs. Although a greater percentage of participants in the school system with than without LD (as diagnosed by the study criteria) had previously been diagnosed as having LD (36.4% versus 20.9%, respectively), these figures indicate a poor rate of identification of this disability. Analysis by age of the participant shows that identification is improving, perhaps as a result of the enactment of the Education for All Handicapped Children Act of 1975 (PL 94-142) (known as the Individuals with Disabilities Education Act [PL 101-476.]). These results are summarized in Table 9.5. The groups are divided by age into 24 years and younger and 25 years and older based on the JOBS program breakdown in service priorities. Under the JOBS program, participants ages 24 and younger were referred primarily for continued education and GED completion.

Sixty-two percent of the participants younger than 25 years of age diagnosed in this study as having LD had been previously identified, compared with 31% of such participants ages 25 years and older. False-positive identifications have also increased somewhat, mostly among the participants diagnosed as having MMR and "slow learner" participants.

Participants between the ages of 17 and 24 left school between 1984 and 1995, with the median year being 1991. Older participants left school between 1953 and 1988, with the median year being 1978.

Table 9.5 shows that about one fourth of the participants 25 years and older at the time of assessment had been diagnosed with LD in school. In comparison, almost one third of the participants in the younger age group received such a diagnosis in school, indicating that participants who attended school more recently are more likely to have a diagnosed learning disability while in school.

Table 9.5 shows an increase in both correct and incorrect school diagnoses of LD. The shaded columns show false positive in-school diagnoses. Participants with a current diagnosis of no special learning need, MMR, LD, or slow learners who were diagnosed with a learning disability in school. The percentage of students who are incorrectly diagnosed with a learning disability increased from 17.4% among students without LD to 30% among the younger participants. Among participants diagnosed with a learning disability, 30.8% of the older students were correctly diagnosed in school, compared with 61.5% of the younger students.

Effect of Age and Learning Disability on Educational Status

The purpose of the next analysis was to examine the effect of learning disability on educational status for those younger than 25 years of age and still eligible for public education and those age 25 years and older. Table 9.6 summarizes educational status by learning disability status and age. Significantly more of the students with than without LD had earned either a high school diploma or a GED (58.1% versus 44.2%, respectively), and significantly more of the students in the older age group had earned either degree (60.0% versus 52.6%, respectively). Just more than half of the individuals without LD who are still eligible for public education have not completed either a high school diploma or a GED. More than three quarters of the students in this age range with a positive learning disability diagnosis have not yet completed either degree.

Educational Achievement and Special Learning Needs

The achievement portion of the psychological evaluation yielded grade-equivalent scores in five areas of academic achievement: writing, math, comprehension, broad reading, and basic reading. For each student, the difference was computed between the grade-equivalent score achieved during the evaluation in each of the five academic areas and the number of years of education completed by that student. The resulting

Table 9.5.   Special learning need by previous diagnosis and age

Diagnosed through project	Percent of LD in school (by age)	
	25+ years	17–24 years
No identified need	8 (19.5%)	6 (20.7%)
Mild mental retardation	0 (0.00%)	3 (100%)
"Slow learner"	2 (16.7%)	3 (37.5%)
Learning disability	12 (30.8%)	8 (61.5%)
Total	(23.8%)	(32.8%)

Table 9.6.   Educational status of project participants with and without LD by age

	Educational status	
Participant group	Completed GED or high school diploma	No completed degree
Total sample (N = 145)		
Without LD (N = 93)	54 (58.1%)	39 (41.9%)
With LD (N = 52)	23 (44.2%)	29 (55.8%)
17–24 years old (N = 54)		
Without LD (N = 40)	19 (47.5%)	21 (52.6%)
With LD (N = 14)	3 (21.4%)	11 (78.6%)
25+ years old (N = 91)		
Without LD (N = 53)	35 (66.0%)	18 (34.0%)
With LD (N = 38)	20 (52.6%)	18 (47.4%)

GED, General Equivalency Diploma; N, total number in the sample.
Note: LD, learning disabilities.

numbers could be negative (meaning that achievement is below what would be expected based on years of education), zero (meaning that achievement is what would be expected based on years of education), or positive (meaning that achievement exceeds years of education). Figure 9.2 displays these differences by special learning need.

The average achievement of the groups with special learning needs (LD, Slow learner, MMR) was from 3 to 6 years less than what would be expected based on their years of education (see Figure 9.2). For the students with LD, the most impaired areas

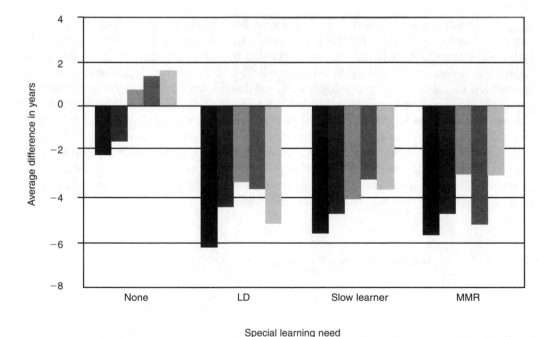

Figure 9.2.   Average difference in years between achievement and education by learning need. (*Key:* ■ = writing; ■ = math; ■ = comprehension; ■ = broad reading; ■ = basic reading; LD, learning disabilities; MMR, mild mental retardation.)

included writing and basic reading. The importance of this finding further strengthens the belief that these individuals demonstrate impairments that are more neurologically related versus being attributable to a lack of achievement or deficient academic exposure. The discrepancy between reported educational level and performance in these two areas was much greater than in those individuals within the MMR or slow learner groups. Furthermore, students demonstrated that, when the information was received, it could be assimilated into overall comprehension. In contrast, the average achievement of those without an identified special learning need ranged from 2 years less than expectation to 2 years beyond expectation based on years of education. Follow-up analyses showed that these gaps between years of education and academic achievement are not related to age, sex, or educational differences between the groups.

Effectiveness of the Special Learning Needs
Inventory for Identifying Individuals with Learning Disabilities

The results of the Payne Learning Needs Inventory were compared with the results of the psychologist's evaluation of learning disability. Table 9.7 summarizes the results of these analyses. Of the 58 participants positively diagnosed as having LD, the Payne tool correctly identified 41 (70.7%), leaving 17 participants without necessary services. Of the 94 participants not diagnosed as having LD, 61 (64.9%) were ruled out with the Payne tool (erroneously qualifying 33 for potentially unnecessary services or evaluation). Further analysis of these "false positives" revealed that the individuals without LD who would have been referred for further evaluation based on the Payne tool tended to have other special learning needs. Eighty-six percent of the participants with MMR, 48% of the "slow learner" participants, and 32% of the participants identified as having no identified special learning need screened positive with the Payne tool.

Those participants who received a positive diagnosis of learning disability but were screened negative by the screening tool tended to be higher functioning than those who were screened positive, and they received higher achievement scores in all five academic areas, most notably in writing, math, and broad reading. These scores are presented in Table 9.8. The participants with LD who screened negative also had consistently smaller gaps between achievement and ability than did the participants with LD who screened positive. Table 9.9 presents the gap between achievement and ability for these participants in each academic area. Except in the area of writing, the participants with LD who screened negative averaged small gaps between ability and achievement. This may suggest that the screening tool is weak at identifying individuals with a writing disability and relatively effective in identifying other types of LD when there is a relatively large gap between achievement and ability.

Table 9.7.   Success of Payne instrument

Screened LD	Assessed LD		Total
	No	Yes	
No	61	17	78 (51.3%)
Yes	33	41	74 (48.7%)
Total	94 (61.8%)	58 (38.2%)	152

LD, learning disabilities.

Table 9.8.   Achievement for participants with learning disabilities (LD) by Payne screen results

Subject area	LD, negative screen		LD, positive screen	
Writing	5.1	(72.8)	3.7	(66.8)
Math	6.5	(83.4)	5.4	(75.5)
Comprehension	8.4	(80.6)	6.4	(72.7)
Broad reading	8.2	(84.7)	6.0	(73.3)
Basic reading	7.1	(80.2)	4.7	(70.2)

Note: Numbers without parentheses represent grade equivalence; numbers with parentheses represent standard scores.

CONCLUSION AND FUTURE DIRECTIONS

The findings of the LDI project can be summarized as follows:

- More than half of the TANF recipients in the study are identified as having some special learning need (learning disability, 36%; slow learner, 13%; MMR, 5%).
- Those participants with a special learning need (39%) had obtained a high school diploma or GED, compared with 63.5% of those without an identified learning need.
- The special learning needs of many of these study participants have not been identified in school. Thirty-six percent of the participants with LD recalled having been identified previously as such, as did 21% of participants *without* a diagnosable learning disability. Special learning needs were not effectively accommodated in the school experience of many of these individuals, and they left school before graduation.
- The average achievement of the groups with special learning needs was from 3 to 6 years less than what would be expected based on their years of education. In contrast, the average achievement of those participants *without* an identified special learning need ranged from 2 years less than expectation to 2 years beyond expectation based on years of education. The academic achievement of the participants with LD was similar to that of the slow learner participants and participants with MMR.
- Two thirds of the participants were correctly screened using the Payne tool. Seventy-one percent of the participants with LD were positively screened, whereas sixty-five percent of the participants without LD were negatively screened. Participants without LD who were positively screened tended to have other learning needs, whereas participants with LD who were negatively screened tended to be higher functioning.

Additional research is currently under way that will

- Replicate the current study on a larger, more diverse sample to improve generalizability

Table 9.9.   Gaps between achievement and ability for participants with learning disabilities (LD) by Payne screen results (average discrepancy scores between full-scale IQ scores and standard achievement scores)

Subject area	LD, negative screen	LD, positive screen
Writing	13.3	15.6
Math	3.4	6.6
Comprehension	3.5	9.1
Broad reading	2.2	8.8
Basic reading	3.2	11.5

- Include outcome evaluations to determine whether the interventions provided to the participants have been effective in helping them to achieve their goals of self-sufficiency
- Validate a brief version of the screening tool developed on the current sample (a brief screen will be more easily and consistently administered than the full Payne instrument, providing social service workers with a consistent and reliable basis for referring individuals for further assessment)

Several policy implications can be drawn from the results of this project. First, a statewide task force should be convened to examine the multiple criteria for service delivery in regard to a specific learning disability (SLD) diagnosis. This committee should include representatives from the state department of vocational rehabilitation, the DSHS, special education, education, mental health, higher educational institutions and technical colleges, and the literacy community; GED representatives; a representative from the disability community; and an expert in the field of LD. The goal of this task force should be to develop statewide regulations regarding consistency in qualifications for services. As of 1998, consumers and students may be qualified under one department and not another. Testing and diagnostic criteria are inconsistent and lead to costly reevaluations, often at the consumer's expense. Yet, without such diagnostics, the individual may not be afforded the accommodations and services necessary to achieve self-sufficiency.

Second, a policy must be established of providing learning disability evaluations for individuals who are flagged as needing additional services. Identifying or developing a consistent funding source to support this policy may involve improved utilization of and access to available resources, or it may require the development of new services. A review should be made of available resources and utilization and accessibility of these resources to consumers for learning disability evaluations. School protocols and guidelines for use of early periodic screening treatment and diagnosis dollars should be examined. The possibility of linking with training programs (e.g., the School of Education at the University of Washington) to establish appropriate internships should be considered.

Third, staff instruction on the impact of LD on services and possible accommodations that can be implemented must be continued. Instruction on an accommodation planning tool for use by social workers to help consumers and employment specialists better understand the strengths and weaknesses of individuals who have LD should be considered.

REFERENCES

American Council on Education. (1992). *GED test accommodations: For candidates with specific learning disabilities*. Washington, DC: Author.

American Psychiatric Association. (1994). *Diagnostic and statistical manual of mental disorders* (4th ed.). Washington, DC: Author.

Education for All Handicapped Children Act of 1975, PL 94-142, 20 U.S.C. §§ 1400 *et seq.*

Frankenberger, W., & Harper, J. (1987). State criterion and procedures for identifying learning disabled children: A comparison of 1981/82 and 1985/86 guidelines. *Journal of Learning Disabilities, 20,* 188–121.

Hallahan, D., Kauffman, J., & Lloyd, J. (1996). *Introduction to learning disabilities*. New York: Simon & Schuster.

Hammill, D. (1990). On defining learning disabilities: An emerging consensus. *Journal of Learning Disabilities, 23,* 84.

Individuals with Disabilities Education Act of 1990, PL 101-476, 20 U.S.C. §§ 1400 *et seq.*

National Center for Learning Disabilities. (1996–97). *Their world.* New York: Author.

Personal Responsibility Act of 1996, PL 104-193.

Stanovich, K.E. (1989). Has the learning disabilities field lost its intelligence? *Journal of Learning Disabilities, 22* (8), 487–492.

Torgensen, J.K., & Wong, B. (Eds.). (1986). *Psychological and educational perspectives on learning disabilities.* New York: Academic Press.

Wechsler, D. (1981). *Manual for the Wechsler Adult Intelligence Scale–Revised.* San Antonio, TX: The Psychological Corporation.

Woodcock, R.W. (1977). *Woodcock-Johnson Psycho-Educational Battery: Assessment Services Bulletin No. 2.* Allen, TX: DLM Teaching Resources.

Washington Administration Code § 392-172-130 (1995).

III

Instructional Strategies

Section III addresses the question of instruction for adults identified with or at risk for learning disabilities (LD) in adult education and literacy education settings. One of the basic assumptions is that the teaching strategies that are effective for individuals with severe reading disabilities, regardless of whether they are identified formally, will benefit all adult learners. Two models that have been used to deliver in-service instruction for tutors and literacy providers are presented in Section III.

Chapter 10 describes a 12-hour course for teaching adults with LD. The course, developed by Blanche Podhajski in Vermont, was designed to be delivered through interactive television. This professional development program, based on research funded by the National Institute of Child Health and Human Development, uses videotaped sessions of teachers demonstrating the program followed by one-to-one coaching. The course is composed of several components: the language continuum (metalinguistics, phonology, semantics, morphology, syntax, and pragmatics), a structured language approach to teaching decoding skills, and specific strategies to teach spelling.

Chapter 11 describes the Wilson Reading Program (WRP), one of the most widely used adult reading programs. The WRP is based on the content and principles of the multisensory structured language education approach of the Orton-Gillingham philosophy. Barbara A. Wilson, the founder of the WRP, describes this 12-step, 1–3 year program in which students master each step in a carefully sequenced progression, with the end result being fluent and accurate decoding and encoding (i.e., reading and spelling) skills. Wilson describes the effectiveness of the WRP at several different sites, including a university with support services for students with LD, a community college, a library literacy center, and a private center for students with dyslexia. The programs in each environment are described in depth, including how each is funded, the student admissions criteria, the methods of program delivery, and the results of program evaluation.

An often neglected area in the curriculum for adults with severe reading and spelling difficulties is the area of math literacy or functional math. This book would be incomplete without Chapter 12, written by James R. Patton, Mary E. Cronin, and Diane S. Bassett. This chapter explains math disabilities and offers methods for teaching the basic math skills that are needed to function independently as an adult. Based on a careful review of the literature, the authors address the questions surrounding the characteristics of individuals with difficulties in math literacy and discuss the implications of these characteristics on achieving various competencies with basic math skills. The authors argue that competencies need to be taught in a life-skills curriculum, regardless of the individuals' disabilities. The authors suggest that difficulties with basic math competencies should be identified on the job, in postsecondary training/education environments, and during everyday life activities. A common thread in each of these settings is the centrality of problem solving. Furthermore, the authors recommend that whenever possible, the life-skills curriculum should be integrated into the other content areas of instruction and should be related to the students' current and future needs.

LD teachers as well as adult education and literary instructors have come to realize that in spite of their best efforts to educate and instruct adults, the difficulties observed in adults with LD in reading, spelling, written expression, and math often persist. Moreover, in spite of the recognition of the importance of program evaluation, there is limited research regarding the most effective instructional approaches. In addition, not all adults with LD have remained in school, and many have become impatient with basic skills programs that require a significant commitment over an extended period of time—a luxury that some adults, if not most, cannot afford. For these reasons, an alternative approach that bypasses the impairment areas rather than striving to improve them, has been suggested—namely, the use of technology.

Chapter 13 describes a variety of assistive technological devices that many adults with LD have found helpful in compensating for their LD. The technology is divided into the following categories: written language, reading, listening, organization/memory, and math. Marshall Raskind provides a method for determining whether a particular device is appropriate for an individual and whether the device will meet the individual's needs. Raskind also provides a model for selecting the right type of assistive technology and discusses cost analysis, the availability of external funding, and the challenge of learning how to use new devices. LD teachers, ABE and ASE instructors, and other literacy providers are encouraged to explore all avenues to assist their students (i.e., instructional intervention as well as bypass strategies through the use of assistive technology).

10

Professional Development in Learning Disabilities for Adult Literacy Providers

Blanche Podhajski

In the past, literacy and learning disabilities (LD) were considered very distinct issues. As literacy providers and policy makers placed greater emphasis on lifelong learning, however, interest in the relationship between literacy and LD intensified. This interest swelled within adult education programs, where individuals wrestling with literacy problems were concentrated. There is increasing evidence that adults with LD constitute a significant percentage of students in adult literacy basic education programs (Bowren, 1981; Gold, 1981; Thistlewaite, 1983).

LITERACY AND ADULT EDUCATION

As the field of LD has matured since its inception in 1963, so too has the group of individuals served. During the 1970s, attention expanded to include the needs of adults as well as children. Early interest in adults with LD focused on individuals who had been identified during childhood (Rogan & Hartman, 1990), particularly those who continued their education beyond high school (Patton & Polloway, 1982; Rogan & Hartman, 1990; Vogel, 1985; White, Schumaker, Warner, Alley, Deshler, 1980). Passage of the Americans with Disabilities Act (PL 101-336) in 1990, establishment of the Goals 2000 initiative in 1991, and publication of results of the National Adult Literacy Survey in 1993 (Kirsch, Jungeblut, Jenkins, & Kolstad, 1993) challenged adult educators to consider the needs of all adults, including those with LD, and rethink their definitions of *literacy*.

Traditional definitions of *literacy* focused on reading and writing, whereas current thinking expands the concept to a broader range of skills considered essential to functioning in work, home, and community environments: "using printed and written information to function in society, to achieve one's goals, and to develop one's knowledge and potential" (Kirsch et al., 1993, p. 2). The National Literacy Act defined *literacy* as "an individual's ability to read, write, and speak in English, and compute and solve problems at levels of proficiency necessary to function on the job and in society and achieve one's goals, and develop one's knowledge and potential" (1991, p. 276). Sturomski (1996) confirmed that literacy definitions have varied according to the manner in which individuals must function: in the workplace, in the home, and in society at large.

Adult education programs have traditionally responded to widely diverse needs. Although research on adult literacy participation has emphasized that literacy development should not be limited to reading instruction (Wikelund, Reder, & Hart-Landsberg, 1992), it would be hard to ignore the important role of efficient reading ability in meaningful literacy. Limitations in basic reading skills are considered the most prevalent and often the most debilitating impairments to both children and adults (*Learning Disabilities: A National Responsibility*, 1995). Research in the area of reading disabilities in both children and adults must be communicated to adult literacy practitioners. In particular, there is a need to focus on improving adults' persistent difficulties with basic word decoding in conjunction with reading comprehension in order to promote literacy.

PROFESSIONAL DEVELOPMENT

Adult literacy providers have recognized that instruction in LD is important to improve their teaching skills and search for techniques and interventions to meet the needs of adults with LD (Osher & Webb, 1994). Although laudable, this quest is not simply fulfilled. LD as a concept defies consensus even at the very basic level of definition (Kavale & Forness, 1985). Furthermore, there is a wide range of instructional methods for addressing LD, many of which lack clinical or scientific validity.

Serious concerns have been expressed about the failure of teacher preparation programs to equip public school educators with sufficient knowledge to meet the needs of students with LD (National Center for Learning Disabilities, 1994–1995). Yet the formal education available to teachers of children far exceeds that typically offered to teachers within adult education programs. In fact, many adult literacy practitioners are volunteers. Students whom they teach have known enormous academic frustration and often present complex learning difficulties. Thus, both students and teachers are vulnerable to failure (Schupack, 1992). Studies have emphasized the important relationships between professionalization of the literacy workforce and curriculum for literacy education (Lytle & Reumann, 1992; Lytle, Belzer, & Reumann, 1993).

Professional development within adult literacy programs has, however, been fraught with problems. Frequent staff turnover and fluctuating degrees of knowledge among the workforce are common. Unfortunately, adults eager to increase their literacy levels enter adult education programs often staffed by individuals with widely varying levels of expertise. Within the broad field of LD, however, knowledge about reading disabilities identification and instruction is becoming increasingly robust for both children and adults (Grossen, 1996). This information needs to be shared with adult literacy providers.

Reading Research

Because the majority of adults seeking assistance from adult education programs are interested in improving their reading skills (Silver & Hagin, 1964), professional staff development should address what is known about successful reading instruction for both children and adults. Research has clearly established that phonological awareness, particularly at the sound level, is a prerequisite oral language process to successful reading and spelling (Blachman, 1991; Lewkowicz, 1980; Liberman & Shankweiler, 1985; Stanovich, 1991). *Phonological awareness* is an awareness of, and the ability to manipulate the word, syllable, and sound segments represented in our language. Although most students develop phonological awareness intuitively or implicitly, a significant percentage of individuals exhibit impaired phonological awareness skills. Both individuals with LD and "garden variety" poor readers (Gough & Tunmer, 1986) show limitations in phonological awareness. Bruck showed that persisting phonological awareness limitations of adults with LD such as dyslexia "remain a crucial stumbling block for the acquisition of fluent word recognition skills throughout their life span" (1992, p. 885). Research specific to the relative effectiveness of various reading approaches to treating adult reading problems is sorely needed (Fowler & Scarborough, 1993). Nonetheless, clinical experience and research findings regarding phonological awareness impairment in adults with reading disabilities provide significant implications for literacy instruction. Studies supported by the National Institute of Child Health and Human Development (NICHD) demonstrated that phonological awareness skills can be taught and that their effectiveness can be enhanced when followed by a code emphasis approach to reading (Lyon, 1995). Adult literacy providers must understand the crucial role of phonological awareness to reading and spelling and how limitations in the area can be identified and addressed educationally.

A DEMONSTRATION PROFESSIONAL DEVELOPMENT PROGRAM

A demonstration project to teach NICHD research-based reading strategies, focusing on phonological awareness and structured language concepts, was developed in Vermont for adult basic education (ABE) tutors. Content for this professional development course, "Teaching Adults with Learning Disabilities," followed a five-part sequence.

- The first part introduced participants to the concept of the language continuum as it affects individuals with LD.
- The next three parts addressed specific strategies for teaching the language skills of decoding (reading) and encoding (spelling).
- The last part specifically concentrated on strategies for encoding.

The program was made available on videotape and is in use in 27 states. This project was based on research findings that adults with LD demonstrate some of the same types of underlying language limitations that are exhibited by children with reading disabilities. In order for adults to learn to read, they must learn how the English language is constructed and how speech maps to print. This professional program taught adult literacy providers how to analyze the language that they and their students use every day.

Adult literacy providers who participated in this professional program varied in experience, skill level, and professional training. None of them, however, were familiar with the most recent research findings from the NICHD and how this information affects assessment and instruction of adults with LD.

Because Vermont is a rural state with a widely dispersed population, instruction was provided through interactive television. The program included 12 hours of instruction to more than 100 ABE tutors throughout the state. A vital component of the program was active participation by selected ABE participants who were videotaped while receiving remedial instruction at the Stern Center for Language and Learning. These videotapes served as accompanying demonstrations for didactic coursework. On course completion, follow-up visits were made to each of the 17 ABE sites to meet individually with tutors to help them implement course content.

The Language Continuum

Language difficulties in adults with LD affect listening, speaking, reading, and writing. They need to be addressed within both auditory and visual contexts across the language continuum. The concept of a language continuum is central to understanding that reading and spelling are as much language functions as are listening and speaking (see Figure 10.1). It is also essential to underscoring the notion that print maps to speech. Johnson (1993) reported that adults with LD experience challenges not just in reading and writing but with one or more aspects of spoken language as well. Adult literacy providers must understand that language disorders associated with LD persist into adolescence and adulthood (Wiig, 1996).

Features of language include metalinguistics, phonology, semantics, morphology, syntax, and pragmatics. These features were described to adult educators in the professional development course, citing characteristic language behaviors and examples. It is known that individuals with reading disabilities experience difficulties with oral language, specifically word finding, short-term verbal memory, and production of multisyllabic words (Catts, 1991).

Metalinguistics   Most adults with LD have difficulties with metalinguistics, or with knowing how language is used. Metalinguistic tasks such as sentence building and using specific words in sentences pose particular difficulties for adults with LD (Johnson, 1993; Johnson & Blalock, 1987). Wiig (1996) cited the following metalinguistic–cognitive abilities as characteristic of mature communicators and impairments among adults with LD:

- Analyzing and talking about language
- Using language as a tool and playing with language (e.g., riddles, jokes)

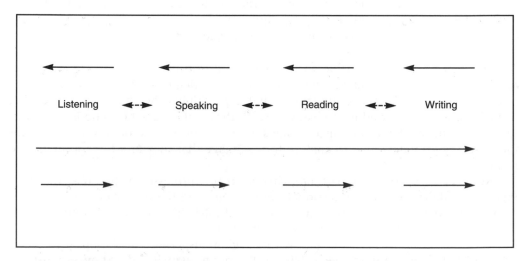

Figure 10.1.   The language continuum. (From Stern Center for Language and Learning. [1994]. *Teaching adults with learning disabilities.* Winooski, VT: Author; reprinted by permission.)

- Interpreting and using double meaning and figurative expressions (e.g., jokes, sarcasm, metaphors)
- Planning for the production of statements, questions, discourse interactions, and narratives
- Making predictions and inferences and forming hypotheses
- Coming up with communication options and selecting which might be most effective (strategic language use)
- Self-monitoring, correcting, and editing speech and writing

Not knowing how one's own language is used is a major impediment to efficient communication.

Phonology   In addition to displaying difficulties in segmenting words into sounds and syllables, adults also show evidence of sound production and sequencing difficulties (Johnson, 1993). These kinds of errors frequently occur in the absence of articulation difficulties (e.g., "pacific"/*specific*, "temptature"/*temperature*). Difficulties with phonology are evident in word-finding errors commonly experienced by poor readers (e.g., "telescope"/*microscope*). Liberman, Shankweiler, and Liberman (1989) described instances of word miscallings in which sounds produced follow the same pattern of syllabification, stress, and vowel use (i.e., "tornado"/*volcano*). Adult educators need to be alert to these kinds of errors in their students' spoken language because such limitations will be mirrored in written language, particularly spelling.

Semantics   Word understanding and usage are difficult for adults with LD. Often their vocabularies are impoverished because they have not read widely (Johnson, 1993). Difficulties with specific kinds of words, such as spatial words (*beneath, next to, left/right*), and relational words, such as prepositions (*with, except*), conjunctions (*since, if, but, or, because, although*), and interrogative pronouns (*who, what, where, when, why*), are common. Chall, Jacobs, and Baldwin (1990) described abstract vocabulary difficulties among poor readers. Solving verbal problems such as analogies taps difficulties with part–whole relationships, synonyms, antonyms, and function words. Verbal ambiguities, multiple meanings, metaphorical language, and use of speech are challenging as well (Johnson, 1993). Wiig (1996) discussed the importance of verbal concept understanding, both for spontaneous, everyday life and for scientific, academic, or vocational purposes. For example, not understanding the phrase *in the ozone* may suggest a difficulty with the multiple meanings of words as they are used in a social context or a lack of knowledge about the actual definition of a scientific term. In either case, language difficulties limit access to social and job opportunities otherwise available to adults who use language effectively.

Morphology   Difficulties with morphology are evident in the language of adults with LD. Most common, the plural marker *s* is used incorrectly. Parts of speech are also often confused (e.g., adjectives for nouns). Vogel (1977) found that college-age students with LD did not respond correctly to every item when tested on a grammatical completion activity assessing the application of morphological rules to nonsense words. Errors included both incorrect and omitted word endings. Adults with language problems often have difficulties in determining word meanings through the analysis of word roots and origins because of difficulties not only with the meanings of base words but also with the meanings of affixes (*pre-, -ment, post-, -tion*).

Syntax   Adults with LD often experience difficulties despite adequate conversational abilities. Johnson (1993) identified specific difficulties with syntax in this group with subject–verb agreement and pronoun reference. Syntax difficulties are more clearly apparent in written language when difficulties with active/passive voice and embedded clauses are evident. Both Gregg (1992) and Johnson (1987) postulated syntax as one of the linguistic processing impairments responsible for the prevalence of written language difficulties in adults.

Pragmatics   Pragmatics, or language in use, is often a difficulty for adults with LD, and one that can affect social relationships. Difficulties in understanding and using slang expressions and idioms are common. Adults also frequently lack a sense of audience to guide them in different listening and speaking situations, such as informal conversation with a spouse as opposed to a formal interview with a prospective employer. Wiig (1996) posited that pragmatic difficulties in adults with LD may result from a lack of linguistic flexibility, difficulty in perspective taking (conceptual or affective), or difficulties in abstracting or internalizing communication maxims and social conventions. Nonverbal communication skills, often called *body language*, may also be underdeveloped.

Strategies for Teaching Language Skills

Commonly used approaches to reading instruction include language experience and whole-language programs. Language experience and whole-language approaches share the belief that the "whole" or textual integrity of reading takes precedence over any structured presentation of the "parts" (i.e., phonics). Practices employed by Literacy Volunteers of America and users of the Laubach Reading System are reviewed briefly here. Rather than beginning with text, structured language programs build from more discrete phonological units of sounds and symbols to generalization of these concepts within connected text. Because the goal of the Teaching Adults with Learning Disabilities course was to share the basic tenets of phonological awareness training and structured language programs with adult literacy providers, these concepts are discussed in greater detail.

Language Experience/Whole Language   Language experience, the older of the two primary reading instruction approaches, achieved its greatest popularity since the 1970s and remains a favorite among teachers of adult learners. In the language experience approach, language of interest to the student guides explanation of how the reading process works. Practitioners view language experience as an attractive way to enable adults to drive their own reading programs. Topics focusing on sports, hobbies, or careers often govern vocabulary selection and the establishment of word patterns.

Whole language, a popular philosophy of teaching reading in the primary grades, is a literature-based approach that links reading to writing. Similar to language experience, it also underscores the importance of student-driven learning goals.

Literacy Volunteers of America   One of the major providers of literacy services to adults, Literacy Volunteers of America (LVA), uses a whole-language approach. LVA emphasizes learner-centered activities when tutoring students both individually and in small groups. LVA practitioners believe that people use their life experiences and knowledge of what makes sense when learning to read and write. In addition to materials tied to the learners' goals and interests, LVA stresses the use of literature and "real-life" materials such as newspapers or employment forms. The learning of reading always occurs within a print context that has meaning for the learner. Word analysis skills in terms of sound–symbol relationships and word patterns are taught implicitly as needed to complete authentic reading and writing tasks selected by the student (Literacy Volunteers of America, 1997).

Laubach Way to Reading   One of the most widely used reading programs within adult literacy centers is the Laubach Way to Reading. As their publishing materials emphasize, a Laubach program is designed for "new readers." It consists of four structured workbooks that present letter–sound correspondences from single consonants to diphthongs. Curtis and Chmelka (1994) modified the Laubach Way to Reading for use with adolescents with LD. Use of this method suggests improvement in reading skills and empathizes with the need to include materials that provide students with opportunities to generalize and extend information learned. The Laubach curriculum has been used to teach adults to read in English as well as in 300 other languages. Combining principles of phonics instruction with whole language, the Laubach curriculum requires minimal teacher preparation and experience. As of 1998, it does not include training in phonological awareness, nor does it explicate rules governing English orthography.

Structured Language Programs   Structured language programs are designed to teach sound–symbol correspondences directly. They follow a systematic sequence from simple to complex and emphasize multisensory instruction whereby targeted print concepts are seen (visual), heard (auditory), and felt (kinesthetic). Popular structured language programs include Orton-Gillingham, Project Read, Recipe for Reading, the Wilson Reading System (see Chapter 11), and the Herman Method.

Structured language programs differ from other reading approaches mainly in the explicitness with which they teach phonology. Whereas other approaches assume that students will learn basic sound–symbol correspondence intuitively, structured language programs explicate how printed symbols map to speech sounds. For those 20% of learners who do not intuit our language code, structured language programs are more effective. Research from the NICHD has shown that structured language programs produce positive results for individuals with LD (Foorman et al., 1998).

Key Concepts for Instruction   Phonological awareness, knowing that spoken language can be broken down into smaller units, has been identified as a skill that is frequently limited among individuals with LD (Stanovich, 1988). Although phonics is often a component part of many reading instruction programs in adult literacy centers, it differs from phonological awareness in that, in phonics instruction, letters accompany sounds. Phonological awareness is a metalinguistic skill that requires that an individual be able to segment words into syllables or sounds auditorily *before* letters are even introduced. Many students do not learn to read even when provided written phonics instruction, because they lack the prerequisite understanding of the basic syllable and sound units within spoken language.

Identification   In the teacher instruction course, adult educators were taught how to assess phonological awareness limitations by using an informal phonological awareness screening test adapted from the Test of Awareness of Language Segments (Sawyer, 1987). This test involves using blocks or chips to divide sentences into words, words into syllables, and syllables into sounds following their oral presentation.

Developing an awareness when listening to the conversation of adult students can supply a further index to phonological awareness difficulties. Difficulties with phonological awareness are frequently seen in the speech patterns of adults who omit, substitute, or transpose syllables or sounds when articulating (i.e., "pacific"/*specific*, "temptature"/*temperature*, "eksalate"/*escalate*).

Training   Students who display significant difficulty on the informal phonological awareness screening test by not correctly using blocks to sequence words, syllables, or sounds are good candidates for phonological awareness training. A series of phonological awareness skills was presented to adult educators to further instruct them in the importance of this developmental sequence and as a guide to educational intervention. This sequence includes

- Sound discrimination
- Sound imitation
- Isolation of initial sounds
- Sound segmentation
- Sound manipulation
- Sound blending

During this course, training procedures were discussed and demonstrated through videotapes of adults being taught using structured language methods. A modified bridge game (Zhurova, 1973) was developed to help adults isolate initial sounds. Elkonin's (1973) procedures were used to develop awareness of sound segments within monosyllabic words using picture cues (see Figure 10.2). Teaching strategies also extended to sound manipulation activities adapted from Lindamood and Lindamood (1975): "If that says *bed*, show me *bet*; if that says *mat*, show me *mit*." Practice in manipulating initial, medial, and final sounds demonstrates the power that a finite number of sounds has to constructing a limitless number of words.

Phonological awareness skills were stressed as essential to the reading and spelling success of adults with LD. The hardest concept for adult educators to grasp was the notion that letters are not introduced until sound units within words are understood. Blocks were thus used to demonstrate knowledge of syllable and sound segmenta-

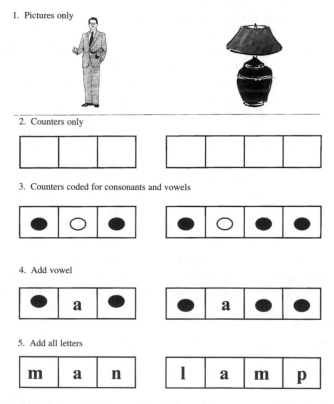

Figure 10.2.   Sample worksheet: Elkonin procedure from the Stern Center for Language and Learning. (Adapted from Elkonin, 1973)

tion within words before letter anagrams were introduced. With adult learners, letter anagrams can be presented more quickly than with children because most adults are already aware that sounds are associated with letters. Being able to identify that /church/ has only three sounds despite having six letters is an important concept that requires careful instruction. Similarly, vowel confusions, particularly between short /e/ and short /i/, frequently are extremely difficult for individuals with a reading disability.

Structured Language Teaching The progression from phonological awareness instruction to the basic rules and concepts of structured language programs is a logical one. The code emphasis approach to reading that structured language programs espouse has been demonstrated to enhance the effectiveness of phonological awareness instruction (Foorman et al., 1998). Research has also established that there is a reciprocal relationship between phonological awareness and reading ability. That is, just as reading skills can be improved through phonological awareness, phonological awareness skills are strengthened as reading abilities increase (Morais, Cary, Alegria, & Bertelson, 1979).

The Language of Language Because individuals with LD have difficulties at the very basic levels of language usage, key vocabulary for phonics instruction must be taught. Concepts such as phonemes, syllables, prefixes, suffixes, and phonics were defined for adult educators. Consonants were identified according to whether they have one or multiple sounds and by consonant blends. The course emphasized that adult educators need to provide their students with the basic rule that governs our alphabetic orthographic system: that each syllable must have a vowel. Syllables are then categorized according to how vowels function within them (see Table 10.1).

Table 10.1. Categorization of syllables according to vowel function

Syllable	Description	Examples
Closed syllable	One vowel, followed by a consonant; **the vowel is short**	*mug, stomp, at, attic*
Silent *e* syllable	Vowel–consonant–silent *e*; **the vowel is long and *e* is silent**	*bake, explode, concrete*
Open syllable	Vowel at the end of a syllable; **the vowel is long**	*she, we, fever, robot, bagel*
R-controlled syllable	Vowel paired with an *r*; **it has a different sound:** /ur/, /er/, /ir/, /or/, /ar/	*murder, thunder, squirrel, barnyard*
Consonant–*le* syllable	Comes at the end of a word; **/le/ sounds like /ul/**	*trample, tackle*
Vowel team syllable	Vowel spelled with two letters	
Vowel teams	/ai + ay/ /ee + ea/ /oa + ow/	*mail, sustain, mayonnaise* *employee, eagle* *approach, growth*
Diphthongs/glided sounds	/ou + ow/ /oi + oy/	*outlaw, power* *oil, ointment, boy, oyster*
Vowel teams with unique sounds	/au + aw/ /oo/ /ue + ew/	*pauper, saw* *moon, cook* *blue, flew*
Syllable oddities	/tion/ + /sion/ /cian/ + /cious/	*action, occasion* *magician, audacious*

Source: Stern Center TIME for Teachers (1996).

Use of a Resource Notebook   Two characteristic features of individuals with LD are poor memory and disorganization. To meaningfully generalize structured language concepts when reading text, students must be able to recall concepts taught. To provide them with a systematic and ordered format within which to do so, adult educators are encouraged to make resource notebooks with each of their students. Important concepts learned can be inserted and become personal dictionaries of information. The student is then able to look up the content of instruction when the instructor is not available, encouraging independence, promoting initiative, and facilitating recall.

Difference Between Synthetic and Analytic Phonics   A common confusion among instructors of individuals with LD is the teaching of analytic phonics instead of synthetic phonics. The difference can be most easily remembered when considering the origin of the words that characterize their differences: analysis and synthesis. Analytic phonics encourages the student to analyze syllables for phonic elements. Synthetic phonics teaches students discrete sounds that they can then synthesize into syllables and words.

Analytic phonics is frequently referred to as a *word family approach.* For many individuals with reading disabilities, analytic phonics is not sufficiently explicit and lends itself to rote memorization of rhyming word patterns. Once the basic concepts of sound–symbol correspondence have been mastered, analytic phonics can be extremely helpful as a tool for generalizing phonics applications.

Advanced Structured Language Concepts   Adult literacy providers were also taught rules governing more advanced structured language concepts. These included rules of syllabification and principles of structural analysis. Participants learned how to teach their students to divide words into syllables, labeling each according to the six syllable types that had previously been taught.

Specific Encoding Strategies

Adults who have histories of reading problems continue to experience difficulty in spelling. The mistaken notion that people are "born spellers" and cannot be taught how to spell correctly must be dispelled. Adult literacy providers were shown how to facilitate the development of spelling skills by using specific teaching strategies. Providers learned the importance of teaching spelling rules for plurals, base words, and suffixes.

Instructional Materials

Participants in this professional development program came from 17 different ABE sites throughout Vermont. To enable them to have assessment and instructional materials available within their own regions, three assessment tools and seven instructional resources were supplied (see Suggested Readings at the end of this chapter).

Family Literacy Library

The vast majority of adults seeking services through ABE programs are in their child-rearing years (Wells, 1985). Therefore, children's literature books were selected as vehicles for encouraging application of concepts taught within text. Although not all children's books conformed to phonetically regular decoding principles, instructors were encouraged to select vocabulary that was rule based, thus demonstrating how many words conformed to structured language principles. We know that 50% of our language is phonetically predictable and that another 37% is usually phonetically predictable (Moats, 1996). Enabling adults to have control over 87% of their language provides them with a powerful tool and offers adult students the opportunity to read the majority of English words to their young families. Children's literature also enriches vocabulary and verbal thinking.

Providing adult learners with materials that they can read to their children was found to be highly motivational and a way to break the cycle of illiteracy that so frequently runs in families. Furthermore, being read to as a child is one of the best predictors of later reading success.

Follow-Up

Because research has shown that didactic instruction in and of itself is insufficient for generalization of skills taught, follow-up consultations were also provided to all adult education participants. Stern Center instructors provided follow-up consultation at each ABE site throughout the state during the 4 months following class participation. These "mentorships" are considered essential to meaningful application of instructional principles.

Outcome evaluations indicated that this course provided significant new information to ABE tutors and was favorably received. Many participants, however, felt that greater time was needed to fully assimilate concepts presented, generalize them, and incorporate them into a regular teaching routine. Further follow-up coursework was requested by participants.

CONCLUSION

As research strides are made with regard to effective teaching methods for people who have not learned how to read, proven approaches to instruction must be shared with teachers. Because the instruction of adult educators in the area of LD is particularly sparse, this kind of information is all the more crucial. Professional development programs need to emphasize language issues that are pervasive among adults with LD. Furthermore, professional development must capitalize on the most efficacious instructional interventions to address language difficulties. Structured instruction programs in research-proven reading instruction methods are essential to address the needs of not only adults with LD but also those who have "fallen through the cracks" with traditional reading curricula.

Instruction models that underscore phonological awareness identification and instruction as well as teach structured language concepts will be important to include within professional development offerings. If traditional coursework is not accessible because of geographic constraints, videotaped courses should be considered. In this way, both providers and recipients of literacy programs will be better served.

Teaching Adults With Learning Disabilities, a professional development program that included both a didactic course and a follow-up mentorship, offered adult literacy providers an opportunity to learn about research findings that affect reading instruction and apply them when teaching adult learners. Information about the importance of phonological awareness and structured language, from the perspective of both assessment and instruction, was well received. Unfortunately, given the high turnover rate among adult literacy providers, ongoing professional development is necessary. The videotape training series that resulted from this professional development initiative was valuable in supplying literacy centers with this kind of ongoing in-service training. Mentorships, however, were not available to adult literacy providers who received the instruction via videotape. Several instructors became so enthused about the information that they themselves sought further instruction and became providers for new or under-serviced staff.

Adult learners were the most obvious beneficiaries of this professional development initiative. As one 37-year-old man perceptively commented: "It's not that no one never taught me how to read before. It's just that no one ever took me back far enough. They didn't know what I didn't know." Teaching Adults With Learning Disabilities provided these individuals with a new opportunity to achieve literacy.

REFERENCES

Americans with Disabilities Act of 1990, PL 101-336, 42 U.S.C. §§ 12101 *et seq.*

Blachman, B.A. (1991). Early intervention for children with reading problems: Clinical applications of the research in phonological awareness. *Topics in Language Disorders, 12*(1), 51–65.

Bowren, F.F. (1981). Teaching the learning disabled adult to read. *Adult Literacy and Basic Education, 5*(3), 179–184.

Bruck, M. (1992). Persistence of dyslexics' phonological awareness deficits. *Developmental Psychology, 28,* 874–886.

Catts, H. (1991). Early identification of reading disabilities. *Topics in Language Disorders, 12*(1), 1–16.

Chall, J.S., Jacobs, V.A., & Baldwin, L.E. (1990). *The reading crisis: Why poor children fall behind.* Cambridge, MA: Harvard University Press.

Curtis, M.E., & Chmelka, M.B. (1994). Modifying the "Laubach Way to Reading" program for use with adolescents with LDs. *Learning Disabilities Research and Practice, 9*(1), 38–43.

Elkonin, D.B. (1973). U.S.S.R. In J. Downing (Eds.), *Comparative reading* (pp. 551–579). New York: Macmillan.

Foorman, B., Francis, D., Fletcher, J., Schatschneider, C., Mehta, P., & Beeler, T. (1998). The role of instruction in learning to read: Preventing reading failure in at-risk children. *Journal of Educational Psychology.*

Fowler, A.E., & Scarborough, H.S. (1993). *Should reading-disabled adults be distinguished from other adults seeking literacy instruction? A review of theory and research* (TR93-7). Philadelphia: National Center on Adult Literacy.

Gold, P.C. (1981). The DI-LEA: A remedial approach for nonreaders with a language deficiency handicap. *Adult Literacy and Basic Education, 5*(3), 185–192.

Gough, P.B., & Tunmer, W.E. (1986). Decoding, reading, and reading disability. *Remedial and Special Education, 7*(1), 6–10.

Gregg, N. (1992). Expressive writing disorders. In S.R. Hooper, G.W. Hynd, & R.E. Mattison (Eds.), *Developmental disorders: Diagnostic criteria and clinical assessment* (pp. 127–172). Hillsdale, NJ: Lawrence Erlbaum Associates.

Grossen, B. (1996). *30 years of research: What we now know about how children learn to read.* Washington, DC: National Institute of Child Health and Human Development.

Johnson, D.J. (1987). Introduction and definition of the problem. In D.J. Johnson & J.W. Blalock (Eds.), *Adults with learning disabilities: Clinical studies* (pp. 1–7). Orlando, FL: Grune & Stratton.

Johnson, D.J. (1993). Relationships between oral and written language. *School Psychology Review, 22*(4), 595–609.

Johnson, D.J., & Blalock, J.W. (Eds.). (1987). *Adults with learning disabilities: Clinical studies.* Orlando, FL: Grune & Stratton.

Kavale, K., & Forness, S. (1985). *The science of learning disabilities.* San Diego: College-Hill Press.

Kirsch, I.S., Jungeblut, A., Jenkins, L., & Kolstad, A. (1993). *Adult literacy in America.* Washington, DC: Educational Testing Service.

Learning disabilities: A national responsibility. (1995). New York: National Center for Learning Disabilities.

Lewkowicz, N.K. (1980). Phonemic awareness training: What to teach and how to teach it. *Journal of Educational Psychology, 72*(5), 686–700.

Lindamood, C.H., & Lindamood, P.C. (1975). *The A.D.D. program: Auditory discrimination in depth* (2nd ed.). Hingham, MA: Teaching Resources Corp.

Liberman, I., & Shankweiler, D. (1985). Phonology and the problems of learning to read and write. *Remedial and Special Education, 6,* 8–17.

Liberman, I., Shankweiler, D., & Liberman, A. (1989). The alphabetic principle and learning to read. In D. Shankweiler & A. Liberman (Eds.), *Phonology and reading disability: Solving the reading puzzle* (pp. 1–33). Ann Arbor: The University of Michigan Press.

Literacy Volunteers of America. (1997). *LVA philosophy and approaches*. (Available: http://archon.educ.kent.edu/LVA/facts.htm.)

Lyon, R. (1995). Research initiatives in learning disabilities: Contributions from scientists supported by the National Institute of Child Health and Human Development. *Journal of Child Neurology, 10*, 120–126.

Lytle, A.B., & Reumann, R. (1992). *Invitations to inquiry: Rethinking staff development in adult literacy education* (TR92-2). Philadelphia: National Center on Adult Literacy.

Lytle, S.L., Belzer, A., & Reumann, R. (1993). *Initiating practitioner inquiry: Adult literacy teachers, tutors, and administrators research their practice* (TR93-11). Philadelphia: National Center on Adult Literacy.

Moats, L.C. (1996, July). Oral presentation at TIME for Teachers, Burlington, VT.

Morais, J., Cary, L., Alegria, J., & Bertelson, P. (1979). Does awareness of speech as a sequence of phonemes arise spontaneously? *Cognition, 7*, 323–331.

National Center for Learning Disabilities. (1994–1995, Winter). Verdict on teachers: Training needed. *NCLD News*, pp. 8.

National Literacy Act of 1991, PL 102-73, 20 U.S.C. §§ 12089a *et seq.*

Osher, D., & Webb. L. (1994). *Adult literacy, learning disabilities and social context: Conceptual foundations for a learner centered approach*. Washington, DC: Pelavin Associates.

Patton, J., & Polloway, E. (1982). Learning disabilities: The adult years. *Topics in Learning and Learning Disabilities, 2*, 79–88.

Rogan, L., & Hartman, L. (1990). Adult outcome of learning disabled students ten years after initial follow-up. *Learning Disabilities Focus, 5*, 92–102.

Sawyer, D.J. (1987). *Test of Awareness of Language Segments*. Rockville, MD: Aspen Publishers.

Schupack, H.M. (1992). Illiteracy. *Network Exchange, 8*(1), 4–7.

Silver, A., & Hagin, R. (1964). Specific reading disability: Follow-up studies. *American Journal of Orthopsychiatry, 34*, 85.

Stanovich, K.E. (1988). Explaining the difference between the dyslexic and the garden-variety poor reader: The phonological-core variable-difference model. *Journal of Learning Disabilities, 21*, 590–612.

Stanovich, K.E. (1991). Cognitive science meets beginning reading. *Psychological Science, 2*(70), 77–81.

Stern Center for Language and Learning. (1994). *Teaching adults with learning disabilities*. Winooski, VT: Author.

Sturomski, N. (1996). Literacy needs for adults who have learning disabilities. In N. Gregg, C. Hoy, & A. Gay (Eds.), *Adults with learning disabilities* (pp. 261–276). New York: The Guilford Press.

Thistlewaite, L. (1983). Teaching reading to the ABE student who cannot read. *Lifelong Learning: The Adult Years, 7*(1), 5–7.

Vogel, S.A. (1977). Morphological ability in normal and dyslexic children. *Journal of Learning Disabilities, 10*(1), 41–49.

Vogel, S.A. (1985). Learning disabled college students: Identification, assessment and outcomes. In D. Duane & C.K. Leong (Eds.), *Understanding learning disabilities: International and multidisciplinary views* (pp. 179–203). New York: Plenum Press.

Wells, G. (1985). Preschool literacy related activities and success in school. In D. Olson, N. Torrance, & A. Hilyard (Eds.), *Literacy, language and learning* (pp. 229–255). Cambridge, MA: Educators Publishing Service.

White, W., Shumaker, J., Warner, M., Alley, G., & Deshler, D. (1980). *The current status of young adults identified as learning disabled during their school career* (Research Report No. 21). Lawrence: University of Kansas Institute for Research in Learning Disabilities.

Wiig, E. (1996). Language and communication disorders in adults with learning disabilities. In N. Gregg, C. Hoy, & A. Gay (Eds.), *Adults with learning disabilities* (pp. 232–260). New York: The Guilford Press.

Wikelund, K.R., Reder S., & Hart-Landsberg, S. (1992). *Expanding theories of adult literacy participation: A literature review* (TR92-1). Philadelphia: National Center on Adult Literacy.

Zhurova, L.E. (1973). The development of analysis of words into their sounds by pre-school children. *Soviet Psychology and Psychiatry, 2*, 17–27.

SUGGESTED READINGS

Assessment

Arena, J. (1982). *Diagnostic Spelling Potential Test.* Novato, CA: Academic Therapy Publications.

Gallistel, E., & Ellis, K. (1974). *Gallistel-Ellis Test of Coding Skills.* Hamden, CT: Montage Press.

Wilkinson, G.S. (1993). *Wide Range Achievement Test–3.* Wilmington, DE: Wide Range.

Instruction

Dynamic ways to teach the fundamentals of reading. (1989). Bloomington, MN: Extend-A-Word Games and Lessons/Hoiland Publications.

Gillingham, A., & Stillman, B.W. (1960). *Remedial training for children with specific disability in reading, spelling and penmanship.* Cambridge, MA: Educators Publishing Service.

Garside, A.H. (1960). *A key to the Gillingham Manual* (7th ed.). Cambridge, MA: Educators Publishing Service.

Gillingham, A. (1992). *Phonics drill card for remedial reading and spelling* (Green 7th ed.). Cambridge, MA: Educators Publishing Service.

Lindamood, C., & Lindamood, L. (1979). *Lindamood Auditory Conceptualization Test.* Austin, TX: PRO-ED.

Sawyer, D. (1987). *Test of Awareness of Language Segments.* Austin, TX: PRO-ED.

Steere, A., Peck, C.Z., & Kahn, L. (1984). *Solving language difficulties: Remedial routines.* Cambridge, MA: Educators Publishing Service.

Stone, J.M. (1997). *Syllable Plus.* Lincoln, NE: Educational Tutorial Consortium, Inc.

Traub, N., & Bloom, F. (1992). *Recipe for reading* (3rd ed.). Cambridge, MA: Educators Publishing Service.

11

Matching Student Needs to Instruction

Teaching Reading and Spelling Using the Wilson Reading System

Barbara A. Wilson

Adults who have great difficulty in learning to read or spell with fluency and accuracy as a result of a language-based learning disability may require direct instruction in English word structure. Many people, regardless of their ages, have not been able to acquire reading and writing skills because their learning needs have never been properly assessed. These students can be identified and taught in a way that addresses their language needs.

MULTISENSORY, STRUCTURED LANGUAGE EDUCATION

One approach for teaching students to read and spell is based on the work of Orton and Gillingham (Orton, 1966). Gillingham, a psychologist, worked with Bessie Stillman, a remedial reading teacher, in writing a manual for teachers based on the beliefs of Orton. The Orton-Gillingham approach (as it has become known) is based on a technique of studying and teaching language to students with dyslexia incorporating an understanding of the language-learning process in individuals. Teachers present the sounds as isolated units and directly teach how to blend these sounds into syllables and words. The students master the concepts by hearing, speaking, seeing, and writing, integrating the senses to form what is called the *language triangle*. The language concepts are taught systematically, progressing from simpler to more complex in an upward spiral of language development.

Several reading and spelling instruction methods have been devised based on the Orton-Gillingham philosophy. The teaching that incorporates this philosophy is referred to as *multisensory structured language education* (MSLE). The International Multisensory Structured Language Education Council (IMSLEC) described the necessary program content and the principles of instruction for MSLE programs (McIntyre & Pickering, 1995). According to IMSLEC, students need to be taught phonological awareness, phonology, sound–symbol association, syllable instruction, morphology, syntax, and semantics. IMSLEC listed the following principles for teaching such content:

- *Simultaneous, multisensory:* Teaching is done using all learning pathways in the brain (visual-auditory, kinesthetic-tactile [VAKT]) simultaneously in order to enhance memory and learning. For example, students might learn to write a letter and say its sound with an awareness of their mouth position while making that sound. They might learn to proofread by looking at a word or sentence as they read aloud and track the text with a pencil point.
- *Systematic (sequential and cumulative) instruction:* Multisensory language instruction requires that the organization of material follows the logical order of the language. Students learn and master the basics of word structure before progressing to more complex words. A word such as *electricity* is easier to read and spell when the student understands that the suffix *-ity* changes the *c* in electric from the hard sound /k/ to the soft sound /s/. In order to understand this, the student must first understand base words with syllables, suffixes, and the two sounds of the letter *c*. With these concepts in place, the structure of a word such as *electricity* can then be taught.
- *Direct instruction:* People who are intuitive language learners will usually read the words *cell*, *city*, and *cycle* accurately whether or not they know that *c* followed by *e*, *i*, and *y* is pronounced /s/. However, students with a language-based learning disability may not be able to read these words. MSLE teachers do not assume that the student will apply the rules of the language without direct instruction. The inferential learning of any concept cannot be taken for granted.
- *Diagnostic teaching:* The teacher must be adept at prescriptive or individualized teaching. The teaching plan is based on careful and continuous assessment of the individual's needs as he or she progresses through a systematic sequence of instruction. The content must be mastered to the degree of automaticity. Students need substantial practice in order to internalize and master each new skill.
- *Synthetic and analytical instruction:* Synthetic instruction presents the parts of the language and then teaches how the parts work together to form a whole. Analytical instruction presents the whole and teaches students how this can be broken down into its component parts. For example, for reading, a student learns to blend the parts of a word together in order to decode. At an easy level, the student blends the sounds /m/, /a/, and /sh/ to form *mash*. At a more complex level, the student combines the syllables *e*, *lec*, and *tric* with the suffix *-ity*. Conversely, students learn to analyze a word into parts in order to spell it. At an easy level, the word *mash* is dictated and a student segments its sounds—/m/, /a/, and /sh/—and then writes the letter(s) that correspond to the segmented sounds. At a more complex level, the student segments the word *electricity* into its parts in order to spell it. An MSLE teacher has students work with the language in both directions. Concepts learned and practiced for decoding are also learned and practiced for encoding.

WILSON READING SYSTEM

One multisensory, structured language method based on the Orton-Gillingham philosophy is the Wilson Reading System (WRS; Wilson, 1988). This program is targeted at helping students who are unable to decode independently with fluency, spelling, or both, even with the help of a spell checker or a dictionary. The WRS teaches students the structure of words and language through a carefully sequenced 12-step program that helps them master decoding and greatly improves encoding in English.

The WRS was developed in 1988 for adult students with dyslexia. It provides a step-by-step method for teachers working with students who require direct, multisensory, structured-language teaching. The WRS directly teaches phonological awareness, phonology, and total word structure in 12 steps that take 1–3 years to complete. Its basic purpose is to teach students fluent decoding and encoding or spelling skills to the level of mastery and automaticity. Each lesson follows a standard format. The procedures of the lesson plan follow a specified multisensory method of instruction (see Appendix A at the end of this chapter).

Sequence of Skills

The WRS teaches a specific sequence of skills (see Appendix B at the end of this chapter). At each step, students master specific reading and spelling skills before progressing to the next step. Steps 1 and 2 teach letter–sound correspondence for closed syllables, the identification of sound units, phoneme segmentation, and blending. A closed syllable, such as *up, cup, clap, clasp*, and *script*, contains a short vowel. The word *up* has two sounds, *cup* has three, *clap* has four, *clasp* has five, and *script* has six. At the end of Step 2, students are able to blend and segment up to six sounds in a syllable. For example, for reading, the student blends the sounds /m/, /a/, and /sh/ to decode the word *mash*. For spelling, a student must segment the sounds in *mash*—/m/, /a/, and /sh/— and then correspond a letter or letters to each of the segmented sounds. The ability to break a word into individual sound units (phoneme segmentation) is taught directly with sound cards and finger tapping. A technique of finger tapping was developed for the WRS. Cards with letters (e.g., *m, a,* and *p*) are put on a table. Students are taught how to say each sound as they tap one of their fingers to their thumbs; as they say /m/, they tap their index fingers to their thumbs; as they say /a/, they tap their middle fingers to their thumbs; and as they say /p/, they tap their ring fingers to their thumbs. They then say the sounds as they drag their thumbs across their fingers, starting with their /m/ (index) fingers. With a word such as *mash*, the student also taps only three times because the digraph *sh* stays together to make only one sound. Students do not progress from three sounds to four or more sounds until they can read and spell the three-sound words *without tapping*.

In Steps 1 and 2, the Wilson program uses a very specific sound-tapping procedure for blending and segmenting sounds for all one-syllable words. This phoneme segmentation training lays essential groundwork for the next 10 steps of the program. The next 10 steps teach "total word structure," including syllabification, syllable types, suffix rules, and sound options. These important elements are taught in a step-by-step way using multisensory procedures and plenty of opportunity to practice with word lists, sentences, and stories.

Beginning in Step 3, syllable segmentation is emphasized. This, too, is taught directly by using sound cards and syllable cards. Step 3 introduces multisyllabic work, combining closed syllables such as *catnip* or *submit*. Steps 4–6 teach vowel–consonant–*e* syllables, open syllables, and suffix endings and consonant–*le* syllables. These syllable patterns are combined with previously taught patterns. For example, the word *reptile* has a closed syllable (*rep*) combined with a vowel–consonant–*e* syllable (*tile*). Words and sentences at this step will be controlled to have only closed syllables and vowel–

consonant–*e* syllables. Anglo-Saxon suffixes are also taught in Step 6. Although Steps 1–6 emphasize decoding and spelling, comprehension is included from the beginning. Word attack skills are taught to mastery so that the student is able to read with fluency and ease. The completion of these six steps might take from 60 hours to several years of instruction, depending on the individual. At the completion of these six steps, students are able to read more text independently, often scoring quite high on standardized word attack subtests. Depending on the student's cognitive ability and background knowledge, a significant increase in comprehension may also be seen at the completion of these initial steps.

Instruction after Step 6 is more balanced, combining continued word attack and spelling work with comprehension and the independent application of the mastered skills. Steps 7–12 teach higher-level word structure. Words containing sound options are introduced for reading and spelling. *R*-controlled and diphthong/vowel digraph syllables are taught, and students do additional work with spelling rules and suffixes.

The careful control of text for both reading and spelling provides extensive opportunity for the student to apply the taught skills. With repeated application, the student is able to break a guessing habit and become more fluent with decoding and encoding. With mastery at one step, the next concept is introduced and practiced, using the multisensory techniques. Thus, when a student is fluently reading and spelling closed syllables, the vowel–consonant–*e* pattern is introduced. The two patterns are combined to form longer words (*reptile, confuse, contemplate*). Because the text has only the patterns taught thus far, the student begins to develop confidence and sees that there are reliable patterns and structure in the English language. Although the text is controlled by patterns of word structure, the content is written for older students. The following are examples of controlled text with closed and vowel–consonant–*e* patterns:

Sentences
- Did the wind subside at last?
- The staff had to compile the list of investments.
- The landscape here is fantastic!

Story: Flipping Pancakes
Jim has a job at the Esquire Pancake Shop. His boss is Mr. Musgrave, but they call him "Bigtime." He has the shop as a franchise. . . .

Student Pretesting

The WRS is intended for students with low- to high-average cognitive ability with a specific language difficulty in decoding and spelling. The WRS Pretest and standardized reading tests are used to determine whether the WRS is appropriate for a student. The cognitive ability of an adult student is not always formally assessed. When funding and staffing are available, adult students are given the Wechsler Adult Intelligence Scale–Revised (WAIS–R) (Wechsler, 1981). When staff and funding are not available in a literacy program, average cognitive ability must be judged on the basis of interviews, past history, and records.

The WRS Pretest includes a questionnaire for use with adult students. The potential student is asked questions about past school history and handedness, language-related questions intended to identify language-related difficulties such as stuttering and word retrieval difficulty, and questions regarding skills and hobbies. The WRS Pretest encompasses a subtest on sound–symbol knowledge, reading words in isolation, reading nonwords, and spelling. This test can be administered in approximately 20 minutes. Students who do poorly on this test can be given further testing with a normed test such as the Woodcock Reading Mastery Test–Revised (Woodcock, 1987). This test is often used because it provides information regarding a student's word attack skills. It is unnecessary to have a formal diagnosis of a language-based learning disability. A student with poor word attack or spelling skills, or both, and average cognitive ability is targeted for Wilson instruction.

Program Training

In 1989, the Wilson Center began to provide training in the use of the WRS to educators beyond its doors. Wilson Language Training (WLT) provides educators with training and certification in WRS techniques. WLT conducts overview workshops, in-service programs, and Levels I and II training in the WRS. Overview workshops provide a solid introduction to the Wilson system and its multisensory structured language-teaching program. Levels I and II training provides teachers with ongoing supervision as they implement the program in one-to-one and small-group settings.

Level I training sites are generally established at public schools or Adult Basic Education (ABE) centers. Ongoing seminars are scheduled at the training site throughout the school year. Each teacher-trainee selects a practicum "case study" student with significant reading and writing difficulties. Once this student is approved, the trainer conducts a demonstration lesson, and then the teacher-trainee begins one-to-one remedial instruction sessions with the student two to three times per week for the duration of the school year. The Wilson Center trainer observes each trainee for the length of a lesson five more times during the year. The trainer provides verbal and written feedback along with suggestions for improving instructional methods. Level I training is also available at selected sites established by WLT in an intensive 4-week summer program. Each day, teacher-trainees work with students in the morning and attend meetings and seminars in the afternoon.

Level II training begins with a full-day seminar and continues with ongoing seminars scheduled at the training site throughout the school year. Each teacher-trainee continues one-to-one remedial instruction with a practicum student two to three times per week throughout the school year. In addition, teacher-trainees implement the program in a group setting of three to six students. The Wilson trainer observes a full lesson four times during the course of the year, providing verbal and written feedback along with suggestions for improvement after each observation. When training is unavailable, programs have used the WRS materials with guidance from videotaped instruction provided by Wilson Language Training.

STUDIES OF WILSON READING SYSTEM EFFECTIVENESS

To date, two studies examining the effectiveness of the Wilson system have been published. In one study, students at Marshall University significantly improved their spelling skills using the WRS program (Banks, Guyer, & Guyer, 1993; Guyer, Banks, & Guyer, 1993). In another study, 220 New England school-age students made significant gains in decoding, total reading, and spelling after an average of 62 lessons (O'Connor & Wilson, 1995). A third, unpublished study was presented at a statewide meeting of adult educators in Maine in the spring of 1992. This study, conducted at the Mechanic Falls/Poland Adult Education Center, concluded that the Wilson approach was effective in teaching reading to individuals with learning disabilities (LD) at that site (Gustavson & Watson, 1995).

Marshall University Study

The purpose of the Marshall University study was to determine whether college students with dyslexia would make more progress when taught with the modified Orton-Gillingham approach (the WRS), with a nonphonetic approach, or with no intervention. Participants in the study were 30 students diagnosed as having dyslexia who were enrolled in the Higher Education for Learning Problems (HELP) program at Marshall University. Their ages ranged from 18 to 32 years, with a mean of 21.2 years. There were 26 men and 4 women divided into three groups.

Group 1 consisted of 10 HELP students who selected no intervention for the semester, randomly selected from a group of 70 students who were not going to receive help for the semester of study. For Groups 2 and 3, 20 students were randomly selected who had contracted to receive remedial assistance through HELP in reading and spelling. Ten of these students were assigned randomly to Group 2 and 10 to Group 3. The students in Group 2 were taught spelling using the WRS. The students in Group 3 were taught spelling using a nonphonetic approach described in Spelling Power (Goodman, 1987). There were two 1-hour sessions per week for the 16 weeks of the semester.

The Spelling subtest of the Wide Range Achievement Test–Revised (WRAT–R) (Jastak & Wilkinson, 1984) was used to measure subjects' achievement in this study. The results seem to indicate that college students with dyslexia will significantly improve in spelling with the WRS (see Figure 11.1). Group 2, which received training with the multisensory phonetic technique of the WRS, was significantly higher on the adjusted posttest scores than were the other two groups. It should be noted that Groups 1 and 3 scored higher on the spelling pretest than did Group 2. At the conclusion of the study, however, the Wilson group was functioning on a higher level than the other two groups.

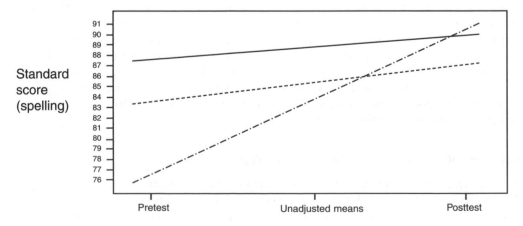

Figure 11.1.   Pre- and posttest results of the Marshall University study on the Wide Range Achievement Test–Revised. Group 1, no remedial instruction; Group 2, Wilson Reading System; Group 3, nonphonetic remedial instruction. (From Guyer, B., Banks, S., & Guyer, K. [1993]. *Spelling improvement for college students who are dyslexic* [p. 191]. Huntington, WV: Marshall University/Orton Dyslexia Society; reprinted by permission.) (*Key:* — = Group 1; —·—· = Group 2; ---- = Group 3.)

School-Age Study

The aim of O'Connor and Wilson's (1995) study was to determine whether special education pull-out programs with teachers instructed in the multisensory instruction of phonological awareness and English word structure yield significant growth in reading and spelling skills. The study examined the effectiveness of multisensory structured language teaching in public school settings using the WRS. Data from pre- and post-tests of students with language-based LD in Grades 3–12 were analyzed.

A total of 220 students were included in the study. Most were from Massachusetts schools, with a small number from Maine and New Jersey. Ninety-two students were in Grades 3 and 4; 128 students were in Grades 5–12. All students had a history of reading and spelling difficulties. Special education assessments identified the students included in the study. These students had a total reading score on the Woodcock Reading Mastery Test (both original and revised version) at least 2 years below their grade placement. Their IQ scores ranged from low to high average. Many also met the criteria for attention-deficit/hyperactivity disorder as outlined in the *Diagnostic and Statistical Manual of Mental Disorders, Third Edition, Revised* (American Psychiatric Association, 1987).

The students selected for this study had not shown progress in other reading programs using a small-group or one-to-one approach. Thirty-five percent had been retained for at least one grade. Most received direct special education services in daily pull-out programs: 48% were in pull-out programs for up to one third of the day; 26% were in such programs for up to three fourths of the day; 18% were in special education classrooms for the entire day; and only 8% were in general classrooms all day. Most had been in special education programs for several years.

The Woodcock Reading Mastery Test–Revised was used to measure growth in word attack, passage comprehension, and total reading. The Word Attack subtest is a measure of decoding ability using nonsense words. This subtest eliminates the possibility of recognized or memorized words and measures the student's word attack skills accurately. The Passage Comprehension subtest provides a measure of reading comprehension. However, slow and inefficient decoding has an impact on the comprehension test scores (Perfetti & Hogaboam, 1975). The total reading score is based on four subtests: Word Attack, Word Identification, Word Comprehension, and Passage Comprehension.

The WRS Test was used to measure spelling growth. This test requires students to spell dictated words. A total of 40 phonetically regular words are presented: *mix, shed, quill, yam, nets, punk, chop, blind, twist, scrimp, extent, compact, mundane, infiltrate, plenty, regulate, spilled, reflectively, razzle, thistle, oblige, infringement, hatchet, compensation, passionately, harmonizing, hurricane, inspector, displaying, discountable, postponing, canned, transmitting, accidental, synthetically, industrial, obedience, achievement, infatuate,* and *graciously.* The examiner ends the test after five consecutive errors. During WRS instruction, spelling words are not memorized and specific lists are not used; rather, a spelling process is learned. Therefore, the spelling posttest does not reflect memorized words; instead, it measures the student's ability to encode words by using the learned spelling process.

At posttesting, the average number of lessons completed was 62. The application of paired *t*-tests to the pre- and posttest raw scores revealed significant gains for all the Word Attack and Passage Comprehension comparisons (Woodcock Reading Mastery Tests) as well as the spelling comparisons (WRS Test). Similar tests applied to the pre- and posttest grade level scores revealed significant gains for all the Total Reading comparisons (see Table 11.1).

Significant gains in word attack skills were obtained; the average gain was 4.6 grade levels. Students had scored lowest on the Word Attack subtest at pretesting. The

Table 11.1. Effect of Wilson Reading System instruction

Test/subtest	Raw scores		Average gain	Grade level scores		Average gain	t scores[a]
	Pretest	Posttest		Pretest	Posttest		
Woodcock							
Word Attack							
A-B forms (n = 97, df = 96)	19.97	38.18	18.21	3.00	7.14	4.41	19.50
G-H forms (n = 123, df = 122)	20.19	32.17	11.98	2.73	7.68	4.95	22.12
All forms (n = 220, df = 219)	20.09	34.84	14.73	2.85	7.44	4.59	26.73
Passage Comprehension							
A-B forms (n = 97, df = 96)	33.01	45.08	12.07	3.69	5.26	1.57	12.86
G-H forms (n = 123, df = 122)	30.21	37.59	7.38	3.28	4.87	1.60	16.20
All forms (n = 220, df = 219)	31.45	40.90	9.45	3.46	5.05	1.59	18.55
Total Reading							
G-H forms (n = 123, df = 96)	N/A	N/A	N/A	2.86	4.25	1.39	12.00
G-H forms (n = 123, df = 122)	N/A	N/A	N/A	3.80	6.03	2.23	13.20
All forms (n = 220, df = 219)	N/A	N/A	N/A	3.38	5.24	1.86	17.88
Wilson Reading System Spelling (n = 220, df = 219)	8	18	10	N/A	N/A	N/A	32.00

From McIntyre, C., & Pickering, J. (Eds.). (1995). *Clinical studies of multisensory structured language education* (p. 253). Salem, OR: International Multisensory Structured Language Education Council; reprinted by permission.

[a]All scores significant at *p* < .001.

average word attack gain of 4.6 grade levels indicates that the WRS greatly improved students' decoding abilities. Significant gains in passage comprehension were also obtained; the average gain was 1.6 grade levels. Comprehension was better than decoding at pretesting. Although the emphasis in instruction was primarily on word attack, students still gained more than 1.5 years in comprehension.

Significant gains in the total reading scores resulted from the significant gains in word attack and comprehension. The average gain was 1.9 grade levels in total reading. These gains are striking because these students had made little or no gain in reading with previous intervention methods. Finally, significant gains in spelling were obtained; the average gain in raw score was 10. Moreover, errors on the spelling posttest were much closer to the correct spelling. Students not only increased their spelling accuracy but also showed significant growth in their understanding of basic written word structures. These results demonstrate the effectiveness of the Wilson system with students who had little success with previous forms of intervention.

Mechanic Falls/Poland Adult Education Center

The objective of Gustavson and Watson's (1995) study was to document the progress of adult students being instructed with the WRS program at an adult education center. Nine students participated in the study. One of the nine elected to use a whole-language approach rather than the Wilson program. Six of the nine were identified as adults with a language-learning disability through formal evaluation by qualified evaluators. The others, although not formally diagnosed, appeared to have average cognitive ability with specific weaknesses in decoding and encoding. Two members of the group appeared to function in the low-average range of cognitive ability, with achievement commensurate with this ability.

Initial participant reading grade levels for words in isolation ranged from 3.2 to 7.6 on the Slosson Oral Reading Test (Slosson, 1963). Following 6 weeks of instruction using Wilson methods, gains ranged from 0.7 to 1.7 grade equivalents on the Slosson. Following 12–18 weeks of instruction, gains from baseline ranged from 1.2 to 4.5 grade equivalents. Following completion of 18 weeks or more of instruction, reading grade equivalents for words in isolation ranged from 5.6 to 10.0. The student who elected the whole-language approach made no significant gains. His baseline scores for words in isolation were 3.2, 3.4, and 3.3. Following 18 weeks of instruction, his score was 3.7. These results appear to indicate that the Wilson approach is effective in teaching decoding to adults with a language-learning disability.

DEMONSTRATION PROJECTS

Programs and settings for delivering services to adults with LD vary tremendously; the programs described in this section are examples of sites that use the WRS to teach students with language-based LD. The environments presented are

- A private center for students with dyslexia
- A community college course
- A library literacy center
- An ABE program

These programs are quite typical examples of adult education environments (see Table 11.2). Administrators of the described programs have chosen to address decoding and spelling needs with the WRS. In addition to the Wilson system, most sites use a variety of other methods. The WRS is usually an additional method available for students with a language-based learning disability.

These programs were selected in order to describe a variety of settings. The private center for students with dyslexia provides an example of a facility with highly trained personnel providing one-to-one instruction, working in cooperation with a state-run organization (the Massachusetts Rehabilitation Commission). The community college–based courses provide an example of identifying and helping students applying to college programs who lack basic skills and thus need reading and writing assistance prior to doing college-level coursework. The library literacy center is an example of a site-based volunteer program involving volunteer training and supervision. The ABE program provides a description of a setting for adults with LD in a large, urban program.

Site Requirements for Wilson Language Instruction

The common element of most of the programs described is the staffing of the program with Level I and Level II personnel who are Wilson-instructed. Some of those individuals received Wilson instruction and then brought their skills to the established program. Others were instructed on site. Some programs using the WRS extensively do

Table 11.2.   Demonstration sites and examples of similar settings

Site	Brief summary
Private centers	
Wilson Language Training 175 West Main Street Millbury, MA 01527 contact: Barbara A. Wilson (508) 865-5699	Private center for students with LBLD. The WRS was developed at this site. Students are referred to the center from various agencies. Adult students receive 1:1 instruction one to two times per week.
Total Learning Center 3297 Route 66 Neptune, NJ 07753 contact: Marge Weiner (732) 922-6655	Private center for both children and adults with LBLD. Instruction for adults is 1:1 once per week.
Learning Techniques Ltd. 1600 Ravinia Place Orland Park, IL 60462 contact: Dawn Hillstrom-Lynn (708) 460-3933	Private center for both children and adults with LBLD. Instruction for adults is 1:1 once per week.
Adult Education centers	
Portland Adult Education 57 Douglas Street Portland, ME 04102 contact: Judy Storer (207) 874-8155	1:1 instruction twice a week, group instruction 1–1.5 hours two times per week; Wilson spelling class meets two times per week for 2.5 hours.
Lowell Adult Education Center 408 Merrimack Street Lowell, MA 01854 contact: Sharon Martin (508) 937-8989	Approximately 30 day and evening students using the WRS. Day students work in a group setting 3 days per week for 2 hours; one group of eight students in an evening class.
Hull Adult Learning Program 812 Nantasket Avenue Hull, MA 02045 contact: Janna Oddleifson (617) 925-0951	Approximately five students using the WRS; one group of three, two times per week; 1:1 instruction two times per week for 3 hours.
Brockton Adult Learning Center 470 Forest Avenue Brockton, MA 02401 contact: Kathy Quinn (508) 580-7475	Approximately 60 students using the WRS; group instruction 2 days per week. Also used with ESL students.
Volunteer programs	
Chula Vista Literacy Team Center South Chula Vista Library 389 Orange Avenue Chula Vista, CA 91911 contact: Meg Schofield (619) 585-5757	Approximately 88 students using the WRS; 1:1 instruction once per week for 1.5 hours; group instruction once per week.

(continued)

Table 11.2.   *(continued)*

Site	Brief summary
Literacy Volunteers of America– Morrill Memorial Library Post Office Box 220 Walpole Street Norwood, MA 02062 contact: Tina Blood (617) 769-4599	Approximately 25 students using the WRS; 1:1 instruction two times per week for 1–1.5 hours.
Literacy Volunteers of America– Northern Rhode Island/Project LEARN 303 Clinton Street Woonsocket, RI 02895 contact: Susan Grislis (401) 769-9046	Approximately 25 students using the WRS; 13 students receive 1:1 instruction one to two times per week; 12 students receive group instruction: four per group, three times per week, for 1 hour each lesson.
Community colleges	
County College of Morris–CPP 214 Center Grove Road Randolph, NJ 07869 contact: Sue Tramaglini (732) 879-0466	Currently, 13 students working in small groups of up to three students per group once per week for 2 hours.
Sussex County Community College College Hill Newton, NJ 07860 contact: Jean Coen (732) 300-2153	Currently, 22 students in groups ranging in size from two to seven students with additional 1:1 support for up to 2 hours per week.
Mount Wachusett Community College Better Effective Skills for Tomorrow (BEST) 444 Green Street Gardner, MA 01440 contact: Marlene McBride (508) 632-6600	Approximately nine students using the WRS; group instruction of four to five students per group for 3 hours.

Note: LBLD, language-based learning disability; ESL, English as a second language program; WRS, Wilson Reading System.

not have a Level I or II instructed person on staff. These programs, however, have reported significant success with in-service workshops and videotape support.

In order for a program to establish a Wilson program on-site and incorporate multisensory instruction with its existing services, the following requirements are necessary:

- Staffing interest and administrative support
- A group of students who would benefit from multisensory, structured language teaching—that is, students who have
  - Decoding and word attack skills well below listening comprehension skills
  - Significant spelling and writing impairments
  - English as a second language group (they can speak and understand the English language but cannot read or write it)
  - Past or present difficulty in learning how to independently decode words despite low-average to high cognitive ability
- Personnel to oversee student selection and placement process through testing
- Staff, volunteers, or both able to devote instructional services initially in one-to-one settings and eventually in small groups once the instructional methodology has been well practiced

Private Center

At the Wilson Language Training Center in Millbury, Massachusetts, adults with dyslexia receive one-to-one, direct, structured multisensory language instruction. Many of the adult students at the center have been referred by counselors at the Massachusetts Rehabilitation Commission Office in Worcester (Mass Rehab). Frequently, Mass Rehab consumers are under- or unemployed because of an inability to read. Vocational training options are limited for consumers with such low reading skills.

Many of the counselors at the Worcester Mass Rehab office have learned to identify adults with potential LD. When such an individual is identified, counselors schedule an initial assessment with a psychologist working under contract to Mass Rehab. This assessment includes the WAIS–R and the WRAT–R tests. Adults with average cognitive ability who score below a fourth-grade level on the reading section of the WRAT–R are then referred to WLT for further assessment. The individual is given a battery of reading tests that may include a selection of the following tests: the WRS Pre-test, the Woodcock Reading Mastery Test, the Decoding Skills Test (DiBenedetto & Richardson, 1985), the Gallistell-Ellis Test of Coding Skills (Ellis & Gallistel, 1974) and the Analysis of Reading Difficulty (Durrell & Catterson, 1980). The Decoding Skills Test and the Gallistell-Ellis test yield further information regarding a student's word attack skills. The Durrell test is used for listening comprehension as well as silent and oral reading of graded passages.

Using results from the Mass Rehab psychologist and the evaluator at the Wilson Center, students are selected for WRS instruction. Students with average cognitive ability, listening comprehension skills higher than basic decoding skills, and poor spelling skills are targeted for one-to-one lessons at the WLC Center. Mass Rehab will fund an average of 30 hours of instruction at $30 per hour. If there are no student openings at the Wilson Center, the student is referred to Wilson-instructed teachers working in private practice. Frequently, students begin instruction at the Wilson Center only to have their Mass Rehab funds run out because the funding is not usually extended beyond 30 hours. In order for work with the student to continue, a scholarship fund has been established at the Wilson Center. Occasionally, the student is able to pay all or a portion of the $30-per-hour fee on his or her own. Often a student and the center agree to trade services, with the student bartering office, painting, or other skills in exchange for instruction. As of 1998, approximately 70 adults have been identified, referred, tested, and served with one-to-one instruction in the WRS through the collaborative efforts of the Worcester Mass Rehab office and the WLT Center.

County College Program

When students graduate from high school with limited reading skills, their chances of success in college courses may be reduced, even when accommodations are made for their LD. Even with accommodations and program modifications, students still need a basic level of competency with the written language in order to succeed in college. The International Dyslexia Association recognized this problem and proposed to address it.

In 1994, the New Jersey Branch of the International Dyslexia Association received a grant from the Kirby Foundation to be used to help students ages 25 years and older whose employability was significantly hampered by difficulties with reading and spelling. The grant was used to develop a reading course at the County College of Morris (CCM). International Dyslexia Association members met with representatives from CCM's Academic, Learning Disabilities, and Adult and Community Services departments. Adult and Community Services agreed to coordinate logistics for a course to be offered on campus in the fall semester of 1994.

Student Selection   In 1994, the CCM administered the New Jersey College Test of Basic Skills (NJCTBS), which is broken into two verbal components: reading and writing. In order to pass, students had to obtain a raw score of 164 on the reading section. That year, CCM offered two reading courses for students who did not pass this test. A course using the WRS was added as a third option for students who did not pass the NJCTBS. If their score was only 5 or fewer points below passing, students were directed to Developmental Reading II. If their score was 6–20 points below passing, they were directed to Developmental Reading I. Students with scores 21 points or more below passing were potentially eligible for the Wilson system course.

Since the first year the Wilson course was offered, entrants have also been referred by social service agencies, private evaluators, and the International Dyslexia Association. Students were then screened with tests including the Woodcock Reading Mastery Test–Revised and the WRS Pretest. These two tests identified students with specific impairments in word attack skills and spelling. Separate interviews were conducted by two Wilson-instructed teachers to collect personal histories and screen out students exhibiting limited cognitive skills. This screening out was based on collaborative decisions by two staff members, who used student responses to questions regarding past and present independent living skills and work experience as well as past assessments available from school records.

Delivery   CCM has continued to offer the course since its inception in the fall of 1994. The course follows CCM's normal calendar and meets for 2 hours once per week during the academic year and twice per week during the summer. The three current instructors in the course are special education teachers with certified training in the Wilson program. The New Jersey branch of the International Dyslexia Association has sponsored Levels I and II training in the WRS; course instructors have been selected from that pool of individuals. As of the fall 1996 semester, there were 13 students at various learning levels working in groups of up to three. As of 1998, students travel to CCM from six different counties in the state to participate in the program.

Funding   The estimated annual cost of the course ranges from $5,000 to $6,000. This includes materials, testing fees, instructors' salaries, and one student scholarship per semester. While the Kirby Foundation grant was used to initiate the course, since its inception the International Dyslexia Association of New Jersey has financed the instructors' salaries. In addition, students pay CCM tuition averaging $150 per semester.

Similar Settings   Sussex County Community College in Newton, New Jersey, also offers an institutional credit course for students with dyslexia: Reading Skills Using Orton Reading Principles. The principal instructor is certified in the Wilson program. The course was first offered in September 1990 with the support of the Academic Affairs Department as a course for college students and people from the community who have difficulties in decoding and spelling. The classes (there are now two each semester) are taught in small groups. There have been up to 22 students in the two classes, with several groups within each class. Groups range in size from two to seven students.

Each new group of students begins at Step 1 of the WRS; students receive individual tutoring outside of class to maintain a pace that is appropriate for each student. Students are eligible for up to 2 hours of tutoring outside of class per week as part of the Project Success Academic Support Program at Sussex County Community College. As of 1998, there are two tutors certified in the Wilson program and one LD teacher tutoring under guidance. Not all students are able to take advantage of this additional support because of time constraints. When possible, students meet with their tutors in the college's Learning Center at a mutually agreeable time. Tutors review and reinforce concepts and submit a written report to the course instructor after each tutoring session. At the semester break, students from the beginning group are divided into separate levels, if necessary, in order to accommodate the relative speed of their progress through the steps. On average, students complete the 12 steps of the program in approximately four semesters.

Mount Wachusett Community College in Gardner, Massachusetts, offers a program called Better Effective Skills for Tomorrow (BEST). This offers a course for basic skills development. Currently, nine students are enrolled in the course, which meets twice per week for 3 hours each session.

Chula Vista Library Literacy Program

The Chula Vista Literacy Team Center, established in 1987, is the adult literacy program of the Chula Vista Public Library. Chula Vista is situated at the southern end of San Diego County, only a few miles from the United States–Mexico border. Tutoring stations, a computer learning lab, small-group classrooms, books, resources, and staff support are all available on site. The services provided by the center include multisensory reading and spelling instruction with the WRS, a family reading program, small-group writing classes, and technology instruction (including workplace literacy training) in the computer lab. All services are confidential and free of charge.

Student Selection/Identification   Eighty-eight of the active learners in the Chula Vista program (69%) have been identified as requiring multisensory structured language teaching. The Chula Vista assessment process now includes the Woodcock Reading Mastery Test–Revised, writing samples, California Adult Learner Progress Evaluation Process (CALPEP) self-report questionnaires (California State Library, 1993), WRS Pretest, and an educational history. Although no formal learning disability diagnoses are made, staff members recognize the characteristics of language-based LD in the phonological domain, and identified students are targeted for WRS instruction.

Delivery   Students are scheduled for one or two 1.5-hour sessions per week with a volunteer tutor or one small-group session per week with a staff member. The program director, who has Level I certification in the WRS, supervises the volunteers. Volunteers receive a 3-hour orientation followed by a 13-hour workshop and a 3-hour practice session. They then enter a 100% grant-funded apprenticeship period. The student's first lesson, taught by a staff member, serves as a demonstration lesson for the volunteer tutor. The staff member then continues to model, coach, and provide the tutor with feedback for the next 3–4 months. Center-based tutoring makes this supervision possible. Ongoing support is provided by staff and through in-house videotapes.

Funding   The program was begun with a 5-year grant from the California State Library under the California Library Services Act. The grant was designed to taper off during the 5 years, requiring local sources to assume 50% of the costs by the fifth year and 100% in the sixth and future years. The center has now been incorporated into the library's budget, so funding comes primarily from the City of Chula Vista general fund and city-administered Community Development Block Grant funds. Funding to support multisensory structured language instruction with the Wilson program comes entirely from outside grants. Sources include the U.S. Department of Education, the California Department of Education, the California State Library, Friends of the Library, the San Diego Council on Literacy, the Altrusa Club of Chula Vista, and corporate and individual donors.

Student Retention Rate   The program's student retention rate indicates that students believe the program works for them. Of the 127 current active students, 70 began instruction during the 1995–1996 fiscal year. Thirty-two students were placed in the core program and thirty-eight students were placed in the Wilson program. Six to eighteen months later, 82% (31 of 38) of the students receiving Wilson multisensory structured language teaching have continued on in the program, whereas only 41% (13 of 32) of those students in a more traditional core program have continued on for the same amount of time.

Similar Settings   The Morrill Memorial Library in Norwood, Massachusetts, has a Literacy Volunteers of America program. Several volunteers completed Wilson Level 1 training. Twenty-five students are learning with the Wilson program. These students receive one-to-one instruction two times per week for 1.5-hour sessions.

Another Literacy Volunteers of America program, the Northern Rhode Island/ Project LEARN, works with approximately 25 students using the WRS. Thirteen students receive one-to-one instruction one or two times per week. Twelve students receive group instruction, four per group, three times a week for 1 hour per session.

The Portland Adult Basic Education Program

The ABE program in Portland, Maine, offers educational opportunities to approximately 6,000 adults throughout the year. More than 15 school and community sites are used for daytime and evening classes. These programs are funded by Portland Public Schools, the state of Maine, registration fees, grants, and contracts. Portland ABE program offers learning opportunities in three areas: vocational, academic, and community life.

Student Selection   In its year-end report of June 1996, the Portland ABE program identified 349 native-born adult students who read below the eighth-grade level. All students go through an intake process with the Portland ABE intake counselor. Tests including the General Equivalency Diploma (GED) reading pretest (GED Testing Service, 1987) or the Test for Adult Basic Education (California Testing Bureau, 1994) are used for initial screening as well as an informal interview. The intake counselor also investigates previous educational experience and medical and work history as appropriate. Students with low scores on the diagnostic tests receive further testing with the Woodcock Reading Mastery Test–Revised and the Wilson Reading Pretest and Questionnaire. Ten percent of these students have been assessed and placed in a WRS class or one-to-one Wilson instruction.

Students with weak decoding-versus-comprehension scores and significantly poor spelling are targeted for the Wilson program. The number of students placed in the Wilson program is limited because of funding and the small number of trained staff. If not placed in a Wilson program, then students are registered for specific reading classes or matched with basic reading tutors (including Literacy Volunteers of America personnel). The Wilson staff have educated other staff members to help them identify and refer students in their classes who demonstrate the characteristics of a language-learning disability. These students can then be placed in a Wilson class as space becomes available.

Delivery   Students identified as having a primary decoding weakness despite strong comprehension are targeted for multisensory structured language teaching. The program employs one salaried teacher who has Level II training in the WRS. This trained instructor supervises an additional salaried teacher with a special education background, one volunteer with Level 1 training, and three volunteers. Students in the program work

- One-to-one with volunteers one to two times per week
- In small groups with trained instructors from 1 to 1.5 hours twice per week
- In a spelling class that meets for 2.5 hours two evenings per week

Funding   Federal funds awarded through the Maine State Department of Education support the ABE program. Students who are Portland residents working toward a high school diploma or GED receive free instruction, paying for materials as needed. Students with a high school diploma pay $40 per semester for the course and materials.

Program Evaluation   On an individual basis, many students have learned to read and write. Two such students were significantly disadvantaged as a result of poor decoding skills. Donna is a 34-year-old woman who was told she would never be able to read. She dropped out of school in the sixth grade, receiving special education services only during her final year of school. She continues to overcome many difficulties in her personal life. At the Portland Adult Education Center, Donna is learning to read with multisensory structured language teaching. Now, with her decoding skills significantly improved (see Table 11.3), she is preparing for the GED test. Donna recently went off of welfare services and secured a full-time job. She is able to use her reading skills on the job and in the job-training program.

Donny is in his early 20s and is a student at the Portland Adult Education Center. He graduated from high school reading at a second-grade level. He received special education assistance throughout his school years. Donny was an athlete in high school; hockey was his favorite sport. His goal is to enter vocational carpentry training offered through the Portland Adult Education Center. In order to be accepted into the program, he needs to read at a ninth-grade level. Donny has progressed significantly in decoding and is now making gains in comprehension and overall reading as well (see Table 11.4). He is highly motivated because of his success thus far.

Similar Settings   At the Lowell, Massachusetts, Adult Education Center, approximately 30 day and evening students are instructed with the WRS. Day students work in groups 3 days per week for 2 hours per day. Evening students work in a group 1 day per week. All students are pre-GED students with pretest reading scores below the grade 4 reading level.

At the Brockton, Massachusetts, Adult Learning Center, approximately 60 students, including some English as a Second Language program students, are learning with the Wilson system with group instruction 2 days per week.

Table 11.3.   Donna's pre- and posttest results: Woodcock Reading Mastery Test–Revised

Subtest	Pretesting date: 9/15/94 (A Woodcock)		Posttesting date: 5/10/96 (B Woodcock)	
	Raw score	Grade level	Raw score	Grade level
Word Identification	46	1.9	108	4.4
Word Attack	4	1.7	44	10.1
Word Comprehension	9	1.8	41	7.1
Passage Comprehension	25	2.8	49	5.4
Total Reading		2.2		5.8

Table 11.4.   Donny's pre- and posttest results: Woodcock Reading Mastery Test–Revised

Subtest	Pretesting date: 5/12/95 (A Woodcock)		Posttesting date: 10/1/96 (B Woodcock)	
	Raw score	Grade level	Raw score	Grade level
Word Identification	107	4.2	122	6.0
Word Attack	25	3.4	47	12.9
Word Comprehension	22	2.9	39	6.3
Passage Comprehension	30	3.1	64	8.7
Total Reading		2.5		6.6

CONCLUSION

Programs and settings for delivering literacy instruction to adults vary greatly, but a factor common to all programs is that many of their students have never learned to read or write because of a learning disability. Often such disabilities have not previously been identified or addressed with appropriate instruction. Research conducted by the National Institutes of Health (NIH) indicates that individuals with a reading disability do not readily acquire the alphabetic code when learning to read because of impairments in the processing of phonological coding. Therefore, such readers must be presented with highly structured, explicit, and intensive instruction in phonics rules and the application of the rules to print. The WRS provides such instruction following Orton-based principles that have proved successful with students with dyslexia for decades.

Adults with language-based LD do not intuitively learn rules governing language decoding and encoding. These students do not make significant gains in their overall reading and writing skills until they are able to understand basic word structure. NIH research shows that the ability to read and comprehend depends on rapid and automatic recognition and decoding of single words. When students do acquire the understanding of basic word structure, they can become fluent at decoding and encoding. They are then equipped to make progress in comprehension, overall reading, and written expression. Our experience shows that students who receive instruction from teachers trained in multisensory language education are able to develop these basic reading and spelling skills, and often express a sense of relief as they begin to understand word structure. The retention rate in Wilson programs is significant: 82% of the students receiving Wilson instruction in the Chula Vista Library program have continued on the program after 6–18 months. This retention rate is rare in adult education programs.

Wilson Language Training's mission is to provide teachers with the materials and skills needed to succeed in teaching reading skills to students with language-based LD. In the future, Wilson Language Training will continue to develop effective training models so that more programs and settings that deliver services to adults can include a component specifically designed to address the needs of such students. With properly implemented multisensory structured language methods such as the WRS, many more adult students should find success in learning to read and write despite their language-based LD.

REFERENCES

American Psychiatric Association. (1987). *Diagnostic and Statistical Manual of Mental Disorders* (3rd ed., Rev.). Washington, DC: Author.

Banks, S.R., Guyer, B.P., & Guyer, K.E. (1993). Spelling improvement by college students who are dyslexic. *Annals of Dyslexia, 43,* 186–93.

California State Library. (1993) *California adult learner progress evaluation process.* Sacramento: Author.

DiBenedetto, B., & Richardson, E. (1985). *Decoding Skills Test.* Timonium, MD: York Press.

Durrell, D., & Catterson, J. (1980). *Analysis reading difficulty.* San Antonio, TX: The Psychological Corporation.

Ellis, K., & Gallistel, E. (1974). *Gallistel–Ellis Test of Coding Skills.* Hamden, CT: Montage Press.

GED Testing Service. (1987). *Predictive GED Test.* Washington, DC: Steck-Vaughn.

Goodman, B. (1987). *Spelling power.* Providence, RI: Jamestown Publishers.

Gustavson, K., & Watson, N. (1995). *Wilson reading and reading to read.* Augusta, ME: Division of Adult & Community Education.

Guyer, B., Banks, S., & Guyer, K. (1993). *Spelling improvement for college students who are dyslexic.* Huntington, WV: Marshall University/The Orton Dyslexia Society.

Jastak, S., & Wilkinson, G. (1984). *Wide Range Achievement Test–Revised.* Wilmington, DE: Jastak Associates.

McIntyre, C., & Pickering, J. (Eds.). (1995). *Clinical studies of multisensory structured language education.* Salem, OR: International Multisensory Structured Language Education Council.

O'Connor, J., & Wilson, B. (1995). Effectiveness of the Wilson Reading System used in public school training. In C. McIntyre & J. Pickering (Eds.), *Clinical studies of multisensory structured language education* (pp. 247–254). Salem, OR: International Multisensory Structured Language Education Council.

Orton, J.L. (1966). The Orton-Gillingham approach. In J. Money (Ed.), *The disabled reader: Education of the dyslexic child* (pp. 245–253). Baltimore: The Johns Hopkins University Press.

Perfetti, C.A., & Hogaboam, T. (1975). The relationship between single word decoding and reading comprehension skill. *Journal of Education Psychology, 67,* 461–469.

Slosson, R. (1963). *Slosson Oral Reading Test.* East Aurora, NY: Slosson Educational Publications, Inc.

Wechsler, D. (1981). *Wechsler Adult Intelligence Scale–Revised.* San Antonio, TX: The Psychological Corporation.

Wilson, B.A. (1988). *Wilson Reading System.* Millbury, MA: Wilson Language Training.

Woodcock, R. (1987). *Woodcock Reading Mastery Test–Revised.* Circle Pines, MN: American Guidance Service.

Appendix A

Wilson Reading System 10-Part Lesson Plan

Parts 1–5: Emphasis on Decoding

1. *Sound cards:* A quick drill of the phonemes with the teacher showing a sound card and the student(s) naming the letter(s) and corresponding sound(s). Key words are always used with vowels and as needed with other sounds.
2. *Teach/review concepts for reading:* Blank cards and letter cards used to teach phoneme segmentation and blending (initially). Students are taught to segment sounds using a finger-tapping procedure. Beyond Step 2, syllable and suffix cards are used to teach total word structure. Every lesson involves this manipulation of cards to teach word structure and practice reading.
3. *Word cards:* Skills learned in Part 2 of the lesson plan are applied to reading single words on flashcards. Review words are included in the stack of cards presented.
4. *Word list reading:* Skills are applied to the reading of single words on a controlled word list in the student reader containing only those elements of word structure taught thus far. In one-to-one lessons, the student is charted daily for independent success. In group lessons, students are charted before progressing to the next substep. The list changes with each lesson so that students never memorize the list.
5. *Sentence reading:* Word attack skills are applied to reading within sentences. All sentences contain only the elements of word structure taught thus far.

Parts 6–8: Emphasis on Encoding

6. *Quick drill (in reverse):* Letter formation is taught as needed. Every lesson includes a phoneme drill with the teacher saying a sound and the student identifying the corresponding letter(s).
7. *Teach/review concepts for spelling:* Initially, the student spells words with phoneme cards and blank cards. Students apply a finger-tapping procedure to segment sounds for spelling. Beyond Step 3, students use syllable and suffix cards. Students spell words using the cards to sequence sounds, syllables, and word parts.
8. *Written work:* Sound, single-word, and sentence dictation are included. The teacher dictates sounds, words, and sentences that are controlled to contain only the word structure elements directly taught thus far. The student repeats the dictation prior to writing. Sounds and words are spelled orally before they are writen. A formal procedure is followed for independent sentence proofreading.

Parts 9 and 10: Emphasis on Reading Comprehension

9. *Passage reading:* The student silently reads a short passage with controlled vocabulary containing only the studied word elements. The student retells the passage in his or her own words linked to visualization of the passage. The student then reads the passage aloud.

10. *Listening comprehension:* In this part of the lesson, the teacher reads noncontrolled text to the student. The student uses visualization and retelling to develop comprehension skills at a higher level than current decoding. As the student progresses in the program (usually beyond Step 6), the student begins to read the noncontrolled text independently with help from the instructor, as needed.

Appendix B

Sequence of Skills in the Wilson Reading System

Step 1: Closed Syllables (Three Sounds)

1.1.   *f, l, m, n, r, s* (initial) and *d, g, p, t* (final); *a, i, o* (blending of two and three sounds)
1.2.   *b, sh; u; h, j; c, k, ck; e; v, w, x, y, z; ch, th; qu, wh* (introduced gradually)
1.3.   Practice with above sounds (*wish, chop, wet*)
1.4.   Double consonants, *all* (*bill, kiss, call*)
1.5.   *am, an* (*ham, fan*)
1.6.   Adding suffix *s* to closed-syllable words with three sounds (*bugs, chills*)

Step 2: Closed Syllables (Four to Six Sounds)

2.1.   *ang, ing, ong, ung, ank, ink, onk, unk* (*bank, pink*)
2.2.   Closed syllables with blends—four sounds only + suffix *s* (*bled, past, steps*)
2.3.   Closed-syllable exceptions—*ild, ind, old, ost, olt* (*mold, host*)
2.4.   Five sounds in a closed syllable + suffix *s* (*blend, trumps*)
2.5.   Three-letter blends and up to six sounds in a closed syllable (*sprint, scrap*)

Step 3: Closed Syllables (Multisyllabic Words)

3.1.   Two-syllable words with two closed syllables combined—no blends, schwa (*catnip, wagon*)
3.2.   Two-syllable words with two closed syllables, including blends (*disrupt, fragment*)
3.3.   Words with two closed syllables ending in *ct* blend (*contract, district*)
3.4.   Multisyllabic words, combining only closed syllables (*Wisconsin, establish*)
3.5.   *-ed, -ing* suffixes added to unchanging base words with closed syllables (*slashing, blended*)

Step 4: Vowel–Consonant–*e* Syllable

4.1.   Vowel–consonant–*e* syllable in one-syllable words (*hope, cave*)
4.2.   Vowel–consonant–*e* syllable combined with closed syllables (*combine, reptile*)
4.3.   Multisyllabic words combining two syllable types (*compensate, illustrate*)
4.4.   *ive* exception: no word ends in *v* (*olive, pensive*)

Step 5: Open Syllable

5.1. Open syllable in one-syllable words, *y* as a vowel (*he, hi, shy*)
5.2. Open syllables combined with vowel–cosonant–*e* and closed syllables in two-syllable words (*protect, decline*)
5.3. *y* as a vowel at the end of two-syllable words when combined with a closed syllable or another open syllable (*handy, pony*)
5.4. Multisyllabic words combining three syllable types: open, closed, vowel–consonant–*e* (*instrument, amputate*)
5.5. *a* and *i* in unaccented, open syllables (*Alaska, indicate*)

Step 6: Suffix Endings (Unchanging Base Words) and Consonant–*le* Syllable

6.1. Suffix endings *-er, -est, -en, -es, -able, -ish, -y, -ive, -ly, -ty, -less, -mess, -ment, -ful* added to unchanging base words (*thankful, classy*)
6.2. Suffix ending *-ed*: /d/, /t/ added to unchanging base words (*thrilled, punished*)
6.3. Combining two suffixes with an unchanging base word (*constructively, helpfulness*)
6.4. Stable final syllable: Consonant–*le, stle* exception (*dribble, whistle*)

Step 7: Introduction to Sound Options, Contractions

7.1. Sound options: *c* {e, i, y} (*concentrate, concede*): *g* {e, i, y} (*gentle, pungent*)
7.2. *ge, ce, dge* (*lunge, indulgence, fudge*)
7.3. New trigraph and digraph: *tch, ph* (*fetch, pamphlet*)
7.4. *tion, sion* (*subtraction, expansion*)
7.5. Contractions (*we've, I'll*)

Step 8: R-Controlled Syllable

8.1. R-controlled syllable: *ar, er, ir, or, ur* in one-syllable words (*firm, turn, barn*)
8.2. *ar, or* in multisyllabic words (*market, cortex*)
8.3. *er, ir, ur* in multisyllabic words (*skirmish, surgery*)
8.4. Exceptions: vowel *rr* (*hurry, barren*); *para*
8.5. Exceptions: *ar, or* in final syllable (*beggar, doctor*); *ard, ward* (*blizzard, onward*)

Step 9: Vowel Digraph–Diphthong Syllable

9.1. *ai, ay* (*plain, display*)
9.2. *ee, ey* (*tweezer, valley*)
9.3. *oa, oe, ue* (*croak, toe, revenue*)
9.4. *oi, oy, au, aw* (*thyroid, employ, saucer, squawk*)
9.5. *ou, ow, oo* (*trousers, drowsy, spoon*)
9.6. *ea* (*eat, bread, steak*)
9.7. *eu, ew, ui* (*Europe, few, suit*)

Step 10: Adding Suffixes to Changing Basewords

10.1. *v-e* exceptions: *ice, ace, age, ate, ile, ite, ine*
10.2. Spelling rule: Adding a suffix to a base word ending in *e* (*taping, lately*)

10.3.   Spelling rule: Adding a suffix to a one-syllable closed or *r*-controlled base word (*starred, shipment*)

10.4.   Spelling rule: Adding a suffix to a multisyllabic base word when the final consonant must double (*regretting, controlled*)

10.5.   Additional suffixes: *-ic, -al, -ible, -ous, -ist, -ism, -ity, -ize, -ary, -ery, -ory, -ent, -ence, -ant, -ance*

Step 11: Additional *I, E, Y* Vowel Work

11.1.   *y* in open, closed, *v-e* syllables (*reply, gym, type*)

11.2.   The *y* spelling rule (*enjoyable, player*)

11.3.   *i* in an open syllable pronounced as /e/ (*orient*); *i* pronounced as /y/ (*genius, million*)

11.4.   *ie/ei* (*piece, ceiling, vein*)

11.5.   *igh, eigh* (*light, eight*)

Step 12: Advanced Concepts

12.1.   Split vowels: vowel team exceptions (*create, violin*)

12.2.   Silent letters: *rh, gh, mb, mn, kn, gn, wr* (*rhyme, ghost, lamb, column, knife, gnat, wrist*)

12.3.   *w* affecting vowels: (*water, worship*)

12.4.   *ch, que* pronounced as /k/ (*chorus, clique*)

12.5.   *ti, ci, tu, ture* (*patient, official, actual, torture*)

12.6.   Chameleon prefixes (*correct, accent*)

12

Math Literacy

The Real-Life Math Demands of Adulthood

James R. Patton, Mary E. Cronin, and Diane S. Bassett

Mathematical competence is a major goal of education and a key element of the curriculum at both the elementary and the secondary levels of school. It becomes a critical necessity in adulthood, because much of everyday life demands the functional application of math skills. Some degree of mathematics proficiency is needed for most jobs; for some jobs, it is the essence of what the worker does (e.g., accountant, cashier). In reality, mathematics pervades almost everything we do as adults. Most of the competence we need, however, does not involve complex, advanced mathematical understanding. Rather, it entails the application of basic arithmetic operations to everyday situations, which is one way to conceptualize basic math literacy.

Given that only 18.1% of youth with learning disabilities (LD) attend 2-year or 4-year colleges (Wagner, Blackorby, Cameto, Hebbeler, & Newman, 1993)—settings in which one may certainly need higher levels of math competence—it is both prudent and necessary to look closely at the noncareer math skills that are needed for survival in everyday living. Those students with LD for whom higher education is possible must be exposed to higher levels of mathematics while they are in high school because such exposure is necessary for dealing with the math demands of their college coursework. However, attention must be given to teaching the math skills that will be used on the job, at home, and in the community as a matter of routine for all students with LD, and especially for those non–college-bound students, who constitute the majority of

This chapter is adapted with permission from Patton, J.R., Cronin, M.E., Bassett, D.S., & Koppel, A.E. (1997). A life skills approach to mathematics instruction: Preparing students with learning disabilities for the real-life math demands of adulthood. *Journal of Learning Diabilities, (30)*, 178–187.

students with LD. The teaching of these math skills should be implemented first in lower education and later in adult education.

An index of the use of various math-related life skills by an individual with LD is available from the findings of the National Longitudinal Transition Study (Wagner et al., 1991). One topic about which data were collected involved the extent to which students performed various financial management activities. Although 44.4% of the young adults with LD in the study who had been out of school for up to 2 years had savings accounts, very few of these individuals had checking accounts (8.1%), a credit card in their own name (8.1%), or other investments (0.4%). These data suggest that students with LD either are not being prepared to take these financial avenues or are choosing not to pursue them. Regardless, all of these areas involve life skills that most adults will need.

Certain recurrent themes underlie the impetus to better prepare students for the realities of adulthood (Polloway, Patton, Epstein, & Smith, 1989). Some of the most important themes are as follows:

- The education programs of many students with LD are not preparing them to meet their current and future needs.
- An overwhelming need exists to reexamine programming for students with LD at the secondary level and to consider more relevant, innovative options to prepare them for various postsecondary contexts.
- In addition to reexamining the secondary programs, professionals must carefully review the elementary and middle school programs of students with LD to determine how preparation for subsequent environments can be systematically included throughout the curriculum and the entire school experience.
- A significant number of students with LD are not finding their present school experience to be beneficial or relevant to their daily lives and thus are dropping out during the early years of high school.
- Students with LD need continuing support services such as adult education even after they systematically exit school—and, in fact, throughout adulthood.
- As noted previously, only a relatively small percentage of students with LD go on to higher education; for those who do, however, life skill competence in these settings is essential.

This chapter discusses teaching the life skills math that nearly every student with LD will need to function successfully as an adult. It is organized into three major sections. The first section provides a discussion of math disabilities and math literacy. The second section identifies the common situations in which most adults need to demonstrate math competence. The third section provides some suggestions for teaching life skills to individuals with LD by examining various curricular and instructional dimensions.

NATURE OF MATH DISABILITIES AND MATH LITERACY

This section focuses on two important topics. The first portion is a general overview of some of the characteristics displayed by individuals with difficulties with math-related literacy. The second focuses on the notion of math literacy, particularly in the context of standards and professional thinking.

Nature of Math Disablilities

A number of individuals struggle with various aspects of mathematics. Many students who have difficulties in mathematics do not have LD. Their difficulties stem from attendance issues (e.g., poor attendance, frequent moves), inadequate math instruction, or lack of motivation.

Students having difficulties in math who do have LD show substantial diversity in their mathematical skills. This diversity can be attributed to personal characteristics, which are discussed later in this section, as well as to the criteria used to determine whether one has a learning disability. This latter point suggests that different types of students with LD may be identified, depending on the setting in which they are being studied. In other words, different criteria are used for identifying individuals as having a learning disability in schools, as part of research projects, or in clinical settings. As a result, one must be careful in comparing data across various settings that use different standards for identification.

Based on a review of the literature, Miller and Mercer noted that "students with learning disabilities experience even greater difficulty in math than their peers without disabilities" (1997, p. 47). The math difficulties displayed by students with LD can be organized in three categories: general characteristics, specific learning-related characteristics, and math areas that are affected. Table 12.1 highlights the most widely cited characteristics found in the literature on students with LD. It is important to note that, although not all students with LD will display all of the features listed in Table 12.1, these students are more likely to show them than their peers without such disabilities.

Emerging Conceptualizations of Math Literacy

Math literacy is somewhat of an elusive construct when it comes down to pinpointing exact domains and levels of competence. Most people have a general understanding of what it means, as already inferred by the notion of successfully dealing with everyday math demands. Unfortunately, no widely accepted set of standards exists for clearly defining math literacy in adult contexts. Without standards, we are forced to look at school-based standards that are used to demarcate the skills and knowledge students should have mastered before leaving school. Although useful to a certain extent, such an analysis does not completely delineate the complexities of the math demands of adulthood.

Table 12.1.   Type of mathematics difficulties demonstrated by students with learning disabilities

Area of math difficulty	Source
General characteristics	
Developmental delays	Cawley and Miller (1989)
Limited mathematics achievement and performance on competency tests	Cawley, Baker-Kroczynski, and Urban (1992)
Specific characteristics	
Cognitive and metacognitive difficulties	Montague and Applegate (1993)
Memory and retrieval difficulties	Bley and Thornton (1995)
Generalization skills	Woodward (1991)
Math areas affected	
Computational proficiency	Miller and Mercer (1997)
Problem-solving abilities	Montague (1992)
Fractions, decimals, measurement, algebra mastery	Rivera (1996)
Reasoning ability	Rivera (1997)

The emergence of new math standards, which are discussed later, has tended to define what many now consider minimum levels of literacy, particularly in light of the increasingly more demanding nature of the workplace and daily living. This scenario, along with a cautionary note regarding curricular focus, was captured nicely by Goldman and Hasselbring:

> Students' deficits in traditionally defined mathematics skills, in combination with the growing awareness of the insufficiency of these skills in preparing individuals for the twenty-first century, create a climate for evolving conceptions of basic mathematical literacy. But specifying new standards is not the same as specifying curricular content and instructional environments. (1997, p. 199)

One of the greatest challenges facing advocates of teaching functional math skills is demonstrating how these everyday math skills relate to the various reform initiatives that are now providing the parameters for defining math literacy. At first glance, a workable relationship may seem strained; however, life skills math (i.e., those skills needed for everyday life by most individuals) and emerging standards for math curricula do not have to be perceived as separate tracks. Central to the Curriculum and Evaluation Standards for School Mathematics document (National Council of Teachers of Mathematics [NCTM], 1989) is the belief that teachers must help students become better problem solvers through the use of interactive, hands-on mathematics instruction. Rote memorization and pencil-and-paper exercises are minimized in favor of "investigating and reasoning, means of communication, and notions of context. In addition, for each individual, mathematical power involves the development of personal self-confidence" (NCTM, 1989, p. 5).

The NCTM standard included statements of what students should learn in grades K–4, grades 5–8, and grades 9–12. This included areas such as mathematics as problem solving, mathematics as communication, mathematics as reasoning, mathematical connections, number systems and number theory, and computation and estimation. In short, NCTM standards constituted a long-awaited reform effort that, if implemented appropriately, would guide students to higher levels of mathematics understanding, reasoning, and application. Although the NCTM content standards would appear to work harmoniously with life skills applications (Marzano & Kendal, 1995), a direct application of life skills instruction in the standards has not been formally explored. A link is also necessary to the real-world demands of adult life.

According to certain professionals (i.e., Hofmeister, 1993; Hutchinson, 1993; Mercer, Harris, & Miller, 1993; Rivera, 1993), the NCTM standards have failed to provide valid, data-based instructional programs for a diverse group of individuals in schools. It goes without saying that little attention has been given to how these standards relate to adult programming. Minimal reference is made to students who may be at risk for math failure, including students with disabilities, regardless of type or severity. Hofmeister noted the "troubling lack of reference to research of any kind" (1993, p. 12) to validate the standards and argued that, unless such research is conducted, validated, and replicated, students most vulnerable to failure will continue in that pattern. This downward spiral may be exacerbated for students with LD who receive the bulk of their instruction in general education settings, where often very few real adaptations or accommodations are made (Rivera, 1993).

Aside from reform efforts aimed specifically at math, other general education reform initiatives address the mathematical needs of students with disabilities. The Goals

2000: Educate America Act of 1994 (PL 103-227) is being implemented by states across the nation as a foundation on which to build instructional practices. Goals 2000 directly addresses the following mathematics competencies to be mastered by students:

- Students in grades 4, 8, and 12 will have demonstrated competency over challenging subject matter, including English, mathematics, science, foreign languages, civics and government, economics, arts, history, and geography.
- U.S. students will be first in the world in mathematics and science achievement.
- Every adult will be literate and will possess the knowledge and skills to compete in a global economy.

Although this legislation does not specifically address the issue of students with special needs, this reform act is applicable to all students, including those with disabilities. Moreover, it also has implications for adults, although its focus is not on math literacy per se. Goals 2000 includes Opportunity to Learn standards, which are specifically targeted at students vulnerable to repeated failure and provide these students with a better chance to master these content standards.

The inclusion of life skills instruction in relevant classroom practices and instruction is critical for meeting not only the standards of Goals 2000 but also those of the NCTM. There are several compelling arguments for including life skills instruction across a K–12 curriculum and into adult education, for both typical learners and learners with disabilities. Life skills instruction can address both the NCTM standards and Goals 2000 in meaningful, relevant ways. All students should master the content standards to progress from grade to grade and to eventually graduate; direct application of life skills instruction can help foster student motivation and subsequent comprehension of mathematical concepts, computation, and application. In addition, life skills instruction directly relates to specific goals delineated in the NCTM standards, including problem solving, reasoning, connections, estimation, measurement, patterns, and functions. Instruction can be enhanced by the consistent integration of life skills topics into existing course content and by using community-based experiences.

In addition to providing relevance and opportunities for real-life applications, life skills instruction in math also bridges the gap between theory and practice. When instruction utilizes real-life situations, such as estimating the costs of going on a date or purchasing supplies for a hobby, it places math into the real world of students' lives. Theoretical constructs take on a new life, which can then be generalized to other situations.

Life skills can help students at all levels to master math content in nontraditional ways. For example, a student with LD is likely to find a meaningful real-life math problem involving square footage calculations to determine how many gallons of paint are needed to cover the exterior of a home. The problem could also include estimation, hourly wages, taxes, budgeting time, and the cost of materials.

The Division of Career Development and Transition of the Council for Exceptional Children developed a position paper that strongly depicts life skills instruction as critical for all students with disabilities, regardless of academic ability or educational setting (Clark, Field, Patton, Brolin, & Sitlington, 1994). Real-life applications of math hold the key to reaching students at risk for failure in traditional mathematics education and should be included as a key component in the development of professional, national, or state reform standards.

COMMON MATH DEMANDS OF EVERYDAY LIFE

Life skills, as briefly addressed in the previous section, can be conceptualized as those specific skills or tasks that contribute to an individual's successful independent functioning across a variety of situations. They are influenced by local and cultural contexts. Life skills competence is needed in a range of domains, including employment, further education, home and family, leisure, health, community involvement, interpersonal relationships, and personal development (Cronin & Patton, 1993).

Math is a significant part of all of our lives and is woven into all of the areas previously identified, affecting successful functioning on the job, in school, at home, and in the community. Most individuals are able to generalize the math they learned in school to the wide variety of real-life situations that require math competence. However, for a significant number of students with LD, this transfer to everyday living remains elusive (see Table 12.1).

An argument for the inclusion of life skills–oriented math content in programs for students with LD has already been made. Although some life skills math topics are generic (i.e., found in most settings), specific content to be included in any instructional program should be based on a thorough analysis of local contexts. Table 12.2 includes a listing of many of the adult situations in which math competence is needed. These situations are typically encountered by most adults and represent areas on which math literacy can be based. The following discussion explores three general adult settings in which basic math literacy is required: in the workplace, in postsecondary training/education settings, and in everyday activities at home and in the community.

Workplace Math

The critical importance of mathematics competence in the workplace is being given a great deal of attention. In a more sophisticated workplace, a higher level of math performance is being demanded. Scott, Quinn, and Daane (1996) pointed out that the average worker in the United States needs to have math skills at the ninth- to twelfth-grade level. Because the skill levels of most workers are lower than what is needed, industry and businesses are spending much money on teaching basic math skills to their employees.

Every job involves some use of mathematical concepts. Entry-level skills identified by employers as critical for success include basic computation; measurement; practical problem solving; the use of fractions, decimals, and percentages; and estimation (Scott et al., 1996). The Secretary's Commission on Achieving Necessary Skills (SCANS) (U.S. Department of Labor, 1991) issued recommendations for strengthening the relationship between education and business. The SCANS report defined the knowledge and skills needed in the workplace by describing 1) foundation skills needed by workers and 2) workplace applications that use the foundation skills (see Figure 12.1). Although this report was concerned with a range of competencies, it underscored the importance of math competence.

Personal interest in job-related math usually is focused on one's financial compensation for work performance. The actual job one holds will determine whether compensation is in the form of hourly wages, a monthly salary, commissions from sales, or some combination of these options. Regardless of how the gross amount on the paycheck is determined, workers have a keen interest in verifying the correctness of the amount of their check after deductions. This would require that they understand how net pay is determined and the reason for the various deductions (e.g., retirement, taxes, insurance, savings) and that they be aware of the amount of their deductions.

Table 12.2. Math skills typically encountered in adulthood

Life demand	Applied math skills					
	Money	Time	Capacity/volume	Length	Weight/mass	Temperature
Employment						
Transportation	x	x		x		
Pay						
• Wages	x	x				
• Deductions	x					
• Taxes	x					
• Retirement	x	x				
• Investment	x	x				
• Savings	x					
Commission						
• Straight or graduated	x					
Hours worked		x				
Overtime	x	x				
Break/lunch	x	x				
Deadlines		x				
Further education						
Budgeting	x	x				
Costs	x					
Financing	x					
Time management						
• Requisite course hours		x				
• Scheduling		x				
• Extracurricular		x				
• Meetings		x				
Home/family						
Budgeting	x	x				
Bills						
• Payment options	x	x				
• Day-to-day costs	x					
• Long-term purchases	x					
Locating a home						
• Rental or purchase	x	x	x	x		
• Moving	x	x	x		x	
• Insurance	x	x				
• Contracts	x	x				
• Affordability	x					
• Utilities	x	x				
Mortgage	x	x				
Home repair/maintenance	x	x	x	x	x	x
Financial management						
• Checking/savings account	x					
• Automated teller machines	x			x		
• Credit cards	x	x				
• Insurance	x	x				
• Taxes	x	x				
• Investment	x	x				
Individual/family scheduling		x		x		
Automobile						
• Payments	x	x				
• Maintenance	x	x	x	x	x	x
• Repair	x					
• Depreciation	x					
• Fuel costs	x		x			
Thermostat		x				x
Cooking	x	x	x	x	x	x
Yard maintenance	x	x	x	x	x	x
Home remodeling	x	x	x	x	x	x
Decorating	x	x	x	x	x	x

(continued)

Table 12.2.   *(continued)*

Life demand	Applied math skills					
	Money	Time	Capacity/volume	Length	Weight/mass	Temperature
Shopping						
• Comparing prices	x	x	x		x	
Laundry	x	x	x			x
Leisure pursuits						
Travel	x	x		x	x	x
Membership fees	x	x				
Subscription costs	x	x				
Reading newspaper	x	x	x	x	x	x
Equipment costs						
• Rental or purchase	x	x				
Sports activities	x	x		x	x	x
Entertainment (e.g., movies videotapes, performances, sporting events, cards, board games, electronic games)	x	x		x		x
Lottery	x	x				
Hobbies	x	x	x	x	x	x
Personal responsibility and relationships						
Dating	x	x				
Scheduling		x				
Anniversaries/birthdays, etc.	x	x				
Correspondence	x	x	x		x	
Gifts	x	x				
Health						
Physical development						
• Weight					x	
• Height				x		
• Caloric intake				x		
• Nutrition	x	x			x	
Physical fitness program	x	x		x	x	
Doctor's visits	x	x		x	x	x
Medications	x	x				
Medically related procedures (e.g., blood pressure)		x	x			x
Community involvement						
Scheduling		x		x		
Voting		x		x		
Directions				x		
Public transportation	x	x		x		
Menu use	x	x				
Tipping	x					
Financial transactions						
• Making/receiving change	x					
• Fines/penalties	x	x				
Telephone usage	x	x				
Using specific community services	x	x		x		
Emergency services	x	x		x		x
Civic responsibilities						
• Voting		x		x		
• Jury duty		x				

From Patton, J.R., Cronin, M.E., Bassett, D.S., & Koppel, A.E. (1997). A life skills approach to mathematics instruction: Preparing students with learning disabilities for the real-life math demands of adulthood. *Journal of Learning Diabilities, 30,* 181; reprinted by permission.

SCANS Skills and Competencies

Workplace competencies—Effective workers can productively use

Resources—They know how to allocate time, money, materials, space, and staff.

Interpersonal skills—They can work on teams, teach others, serve customers, lead, negotiate, and work well with people from culturally diverse backgrounds.

Information—They can acquire and evaluate data, organize and maintain files, interpret and communicate, and use computers to process information.

Systems—They understand social, organizational, and technological systems; they can monitor and correct performance; and they can design and improve systems.

Technology—They can select equipment and tools, apply technology to specific tasks, and maintain and troubleshoot equipment.

Foundation skills—Competent workers in the high-performance workplace need

Basic skills—reading, writing, arithmetic and mathematics; speaking and listening.

Thinking skills—the ability to learn, to reason, to think creatively, to make decisions, and to solve problems.

Personal qualities—individual responsibility, self-esteem and self-management, sociability, and integrity.

Figure 12.1.   Skills and competencies needed in the workplace. (From Secretary's Commission on Achieving Necessary Skills, U.S. Department of Labor. [1991]. *What work requires of schools: A SCANS report of America 2000.* Washington, DC: U.S. Government Printing Office; reprinted by permission.)

Even though the type and complexity of math needed for specific job duties will vary with the nature of the job, almost all jobs demand the math competence noted previously. For example, salespeople and cashiers need to know how to give correct change to buyers, calculate total sales for the day, and balance the cash drawer with receipts. A person who works for a delivery service must be very skillful at knowing addresses, managing time, and maintaining a log—all of which require math.

The point is that certain general math skills are part of most jobs, and additional, vocation-specific math skills are also usually required, depending on the type of job. Preparation for both the generic skills and the more specific skills is critical to success. Generic math skills should be covered in a general mathematics curriculum; the career-specific math skills need to be refined via vocational preparation. One way in which many instruction programs are teaching various math skills is through integrative approaches within the context of vocational classes (Barbieri & Wircenski, 1990; Pickard, 1990).

Math in Postsecondary Training or Education

Any type of postsecondary education, from a few months of vocational training to several years of undergraduate/graduate education, will require various types of mathematical competence related to the nature of the instruction or the particular field of study. Everyday math life skills will also be needed.

Postsecondary vocational instruction programs are designed to prepare the individual for specific jobs. Within this instruction, the student will be exposed to different facets of the job that involve math performance. For example, an individual studying to become an automobile mechanic will need to become skilled at recognizing and using different tools that are calibrated in either standard or metric units. The general education requirement of higher education programs typically has mathematics requirements, such as algebra courses. As a result, a sound foundation in mathematics can be beneficial to students as they pursue a given degree program. Even programs of study that on the surface do not seem to be math-laden (e.g., social work) will involve some amount of applied math.

Everyone in postsecondary education, regardless of program orientation, will need to deal with the everyday math identified previously and discussed in the next section. Areas such as time management and personal finance are very much a part of the lives of young adults pursuing postsecondary instruction or education. As stressed, various measurement demands pervade a person's everyday life.

Everyday Math in the Home and Community

Much of the math that we use on a daily basis involves in-home or community routines. Much of Table 12.2 highlights areas in which people will need to demonstrate math proficiency. Without question, some math must be worked on independently (e.g., paying for groceries, estimating how long it will take to run an errand). Other everyday tasks involving math, however, can be accomplished with the support of others (e.g., tax preparation, landscaping). Nevertheless, it seems logical that many of these types of topics would be covered comprehensively in the math curriculum.

An important point to remember is that much of the math that we use on a daily basis involves estimation rather than precise calculation. Certainly precision is useful in maintaining a checkbook; but, for most situations, estimation skills are used and therefore essential. For instance, scheduling one's day demands estimates of the time it will take to travel or how long a meeting will take. The number of grocery items one buys is guided by judging their estimated cost against available funds.

Another important point is that almost all of the situations identified in Table 12.2 require the individual to apply math skills in problem-solving situations. The more prepared a student is for the typical events of adulthood that require math and the more proficient the student is at using the basic skills of arithmetic, the more likely it will be that he or she will solve the math-related challenges of adulthood. The educational challenge is to prepare students within existing curricular structures for real-life situations.

CURRICULAR AND INSTRUCTIONAL CONSIDERATIONS

It is crucial for instructors to find ways to include functional math topics in the curricula of students with LD. The overriding theme of this philosophy of instruction is the achievement of problem-solving proficiency, because daily life presents one problem to solve after another. This section offers some suggestions for teaching the life skills needed to be a literate citizen within the parameters of current educational practice.

Problem Solving

As has been stressed throughout this chapter, a significant amount of instructional time should be dedicated to solving real-life problems. As has been emphasized since the early 1980s by the National Council of Teachers of Mathematics (1980) and as clearly noted in reform initiatives, mathematics curricula should be organized around problem solving. Figure 12.2 suggests that all the major areas of mathematics must lead to functional problem solving.

All adults need to become proficient problem solvers in dealing with real-life situations. Most of the mathematics needed on a day-to-day basis involves the application of basic arithmetic principles to a variety of daily encounters—primarily measurement, as highlighted in Table 12.2. It is extremely important to note that life skills mathematics is not restricted solely to arithmetic operations in the area of measurement; competence in other areas of mathematics may also be needed (see Table 12.3).

Changing Curricular Focus as a Function of Age

Instructional attention to math-related life skills varies as a function of the level of schooling. At the elementary level, math instruction is focused on basic skill development, giving direct attention to or laying the foundation for the different areas of mathematics depicted in Figure 12.2. The challenge at this level is to relate math content to real-life situations as often as possible.

At the secondary level, math instruction typically is determined by the nature of one's program (college preparation; general, vocational, or special education). Life skills can be covered in a number of ways. Functional content can be integrated in courses that are not inherently life-skills oriented. Additional life skills topics can enhance other courses that are already functionally oriented (e.g., consumer math). However, a significant number of students may not be exposed to this type of coursework. Furthermore, the quality of these courses will depend on the specific content covered, the textbook used, and the teacher's knowledge and skills.

At the adult education level, the focus of math instruction can vary, much like at the secondary level, depending on the needs of the individual. Courses can range

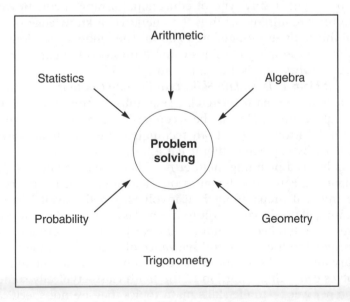

Figure 12.2.   Relationship of areas of mathematics to problem solving. (From Patton, J.R., Cronin, M.E., Bassett, D.S., & Koppel, A.E. [1997]. A life skills approach to mathematics instruction: Preparing students with learning disabilities for the real-life math demands of adulthood. *Journal of Learning Disabilities, 30,* 184; reprinted by permission.)

Table 12.3.   Functionality of various areas of mathematics

Area of mathematics	Definition	Example of functional application
Arithmetic	Real numbers and computations involving them	(Most of Table 12.2)
Algebra	Generalization of arithmetic	Ratios—scale on map Cooking—adjusting recipes Income tax formulae
Geometry	Measurement, properties, and relationships among points, lines, angles, surfaces, and solids	Gift wrapping Map reading Wallpaper hanging
Trigonometry	Relationships between the sides and angles of triangles	Miniature golf Putting up a tent Interior design
Probability	Mathematical basis for prediction	Planning food for a party Card and board games Selecting which cashier's line to get into
Statistics	Collection, analysis, interpretation, and presentation of masses of numerical data	Price comparisons Baseball information Stock market Diet/nutrition Monitoring temperature of sick child

From Patton, J.R., Cronin, M.E., Bassett, D.S., & Koppel, A.E. (1997). A life skills approach to mathematics instruction: Preparing students with learning disabilities for the real-life math demands of adulthood. *Journal of Learning Disabilities, 30,* 184; reprinted by permission.

from General Equivalency Diploma test preparation to those with a clear consumer orientation. The difference in adult education settings is that more freedom is available to create course offerings that are topical and related to specific goals. Regardless of the type of course being offered, all should stress real-life problem solving.

Addressing Life Skills Content

Life skills can be taught in any type of educational arrangement. However, to do so effectively, two basic requirements must be operative: a knowledge of what needs to be covered and the motivation/mandate to do so. The following sections highlight specific methods for incorporating life skills content into existing curricular structures or creating new coursework that is life skills focused.

Integration of Math-Related Life Skills into Existing Content   The overriding characteristics of integration of math-related life skills into existing content is the utilization of existing curricular content. This can be accomplished through either augmentation or infusion (Cronin & Patton, 1993). Both techniques use the already-prescribed math scope and sequence by supplementing it with life skills content. Although both techniques require advanced planning, neither need become overwhelming to instructors who already have a great many demands on their time. Instructors are likely to find that, with the minimal preparation time involved and the availability of useful resources, integrating life skills content into math classes is beneficial to them and their students. Instructors often become more enthusiastic about covering traditional topics, and students respond to the newfound relevance of these same topics to their lives.

An arbitrary and fine distinction exists between augmentation and infusion. *Augmentation* involves dedicating a portion of the math class—typically some prespecified amount of time per week—to life skills math topics that are not specifically indicated but that relate to the content being covered. This way of covering life skills topics is similar to the unit approach. The life skills topics that are chosen are based on their relationship to the content being taught and the importance of the topic to students' lives. *Infusion* differs from augmentation in that life skills topics are addressed on an opportunistic basis. Based specifically on content covered in the math class, the infusion technique works by relating real-life applications to the content of the textbook, or other materials, being used in the class. Table 12.4 provides a variety of examples of augmentation and infusion techniques.

Life Skills Mathematics Coursework   Some instructional settings offer specific subject area coursework that is tailored completely to everyday living needs. In the past, such coursework in lower education has been associated with noncredit, alternative programs of study, in self-contained, special education settings with students who were not in diploma-track programs. However, variations of this type of coursework for a range of students exist in certain schools where innovative practices have been initiated (see Helmke, Havekost, Patton, & Polloway, 1994).

Life skills coursework in the area of mathematics can be developed along a number of strands. Nearly all secondary schools in the United States typically have offered courses entitled "Practical Math" or "Consumer Math," which can be very functional and appropriate for the non–college-bound student. However, it should be noted that as a reaction to increasing graduation standards, some school districts are no longer providing these courses. Nevertheless, when offered, these courses can be made more relevant to students if locally derived content is integrated into them. When this is the case, little reason exists for arguing that other math-related life skills coursework is needed.

Other types of math courses or programs can be developed with a clearly functional, life skills orientation. For instance, a comprehensive life skills curriculum,

Table 12.4.   Augmentation (A) and infusion (I) examples

Source	Topic covered	A/I	Sample activities
Practical math textbook (secondary level)	"Budgeting for Recreation"	A	Add coverage on the "economics" of dating
		I	Identify best time and cost for going to a movie
	"Credit Card Math"	A	Add coverage of how to get the best deal on a credit card (e.g., low annual percentage rate, no annual fee)
		I	Present ways to get a lower annual percentage rate or waiver of annual fee
	"Maintaining a Vehicle"	A	Add coverage of the realities of being involved in an accident and what one needs to do
		I	Discuss the importance of keeping tires inflated at the proper levels
Basic math textbook (elementary level)	"Using Decimals: Adding & Subtracting Money" —buying a sleeping bag	A	Add coverage of costs of purchasing or renting camping gear
		I	Discuss where one can buy or rent a sleeping bag
	"Using Tables to Solve Problems"	A	Add coverage on how to use the weather map from the newspaper
		I	Identify other tables that have numbers

From Patton, J.R., Cronin, M.E., Bassett, D.S., & Koppel, A.E. (1997). A life skills approach to mathematics instruction: Preparing students with learning disabilities for the real-life math demands of adulthood. *Journal of Learning Disabilities, 30,* 185; reprinted by permission.

whether it is part of adult education or lower education, might include such math classes as "Personal Finance" (in which the focus is in personal money transactions and management) or "Survival Math" (a class dedicated to the nonmonetary math needed at home and in the community). Some schools have developed 2- to 3-year math programs for non–college-bound students that focus on the functional math required in daily situations. Table 12.5 describes programs employing both these options.

The concern frequently associated with life skills courses is that they are watered-down versions of more traditional courses. Although this can happen in some circumstances, it is also possible to develop comprehensive, challenging courses that do differ in orientation from the more traditional math courses but cover essential life skills content.

Table 12.5.   Sample applied life skill math programs

Program	Purpose	Features
Applied Mathematics Program (Chambers & Kepner, 1985)	Description of an integrated mathematics program for non–college-bound students in the last 3 years of high school	• Integrated curriculum approach • Covers goals for arithmetic, algebra, geometry, statistics, probability, and problem solving • Emphasizes use of calculators and computers • Emphasizes applications to real-world difficulties
This Is Your Life (Lindsay, 1979)	Students project themselves into the 2 years after leaving high school with no plans for further education but holding down a job and living. Exposes them to true and familiar situations from the adult world; helps students realize the skills they need	• Ongoing "payday" theme • Six units simulating adult responsibilities (i.e., shopping, $1,000 facelift, "wheels for real," spring vacation, first place, and career bound)
Economics and the Real Life Connection (Murphy & Walsh, 1989)	Description of a program that describes the impact of economics and consumerism on day-to-day life	• Introduction of basic economic concepts • Impact of choices we make on economics • Decision-making process
Integrating Math Skills Into Vocational Education Curricula (Pickard, 1990)	Description of classroom math instruction in a vocational setting	• Reinforces academic concepts and suggests hands-on activities
Noncareer Mathematics (Sonnabend, 1985)	Description of the most common noncareer mathematics topics that adults need (consumer math, media math, applied math in leisure and theme, and mathematical content and processes)	• Outlines several noncareer mathematics units, such as surveys, federal taxes and budget, economics, world population growth, inductive and deductive reasoning, diet, and games
Civics Mathematics (Vatter, 1994)	Description of a program designed to teach math in the context of important social issues of concern to teenagers	• Employs current data • Emphasizes newspapers • Students are encouraged to pursue projects that may be of service to the community • Students gain the understanding that they are part of school, local, and world communities

From Patton, J.R., Cronin, M.E., Bassett, D.S., & Koppel, A.E. (1997). A life skills approach to mathematics instruction: Preparing students with learning disabilities for the real-life math demands of adulthood. *Journal of Learning Disabilities, 30,* 186; reprinted by permission.

The argument made in this chapter is that all students should be exposed to life skills math courses in addition to more traditional math coursework. Such coursework that is distinctively relevant to students' current and future needs is highly desirable— and a balance between the real-life needs (functional literacy) of students and the mathematics standards identified by schools (standards-based literacy) is desperately needed. Having such coursework available as part of the curricular menu makes sense, given what we know about the outcomes and adult needs of students with LD (Wagner et al., 1993).

CONCLUSION

The time is right for reexamining how we prepare students with LD for the demands and challenges of adulthood. Life skills instruction can and should be included in the curriculum for all students from kindergarten through adult education. Students, in general, need to find meaning in their math education (Kloosterman, Raymond, & Emenaker, 1996). Similarly, students with LD can greatly benefit from math content that is meaningful and characterized by the following features:

- Related to student's current and future needs
- Presented in a cohesive fashion
- Tailored to a broad range of students, from those who are gifted to those with significant challenges
- Integrative by nature—blend well into other content areas
- Utilizes classroom as well as community-based settings—particularly ones in which the individual will probably function
- Emphasizes everyday problem solving

It makes sense to ensure that students with LD are competent in applying the math skills needed to survive the daily struggles of life and to be successful in their everyday existence—however those individuals define personal success. The message is simple. The math needs of students with LD must be addressed realistically, functionally, comprehensively, and longitudinally. If these ideas become operative guiding principles, then it is extremely likely that a more sensitive and enlightened view of mathematics programming for students with LD will emerge.

REFERENCES

Barbieri, M.M., & Wircenski, J.L. (1990). Developing integrated curricula. *Journal for Vocational Special Needs Education, 13*, 27–29.

Bley, N., & Thornton, C. (1995). *Teaching mathematics to students with learning disabilities* (3rd ed.). Austin, TX: PRO-ED.

Cawley, J.F., Baker-Kroczynski, S., & Urban, A. (1992). Seeking excellence in mathematics education for students with mild disabilities. *Teaching Exceptional Children, 24*, 40–43.

Cawley, J.F., & Miller, J.H. (1989). Cross-sectional comparisons of the mathematical performance of children with learning disabilities: Are we on the right track toward comprehensive programming? *Journal of Learning Disabilities, 23*, 250–254, 259.

Chambers, D.L., & Kepner, H.S. (1985). Applied mathematics: A three-year program for non–college-bound students. In C.R. Hirsch & M.J. Zweng (Eds.), *The secondary school mathematics curriculum* (pp. 211–229). Reston, VA: National Council of Teachers of Mathematics.

Clark, G.M., Field, S., Patton, J.P., Brolin, D.E., & Sitlington, P.L. (1994). Life skills instruction: A necessary component for all students with disabilities (Position statement of the Division on Career Development and Transition). *Career Development for Exceptional Individuals, 17*, 125–133.

Cronin, M.E., & Patton, J.R. (1993). *Life skills instruction for all students with special needs: A practical guide for integrating real-life content into the curriculum.* Austin, TX: PRO-ED.

Goals 2000: Educate America Act of 1994, PL 103-227, 20 U.S.C. §§ 5801 *et seq.*

Goldman, S.R., & Hasselbring, T.S. (1997). Achieving meaningful mathematics literacy for students with learning disabilities. *Journal of Learning Disabilities, 30,* 198–208.

Helmke, L., Havekost, D.M., Patton, J.R., & Polloway, E.A. (1994). Life skills programming: Development of a high school science course. *Teaching Exceptional Children, 26,* 49–53.

Hofmeister, A. (1993). Elitism and reform in school mathematics. *Remedial and Special Education, 14,* 8–13.

Hutchinson, N. (1993). Students with disabilities and mathematics education reform: Let the dialogue begin. *Remedial and Special Education, 14,* 20–23.

Kloosterman, P., Raymond, A.M., & Emenaker, C. (1996). Students' beliefs about mathematics: A three-year study. *The Elementary School Journal, 97,* 39–56.

Lindsay, E.R. (1979). This is your life: An applied mathematics curriculum for young adults. In S. Sharron & R.E. Reys (Eds.), *Applications in school mathematics* (1979 Yearbook, pp. 70–81). Reston, VA: National Council of Teachers of Mathematics.

Marzano, R.L., & Kendall, J.S. (1995). The McREL database: A tool for constructing local standards. *Educational Leadership, 52,* 42–47.

Mercer, C.D., Harris, C.A., & Miller, S.P. (1993). Reforming reforms in mathematics. *Remedial and Special Education, 14,* 14–19.

Miller, S.P., & Mercer, C.D. (1997). Educational aspects of mathematics disabilities. *Journal of Learning Disabilities, 30,* 47–56.

Montague, M. (1992). The effects of cognitive and metacognitive strategy instruction on the mathematical problem solving of middle school students with learning disabilities. *Journal of Learning Disabilities, 25,* 230–248.

Montague, M., & Applegate, B. (1993). Middle school students' mathematical problem solving: An analysis of think-aloud protocols. *Learning Disabilities Quarterly, 16,* 19–30.

Murphy, S., & Walsh, J. (1989). Economics and the real life connections. *Social Studies and the Young Learner, 2,* 6–8.

National Council of Teachers of Mathematics. (1980). *Agenda for action.* Reston, VA: Author.

National Council of Teachers of Mathematics. (1989). *Curriculum and evaluation standards for school mathematics.* Reston, VA: Author.

Patton, J.R., Cronin, M.E., Bassett, D.S., & Koppel, A.E. (1997). A life skills approach to mathematics instruction: Preparing students with learning disabilities for the real-life math demands of adulthood. *Journal of Learning Disabilities, 30,* 178–187.

Pickard, S. (1990). Integrating math skills into vocational education curricula. *Journal for Vocational Special Needs Education, 13,* 9–13.

Polloway, E.A., Patton, J.R., Epstein, M.H., & Smith, T. (1989). Comprehensive curriculum for students with mild handicaps. *Focus on Exceptional Children, 21*(8), 1–12.

Rivera, D.M. (1993). Examining mathematics reform and the implications for students with mathematics disabilities. *Remedial and Special Education, 14,* 24–27.

Rivera, D.P. (1996). Effective mathematics instruction for students with learning disabilities: Introduction to the two-part series. *LD Forum, 21*(2), 4–9.

Rivera, D.P. (1997). Mathematics education and students with learning disabilities: Introduction to the special series. *Journal of Learning Disabilities, 30,* 2–19, 68.

Scott, B.H., Quinn, R.J., & Daane, C.J. (1996). Are we teaching the mathematics skills students will need for work in the twenty-first century? *The Clearing House, 69,* 354–357.

Secretary's Commission on Achieving Necessary Skills, U.S. Department of Labor. (1991). *What work requires of schools: A SCANS report for America 2000.* Washington, DC: U.S. Government Printing Office.

Sonnabend, T. (1985). Noncareer mathematics: The mathematics we all need. In C.R. Hirsch & M.J. Zweng (Eds.), *The secondary school mathematics curriculum* (pp. 107–118). Reston, VA: National Council of Teachers of Mathematics.

Vatter, T. (1994). Civic mathematics: A real-life general mathematics course. *The Mathematics Teacher, 87,* 396–401.

Wagner, M., Blackorby, J., Cameto, R., Hebbeler, K., & Newman, L. (1993). *The transition experiences of young people with disabilities: Findings from the National Longitudinal Transition Study of Special Education Students.* Menlo Park, CA: SRI International.

Wagner, M., Newman, L., D'Amico, R., Jay, E.D., Butler-Nalin, P., Marder, C., & Cox, R. (1991). *Youth with disabilities: How are they doing?* Menlo Park, CA: SRI International.

Woodward, J. (1991). Procedural knowledge in mathematics: The role of the curriculum. *Journal of Learning Disabilities, 24,* 242–251.

13

Literacy for Adults with Learning Disabilities Through Assistive Technology

Marshall H. Raskind

Estimates of the number of individuals with learning disabilities (LD) in literacy and adult education programs range between 50% and 80% (Nightengale, 1991). Unfortunately, adults with LD often leave the literacy programs because their needs are not being met (Malicky & Norman, 1989). Sturomski emphasized that literacy programs are often not equipped to deal with adults who have specific LD and stated that "when programs cannot meet the needs of students with learning disabilities, frustration and failure continue, often with little hope of meaningful change" (1996, p. 263).

Recognition of the substantial number of adults with LD in literacy programs, coupled with the difficulties encountered when serving this group of individuals, has prompted literacy service providers and professionals from the field of LD to form partnerships in an effort to better address the literacy needs of adults with LD. Collaborations have been formed between various learning disability (e.g., International Dyslexia Association, Learning Disabilities Association of America, National Center on Learning Disabilities) and literacy (e.g., Literacy Volunteers of America, Laubach Literacy Action, Project Literacy U.S. [PLUS]) organizations and have resulted in a number of conferences, publications, and programs. Awareness of the need to find more effective ways of serving the literacy needs of adults with LD has also led to the establishment of the National Adult Literacy and Learning Disabilities (NALLD) Center, a program funded by the National Institute for Literacy, whose goal is to raise national "awareness about the relationship between adult literacy and learning disabilities" and to help "literacy practitioners, policymakers, and researchers better meet the needs of adults with learning disabilities" (NALLD, 1995a).

As can be expected, the methods suggested by learning disability professionals that are aimed at helping literacy providers better meet the needs of adults with LD are reflective of traditional instructional approaches within the field of LD. For example, a PLUS publication entitled *Literacy/Learning Disabilities Collaboration Project* (1992), which reviewed several joint learning disability and literacy service programs, makes frequent references to the use of such approaches as *multisensory teaching techniques, Orton-Gillingham approaches, phonics, language experience, sight-word teaching,* and *basic skills.* Gottesman (1994) noted that both whole-word and phonics approaches are used by literacy providers to teach adults with LD to read; however, whole-word approaches are used most often. Although specific instructional approaches may vary, taken as a whole, the wide variety of approaches used by literacy providers to enhance the literacy skills of adults with LD are aimed at improving basic skills impairments in the areas of reading and writing.

INSTRUCTIONAL APPROACHES FOR INDIVIDUALS WITH LEARNING DISABILITIES

Research in LD indicates that children with LD grow up to be adults with LD (e.g., Gerber, Ginsberg, & Reiff, 1992; Kavale, 1988; Raskind, Goldberg, Higgins, & Herman, 1996; Spekman, Goldberg, & Herman, 1992; Werner & Smith, 1992). Unfortunately, despite early instructional interventions intended to improve impairments in skills, adults with LD continue to have persistent difficulties in such areas as reading, writing, spelling, mathematics, organization, and memory. LD in these areas remain (although some improvement may be made) regardless of the specific instructional approaches used (Poplin, 1988). Furthermore, even when specific skills appear to have been learned, they often are not maintained over time (Poplin, 1988).

In addition to the questionable efficacy of traditional instructional approaches for dealing with LD, it is also important to recognize that many adults with LD may be reluctant to participate in such instructional efforts because past experience with such programs may have yielded little or no results. Furthermore, adults with LD may become impatient with instructional programs because such programs cannot provide immediate solutions to literacy-based difficulties. Adults with LD often do not have the "luxury" of time to improve the literacy skills necessary to accomplish specific tasks within specific contexts.

It is also important to note that traditional instructional approaches are generally "deficit driven," focusing on the individual's area(s) of impairment. According to several authorities in the field of LD (e.g., Heshusius, 1989, 1991; Poplin, 1988), instructional approaches that emphasize impairments over strengths and special abilities generally fail to promote learning and often lead to learner boredom, disinterest, and poor self-concept. In contrast, programs that focus on strengths (over weaknesses) and special abilities (over disabilities) tend to maintain the learner's interest, sustain participation in instructional efforts, and enhance self-concept and learning outcomes. The importance of emphasizing strengths and abilities has also been supported by longitudinal research (Raskind et al., 1996) that has shown that successful adults with LD learn to work around their impairments and to develop and effectively use their strengths and special abilities in their chosen life pursuits (see also Chapter 16).

COMPENSATORY APPROACHES FOR INDIVIDUALS WITH LEARNING DISABILITIES

The problems associated with traditional instructional approaches have led several authorities in the field of LD (e.g., Gray, 1981; Vogel, 1987) to consider alternative approaches to dealing with the literacy difficulties of adults with LD. One approach that is gaining increasing popularity is the "compensatory" approach. The compensatory approach strives to bypass, circumvent, or work around specific LD, in contrast to attempts to improve areas of impairment. For example, in a compenstory approach, a college student with a reading disability might be provided with a tape recorder and audiotaped text, whereas a course on reading improvement might focus on word attack skills and reading comprehension strategies. It is important to emphasize that compensatory approaches do not preclude concurrent instruction. In many instances, it may be helpful to develop compensatory strategies at the same time the individual is receiving instruction aimed at improving specific skill impairments.

ASSISTIVE TECHNOLOGY AS A COMPENSATORY APPROACH TO LITERACY

There has been increasing interest within the field of LD regarding the use of technology to compensate for LD. Technology used to compensate for disabilities has been termed *assistive technology*. According to the Technology-Related Assistance for Individuals with Disabilities Act of 1988 (PL 100-407), *assistive technology* refers to "any item, piece of equipment, or product system, whether acquired commercially off-the-shelf, modified, or customized, that is used to increase, maintain or improve the functional capabilities of individuals with disabilities" (p. 102). In regard to LD, Raskind further delineated *assistive technology* as

> Any technology that enables an adult with a learning disability to compensate for specific deficits. In some instances the technology may assist, augment, or supplement task performance in a given area of disability, whereas in others it may be used to circumvent or "bypass" specific deficits entirely. Assistive technology is not intended to "cure," "fix," or remediate learning disabilities, nor is it intended to teach or instruct (as is computer-aided instruction [CAI]). Furthermore, it strives to accentuate strengths rather than weaknesses, to enable expression of abilities at a level commensurate with intelligence, and, ultimately, to enhance the quality of life of persons with learning disabilities. (1994, p. 152)

Raskind (1994) emphasized that there are several reasons for using assistive technology with individuals with LD, including the use of assistive technology as a means to compensate for difficulties that persist throughout the life span, as well as to accomplish tasks independently across a variety of settings and contexts.

Research on assistive technology has also shown it to be a viable approach for addressing the reading and writing difficulties experienced by adults with LD. Higgins and Raskind (1997) reported that a group of postsecondary students with reading disabilities were able to comprehend written passages significantly better when using an optical character recognition (OCR)/speech synthesis system (this and other assistive technologies mentioned in this section are described later in this chapter) as compared with reading the passages on their own (without the technology) and that the more severe the reading disability, the more the technology was likely to assist the student. However, the authors also noted that the use of the system interfered with the reading comprehension of individuals with mild reading difficulties and, therefore, suggests that a careful analysis of an individual's reading ability be made before recommending OCR/speech synthesis. Similarly, Elkind, Black, and Murray (1996) studied OCR/ speech synthesis as a compensatory tool for adults with dyslexia. According to these researchers, the technology enhanced reading rate and comprehension as well as enabling the subjects to sustain reading longer (as compared with unaided reading). Similarly, Elkind and colleagues also caution that the technology may not be helpful to all adults with dyslexia and, in some cases, may even degrade reading.

Raskind and Higgins (1995) found that the use of speech synthesis/screen review enabled adults with LD to find significantly more overall errors in their self-generated written language samples as compared with having the text read out loud to them by another person or proofreading the text on their own. In addition to overall errors, speech synthesis/screen review enabled individuals to locate significantly more specific types of errors than either of the other two conditions, including errors of capitalization and usage. Significantly more typographical and spelling errors were also found when using speech synthesis as compared with individuals proofreading text on their own. Participants, however, found significantly more "grammar-mechanical" errors by having the text read out loud to them by another person as opposed to using this technology. Therefore, Raskind and Higgins emphasized that speech synthesis/screen review should not be considered the best proofreading strategy for all types of errors and recommended that individuals with LD be encouraged to select from a repertoire of proofreading strategies, each matched to the search for specific types of errors.

Higgins and Raskind (1995) also found that postsecondary students with LD were able to improve their written compositions when using speech recognition technology. Students who wrote essays when using a speech recognition system received significantly higher holistic scores as compared with essays written by hand or on a word processor alone. The authors suggested that the technology may have been successful because it "encouraged" the use of longer words, a powerful predictor of holistic scores.

Additional research also supported the use of word processors and spell checkers as a means by which to compensate for the writing and spelling difficulties experienced by many adults with LD. Collins (1990) conducted a 3-year study on the impact of word processing on the writing performance of college students with LD in a required first-year writing course. Results suggested that the use of word processors helped students with LD complete the writing course at rates similar to peers without such disabilities, achieve grades at least comparable with those of these peers, and improve writing fluency. According to Collins, the use of word processors also led to a significant reduction in writing apprehension among students with LD. Similarly, Primus (1990) studied the impact of word processing on grades and grade point averages of university students with LD. Results of that study indicated that freshman English grades and semester and cumulative grade point averages were higher for students with LD who used word processors while taking freshman English as compared with students with LD who did not use computer technology. However, Primus emphasized that the trend toward higher academic performance was not sustained throughout the students' academic careers.

McNaughton, Hughes, and Clark (1993) investigated the effect of five writing conditions on the spelling performance of college students with LD: handwriting, handwriting with a conventional print dictionary, handwriting with a handheld spell checker, word processing, and word processing with an integrated spell checker. Results indicated that the word processor with an integrated spell checker provided a statistically significant advantage over the other four conditions in the detection of spelling errors. The word processor with an integrated spell checker also showed a statistically significant advantage over handwriting and word processing (but not over the other conditions) in "correction activities." The authors also reported that the word processor with spell checker demonstrated a significant advantage in detecting spelling errors over handwriting and word processing but not over handwriting in combination with a spell checker or conventional dictionary.

Ethnographic research on adults with LD also indicated that assistive technology is a viable compensatory strategy. A study by Raskind, Higgins, and Herman (1997) found that adults who used assistive technology in the workplace believed the technology was instrumental in achieving job independence, satisfaction, and success. Similarly, Gerber et al. (1992) reported that highly successful adults with LD tend to be users of technology.

Again, it is important to emphasize that the use of assistive technology (like other compensatory strategies) and instructional approaches are not mutually exclusive. In fact, there is some evidence to suggest that assistive technology may actually serve to improve specific skill impairments. For example, Kerchner and Kistenger (1984) found that children with LD who used word processors to compensate for writing difficulties also became better writers when using pencil and paper. Similarly, Raskind and Higgins (1998) found that postsecondary students with LD who used speech recognition to compensate for writing difficulties also tended to become better writers even when the technology was not used. Raskind and co-workers (1997) also found that adults with LD who used spell checkers on a regular basis reported improvement in spelling even in the absence of spell-checking technology.

Although research has shown assistive technology to be a viable strategy for addressing the literacy needs of adults with LD, literacy programs have given relatively little attention to assistive technology. When technology is used by literacy providers, it tends to be primarily CAI designed to teach or practice specific skills (e.g., phonics) (Office for Technology Assessment [OTA], 1993), rather than assistive technology aimed at circumventing literacy difficulties. Furthermore, despite the fact that several publications mention assistive technology in regard to literacy and learning disabilities (e.g., *Literacy/Learning Disabilities Collaboration Project* [PLUS, 1992]; *Techniques: Working with Adults with Learning Disabilities* [NALLD Center, 1995b]; *Adult Literacy and New Technologies: Tools for a Lifetime* [OTA, 1993]) and that a NALLD Center publication (*Assistive Technology: Meeting the Needs of Adults with Learning Disabilities* [Riviere, 1996]) has been devoted exclusively to the subject, literacy providers have little knowledge of and rarely use such technologies (OTA, 1993). According to the OTA, the "potential of [assistive] technology for [literacy] programs has barely been exploited" (1993, p. 221). This is true even of the simple and inexpensive technologies such as handheld spell checkers/dictionaries and tape recorders, which are "largely ignored" (1993, p. 200).

TYPES OF ASSISTIVE TECHNOLOGY[1]

This section provides a brief description of a number of technologies available that may help people with LD compensate for their literacy (and related) difficulties. Technologies appear under general headings according to primary areas of difficulty experienced by people with LD. Some technologies may appear under more than one heading because they may be of benefit in more than one area of difficulty.

---

[1]It is important to emphasize that not all technologies are appropriate for all individuals. People with LD have their own unique sets of strengths, weaknesses, interests, experiences, and special abilities. Therefore, a technology that may be a blessing for one person may be a curse for another. Similarly, a technology that is appropriate for one purpose in a particular setting may be of little value in another situation. This section draws from several of the author's previous publications, including Raskind (1994) and Raskind and Scott (1993).

Written Language

Word processors are computer-based writing systems that enable the user to view text on a computer screen before it is printed on paper. In this way, the user can easily delete or add words, move sentences around, and correct punctuation and spelling. Text is also easily underlined, boldfaced, and centered. The ability to manipulate text in these ways may help reduce a writer's fear of making errors, because text is easily changed before it is permanently put on paper. The user can also focus on what he or she wants to express, rather than on having to make the paper error free. In addition, the writer can be confident that his or her efforts will result in a neat, clean, and presentable document.

Spell checkers are part of most word-processing programs and are also available as stand-alone desktop and pocket-size devices. Spell checkers attached to word processors scan a written document and alert the user (usually by visually highlighting the word) to misspelled words. Stand-alone spell checkers require users to enter the word (the way they think the word is spelled) by means of a small keyboard. Some devices will simply verify and correct the spelling on a small screen, whereas others offer a complete dictionary and thesaurus. Other devices actually "speak" the words by means of a speech synthesizer (see section on Speech Synthesizers), allowing the user to hear as well as to see text.

Proofreading programs (sometimes referred to as grammar checkers) are used in combination with word-processing programs to check for errors in grammar, punctuation, capitalization, and word usage. Suspected errors are identified on the computer monitor, and the user is given the opportunity to correct them prior to printing the document. Unfortunately, many proofreading programs are not completely accurate and may miss a large number of errors. They may also prompt the user to alter portions of text that are not incorrect.

Speech synthesizers, together with *screen review* software, enable the user to hear text on a computer screen spoken aloud. Words are spoken in a computerized or "synthetic" voice through a synthesizer device installed either inside or outside the computer. Users are able to review text that they have written by reading it on the computer screen while hearing the words read out loud. Hearing written text may assist them in detecting writing errors (e.g., difficulties with grammar, omitted words) that might otherwise go unnoticed. Similarly, listening to text may also help users determine whether their writing "makes sense" and whether it reflects what they are really trying to say. Speech synthesis may be especially helpful to individuals who are better listeners than readers.

Speech recognition systems allow a person to operate a computer by speaking to it. In combination with a word processor, the user dictates to the system (through a microphone), and the spoken words are converted to text on the computer screen. For most systems, a pause of approximately $\frac{1}{10}$ of a second is required between words. ("Continuous speech" systems released in the 1990s do not require a pause.) If the system incorrectly recognizes a word, the user has the option of choosing the correct word from a list of similar sounding words displayed on the screen. The more the system is used, the more accurate it becomes in recognizing the user's spoken language. Speech recognition systems may be particularly helpful to those individuals who have oral language abilities that are superior to their written language abilities.

Outlining programs (now included as part of many word-processing programs) help the user create outlines. By using a few simple keystrokes (or a mouse), the program automatically creates Roman numerals for major headings and letters and numbers for subordinate headings. If the user decides to move text around, then the program automatically reorganizes the Roman numerals, letters, and numbers that had been designated for specific headings. Users are able to freely "dump" their ideas into the computer without having to worry about order, level of importance, or category, because text can be easily moved (and automatically reorganized) at a later time. These programs may be of value to those individuals who have great ideas but experience difficulty in getting them down on paper. Outlining programs may also be helpful to people who, even if they can get started, may not know how to keep going.

"Brain storming"/"mind mapping" programs enable writers to create a diagram of their ideas before writing an outline. The user first types a main idea into the computer. The main idea is displayed on the computer screen. The user then types in related ideas that appear as specified geometric shapes (e.g., circles, ovals, rectangles) surrounding the main idea. Ideas may be linked with the main idea (and each other) by lines. Ideas are easily moved, rearranged, and categorized. After the diagram is completed, it can be automatically changed to an outline. Some individuals who have difficulty in expressing their ideas in writing may find this free-form graphic approach more helpful than simple text-based outlining.

Word prediction programs work together with word processors to "predict" the word a user wants to enter into the computer. The user types the first letter of a word and the program offers a list of words beginning with that letter. If the desired word appears, it can be chosen from the list (by pressing a corresponding number on the keyboard or pointing and clicking with a mouse), and it will be automatically inserted into the sentence. If the desired word does not appear in the list, the user continues to type the next letter until it does appear. After a word is chosen, the next word in the sentence is predicted (again offering a list of possible words), even before the first letter is typed. Predictions are based on syntax and spelling, as well as word frequency, redundancy, and recency factors. Word prediction may be helpful to individuals who experience difficulties with keyboarding, spelling, or grammar or experience difficulty in coming up with the appropriate word to use in a sentence.

Alternative keyboards allow the user to individualize the keyboard by changing the layout and appearance of the keys. For example, the position of the keys can be changed from the standard QWERTY layout to an alphabetical arrangement, and the size of the letters can be made larger. The availability of specific options depends on the particular product. Individuals who experience difficulty in keyboarding/typing may find these devices helpful.

Reading

Optical character recognition systems, when combined with speech synthesis, might be thought of as "reading machines." Along with a scanner (a device used to input images from a printed page into a computer file), the OCR (hardware, software, or both that changes the printed text input by the scanner into computer/electronic text) enables the user to input "hard copy" text (e.g., books, letters) directly into a computer, which can then be read back—out loud—by means of the speech synthesizer. In this way, the individual can hear as well as see the text. OCR systems are available as self-contained units (which act solely as reading machines) or as systems that work together with personal computers. These systems are particularly helpful to individuals who experience difficulty in reading printed words and can better understand what they hear than what they read.

Speech synthesis/screen review systems may also function as reading machines independent of an OCR system if the text is available on a computer disc. Several agencies, including the American Printing House for the Blind in Louisville, Kentucky, and Recordings for the Blind and Dyslexic (RFBD) in Princeton, New Jersey, have begun producing electronic text (i.e., "books on disk") that may be loaded directly into a computer (bypassing the OCR) and then read back by means of a speech synthesis/screen review system.

Tape recorders can be used to play back audiotaped text. People with reading difficulties can work around their problems by listening to prerecorded text (books, journals, newspapers) rather than reading the hard copy. Taped text (e.g., books on audiotape) is available from a number of sources, including local book, toy, and record stores, as well as the Library of Congress National Library for the Blind and Physically Handicapped in Washington, D.C., and RFBD. Organizations that offer audiotaped text generally require verification of a learning disability from a qualified professional. It is important to keep in mind that not all audiotapes will work on all tape recorders because they may have varying speeds (1 7/8ths or 15/16ths inches per second) and formats (two track, four track). Care should be taken to ensure that there is a match between the playback unit and the tapes.

Variable speech control (VSC) tape recorders enable the listener to play back audiotaped text (either two- or four-track format, depending on the device) at rates that are faster or slower than originally recorded, without a loss of intelligibility. This feature may be quite useful for people who are better able to comprehend spoken language (in the case of reading, audiotaped text) when the material is presented at a slower pace. Conversely, some individuals may find that they are able to review material faster by speeding up the audiotape. VSC audiotape recorders typically allow slowdown by 25% of the original recording speed and an increase in playback speed of up to 100%.

Listening

Personal FM listening systems place a speaker's voice directly into a listener's ear by means of a small transmitter unit (with a microphone) and a receiver unit (with head- or earphone). Both units are about 2 inches by 3 inches. These wireless systems make the speaker's voice more prominent, which may be of particular benefit to those individuals with learning problems who have difficulty in focusing on what a speaker is saying. Volume is controlled by a dial on the receiver unit.

Tape recorders can be used to permanently record spoken information such as a teacher's instructions or a classroom lecture. Having a permanent record provides an individual with the ability to refer back to an oral presentation in the event that there was difficulty in processing or comprehending the initial presentation. It may also be helpful to people who have difficulty in remembering what they hear. A VSC audiotape recorder may be particularly helpful because it allows the user to slow down or speed up recorded presentations (in the same way that one might be useful with prerecorded text).

Organization/Memory

Personal data managers (available as software packages or electronic handheld devices) may be useful to people with organizational or memory difficulties, or both, because they provide the user with a means to easily store and retrieve large amounts of personal information (e.g., telephone numbers, addresses, important dates, appointments, reminders). Information is entered and retrieved by means of a keyboard/keypad and displayed on a computer monitor or small liquid crystal display (LCD). Features and capabilities vary considerably. Some handheld units are available that allow the user to enter and retrieve information by speaking into the device. Stored information is spoken back in the user's own voice.

Free-form databases are software programs that enable the user to type notes into the computer in much the same way as a person might write them down on a notepad or a piece of paper. The note is displayed on the computer monitor and can be stored in the computer's memory. Specific notes are retrieved by typing in any bit of information contained in the note. For example, "Mike," "birth," or "Dec" could be used to retrieve the note "Mike's birthday is on December 8." Such systems may be helpful to those individuals who have difficulty organizing and remembering important information.

Math

Talking calculators use a built-in speech synthesizer to speak number, symbol, or operation keys as they are pressed as well as to read back answers from completed calculations. Hearing the numbers or symbols may assist some people in catching errors at the "input" level, such as pressing the wrong key. Similarly, having the answer read out loud may help the user double-check for errors (e.g., transpositions [91 for 19], inversions [6 for 9]) that may have been made when copying numbers from the calculator display onto paper.

SELECTING THE APPROPRIATE ASSISTIVE TECHNOLOGY

As previously mentioned, not all assistive technologies are appropriate for all individuals in all situations. People with LD have their own unique sets of strengths, weaknesses, special abilities, interests, and experiences. Therefore, a technology that may be appropriate for one person may be inappropriate for another. Similarly, a technology that is helpful for one purpose in one particular setting may be of little value in another situation or setting. Consequently, selecting the appropriate technology for an individual with a learning disability requires careful analysis of the interplay between 1) the individual, 2) the specific task/functions to be performed, 3) the specific technology, and 4) the specific contexts of interaction (Raskind & Bryant, 1996). A model for assistive technology selection is displayed in Figure 13.1 and is discussed in the following section.

The Individual

First, it is imperative to consider the individual's strengths and weaknesses in regard to such areas as reading, writing, spelling, listening, speaking, match, memory, organization, and physical/motor abilities. Examining these areas will enable the literacy provider to identify the areas of difficulty that may be circumvented by the use of assistive technology. Such examination will aid in determining the areas of strength on which an assistive technology may capitalize in order to bypass a specific difficulty. Information of this nature may be gathered from school records, prior diagnostic assessments (informal and formal), and interviews with individuals who are familiar with the person (e.g., teachers, parents, employers, as appropriate). In addition (as appropriate and as resources permit), data may be obtained from the administration of formal (e.g., standardized instruments) and informal diagnostic assessments (including observations) that focus on the previously mentioned areas (e.g., reading, writing, spelling). The person being evaluated for technology use should also be considered a key member of the technology evaluation team and should be thoroughly interviewed

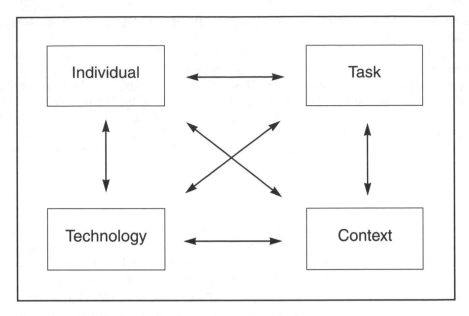

Figure 13.1.   Model for the selection of appropriate assistive technology.

as to his or her own understanding of the nature of his or her learning disability, including his or her strengths, weaknesses, and special abilities.

Second, the potential effectiveness of a technology requires an understanding of not only the individual's strengths and weaknesses but also the individual's prior experience with and interest in technology. Such information is needed to plan appropriate technology instruction/training as well as to help determine the individual's interest in pursuing a technological approach to literacy. The literacy provider can gather such information from prior records; interviews with individuals familiar with the person under evaluation; an interview with the individuals familiar with the person under evaluation; an interview with the individual him- or herself; and, if possible, observation of technology use by the individual. The literacy provider will need to consider the individual's technology experience and interest relative to the specific areas of difficulty (e.g., prior experience with/interest in a word processor to compensate for writing problems, or an OCR system for a reading difficulty), as well as the individual's general technological literacy, working knowledge of technology, and overall interest. Again, such information is needed to select the most appropriate/effective technology and to develop a plan for helping the individual learn to use the technology.

The Task–Individual–Technology Match

The literacy provider should also gather information on the individual's use of a technology to compensate for a specific difficulty through direct observation. Only by observing the interplay between the individual and the technology while a specific task is performed can the literacy provider be assured that the technology is appropriate for the individual. In many instances, the literacy provider will not have the technological resources to make such observations and may find it necessary to collaborate with assistive technology professionals who possess the necessary resources. (The appendix at the end of this chapter may be helpful in finding such professionals.) Manufacturers' representatives can also be brought in to demonstrate and provide an opportunity for the individual to try out a technology. As the individual experiments with the technology to perform specific tasks, consideration should be given to the following areas: 1) the effectiveness of the technology in compensating for specific difficulties as compared with alternative strategies (e.g., "no-tech" strategies); 2) the individual's ease in learning and using the technology; 3) the individual's interest in and comfort with the technology; 4) the degree to which the technology taps into the individuals strengths; 5) the extent to which the individual was able to use the technology independently and troubleshoot as necessary; and 6) the individual's overall psychological and behavioral response to the technology.

The Technology

A number of elements specific to the technology itself should be considered in the selection process. Particular attention should be given to 1) the technology's effectiveness in accomplishing its primary compensatory purpose (e.g., does a speech recognition system accurately convert an individual's oral language to written text and improve the quality of the written product?); 2) the reliability/dependability of the product over time; 3) the compatibility of the product with other technologies; 4) the ease of learning and using the technology; 5) the ease of installing/setting up the technology; 6) the availability and ease of accessing technical support; and 7) the cost of the technology. Information regarding these characteristics may be found by talking to past and current users, as well as by contacting the assistive technology resources listed in the appendix at the end of this chapter. Technology magazines may also provide critical reviews and comparisons of selected products. For an in-depth discussion of these selection elements, see Raskind and Scott (1993).

Context of Interaction

Literacy skills are required in numerous contexts. Therefore, it is important to consider the selection of technology appropriate for people with LD relative to a number of settings, including school, work, home, social, and recreational/leisure environments. Technology that is appropriate in one environment may be quite inappropriate in another. As previously discussed, it is imperative to consider the compensatory effectiveness of a particular technology. It is also critical to consider the compensatory effectiveness of the technology relative to different settings. The fact that a technology successfully compensates for a learning disability in one context does not necessitate that it will be effective in another. For example, a speech recognition system may work quite effectively at home, where the user can work alone. However, the use of the technology in a classroom setting where there is considerable extraneous noise may interfere with the technology's operation.

Similarly, the social appropriateness of an assistive technology may change from one context to another. For example, the use of a calculator to compensate for a math disability in a work setting may blend in quite nicely, without any negative social ramifications among co-workers. However, using a calculator to keep the score of a board game in a social setting may appear inappropriate to peers. In addition to the context-dependent compensatory effectiveness and social appropriateness of an assistive technology, there are a number of other contextual elements that should be considered when selecting the appropriate assistive technology for an individual with a learning disability, including 1) portability of the technology between contexts, 2) compatibility with other technologies in various contexts, 3) space availability and appropriateness for specific technologies within specific contexts, and 4) availability of and access to technical support. It is also important to keep in mind that the contexts in which the technology will be used may change over time. Therefore, some consideration should be given to projecting the appropriateness of the technology for the contexts of inter-actions that may evolve across time—in both the short (e.g., within 1 year) and long (e.g., within several or more years) terms.

AVAILABILITY OF ASSISTIVE TECHNOLOGIES

There is no one central location where assistive technology can be purchased for an individual with a learning disability. In general, assistive technology is available from two primary sources: 1) companies and their representatives that specialize in tech-nologies for people with LD; and 2) companies and their representatives (retailers) that supply "standard" technology to the general public.

As of 1998, there is no single company that specializes solely in the development, manufacture, or sale of products exclusively for people with LD. However, a limited number of companies have added technologies to their product lines that are targeted specifically at people with LD (e.g., Xerox Adaptive Technologies, Franklin Learning Resources). Assistive technology companies are increasingly taking products initially developed for other disabilities and, because of their potential usefulness, marketed them as products for people with LD.

Many products from companies offering standard technologies to the general pub-lic (as opposed to focusing on groups with disabilities) have been recognized as assis-tive technology because of their compensatory potential. For example, the wide vari-ety of personal data managers produced by Sharp Electronics and spell checkers from Texas Instruments, although not specifically developed for people with LD, can be valuable in their working around difficulties. Technologies of this type are widely avail-able at local electronics and computer retail outlets.

COST OF ASSISTIVE TECHNOLOGIES

The cost of assistive technology varies widely, ranging from as little as $15 for a "low-end" personal data manager to as much as $4,500 for an OCR system. Fortunately, the cost of many assistive technologies has been decreasing. A speech recognition system (without the computer) introduced on the market for approximately $5,000 has dropped in price to about $100.

However, there is no doubt that in some cases the required technology may be too expensive to purchase (either by the literacy providers or by the individual). In such situations, a "lower tech" or "no-tech" compensatory strategy should be investigated because in many instances, such a strategy may work just as well as more expen-sive "high-tech" solutions. For example, a book on tape may work just as well as (and in some cases better than) an expensive OCR system in compensating for reading problems.

Before a purchase is made, it is advisable to try out a specific technology. Depend-ing on the product, it is possible to learn the strengths and weaknesses of a specific product through such sources as assistive technology centers, schools/universities, computer shows, assistive technology conferences, learning disability conferences, friends, and retail outlets. In addition, most manufacturers/representatives of assistive technology are willing to provide demonstrations, and some will even lend the tech-nology on a trial basis.

Although no widespread funding is available for purchasing assistive technology, there are some sources that may help offset the costs for individuals with an official diagnosis of learning disability. For children with LD in elementary and secondary schools, the Individuals with Disabilities Education Act (IDEA) of 1990 (PL 101-476) states that it is the school's responsibility to provide assistive technology—at no cost to the child's family—if the technology is required as part of the child's special education program.

In some instances, postsecondary institutions might be responsible for providing assistive technology to students with LD under the Rehabilitation Act of 1973 (PL 93-112) if a specific technology is found to be the only viable solution for ensuring full access to the institution. Some postsecondary institutions have already recognized their obligation and the importance of assistive technology for students with LD and have set up assistive technology programs on their campuses. State departments of rehabilitation also may provide assistive technology funding for an individual with a learning disability if the person is a consumer of the agency's services. Funding is handled on a case-by-case basis, with specific funding requirements varying widely between individual state agencies and district offices.

Depending on the particular employment setting, employers of people with LD also may be responsible for picking up the cost of assistive technology under Sections 503, 504, or 508 of the Rehabilitation Act of 1973 or under the Americans with Disabilities Act (ADA) of 1990 (PL 101-336) in order to meet the legal obligation of providing "reasonable accommodation." Once again, determining whether an institution, agency, or employer is responsible for purchasing technology for an individual with a learning disability is handled on a case-by-case basis and may at times require legal counsel. Many of these waters have yet to be tested.

There is also the possibility of obtaining funding from Medicare, Medicaid, and private insurance. These sources, however, require that the technology serve a medical rather than an educational purpose. These sources also require that the technology be prescribed by a physician or other licensed practitioner (e.g., a licensed speech-language pathologist). Other possibilities for financial support include private foundations and service clubs. It may also be possible to contact manufacturers of technology directly for donations or discounts. In addition, a number of reference books available in local and university libraries list possible sources of financial assistance for people with disabilities and their families.

LEARNING TO USE ASSISTIVE TECHNOLOGY

There are a number of different ways an individual with a learning disability can learn to use assistive technology, again depending on the particular technology, setting, and person. Of course, the literacy provider's level of technological expertise will play a major role in determining the most appropriate channels (which may include the literacy provider him- or herself) for helping the individual learn to use the technology. In some instances, such as the purchase of a audiotape recorder or handheld spell checker, a few minutes with the retail saleperson may be all that is needed. The instruction booklet may even be sufficient for such technologies. In contrast, 4–5 hours of specialized training from a manufacturer's representative or an assistive technology specialist may be required to learn to use a speech recognition system. Training may or may not be provided as part of the purchase price, depending on the particular sales agreement. It is important to emphasize that "low" technology is not necessarily easier to learn than "high" technology. For example, some personal data managers may take many hours to master, whereas a speech synthesis/screen review system might be learned reasonably well within half an hour.

If instruction in a standard technology is required (e.g., a word-processing program like WordPerfect), a friend or relative may have the necessary expertise. If not, then a computer consultant or tutor may need to be hired. Other possibilities include learning how to use a technology from a manual (although in some situations this can be quite difficult) and on-line tutorials. Some companies now provide tutorials on videotape. Again, the manner in which a technology is taught depends on the technology itself and the needs of the individual.

The literacy provider may also need to consider collaborating with outside sources. There are a number of public and private centers that have been established to provide assistive technology services for people with disabilities (e.g., The Alliance for Technology Access; see the appendix at the end of this chapter). Although some provide services for individuals with LD, most focus on other disabilities. The services offered by these centers, as well as eligibility for services and fees, vary considerably and must be investigated on an individual basis.

A new group of professionals referring to themselves as "assistive technology specialists" has emerged. As is the case with all professionals, some are better qualified than others. Unfortunately, there is no credentialing or licensing required to practice as an assistive technology specialist. Consequently, the literacy provider should inquire as to the specific qualifications of the assistive technology specialist, including questions regarding the specialist's educational background, training, and experience (in regard to both LD and technology).

CONCLUSION

The significant number of adults with LD in literacy education programs has prompted numerous collaborations between literacy service providers and learning disability professionals. These collaborations are aimed at establishing literacy service practices that are designed to meet the specific needs of individuals with LD. The instructional approaches emerging from these collaborations are generally intended to "correct" or improve specific skill impairments in such areas as reading, writing, and math.

Although reflective of the LD field as a whole, the instructional methods often being used in literacy service programs to address the needs of individuals with LD are of questionable efficacy. Consequently, an alternative approach to meeting the literacy needs of adults with LD has been presented in this chapter—the use of assistive technology as a means to compensate for, or bypass, specific impairments. It is not the intention of the chapter to suggest that instructional approaches should not be used by literacy providers in an attempt to improve the skills of adults with LD. Rather, the use of assistive technology is introduced as an additional, supplemental approach to meeting the literacy needs of adults with LD—an approach that has proved to be effective in enabling individuals with LD to circumvent their difficulties while accentuating their strengths and special abilities, an approach that has the potential to help people with LD reach their full potential and live satisfying and rewarding lives, now and in the years to come.

REFERENCES

Americans with Disabilities Act of 1990, PL 101-336, 42 U.S.C. §§ 12101 *et seq.*
Collins, T. (1990). The impact of microcomputer word processing on the performance of learning disabled students in a required first year writing course. *Computers and Composition, 8,* 49–68.

Elkind, J., Black, M.S., & Murray, C. (1996). Computer-based compensation of adult reading disabilities. *Annals of Dyslexia, 46,* 159–186.

Gerber, P.J., Ginsberg, R., & Reiff, H.B. (1992). Identifying alterable patterns of vocational success in highly successful adults with learning disabilities. *Journal of Learning Disabilities, 25,* 475–485.

Gottesman, R.L. (1994). The adult with learning disabilities: An overview. *Learning Disabilities: A Multidisciplinary Journal, 5,* 1–14.

Gray, R.A. (1981). Services for the LD adult: A working paper. *Learning Disability Quarterly, 4,* 426–431.

Heshusius, L. (1989). The Newtonian mechanistic paradigm, special education, and contours of alternatives: An overview. *Journal of Learning Disabilities, 22,* 403–415.

Heshusius, L. (1991). Future perspectives. In D.K. Reid, W.P. Hresko, & L. Swanson (Eds.), *A cognitive approach to learning disabilities* (pp. 431–467). Austin, TX: PRO-ED.

Higgins, E.L., & Raskind, M.H. (1995). An investigation of the compensatory effectiveness of speech recognition on the written composition performance of postsecondary students with learning disabilities. *Learning Disability Quarterly, 18,* 159–174.

Higgins, E.L., & Raskind, M.H. (1997). The compensatory effectiveness of optical character recognition/speech synthesis on reading comprehension of postsecondary students with learning disabilities. *Learning Disabilities: A Multidisciplinary Journal, 8,* 75–87.

Individuals with Disabilities Education Act (IDEA) of 1990, PL 101-476, 20 U.S.C. §§ 1400 *et seq.*

Kavale, K.A. (1988). Adult outcomes. In K.A. Kavale, S.R. Forness, & M. Bender (Eds.), *Handbook of learning disabilities* (Vol. III, pp. 199–208). Boston: College Hill.

Kerchner, L.B., & Kistenger, B.J. (1984). Language processing/word processing: Written expression, computers, and learning disabled students. *Learning Disability Quarterly, 7,* 329–335.

Malicky, G., & Norman, C.A. (1989). The reading concepts and strategies of adult nonreaders. *Journal of Reading, 33,* 198–202.

McNaughton, D., Hughes, C., & Clark, K. (1993, February). *An investigation of the effect of five writing conditions on the spelling performance of college students with learning disabilities.* Paper presented at the 30th International Conference of the Learning Disabilities Association of America, San Francisco.

National Adult Literacy and Learning Disabilities Center. (1995a). *Linkages: Linking Literacy & Learning Disabilities.* Washington, DC: Author.

National Adult Literacy and Learning Disabilities Center. (1995b). *Techniques: Working with adults with learning disabilities.* Washington, DC: Author.

Nightengale, D. (1991). *The learning disabled in employment and training programs* (Research and Evaluation Report Series 91-E). Washington, DC: The Urban Institute.

Office for Technology Assessment. (1993). *Adult literacy and new technologies: Tools for a lifetime.* Washington, DC: Author. (Available from U.S. Government Printing Office [GPO No. S/N 052-003-01330-4]

Project Literacy U.S. (1992). *Literacy/Learning Disabilities Collaboration Project.* Pittsburgh, PA: Author.

Poplin, M. (1988). The reductionist fallacy in learning disabilities: Replicating the past by reducing the present. *Learning Disability Quarterly, 7,* 389–400.

Primus, C. (1990). *Computer assistance model for learning disabled* (Grant No. G008630152-88). Washington, DC: U.S. Department of Education, Office of Special Education and Rehabilitation Services.

Raskind, M.H. (1994). Assistive technology for adults with learning disabilities: A rationale for use. In P.J. Gerber & H.B. Reiff (Eds.), *Adults with learning disabilities* (pp. 152–162). Austin, TX: PRO-ED.

Raskind, M.R., Goldberg, R.J., Higgins, E.L., & Herman, K.L. (1996, November). *Children with learning disabilities grow up: Results of a twenty-year longitudinal study.* Paper presented at the Council for Learning Disabilities International Conference, Nashville, TN.

Raskind, M.H., & Higgins, E.L. (1995). The effects of speech synthesis on proofreading efficiency of postsecondary students with learning disabilities. *Learning Disability Quarterly, 18,* 141–158.

Raskind, M.H., & Higgins, E.L. (1998). Assistive technology for postsecondary students with learning disabilities. *Journal of Learning Disabilities, 31,* 27–40.

Raskind, M.H., Higgins, E.L., & Herman, K.L. (1997). Technology in the workplace for persons with learning disabilities: Views from the inside. In P.J. Gerber & D.S. Brown (Eds.), *Learning disabilities and employment* (pp. 307–330). Austin, TX: PRO-ED.

Raskind, M.H., & Scott, N. (1993). Technology for postsecondary students with learning disabilities. In S.A. Vogel & P. Adelman (Eds.), *Success for postsecondary students with learning disabilities* (pp. 240–279). New York: Springer-Verlag.

Raskind, M.R., & Bryant, B. (1996, November). *Assistive technology evaluation for persons with learning disabilities.* Paper presented at the Council for Learning Disabilities International Conference, Nashville, TN.

Rehabilitation Act of 1973, PL 93-112, 29 U.S.C. §§ 701 *et seq.*

Riviere, A. (1996). *Assistive technology: Meeting the needs of adults with learning disabilities.* Washington, DC: National Adult Literacy and Learning Disabilities Center.

Spekman, N.J., Goldberg, R.J., & Herman, K.L. (1992). Learning disabled children grow up: A search for factors related to success in the young adult years. *Learning Disabilities Research & Practice, 28,* 602–614.

Sturomski, N.A. (1996). Literacy needs for adults who have learning disabilities. In N. Gregg, C. Hoy, & A.F. Gay (Eds.), *Adults with learning disabilities* (pp. 261–276). New York: The Guilford Press.

Technology-Related Assistance for Individuals with Disabilities Act of 1988, PL 100-407, 29 U.S.C. §§ 2201 *et seq.*

Vogel, S.A. (1987). Issues and concerns in LD college programming. In D.J. Johnson & J.W. Blalock (Eds.), *Adults with learning disabilities: Clinical studies* (pp. 239–275). Orlando, FL: Grune & Stratton.

Werner, E.E., & Smith, R.S. (1992). *Overcoming the odds: High risk children from birth to adulthood.* Ithaca, NY: Cornell University Press.

Appendix

Resources

The following organizations, agencies, centers, and conferences should be helpful in obtaining further information on assistive technology and learning disabilities.

Alliance for Technology Access (ATA)
2175 East San Francisco Boulevard
Suite L
San Rafael, CA 94901
(415) 455-4575
e-mail address: atainfo@ataccess.org

American Printing House for the Blind
1839 Frankfort Avenue
Post Office Box 6085
Louisville, KY 40206
(800) 223-1839
(502) 895-2405
e-mail address: info@aph.org

Center for Applied Special Technology (CAST)
39 Cross Street
Peabody, MA 01960
(508) 531-8555
e-mail address: cast@cast.org

Council for Learning Disabilities (CLD)
Post Office Box 40303
Overland Park, KS 66204
(913) 492-8755

Closing the Gap (conference)
Post Office Box 68
Henderson, MN 56044
(507) 248-3294
e-mail address: info@closingthegap.com

Frostig Center for Technology and Learning Disabilities (CTLD)
971 North Altadena Drive
Pasadena, CA 91107
(818) 791-1255

International Society for Augmentative and Alternative Communication (ISAAC)
Post Office Box 1762
Station R
Toronto, ON M4G 4A3
CANADA
(905) 737-9308

Learning Disabilities Association of America (LDA)
4156 Library Road
Pittsburgh, PA 15234
(412) 341-1515
e-mail address: liz_baer@mail.cepp.org

**National Adult Literacy and
Learning Disabilities Center**
1875 Connecticut Avenue, NW
Washington, D.C. 20009
(202) 884-8185
e-mail address: info@nalldc.aed.org

**National Center for Learning
Disabilities**
381 Park Avenue S, Suite 1420
New York, NY 10016
(212) 545-7510

The Orton Dyslexia Society
Chester Building
Suite 382
8600 La Salle Road
Baltimore, MD 21286
(800) 331-0688
(410) 296-0232

**Parents' Educational Resource
Center**
1660 South Amphlett Boulevard
Suite 200
San Mateo, CA 94402
(415) 655-2410
e-mail address: perc@netcom.com

Recording for the Blind and Dyslexic
20 Roszel Road
Princeton, NJ 08540
(800) 221-4792
(609) 452-0606
e-mail address: info@rfb.org

**RESNA Technical Assistance
Project**
1700 N. Moore Street
Suite 1540
Arlington, VA 22091
(703) 524-6686 Ext. 313

Technology and Media (TAM)
Council for Exceptional Children
1920 Association Drive
Reston, VA 22091
(703) 620-3660

**Technology and Persons
with Disabilities (conference)**
California State University, Northridge
Center on Disabilities
18111 Nordhoff Street
Northridge, CA 91330
(818) 885-2578
e-mail address: ltm@csun.edu

**Technology, Reading and
Learning Difficulties (conference)**
Education Computer Conferences
1070 Crows Nest Way
Richmond, CA 94803
(510) 594-1249

IV

Employment Issues

Sections I–III address some of the issues in defining, describing, screening, and teaching adults with learning disabilities (LD). Section IV focuses on a critical (some would describe it as the most critical) application of this knowledge: helping adults with LD to identify, secure, and succeed in careers that match their interests and abilities. The chapters in Section IV address different aspects of and provide complementary insights into these employment concerns.

In Chapter 14, Rob Crawford addresses the disparity between the lofty goals of national training and employment initiatives and the lack of effective assessment, training, and placement for adults with LD. Crawford details a number of specific problems and limitations with employment initiatives such as the U.S. Department of Labor's common "learning and earning system." Many of these limitations originate in the standardized testing systems and associated curricula that have dominated workforce training and employment programs for decades. After pointing out how traditional assessments provide little information about the strengths, weaknesses, and instructional needs of adults with LD, Crawford describes promising new abilities-based approaches to assessment and training. These new systems are based on principles of authentic assessment and customized instruction designed to meet adults' individual learning needs and goals in three broad areas required for success in the workplace: academic skills, social skills, and career awareness. Crawford illustrates how such concepts can be shaped into effective programs serving adults with LD and literacy difficulties. Crawford describes the design, operation, and results obtained by the Life Development Institute, a community-based residential program providing assessment, training, and placement services for adults with LD.

In Chapter 15, James R. Koller and Gregory A. Holliday look carefully at the transition support system for youth and young adults with specific LD as they move from one system (school) into another (the workplace). As is Crawford, Koller and Holliday are concerned that the increasing technological requirements of work are heightening demands for more effective diagnostic and intervention services for individuals with LD. Although Koller and Holliday find empirical support for the notion that an increasing proportion of workforce entrants have specific LD, Koller and Holliday are concerned with the lack of effective transition support. A particular problem is the lack of effective collaboration between different components of the transition support system, particularly those of school and those of vocational rehabilitation. Chapter 15 (similar to Chapter 14) contrasts situational or authentic assessment practices with more traditional approaches, and Koller and Holliday conclude that the newer approaches maximize the chances for adults with LD to find satisfying and rewarding work roles. Chapter 15 reviews field-tested outcome studies and identifies a number of promising approaches and practices. The optimal approach to workplace transition support, which draws on a variety of these effective practices, is described as a functional, holistic, and authentic self-advocacy model.

Chapter 16, written by Henry B. Reiff, formulates the "road to employment success" for adults with LD in somewhat different terms than do Crawford and Koller. Similar to each of the preceding chapters in this section, this chapter describes the changing market forces that are reshaping the employment contexts encountered by adults with LD. The chapter then shifts to examining the ingredients in employment success experienced by adults with LD. Profiles of three vocationally successful adults with LD are used to illustrate the pathways to successful employment identified in a major study of successful adults with LD. Using the metaphor of a road less traveled, Reiff locates the successful life trajectory of an adult with LD as being "off the beaten path," traveling through well-developed regions of self-awareness and self-advocacy. Seeing successful adjustment in the workplace being realized partly through effective coping mechanisms and partly through a heightened sense of identity, Reiff eloquently sketches the vital role that humor plays in the successful adjustment of individuals with LD. Although adults with LD may have to travel off the beaten path, they can reach the same destinations as everyone else.

14

Developing Abilities-Based Literacy and Employment Services for Adults with Learning Disabilities

Rob Crawford

The demands of today's workplace, with its emphasis on high technology, strong inter-personal skills, and maintaining market share against global competition, are driving forces behind reform themes in adult and workplace education programs. The higher expectations of the workplace should have changed the way that assessment and placement of adults with learning disabilities (LD) and literacy problems into education, instruction, and employment programs are conducted. In general, the exact opposite is typically the case.

Most employment and education reform initiatives continue to display a lack of awareness of, sensitivity to, or acknowledgment of adults with LD, who represent the largest identified group of learners with special needs seeking employment and adult education services. Many of these individuals are nontraditional learners who do not accurately present their maximum capabilities with traditional assessments and academic approaches. The ability of practitioners to accurately predict how an individual who is a nontraditional thinker knows, understands, perceives, learns, and processes information can result in prescriptive, individualized instruction that would benefit the entire lifelong learning community. This chapter identifies and focuses on techniques that facilitate abilities-based reflections of individual interests, capabilities, and aptitudes combined with demands of the targeted employment objective.

AUTHENTIC ASSESSMENT

Typically, instructional needs are identified through the use of criterion-referenced ability assessments. Of the many shortcomings associated with these instruments for the purpose of counseling, employment placement, and postsecondary education of students with LD, there are three in particular that are problematic.

First, standardized testing generates situations in which abilities being measured are tested in formats not typical of contextual or "real-world" situations. Wiggins characterized the inadequacy of this testing approach as "removing what is central in intellectual competence: the use of judgment to recognize complex problems and use one's discreet knowledge to solve them" (1989, p. 89).

Second, standardized testing provides, at best, superficial information limited in relationship to the full potential of the individual. Accurate measurement using standardized instruments falls short of examining the "whole" individual because it provides limited understanding of the social, emotional, physical, aesthetic, and intellectual development that is unique to that individual (Ulrey & Ulrey, 1992).

Finally, standardized testing focuses on the content of test responses instead of the learning process used to formulate a response (Lazear, 1994). Living in an information-age society, in which the sheer volume of available knowledge is growing beyond our capability to acquire, make meaningful, store, and situationally select it, should promote efforts to look beyond mastering academic content as the primary benchmark of testing. Increased attention should be given to designing instruments that identify the processes associated with developing and utilizing the capacity to be a creative thinker and problem solver—how to adapt, transfer, and integrate classroom content into daily living/employment tasks.

The authentic assessment process has been developed to provide an abilities-based evaluation of such processes. Authentic assessments are realistically structured, taking into account real-world constraints typically encountered outside the learning environment (e.g., time, production-level requirements). Academic design factors for authentic assessment require that testing occur in the context of actual learning situations that are relevant to students. By focusing on the mastery and measurement of true essential skills and competencies, which are the basis of the course of study, the ability to uncover students' working knowledge, skillful utilization of course competencies, and transferability of applied learning into real-life situations is facilitated.

Lazear (1994) suggested a schema that consists of three primary criteria that promote authentic assessment and can be used in conjunction with standardized testing (see Figure 14.1). A brief description of the academic design, examination structure, and scoring criteria of authentic assessment is provided here. For further information on authentic assessments, the reader is referred to the description of multiple intelligence approaches to authentic assessment by Lazear (1994).

Components of Authentic Assessment

The structure of an authentic assessment is similar to an apprenticeship program in that it is developmentally designed to move a student from the novice to the master level through demonstration of the knowledge, understanding, and skill development required for the subject discipline. The academic design for authentic assessment is constructed by instructional personnel involved in teaching the curriculum and is directly related to the actual curriculum. It takes into consideration the personal motivation of students who want to improve their individual performance and are, in essence, competing with themselves. Academic design also takes into consideration realistic, typical, hands-on performance situations students will encounter in life beyond school. Authentic assessment thus benefits all stakeholders through challenging

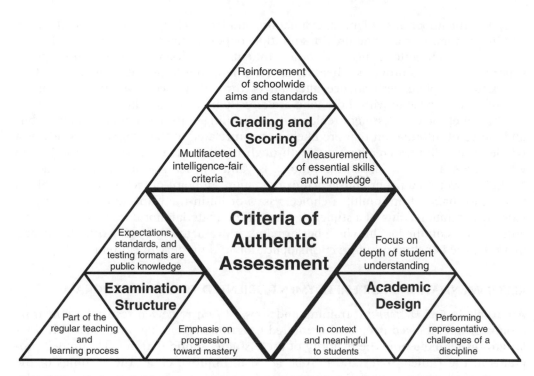

Figure 14.1.   Criteria of authentic assessment. (From Lazear, D. [1994]. *Multiple intelligence approach to assessment* [p. 15]. Tucson, AZ: Zephyr Press; reprinted by permission.)

assessment situations that lead to higher levels of achievement measurable in terms of both program/industry requirements and student satisfaction/performance.

The examination structure of authentic, intelligence-based assessment becomes part of the daily teaching and classroom process rather than an event that occurs apart from or in isolation from daily instruction. Interaction between students and instructors is an active process in which all parties know before testing what the assessment will cover and that testing situations will be structured to allow multiple opportunities for students to fully demonstrate mastery of education and instruction competencies as they occur within a specific discipline. Demonstration of mastery would include development of portfolio-like products reflecting learning progress over a period of time, with examples of best work completed, descriptions of skills developed, and students' introspective commentary on how their lives have been affected as a direct result of their efforts.

The structure of authentic examinations emphasizes individual student progress in terms of discipline content, processes, and applications of materials—regarding both program requirements and the outside world. Evaluations are constructed using a developmental spiral to represent differing stages of achievement (e.g., content, process, product, skill level), resulting in tests worth taking and repeating until material is mastered.

All assessment testing standards and formats are known to each stakeholder of the learning community. This means that the results of the examinations are evaluated by experts in both education and industry for their reflection of the knowledge, skills, and aptitudes necessary for success in the desired occupation.

The guidelines for scoring authentic assessments recognize and value the fact that all students learn differently and at different rates. The validity of grading and scoring considers the importance of input, evaluation, and feedback from the individual, peers, and instructors. This method provides multiple opportunities for students to reflect on and discuss their performance with other students (co-workers) and evaluators (work supervisors). It also provides a healthy environment to improve performance, reduce errors, and explore performance alternatives through nonconfrontational feedback and real-time dialogue with those who are directly involved on-site.

This method of assessment replaces the rewarding of retrieval of disconnected bits and pieces of information that are likely to be unrelated to the program of study as a whole. The ability to creatively work through problems encountered on the job, to which there are many possible solutions, is valued at least as much as getting the "right" answer on a paper-and-pencil examination. In point of fact, just being able to recall information from multiple-choice, essay, or fill-in-the blank tests does not provide an accurate reading of a student's grasp of the material, nor does this alone guarantee success on the job, in which performance is evaluated through work quality and quantity, the benchmarks of practical application and mastery of content.

RECOMMENDATIONS FOR EMPLOYMENT-ORIENTED TRAINING PROGRAMS

An article in *The Economist* ("Training and Jobs," 1996) reviewed research comparing groups of unemployed people who entered government training programs with similar groups who did not. The majority of these studies found that publicly funded programs in the United States and Europe failed to improve either the earnings or the employment prospects of their consumers. Job-training programs in these countries were unable to produce skilled and flexible workers able to switch easily from one task to another. One major British employer said that what he really needed was not more skills training but people able to address an envelope. Complaints concerning a lack of basic literacy skills are widespread even in countries with nominally high levels of literacy. In Sweden, 1 in 12 men were unable to understand the directions for use on an aspirin bottle; in the Netherlands, the figure was 1 in 10, in Germany 1 in 7, and in Canada and the United States 1 in 5 ("Training and Jobs," 1996).

The conclusion of the article indicated that publicly funded training programs conducted through government entities are generally inadequate in meeting industry-specific contextual literacy needs. Many employers prefer to hire employees with no prior industry knowledge and instruct them "the company way," rather than hire graduates of government-funded training programs. However, government-funded training programs have succeeded in situations in which their efforts are focused on teaching people how to conduct job searches or providing basic contextual literacy instruction.

Despite numerous blue-ribbon task forces and resulting legislation (Goals 2000: Educate America Act of 1994, PL 103-227), research efforts (National Longitudinal Transition Study; Office of Special Education Programs, 1992), and public/private funding dedicated to investigating methods to improve the workplace literacy of the U.S. work force (National Adult Literacy Survey, 1993), recommendations for creating a tighter linkage between instructional methods, outcomes that accurately reflect instruction, and employment situations have been largely ignored. One of the most significant of these efforts was the U.S. Department of Labor's (1992) vision of a common "learning and earning system" based on the results of the Secretary's Commission on Achieving Necessary Skills (SCANS). The workplace know-how identified by SCANS is made up of five competencies and a three-part foundation of skills and personal qualities needed for solid job performance (Figure 14.2). SCANS recommendations, such as students being introduced to workplace know-how by 14 years of age, a national competency-based assessment system certifying work-based competencies achieved, and employment-based assessments diagnosing individual learning needs, have merit but are yet to be systematically implemented.

Three-Part Foundation

I. **Basic skills:** Reading, writing, arithmetic/mathematics, listening, speaking

II. **Thinking skills:** Creative thinking, decision making, problem solving, seeing things in the mind's eye, knowing how to learn, reasoning

III. **Personal qualities:** Responsibility, sociability, self-esteem, self-management, integrity, honesty

Five Competencies

1. Planning resources (budgeting, scheduling and allocating staff and space)

2. Using information (finding and evaluating data, communicating in oral and written form, using computers)

3. Interpersonal skills (working in teams that may be multicultural, negotiating, and teaching

4. Understanding systems (applying total quality management and statistical process control)

5. Applying technology (selecting, using, and maintaining equipment)

Examples of SCANS at School and Work

- Learning, planning, and scheduling in math class; scheduling a work shift at a restaurant

- Using information by analyzing data in a geography class; collecting and analyzing data on customer preferences

- Learning interpersonal skills by reading about cultural diversity in English; working on a multicultural team

- Understanding systems by studying social change in history; evaluating error rates in food shipments

- Applying technology by using test instruments in science; using test instruments to maintain equipment

Figure 14.2. The SCANS workplace know-how model. (From Packer, A. [1993]. Earning and learning: Major links to better living. *HR Magazine, 38*[4], 52; reprinted by permission of the Society for Human Resource Management, Alexandria, VA.)

The National Longitudinal Transition Study underscored the academic under-achievement of students with LD in traditional educational settings. Thirty-nine percent of the students identified with LD in this study left school without graduating (Marder & D'Amico, 1992). These young adults fare horribly in adult education programs, where less than 3% obtain a high school diploma or General Equivalency Diploma. The inability of the system to provide prescriptive remediation and support tutorial instruction results in fragmented service delivery in which the skill focus is limited or is taught in isolation from an applied real-world contextual basis. Improving this dismal situation requires teachers who have an understanding of the demands of the workplace; a creative grasp of how to develop compensatory learning strategies that address workplace requirements; an appreciation of the need for individualized, comprehensive instruction as a result of the heterogeneity of LD; and classroom instructional tools and techniques based on interests, abilities, and aptitudes identified through vocational assessment.

Sitlington (1996) argued that transition education programming for individuals with LD must be infused into the college and university programs that prepare teachers to work with individuals with LD of all ages. She pointed out that the competencies for teachers of students with LD identified by the Division for Learning Disabilities of the Council for Exceptional Children (Graves et al., 1992) do not fully integrate life skills and transition-planning issues beyond those found in traditional academic content areas (i.e., primarily those related to written language skills). Sitlington stressed that life skills and transition planning must be fully integrated into all instructional and curricular activities currently being used with individuals with LD.

ABILITIES-BASED PROGRAM MODEL:
THE LIFE DEVELOPMENT INSTITUTE PROGRAMS

Research outcomes in adult postsecondary education indicate that the goal of such training programs for people with LD should be to enhance their ability to successfully make the transition into independent living, enhance functional literacy, and help them to achieve competitive employment commensurate with their peers without LD when holistic quality-of-life planning, instruction, and employment are provided. To this end, two field-based demonstration projects, Project MEAL (Model for Employment and Adult Living; D'Alozo, Fass, & Crawford, 1987) and Project SMILE (Successful Moves to Independence, Literacy, and Employment; Crawford & Crawford, 1992), were funded by the Office of Special Education and Rehabilitation Services of the U.S. Department of Education. The grants for these projects were administered through the Life Development Institute (LDI), a private, nonprofit organization.

The LDI was established in 1982 as a community-based program in a residential setting to assist individuals with LD and other related conditions to gain literacy skills for the workplace, achieve careers through competitive employment commensurate with their capabilities, and attain independent status. The LDI continues to conduct two 2-year programs for adolescents ages 16 and older and adults. One focuses on postsecondary literacy, social skills, and job placement. The LDI is authorized under federal law to enroll nonimmigrant alien students. Also, the LDI has contracts with the Rehabilitation Services Administration and the Administration for Children, Youth, and Families, and serves students from private referrals through a variety of sources. Extensive interagency linkages with area employers, adult education providers, the community college system, and state agencies are utilized by the LDI to facilitate holistic service provision for program participants. The LDI has successfully placed more than 1,500 individuals with LD and related disorders into mainstream, competitive employment and is recognized throughout the United States for its exemplary literacy program for adults with learning and literacy disorders. In 1992, the LDI was a recipient of a coveted Points of Light Award (1 of 21 recipients selected out of 4,500 nominated) presented by former President George Bush and First Lady Barbara Bush.

The facility is a unique residential setting that enables program participants to live in an apartment community with a minimum of staff supervision and a moderate amount of structure. LDI program participants are housed in a complex of 44 two-bedroom, two-bath apartments located in a central Phoenix middle-class, culturally diverse neighborhood. The complex has two clubhouses; a swimming pool with a Jacuzzi; a basketball half-court; washers, dryers, and telephones in most apartments; training rooms; and computer labs. The usual limiting factor of most residential training situations is that they are "sheltered" or "institutional" in their orientation. At the LDI, the setting is an actual apartment complex and not a dormitory, institutional setting, or group home. The LDI is thus part of the community, not an "island."

The LDI Postsecondary Program: A Team Approach to Literacy and Employment

The overall mission of the LDI is to provide older adolescents and adults with LD, attention-deficit/hyperactivity disorder (ADHD), or both with workplace literacy skills and the ability to make appropriate choices in order to compete in the global job market, thereby achieving an enhanced quality of life. The LDI defines *workplace literacy* as the necessary basic academic skills that can be applied in the functional context of the job plus demonstrated abilities in communications, problem solving, decision making, anger control, and developing teamwork skills.

In order to facilitate the goals of the LDI postsecondary program, mission-based teams of students are formed. Using the model adapted by McCollough (1993), this process is an effective way to enhance student learning through application. These teams organize their efforts around project-driven activities that are compatible with the overall mission of the program. For example, a major goal of the program is to secure mainstream competitive employment commensurate with individual capabilities. A vocational research project is therefore conducted to obtain necessary background information that would enable a program participant to make an informed decision regarding necessary education, training, and employment steps that are part of a career path.

Instructional staff knowledgeable in the tools and concepts of quality improvement (Deming, 1981; Langford, 1992) facilitate approaches that help the team conduct the project. They facilitate coaching team members in how to establish team goals, observe the team's progress, evaluate how the team functions, and help eliminate barriers to team progress. The effectiveness of various approaches in terms of project standards can be measured and analyzed by these instructor-facilitators as benchmarks of achievement or areas needing change.

Project Mission Statement   The project-driven activities of each team are supported by instructing all individuals involved in these activities about their purpose. A project mission statement is then developed that is the focus of all work that is done, both as teams and as individuals. For example, a team might develop the following mission statement: "It is the commitment of this team to determine, establish, and obtain mainstream competitive employment while supporting individual goals." By keeping the mission statement as the guideline for developing new strategies, implementing new policies and procedures, and addressing the need for change, students are empowered to contribute talents and ideas to the project.

Team Charter   Mission-based, project-driven teams develop a charter that specifically outlines the "scope" of a team (McCollough, 1993). The charter focuses on the scope, which enables the team to have a fuller understanding of what the "team" is all about. The charter is developed in conjunction with the overall LDI mission statement and the individual teams' mission statements. Each team of students and staff facilitators can develop their own charter as long as it directly reflects the values incorporated in these mission statements. Based on the mission, the team, with the assistance of the instructional staff, develops a supportive statement to define more specifically that mission; for example,

> Our team [insert team name] will work toward obtaining mainstream competitive employment using classroom instruction, research, discussion, individual and group projects, and informational interviews. This function will serve as a guideline toward meeting both our group and individual goals, which will allow us a successful transition into the competitive workplace. The charter would include a more detailed statement of the "how-tos" in obtaining the goal established in the project mission statement. (Lieb, 1997, p. 2).

Team Roles   Roles for team members are established through a series of self-assessments that inventory personal learning styles, leadership traits, and individual personality traits. Based on each team member's relative strengths, assignments for work duties related to the vocational research project are given. For example, a student proficient in oral communication skills might be responsible for setting up job shadowing tours. Another student with organizational strengths would be responsible for scheduling and reminding team members of deadlines and due dates. A third student who has the ability to synthesize the group's collected information would be responsible for acting as a spokesperson/team leader to instructor-facilitators and team members.

Team Goals   Specific project goals are identified and given a time line for completion. The charter is considered when establishing these goals (Lieb, 1997). It is critical that team members have a clear sense of what is to be accomplished and by what date. This understanding is ensured by instructional staff and student team members, who reach consensus on project goals after the charter is established and team goals are confirmed.

Standard Operating Procedures   Standard operating procedures (SOPs) serve as the ground rules for the team working together. Team members decided on issues related to enforcement, reward, and recognition of effort as ways to guarantee that these ground rules are effective. This process assists the team in two ways: 1) It helps to establish a stronger team base, and 2) it reinforces understanding of the demands placed on adults in the workplace by using rewards and consequences for following or failing to follow procedures and policies. For example, one team determined that a reward for adhering to team SOPs would be a casual day and the consequence for not doing so would be cleaning the classroom. It should be mentioned that, although this process is very helpful in promoting communications skills, decision making, and team cohesiveness, it is critical that there be guidance from and final approval by the instructors (Lieb, 1997).

Vocational Research Project

The student team and instructional facilitators decide on vocational research project course competencies and design evaluation methods to track individual performance, field experiences, group and individual report writing, and use of computer systems to identify appropriate vocational and educational goals. Content is built around performance areas outlined in the five SCANS competencies (see Figure 14.2). Potential course competencies include

- Describing a system, its parts, and their relationship to the whole
- Assessing personal knowledge, skills, and abilities in relationships to those needed in a work and an educational environment
- Demonstrating use of appropriate technology tools to complete portions of the final project
- Evaluating personal performance as a team member and on written material
- Demonstrating efficient use of time and ability to set up a schedule that includes goal-relevant activities
- Participating as an active member of a team as well as a team leader
- Providing feedback to the team on individual progress toward meeting team expectations
- Acquiring, evaluating, and organizing information effectively
- Demonstrating clear written and oral communication skills
- Predicting project outcomes
- Identifying work fields, career ladders, national employment outlook, and educational opportunities in areas commensurate with identified individual skills, interests, and abilities
- Developing job bank of potential employers from job shadowing experiences
- Identifying, prequalifying for, selecting, and enrolling in postsecondary program to operationalize vocational research project
- Securing and maintaining competitive employment in the field of postsecondary training or education

The team is thus armed with a specific, targeted agenda and course outcomes. They are ready to combine personal understanding of learning styles, leadership traits, and communication preferences with data derived from occupation-specific vocational assessments. Such assessments will result in an objective picture of a targeted career cluster, career ladders within the cluster, and range and requirements of the specific vocational preparation needed to compete as a qualified worker in relationship to individual career goals.

Vocational Assessment

The Vocational Research Institute's (1988) APTICOM AF System has been used with great effectiveness to provide initial objective information concerning team members' individual interests, abilities, and aptitudes. The system consists of three test batteries: The Aptitude Test Battery, the Occupational Interest Inventory, and the Educational Skills Development Battery. The APTICOM Aptitude Test Battery and General Aptitude Test Battery are designed to assess cognitive, perceptual, and motor skills. The relationships between aptitude test scores and jobs are established by using the battery's Occupational Aptitude Pattern structure. Its listings are closely related to work groups from the *Guide for Occupational Exploration* (GOE, 1989).

The Educational Skills Development Battery screens for levels of required literacy as defined by the U.S. Department of Labor's (1994) *Dictionary of Occupational Titles* (DOT). Every one of the 12,000+ jobs in the DOT has been evaluated in terms of employment-required levels of mathematical development and language development. Scores derived from the Educational Skills Development Battery allow for general estimates of individual team members' abilities to meet the workplace literacy demands of a given occupation. Information obtained from both the educational and aptitude batteries provides important indicators of how team members are performing relative to all other job seekers. An emphasis on becoming aware of what constitutes a qualified worker revolves around finding what requirements and expectations an employer has of any applicant, with or without disabilities.

The APTICOM Occupational Interest Inventory measures team members' interests according to the GOE, which classifies all U.S. Department of Labor titles recognized in the DOT. The objective of this measurement is to facilitate team members' vocational exploration by identifying occupational possibilities that are compatible with expressed personal preferences. Because of the uncertainty that many team members may have regarding their vocational goals, information collected from this inventory provides opportunities for broader exploration of potential vocational futures.

Occupational Awareness System   The outcomes from these batteries and interest inventories are entered into the Occupational Awareness System (OASYS; Vertek, Inc., 1989). OASYS is a computer-aided resource that matches a person's skills and abilities to employer job requirements. The database in OASYS contains the entire DOT, including all job descriptions, job performance criteria, and operational definitions of job performance variables. The version used by team members at the LDI complies with the criteria of the Americans with Disabilities Act of 1990 (PL 101-336), which establish essential functions of each job, physical demands required, environmental conditions, and the frequency with which tasks and functions are performed.

Information entered into the OASYS system also includes individual work histories, personal skills, and present work abilities. A computer search for job matches is conducted. The type of job matches found in the search process depends on the individual's highest demonstrated skills from previous work history, levels of demonstrated performance from the aptitude and educational batteries, and identified areas of occupational interest derived from the various inventories.

Each job match contains a complete description of all tasks required to perform the job and of related jobs listed under alternative titles. This information allows the development of a career ladder made up of an occupational cluster of jobs directly related to the target position. Each job match states the Specific Vocational Preparation (SVP) required to learn the necessary skills, achieve the level of workplace literacy, and develop the facilities needed for average performance in a specific work situation. There is a hierarchy of nine SVP levels ranging from unskilled jobs requiring no previous work experience to professional skilled positions requiring more than 10 years to master.

OASYS can compare an individual's skills and abilities to DOT job performance variables. In situations in which the person has a career goal or knows about a potential job opening, OASYS's Occupational Goal Analysis (OGA) allows comparison of the skills and aptitudes possessed by the team member to each job performance variable required for the job. This comparison makes it possible to identify potential barriers to instruction and employment that may exist for a particular occupation. The barrier may be significant, such as the individual's having a much lower level of workplace literacy than the job requires, or may be relatively insignificant, such as his or her having no previous work history for the desired occupation.

Combining career ladder and OGA information allows the student and LDI instructor-facilitators to explore hunches about different kinds of jobs the team member could perform. Frequently, individuals at the LDI need a career goal "reality check" in order to be candid with themselves about whether their present abilities meet the requirements of a particular job they are considering. This initial career goal may involve more training or experience than they presently possess, and it is important to identify all potential vocational barriers involving academic enrichment, job modification, or skill development that must be overcome in order to achieve this career goal. Self-realization allows the individual investigating the occupation to recognize present limitations with respect to this choice while encouraging him or her to develop alternative vocational strategies.

Relating Job Requirements to Team Members' Abilities   At every stage of the OASYS analysis, emphasis is placed on the team members' capabilities. Employers recruit, hire, instruct, and employ workers based on their abilities to make the company profitable, fit in with the corporate culture, and become a functioning member of the company. The priority, then, should first be on the bigger picture of what the student *can* do for the employer; then any areas in the OGA that are found deficient or in need of further enhancement should be reviewed.

Literacy Skills Enhancement

Once the students have a detailed description of their targeted careers, their next step is to undertake a sequence of tutorial instruction in vocation-related literacy, emphasizing contextual academics that promote learning by doing. Incorporating technical and industry-specific terminology, acronyms, jargon, and other work-related vocabulary into computer-assisted instruction and learning strategies allows the development of career projects and demonstrations that mirror the world of work that students would experience in their desired occupations. Strategies (Deschler, 1993) developed by the University of Kansas Institute for Research in Learning Disabilities are taught in order to enhance the team member's ability to acquire information for later use, to express information in writing, and to demonstrate competence on tests and assignments.

Additional literacy skills enhancement is provided by a customized computer curriculum supported through the Invest Learning System (Josten's Learning, 1994), used to teach specific skill subject areas in which the student needs to improve. Occupational objectives are grouped without regard to instructional level. This provides complete instruction based on the individual's presenting literacy skills and allows progress toward the required levels of literacy demanded by a particular job. Third-party software such as OASYS can be combined with this system to correlate the results of the computer-assisted instruction with occupational objectives for the desired career.

Individual Needs Assessment

Efforts to extend personal awareness of LD and their impact on the job are implemented, resulting in a series of related written and oral projects. Students become familiar with the specific manifestations of their particular learning impairment through the use of a checklist (Dowdy, 1994). Determinations of the effect these characteristics might have in a potential occupation are made, and specific compensations, accommodations, modifications, and strategies that could be utilized to circumvent the barriers presented by the impairment are identified. This information is formatted into a draft cover letter to a potential employer within the desired occupational cluster outlining the position the student wants, discussing the nature of his or her learning disability, outlining specific instruction interventions he or she will use to neutralize its impact, and emphasizing his or her expectations to be evaluated by the same standards as co-workers.

When the document is completed, the team member presents it orally to his or her classmates and instructor-facilitators, with the presentation being videotaped for feedback and an evaluative review of the approach. This exercise helps team members become proficient in correctly identifying the time and place to disclose a disability or to advocate for accommodations in postsecondary instruction or in employment settings. Taking personal responsibility for identifying their own accommodations will facilitate the team members' learning and communication styles as well as promote academic success and corporate profitability through their enhanced performance.

Accessing Community-Based Resources

The initiation of field experiences to explore local employers is the next step in the LDI program. A series of letters and forms are developed by the team requesting job-shadowing tours of local companies. The team must reach agreement on its expectations of what will occur during these company tours. Instructor-facilitators help team members to anticipate the type of information needed from employers to use as a basis of comparison for individual abilities, aptitudes, and interests. The team develops a telephone script to use for prescreening employers for potential tours and setting up job shadowing experiences. A follow-up cover letter is developed by the team confirming a tour appointment and including a list of questions covering details about the company that team members will be asking during the tour. This way there are no surprises for the employer because the questionnaire allows ample time for employers to organize appropriate responses and collect requested information from corporate resources prior to the tour. This also allows the team to collect consistent information on each employer for the purpose of developing a job bank.

Topics that could be covered in a formalized questionnaire include

- Job descriptions
- Levels of employment, SVPs
- Range of academic and skill levels needed
- Employer expectations with regard to appropriate behavior, dress, and so forth
- Overview or schematic of day-to-day business operations
- How employees work together and alone
- How the organization fosters team development
- How employee discipline is handled
- Levels and types of technology used
- Methods of job recruitment (e.g., job fairs, internships)

Job shadowing provides an excellent opportunity to validate classroom instruction by getting team members out into the corporate community and allowing them to meet with key decision makers who are in a position to make a future hiring decision. Observations of the workplace are easier to tie in to personal interests, career goals, and abilities and tend to either eliminate or illuminate a student's interest in a prospective company.

These tours are followed up with thank-you letters from each participant to the employer contact, and the information gathered is discussed in a team brainstorming session in which consensus tools are used to develop a report of each company toured. Although there could be situations in which no team member was particularly interested in the visited company, data collected and reported could assist future team members by providing reliable information and key contacts. These report debriefings are used in conjunction with educational field experiences prior to operationalizing the vocational research project.

The educational field experience begins with making arrangements to visit area postsecondary instruction and educational facilities. The team members decide on information to be gathered by identifying pertinent factors that will assist them in making informed decisions on which institution is the best fit for their present and future needs. Learning to differentiate between student services and program services will help team members to identify available resources, support services, and any institutional experience providing accommodations for nontraditional learners. Finding out the literacy level of entrance and placement exams will provide insight as to whether the student meets the academic criteria of "ability to benefit."

The term *ability to benefit* refers to a student's being able to function at the literacy level of instruction utilized by the institution. Although not intended to be biased toward applicants with learning or literacy difficulties, this approach can screen out students who otherwise would be successful in postsecondary training and educational programs. Such screening out would not automatically occur if alternative assessment germane to that specific level of instruction were available. Entrance and placement exams cannot be circumvented but must be planned and prepared to provide academic evidence that applicants with LD can achieve at the same level as their peers without LD. Opportunities to observe classes and potential instructors and to witness how instruction is provided can later be compared with individual learning styles and preferences.

The ability to meet with current students, faculty, recent graduates, and businesses who have hired graduates provides another source of information from parties who have no agenda to enroll students because of commission potential. Requests are made to receive and review textbooks and course syllabi for preview purposes to facilitate identification of needs for tutorial support services. This information is included in both the individual team member's portfolio and the LDI's postsecondary resource bank. Future team members interested in a prospective program are thus able to ascertain the literacy requirements and instructional methods central to a given postsecondary institution. This allows for additional time to provide extra literacy instruction to prepare the student for the educational requirements of the targeted institution. Sorting out the pros and cons of different but equal educational programs requires identifying program strengths in meeting personal requirements for the team member's career.

In addition, it is frequently necessary to compare and contrast a traditional college program with a similar vocational school program. Many vocational and technical schools offer accelerated degree programs in which changes in technology are often more realistically addressed in the curriculum. This means that the educational services are driven by the changing nature of the world of work and that instruction is state-of-the-art. Because instruction and training are accelerated, however, such institutions require above-average organizational skills, ability to meet deadlines, and student availability to work in externship programs.

Vocational Research Project

The culminating project in the LDI postsecondary program outlines vocational goals and a plan of action, complete with supportive details for each team member.

Information-age technology in the form of computer software is used by students to complete this project. *Microsoft Office* (Microsoft, 1993b) software assists in compiling the final report. Spreadsheets using the *Excel* (Microsoft, 1993a) program allow students to prepare and formalize financial aid plans, chart the pros and cons of various programs, graph the occupational outlook of targeted employment, and develop a time line for goals in education and career areas. *Microsoft Word* (Microsoft, 1993d) is used to document all written report activities. *Microsoft Word* allows tremendous flexibility for nontraditional learners to get ideas down on paper without the frustration of worrying about grammar, spelling, or illegible handwriting. Development of a multimedia presentation using the *Microsoft PowerPoint* (Microsoft, 1993c) program incorporates information about the overall project in a creative format. The information is divided into slides on which students insert key phrases, original designs and pictures, embedded photographs of schools and corporations, videotape clips related to the career goal, background music that the team members identify with their individual projects, and many other options to represent the results of the vocational research project.

Postsecondary Placement

If the results of the student's vocational research project are considered valid, placement into the selected postsecondary program occurs subsequent to successfully passing entrance exams. Weekly program performance tracking by LDI staff permits timely tutorial or crisis intervention for students struggling in a particular course. Although many vocational and technical programs claim expertise in working with nontraditional learners, few have either formal or informally trained staff available to implement a sequence of support tutorial instruction appropriate for adults with LD and ADHD. The collaboration between the LDI and the community-based training program augments the student's learning by providing additional literacy tools and techniques appropriate for the individual's needs without diminishing the requirements of the school.

Externship placements provide the opportunity to link classroom instruction with the daily demands of a workplace setting. Key contacts and decision makers have an opportunity to see the student in action. The student extern develops an appreciation for and competency in the essential functions necessary to become a qualified applicant for that particular employer's work setting.

Job Placement

Competitive job placement is initiated by the student, who utilizes telephone informational interviews with prescreened prospective employers to schedule appointments for tours of the companies and to present his or her qualifications in person. Once employment is obtained, an individual financial plan is developed to prepare the student for managing his or her expenses. Continued residency at the LDI for a minimum of 6 months allows for follow-up and follow-along maintenance efforts to ensure competency in financial planning and retention of employment. Supportive employment efforts are provided by staff if transitional difficulties occur in the process of adjusting to the new work environment. These efforts can include weekly telephone calls for job tracking, site visits to observe seasoned employees' work performance in comparison with that of the newly placed LDI team member, and additional instructional support at the LDI through debriefings following workplace situation assessments.

Life Development Institute Learning Matrix

Final determination of team members' success and competency is accomplished by the documentation of skills in a matrix format tied in to the five SCANS competencies.

The LDI learning matrix is based on Langford's (1992) model of total quality learning. The matrix is a tool for self-assessment and measurement of knowledge. It returns the responsibility for learning to the student and provides a method to ensure quality and continuous learning. This evaluation process is based on continual analysis, critical thinking, and reflection.

As a student moves through a course, he or she can request that an instructor-facilitator initial the corresponding block indicating the current level of learning and understanding. The student can also initiate review and update of the matrix. Each level initialed across the matrix must be accompanied by one or more of the following:

- Documentation (assignment, handout, written proof)
- Demonstration (role-play, actions)
- Defense (questions, discussions, debate)

Various project documents are filed in the student's portfolio. One documented project can reveal competencies in several areas in the matrix. If a project required drafts, those are included with the finished copy to show improvement.

Instructor-facilitators assist students in recognizing their levels of learning by using the vocabulary and techniques outlined in the appendix at the end of this chapter. These words and techniques are also explained to the students and appear in their program handbooks. By using consistent and familiar language, students become proficient with what is expected while they learn to recognize corresponding levels of the matrix. No area is to be initialed without an instructor's verifying the documentation. Students may suggest changes in the language content of their handbook if this makes the matrix system more understandable to them.

CONCLUSION

This chapter has examined factors driving today's workplace and suggestions for improving assessment and placement into postsecondary programs for adults with LD and related literacy difficulties. Use of a variety of assessments, instructional methods, and team approaches that center around unifying themes and are project driven allows the individual to competently identify his or her vocational preferences and work abilities and develop plans to achieve successful postsecondary instruction and competitive employment.

The key ingredient in achieving successful outcomes using these approaches is the linkage of learning to know with learning to do. Providing multiple opportunities to practice and become proficient in the areas described in this chapter requires instructors knowledgeable in the ever-changing demands of Corporate America. In addition, both students and teachers must develop an appreciation of the barriers adults with LD and related literacy difficulties will face in gaining access to appropriate programs that use criterion-referenced assessments and traditional instructional techniques. Adult educators should not shy away from these challenges but rather approach them with the expectancy of finding the right niche for each student through development of educational, instructional, and employment curricula that match the essential functions of targeted careers with the individual's expressed desires, abilities, and impairments, as well as available local resources.

REFERENCES

Americans with Disabilities Act of 1990, PL 101-336, 42 U.S.C. §§ 12101 *et seq.*

Crawford, R., & Crawford, D. (1992). *Project SMILE: Successful moves to independence, literacy, and employment.* Washington, DC: U.S. Department of Education, Office of Special Education Programs.

D'Alozo, B., Fass, L., & Crawford, D. (1988). *Project MEAL: Model for employment and adult living.* Washington, DC: U.S. Department of Education, Office of Special Education Programs.

Deming, W.E. (1981). *Out of the crisis.* Cambridge: Massachusetts Institute of Technology, Center for Advanced Engineering Study.

Deschler, & Donald, D. (1993). *Intervention methods* (Rev. ed.). Lawrence: The University of Kansas, The Center for Research on Learning.

Dowdy, D. (1994). *LD characteristics checklist.* Birmingham: University of Alabama at Birmingham.

GOALS 2000: Educate America Act of 1994, PL 103-227, 20 U.S.C. §§ 5801 *et seq.*

Graves, A., Landers, M., Lockerson, J., Luchow, J., Hovarth, M., & Barnett, K. (1992). *The Division on Learning Disabilities competencies for teachers of students with learning disabilities.* Reston, VA: Division for Learning Disabilities, Council for Exceptional Children.

Guide for occupational exploration. (1989). Washington, DC: U.S. Department of Labor.

Josten's Learning. (1994). *Invest Learning System* [Computer software]. San Diego, CA: Author.

Lazear, D.P. (1994). *Multiple intelligence approach to assessment.* Tuscon, AZ: Zephyr Press.

Langford, D.P. (1992). *Quality learning.* Billings, MT: Langford International, Inc.

Lieb, V.J. (1997). *Setting up a simulated team-based environment.* St. Louis: P.A.R.T.

Marder, C., & D'Amico, R. (1992). *How well are young people with disabilities really doing? A comparison of youth with disabilities and youth in general.* Menlo Park, CA: SRI International.

McCollough, F. (1993). *Building effective teams.* St. Charles, MO: Foundations for Excellence.

Microsoft. (1993a). *Microsoft Excel* [Computer software]. Redmond, WA: Author.

Microsoft. (1993b). *Microsoft Office* [Computer software]. Redmond, WA: Author.

Microsoft. (1993c). *Microsoft PowerPoint* [Computer software]. Redmond, WA: Author.

Microsoft. (1993d). *Microsoft Word* [Computer software]. Redmond, WA: Author.

National Adult Literacy Survey. (1993). Washington, DC: National Center for Education Statistics.

Office of Special Education Programs. (1992). *National longitudinal transition study.* Menlo Park, CA: SRI International.

Packer, A. (1993). Earning and learning—major links to better living. *HR Magazine, 38*(4), 52. (Published by the Society for Human Resource Management, 606 North Washington Street, Alexandria, VA 22314)

Sitlington, P. (1996). Transition to living: The neglected component of transition programming for individuals with learning disabilities. *Journal of Learning Disabilities, 29,* 31–39.

Training and jobs: What works? (1996, April 6). *The Economist,* 19–23.

Ulrey, D., & Ulrey, J. (1992). Developmentally appropriate practices meet multiple intelligences. *Intelligence connections, 2*(1), 4–6.

U.S. Department of Labor. (1994). *Dictionary of occupational titles.* Washington, DC: Author.

U.S. Department of Labor. (1992). Secretary Commission on Achieving Necessary Skills. Washington, DC: Author.

Vertek, Inc. (1989). *Occupational Awareness System* (OASYS) [Computer software]. Bellevue, WA: Author.

Vocational Research Institute. (1988). *APTICOM* [Computer software]. Philadelphia: Author.

Wiggins, G. (1989). Creating tests worth taking. *Educational Leadership, 49*(8), 26–33.

Appendix

Life Development Institute Academy of Lifelong Learning Guide for the Learning Matrix

Across the top of each Learning Matrix appear several levels of learning:

I. I Know This
II. Do with Help
III. Can Explain/Discuss
IV. Break into Parts
V. Know When to Use
VI. See Life Applications
VII. I Appreciate This

Each level of learning requires increasingly more complex demonstrations of knowledge. When a student feels ready to move to a higher level, the instructor-facilitator is asked to sign off on the documentation. This can be done by reviewing the work with the student one-to-one after the particular class assignment. If it meets the requirements of that level, the work is initialed and the appropriate block on the matrix is filled with the students' work and placed in a portfolio. If the student is demonstrating or defending his or her knowledge at a particular level and it meets the requirements of that level, the instructor-facilitator initials the appropriate block.

Periodic review of each matrix is critical. The last 15 minutes of class on the last class day of the week are used for matrix review and evaluation.

Explanation of Levels of Learning

At each level of learning, students' specific abilities should be apparent. These abilities are listed here for each level, along with suggestions to instructor-facilitators for determining student competency.

---

1. I KNOW THIS
KNOWLEDGE: Information (remember)

A STUDENT AT THIS LEVEL WILL

- Remember information
- Remember the right material at the right time
- Respond to simple questions

IN THE CLASSROOM, TEACHERS CAN TEST COMPETENCY BY ASKING STUDENTS TO (vocabulary):

1. Repeat
2. List, tell
3. Define
4. Who? When? What?
5. Yes or no questions: "Did . . . ?": "Was . . . ?" "Is . . . ?" "Will . . . ?"
6. How many, how much?
7. Recall, identify terms
8. What did the book/article/handout say?
9. Key word meanings

---

2.   DO WITH HELP
KNOW-HOW: Understanding/Comprehension

A STUDENT AT THIS LEVEL WILL

- Understand what is being said (may not yet understand fullest meaning)
- Use the ideas being taught
- Rephrase the ideas in his or her own words
- Understand what others are discussing about the idea

METHODS/TECHNIQUES TO USE IN THE CLASSROOM THAT WILL TEST COMPETENCY:

1. Give an example . . .
2. What is the most important idea?
3. What will probably happen?
4. What was the cause?
5. Compare/contrast
6. Why did you say that?
7. Using correct terms

---

3.   CAN EXPLAIN/DISCUSS
KNOW-HOW: Application (solve the problem)

A STUDENT AT THIS LEVEL WILL

- Have the ability to use what is learned in new situations
- Use what is learned in new situations
- Know that a task, question, project, or concept is beyond current capabilities
- Ask for more explanation, information, and/or help from appropriate person
- Be able to identify correct resources for information

ASK STUDENTS TO

1. Solve problems
2. Find answers on their own (appropriate resources)
3. Explain how to use this information in other situations

---

4. BREAK INTO PARTS
KNOW-HOW: Analysis (logical order, components)

A STUDENT AT THIS LEVEL WILL

- Look at the details of ideas and writings and separate them into parts or basic ideas
- Break down information into parts in order to understand the whole

AS AN INSTRUCTOR-FACILITATOR, I SHOULD

- Ask the student to give reasons for a conclusion (why does he or she believe it?)
- Have the student give evidence to support a conclusion
- Expect the student to be able to see bias or emotion in an article, paper, book, quote, television program, or movie
- Expect the student to recognize methods of persuasion
- Ask the student to explain what an author believes
- Have the student argue a point as being fair or unfair
- Find out if the student knows whether a conclusion is supported by fact or by opinion

All arguments/discussions or conclusions should use a variety of methods of persuasion. The student should be able to make a good case to support his or her conclusions.

---

5. KNOW WHEN TO USE
WISDOM: Judgment (discern)

A STUDENT AT THIS LEVEL WILL

- Understand the right time to apply knowledge
- Be able to apply knowledge in new situations
- Know that, by using this information, he or she will move ahead
- Not use information when it may hurt others

AS AN INSTRUCTOR-FACILITATOR, I WILL NOTICE THE STUDENT

- Being proactive
- Taking what is learned in the classroom and applying it during time outside of the classroom
- Using information and then being able to tell why it was a good decision

---

6.   SEE LIFE APPLICATIONS
WISDOM: Synthesis (create)

A STUDENT AS THIS LEVEL WILL

- Put together parts of information into an organized whole
- Create an original idea fully thought out and explained
- Recognize new problems and develop strategies to solve them
- Create a personal plan that includes possible problems and their solutions

I CAN ASK AND EXPECT STUDENTS TO BE ABLE TO

- Create a plan
- Develop a model (examples)
- Combine parts of plans and models

---

7.   I APPRECIATE THIS
WISDOM: Application/Evaluation

A STUDENT AT THIS LEVEL WILL

- Have the ability to judge the value of ideas, procedures, and methods using appropriate criteria
- Be able to tell if an idea or method is good or bad and explain why

I CAN ASK STUDENTS AT THIS LEVEL TO

- Evaluate an idea in specific terms
- Explain why they agree with the idea or concept
- Explain why a policy/rule/law is in effect
- Compare and contrast the good/bad parts of an idea or concept
- Develop ideas, concepts, laws, and policies that would benefit the most people

15

Learning Disability Characteristics and Job Success

A Holistic Situational Assessment Model for Vocational Planning

James R. Koller and Gregory A. Holliday

It has become increasingly evident that the rates of individuals with learning disabilities (LD) entering the general workforce are continuing to rise. For example, the U.S. Department of Education (as cited in Coutinho, 1995) reported a 200% increase in public school students diagnosed with LD between 1977 and 1993. As the adolescent with LD makes the transition to adulthood and eventual employment, both the opportunities and corresponding challenges magnify. Just as individuals without disabilities face increasing barriers to employment (e.g., vocational/technical certification, college degree requirements, job downsizing), the individual with LD must compete with people without such disabilities not only in the job market but also in the current workforce.

Presuming that one ultimate goal of education is to secure and maintain meaningful employment and because individuals with LD aspire to jobs requiring increased technological skills, it can be assumed that a positive vocational outcome is far from guaranteed, even with appropriate vocational planning. The movement from a relatively supportive and sheltered academic environment to the highly competitive labor market can exacerbate the problems of employment survival, underemployment, and job dropout (Koller, 1994). With the realization that LD persist into adulthood and that the manifestations of the disabilities have significant implications for adult daily living, including employment (Vogel, 1989), the responsibility to prepare individuals for an effective and smooth transition is paramount.

Furthermore, as individuals make the transition into employment from other settings, including welfare-to-work, literacy, and corrections programs, numerous additional barriers may prevent occupational success. Commonly overlooked factors that often impede progress include hidden disabilities such as LD. Therefore, recognizing and addressing all of those variables that present as barriers to employment will improve the individuals' occupational outcome.

The study of the vocational success of adults with LD in the labor market is only beginning, yet data suggest that these individuals with LD are often underemployed or unemployed and significantly at risk for job failure (Berkeley Planning Associates, 1989; Tillman & Abbott, 1992; Zigmund, 1990). For individuals in the U.S. workforce as well as those in transition from school to work, successful long-term employment outcomes are often problematic. Fortunately, those individuals who present with LD as a significant or substantial impediment to employment may be eligible for services through their state vocational rehabilitation (VR) system, under the aegis of the federal Rehabilitation Services Administration (RSA). The determination of eligibility through VR for LD services is based on the following criteria (State Rehabilitation Services Program Rule, § 361.42[a], 1997):

- The applicant has a mental impairment.
- The applicant's mental impairment constitutes or results in a substantial impediment to employment.
- A presumption that the applicant can benefit in terms of a positive employment outcome from the provision of VR services.
- A determination that the applicant requires VR services to prepare for, enter into, engage in, or retain gainful employment consistent with the applicant's strengths, resources, priorities, concerns, abilities, capabilities, and informed choice.

LD is considered the fastest growing of all disability groups served through the U.S. state/federal system of the RSA (Koller, 1997; N. Nair, personal communication, 1997; RSA statistician, personal communication, 1997).

Preliminary follow-up adult LD studies with successful Status 26 VR participants (those who were determined eligible, received services, and were suitably employed for at least 60 days) and nonsuccessful Status 28 participants (those who were determined eligible for VR services but for some reason did not progress to the point of rehabilitation) reveal significant implications for individuals involved in transition (Dunham, Koller, & McIntosh, 1996). Of the 613 VR participants studied, a significant number were men (71%) who did not have a high school diploma. In addition, these individuals demonstrated achievement levels significantly below their counterparts without LD. Status 28 closures were more likely to have a comorbid and significant psychiatric disorder diagnosable by the *Diagnostic and Statistical Manual of Mental Disorders, Fourth Edition* (DSM–IV; American Psychiatric Association, 1994), especially with varying degrees and types of depression and attention-deficit/hyperactivity disorder (ADHD), compared with Status 28 closures. Major conclusions of this study included the necessity for individuals in transition to secure desirable preemployment skills as well as academic preparation, the need to ensure that the school-based curriculum is geared toward vocational readiness, and the importance of recognizing the influence of significant personal, social, and emotional functioning, secondary to the learning disability, on subsequent job-seeking and job maintenance skills.

Clearly, a learning disability is more than just an academic difficulty and manifests in a variety of ways to significantly impede both a personal and positive employment outcome (Koller, 1994). A federal/state demonstration project (Koller, 1996) by the authors generated strong evidence that effective transition and employment outcomes can be substantially enhanced with the implementation of a more holistic, comprehensive approach to transition assessment, incorporating the full range of skills, expertise, and tools of the school psychologist, the rehabilitation counselor, educators, family members, and the individuals themselves. This chapter describes the outcomes and results of that project (Koller, 1996), illustrating those characteristics of learning disability that have a critical impact on job success as individuals enter adulthood and the world of work.

TRADITIONAL ASSESSMENT PRACTICES

Traditional assessment services provided to individuals with LD are often fragmented, discipline bound, and focused on a subset of the numerous variables influencing both current performance and future vocational potential. These compartmentalized assessments reflect the limited perspectives often held by various professionals, including those in the VR arena who often have a restricted view of their potential role as part of the transition system for adolescents with LD. It is not surprising, therefore, that assessment practices reflect those limited, fragmented, and even contradictory perspectives. To be effective, assessment practices must be based on a holistic view of the adolescent in transition and should address all developmental systems that have an impact on his or her academic and vocational functioning.

Unfortunately, collaborative practices between and among the various elements of the transition support system are limited by a number of basic issues. Historically, schools defined *learning disability* narrowly (e.g., as an academic deficiency), providing services intended to remediate those deficiencies while the student is in school. Vocational rehabilitation systems endorse a broader definition designed to focus on the vocational impact of the disability. Thus, the RSA defined *learning disability* as follows:

A specific learning disability is a disorder in one or more of the central nervous system processes involved in perceiving, understanding, and/or using concepts through verbal (spoken or written) language or nonverbal means. This disorder manifests itself with a deficit in one or more of the following areas: attention, reasoning, processing, memory, communication, reading, writing, spelling, calculation, coordination, social competence, and emotional maturity. (1985, p. 2)

Disparate assessment methodologies, diagnostic decisions, and service delivery decisions are bound to arise from such contrasting operational definitions. Unfortunately, the assessment information that is generated within each of those systems is seldom fully used to optimize individual transition and employment outcomes. For example, school psychologists are often called on to complete the school's initial diagnostic evaluation, which, in part, typically consists of the administration of an individual cognitive ability test (e.g., the Wechsler Adult Intelligence Scale III–Revised [Wechsler, 1997]) and an individual academic achievement test (e.g., the Woodcock-Johnson Tests of Achievement–Revised [Woodcock & Johnson, 1989]). Resultant scores are then examined for discrepancies significant enough to meet a predetermined statistical criterion for classification of learning disability, and to determine the academic areas in need of remediation. Test scores (e.g., IQ scores, grade levels, standard scores, percentiles) assume an overwhelming influence because school personnel are required to comply with federal/state guidelines demanding explicit discrepancy criteria and rigidly defined 3-year reevaluations. Often that is the extent of use of the psychometric assessment data gathered, although these data are potentially a rich source of information about individual strengths and weaknesses that could be highly relevant vocationally. In essence, the scores are often utilized for compliance or categorization purposes rather than as an indication of functional abilities.

Additional informal assessment by teachers charged with academic remediation further measures the type and extent of the academic skill impairment, and the progress made as a result of the provision of special services, generally with little reference to the information gathered through the more formal diagnostic, psychometric assessment. Thus testing becomes mechanical and automated, as does the individualized education program (IEP) meeting that culminates the assessment process. Furthermore, most traditional interventions are oriented toward specific academic remediation rather than the development of vocationally relevant accommodation strategies targeted directly toward specific school-to-work transition efforts.

In contrast, the typical school-based transition specialist often takes an alternative assessment perspective, measuring student career interests and maturity, vocational readiness, and transition support needs. Koller (1994) amply described the use and value of various assessment tools utilized for those purposes. Individuals with LD as well as other students clearly benefit from exposure to that type of relevant information followed by field-tested interventions and realistic experiences designed to increase work preparedness and career decision-making ability.

As the individual seeks assistance through the VR system, however, an additional assessment orientation is imposed. At this point, the goal changes from the remediation of academic limitations to accommodation (e.g., the identification of compensatory strategies) for those functional limitations that will impede employment success. If sufficient diagnostic information is not available, the individual will most likely be given a comprehensive psychological evaluation, including measures of intelligence, achievement, and personality, with the primary intent of diagnosing the presence or absence of a learning disability and identifying those functional limitations that will have a negative impact on a positive vocational outcome. Even after this evaluation, it may still be unclear exactly how the identified LD and accompanying functional limitations will affect the individual's actual vocational performance. For example, it is not enough to determine that an individual has a learning disability. We must also know what type(s) of learning disability is present, how it affects his or her vocational goal, and to what extent the disability represents a significant impairment to employment. Thus, all too often, learning disability is seen as a homogeneous rather than a heterogeneous condition.

Various vocational evaluation methods traditionally are employed to assess functional capability regarding particular job tasks. These typically involve paper-and-pencil tests, work samples, and laboratory-based assessment activities. Increasingly, VR personnel are expected to utilize more authentic (e.g., functional, situational, contextually relevant) assessment measures to predict vocational success for individuals with LD. Indeed, the Rehabilitation Act Amendments of 1992 (PL 102-569) required that the vocational assessment be clearly functional or situational in nature. Thus, although traditional psychometrically driven procedures are used as a baseline, the individual is placed directly on the job, which allows the evaluator a chance to observe how the individual's strengths and weaknesses will manifest on the particular job tasks in question.

COMPREHENSIVE FUNCTIONAL ASSESSMENT

Evaluations conducted from many professional perspectives unfortunately offer a limited view of the elements that actually contribute to the educational and vocational success of individuals with LD in transition to employment. Ultimately, optimal transition assessment procedures should take into consideration all relevant variables that are known to have an impact on individual performance. For example, the success or failure of an individual is influenced by his or her work attitude; experience; cognitive attributes; type and severity of learning disability; social and personality characteristics; and other environmental demands, including family, job expectations, and cultural barriers (Koller, 1997). Within any individual, numerous characteristics represent strengths, weaknesses, attributes, and detriments as he or she engages in particular activities. As an individual attempts a task, those variables interact simultaneously to compose his or her functional ability. As task demands and situational factors change, the complex interplay of these individual characteristics often has a unique and unpredictable impact on individual performance.

Those practitioners sincerely concerned with assisting individuals with LD in the transition to appropriate vocational futures have a difficult task in understanding the broad and pervasive functional implications of the LD without underestimating individual potential. Often assessment procedures or policies focus on what is wrong with an individual, not on what is right. Based on the identified limitations, individuals with LD are then frequently channeled into low-level jobs in which their strengths and capabilities are not engaged but their limitations are less likely to be problematic. Underemployment is a serious concern, particularly for those individuals who have high levels of aptitude concurrent with the learning disability (Koller, 1994).

In the traditional psychometric evaluation process, interviews and tests generate data that are designed to formulate conclusions leading to diagnostic decisions and recommendations. In some instances, a diagnostic pattern emerges that sufficiently accounts for the observed performance difficulties that precipitated the assessment. In other instances, further information is needed to confirm the diagnostic conclusions. In nearly all instances, however, traditional assessment approaches have not provided sufficient insight into the vocational implications of the specific learning disability, and these procedures have not successfully predicted long-term vocational outcomes (Koller, 1994). Seldom are data from the various perspectives integrated and utilized in a holistic fashion designed to assist the adolescent in becoming optimally prepared not only to make appropriate career decisions but also to transition to employment successfully.

RSA-FUNDED DEMONSTRATION TRANSITION PROJECT

The University of Missouri Assessment and Consultation Clinic (MUACC) was created in 1992 in response to a nationally expressed need for improved transition assessment methodology to facilitate positive vocational outcomes for adolescents and adults with LD. Supported by grants form the state of Missouri (Division of Vocational Rehabilitation) and the RSA (Grant No. 84.235, Special Projects and Demonstrations for Providing Vocational Rehabilitation Services to Individuals with Severe Disabilities), the MUACC was charged with implementing a model demonstration project designed to enhance the employability and school-to-work transition success of adolescents and adults with LD, based on a comprehensive and more realistic functional assessment.

Several themes guided the project's design, implementation, and subsequent clinic activities. Foremost was the recognition that a systems approach is vital to ensure the engagement of all subsystems that play a role in the eventual attainment of positive employment outcomes. Second, successful work performance is the result of a complex interaction of a multitude of variables, both individual and environmental, and an adequate assessment must address functional attributes in all areas, culminating in a holistic, integrated representation of the individual and his or her characteristics. Third, assessment methods that generate information about individual strengths, assets, preferences, resources, and supports will be more useful than the traditional impairment-driven model. Fourth, human function is too complex to be adequately measured solely through traditional standardized methods. Finally, the utility of any assessment data is a product of their relevance, meaningfulness, comprehensibility, and applicability to their recipients, in particular the individual being assessed.

The transition assessment procedures that were developed and field tested through project activities were specifically designed to:

- Identify not only student academic weaknesses but also individual strengths and vocationally relevant functional limitations
- Provide relevant diagnostic information to service providers and employers
- Investigate the interaction of all variables that contribute to educational and vocational performance (e.g., personality, belief systems, past experiences)
- Directly observe the impact of the specific learning disability as the individual encounters environmental variables (e.g., job demands, work settings, social interactions)
- Evaluate the appropriateness of specific educational and vocational goals; and identify and field test effective accommodation strategies
- Generate appropriate recommendations for the individual with LD, educators, and VR personnel
- Encourage the development of greater self-knowledge and self-advocacy on the part of the individual assessed

The acquisition of this information becomes the basis for assisting teachers and counselors to design prescriptive, individually customized transition services and to facilitate informed vocational decision making by youth with LD. In addition, the project emphasized the creation of a seamless and collaborative transition support system that reduces barriers to employment, thereby increasing employment opportunities.

As a first step, a careful background exploration is conducted through records review, interviews, and the collection of developmental, familial interest, and behavioral data in order to generate a baseline for the planning of a more in-depth investigation. This occurs during the basic psychoeducational phase of the assessment, which typically lasts 1–2 days and includes advanced measures of cognition, achievement, memory, and personality. Formal testing procedures are selected and adapted based on known individual characteristics, past evaluation history, and referral questions. Care is taken to utilize appropriate alternative measures, to assess other areas (e.g., language, attention, neuropsychological function), to employ clinical procedures, and to initiate more specialized measures as warranted. Throughout, attention is directed toward identifying student strengths, preferences, assets, and resources that can be engaged to facilitate optimal decision making and performance.

SCREENING FOR LEARNING DISABILITY

Advocates charged with assisting adolescents and adults in becoming more successful and self-sufficient educationally, vocationally, and financially quickly become aware of the multitude of barriers that impede expected progress. Personality structure, behavioral patterns, family context, personal history and experience, and social and cultural variables, as well as cognitive capabilities, all help or hinder an individual seeking to improve his or her success in education, training, or employment. Professionals advocating for these individuals need access to tools that will reliably assist them to understand the relevant variables and make decisions as to realistic recommendations, interventions, and referrals for further assessment. Unfortunately, most existing rating scales have not been validated through psychometric research, which often leads to a potential misdiagnosis or at least incorrect decision making as a part of the screening process.

Because traditional assessment methodology has proven insufficient in meeting the transition and vocational needs of adolescents and adults with LD, extensive efforts have been devoted to developing alternative measures. For example, the Koller Adolescent and Adult Behavior Scale–Revised (KAABS–R; Koller, Holliday, & Multon, 1996) is a statistically derived 36-item measure of observed behavior of adolescents and adults with suspected LD, ADHD, and accompanying personality/behavioral correlates. In contrast to traditional screening or rating scales, it is the product of psychometrically driven revisions of a number of previous editions (Holliday, Multon, & Koller, 1994) designed to identify, with increasing accuracy, those characteristics known to predict learning disability, ADHD, and accompanying behaviors. A significant feature of the KAABS–R is the provision of a scoring procedure that allows the test administrator to place increased confidence in documenting observed individual characteristics. It has also been designed to be user friendly and economical, both in time and in cost, as well as clinically predictive. The respondents to the KAABS–R may be parents, spouses, teachers, counselors, or any significant other who has had the opportunity to observe the target individual over time and in a variety of situations. The KAABS–R has six statistical, or empirically derived, field-tested subscales:

1. Behavior problems
2. Information-processing problems
3. Perceptual organization problems
4. Poor task persistence
5. Negative self-evaluations
6. Social isolation

Psychometrically, the KAABS–R is an instrument with good internal consistency, with the subscales accounting for a high proportion of overall variance. Continuing empirical investigations of construct validity appear promising. The KAABS–R has been demonstrated to be useful as an assessment measure in disability determination and service delivery as well as in screening groups of individuals at high risk. In addition to the 36-item scale, supplemental items have been included that have proven valuable for clinical use.

In addition to its value as a screening device, the KAABS–R has proven useful in clinical diagnostic and prescriptive efforts. The accuracy of the diagnosis and accompanying emotional and behavioral manifestations is enhanced when standardized psychodiagnostic instruments are supplemented with specific behavioral observations. Accurate knowledge of individual behavioral characteristics is very helpful in developing the most effective educational, vocational, and/or psychosocial interventions. Individual information that is based on the direct observations of significant others provides a unique perspective that can increase the validity of the entire evaluation process.

Items on the KAABS–R were constructed to reflect characteristics identified by the research literature and other existing instruments as being known to be associated with LD and subsequent educational and vocational progress. The two major behavioral domains targeted were those reflecting actual learning disability symptomology (e.g., auditory processing, perceptual organization) and those related to affective, personality, or psychosocial functioning (e.g., depression, social isolation), because both are critical to effective educational and work functioning. Clearly personal/social/emotional development and corresponding personal adjustment issues are essential areas of functioning in learning and work settings. These often-overlooked areas frequently determine the actual vocational or educational success of the individual. In contrast to inferences inherent in the interpretation of standardized tests, the KAABS–R relies on actual, more realistic behaviors that have been observed in natural settings.

SITUATIONAL OR AUTHENTIC ASSESSMENT

Assessments designed to examine an individual's authentic functioning in the community, workplace, or classroom have become an integral part of efforts to maximize the opportunity and potential of individuals with disabilities. As stated previously, federal legislation requires that assessments be applicable to the actual demands of the setting and mandates the use of situation-specific, criterion-based evaluation techniques (Rehabilitation Act Amendments of 1992). People with cognitive impairments such as LD or ADHD present a particular challenge to assessment. McCue emphasized that "the assessment process (for people with LD) must be able to yield a diagnosis and specify the specific functional impediments or impact of the disability" (1995, p. 59). However, many assessment devices used in vocational or educational assessments are designed for administration through media that may conflict with the functional limitations imposed by an individual's cognitive disability, just as devices incorporating auditory stimuli conflict with the functional limitations of an individual with an uncorrected hearing impairment.

Logically, it follows that the use of these devices may result in a skewing (typically an underestimation) of predicted abilities. For example, if an individual with a visual processing disorder is evaluated for knowledge of mechanical properties through the Bennett Mechanical Comprehension Test, the resulting score is likely to reflect the individual's visual processing disabilities as well as his or her mechanical knowledge. This potentially biased assessment could be a factor in closing vocational or educational opportunities. Even when nomothetically standardized psychometric measures have been effectively and properly used to diagnose the existence of an impairment, the derived norm-referenced scores may not predict the impairment's actual impact on the individual's performance in specific "real-life" situations (Dunham et al., 1996). To combat this difficulty, the MUACC uses a technique known by various terms, including *community-based, functional, authentic,* or *situational assessment* (SA).

Traditional vocational evaluations typically use norm-referenced intelligence, aptitude, personality, and achievement testing to determine which occupations best fit the attributes of the individual or are least affected by that person's disability. Lists of occupational possibilities are then compared to the individual's interests in order to narrow down an individual's vocational choice to one or a few that would be supported as feasible given the functional limitations assumed from the person's diagnosis. SA starts with an individual's initial interests and bases preliminary decisions regarding the feasibility of success on the congruence between the individual's choice and the skills and behaviors demonstrated in the setting associated with that choice. Thus, instead of theorizing from lists of contrived functional limitations about possible accommodations necessary for success, SA enables the individual to try out accommodations in authentic settings, enabling the evaluator to judge directly the effectiveness of those accommodations and, if necessary, devise more effective ones.

Instead of looking for ways in which the individual is different from the norm (what the individual *cannot* do), SA seeks behaviors and skills matching the requirements of the situation (what the individual *can* do). That being said, SA frequently results in a decision to refocus vocational plans. The key difference is that this method of assessment enables individuals to view occupations from a skills-based perspective (perhaps for the first time in their lives) in light of their personal experiences in authentic settings. SA does not eliminate all of the disagreements between the evaluator and the individual, but it does facilitate a discussion with reference to more tangible and defensible criteria than the occupational task description provided by the *Dictionary of Occupational Titles* (U.S. Department of Labor, Division of Employment and Training, 1991) or even the evaluator's or counselor's knowledge of the world of work. In addition, the individual gains an understanding of his or her disability in functional terms, as contrasted with vague numerical descriptions based on statistical variability from predicted values.

SA is designed to obtain relevant reality-based information, to establish a basis for comparison, to create an opportunity for description, and to provide a complement for traditional normative assessment devices. Its primary contention is that behavioral observations can provide valuable information regarding an individual's ability to meet the requirements of a given situation. In addition, when criteria can be established for a minimum acceptable performance, those criteria provide a more informative and realistic basis for comparison than a comparison with a normative sample. Furthermore, SA enables evaluators to describe the strengths and limitations an individual possesses in terms of his or her interaction with the actual demands of life situations. Thus, the use of SA and traditional psychometric measures in a reciprocal relationship is a powerful tool in assisting an individual to meet his or her vocational, training, and social goals. Situational and psychometric assessments complement each other by providing a more thorough, descriptive, and relevant evaluation of an individual's functioning. This combination creates the opportunity to assess how strengths and limitations suggested by psychometric testing affect the individual in situations relevant to current and planned activities. If desired, behaviors noted through direct observation by staff during an individual SA can be further quantified by more traditional paper-and-pencil measures, including measures of visual or verbal memory and other psychosocial behaviors (e.g., interpersonal relationships, client insight, courtesy, stress tolerance).

SA is typically implemented to generate authentic samples of individual functioning in relevant job or classroom settings. Hands-on SA procedures are customized in each situation to answer the specific questions relevant to that individual and to test hypotheses developed through available data. In light of the presence of LD, typical SA referral requests include questions as to appropriate career directions, differentiating between the effects of multiple disabilities, assessing an individual's suitability for a particular job, and clarifying diagnostic patterns when individuals present with particularly involved situations.

Depending on the specific referral question, different SA strategies are used. These strategies are classified into five types. *Job shadowing* strategies are designed to provide the participant with the opportunity to obtain vocational and career information from actual jobsites, to estimate the vocational implications of the functional limitations, and to gain an understanding of the essential tasks corresponding to his or her vocational interests. For example, an individual is given an opportunity to directly observe and ask questions of a heavy equipment operator on the job. This provides the evaluator with an opportunity to directly assess (versus infer) the participant's preliminary basic workplace behaviors and psychosocial skills. *Functional skill evaluations* address the need to explore strengths and limitations suggested by previous psychometric assessment in terms of their impact on specific functional domains. For example, this technique assists in exploring how a reading comprehension impairment, indicated by psychometric testing, is expressed in terms of an individual's ability to complete a typical college-level writing assignment or to obtain information from a technical manual on the job. At the same time, alternative strategies for securing information are field tested as to their efficacy. *Position evaluation* and *approximated position evaluation* strategies assess an individual's ability to perform the essential task functions of a chosen occupation. Both types of strategies require a preassessment position evaluation and an extended assessment time line in order to gain insight into an individual's probability of occupational success. The difference between the two types resides primarily in the ability of the evaluator to schedule an assessment on an actual jobsite versus the need to approximate a position because of safety, contract, or time management conflicts. For example, an individual interested in a position as a police dispatcher may not have the opportunity to take direct emergency calls from the field. Therefore, a simulation can be created in which the individual is required to field similar types of calls. The evaluator is then able to manipulate the frequency and urgency of the calls to test individual responses. *Interview and role-play activities* rely on specifically designed structured interviews and role-play situations to obtain information relevant to an individual's functioning. For example, both mock and actual job interviews are conducted to directly observe individual self-advocacy needs.

Based on all available data, clinicians use these opportunities to assess performance on work tasks most relevant to the individual's vocational future. Job shadowing is frequently effective in revealing a good or bad fit between the individual and a particular job interest. For example, it is not unusual for high school students with LD, when transitioning to the world of work, to have unrealistic career expectations, be driven by parents who advise that they can "do whatever you set your mind to do," or to possess positive skills enabling them to achieve at levels higher than their expectations. In addition, an opportunity to actually experience parts of a real (versus contrived workstation) job through a functional skill evaluation in an authentic work setting provides valuable information that often influences diagnostic decisions, thus allowing for more realistic career choices. Frequently, individual strengths emerge during the SA that had not been previously identified, especially with traditional assessment procedures geared to identify weaknesses. Finally, interview and role-play activities are designed to help both the evaluator and the individual gain an understanding of the individual's ability to self-advocate, apply recommended accommodation strategies, and demonstrate job-seeking and job-keeping skills, thereby increasing his or her ability to make informed career choices.

SA specialists are trained to work in partnership with individuals and with employees on actual worksites as individuals receive actual experience on the job. This allows for direct observation of the impact that a specific learning disability will have on the job as well as other relevant work-related behaviors, including the individual's ability to receive supervision, follow directions, complete a time sheet and the like. Realistic accommodation strategies are then designed, implemented, tested on the job or in the classroom, and modified. Career development issues are clarified as vocational interests are considered in the context of a specific learning disability and other pertinent factors regarding the individual. Evaluation conclusions and recommendations, therefore, are based on a series of individually tailored, environmentally specific, dynamic, flexible, and goal-directed assessment activities that generate ecologically valid, integrated, relevant results that are meaningful to the individual and to those in the individual's support system. Finally, conclusions and recommendations are discussed fully with those involved, with particular emphasis on ensuring that the individual assessed has a full understanding of the findings and is capable of applying them to make informed educational and vocational choices.

Following the comprehensive functional assessment, project participants (educators and VR personnel) assume responsibility for implementing the transition support activities based on the evaluation results. Increasingly, schools and agencies have established transition classes wherein students with LD are provided with continuing opportunities to develop self-advocacy skills and implement accommodation strategies with the help of transition specialists (Koller, 1994). In addition, they work to provide more vocationally relevant out-of-school experiences, including job shadowing and part-time work experiences.

FIELD-TESTED SITUATIONAL ASSESSMENT OUTCOMES

As described previously, the MUACC conducted a 3-year project designed to improve the vocational outcomes of rural adolescents with LD who were in transition from school to work. A total of 120 adolescents were included in the 3-year project. Based on the SA model, the following highlights typify results achieved on completion of the state/federal project.

Selected Major Project Findings

Standard VR system procedures (including project student referrals and the determination of individual eligibility for services described previously) were used throughout the project. Following this process, a highly significant 98% of all project students were successful in completing the eligibility determination process to become VR students (Berkeley Planning Associates, 1989). This statistic is in stark contrast to an earlier RSA-sponsored study that found that 37% of applicants with LD *failed* to complete the process of eligibility determination (Berkeley Planning Associates, 1989). The major perceived difference was the effort of project and VR staff, as well as school referral personnel, to proactively involve the student and his or her teacher and parents step by step through the referral and evaluation process. By so doing, the focus was on enhancing student empowerment, thus allowing the student to make better-informed decisions.

Self-advocacy was a major project objective. Eighty-eight percent of the project students reported that the SA approach significantly helped improve self-advocacy competencies (Berkeley Planning Associates, 1989). This was accomplished primarily by increasing student understanding as to how specific types of LD affect their own lives, not just in school. One interesting residual by-product was that 48% of the students independently requested a more active involvement in their own IEP development (Berkeley Planning Associates, 1989).

Previous research (Wagner, 1989) documented that, of all the disability groups served, students with LD have the second-highest school dropout rate (32%). In this particular project, however, 95% of the project students with LD who were eligible to graduate during the course of the project remained in school through its 3-year completion. This rate more than doubles the national rate reported for graduation of students with LD (Berkeley Planning Associates, 1989). In fact, one project school reduced its anticipated student "high-risk" dropout rate among those students referred by 75%. It is a well-documented finding that graduation from high school is positively associated with better transition outcomes (Wagner, 1989). Therefore, by staying in school and proactively advocating for their individual needs, a significant 92% of the students reported that their personal academic coursework had been modified to focus more toward a vocational emphasis than to satisfy an academic requirement.

It is interesting to note that, prior to participating in the project, less than 5% of the participating students were able to elaborate on individual strengths. Many denied that they had LD, believed their difficulties would go away on leaving high school, or did not see how their functional limitations would affect employment. However, on completion of the project, 85% of the students were able to verbally list four or more of their learning and working strengths, as well as weaknesses, through mock employment job interviews.

Following an attempt to increase the number of realistic educational and vocational goals and objectives in the project students' IEPs, 47% of the students reported that their preferred career and vocational goals had been added to their IEPs. This rate increased the number of career and vocational goals by 300% based on a random review of past IEPs. In point of fact, it was not unusual before the project began to see the school IEP transition plan written only as "refer to VR."

In addition, as a result of the project activities, 85% of project students reported that school personnel, including the vocational adjustment coordinator, vocational resource educator, teachers, and counselors, had helped them to better understand their LD. Many students (76%) related that, prior to the project, all that they were told was what they could not do rather than being given examples of tasks at which they were capable. In addition, 73% of project students reported that the vocational rehabilitation counselors (VRCs) helped them to better understand how their specific LD would affect postsecondary training and employment. Likewise, 100% of the VRCs voiced a much better understanding of their students, especially individual strengths, based on the evaluations conducted.

All of the participants agreed that these increases were primarily a result not only of the types of evaluations conducted but also of the transmission of practical individual results and recommendations that teachers, counselors, and parents could implement in meaningful ways. Most important, although the evaluation was designed to be comprehensive, all project participants were pleased with the focus on student strengths and their relevance to employment, not just weaknesses. Fifty-one percent of the project students reported that their teachers, counselors, and VRCs became significantly more interested in student career planning as a result of the evaluation. One-hundred percent of the teachers reported an increase in the necessity for realistic student assessment and planning for all students with LD who transition from school to work. Furthermore, 100% of the VRCs surveyed thought that getting involved with the student earlier than the second semester of the senior year had increased their ability to improve the student's long-term employment outcomes.

Following the project, only 2 of the 120 project students reported that they would join the military after leaving high school because of lack of a career focus. Prior to participating in the project, school counselors reported that as many as 30% of students with LD who were undecided as to career had been expected to join the military.

A significant project objective was to improve the working relationship among schools, VRCs, parents, and employers. As a result of this model approach, 100% of the project site administrators (e.g., principals, superintendents, directors) reported significantly improved relationships with VRCs, parents, and employers. Each reported a better understanding of transition issues and differences in agency and school policies, and the need for a closer working relationship and a better grasp of VR policy by school and parent groups alike. In addition, 75% of the project site VRCs reported improved relationships with schools, parents, and employers. Correspondingly, 87% of the parents reported significantly improved relationships with schools, VRCs, and employers, primarily as a result of an increased resiliency on the part of school academic requirements (to make coursework more vocationally relevant) and VR reaching out to proactively interact with all personnel involved.

Because one goal of education is to seek and maintain employment, a major focus of the SA model relates to the employment community. Sixty-six percent of the teachers and VRCs involved in placement reported improved interactions with employers. Specifically designed workshops conducted with community employers focused on a better understanding of learning disability as a disability, as well as the realization that such disabilities can be accommodated to meet employer needs. This allowed employers an opportunity to better assist the students in transition to employment.

It is common knowledge that LD are often characterized as "hidden" disabilities and that individuals with LD who are in transition often have unrealistic career expectations (Koller, 1997). It is interesting to note that the functional or SA model helped create more authentic and realistic expectations of student career options. To illustrate, at the start of the project, only 10% of the students were perceived by school personnel and their VRCs as having a realistic career focus, given their disabilities. With the SA format, however, 78% of the students who completed the project had a more realistic appraisal of their strengths and weaknesses, as well as having acquired several individualized, field-tested accommodation strategies for use with their chosen career path.

Perhaps most important, the attitudes and opinions of project parents underwent dramatic change. Ninety-two percent reported a more realistic attitude toward their child's difficulties, a better understanding of the disability, and an increased willingness to work cooperatively with the school and VRC.

At the completion of the 3-year state/federal project, only 2 of the 120 individuals had Status 28 closures (unsuccessful) by the Division of Vocational Rehabilitation. Project efforts are under way to monitor the long-term outcomes of all student participants as they continue through the world of work.

Project Recommendations

Based on experience with a more authentic and holistic approach to transition as individuals with LD seek realistic employment, the following suggestions are recommended for consumers and advocates alike

1. It is imperative that ideological differences among the various stakeholders, including VR, the school, and other agencies (e.g., adult literacy, welfare to work), relating to transition referral, assessment, planning, and the preparation process be recognized early. It is not unusual to see conflict between the various agencies as to the role and function of each. Merely writing an individualized transition plan (ITP) that states

"refer to VR" is not enough. Likewise, VR needs to become actively involved in IEP development as a vocational expert for the IEP team in the school or agency setting.

2. Talk is often seen as nonproductive, but the development of truly effective lines of communication is essential. This can be accomplished only through intensive and positive relationship-building efforts among agencies, schools, the VRC, parents, consumers, and employers. It is imperative that all stakeholders be actively involved in the common goal of preparing individuals with LD for employment.

3. It is essential to initiate VRC involvement with schools long before the second semester of the senior year, thereby increasing the likelihood that the student will have the opportunity to acquire significant prevocational preparation skills prior to entering the VR system. By becoming involved in the IEP/ITP process earlier—for example, when the student is determined to be "at risk" or is starting the formal transition process—the additional benefits of added time and cooperative team management with parents and employers are enhanced.

4. Schools and agencies must implement a comprehensive functional assessment system that examines student functioning influenced by cognitive, achievement, personality, career interest, family, and other support system variables. The key operative word is *comprehensive*. Behavior does not occur in a vacuum or follow a recipe. To assess only part of the student's skills and abilities (e.g., intelligence, achievement) is to neglect the overall influence that other developmental variables, dynamics, and interests have in that individual's life. However, because of the sheer volume of numbers and time constraints, schools and other agencies often are forced to focus exclusively on academic variables. Likewise, the VRC is increasingly pressured to determine eligibility before the student has been thoroughly evaluated. An important consideration for all stakeholders is not just the determination of learning disability but the determination of the type(s) of learning disability and of any coexisting conditions (e.g., affective) that often accompany a learning disability. Learning disability is not a generic disabling condition because many combinations and permutations of this disorder exist that increase its heterogeneity. Furthermore, it is imperative that all functional limitations be identified, and not just academic limitations, because each limitation has a different impact on the student. By identifying the type or types of learning disability, any concomitant secondary conditions, and the corresponding functional limitations (and strengths), a VRC will significantly improve the student's chances for a successful Status 26 closure. Admittedly, because of variables often beyond the control of the VRC (e.g., 60-day determination of eligibility limit, Order of Selection), the student is often placed in a compromised position when dealing with school and agency referrals. Nonetheless, a balance must be achieved among referral, assessment, determination of eligibility for services, and the provision of those services.

5. It is important to use SA to gain an authentic understanding of student functioning in diverse real-life settings and to provide insight regarding career appropriateness. Formal, more psychometric procedures are typically used to determine the existence not only of LD and placement for special education and adult education services but also VR eligibility. Although these traditional procedures yield a considerable amount of information, they do not reliably predict long-term vocational success. By supplementing the student's formal standardized testing with more realistic SA, a more accurate picture of his or her strengths and weaknesses is established. Although traditional psychometric procedures alone may moderately predict future vocational success, a successful prediction can be increased significantly with more authentic, realistic SA in combination with regular testing.

6. The likelihood of long-term positive vocational outcomes will be enhanced by providing an in-depth description of student functional strengths. The Division of Vocational Rehabilitation traditionally follows the medical model approach, in which the primary focus is on functional limitations. However, with LD, although a specific area of brain–behavior functioning may present with limitations, it is not unusual to see other sensory processing skills emerge as strengths. By formally identifying student strengths, not just weaknesses, advocates are in a better position to bring about positive accommodations. Clearly, the focus should be not just on "what's wrong" but also on "what's right" with the student. It is important to empower students to advocate for their own needs by providing realistic and meaningful information that will lead to increased self-awareness and knowledge of individual strengths, weaknesses, needs, and resources.

7. The creation of intensive school- and community-based vocational preparation activities must be promoted as a part of the school experience, including active job shadowing, SA, and skill-building activities. The community-based transition support system can be strengthened by building relationships and reducing barriers to collaboration across all stakeholders involved in the student's life.

8. We must establish an effective evaluation system that provides for the collection of formative and summative data that can be used to make adjustments in policy and procedures not only at a local but also at a state level. A follow-along system is needed to support individuals at risk for dropping out across all referring agencies in forthcoming transitional planning.

9. LD are clearly more than an academic issue. As a result, if only achievement variables are considered, then the student stands at a clear disadvantage as he or she enters the workforce. For this reason, a reconciliation as to the definition of *learning disability* must be made between and across agencies. From an employment perspective, the RSA definition is by far the most comprehensive and realistic definition. If a student has a specific type of memory problem in school, why should it be presumed that it would not exist on the job? Clearly, therefore, a barrier to interagency cooperation lies in the definition of *learning disability* to which each agency subscribes.

10. A significant number of professionals are under the assumption that learning disability is a fad, that it cannot be severe, or that it will go away as the individual matures. None of these assumptions is correct, but each produces a significant barrier preventing the student from realizing vocational success. Although the student with LD is still in school or in training, concerted efforts should be enforced to require that the individual's training curriculum be geared toward a realistic vocational outcome.

11. Personality and social functioning play far greater roles in understanding the individual with LD than has ever been assumed (Koller, 1994, 1997; Vogel & Forness, 1992). Because individuals with LD often present with coexisting psychiatric diagnoses, especially depression, it is important for the schools and agencies to determine the student's strengths and weaknesses in this area. Even though a student may not have a coexisting psychiatric disorder sufficient to constitute a DSM-IV diagnosis, the basic parameters of an individual's personality are established early regardless of whether he or she has a cognitive disability. Thus, it is apparent that personality variables alone may help to contribute to learning disability's being a hidden disability. If an individual has a poor self-concept, is subservient, and is prone to feelings of isolation, should not these characteristics be considered as he or she transitions to employment? In addition, if accommodative strategies are not learned early, their personality correlates alone will present as significant barriers to a successful employment outcome.

12. Learning disability should be recognized as the most significant piggybacking disability in all the disability groups served by schools, agencies, and VR. For example, it is obvious when we see an individual who is quadriplegic that there is a likelihood of a significant motor problem, but how obvious is it that a learning disability coexists? In point of fact, we must infer its existence somehow through performance. Because it is possible that the quadriplegic might also have a coexisting learning disability, should not such a disability at least be ruled out as advocates try to find training and subsequent employment for this individual?

13. With the increased pressure to determine a disability as expeditiously as possible, the need exists to develop better screening tools standardized on those known variables that predict learning disability. Many useful diagnostic tests that are available are time consuming and expensive. Developing low-cost, brief predictive screening procedures would facilitate the eventual diagnostic process.

14. A growing concern is the relationship of ADHD between LD and other debilitating conditions. Significant differences exist among states and among state agencies and schools as to coding, diagnosis, severity determination, and service delivery for ADHD. There is incongruity between VR, school and agency, and the medical/psychological community's interpretations. VR has not correctly established a unitary coding system to track the incidence of ADHD, and school policies are likewise inconsistent, making it possible for a student to be diagnosed as having ADHD in one school but not another in the same state. Increasing the effective communication among agencies will help to resolve the growing ADHD dilemma.

15. When there is a lack of investment by any significant partner in the transition support system, progress on behalf of the student stalls. Unfortunately, the student with LD who is in transition is the individual who ultimately suffers.

CONCLUSION

As the numbers of individuals with LD increase in the U.S. workforce and because a corresponding increase in technological skills will be prerequisite for individuals with LD to succeed, we must continue to develop better, more effective diagnostic and intervention models capable of improving effective service delivery. This chapter has described a functional, holistic, more authentic SA model that focuses on student strengths and weaknesses and appears to hold considerable promise as a means of improving employment outcomes and strengthening the student support system.

REFERENCES

American Psychiatric Association. (1994). *Diagnostic and statistical manual of mental disorders* (4th ed.). Washington, DC: Author.

Berkeley Planning Associates. (1989). *Evaluation of services provided for individuals with specific learning disabilities: A final report* (Vols. I and II) (Report prepared for U.S. Department of Education under Contract No. 300-87-0112). Berkeley, CA: Author.

Coutinho, M.J. (1995). The national profile and recent studies regarding characteristics, integration, secondary school experiences and transitions of youth with specific learning disabilities: Summary and implications. In *Secondary education and beyond: Providing opportunities for students with learning disabilities* (pp. 1–37). Pittsburgh: Learning Disabilities Association of America.

Dunham, M.D., Koller, J.R., & McIntosh, D.E. (1996, Winter). A preliminary comparison of successful and nonsuccessful closure types among adults with specific learning disabilities in the vocational rehabilitation system. *Journal of Rehabilitation, 6,* 42–47.

Holliday, G.A., Multon, K.D., & Koller, J.R. (1994). Behavioral assessment of vocational rehabilitation clients with learning disabilities: Development of the Koller Adolescent and Adult Behavior Scale. *Journal of Assessment in Rehabilitation and Exceptionality, 1*(4), 277–288.

Koller, J.R. (1994, Summer). Improving transition outcomes for persons with specific learning disabilities. *Journal of Rehabilitation,* 37–42.

Koller, J.R. (1996). *SWRLD: School to Work Rural Disabilities Project* (CRD-84-235A) (1–260). Washington, DC: U.S. Office of Education.

Koller, J.R. (1997). Vocational rehabilitation: Best practices for work preparation. In P.J. Gerber & D.S. Brown (Eds.), *Learning disabilities and employment* (pp. 1–25). Austin, TX: PRO-ED.

Koller, J.R., Holliday, G.A., & Multon, K.D. (Eds.). (1996). *Koller Adolescent and Adult Behavior Scale–Revised (KAABS–R).* (Available from the Assessment & Consultation Clinic, University of Missouri–Columbia, 223 Townsend Hall, Columbia, MO 65211.)

McCue, M. (1995). Assessing vocational rehabilitation services for individuals with specific learning disabilities. In *Secondary education and beyond: Providing opportunities for students with learning disabilities* (pp. 57–61). Pittsburgh: Learning Disabilities Association of America.

Rehabilitation Act Amendments of 1992, PL 102-569, 29 U.S.C. §§ 701 *et seq.*

Rehabilitation Services Administration. (1985, March). Program policy directive (RSA-PPD-85-7). Washington, DC: Office of Special Education and Rehabilitation Services.

State Vocational Rehabilitation Services Program Rule. 34 C.F.R. § 361. (1997).

Tillman, Z., & Abbott, J. (1992). *Transition of youth with learning disabilities (working papers).* Washington, DC: U.S. Department of Education, Rehabilitation Services Administration.

U.S. Department of Labor, Division of Employment and Training. (1991). *Dictionary of occupational titles* (4th ed.). Washington, DC: Author.

Vogel, S.A. (1989). Adults with language learning disabilities: Definitions, diagnosis and determination of eligibility for postsecondary and vocational rehabilitation services. *Rehabilitation Education, 3,* 77–90.

Vogel, S.A., & Forness, S.R. (1992). Social functioning in adults with learning disabilities. *School Psychology Review, 21*(3), 375–386.

Wagner, M. (1989). *The transition experience of youth with disabilities: A report from the National Longitudinal Transition Study.* Menlo Park, CA: SRI International. (ERIC Document Reproduction Service No. ED 303 988)

Wechsler, D. (1997). *Wechsler Adult Intelligence Scale–III.* New York: The Psychological Corporation.

Woodcock, R.W., & Johnson, M.B. (1989). *Woodcock-Johnson-Revised Test of Achievement.* Chicago: Riverside.

Zigmund, N. (1990). Rethinking secondary school programs for students with learning disabilities. *Focus on Exceptional Children, 23,* 1–22.

16

Off the Beaten Path

A Model for Employment Success for Adults with Learning Disabilities

Henry B. Reiff

Many of us have heard about successful people with learning disabilities (LD). From Edison to Einstein, DaVinci to Rodin, Churchill to Patton, it seems that many of the most famous, noteworthy, and colorful figures of history had some type of learning disability. We have only to turn to the tabloids to discover that a current crop of celebrities, such as Cher, Henry Winkler, Tom Cruise, and Greg Louganis, are also among the growing legion of highly successful adults with learning and reading difficulties.

CREATING A CONTEXT

The disclosure that such stellar and glamorous people have LD is perhaps quite reassuring, even uplifting, to many individuals with LD. Who would not want to be in the company of Einstein? Yet our search for successful adults with LD need not be confined to history or entertainment. In fact, we might consider taking a slightly more ordinary path in looking for successful adults with LD. First, the dead may not serve as the best role models. Surely we can find living examples of individuals with LD whose accomplishments should inspire us. Also, as Adelman and Adelman (1987) warned, relying on posthumous diagnoses of LD from anecdotal and sometimes apocryphal sources may sound similar to an inadvertent admission; "real" successes are so limited that we have to make them up. Second, although contemporary entertainers and athletes may provide better credentials of learning difficulties (notwithstanding doubt about authen-

The author expresses sincere appreciation to Dr. Paul J. Gerber of Virginia Commonwealth University for his invaluable assistance in the preparation of this chapter.

ticity in many instances), how many of us are likely to realize stardom in sports or entertainment? In the same way that many leaders have questioned the worthiness of professional athletes as the major role models for adolescent African American boys, we must attempt to offer more realistic career aspirations to people with LD.

The good news is that a multitude of living individuals with LD live all around us, excelling in careers from accounting to astrophysics, banking to biology, politics to paleontology. We have discovered that some incredibly successful people can barely read. Their success may surprise or impress us; but, more important, it may suggest a direction for others to follow. Most people with LD do not become successful by doing things like everyone else. They often have to travel off the beaten path to find employment success; they often must overcome significant obstacles to achieve this goal. In this chapter, we learn about the journeys of some adults with LD, consider the commonalities of their experiences, and listen to their advice. We will not find a magical formula that guarantees employment success, but we can develop a practical understanding of what the issues are for people with LD.

Understanding the Workplace

Before we examine individual stories of adults with LD in the workplace, we need to develop a basic context of essential issues related to employment. The workplace is a complex setting—made even more complex when we consider the added element of LD. The success of individuals with LD is dependent to a large extent on the larger market forces in the workplace. When the economy is strong, more employment opportunities exist for all people, with and without LD. In addition, in a strong economy, employers are more willing to take risks by hiring and accommodating people with LD. When the economy is weak, fewer opportunities exist and employers tend to develop a more conservative frame of mind regarding qualifications.

Of course, the American with Disabilities Act (ADA) of 1990 (PL 101-336) was intended to prohibit decisions about employability based on disability, as long as the prospective employee is "otherwise qualified." Nonetheless, unlike the protected experience of the school environment, the employment world represents a social system that is generally barely knowledgeable about the issues of disability. Negative perceptions and misinformation are rampant. It is not uncommon for employers to believe that LD are a kind of mental retardation. Moreover, the hidden and often subtle manifestations of LD tend of obscure disability discrimination issues. Many employers doubt the very existence of LD. An employer may wonder, "You look normal and seem normal when you work. What do you mean you need special considerations?" As of 1994, few discrimination suits had successfully redressed grievances of employees with LD under the ADA (Anderson, Kazmierski, & Cronin, 1995).

The increasing job mobility of many Americans also has significant implications for people with LD. The era of a single lifetime job has all but ended. Not only do most adults change jobs but also many change careers. Such change can create opportunities and possibilities; it can also be negative for individuals with LD because of the flexibility needed in all areas of employability, from job entry to job advancement.

What Happens to People with Learning Disabilities at Work?

What do we know about actual job outcomes of people with LD? Overall, employment and unemployment rates for individuals with LD do not differ significantly from the rates of the population in general (Blackorby & Wagner, 1996). What does seem to be different, however, is the level or status of employment. Many studies indicate that people with LD tend to be underemployed—either in the sense of menial or part-time employment or in positions that underutilize their qualifications, or both (White, 1992). The same difficulties that plagued individuals with LD in school and other areas of childhood often surface on the job and throughout adulthood. In spite of the common perception that LD are easier to hide once one is out of school, many adults with LD are finding the converse to be true. Chris Lee, an adult with LD and author of *Faking It* (1992), a book about the frustrations of growing up with LD, hid his learning difficulties relatively well in school. "Although I managed to get through school," he confides,

> It wasn't long before I was hit with the reality that faking it wouldn't work in the "real world." I couldn't fake it when I needed to write checks. I couldn't fake it when I took the test to get a driver's license. I couldn't fake it when I wanted to apply for jobs and the potential employer demanded that I fill out the application on the spot. As much as I tried to hide [from] my learning disabilities, it became apparent that I was going to have to deal with having learning disabilities in every aspect of my life—academically, socially, and in the workplace. (Lee, 1995, p. 8)

One reason why employed adults with learning and reading difficulties cannot hide is the increasing demand for literacy in the workplace. According to Mikulecky (1995), the National Adult Literacy Survey of 26,000 adults found that almost all workers, including those in labor positions, must read and write forms, reports, and memos on at least a weekly basis. Today's jobs typically require employees to gather information from charts and graphs; to measure, calculate, graph, and record information; and to problem solve in written reports. The majority of jobs require more than basic or functional literacy skills; most materials, such as manuals, directions, and new product information, are written at the high school or college level (Mikulecky, 1995). Even entry-level employment, such as working as a cashier, typically requires computer literacy skills.

Gerber and Reiff (1991) interviewed nine adults with LD in a variety of occupations and levels of accomplishment. One young man discovered that his reading impairments hindered his ability to perform in what he considered to be a menial occupation, driving a delivery truck. He often made mistakes in reading his delivery orders and in using maps. A young woman with LD related that writing and spelling continued to pose uncomfortable challenges in her job: "The girl behind me had to proofread my writing. There were even small mistakes like 'wait' for 'want.' She was frustrated with me. . . . She did yell at me a couple of times" (1991, p. 57). Similarly, another young adult could not hold her job at an exercise center: "I had to write down how much this person weighed. . . . But I couldn't really spell well or measure the weight" (1991, p. 61). Reversing letters, words, or numbers—perhaps the stereotypical feature of dyslexia—presented inordinate difficulties for another individual. Working at a gas station, he charged customers incorrect amounts of money, gave the wrong time, and created a number of confusing situations. "It happens all the time, on license plates and credit cards. It also happens with words—everything" (1991, pp. 63–64).

Moody (1995) reminded us that individuals with LD face more than difficulties with just reading and writing in the workplace. They may miss appointments, write down telephone numbers incorrectly, forget to pass on messages, find report writing overwhelming, or miss key points at meetings. They may forget instructions; have difficulties in copying, filing, and organizing; take too long to get things done; and express themselves poorly in speech or in writing. It is easy to imagine that coping with one or more of these situations can be frustrating; the frustration may be internalized and generalized.

These persisting difficulties are not limited to individuals with LD who are having a tough time "making it"; successful adults with LD also contend with pervasive obstacles. A high-powered real estate lawyer related that, even after years of successful practice, "I was constantly anxious, and I was constantly under the gun because there were a lot of things that I had to read" (Gerber & Reiff, 1991, p. 50). An assistant dean of student affairs at a large university realized that her writing skills simply did not meet the typical expectations in an academic setting:

> There's no way I can hide it. . . . Even now I write with two-cent words when in an academic setting. If it takes a five dollar word, I use a two-cent word because I can spell the two-cent word. I can't spell the five-dollar word. (Gerber & Reiff, 1991, p. 53)

As the two preceding examples demonstrate, many adults with LD do achieve employment success and a significant degree of satisfaction in their lives, even though their dyslexia or LD clearly do not disappear. They often do relatively well in school and higher education despite their learning and reading difficulties, work in professional settings, and have a very good understanding of their strengths and limitations (Gerber & Reiff, 1991). They are able to find employment they like and in which they can do well and thus remain employed in (Rogan & Hartman, 1990) and develop compensatory strategies (Adelman & Vogel, 1990). These findings reveal that a number of adults with LD are able to beat the odds. Their stories may help others to cope with a persisting difficulty that has implications for employment as well as overall adult functioning.

ON THE ROADS LESS TRAVELED: THREE STORIES OF EMPLOYMENT SUCCESS[1]

KD

A clinical psychologist with a thriving practice, KD has authored a best-selling book on men's issues and writes features for prominent magazines, has his own local television show, has appeared on the talk show circuit, and is in demand as a speaker at national and international conferences. His lucrative career has brought him not only material wealth but also the freedom to control much of his time. To a great extent, KD can do what he wants. Yet bubbling just below the surface of these untroubled waters are

> major and ever present difficulties—those demons coming back and saying. "You're the imposter here. You're going to get found out. You're a big phony. You're not smart enough." It's a small miracle that I write with fluidity and proper punctuation. (p. 22)

KD seems genuinely self-assured, a naturally empathic psychologist; it is hard to reconcile this image with such self-doubt and insecurity. The pervasive hurt and pain are the legacy of his LD, or, perhaps more accurate, the interaction between his LD and his schooling. Never formally identified as having LD in childhood, he struggled with D and F grades, habitually attended summer school, and was generally regarded as a "dummy." KD's learning difficulties were treated as a source of embarrassment and largely ignored. "Mostly school was a horrible, humiliating experience" (p. 23).

---

[1]The stories presented in this section have been adapted from Reiff, Gerber, & Ginsberg (1997). These stories are adapted by permission from PRO-ED.

School was exasperating because KD had so much difficulty reading: "I could read a sentence, and I had no comprehension. I could read it ten times, and I still wouldn't get it" (p. 23). Today, "the process of reading just still doesn't click with me. I enjoy the process of reading and learning now, but I'm still very slow" (p. 23). Ironically, his writing career has blossomed in many ways because of his reading style. KD writes at a level at which he can read, which turns out to be simple, clear, and accessible, just the ticket for popular success. His writing has also rewarded him with a unique method of improving his reading: "I'm learning how to read by reading my own writing, things that I'm making intelligible to me. And as I make myself a better writer, I'm going to train myself to be a better reader" (p. 24).

KD managed to graduate from high school and eventually earned a bachelor's degree in sociology, a master's degree in counseling psychology, and a doctorate in clinical psychology. He did not suddenly learn to read well. Instead, he decided that, if he worked hard enough, he could meet the requirements. "I never stop trying. I have an incredible amount of persistence. . . . I would adapt by doing extra work" (p. 23). He needed to prove himself, to be accepted and recognized. Higher education gave him that opportunity because it provided a more flexible means for him to show what he could do. KD used his wisdom and charm to find people to support and teach him. It was still a struggle, but it helped develop the learned creativity so useful to him in later life.

> The ways I've been asked to learn, with very few exceptions, were not native to me. I was always having to change the situation to show what I knew or to show how I learned. So I learned how to struggle adversely with the system. (p. 23)

He learned to trust himself and not to get too emotionally involved in what others said he could or could not do. "At times it was extremely lonely and painful, but I think I got to know myself in that loneliness. I think I had to really pull for myself" (p. 23). KD also has used the painful experiences of struggling with LD to provide a major foundation for his success as a psychologist.

> I think I identify with people in low self-esteem positions or people who are struggling to believe in themselves because I had that experience so intimately. . . . The struggle has taught me something. I'm now drawing from that wisdom to help other people. I draw from that wisdom for perspective. (p. 22)

KM

A popular faculty member in the art department at a major campus of a state university, KM has established a reputation as an innovative visual artist and sculptor. Three years ago she was diagnosed as having LD. As a child in school, she was always the first to sit down in the spelling bee. She was the one child in kindergarten who could not learn to spell her own name. Math and reading were difficult, too. She generally did not fail; instead, she managed to eke out C grades. KM did not present a problem to her teachers, but she did suffer. The spelling bees were "always excruciating" (p. 27) and embarrassing. She remembers looking for the skinniest book to assuage her anxiety about doing book reports. She persevered, buoyed by her talent and interest in art. When she got to community college, however, she was almost destroyed by a psychologist's response to her vocational testing. He imperiously informed her, "You have third-year college-level visual perception, but you are retarded in all other areas" (p. 27). She felt as if she had been slapped in the face.

Similar to most adults with LD who have found employment success, KM refused to let one blow keep her down. Rather, it strengthened her resolve to succeed, to prove that she was a capable and talented person. "I know he's wrong" (p. 27), she repeated to herself. She dropped out of the community college and transferred to a well-known art institute. As she was able to specialize more and more in art courses and less and less in basic educational requirements, her grades improved. KM eventually made the dean's list and went straight to graduate school, where she received a fellowship. She has not looked back. She succeeded because she persisted, because she was stubborn, because she refused to allow someone else tell her that her expectations were too high. She exceeded that psychologist's expectations, but not her own.

KM believed in herself even though others did not. She credits much of her resolve to her parents. They saw her talent as an artist, nurtured it, and emphasized her artistic strengths.

> So although I wasn't feeling good until third grade, from then on, when I started to get this praise with the art, it just seemed to. . . . it clicked for me. If I didn't have art, I don't know how I'd feel about myself. (p. 27)

Her successful career in art has not obliterated the impact of her learning difficulties. KM has had a long-time interest in the biomedical field but never felt she was capable of pursuing such a career. In her teaching, she finds it nearly impossible to memorize her students' names. She makes mistakes writing on the board, although she encourages her students to correct her. Her forthrightness not only makes students comfortable but also works as an effective strategy to get them to pay attention. She has a large library collection at her home, not because she has become a good reader but because, if she does not understand one book, she can go to another. Writing also continues to be a problem.

KM is not overwhelmed by her LD in her profession or in day-to-day life. For the most part, her strengths rather than her weaknesses drive her career. Overall, she has created environments that only minimally exacerbate her LD. KM is quite satisfied with her career and professional life.

JC

At the age of 47, in spite of immense success in his self-developed contracting and building business, JC had a harrowing secret:

> I always had a horrendous inferiority complex. It affected me every moment of my waking hours that I could neither read nor write. . . . I didn't think I could feel successful unless I could learn to read and write. And in this society learning how to read and write is very basic and you learn it when you're a child. So psychologically and emotionally we're left in our childhood. And we're left in the emotions and fears of our childhood. No matter how much intellectual power and success that people might have, it's always been superficial to me. (pp. 30–31)

As a child, JC started out with a sense of wholeness and confidence. His parents loved him, supported him, and told him he was a winner. Until he was 6 years old, he had no reason to doubt them. Then "I went to school only to find out that I was a loser" (p. 31). He did not learn to read and write like the other children. He felt inferior and weak: "I went through a time where they were calling kids like me mentally retarded. I don't even know what the other names were but they all came out being subhuman" (p. 31). Yet JC did not give up on himself. Instead, he quickly learned to compensate.

In fact, he learned to compensate so well that he fooled most people. He acted much too self-assured to have an inferiority complex. He even fooled the system. In spite of not learning to read, he kept on getting promoted. He learned how to survive, how to play the game. He was able to succeed and pass because "I'm an athlete, six foot four, blue eyed, and I had adapted socially" (p. 31).

On the outside, JC was making it. He became a fighter who decided he simply was not going to be held back no matter what he had to do. If that meant deception, so be it.

> It was easy to deceive the system because they were continuing to deceive themselves. So all I did was to find out where their deceptions were, where their weaknesses were. I was at war every single day with my world. That gave me some discipline. . . . The literate world was my enemy. . . . I took a psychological posture of who the good guys were and who the bad guys were. I wasn't going to let the literate world beat me. (p. 31)

JC managed to get through high school, partially through sheer force of will (he took science eight times until he passed it as a senior) and partially through his nonacademic talents. His social charm and obvious brightness may have overwhelmed his teachers and obfuscated his academic impairments, and it did not hurt that he lettered in three sports.

His athleticism led to a college scholarship. By then, JC had honed his survival skills to a fine edge. Not only did he graduate, but he also took a job as a high school teacher, still not being able to read. Paradoxically, his strategies to hide his illiteracy may have made him a better teacher. Instead of reading the daily bulletin, he let the kids read it. To cope with taking roll, he used assigned seating; and for the first week of class, the students would introduce themselves to each other each day. JC memorized the roll list, and the students got involved in positive social interactions. Debates and discussions became the hallmarks of his teaching approach. He worked with the students whom other teachers could not handle, perhaps a sure way to endear oneself to the administration. He told the students that they were his teachers, and he did not want to be bored. He challenged his students to grow and learn, and they responded. "A good teacher is somebody that is sensitive and cares, and I did that, even though I was illiterate" (p. 32).

JC had realized that, to evolve in the workplace, he would have to face "the paper"; he would have to deal with reading and writing. He became the consummate manipulator but paid a heavy price. His deception haunted him. "My conscience was clear, but I still had that terrible fear of being caught." He was constantly fearful of being revealed as illiterate.

While he was teaching, JC took a leave of absence, built an apartment building in 9 months, and made several hundred thousand dollars. He has never looked back. If he had learned to cope as an illiterate in one of the most literate environments imaginable, then he could certainly handle the world of business. He also found that a wide array of his other qualities had a particularly good fit for contracting, developing, and building. "The reason I'm an entrepreneur and have my own business is because I couldn't work for somebody else's system because their system wasn't fixed for me" (p. 32). A man who built his own house with no previous experience, JC has a hands-on knowledge and understanding of his business. His natural learning style is well suited to an enterprise that literally requires the vision to turn ideas into tangible form. "I'm a visual person. I'm a conceptual person. That's how I work" (p. 32). His illiteracy may have helped him develop these talents. He had to tap into parts of his brain that many literate people never need to discover.

JC has achieved success. His company has done as much as $50 million worth of business in a year. He likes what he does. He regards the longevity of his marriage and raising his children as significant achievements. His greatest sense of accomplishment, however, stems from a catharsis that began 2 years before we spoke. "It wasn't until I was 48 years old that I stopped running, by going to a library and asking for help. . . . I found out that it was even possible for me to read" (Corcoran, 1994, p. 216). He works with a tutor, someone who allows him to acquire basic skills at this own pace and in his own way. "I define success by learning how to read and write. That's my definition" (p. 33). Slowly, painstakingly, JC is entering the previously inaccessible literate world. After a lifetime as a fugitive from literacy, "learning how to read and write for me has meant coming home and being able to be whole" (p. 33).

A MODEL FOR EMPLOYMENT SUCCESS

These three examples of adults with LD who have found employment success are not rare. Many other individuals with LD have similar stories to tell. Gerber, Ginsberg, & Reiff (1992) discovered clear commonalities in the ways these individuals had achieved success. Although these individuals did not all use identical strategies, they all headed in the same direction. Through analyzing this process, Gerber et al. (1992) developed a model for employment success—a systematic analysis that others may use to increase the likelihood of their own success.

The adults in this study had managed to gain a considerable amount of control over their professional lives. "Taking control" has particular import for people with LD. First, the experience of growing up with LD often leads to a loss of control. After all, children with LD routinely hear that they could (and should) do better and that they are not trying hard enough. The very existence of an information-processing difficulty may be greeted with suspicion and doubt. If the "system" decrees that these students really do have a legitimate difficulty, decisions are made for them regarding the type of education that is appropriate, with a subtle if unintended message that they somehow are not quite intact as learners. The list goes on. In almost all instances, the autonomy of people with LD is undermined, especially as they find they have great difficulty with tasks that others take in stride, and their self-concept and confidence are thus eroded. In the worst instances, people with LD may learn to be helpless. They feel that they do not control their own destinies; rather, they are simply adrift, capriciously vulnerable to any current, wave, or whirlpool. In short, they feel that life is out of control.

How did these successful adults with LD get back in control? Over a period of time, they made three significant internal decisions: 1) They developed a desire to succeed; 2) they adopted a clear sense of goal orientation, and 3) they engaged in a process of reframing (in a sense, redefining) the LD experience such that they recognized, accepted, and understood their LD and consequently developed a sense of how to use their unique abilities, being mindful of both their strengths and their weaknesses. They were able to transform these decisions into four behaviors or external manifestations, typified by a high degree of adaptability:

1) They exhibited extraordinary persistence and resilience.
2) They found a goodness of fit between their abilities and their work environments.
3) They developed and relied on many kinds of learned creativity to cope with, compensate for, and overcome the challenges their LD presented.
4) They created favorable social ecologies or interpersonal and interdependent support networks.

As adults with LD incorporate these characteristics, they should increase the likelihood of attaining employment success.

The proportions, sequencing, and interactions of the components of the model for employment success will vary with each individual. Adults with LD cannot expect a "one size fits all" cookbook-type recipe of a simple set of concrete steps to lead to success. In addition, because the model is so interactive, it is difficult to predict its development in any given situation. However, it is believed that some general advice about the model will be useful to most individuals with LD.

In terms of internal decisions, the process of reframing may be the engine that powers people down the road to success. Desire to succeed fuels the engine, and goal orientation sets the direction; but reframing ultimately empowers individuals to utilize behaviors that will determine employment outcomes. In order to find success, an applied understanding of strengths and weaknesses is of critical importance. Knowing what one can and cannot do will lead to more realistic goal orientation; a sense of personal strength is often the foundation of desire. People with LD must honestly and objectively assess their abilities in order to make effective decisions about types of employment they will pursue, how they will present themselves in the application process, and what they will need to do to perform the job successfully. One adult in this study captured the essence of the reframing process in this straightforward self-assessment.

> You must learn where your strengths are and how to use them and where your weaknesses are and how to avoid them or compensate. I have learned to accept who I am, what I can do, what I cannot do, who I should try to be, and who I should not try to be. (Gerber, Ginsberg, & Reiff, 1992, p. 481)

Reframing also directly affects the external manifestations. Clearly, *goodness of fit* (i.e., choosing employment that maximizes strengths while minimizing weaknesses) directly correlates with self-understanding and awareness. *Learned creativity,* the special strategies and mechanisms that people with LD use to meet work demands, must again evolve from a careful analysis of one's own abilities and determination of how to use one's strengths to compensate for one's weaknesses. Even the development of favorable social ecologies depends on the reframing process, because it gives the individual a sense of what types of support are necessary and what kinds of support the individual can give in return.

As a kind of reality check, individuals with LD must accept or even embrace the notion that they have to work harder than their counterparts without LD to succeed in most areas of employment. One adult encouraged employees with LD to view hard work as a gift: "Take the hard work to be your friend. You will be able to think, to function, to succeed at a level a normal person could never reach for." In the Gerber et al. (1992) study, the successful adults with LD stressed over and over again that they rose above the limitations of their disabilities, the expectations of their employers, and the performance of their competitors—simply by being the hardest worker.

Many indicated that working harder and longer was a deeply ingrained personal characteristic that they had developed as a survival mechanism in school. In fact, some went on to credit the trials and tribulations of growing up with LD as laying the foundation for a ferocious work ethic: "The learning disability positively affected my success. . . . I learned to persist, to deal with pain and frustration. . . . Things don't come easy to me, but I work long and hard. This is central to my being." They occasionally reasoned that, if they could survive school, they could survive anything. Moreover, they remarked that they believed themselves to be at an advantage over schoolmates who did not have to work hard because everything came easily; those individuals were oftentimes unprepared to cope with the real-life demands of adulthood and the world of work. Adults with LD cannot afford to overlook the power of persistence and the edge it may give them. As one successful adult in the study wryly observed, "There's always a place for someone who wants to work hard because most people in the world do not want to work at all."

The Role of Self-Esteem in Employment Success

It is no coincidence that many successful adults with LD emphasize the importance of self-esteem as the primary component of success. Conversely, a sense of personal inadequacy may severely thwart the efforts of adults with LD in the workplace. Building positive self-esteem is a lifelong process that does not readily lend itself to a simple list of *do*s and *don't*s. Nevertheless, gaining access to counseling or similar services may constitute a critical factor in the employment success of some adults with LD. This process can begin in elementary school. It should focus on helping individuals with LD become self-sufficient, independent thinkers who can self-advocate and be responsible for their actions (Shaw, 1991).

As Blocher (1989) pointed out, the basis for building self-esteem lies in an acceptance and awareness of "simple strengths," part of the reframing process. Many individuals with LD do not have a good sense of their strengths because they have not had the opportunity to discover "strength situations"—those areas in which they can succeed. In addition, it is all too human to deny our strengths; in many ways, it is easier not to accept the responsibility and risk that come with the potential to succeed. Blocher (1989) suggested that we will be more likely to recognize our strengths if we self-assess in terms of meaningful and realistic goals we set for ourselves rather than in terms of society's expectations. He called this process assessing on the *horizontal* rather than *vertical* dimension. Clearly this approach can be useful to people with LD, who often must reframe their sense of personal strengths and weaknesses, largely because the vertical expectations of the school system tend to work against people with LD. Learning to advocate for oneself presents formidable challenges as described in the next section. Effective self-advocacy is related to positive self-esteem. We are more ready to stand up for ourselves when we feel good about ourselves. Others will believe in us only when we believe in ourselves. As one of the successful adults from the Gerber et al. (1992) study advised,

> You need to look in the mirror and say, "Ok, I can live with you, good and bad; I can live with you." Maybe then you're on the road to success. You can't get other people to respect or love you when you can't do the same to yourself. (p. 481)

Emotional Intelligence: Reframing the Concept of Intelligence in the Workplace

Consensus is mounting that success does not necessarily depend on our traditional conceptions of intelligence, especially the kinds of intelligence typically associated with reading and writing prowess per se. Most employers would probably agree that school smarts do not predict who will be a highly valued employee. In fact, the characteristics described in the model for employment success would seem advantageous to almost any work situation. The reading and writing difficulties that were so debilitating in school to many people with LD need not prohibit achievement in the workplace. Adults with LD can draw on many other skills, abilities, and sources of strength.

A growing body of research supports this view of employment success. In the best-selling book *Emotional Intelligence*, Goleman (1995) made a compelling argument that self-awareness and impulse control, persistence, zeal and self-motivation, empathy, and social deftness represent the qualities of people who do well in life. The parallels to the model for employment success are striking. Perhaps the successful adults with LD of the Gerber et al. (1992) study were tapping into the components of Goleman's construct. The good news is that people with LD are in no way disadvantaged when it comes to emotional intelligence; in some ways, simply enduring in the face of the many obstacles that LD present may be a building block of emotional intelligence.

Goleman (1995) and Reiff, Gerber, and Ginsberg (1994) further contended that such qualities, unlike our conventional representation of IQ score, are neither predetermined at birth nor static. The educational and psychological literature are replete with evidence and examples. We need not look far to find suggestions for learning how to improve self-motivation and persistence, for determining and setting goals by controlling impulses and delaying gratification, for increasing our awareness of who we are. According to Goleman (1995), the more we can find pleasure in and develop enthusiasm for what we do, the more we master the aptitude of emotional intelligence. Not coincidentally, Gardner (1983), whose theory of multiple intelligences dovetails with and supports the concept of emotional intelligence, provides a succinct, albeit idealistic, commentary on how to nurture a positive, optimistic, and success-oriented approach to the workplace:

> The single most important contribution education can make to a child's development is to help him toward a field where his talents best suit him, where he will be satisfied and competent. . . . We should spend less time ranking children and more time helping them to identify their natural competencies and gifts, and cultivate those. There are hundreds and hundreds of ways to succeed, and many, many different abilities that will help get you there. (Gardner, as cited in Goleman, 1995, p. 37)

The educational system has the potential to create an inclusive mainstream. Education can become a journey that accommodates entries from many different directions while continually moving forward. If Gardner's dream can be realized, people with LD will not need to travel off the beaten path to find employment success.

AN ADDENDUM TO THE MODEL: SELF-ADVOCACY IN A CHANGING WORKPLACE

The workplace is beginning to be more receptive to working proactively with adults with LD. For example, Carter and Maher (1995) described a pilot project called "Learning Disabilities in the Workplace," an on-site workplace education program that trains educators to assist workers with special learning needs. The educators learn to identify employees who have possible LD or dyslexia. Informal and formal assessment follow wherein the worker is interviewed and completes a learning inventory, a basic written skills inventory, and an oral screening test. The educator evaluates this information; identifies strengths, weaknesses, and needs; and discusses these results, possible accommodations, and the like with the employee. The educator then monitors progress and revises the plan as necessary. Carter and Maher (1995) stated that any industry-based program in any state can replicate this project and ultimately save money by developing a more productive workforce.

Brenda, a worker at a major food processing corporation, credits a workplace literacy program with improving not only her job skills but also her overall outlook

(Sweigart-Guist & Washington, 1995). Diagnosed as having LD in elementary school, she attended both general and special education classes but believed she did not learn much and dropped out after eighth grade. Her company's literacy program gave her the options of enrolling in Adult Basic Education, General Equivalency Diploma (GED) classes, or computer literacy classes. Moreover, her company offered cash incentives for completing programs and demonstrating progress in math and reading skills. Since enrolling in GED classes, Brenda has improved her math, reading, and social skills; has learned to fill out forms and applications; and has begun to advocate for accommodations and help on the job as needed. The proactive approach of her company toward workers with special needs has not only resulted in a more effective employee but also changed Brenda's overall outlook and self-esteem (Sweigart-Guist & Washington, 1995). Brenda's workplace was receptive to working with employees with LD; but, of at least equal importance, Brenda also advocated for herself and took advantage of the available opportunities.

Self-Disclosure as a Means of Self-Advocacy

Embedded in the model of employment success is the necessity of self-advocacy. From finding a job to attaining a leadership role, the process of self-advocacy, when done effectively, demonstrates individual initiative, accountability, and responsibility and encourages the system to be responsive in turn. As one adult with LD succinctly summarized, self-advocacy may be a basic survival issue: "If I hadn't been able to stand up for myself, nobody else would have" (Shessel, 1995, p. 146).

The first issue of self-advocacy is that of self-disclosure: Is the individual willing to be identified as having a learning disability? The ADA clearly protects individuals from being required to identify themselves as having a disability. However, reasonable accommodations and other job modifications are generally restricted to individuals with documented disabilities. Depending on the needs of the individual, self-advocacy may take either form. Therefore, effective self-advocacy requires, at the outset, a clear understanding of what it will take (or will not take) to succeed on the job.

This process of understanding the practical implications of one's strengths and weaknesses (previously termed *reframing*) can and should begin well before the initial foray into the world of work. Children with LD often find their weaknesses are amply evident in a school setting. Parents need to provide a variety of opportunities and experiences to help children find areas in which they can succeed. In this way, they will facilitate a recognition of strengths that may eventually lead to career preferences. Teachers can promote self-evaluation by consistent feedback on what works for a student and what does not; Adelman and Vogel (1990) suggested that the individualized education program conference presents an ideal time for such discussions. Finally, support services to students with LD in college often emphasize this component of self-advocacy. In some programs, the initial meeting between the service provider and student centers on role playing in which the student practices explaining his or her needs and strengths in a concrete and practical manner to the professor.

An inability to articulate one's needs may discourage an individual with LD from self-disclosure on the job, oftentimes with unfortunate results. For example, one young man with LD was having consistent difficulty in maintaining employment, bouncing from one job to another, often unable to meet even modest expectations of his employers. His reading and short-term memory difficulties interfered with completing tasks because

> You read a work order, and you have to remember everything on it, everything to do. . . . So many things to do that I'd leave a few things and forget them and not even know they were there. And somebody would say, "What about this?" (Gerber & Reiff, 1991, p. 64)

He might have found his employer willing to help him compensate had he been willing to disclose and explain his needs. Yet he resisted because "If I did say something, then they would ask me all kinds of details, and I would never be able to answer them. So I just don't let them know" (Gerber & Reiff, 1991, p. 64).

In contrast, effectively communicating one's needs can transform a potential defeat into a victory. Another young man with LD completed training as an electrician. When he interviewed for his first job, he brought up the issue of LD with his prospective employer. "I told him up front that when it comes to writing up service tickets, I guess you should know I'm not retarded, I'm not brain damaged, but I have a problem. . . . In everything I do, my learning disability is there, but that isn't any major reason for things not working out" (Gerber & Reiff, 1991, p. 55). He was hired, and his boss readily supported adjustments and accommodations, largely because this young man was able to communicate his needs. For example, his boss realized that reading the names of parts could be difficult. At his suggestion, his boss "changed parts' names to parts' numbers in the computer for me, only to discover it was a better system for the company altogether" (Gerber & Reiff, 1991, p. 55).

The Potentize course, developed by E. Arnold (personal communication, March 1996), helps adults with LD cope with self-disclosure on the job. Knowing when and how to self-disclose often dictates the outcome of the exchange. The 12-hour seminar teaches strategies for reading or "feeling out" the social dynamics of the workplace, for learning how to ask, and for using a formal expression of self-disclosure in the form of a letter or a brochure. This self-testimonial usually includes the individual's strengths, weaknesses, and compensatory strategies; accommodations needed; and a self-affirming statement.

People with LD who choose to disclose their disability should be aware that the ADA protects them in all aspects of the employment process, including application, testing, hiring, assignments, performance assessment, disciplinary actions, training promotion, medical examinations, layoff/recall, termination, compensation, leave, and benefits. Nevertheless, the effectiveness of the law depends on several types of self-advocacy. In order to utilize these protections, individuals with LD should understand legal concepts such as "qualified" and being able to perform "essential functions," and, when it is necessary, to request "reasonable accommodations." In addition, they must be prepared to answer the following questions when they explain their disability or express their needs to employers:

- What exactly is your disability?
- What does *learning disability* or *dyslexia* mean?
- What kinds of modifications do you need in your work environment?
- What reasonable accommodations do you need? Why/how do you see them as reasonable?
- How can you best be efficient?
- Will your learning disability interfere with your productivity?
- If we need to train you, how do you learn best?
- Can you work well on team?
- Can you be given a lead role in a work group?
- Why should I hire you when I can hire another person who does not have a disability? Aren't I taking a risk? (Gerber, Reiff, & Ginsberg, 1996, p. 101)

Self-Advocacy and Reciprocity

If the individual with LD decides that accommodations are necessary, then self-advocacy plays a critical role in developing both goodness of fit and learned creativity. Self-advocacy may help the adult with LD find an optimal work environment. Self-advocacy also provides a mechanism by which to adapt and change the work environment. Sim-

ilarly, the particular compensatory strategies and modifications necessary for employment success usually depend on the employee with LD advocating for such adaptations. Finally, the process of developing a favorable social ecology in the workplace is
largely predicated on the initiative of the employee with LD. In order to build an interdependent interpersonal support system, employees with LD must be able not only to
express their needs but also to sell themselves as contributing members of the workplace. For example, a person with LD who asks another employee to offer help with a
difficult job task should be prepared to offer some kind of help in return.

M. Radford (personal communication, March 1996), speaking of disabilities in
general, gave an insightful analysis of the workplace dynamics that affect this process:

> Most people underestimate people with disabilities and try to think for them. They have brains
> of their own and usually know best how to cope with their disability. If you tell them the end
> result you want, they will find their own way of getting there. Make sure someone is on hand
> to help them find another way, usually someone with a creative mind, like the "arty" person
> in the department or someone who has suffered the loss of limb or sight or whatever at some
> time in their past. If the person allocated to include the person with the disability in the depart-
> ment is not receptive then it is a no-win situation, and you might as well not attempt it.

Clearly, self-advocacy skills work best in a receptive environment. The young electrician mentioned previously made a determined effort to prove his worth to his business. He can do things that others cannot:

> When my boss, who's worked in the field for years, gets a schematic that's hard to read, he'll
> ask me to help. I don't know what it is, but as far as blue prints and schematics go, I can mas-
> ter that almost immediately. Sometimes I get lost in a schematic, but I am better than the oth-
> ers. (Gerber & Reiff, 1991, p. 56)

His boss was supportive and open to making accommodations largely because this
young adult with LD was such an asset, but he was able to become an asset because
his boss gave him the opportunity. An employer who takes the initiative to understand
the needs of employees with LD offers an environment that encourages self-advocacy.

TALES FROM THE ROADS LESS TRAVELED

Thoughts and Advice from KD, KM, and JC

KD credited much of his own success to tenacity: falling down and getting back up. He
has used his understanding of his strengths, wisdom, and charm by finding people to
support and teach him. His advice to people with LD who are striving for employment
success is simple and succinct: Be true to yourself, but make sure you know what
works best for you. "Make sure you're in the right place. It's not a matter of money or
prestige." KD recognizes that adults with LD are capable of achieving much more than
conventional wisdom would dictate. People with LD should follow their dreams. Nevertheless, he cautions adults with LD to be careful not to choose a profession merely to
prove others wrong, merely to prove that they can do what others told them they
could not. "You're just going to tie yourself into a vicious cycle of proving over and
over again. Rather, put yourself in a situation where you find intensive value in what
you're doing and you're doing it for the right reasons." KD is intimately acquainted
with the struggles that so many people with LD endure. He knows firsthand the associated pain, frustration, and even humiliation; but he realizes that any successful indi-

viduals with LD will have to move beyond any feelings of self-pity, no matter how valid they may seem. "None of us are victims."

KM sees herself as a work in progress who is only beginning to understand the pervasive nature of LD in adulthood:

> I'm just finding out; I'm starting to realize the coping skills or the strategies. I find as I listen to other people I'm starting to learn myself how to deal with it. One is just to recognize it. For myself that has lifted a great deal of pressure or stress. (p. 26)

Somewhat paradoxically, KM's self-exploration of LD has led her to question the very meaning of the label: "If some people can't read or write or do mathematics, but they can do art, they're labeled learning disabled. But what about people who can't do art or music? What are they labeled? They're not labeled anything."

We might be tempted to explain KM's success as the result of "natural artistic talent"; but such rationalizing, as comforting as it may be to those of us who cannot draw a straight line, tends to trivialize KM's arduous journey from "retarded" to respected. She has used a combination of two personal strengths or attributes, forged from her determination to prove herself, to great advantage—persistence and learned creativity. She has been willing to try many solutions to any problem. If one does not work, she switches to another; she does not give up. "I find there's creative ways to problem solve, and it's just trying and being persistent." This approach has worked beautifully in art. KM is goal oriented, even if the goal is process rather than product. Certainly, she exemplifies the construct of goodness of fit; she has found a career that absolutely allows her to exploit her strengths without emphasizing her weaknesses. Success to KM is not a product per se but being involved in the creative process itself. "Coming up with ideas is rewarding. Making them into reality, the blood, sweat and tears is important" (p. 26). Once the vision is realized, it is time to move on to the next project. Perhaps most important, "success is doing something that I like" (p. 26)—and she clearly and dearly loves what she does.

The reasons for JC's success are varied; nevertheless, he believes the driving force is relatively simple to explain:

> The key to success is hard work. Tenacity is more valuable than knowledge and skills. The difference between success and failure is that when you fall down a million times and fail and you get up one million and one times and you succeed—that's all you need is one. (p. 33)

However, for someone with LD, hard work is more likely to pay off when combined with special strategies and compensations. JC learned early on to find advantages in even the most seemingly disadvantageous situations.

> I identify other people's skills and abilities. When I was a teacher in the classroom I found out who the best reader was in the class—and quick! I used those people to read the instructions. So I found readers, and it was my link to the literate world that I would look for other people's strengths. They thought I was the leader. All I did, and any good manager does the same thing, I did everything any good manager would do to tap into the natural resources at his disposal. (p. 32)

JC believed much of his struggle would have been mitigated had employers been more responsive to his needs. Consequently, he aimed much of his advice not only to others with LD but also to the people who employ and work with them:

> The reality may be that it is time for employers to become active in the educational process for personal survival. A change of attitudes is called for. . . . Employers need to develop a spirit

that supports the ongoing learning process and to accept the reality that everyone needs to participate in the teaching process. . . . Education need not end with a diploma, valid or not. Education should be a lifelong process. (Corcoran, 1994, pp. 215–216)

Having the Last Laugh

In many ways, the successes of adults with LD reflect a concerted effort simply to be taken seriously in the workplace. Although we indeed recognize the gravity and earnestness of this endeavor, we need to remember not to take ourselves too seriously. Are we sinking to the level of cliché-ridden platitudes, drawing more on Erma Bombeck than Steven Covey? Research (Gerber & Reiff, 1991; Shessel, 1995) actually indicated that adults with LD not only value a sense of humor but also believe it is a necessary survival strategy. Shessel's (1995) interviews with 14 adults with LD, while depicting a path to employment success consistent with other research, offered the additional strategy of the presence of laughter and humor in day-to-day living. These adults used humor to diffuse anxiety; reduce stress; relieve pressure; and, perhaps most important, regain a balanced and functional perspective on frustrating life events. The simple act of being able to laugh at oneself can be the most effective way of coping with momentary failures and setbacks. People who lack this ability may inadvertently sabotage their own best efforts. As one of Shessel's participants revealed, "One of my biggest personal problem(s) is that I have very impeded difficulty in laughing at myself. I take the world too seriously. Myself I'm much too serious" (Shessel, 1995, p. 158).

The easygoing, upbeat, and cheerful attitudes of adults with LD interviewed by Gerber and Reiff (1991) supported them in employment situations. One woman commented that being "bubbly" was a coping mechanism. Moreover, she reasoned that her ability to laugh at herself helped her deal with the inevitable slipups and allowed her to keep going. We may wonder how some people are able to develop such positive outlooks on life. Although we cannot summarily dismiss some kind of innate predisposition, we must not overlook the effects of environment and upbringing in forging an optimistic approach to life's vicissitudes. Gerber and Reiff (1991) commented that these positive adults shared one experience or critical incident: They all had a favorable recollection of at least one part of their education. Despite any number of negatives in school, eventually having a redemptive experience seemed to reshape and reaffirm their feelings about themselves and their approach to life.

Maintaining a sense of humor is affirming. The ability to laugh at oneself ultimately means that one has enough self-confidence to face momentary setbacks and then move on. When we realize that our own difficulties are probably not the most overwhelming in the history of humankind, we escape the destructive self-centeredness of self-pity. This process can empower people with LD, for it places less emphasis on the difference of having a disability. Instead, it offers the chance to reconnect, to see oneself as similar to anyone else. In the final analysis, the similarities far outweigh the differences. As adults with LD establish such an identity in the workplace, they will stand on an even playing field with all other employees. They may have to travel off the beaten path, but they can reach the same destination.

CONCLUSION

The road less traveled to success for adults with LD is becoming more familiar. The characteristics of working hard; devising strategies; developing good support systems; setting and attaining goals; and knowing, accepting, and understanding one's strengths and weaknesses have surfaced in a number of additional studies investigating success-ful outcomes of adults with LD (see Adelman & Vogel, 1990; Gerber & Reiff, 1991; Rogan & Hartman, 1990; Spekman, Goldberg, & Herman, 1993; Werner, 1993). Devel-oping and applying these characteristics or behaviors will not guarantee success, but adults with LD should be reasonably confident that following the advice of those who have succeeded surely increases the likelihood of achieving in the workplace. Con-versely, ignoring the experiences of others will make the road to success less familiar and predictable and probably more treacherous.

REFERENCES

Adelman, K.A., & Adelman, H.S. (1987). Rodin, Patton, Edison, Wilson, Einstein: Were they really learning disabled? *Journal of Learning Disabilities, 20,* 270–279.

Adelman, P.B., & Vogel, S.A. (1990). College graduates with learning disabilities: Employment attainment and career patterns. *Learning Disability Quarterly, 13,* 154–166.

Americans with Disabilities Act (ADA) of 1990, PL 101-336, 42 U.S.C. §§ 12101 *et seq.*

Anderson, P.L., Kazmierski, S., & Cronin, M.E. (1995). Learning disabilities, employment dis-crimination, and the ADA. *Journal of Learning Disabilities, 28,* 196–204.

Blackorby, J., & Wagner, M. (1996). Longitudinal postschool outcomes of youth with disabilities: Findings from the National Longitudinal Transition Study. *Exceptional Children, 62,* 399–413.

Blocher, D.H. (1989). *Career actualization and life planning.* Denver, CO: Love Publishing.

Carter, J., & Maher, P. (1995). Joint efforts in training. *Linkages, 2*(1), 5–6.

Corcoran, J. (1994). Personal perspective on vocational issues. In P.J. Gerber & H.B. Reiff (Eds.), *Learning disabilities in adulthood: Persisting problems and evolving issues* (pp. 214–218). Austin, TX: PRO-ED.

Gardner, H. (1983). *Frames of mind.* New York: Basic Books.

Gerber, P.J., Ginsberg, R., & Reiff, H.B. (1992). Identifying alterable patterns in employment suc-cess for highly successful adults with learning disabilities. *Journal of Learning Disabilities, 25,* 475–487.

Gerber, P.J., & Reiff, H.B. (1991). *Speaking for themselves: Ethnographic interviews with adults with learning disabilities.* Ann Arbor: The University of Michigan Press.

Gerber, P.J., Reiff, H.B., & Ginsberg, R. (1996). Reframing the learning disabled experience. *Jour-nal of Learning Disabilities, 29*(1), 98–101.

Goleman, D. (1995). *Emotional intelligence.* New York: Bantam Books.

Lee, C. (1992). *Faking it.* Portsmouth, NH: Boynton-Cook.

Lee, C. (1995). You can't "fake it" in the real world. *Linkages, 2*(1), 10–11.

Mikulecky, L. (1995). Literacy practices in today's workplace. *Linkages, 2*(1), 1–2.

Moody, S. (1995). *Dyslexia at work.* Kensington, England: The Adult Dyslexia Organisation.

Reiff, H.B., Gerber, P.J., & Ginsberg, R. (1994). Instructional strategies for long-term success. *Annals of Dyslexia, 44,* 270–288.

Reiff, H., Gerber, P., & Ginsberg, R. (1997). *Exceeding expectations: Successful adults with learning dis-abilities.* Austin, TX: PRO-ED.

Rogan, L.L., & Hartman, L.D. (1990). Adult outcomes of learning disabled students ten years after initial follow-up. *Learning Disabilities Focus, 5,* 91–102.

Shaw, S.F. (1991). Preparing students with learning disabilities for postsecondary education: Issues and future needs. *Learning Disabilities: A Multidisciplinary Journal, 2*(1), 21–26.

Shessel, I. (1995). *Adults with learning disabilities: Profiles in survival.* Unpublished doctoral disser-tation, University of Toronto, Ontario, Canada.

Spekman, N.J., Goldberg, R.J., & Herman, K.L. (1993). An exploration of risk and resilience in the lives of individuals with learning disabilities. *Learning Disabilities Research and Practice, 8*(1), 11–18.

Sweigart-Guist, B., & Washington, C.W. (1995). Brenda's TIPs on workplace literacy. *Linkages, 2*(1), 11.

Werner, E.E. (1993). Risk and resilience in individuals with learning disabilities: Lessons learned from the Kauai longitudinal study. *Learning Disabilities Research and Practice, 8*(1), 28–34.

White, W.J. (1992). The post school adjustment of persons with learning disabilities: Current sta-tus and future projections. *Journal of Learning Disabilities, 25,* 448–456.

V

Future Directions in Learning Disabilities, Literacy, and Adult Education

In Section V, Stephen Reder reflects on the contributions of this book to our emerging understanding of the relationship between learning disabilities (LD) and adult literacy. Writing from the perspective of an expert in adult literacy, Reder reviews what has been learned—and what remains to be understood—about LD as applied to future practice and research in adult literacy education. Drawing on the contributions in this book as well as on other research, Chapter 17 examines the relationship between adult literacy and LD in terms of some key questions frequently discussed among experts in adult literacy:

- What is the evidence that there are students with LD in adult education settings? How common are such students?
- (How) should adult education students with LD be identified?
- (How) should adult education students with LD be taught differently?
- What types of instructional interventions are effective for adult education students with LD?
- What types of noninstructional support services are needed to serve adult education students with LD?
- What resources are available to assist service providers serving adult education students with LD?

In considering these issues, Chapter 17 addresses the nature of the controversy—and some of its scientific and philosophical origins—that has emerged among service providers who provide LD services to school children. Reder discusses how this controversy has been carried over into the field of adult literacy education. He suggests productive ways in which research can be used to resolve this controversy and to bring about effective services and learning supports for adults who have LD.

17

Reflections on Theory, Practice, and Research

What We Have Learned and What We Still Need to Know

Stephen Reder

Adult literacy educators increasingly hear about the prevalence and special needs of their students who have learning disabilities (LD). However, many encounter conflicting accounts and descriptions of the nature and extent of the "LD problem" as well as contradictory advice about whether to treat such learners differently from other adult education students. How should adult literacy teachers understand LD in their day-to-day thinking about and practice of adult literacy education? As a specialist in adult literacy education, I bring to this book a number of important questions:

What is the evidence that there are students with LD in adult education settings? How common are such students?

(How) should adult education students with LD be identified?

(How) should adult education students with LD be taught differently?

What types of instructional interventions are effective for adult education students with LD?

What types of noninstructional support services are needed to serve adult education students with LD?

What resources are available to assist service providers serving adult education students with LD?

This chapter reflects on these questions in light of the many insights and resources provided by the authors of this book. The chapter is a reflective essay, beginning with a review of some of the contributions of this book toward understanding these issues and posing new questions arising from current understandings, questions calling for additional research, and experimentation with promising interventions. The chapter ends with a speculative vision of the directions in which the field of adult literacy education needs to head in order to better serve adult students with LD.

Despite growing attention to LD in adult education (e.g., the description by Sturomski, Lenz, Scanlon, and Catts of the National Center for Adult Literacy and Learning Disabilities; see Chapter 5), practitioners still lack a solid base of knowledge and understanding about definitions, identification criteria, and intervention techniques for LD among adults. Although professional development and dissemination efforts such as those described by Sturomski and colleagues and by Podhajski (see Chapters 5 and 10) are helping to address this gap, the needed research base is still inadequate. Part of the difficulty is that research on adult LD carries many of the complexities of research on LD in children (Fowler & Scarborough, 1993).

Research on LD in children has been impeded by several factors, including diverse definitions, identification and assessment procedures, and theoretical perspectives on LD among such fields as education, neurology, psychology, and speech-language pathology (Cousin, Diaz, Flores, & Hernandez, 1995; Lyon, Gray, & Kavanagh, 1993; Moats & Lyon, 1993). The relatively recent establishment of LD as a federally designated category of handicap has limited the time that has been available for systematizing clinical experience and compiling and analyzing data for research. Consensus about operationalizing the definition and characterization of LD thus has not yet emerged from research with children, which has tended to undermine the credibility of the concept of LD. These circumstances have led many critics to doubt its scientific validity and its clinical and educational utility (Coles, 1987; Cousin et al., 1995; McDermott, 1993; Stanovich & Siegel, 1994; Sternberg, 1997). Significant progress is taking place, however, with systematic funding from the National Institute of Child Health and Human Development and other agencies. These research programs impose more rigorous and systematic criteria on the definition, diagnosis, and treatment of LD and follow its development in children over time (Lyon, 1995; Lyon et al., 1993; Moats & Lyon, 1993).

Research on LD among adults is even less well-developed (and has been very poorly funded). It is clear that many children with school-identified LD continue to have as many poor literacy skills as adults, whereas others with LD may not have been identified either by schools or clinically (Reder, 1995; Vogel & Reder, 1997; see also Chapters 3 and 9). Adults with LD do participate in basic skills classes, although the numbers involved are extremely uncertain.

Some adult literacy educators, believing that many of their students may well have LD, have tried to apply school-derived concepts, terminology, and methodologies of LD. In so doing, they have sometimes encountered the aforementioned uncertainty and skepticism expressed by some researchers and practitioners about LD. This chapter considers how this book's contributions can help adult literacy educators begin to answer some of these important questions about LD that arise in their everyday practices.

SIX ISSUES

This chapter is organized around the six major issues noted in the previous list of questions.

What Is the Evidence That There Are Students with LD in Adult Education Settings? How Common Are Such Students?

The LD debate described previously, "following" students as they move from schools to adult education, remains at the background of ongoing research and discourse among adult educators. The uncertainties about how many adults have LD (including how many in adult education programs or other service delivery streams) cannot be easily separated from more general questions about the various definitions and ways of assessing LD. A number of problems concerning the definition and extent of LD are typically raised by careful (and sometimes skeptical) researchers.

Some researchers have called into question the validity and utility of school-based identification of LD (e.g., Coles, 1987; Cousin et al., 1995; Fowler & Scarborough, 1993; McDermott, 1993). These writers and many others have pointed out the many problems associated with the categorical identification of and funding for individuals with LD within special education. The enhanced resources available for students identified as having LD have, according to many researchers, resulted in the confounding of LD with diverse, partially overlapping, and/or co-occurring difficulties such as attention difficulties, general reading difficulties, cultural differences, and behavioral difficulties. Once officially identified as having a learning disability, most students remain in this categorical state and may receive educational services neither designed nor well suited to their specific needs. McDermott (1993), for example, described this fiscally motivated and administratively driven (mis)classification process as "the acquisition of a student by a learning disability."

These well-known difficulties within school identification of LD do not constitute sufficient reason, as some critics have suggested, to abandon the concept of LD and associated special instructional, protective, and supportive services that do make a difference for many students. These difficulties do point out, however, the need for improved definition, identification, and implementation of educational programs to better serve children with LD. Chapters 1 and 3 in this book describe the history of various definitions of LD and note some of the characteristic differences among school-, clinically, research-, and self-identified ways of assessing LD. Vogel notes in Chapter 1 that there really can be no single definition suitable for all purposes, and thus there can be no single enumeration of individuals with LD nor any one answer to questions such as the two posed in this section about how many adults or how many adult education students have LD.

Many researchers have expressed skepticism in the face of multiple definitions and assessment techniques for LD. Without standard definitions and assessment techniques, it is undeniably more difficult to compare and replicate results of disparate studies and synthesize evaluations of interventions based on differing criteria. Other researchers have taken a somewhat different stance regarding multiple definitions and assessments, seeing them not as evidence of poorly operationalized scientific constructs but as indicative of complex, multidimensional phenomena. Rossi and Wolman (1996), for example, analyzed the overlap among multiple measures of disability in schoolchildren, some provided by students, some by their parents, some by their teachers, and some by their school administrators. Although there was relatively little overlap among these multiple measures of disability, Rossi and Wolman did not interpret these results as reflecting a lack of reliability or validity but rather as a multidimensional construct of student disability that appeared differently from the multiple perspectives of students, parents, teachers, and school officials (Rossi & Wolman, 1996; Rossi, Herting, & Wolman, 1997).

Other researchers have suggested reframing the study and understanding of LD in terms of culturally patterned differences among the individuals' ways of learning and society's ways of responding to individual differences. The VODD Group, for example, argued for replacing what it termed the *reductionist* (or what Coles [1987] termed the *medical*) paradigm for LD with a *constructivist* paradigm based on sociocultural models of contexts for teaching and learning (Cousin et al., 1995). Rather than attempting to locate the phenomenon of learning disability as a deficiency or disability in the individual, they proposed a nested set of sociocultural contexts for teaching and learning: *social/ cultural/community; district/school; classroom/teacher; group;* and *mind.* The VODD Group approach offers considerable insight into how society in general—and how schools in particular—are organized to deal with LD, an instance of how the dominant culture more generally interprets and organizes differences and diversity among people.

This approach explicitly rejects the *individual* locus of LD as superfluous and even harmful. McDermott, for example, believed that "without the social arrangements for making something of differential rates of learning, there is no such thing as LD" (1993, p. 3). Osher and Webb (1994) offered something of a middle ground between the radical constructivist position and the "medical" model for LD. They argued that LD are a subset of a broader class of *learning difficulties,* which are in turn a subset of a broader class of *learning differences.* Within this framework, it is possible to locate both the classical LD concept, which maintains that the uniqueness of learning disability stems from a presumed central nervous system disorder, and the constructivist position, which holds that contextual factors determine which of a wide variety of learning differences are taken to be learning difficulties (or even LD).

Ultimately the critical difference among positions—and the key point in considering the nature and extent of LD among adults—probably comes down to two considerations: 1) whether learning disability is taken to be an underlying neurological condition, manifested as a series of difficulties in learning to read, write, and compute; and 2) whether there are interventions that are differentially effective for adults identified as having LD as opposed to other adults presenting similar difficulties in reading, writing, and so forth. Let us look briefly at each of these points.

On the first point, there is a persuasive body of evidence from a large, long-term longitudinal study in Connecticut (Shaywitz, Shaywitz, Fletcher, & Escobar, 1990) of reading disabilities in representative samples of children conducted in a way that is independent of how schools classified or treated them. There is strong evidence that reading disabilities represent a persistent impairment rather than a developmental lag within typical development; the preponderance of children who have dyslexia in third grade continue to have dyslexia in ninth grade (Lyon, 1994; Lyon et al., 1993; Stanovich & Siegel, 1994). Reading disabilities (i.e., dyslexia) affect approximately one child in five (Shaywitz, Escobar, Shaywitz, Fletcher, & Makuch, 1992). The core impairment in dyslexia appears to be phonological awareness and its attendant abilities to segment and blend constituent sound units. There is strong evidence for a genetic etiology for reading disability, with impairments in phonological awareness having the greatest degree of heritability (Duane & Gray, 1991; Lyon, 1995).

On the second point, there is also growing evidence that certain types of educational interventions are differentially effective (and often bring about long-term success) for children with dyslexia. The interested reader is referred to Duane and Gray (1991) and Lyon (1995) for further details about this important, emerging line of research.

So what does all this have to say about our question concerning the prevalence of LD in adults, particularly those in adult education programs? Because it is widely believed that children with LD have these disabilities on a lifelong basis (Fink, 1995; Gerber & Reiff, 1991; see also Chapter 16), the 20% prevalence figure for children in the research-identified samples of children in the large-scale Connecticut study (Shaywitz et al., 1990) described is one reasonable prevalence estimate for adults. Vogel reviews in Chapter 1 a range of such prevalence estimates, finding that they vary according to the definition and method of identification used. The school-identified rate is approximately 5%, and the self-reported rate among adults 16 years of age and older is approximately 3%, both of which are understandably lower than the 20% figure from the research-based studies of children *affected* by dyslexia. Clearly further research is needed to better characterize the prevalence in adults. Longitudinal studies such as the Connecticut study are now following their research-identified population of children with dyslexia into their early 20s, making it far easier to estimate adult prevalence.

The prevalence of LD among adults with lower levels of literacy proficiency and lower levels of educational attainment should be much higher. Analyzing self-identified LD rates from the National Adult Literacy Survey, Reder (1995) and Vogel and Reder (in press; see also Chapter 3) found elevated prevalence rates for adults at the lower literacy and educational attainment levels. Among U.S.-born adults at the lowest level of literacy and without a high school diploma, the prevalence rate is 11% (by my calculation). This is somewhat lower than the range of generally informal prevalence estimates for adults in adult education and various social service programs, which have been reported to be as high as 40%–80% (Osher & Webb, 1994; see also Chapter 1). Nevertheless, there has been a dearth of clinical validation data to substantiate such reports of particular prevalence rates for LD in specific service streams or in other subgroups of adults.

The Washington state study described by Giovengo, Moore, and Young is a major contribution in this regard (see Chapter 9). Among its many groundbreaking features, this study screened a random sample of adults in Aid to Families with Dependent Children (AFDC; now called the Temporary Assistance for Needy Families) for LD and then validated the screening (regardless of the screening outcome) against a full clinical diagnostic assessment. The overall results are that 36% of the AFDC clients were diagnosed as having a learning disability. Only about one third of those diagnosed as having a learning disability recall being previously identified; conversely, about one fifth of those not diagnosed as having a learning disability recall being previously so identified. This study thus not only provides firm evidence of a relatively high prevalence rate in clients of an important social service program but also confirms the substantial misidentification and misdiagnosis of LD in schools. Other aspects of this important study will be subsequently considered.

Unfortunately, there are no comparable data for clientele of other adult programs, including adult education and literacy programs. There are, to be sure, a few large-scale national surveys that ask adults to self-report on LD, including the National Adult Literacy Survey and the National Educational Longitudinal Study. Unfortunately, such broad population studies do not sufficiently sample the subgroup of interest: adults who participate in basic skills education programs. As a result, the subsample sizes of current or recent program participants are too small to accurately estimate prevalence rates for adult education students. It should be possible, and would be highly desirable, to conduct special studies modeled after the Giovengo et al. study (see Chapter 9), in which representative samples of adult learners are given full diagnostic assessments for LD. Such studies—if appropriately designed—could go a long way toward clarifying not only overall prevalence rates but also the interaction of LD with learner recruitment, participation, and retention in programs.

(How) Should Adult Education Students with LD Be Identified?

This question is worded as "(How) should . . . " to remind us that there are two nested questions here: Should adult education students be identified as having LD in the first place, and, if so, how would this identification process best be accomplished? The question of whether individual adults should be identified is, of course, a complex matter that involves significant legal, ethical, and educational issues. As Rothstein discusses in detail, individuals have rights both to confidentiality (i.e., nonidentification, nondisclosure) and to the protections and resources afforded by the law should they choose to have themselves identified as having a learning disability (see Chapter 2). Vogel carefully considers the ethical and pedagogical issues involved in deciding whether to screen/assess/identify LD among adult learners (see Chapter 1). Together, these chapters indicate that any screening, diagnostic assessment, or other identification procedures should be implemented in programs carefully and sensitively in relation to the ethical and legal considerations involved. It would be useful for programs and practitioners to have specific guidelines and illustrative implementations of such procedures. This is an important area for further development.

Given that appropriate procedures and safeguards are in place, and that individuals choose to be evaluated or identified for LD, or both, how should such identification take place in adult education programs? Contributors to this volume offer a number of promising approaches, techniques, and resources. The Tool Kit described by Sturomski et al. offers important standards and stages for developing effective screening practices and tools (see Chapter 5). Readers should be watching for the official release of the Tool Kit by the National Adult Literacy and Learning Disabilities Center—the preview presented in Chapter 5 suggests the Tool Kit will contain a host of useful and effective tools and resources.

Other chapters in this volume describe specific tools for screening adults for LD. The particular examples included in this volume were selected because of previously conducted or ongoing empirical studies to validate the screening process in relation to full clinical diagnosis. Payne describes one such promising tool, an easily administered checklist and informal assessment process for screening adults likely to have LD (see Chapter 6). The previously mentioned validation study conducted in Washington state (see Chapter 9) found that the Payne screening system correctly identified 71% of individuals clinically diagnosed as having LD. This indicates that it could be a highly cost-effective and relatively unobtrusive component of a more comprehensive screening and assessment system in adult education and other social service programs. The Power-Path system described by Weisel offers another promising, field-tested screening procedure (see Chapter 7). The PowerPath, which includes techniques and tools for client intake, a behavior checklist, learning inventories, and a number of programmatically useful reporting capabilities, has been subjected to a number of validation studies over a long period of time. Fawcett and Nicolson describe a third promising screening resource, the Dyslexia Adult Screening Test (DAST; see Chapter 8). Developed in the United Kingdom, the DAST consists of 11 performance tasks, the results of which generate a "risk" score for adults in need of full assessment. Validation studies of the DAST are under way.

Practitioners may find these and other such resources and tools very helpful. The specific chapters provide further details on the various resources and their use and some basic results from validation studies of the screening instruments. Further validation will likely be helpful to practitioners, particularly if it helps link results of screening to needed full assessment and if the results of such assessments are carefully articulated to appropriate instructional designs. Some of the tools described—and many more are expected in the Tool Kit released by the National Adult Literacy and Learning Disabilities Center—have interfaces to recommended teaching procedures and tools. The careful linking of assessment to effective instruction, certainly one of the key reasons for identifying adult education students with LD, remains an area in which further research and development is vitally needed.

(How) Should Adult Education Students with LD Be Taught Differently?

This question is also expressed in a "(How) should . . ." format because of its two essentially nested parts: *Should* adult education students with LD be given different instruction than other adult education students, and, if so, which different instructional interventions should be used? Although several chapters in this book deal with the second part of the question, it is important to review our assumptions regarding the first part.

There are many researchers and some adult educators who strongly believe that there is no good reason why adult literacy instruction should be different for adults with LD than for other adults. There are, of course, those who hold the opinion that there really is no such thing as LD—there are just difficulties and differences in learning and literacy abilities. Such arguments were considered in detail previously and need not be repeated here. However, even among those who recognize the distinctiveness of LD in children, there is a subgroup of researchers who believe that such differences are not relevant to adult literacy instruction. Fowler and Scarborough (1993), for example, argued exactly such a position. They believed that poor adult readers, *regardless of the etiology of their reading problems*, should all be given the same literacy instruction as other adult students. Fowler and Scarborough argued that, regardless of why young children may have initially encountered difficulty in learning to read (e.g., because of possible LD or because of social or cultural differences), the results are practically indistinguishable by the time they reach adulthood as poor readers. Their accumulated history of extremely poor or even no reading throughout their school years leaves them with relatively little academic knowledge, skill, and vocabulary, all of which combine (in what Stanovich [1986] has termed the *Matthew effect*) into a "garden variety" poor adult reader whose etiology is largely irrelevant for purposes of instructional interventions (Fowler & Scarborough, 1993). Fowler and Scarborough suggested that the same type of instructional remediation is equally effective with all such poor readers as adults, regardless of whether they may have had specific LD in childhood.

On this point, many adult educators seem to agree. Although some may believe that adults with LD constitute a distinguishable subtype of poor readers, they still believe that good instructional interventions for such adults will work equally well with all adult students. Ross-Gordon (see Chapter 4 as well as her earlier work [1989]) has identified a number of teaching practices that are described as being equally effective for adult literacy students with and without LD. Multisensory teaching and experiencing of written materials, for example, are techniques frequently mentioned as effective for all adult literacy students, with or without LD.

There is undoubtedly a great deal of pedagogical and clinical experience underlying beliefs that good teaching will be effective for all adult literacy students. Additional research is certainly needed, however, to identify more effective instructional practices for adult education students with and without LD and to determine the extent to which specialized instructional practices may benefit students with particular needs and difficulties.

What Types of Instructional Interventions Are
Effective for Adult Education Students with LD?

Several of the specific instructional programs described in this volume are based on the assumption discussed previously, that teaching strategies effective with adults with reading difficulties will benefit all adult literacy students. Podhajski's professional staff development program and Wilson's Reading Program (described in Chapters 10 and 11, respectively), are two well-known examples of such an approach. The forthcoming Tool Kit described in Chapter 5 will include, in addition to the aforementioned screening techniques and tools, additional examples of effective instructional practices and resources for adults with LD.

Patton, Cronin, and Bassett emphasize, in discussing the numeracy abilities and needs of adult students, that these competencies must be blended into a curriculum that derives directly from everyday experience and needs originating in other environments—such as the workplace or education and training environments (see Chapter 12). They advocate a life-skills approach for students both with and without LD. It seems important that model curricula embodying these various pedagogical principles be developed and carefully evaluated. Many researchers have found the life skills and the phonologically oriented teaching approaches to be philosophically at odds with one another. At the same time, many practitioners, in this writer's experience, informally blend the two approaches into their everyday classroom practices. Further research, documentation, and evaluation of actual instruction and learning processes would be helpful in this area.

An important adjunct to direct instruction for many adult students with LD are various assistive technologies that learners find helpful to compensate for the LD. Raskind carefully separates these assistive technology devices into a number of categories, including those that help with producing written language, with reading, with listening, with memory and organization, and with math (see Chapter 13). In thinking about these technologies, it may be instructive and helpful for us to think in terms of the broad continuum between learning and performance in the everyday functioning of adults. Emerging research on informal learning in the workplace, for example, suggests that learning and doing are often inseparable components of everyday activities at work. The design and application of assistive technologies should therefore be explored not only for instructional support but also for supporting both performance and learning that involves written materials in workplace and other noninstructional settings. Bypass strategies for adults with LD, in this conception, may also offer promising new approaches for contextualized learning in everyday environments.

What Types of Noninstructional Support Services Are
Needed to Serve Adult Education Students with LD?

It was suggested previously that assistive technology devices be adapted for support of students in the workplace and other noninstructional environments. This is one promising possibility for active research and development. Other support services are essential to facilitating the education and life chances of adults with LD. Several authors in this volume describe particular forms of support that have been effective in helping adults with LD experience successful transitions into the workforce and, more generally, into adult life. Crawford—based on years of operating a successful employment readiness and training program—points out how important customized approaches to assessment and training are in preparing adults with LD for employment and self-sufficiency (see Chapter 14). He argues persuasively that the standardized approaches to assessment and training envisioned in larger-scale training and employment initiatives are generally ineffective for adults with LD. These approaches need to be replaced with new *abilities-based* approaches based on principles of authentic assessment, which are able to customize needs assessment and training in terms of individual strengths, weaknesses, and interests in relation to employment opportunities.

There are, of course, different models of transition support programs that incorporate principles of authentic assessment. Crawford's program is a residential, community-based model. Although highly effective for its participants, other models may be more appropriate for some adults with LD. Koller and Holliday consider a different model of transition support based on principles of authentic assessment (see Chapter 15). Their approach, which blends a variety of field-tested program features and effective practices, is described as functional and holistic and is organized by an *authentic self-advocacy* model. The central importance of supporting self-advocacy is also clear in Reiff's discussion of employment success (see Chapter 16). Reiff examined the key factors in the life experiences of individual adults with LD who had achieved vocational success. A common ingredient was heightened self-awareness and self-advocacy. It is clear in his study and in other studies of successful adults with LD (e.g., Fink, 1995; Gerber & Reiff, 1991; Vogel & Adelman, 1992) that effective adaptations to both educational and workplace environments generally depend on adults making good decisions, compensating for their weaknesses, and taking advantage of their strengths. The key roles of self-awareness and self-efficacy are clear in all of these cases.

A priority area for future development, experimentation, and research is therefore the development of new kinds of resources and tools to help support adults with LD to make such adaptations and transitions successfully. Chapter 5 describes the forthcoming Tool Kit that will compile effective screening and teaching tools. There is an equally important need to develop effective tools and resources into what might be termed an "Identity Tool Kit." Such an effort would synthesize relevant research and bring together demonstrably effective practices for helping adults with LD to develop better self-understanding, self-advocacy, and strategies for taking advantage of their strengths and interests while compensating for their weaknesses. The contributions of Crawford, Koller and Holliday, and Reiff to this volume constitute an excellent beginning to such an endeavor.

What Resources Are Available to Assist Service Providers Serving Adult Education Students with LD?

There are many resources available to assist adult education practitioners to better serve their students who have LD. Ross-Gordon offers an excellent overview (and points to a range of resources) regarding the programmatic context for serving students in adult education programs who have learning disabilities (see Chapter 4). Legal issues and resources are considered by Rothstein (see Chapter 2). State-of-the-art screening and assessment techniques are presented by Sturomski et al.; Payne, Weisel, Fawcett, and Nicolson; and Giovengo et al. (see Chapters 5–9). Promising instructional delivery models are examined by Podhajski, Wilson, Patton, et al., and Raskind (see Chapters 10–13). Models for integrating needs assessment and transition support are presented by Crawford, Koller and Holliday, and Reiff (see Chapters 14–16). The appendices to this book offer a wealth of other information, resources, and suggestions for additional information and resources.

CONCLUSION

Given the aforementioned contributions and suggestions for additional research and development, what else is needed to be better able to serve students with LD in adult literacy and education programs? Undoubtedly practitioners in adult education and literacy need a better information base about the issues in and methods for identifying and teaching adults with LD. Although national training and dissemination efforts such as the National Adult Literacy and Learning Disabilities Center are making some headway, the research base must be strengthened before such efforts go to full scale and can have their desired impact on the field. Better data are needed concerning the outcomes associated with the many options in screening, assessing, remediating, and/or accommodating the range of LD. It is unlikely that sufficient high-quality data will become available to the field for addressing such questions until there is a major commitment to funding the needed research. The investment of the National Institutes of Health in sophisticated research programs on LD among children has added extremely important theoretical and practical information to the research base. It is already helping schools and other professionals to work more effectively with children and adolescents. Similar investments are needed to study carefully the extent, scope, and impact of LD among adults and the effectiveness of various interventions.

In terms of improving service delivery to adults with LD, there are two major areas needing attention that have not been mentioned yet. First, we need to think carefully about how best to provide an integrated framework for assisting adults with LD. Existing services are generally too fragmented and place too much of a burden on the individual to integrate disjointed and often uncoordinated services into meaningful wholes. Too often the adult education student with a strong likelihood of having a learning disability—if screened at all—is referred to another service provider or another agency for assessment, then to another entity for accommodation or advocacy support, with little communication between professionals working in these niches and adult literacy instructors. Although a shared set of tools and resources—which seems to be the focus of current development efforts—may certainly alleviate some of these difficulties, services are all too likely to remain fragmented, with the burden of integration and coordination being left to the individual learner. Although we have seen some promising model programs that integrate services in this way, systemic change among relatively fragmented existing providers and agencies is undoubtedly required to implement such models on a large scale. We certainly can advocate for and work toward this possibility, but it may be unrealistic to rely entirely on this approach. Another promising strategy may be to develop tools and resources directly for the adult learner with LD. Although screening and teaching tools being developed to assist practitioners will be very helpful, tools that learners can use directly to enhance their capacity to integrate resources and services are also essential. The "identity tool kit" described previously is one conception of such a strategy.

Another important consideration is that researchers and practitioners in the fields of adult literacy, education, and LD must come to see a continuum of programmatic possibilities between improving a person's skills (heretofore the province of adult literacy education) and improving environmental supports (accommodation, heretofore the province of LD specialists). In between these two endpoints lies a largely unexplored domain of programmatic possibilities that may be understood as improving the fit of individuals with LD to their environment. I believe this volume offers some glimpses of this rich, uncharted territory that we now must explore together.

REFERENCES

Coles, G. (1987). *The learning mystique*. New York: Pantheon.

Cousin, P.T., Diaz, E., Flores, B., & Hernandez, J. (1995). Looking forward: Using a sociocultural perspective to reframe the study of learning disabilities. *Journal of Learning Disabilities, 28*(10), 656–663.

Duane, D.D., & Gray, D.B. (Eds.). (1991). *The reading brain: The biological basis of dyslexia*. Timonium, MD: York Press.

Fink, R.P. (1995). Successful dyslexics: A constructivist study of passionate interest reading. *Journal of Adolescent & Adult Literacy, 39*(4), 268–280.

Fowler, A.E., & Scarborough, H.S. (1993). *Should reading-disabled adults be distinguished from other adults seeking literacy instruction? A review of theory and research*. Philadelphia: National Center on Adult Literacy, University of Pennsylvania.

Gerber, P.J., & Reiff, H.B. (1991). *Speaking for themselves: Ethnographic interviews with adults with learning disabilities*. Ann Arbor: The University of Michigan Press.

Lyon, G.R. (1995). Research initiatives in learning disabilities: Contributions from scientists supported by the National Institute of Child Health and Human Development. *Journal of Child Neurology, 10*(Suppl. 1), S120–S126.

Lyon, G.R., Gray, D.B., & Kavanagh, J.F. (Eds.). (1993). *Better understanding of learning disabilities: New views from research and their implications for education and public policies*. Baltimore: Paul H. Brookes Publishing Co.

McDermott, R. (1993). The acquisition of a child by a learning disability. In S. Chaiklin & J. Lave (Eds.), *Understanding practice: Focus on activity and context* (pp. 269–305). Cambridge, England: Cambridge University Press.

Moats, L.C., & Lyon, G.R. (1993). Learning disabilities in the United States: Advocacy, science, and the future of the field. *Journal of Learning Disabilities, 26*, 282–294.

Osher, D., & Webb, L. (1994). *Adult literacy, learning disabilities, and social context: Conceptual foundations for a learner-centered approach*. Washington, DC: Pelavin Associates.

Reder, S. (1995). *Literacy, education and learning disabilities*. Portland, OR: Northwest Regional Educational Laboratory.

Reder, S., & Vogel, S.A. (1997). Lifespan employment and economic outcomes for adults with self-reported learning disabilities. In P. Gerber & D. Brown (Eds.), *Learning disabilities and employment* (pp. 371–394). Austin, TX: PRO-ED.

Ross-Gordon, J.M. (1989). *Adults with learning disabilities: An overview of the adult educator*. Columbus: Ohio State University.

Rossi, R., Herting, J., & Wolman, J. (1997). *Profiles of students with disabilities as identified in NELS: 88*. Technical Report 97-254. Washington, DC: U.S. Department of Education, National Center for Education Statistics.

Rossi, R., & Wolman, J. (1996). *Characteristics, experiences and educational outcomes of students with disabilities*. Washington, DC: U.S. Department of Education.

Shaywitz, S.E., Escobar, M.D., Shaywitz, B.A., Fletcher, J.M., & Makuch, R. (1992). Evidence that dyslexia may represent the lower tail of a normal distribution of reading ability. *New England Journal of Medicine, 326*, 145–150.

Shaywitz, S.E., Shaywitz, B.A., Fletcher, J.M., & Escobar, M.D. (1990). Prevalence of reading disability in boys and girls: Results of the Connecticut Longitudinal Study. *JAMA, 64*, 998–1002.

Stanovich, K.E. (1986). Matthew effects in reading: Some consequences of individual differences in the acquisition of literacy. *Reading Research Quarterly, 21*, 360–407.

Stanovich, K.E., & Siegel, L.S. (1994). Phenotypic performance profile of children with reading disabilities: A regression-based test of the phonological-core variable difference model. *Journal of Educational Psychology, 86*, 24–53.

Sternberg, R.J. (1997, August 25). Extra credit for doing poorly. *New York Times*, (p. A15)

Vogel, S.A., & Adelman, P.B. (1992). The success of college students with learning disabilities: Factors related to educational attainment. *Journal of Learning Disabilities, 25*(7), 430–441.

Vogel, S.A., & Reder, S. (in press). Literacy proficiency among adults with self-reported learning disabilities. In M.C. Smith (Ed.), *Literacy for the 21st century: Research, policy and practice*. Westport, CT: Greenwood Publishing (Praeger).

Appendix A

Accommodations

It is generally accepted that Section 504 of the Rehabilitation Act of 1973 (PL 93-112) defines *accommodations* as those measures that provide individuals with learning disabilities (LD) access to educational programs or activities. These accommodations are mandated for individuals with diagnosed LD. However, there are many adults in literacy, adult secondary education, and adult education instructional environments who are unaware that they have a learning disability for a variety of reasons (see Chapter 1). This appendix identifies some characteristics of adults with LD and lists a variety of accommodations that may be helpful if the student has a suspected or identified learning disability.

SECTION I—IDENTIFICATION OF ADULTS WITH CHARACTERISTICS OF LEARNING DISABILITIES

Section I is directed toward teachers who observe the characteristics of adults with LD among their students, but these students have not disclosed that they have been formally identified in the past.

1. Discuss your observations with a student when you suspect that he or she may have a learning disability.
2. Explore whether the student had been previously identified as having a learning disability or has been receiving special education services.
3. Explain the concept of LD in nontechnical language.
4. Explain how it may be beneficial to the student and you, as the teacher, to know whether the student has a learning disability.
5. Determine whether the student seems to have a learning disability, and, if so, refer the student for screening and, if warranted, evaluation.

SECTION II—INSTRUCTIONAL ACCOMMODATIONS

There are two basic types of accommodations that teachers can provide for students with LD: instructional and testing. However, regardless of whether students are formally identified as having a learning disability, the following instructional recommendations may facilitate all students' learning:

1. Make the goals of the instructional program and/or course available 4–6 weeks before the beginning of class, and, when possible, be available to discuss the goals with students who are considering the course.

2.   Begin class with a review of the previous session and an overview of topics/activities that will be covered that day.
3.   Use the chalkboard or overhead projector to outline material, being mindful of legibility and the necessity to read what is written aloud.
4.   Explain technical language, specific terminology, and foreign words.
5.   Emphasize important points, main ideas, and key concepts orally, and/or highlight them with colored pens on an overhead machine.
6.   Speak distinctly and at a relaxed pace, pausing occasionally to respond to questions, for students to interact, and for students to discuss how the skill or information you are discussing may be helpful to them in their job, at home, or in the community.
7.   Notice and respond to nonverbal signals of confusion or frustration.
8.   Try to eliminate or at least diminish auditory and visual classroom distractions such as background noise or a flickering fluorescent light.
9.   Leave time for a question-and-answer period and/or discussion periodically and at the end of each segment of the class.
10.   Try to determine if students understand the material by periodically asking for students to volunteer to give an example, a summary, or a response to a question.
11.   Limit lectures to 10- to 15-minute segments, and alternate minilectures with activities, discussion, or question-and-answer periods.
12.   Give assignments in writing as well as orally, and be available for clarification.
13.   Provide a suggested timeline when making long-range assignments, and suggest appropriate checkpoints.
14.   Be available before and/or after class for clarification of material, assignments, and/or readings.
15.   Select a textbook with a study guide (if available) that offers question-and-answer sessions, review sessions, and frequent practice quizzes.
16.   Help students find study partners and organize study groups.
17.   Provide study questions for exams that demonstrate the format that will be used as well as the content. Provide a model exemplary answer that delineates what comprises a good response.

Note: Students with LD often have difficulty reading aloud despite good silent reading comprehension. Calling only on students who volunteer to read aloud will avoid unnecessary embarrassment.

SECTION III—SUGGESTED TESTING/EVALUATION ACCOMMODATIONS

The specific testing and/or evaluation accommodations should be provided on an individual basis after considering the student's type of learning disability, the severity of the disability, the specific course content, and the course objectives. Suggested accommodations include the following:

1.   Allow extended time on exams.
2.   Provide a reader or tape-recorded exam when the exam entails a lot of reading (e.g., a multiple-choice exam).
3.   Provide the exam in an alternative format (if appropriate to subject matter); for instance, objective instead of essay or vice versa.

4. Allow students to take exams in a separate room that is free from disturbances.
5. Allow students to answer exam questions using methods other than writing (e.g., orally, taping, typing).
6. Allow students to clarify or rephrase exam questions in their own words as a comprehension check before answering the questions.
7. Analyze not only the final solutions to problems (e.g., math word problems) but also the process the student used to reach the solution.
8. Allow alternative methods to demonstrate mastery of class objectives (e.g., using a demonstration, construction, drawing, or presentation).
9. Allow students to use adaptive technology such as a hand-held spell checker or a word processor.
10. Avoid unduly complex sentence structure such as double negatives and embedded questions within questions.
11. Provide ample blank space or additional exam booklets for students with large handwriting.
12. Provide alternatives to computer-scoring answer sheets (e.g., allowing students to indicate their answers directly on the examination).

REFERENCES

Rehabilitation Act of 1973, PL 93-112, 29 U.S.C. §§ 701 *et seq.*

Appendix B

Technology for Adults with Learning Disabilities: A Product Resource List

This product list is provided strictly as a resource. It is in no way intended as an endorsement of any specific product. In addition, this is not an exhaustive compilation of all technologies available for individuals with learning disabilities (LD) but rather provides a representative sampling for each technological category. The author of this appendix apologizes for the omission of any specific products. It is also important to emphasize that selection of appropriate technologies requires a careful analysis of the interplay among specific tasks to be performed; contexts of use; and the individual's strengths, weaknesses, special abilities, and interests. Whenever possible, prior to selection and purchase of any technology, consultation should be sought from a qualified professional in LD and technology.

Technology category	Product name	Source
Alternative Keyboard	IntelliKeys	IntelliTools 55 Leveroni Court Suite 9 Novato, CA 94949 (800) 899-6687
Abbreviation Expansion Software	TextHelp	Lorien Systems Enkalon Business Center 25 Randalstown Road Antrim CO. Antrim BT 41 4LJ Northern Ireland (800) 747-0429
Keyboard/Mouse Interface Software	Access Pack for Microsoft Windows	Microsoft Corporation One Microsoft Way Redmond, WA 98052 (206) 882-8080
	Easy Access	Apple Computer 20525 Mariani Avenue Cupertino, CA 95014 (408) 996-1010
Word Prediction Software	Co: Writer	DJDE Post Office Box 639 1000 N. Rand Road, Building 115 Wauconda, IL 60084 (800) 999-4660 e-mail: djde@aol.com http://www.donjohnston.com

This appendix is courtesy of Marshall R. Raskind, The Frostig Center, Pasadena, CA.

Technology category	Product name	Source
	TextHelp	Lorien Systems Enkalon Business Center 25 Randalstown Road Antrim CO. Antrim BT 41 4LJ Northern Ireland (800) 747-0429
	Aurora 2 for Windows	Aurora Systems, Inc. 2647 Kingsway Vancouver, BC V5R-5H4 Canada (800) 361-8255
"Talking" Word Processors	Write: Outloud	DJDE Post Office Box 639 1000 N. Rand Road, Building 115 Wauconda, IL 60084 (800) 999-4660 e-mail: djde@aol.com http: //www.donjohnston.com
	IntelliTalk	IntelliTools 55 Leveroni Court Suite 9 Novato, CA 94949 (800) 899-6687
Spell Checkers, Dictionaries, Thesauruses (stand alone)	Franklin Learning Resources Product Line	Franklin Electronic Publishers 1 Franklin Plaza Burlington, NJ 08016-4907 (800) 525-9673
Proofreading Software	Correct Grammar	The Learning Center One Athenaeum Street Cambridge, MA 02142 (617) 494-1200 (800) 852-2255
Outliner/Brainstorming Software	Grandview MORE	Symantec Corporation 10201 Torre Avenue Cupertino, CA 95014 (408) 253-9600 (800) 441-7234
Semantic Mapping	Inspiration	Inspiration Software®, Inc. 2920 S.W. Dolph Court Suite 3 Portland, OR 97219 (800) 877-4292
Speech Recognition	DragonDictate NaturallySpeaking	Dragon Systems 320 Nevada Street Newton, MA 02160 (617) 965-5200
	Kurzweil Voice	Kurzweil Applied Intelligence, Inc. 411 Waverly Oaks Road Suite 330 Waltham, MA 02154 (617) 893-5151 (800) 238-6423
	IBM Voice Type ViaVoice	International Business Machines Corp. Special Needs Systems IBM PC Company 11400 Burnet Road Austin, TX 78758 (512) 823-0000 http: //www.ibm.com

Technology category	Product name	Source
	Power Secretary	Articulate Systems 600 W. Cummings Park Suite 4500 Woburn, MA 01801
Speech Synthesizer	DecTalk Products	Digital Equipment Corp. Digital Drive MK02-1/K06 Merrimack, NH 03054 (603) 884-4047
	Keynote Gold Products	HumanWare, Inc. 6245 King Road Loomis, CA 95650 (800) 722-3393
	SoundBlaster	Creative Labs 1523 Cimarron Plaza Stillwater, OK 74075 (800) 998-5227
Screen Reading Software	Outspoken	Berkeley Systems, Inc. 2095 Rose Street Berkeley, CA 94709 (510) 540-5535
	JAWS	Henter-Joyce, Inc. 2100 62nd Avenue North St. Petersberg, FL 33702 (800) 336-5658
	SoundProof	HumanWare, Inc. 6245 King Road Loomis, CA 95650 (800) 722-3393
	Ultimate Reader	Universal Learning Technology 39 Cross Street Peabody, MA 01960 (508) 538-0036
	Aurora for Windows	Aurora Systems, Inc. 2647 Kingsway Vancouver, BC V5R-5H4, Canada (800) 361-8255 or (604) 436-2694
	TextHelp	Lorien Systems Enkalon Business Center 25 Randalstown Road Antrim CO. Antrim BT 41 4LJ Northern Ireland (800) 747-0429
	pwWebSpeak	The Productivity Works, Inc. 7 Belmont Circle Trenton, NJ 08618 (609) 984-8044
Optical Character Recognition	Bookwise	Xerox Adaptive Products 9 Centennial Drive Peabody, MA 01960 (508) 977-2000 (800) 343-0311
	Wynn	Arkenstone, Inc. 555 Oakmead Parkway Sunnyvale, CA 94086-4023 (408) 245-5900 (800) 444-4443 e-mail: info@arkenstone.org http://www.arkenstone.org

Technology category	Product name	Source
	Omni 3000	Kurzweil Educational Systems 411 Waverly Oaks Road Waltham, MA 01254 (617) 893-5151 (800) 238-6423
Free-Form Database	InfoSelect	Micro Logic Corporation 89 Leuning Street S. Hackensack, NJ 07606 (201) 342-6518
Books on Disk	BookManager	Recordings for the Blind and Dyslexic, Inc. 20 Roszel Road Princeton, NJ 08540 (609) 452-0606
Books on Tape		American Printing House for the Blind 1839 Frankfort Avenue Post Office Box 6085 Louisville, KY (502) 895-2405
	Recorded Books	Library of Congress National Library Service for the Blind and Physically Handicapped 1291 Taylor Street, NW Washington, DC 20542 (202) 707-5100
		Recordings for the Blind and Dyslexic, Inc. 20 Roszel Road Princeton, NJ 08540 (609) 452-0606
		American Printing House for the Blind 1839 Frankfort Avenue Post Office Box 6085 Louisville, KY (502) 895-2405
Variable Speech Control Tape Recorder	Handi-Cassette II	American Printing House for the Blind 1839 Frankfort Avenue Post Office Box 6085 Louisville, KY (502) 895-2405
Listening Aids	Easy Listener	Phonic Ear 3880 Cypress Drive Petaluma, CA 94954 (800) 772-3374
Talking Calculators	Radio Shack Talking Calculator Model EC-208	Radio Shack A Division of Tandy Corporation Fort Worth, TX 76102 (800) 433-5502
	Big Calc	DJDE Post Office Box 639 1000 N. Rand Road, Building 115 Wauconda, IL 60084 (800) 999-4660 e-mail: djde@aol.com http://www.donjohnston.com

Appendix C

Information Resources and Clearinghouses

This list of information resources, clearinghouses, and organizations is not meant to be all inclusive or an endorsement of any particular entity. The author apologizes in advance for any inaccuracies or omissions. E-mail addresses, surface addresses, and telephone and fax numbers frequently change, as does availability. Therefore, it is recommended that users of these sites verify the information provided and be prepared to evaluate the sites for quality, ease of accessibility, frequency of being updated, and determination of the match between the site and their own purpose and special interests.

I. CLEARINGHOUSES AND RESOURCE CENTERS

Center for Literacy Studies
University of Tennessee
600 Henley Street, Suite 312
Knoxville, TN 37996-2135
423-974-4109
Fax: 423-974-3857
E-mail address: ncsall@utk.edu
World Wide Web site:
http://www.coe.utk.edu/literacy

ERIC Clearinghouse on Adult,
Career, and Vocational Education
1900 Kenny Road
Columbus, OH 43210-1090
800-848-4185 ext. 4768
Fax: 614-292-1260
World Wide Web site:
http://www.coe.ohio-state.edu/
cete/ERICacve/indx.html

Higher Education and Adult Training
for People with Handicaps
(HEATH) Resource Center
One Dupont Circle, NW Suite 800
Washington, D.C. 20036-1193
800-544-3284 (information tape)
202-939-9320
Fax: 202-833-4760
E-mail address: heath@ace.nche.edu
World Wide Web site:
http://www.acenet.edu

Learning Resources Network (LERN)
1550 Hayes Drive
Manhattan, KS 66502
800-678-5376
913-539-5376
Fax: 913-539-7766
E-mail address: hq@lern.com
World Wide Web site:
http://www.lern.org

This appendix is courtesy of Susan A. Vogel.

National Adult Literacy and
  Learning Disabilities Center
Academy of Educational
  Development
1875 Connecticut Avenue, NW,
  Suite 800
Washington, D.C.   20009-1202
800-953-2553
202-884-8185
Fax: 202-884-8422
E-mail address: info@nalldc.aed.org
World Wide Web site:
  http://novel.nifl.gov/nalldtop.htm

National Center for Family Literacy
325 W. Main Street, Suite 200
Louisville, KY 40202-4251
502-584-1133
E-mail address: ncfl@famlit.org
World Wide Web site:
  http://www.famlit.org

National Center for
  Learning Disabilities (NCLD)
381 Park Avenue South
Suite 1401
New York, NY 10016
Toll-free information/referral:
  888-575-7373
212-545-7510
Fax: 212-545-9665
World Wide Web site:
  http://www.ncld.org

National Clearinghouse on
  ESL Literacy Education
Center for Applied Linguistics
1118 22nd Street, NW
Washington, D.C.   20037
202-429-9292
Fax: 202-659-5641
E-mail address: ncle@cal.org
World Wide Web site:
  http://www.cal.org/ncle

National Clearinghouse on
  Women and Girls with Disabilities
Educational Equity Concepts, Inc.
114 East 32nd Street, Suite 701
New York, NY   10016
212-725-1803

National Governors' Association
444 North Capitol Street, NW,
  Suite 267
Washington, D.C.   20001-1572
202-624-5394
Fax: 202-624-5313
E-mail address: eganzglass@nga.org
World Wide Web site:
  http://www.nga.org

National Information Center for
  Children and Youth with
  Disabilities (NICHCY)
Post Office Box 1492
Washington, D.C.   20013-1492
800-695-0285
202-884-8200 (voice/TTD)
Fax: 202-884-8441
E-mail address:
  nichcy@aed.org/nichcy
World Wide Web site:
  http://www.nichcy.org

National Institute for Literacy (NIFL)
800 Connecticut Avenue, NW,
  Suite 200
Washington, D.C. 20006
800-552-9097
202-632-1506
Fax: 202-632-1512
World Wide Web site:
  http://www.nifl.gov

National Rehabilitation
  Information Center (NARIC)
8455 Colesville Road, Suite 935
Silver Spring, MD   20910
800-346-2742

Office for Civil Rights (OCR)
400 Maryland Avenue, SW
Washington, D.C.   20202-1100
202-205-5413

Office of Special Education and
  Rehabilitative Services (OSERS)
U.S. Department of Education
Switzer Building, 330 C Street, SW,
  Suite 3006
Washington, D.C.   20202
202-205-5465
Fax: 202-205-9252
World Wide Web site:
  http://www.ed.gov/office/OSERS/

Office of Vocational and
   Adult Education
U.S. Department of Education
600 Independence Avenue, SW
Washington, D.C.   20202
202-205-5451
Fax: 202-205-8748
E-mail address: ovae@inet.gov
World Wide Web site:
   http://www.ed.gov/offices/OVAE/

President's Committee on
   Employment for People with
   Disabilities
1331 F Street, NW
Washington, D.C. 20004-1007
202-376-6200

U.S. Department of Education
600 Independence Avenue, SW
Washington, D.C.   20202
800-USA-LEARN
Fax: 202-401-0689
E-mail address:
   CustomerService@inet.ed.gov
World Wide Web site:
   http://www.ed.gov

II.   EMPLOYMENT RESOURCES

AFL-CIO Education Department
815 16th Street, NW
Washington, D.C.   20006
202-637-5144
Fax: 202-508-6987
E-mail address: asarmien@capcon.net
World Wide Web site:
   http://www.aflcio.org

Center on Education and Work
School of Education
University of Wisconsin–Madison
1025 West Johnson Street, Room 964
Madison, WI   53706-1796
800-446-0399
608-263-3696
Fax: 608-262-9197
E-mail address:
   aphelps@soemadison.wisc.edu
World Wide Web site:
   http://www.cew.wisc.edu

Equal Employment Opportunity
   Commission (EEOC)
1801 L Street, NW
Washington, D.C. 20507
800-669-4900
202-275-7377
Fax: 202-663-4912
World Wide Web site:
   http://www.eeoc.gov

Job Accommodation Network
West Virginia University
Box 6080
Morgantown, WV   26506-6080
800-232-9675
904-293-7186
Fax: 304-293-5407
E-mail address: jan@jan.icdi.wvu.edu
World Wide Web site:
   http://janweb.icdi.wvu.edu/

National Alliance of Business
1201 New York Avenue, NW
Suite 700
Washington, D.C.   20005
202-289-2934
Fax: 202-289-2875
E-mail address:
   McClendonW@nab.com
World Wide Web site:
   http://www.nab.com/

National School-to-Work Office
400 Virginia Avenue, SW
Room 210
Washington, D.C.   20024
202-401-6222
Fax: 202-401-6211
E-mail address: stw-lc@ed.gov
World Wide Web site:
   http://www.stw.ed.gov

SER-Jobs for Progress National, Inc.
100 Decker Drive
Suite 200
Irving, TX   75062
972-650-1860
Fax: 972-650-1860
E-mail address:
   Cjohnson@sernational.org
World Wide Web site:
   http://www.sernational.org

III.   FINANCIAL SERVICES

Federal Student Aid Information
   Center
Post Office Box 84
Washington, D.C.   20044
800-433-3243

Social Security Administration
6401 Security Boulevard
Baltimore, MD 21235
800-772-1213
410-965-8882
800-325-0778 (TTD)
World Wide Web site:
   http://www.ssa.gov

IV.   FOUNDATIONS

Barbara Bush Foundation for
   Family Literacy
1002 Wisconsin Avenue, NW
Washington, D.C.   20007
202-338-2006
Fax: 202-337-6754
E-mail address: sooc@erols.com
World Wide Web site:
   http://www.bushfoundation.com

The John S. & James L. Knight
   Foundation
2 South Biscayne Blvd.
Suite 3800
Miami, FL   33131
305-908-2600
Fax: 305-908-2698
World Wide Web site:
   http://www.knightfdn.org

Lila Wallace–Reader's Digest Fund
Two Park Avenue
New York, NY   10016
212-251-9800
Fax: 212-679-6990
E-mail address:
   lwrd@wallacefunds.org
World Wide Web site:
   http://www.lilawallace.org/index.
   htm

Newspaper Association of
   America Foundation
1921 Gallows Road
Vienna, VA   22182
703-902-1730
Fax: 703-620-1265
E-mail address: guntr@naa.org
World Wide Web site:
   http://www.naa.org/foundation/

Starbucks Foundation
Post Office Box 3824
Seattle, WA   98134
206-748-8602
Fax: 206-447-3028
E-mail address:
   pblomqui@starbucks.com

V.   GOVERNMENT AGENCIES

Americans with Disabilities
   Information Hotline
Disability Rights Section,
   Civil Rights Division
U.S. Department of Justice
Post Office Box 66738
Washington, D.C.   20035-6738
800-514-0301
202-514-0301
World Wide Web site:
   http://www.usdoj.gov/crt/ada/
   adahom1.htm

America Reads Challenge
Office of Secretary
U.S. Department of Education
600 Independence Avenue, SW
Washington, D.C.   20202-7240
202-401-8888
Fax: 202-401-0596
World Wide Web site:
   http://www.ed.gov/inits/
   AmericaReads/

Division of Adult Education &
   Literacy (DAEL)
U.S. Department of Education
600 Independence Avenue, SW
Washington, D.C.   20202-7240
202-205-8270
Fax: 202-205-8973
E-mail address:
   ronald_pugsley@ed.gov
World Wide Web site:
   http://www.ed.gov/offices/OVAE

Even Start and Family Literacy
Programs
Office of Elementary and
Secondary Education
U.S. Department of Education
600 Independence Avenue, SW
Washington, D.C.   20202-7240
202-260-0991
Fax: 202-260-7764
World Wide Web site:
http://www.ed.gov/

Office of Correctional Education
U.S. Department of Education
600 Independence Avenue, SW
Washington, D.C.   20202-7240
202-205-5621
Fax: 202-205-8793
E-mail address:
richard_smith@ed.gov
World Wide Web site:
http://www.ed.gov/offices/OVAE/

Office of Family Assistance
U.S. Department of Health and
Human Services
370 L'Enfant Promenade, SW
5th Floor, E
Washington, D.C.   20447
202-401-4619
Fax: 202-205-5887
E-mail address:
yhoward@acf.dhhs.gov
World Wide Web site:
http://www.dhhs.gov/

Office of Research and
Demonstration
U.S. Department of Labor
200 Constitution Avenue, NW
Room N5637
Washington, D.C.   20210
202-219-7674
Fax: 202-219-5455
E-mail address: wandners@doleta.gov
World Wide Web site:
http://www.doleta.gov/

Office of Special Education and
Rehabilitative Services (OSERS)
U.S. Department of Education
Switzer Building
330 C Street, SW, Suite 3006
Washington, D.C.   20202
202-205-5465
Fax: 202-205-9252
World Wide Web site:
http://www.ed.gov/office/OSERS/

Office of Vocational and
Adult Education
U.S. Department of Education
600 Independence Avenue, SW
Washington, D.C.   20202-7240
202-205-5451
Fax: 202-205-8748
World Wide Web site:
http://www.ed.gov/offices/OVAE

U.S. National Commission on
Libraries & Information Science
1110 Vermont Avenue, NW
Suite 820
Washington, D.C.   20005-3522
202-606-9200
Fax: 202-606-9203
E-mail address: js_nclis@inet.ed.gov
World Wide Web site:
http://www.nclis.gov/

VI.   HOTLINES

Americans with Disabilities Act
Information Hotline
Regional Technical Center
800-949-4232
Americans with Disabilities
Information Hotline
(U.S. Department of Justice)
800-514-0301
202-514-0301

Federal Student Aid Information
Hotline
800-433-3243

GED Hotline
800-626-9433

National Literacy Hotline
800-228-8813

VII.   INTERNET/WORLD WIDE WEB
SITES FOR LEARNING DISABILITIES
(LD), LITERACY, AND
ATTENTION-DEFICIT/
HYPERACTIVITY DISORDER
(ADHD)

Americans with Disabilities
(ADA) Document Center
World Wide Web site:
http://janweb.icdi.wvu.edu/kinder

Americans with Disabilities
Information Line
(U.S. Department of Justice)
World Wide Web site:
http://www.usdoj.gov/crt/ada/
adahom1.htm

AskERIC Virtual Literacy
World Wide Web site:
http://ericir.syr.edu/

Disability Resources, Inc.
World Wide Web site:
http://www.geocities.com/~drm

Educational Resource
Information Center (ERIC)
World Wide Web site:
http://www.ed.gov/databases/
ERIC_Digests/index

Equal Access to Software and
Information (EASI)
World Wide Web site:
http://www.isc.rit.edu/~easi

Higher Education and Adult Training
for People with Handicaps
(HEATH)
World Wide Web site:
heath@ace.nche.edu
gopher://bobcat.ace.nche.edu

LD Info Center thru the
Reading Group
World Wide Web site:
http://www.soltec.net/~reading

LD Online
World Wide Web site:
http://www.ldonline.org

LD Resources
World Wide Web site:
http://www.ldresources.com

Middle Tennessee State University
Dyslexia Center
World Wide Web site:
http://www.mtsu.edu/Academic/
Dyslexia/index.html

National Adult Literacy and Learning
Disabilities Center (NALLDC)
World Wide Web site:
http://novel.nifl.gov/nalldtop.html

National Attention Deficit
Disorder Association
World Wide Web site:
http://www.add.org

National Center for Education
Statistics (NCES)
World Wide Web site:
http://www.ed.gov/NCES

National Information Center for
Children and Youth with
Disabilities (NICHCY)
World Wide Web site:
http://www.nichcy.org

National Skill Standards Board
World Wide Web site:
http://www.nssb.org

National Workforce Assistance
Collaborative
World Wide Web site:
http://cac.psu.edu/institutes/nwac

O*Net—The Occupational
Information Network
World Wide Web site:
http://www.doleta.gov/programs/
onet

Rebus Institute
World Wide Web site:
http://www.cenatica.com/rebus/

Roads to Learning
World Wide Web site:
http://www.ala.org/roads

U.S. Department of Labor
World Wide Web site:
http://www.dol.gov

VIII. LISTSERVS

ADAPT-L
Adaptive technology and libraries
E-mail address to
    listserv@american.edu
"subscribe adapt-l (yourfirstname
    yourlastname)"

Adult Attention Deficit Disorder List
Discussions for adults with
    ADD/ADHD
E-mail address to
    listserv@sjuvm.st.johns.edu
"subscribe ADULT (yourfirstname
    yourlastname)"

LD List
General discussions of LD issues
    including people with LD
E-mail address to
    majordomo@curry.edu
"subscribe ld-list (yourfirstname
    yourlastname)"

NIFL-LD
For adults with LD and discussion of
    LD and adult literacy
E-mail address to
    listproc@literacy.nifl.gov
"subscribe nifl-ld (yourfirstname
    yourlastname)"

PLLD-L
Information on libraries and LD,
    all welcomed
E-mail address to listproc@ala.org
"subscribe to PLLD-L
    (yourfirst name
    yourlastname)"

Post-Secondary
LD-List
For postsecondary students with LD
E-mail address to
    listserv@listserv.acsu.buffalo.edu
"subscribe Swdhe-1"

Teaching Writing and LD/ADHD List
For professionals engaged in the
    challenges and rewards of teaching
    writing skills to individuals with
    LD and/or ADHD
E-mail address to
    listserv@home.ease.lsoft.com
"subscribe WLDADD (your name)"

Women and LD/ADHD
For professionals in the fields of
    education, student services,
    psychology, and health services,
    with emphasis on postsecondary
    education
E-mail address to
    listserv@home.ease.lsoft.com
"subscribe WLDADD (your name)"

IX. LAW SERVICES

American Bar Association
740 15th Street, NW, 11th Floor
Washington, D.C.   20005
202-662-1024
Fax: 202-662-1032
E-mail address:
LynchD@staff.banet.org

Americans with Disabilities
    Information Hotline
Disability Rights Section,
    Civil Rights Division
U.S. Department of Justice
Post Office Box 66738
Washington, D.C.   20035-6738
800-514-0301
202-514-0301
World Wide Web site:
    http://www.usdoj.gov/crt/ada/
    adahom1.htm

Disability Rights Education and
    Defense Fund, Inc. (DREDF)
2212 Sixth Street
Berkeley, CA   94710
800-466-4232
510-644-2555
Fax: 510-841-8645

National Association of Protection
    and Advocacy Systems
900 2nd Street, NE, Suite 211
Washington, D.C.   20002
202-408-9514
Fax: 202-408-9520
E-mail address:
    hn4537@handsnet.org

Office of Civil Rights (OCR) of
  the U.S. Department of Education
600 Independence Avenue, SW
Washington, D.C. 20202
800-421-3481
202-205-5413
Fax: 202-205-9862
E-mail address: ocr@ed.gov
World Wide Web site:
  http://www.ed.gov

X.   PROFESSIONAL ORGANIZATIONS

A.   Adult Education

American Association for
  Adult & Continuing Education
1200 19th Street, NW, Suite 300
Washington, D.C. 20036
202-429-5131
202-223-4579
E-mail address:
  Drew_Allbritten@sba.com

American Association of
  Community Colleges
One Dupont Circle, NW, Suite 410
Washington, D.C. 20036-1176
202-728-0200
202-728-7851
Fax: 202-833-2467
E-mail address:
  lbarnett@aacc.nche.edu
World Wide Web site:
  http://www.aacc.nche.edu

Association for Community
  Based Education
1805 Florida Avenue, NW
Washington, D.C. 20009
202-462-6333
Fax: 202-232-8044
E-mail address: acbe@aol.com

Association on Higher Education
  and Disability (AHEAD—formerly
  AHSSPPE)
Box 21192
Columbus, OH 43221-0192
614-488-4972
Fax: 614-488-1174
World Wide Web site:
  http://www.ahead.org

Correctional Education Association
4380 Forbes Boulevard
Lanham, MD   20706
301-918-1915
Fax: 301-918-1846
E-mail address: Steurer1@aol.com
World Wide Web site:
  http://sunsite.unc.edu/icea/index.
  htm

National Adult Education
  Professional Development
  Consortium
444 North Capitol Street, NW,
  Suite 706
Washington, D.C.   20001
202-624-5250
Fax: 608-267-1690
E-mail address: koloski@otan.dni.us

National Council of State
  Directors of Adult Education
c/o Wisconsin Technical College
  System
310 Prince Place
Post Office Box 7874
Madison, WI   53707-7874
608-267-9684
Fax: 608-267-1690
E-mail address:
  jackson@board.tec.wi.us
World Wide Web site:
  http://www.otan.dni.us

B.   English as a Second Language
     (ESL) (Multicultural)

Center for Applied Linguistics
1117 22nd Street, NW
Washington, D.C.   20037
202-429-9292 ext. 200
Fax: 202-659-5641
E-mail address: fran@cal.org
World Wide Web site:
  http://www.cal.org/ncle/

National Clearinghouse on ESL
  Literacy Education (NCLE)
Teachers of English to Speakers
  of Other Languages
1600 Cameron Street, Suite 300
Alexandria, VA   22314
703-836-0774
Fax: 703-836-7864
E-mail address: tesol@tesol.edu
World Wide Web site:
  http://www.tesol.edu/index.html

C.   LD/Dyslexia/ADHD

Children and Adults with Attention
   Deficit Disorder (CHADD)
499 NW 70th Avenue, Suite 101
Plantation, FL   33317
954-587-3700
800-233-4050
Fax: 954-587-4599
E-mail address: national@chadd.org
World Wide Web site:
   http://www.chadd.org

Council for Learning Disabilities
   (CLD)
Post Office Box 40303
Overland Park, KS   66204
913-492-8755
Fax: 913-492-2546
World Wide Web site:
   http://www.winthrop.edu/cld/

Division for Learning Disabilities
   (DLD)
The Council for Exceptional
   Children (CEC)
1920 Association Drive
Reston, VA   22091
800-845-6232
703-620-3660
Fax: 703-264-9494
World Wide Web site:
   http://www.cec.sped.org

International Dyslexia Association
Chester Building, Suite 382
8600 LaSalle Road
Baltimore, MD   21286-2044
800-222-3123
410-296-0232
Fax: 410-321-5069
E-mail address: info@interdys.org
World Wide Web site:
   http://www.interdys.org

Learning Disabilities Association
   of America
4156 Library Road
Pittsburgh, PA 15234-1349
412-341-1515
412-341-8077
Fax: 412-344-0224
E-mail address: ldnatl@usaor.net
World Wide Web site:
   http://www.ldanatl.org

Learning Disabilities Association
   of Canada (LDAC)
323 Chapel Street, Suite 200
Ottawa, Ontario K1N 7Z2
CANADA
613-238-5721
Fax: 613-235-5391
E-mail address: ldactaac@fox.nstn.ca
World Wide Web site:
   http://educ.queensu.ca/~lda

The Attention Deficit Information
   Network, Inc. (AD-IN)
475 Hillside Avenue
Needham, MA 02194
617-455-9895
Fax: 617-444-5466
E-mail address: adin@gis.net

The National Attention Deficit
   Disorder Association (NADDA)
Post Office Box 972
Mentor, OH 44061
800-487-2282
216-350-9595
Fax: 216-350-0223
E-mail address: natladda@aol.com
World Wide Web site:
   http://www.add.org

D.   Literacy

American Library Association
Roads to Learning
50 East Huron
Chicago, IL   60611-2795
800-545-2433 ext. 4027
Fax: 312-280-3211
E-mail address: agoman@ala.org
World Wide Web site:
   http://www.ala.org

National Alliance of
   Urban Literacy Coalitions
600 Jefferson Street, Suite 600
Houston, TX   77002
713-659-8700 ext. 3022
Fax: 713-659-8752
E-mail address: naulc@bcicorp.com

National Association of
State Literacy Resource Centers
c/o D.C. Literacy Resource Center
Martin Luther King Memorial
Library, Room 300
901 G Street, NW
Washington, D.C.   20001
202-727-1616
Fax: 202-727-1129
E-mail address:
marcia_harrington@csgi.com

National Center for
Family Literacy, Inc.
325 West Main
Waterfront Plaza, Suite 200
Louisville, KY   40202-4251
502-584-1133
Fax: 502-584-0172
E-mail address: skdarling@aol.com
World Wide Web site:
http://www.nifl.gov/ncfl/

National Institute for Literacy
800 Connecticut Avenue, NW,
Suite 200
Washington, D.C.   20006-7560
202-632-1422
Fax: 202-632-1512
E-mail address: ahartman@nifl.gov
World Wide Web site:
http://www.nifl.gov

XI.   RECORDING BOOK SERVICES

American Printing House for
the Blind
1839 Frankfort Avenue
Post Office Box 6085
Louisville, KY   40206-0085
800-223-1839
502-895-2405
E-mail address: info@aph.org
World Wide Web site:
http://www.aph.org

National Library Service for the
Blind and Physically Handicapped
Library of Congress
1291 Taylor Street, NW
Washington, D.C. 20542
800-424-8567
202-707-5100
Fax: 202-707-0712
TDD: 202-707-0744
World Wide Web site:
http://www.loc.gov/nls

Recording for the Blind and
Dyslexic (RFBD)
20 Roszel Road
Princeton, NJ   08540
800-221-4792
609-452–0606
Fax: 609-987-8116
E-mail address: custserv@rfbd.org
World Wide Web site:
http://www.rfbd.org

XII.   RESEARCH CENTERS

Institute for the Study of
Adult Literacy
College of Education
The Pennsylvania State University
102 Rackley Building
University Park, PA   16802-3202
814-863-3777
Fax: 814-863-6108
World Wide Web site:
http://www.ed.psu.edu/isal/index.
html

National Center on
Adult Literacy (NCAL)
University of Pennsylvania
3910 Chestnut Street
Philadelphia, PA 19104-3111
215-898-2100
Fax: 215-898-9804
E-mail address:
encal@literacy.upenn.edu
World Wide Web site:
http://ncal.literacy.upenn.edu

National Center on the
Study of Adult Literacy and
Learning (NCSALL)
Nichols House, Harvard University
Harvard Graduate School of
Education
Cambridge, MA   02138
617-496-0516
Fax: 617-495-4811
E-mail address:
comingjo@hugse.1.harvard.edu
World Wide Web site:
http://hugse1.harvard.edu/~ncsall

National Center for Research in
  Vocational Education
University of California at Berkeley
2030 Addison Street, Suite 500
Berkeley, CA 94720-1674
800-762-4093
Fax: 510-642-2124
World Wide Web site:
  http://ncrve.berkeley.edu/
  gopher://ncrve.berkeley.edu/

National Institutes of Health
Building 31, Room 10A31
Bethesda, MD   20892-3100
301-496-6631
Fax: 301-402-4945
E-mail address:
  burklowj@occ.nci.nih.gov
World Wide Web site:
  http://www.nih.gov

XIII.   TECHNOLOGY

Adult Literacy and
  Technology Network
301 South Geneva Street, G-10
Ithaca, NY 14850
607-273-0634
Fax: 607-273-0840
E-mail address: ccarlin@lightlink.com

Alliance for Technology Access
2175 East San Francisco Boulevard
  Suite L
San Rafael, CA   94901
415-455-4575
E-mail address: atainfo@atacess.org

Center for Applied Special
  Technology (CAST)
39 Cross Street
Peabody, MA   01960
508-531-8555
E-mail address: cast@cast.org
World Wide Web site:
  http://www.cast.org

Frostig Center for Technology
  and Learning Disabilities (CTLD)
971 North Altadena Drive
Pasadena, CA   91107
818-791-1255

Technology and Media (TAM)
Council for Exceptional Children
1920 Association Drive
Reston, VA   22091
703-620-3660
Fax: 703-264-9494
World Wide Web site:
  http://www.cec.sped.org

XIV.   TESTING SERVICES

ACT Universal Testing
Post Office Box 4028
Iowa City, IA   52243-4028
319-337-1332
Fax: 319-337-1285
E-mail address:
  turne@act-act4-po.act.org
World Wide Web site:
  http://www.act.org

Educational Testing Service (ETS)
Rosedale Road
Princeton, NJ   08541
Tests administered include:
  SAT, GRE, GMAT
609-771-7670
Fax: 609-771-7906
World Wide Web site:
  http://www.ets.org

The General Educational
  Development Testing Service
  (GEDTS)
One Dupont Circle, NW, Suite 250
Washington, D.C.   20036
800-528-9800
202-939-9490
Fax: 202-775-8578
E-mail address: web@ace.nche.edu
World Wide Web site:
  http://www.acenet.edu

Law School Admission Council
Post Office Box 2000-T
Newtown, PA   18940-0998
215-968-1001
Fax: 215-968-1277
E-mail address: lsacinfo@lsac.org
World Wide Web site:
  http://www.lsac.org

SAT Services for Students with
Disabilities
Post Office Box 6226
Princeton, NJ   08541-6226
609-771-7780

The Comprehensive Adult Student
Assessment System (CASAS)
8910 Clairemont Mesa Blvd.
San Diego, CA 92123
800-255-1036
619-292-2900
Fax: 619-292-2910
E-mail address: casas@casas.org
World Wide Web site:
http://www.casas.org

XV.   VOLUNTEER ORGANIZATIONS

Laubach Literacy Action
Post Office Box 131
1320 Jamesville Avenue
Syracuse, NY   13210
315-422-9121
Fax: 315-422-6369
E-mail address: info@laubach.org
World Wide Web site:
http://www.laubach.org/

Literacy Volunteers of America (LVA)
635 James Street
Syracuse, NY 13203
315-472-0001
Fax: 315-472-0002
E-mail address: lvanat@aol.com
World Wide Web site:
http://archon.educ.kent.edu/LVA

Student Coalition for Action in
Literacy Education
140 East Franklin Street,
Campus Box 3505
University of North Carolina
Chapel Hill, NC   27599-3505
919-965-1542
Fax: 919-965-1533
E-mail address: scale@unc.edu
World Wide Web site:
http://www.unc.edu/depts/scale/

Index

Page numbers followed by "f" indicate figures; those followed by "t" indicate tables.